THEN
AND
NOW

THEN AND NOW

How the World Has
Changed Since
WWII

TAD SZULC

WILLIAM MORROW AND COMPANY, INC.
New York

Recognizing the importance of preserving what has been written, it is the policy of William Morrow and Company, Inc., and its imprints and affiliates to have the books it publishes printed on acid-free paper, and we exert our best efforts to that end.

Library of Congress Cataloging-in-Publication Data

Szulc, Tad.
    Then and now : how the world has changed since WW II / Tad
Szulc.
        p.   cm.
    ISBN 0-688-07558-4
    1. History, Modern, 1945–   I. Title.
D840.S98   1990
909.82—dc20   90-5617
                                                                           CIP

Printed in the United States of America

First Edition

1 2 3 4 5 6 7 8 9 10

BOOK DESIGN BY MANUELA PAUL

This book is for all the people

in the world who deserve a happier

human condition

PREFACE

A s an esteemed colleague of mine has remarked, journalism is the first draft of history.

This book, therefore, is written as a reporter's narrative of things lived, seen, heard, and read and of great events I was privileged to witness in the years since the end of the Second World War. It does not purport to be a scholarly work of history although I have endeavored to frame my account in a historical perspective.

My professional career has paralleled the postwar years since 1945 to the present time. I was given the extraordinary opportunity to travel the world, first on behalf of *The New York Times*, which employed me for nearly twenty years, then as an independent writer. I have reported and written news from Washington, D.C., the United Nations in New York, and sixty-eight countries in North, South, and Central America, the Soviet Union, Eastern and Western Europe, East Asia (including China) and Southeast Asia (including Vietnam), the Indian subcontinent, the Middle East, North Africa, and the Republic of South Africa.

It was a magnificent experience to be directly exposed to the processes of change and evolution in Washington and at the United Nations, to observe the postwar reconstruction of Western Europe under the Marshall Plan and then the birth and the growth of the European Community, to see the astounding transformations in the Communist world—from rise to debacle—and to watch the emergence and the travails of the Third World from Brazil to India and to Algeria. And I was there to report on the great revolutions, uprisings, and violence in Cuba, the Philippines, and Lebanon.

I was fortunate to be on hand for some of the milestone events of the second half of the twentieth century: the Vietnam War, the American interventions in Cuba and the Dominican Republic, the Soviet invasion of Czechoslovakia, the birth, fall, and ultimate triumph of Solidarity in Poland, the incredible mutations of Marxism in China and the Soviet Union, its sudden collapse in Eastern Europe in the autumn of 1989—and the apparent end of the Cold War.

I have followed and tried to understand the high technology revolution and its consequences, along with key developments in science and medicine and in nuclear energy and space missions. My scientific background is vir-

7

tually nonexistent, and I have relied greatly on the advice of friendly specialists and on published materials. I was lucky to find fine mentors in music, the arts, literature, history, popular culture, television, and cinema.

My assignments permitted me to see in action some of the towering figures of the postwar period: Presidents Truman and Eisenhower, Winston Churchill and Charles de Gaulle, Jean Monnet and Konrad Adenauer, Andrei Vishinsky and Andrei Gromyko.

I have met personally other remarkable personages of our time, having interviewed many of them: John F. Kennedy and Robert F. Kennedy, Lyndon B. Johnson, Richard Nixon and George Bush, Henry Kissinger, Zhou Enlai, Aleksandr Yakovlev, Jawaharlal Nehru and Indira Gandhi, Josip Broz Tito, Fidel Castro, Zulfikar Ali Bhutto, Mohammad Zia ul-Haq, François Mitterrand, Michel Rocard, Brian Mulroney, Francisco Franco, Antônio de Oliveira Salazar and Mário Sores, Golda Meir, Yitzhak Rabin, Chaim Herzog, Yasir Arafat, Alexander Dubček, Wojciech Jaruzelski, Lech Wałęsa, Paul VI and John Paul II, Juan Perón, Juscelino Kubitschek, Oscar Arias Sánchez, Omar Torrijos, and King Jigme Singye Wangchuk. It is a privilege and a pleasure to engage in such name-dropping.

These postwar years, I believe, were the most exciting, fascinating, frightening, and promising era in contemporary history. The period from the start of World War II has unquestionably marked the deepest and most rapid changes in human society in recorded memory.

I was able to watch it in Washington, Paris, London, and Moscow policy-making centers and in hi tech centers in the United States and France and in state-of-the-art hospitals in America and Western Europe. I saw it in the slums of São Paulo, Mexico City, Calcutta, and Cairo; in the Amazonas jungle, where settlers slash and burn primeval rain forests, and in southern Spain, where the United States lost four hydrogen bombs; in Afghan, Palestinian, and Nicaraguan refugee camps; in Jerusalem and the occupied West Bank and Gaza territories; in South Africa's Soweto township; in wartime Saigon; in rural western China, where farmers were growing rich under market economy reforms; in the revolutionary Sierra Maestra and Havana; in Polish revolutionary Gdańsk; in hungry Indian villages and along the Khyber Pass; and in the Himalayan mountains of the kingdom of Bhutan, where time stands still.

I covered civil wars, revolutions, the overthrow of hated Latin American tyrants, and I watched unspeakable violence, cruelty, paroxysms of racism and religious intolerance, starvation and deprivation, the grief of infant mortality, and violations of human rights on a monumental scale.

But I was also given the opportunity to see and admire human faith, courage, genius, resilience, sacrifice, optimism, and inspiring acts of love. I observed unbelievable attachment to the ideals of freedom and democracy, often at any cost, and the determination to improve the human condition.

On balance—as a reporter and as a citizen—I am optimistic about the future at this juncture although I know how hard it will be to attain all the goals, how long it is bound to take, and how painful will be the inevitable disenchantments, frustrations, and defeats along the way. Is there really a choice?

In preparing this book, I turned to friends and strangers (many of whom then became friends) to help me understand the quandaries, the issues, and the nuances of our time. I am grateful for the time and the gift of marvelous conversations given me, among many others, by the following persons:

In politics, history, and ideology:

Sir Isaiah Berlin in London; Leszek Kołakowski in Chicago, Prime Minister Michel Rocard, François Furet, Michel Jobert, and Régis Debray in Paris; Emmanuel de Margerie in Washington; President Mauno Koivisto of Finland in Helsinki; President Arias of Costa Rica in San José; Foreign Minister Sahabzada Yakub Khan of Pakistan in Islamabad; President Chaim Herzog of Israel in Jerusalem; Palestine Liberation Organization Chairman Yasir Arafat in Tunis; Wojciech Jaruzelski, Mieczysław Rakowski, Bronisław Geremek, Adam Michnik, and the late Edmund Jan Osmańczyk in Warsaw and Lech Wałęsa in Gdańsk; Jacques Chaban-Delmas in Bordeaux; Aleksandr Yakovlev and Sergo Mikoyan in Moscow; the late Ernesto "Che" Guevara and Fidel Castro in Havana; and Daniel Davidson and the late Jan Victor Mladek in Washington. Among my professional friends: Flora Lewis and Karl E. Meyer of *The New York Times*, Michel Tatu of *Le Monde* in Paris, Philip Geyelin in Washington, and Stanley Sheinbaum in Los Angeles.

In themes touching on the human condition:

Dr. Samuel O. Thier, president, Institute of Medicine, National Academy of Sciences, Dr. Alfred Baer, and Dr. Joseph Fleming in Washington; Werner Fornos, president, the Population Institute, Washington; Pat Rengle, Amnesty International, Washington; Aryeh Neier, Human Rights Watch, New York; Marjorie Sonnenfeldt, Washington; Richard Schifter and Mark L. Schneider, Washington; Alfred H. Edelson in Washington; James P. Grant, executive director, UNICEF, New York; Razia Ismail, UNICEF, New Delhi; Robert Douglas, president, National Center for Therapeutic Riding, Washington; and Dr. William J. Cousins, Washington.

In music and literature:

Byron Janis in New York; Eugene Istomin and Henry Raymont in Washington; and the late Henryk Szeryng in Mexico City; Gabriel García Márquez and Carlos Fuentes in Mexico City; and Steve Wasserman in New York.

The most important source materials are identified in the text with the names of authors of books and articles as they are in the Bibliography. Except when discretion was requested, I have clearly identified the origin of information provided to me directly by participants in the great events of the last half century: statesmen, military leaders, scientists, politicians, thinkers, economists, and so forth. Visits to Poland and the Soviet Union in the late eighties have offered me the opportunity of making new discoveries about the past, recent and not, through conversations with men and women possessing significant knowledge—and now free to speak. The increasingly free press in Poland and the Soviet Union was an invaluable source of new information. And, of course, I drew heavily on *The New York Times, The Washington Post, The Wall Street Journal, The Los Angeles Times, Time, Newsweek, Foreign Policy,* and *Foreign Affairs* in the United States; *Le Monde, L'Exprès,* and *Le Point* in France; and *The Economist* in Britain. I have concluded that in this draft of history the reader would glean little that would be useful from detailed and pedantic Chapter Notes; therefore I chose not to inflict them on you.

This book has also been made possible as a result of foreign assignments by friendly editors of major United States publications:

Walter Anderson, editor, *Parade,* New York; Wilbur E. Garrett, editor, and Charles McCarry, editor at large, *National Geographic,* Washington; Charles William Maynes, editor, *Foreign Policy,* Washington; Arthur Seidenbaum, editor, Opinion, Los Angeles *Times;* Jesse Levine, president, Los Angeles Times Syndicate; and Peter Bloch, executive editor, Penthouse International, New York. To them, my appreciation.

As usual, my wife, Marianne, has read, corrected, constructively criticized, and edited the book manuscript in addition to her year-round support in organizing the material and engaging in research that often required patience and inventiveness. As usual, I am grateful to her.

Lisa Drew, my editor at William Morrow & Company, provided all the possible encouragement during the three years this project had been in the works. My literary agents and friends—Morton L. Janklow and Anne Sibbald—were quarterbacks extraordinary in all the phases of *Then and Now.* Again, I thank them profusely.

CONTENTS

BOOK ONE

SETTING THE SCENE

There are, in my view, two factors that, above all
others, have shaped human history in this century: one
is the development of the natural sciences and
technology. . . . The other, without doubt, consists in
the great ideological storms that have altered the lives
of virtually all mankind: the Russian Revolution and its
aftermath—totalitarian tyrannies of both right and left,
and the explosions of nationalism, racism, and . . .
religious bigotry. . . .

—ISAIAH BERLIN

I

*F*riday, September 1, 1939, a lovely late-summer day with the fragrance of harvests floating gently across the fields of Europe, marked the most important turning point in the history of the twentieth century.

At dawn of that day, at exactly 4:45 A.M., German panzer divisions invaded Poland from the west, north, and south as Luftwaffe dive bombers struck Warsaw and other Polish cities. This was Adolf Hitler's Operation White, the attack that launched the Second World War, which was to last six years, cause at least 50 million deaths (two thirds of them civilians), and alter beyond all imagination the concepts of life on the globe.

The war set in motion, directly and indirectly, fundamental societal changes along with an extraordinary surge of scientific, intellectual, and political advances and progress that continued at an ever-quickening rate over the next half century. This process of immense transformation would not have occurred on an even remotely similar scale without the unprecedented mobilization of human talent and genius as well as material and financial resources that the war triggered on both sides of the Atlantic, most notably in the United States, Great Britain, and Germany. Ultimately the Allied victory was the triumph of the democracies' technological and industrial might over the enemy in both Europe and the Pacific. It was the triumph of the nuclear weapon, air superiority, armor and landing-craft production in huge numbers, technical and scientific intelligence, and dazzling medical discoveries. They complemented the vast human effort and sacrifice on the part of millions in the Allied armies in the West and the Red Army in the East.

And it was a triumph of morale, faith, and leadership.

Wartime breakthroughs in science and medicine were primarily intended, of course, for military advantage. It was for reasons of the battlefield that the Allies and the Germans (the Japanese and the Italians counted for little in scientific innovation) had embarked on grandiose crash programs in the research and production of sophisticated weaponry.

Curiously, such research was almost entirely theoretical everywhere in the prewar years—including quite incredibly the success in atomic fission first achieved by German physicists in Berlin in 1938—and it was severely limited by the lack of adequate funding. With victory or defeat at stake, however, brains and resources were harnessed to develop and produce everything from the atomic bomb to penicillin and from radar to rocketry and jet engines, plastics, antibiotics, antimalarial drugs, and reconstructive surgery.

Once unleashed, the new technology acquired its own momentum, and with research funds now massively available from governments and the private sector, the amazing technological revolution of our time—comparable in scope only with the Industrial Revolution of the nineteenth century—has burst upon us. The spin-off for civilian uses of the wartime discoveries and the subsequent defense research (as the Cold War followed the hot one) gave us industrial nuclear power and nuclear medicine, medical lasers, and organ transplants. It gave us the magic of transistors, computers, manned space travel, with scientific horizons still beyond our understanding, satellite communications, airline jet transportation that shrinks the world, genetic engineering, and artificial intelligence. It also blessed us with ballpoint pens (fountain pens leaked at high altitudes as air travelers, from Churchill to flying crews, soon discovered) and Teflon to coat kitchenwares (the material was developed at the University of Chicago for the first nuclear reactor). Finally, there is the emergence of the information society destined to dominate the new century, replacing the industrial society, with the knowledge worker displacing the blue-collar worker.

Ironically, Japan and Germany, the nations defeated by technology in the Second World War, are exacting their technological revenge by becoming leaders in high technology, capturing markets for their products around the planet as international economy realigns itself in their favor. Between 1950 and 1980, for example, Japan spent ten billion dollars to acquire Western technology in order to apply it to its own industry. In 1990 Japan had the world's biggest bank, and it owned a large share of the American entertainment industry.

Great human and political movements too exploded in the aftermath of World War II. Unlike the 1914–18 war—then known as "the Great War"— the 1939–45 conflict shattered traditional economic and political structures in much of the world. Russia's defeat in 1917 opened the way for the October Revolution and the establishment of the Communist system in what became transformed into the Soviet Union, but communism remained confined to its borders. In 1945, on the other hand, Marxism-Leninism engulfed Eastern Europe in the wake of the conquering Soviet armies, threatening to spread to Western Europe and the nascent Third World. In the aftermath of the war, communism appeared to great numbers of people to be the way of the future, notably among the hundreds of millions in the underdeveloped regions who craved national identity and independence as well as social justice. This led to "wars of national liberation" and countless revolutions across the globe.

But if the postwar rise of Marxism-Leninism was spectacular in many ways, so was its sudden disappearance in the late 1980's as a commanding ideological-political force of the twentieth century. The year 1989 marked, indeed, the end of the Communist era: The unbelievable and spontaneous Autumn of the Peoples represented the collective conclusion in Eastern Europe and much of the Soviet Union, especially in the non-Russian republics, that Marxism-Leninism was a cruel fraud perpetrated on the populations in whose name it purported to exist. The Communist party lost its monopoly of power in all the former Soviet satellites almost overnight. The Soviet Communist party gave up voluntarily this political monopoly in February 1990 in a formal farewell to the Marxist-Leninist Era. It took the ouster of the Eastern European regimes and the fall of its tyrants to expose and demonstrate the extent to which the practice of this ideology had led to murderous repression on a gigantic scale, catastrophic destruction of the economies, and the unspeakable corruption of the Communist ruling class. This realization, of course, was at the root of the rejection of orthodox communism in the Soviet Union under Mikhail S. Gorbachev, its first post-war-generation leader, as it was behind the frightening convulsions of communism in China. In the West, the peril of "Eurocommunism" was barely a memory.

The rise and the fall of Marxism-Leninism were the two historical landmarks of the postwar epoch: The first defined the onset of the Cold War, and the second, forty-five years later, its demise.

Decolonization, an inescapable consequence of the war the Allies had fought in the name of democracy, meant the birth of nearly a hundred new nations in Asia, Africa, the Middle East, and the Caribbean. But their terrible birth pangs never seem to cease, and the impoverished postcolonial Third World exists in permanent crisis with its living standards deteriorating in the most recent years instead of improving. The World Health Organization has estimated that in 1989 about 1.3 billion people, which is more than 20 percent of the global population, were seriously ill or malnourished (500 million were in South and East Asia). In Africa the per capita annual income was $450, and the World Bank reported in a study released in 1989 that incomes in sub-Saharan Africa have been actually dropping during the eighties—and that people there were almost as poor as they were thirty years earlier. The new nations have inherited freedom and poverty, democracy usually being an alien concept.

The United Nations was formed at the war's end to guarantee the maintenance of peace, which *has* survived globally for forty-five years (more than twice as long as the peace between the two world wars). International financial institutions were created at the same time to reconstruct nations ravaged by the conflict and to build up the new ones. Prosperity has touched most of Western Europe and the United States and parts of Asia, molding new middle classes and life-styles. And democracy was asserting itself toward the close of the 1980's at the expense of waning Marxism-Leninism and rightist dictatorships. There has been fantastic flourishing in the arts, culture, and ideas, and more people than ever before have had ample access to the written word, music in all its manifestations, magnificent paintings and sculpture in ancient and supermodern museums, and philosophical thought in every dimension.

For Americans the war and its aftermath created a new nation and a new culture. Nearly eight million servicemen were educated under the GI Bill of Rights, while other millions benefited from veteran housing loans and medical care. The war established a new middle class in America, with suburban lives, consumer goods they could afford, comfortable life-styles, and a stake in society. The Great Depression was forgotten. And the time overseas spent by Americans in uniform taught them so much about the world beyond their oceans that isolationism ended forever and America was ready to assist war-devastated nations, even the enemy, to rebuild.

The postwar world was blessed in its formative decades by leaders of immense courage and vision. In the United States the first postwar Presidents—Harry Truman and Dwight Eisenhower—and George C. Marshall, the military statesman and superb peacetime thinker, belonged to that category. They influenced firmly and dramatically the second half of the century.

Winston Churchill, France's Jean Monnet and Robert Schuman, and Germany's Konrad Adenauer first visualized a unified Europe, which would become an integrated common market—and the world's largest trading bloc—by January 1, 1993. Charles de Gaulle restored the self-confidence of France after generations of defeats and humiliations. Douglas MacArthur, the American proconsul in Tokyo, set the foundations for a democratic and stunningly affluent Japan after the demolition of Hiroshima and Nagasaki by atomic bombs and the massive firebombing of Tokyo. In Brazil the greatest Latin American visionary was President Juscelino Kubitschek, who built the new capital of Brasília in the center of his gigantic country, opened the hinterland to civilization for the first time since the Portuguese conquest in 1500, and hurled Brazilians into modernity. In Indian Jawaharlal Nehru guided the nation to independence through awesome bloodshed and made the Indian voice heard strongly on the international scene. Josip Broz Tito unified Yugoslavia, then became the first Communist chief to challenge the sway of Stalinism and orthodox Marxism-Leninism.

Pope John XXIII moved the Roman Catholic Church toward the realities of the second half of the twentieth century with the Second Vatican Council from 1962 to 1965. He was a much beloved man who died much too soon.

All of them were immensely optimistic men; without optimism they could not have wrought the great changes of the postwar world. The murderous Communist emperors—Joseph Stalin in the Soviet Union and Mao Zedong in China—likewise affected profoundly the world's fate. It was the age of giants, a vanishing species. I was privileged as a reporter to have dealt with all of them except for Stalin and Mao.

Today, as the century nears its end, the scene reflects the spirit of transition and change. Gorbachev has the great opportunity to refashion the Soviet Union into a modern society for the first time since the Russian Revolution in 1917, and if he succeeds, he will have earned his place in the pantheon of universal history. In the United States, George Bush was devoid of exceptional vision and appeared uncertain in his leadership qualities. He seemed unable to match Gorbachev's sense of epochal change and to act accordingly; in December 1989, as Romanians rose in awesome and bloody revolt to topple their maniacal Communist ruler, the President dispatched American forces to invade Panama to remove a tinhorn dictator and to satisfy his personal obsession with him at a cost of hundreds of innocent civilians' lives.

In China the very aging Deng Xiaoping has brought vast economic improvements and reforms for his billion-plus fellow citizens. But tragically, he will also loom in Chinese history as the leader who ordered army tanks and machine gunners to liquidate the new democracy movement with the massacre of students on Beijing's Tienanmen Square in June 1989. At the end of that year, over ten thousand students were still in prisons. In Western Europe only François Mitterrand stands out as a worthy successor of General de Gaulle as a man with a sense of history and a sense of human culture. The Polish pope, John Paul II, remains theologically a question mark.

Margaret Thatcher will be the longest-sitting British prime minister, but she is singularly uninspiring in a nation that produced Disraeli, Gladstone, and Churchill. In Israel no towering influences have emerged to follow David Ben-Gurion and Golda Meir. In West Germany Chancellor Helmut Kohl pales in comparison with the memory of Konrad Adenauer. In Poland, where the Communist system has suffered its greatest defeat with the 1989 formation of a coalition government led by a Solidarity prime minister, General Wojciech Jaruzelski, the Communist president of the country, has not achieved the stature of Marshal Józef Piłsudski, who led his country to independence in 1918 and remains cherished a half century after his death. Lech Wałęsa was a better leader in opposition than as a democratic statesman. In Cuba Fidel Castro, once the romantic inspirer of revolution and social justice, betrayed and lost his chance for greatness when he evolved into a tragic figure of dictatorial megalomania. Elsewhere the cast of leading characters is even more ludicrous and depressing and certainly highly uninteresting.

In the fifty years that have elapsed since the outbreak of the Second World War, humanity has undergone transformations more overwhelming, dramatic, and enriching than during any other half century period in history. After the horrors of the war—from the Holocaust in Europe to the nuclear obliteration in Hiroshima and Nagasaki—it should have been the new golden age.

Yet notwithstanding all the incredible accomplishments since 1939, this half century has become an age of contradiction that is bound to persist in our time. World War III has been avoided, partly because the rival superpowers own huge nuclear arsenals acting as deterrents to conflict and partly because catastrophic blunders of the kind that resulted in World War II were not committed (though during the Cuban missile crisis in 1962 both the United States and the Soviet Union pulled back just in time from the brink of nuclear war). But we have lived through four decades of the bruising and dangerous Cold War, and we have witnessed totalitarian rule of one type or another in much of our world for much of the time.

We have seen the endless bloodbaths of revolutions across the Third World and nearly a hundred regional, guerrilla, civil, and religious wars, costing as many as seventeen million lives (one third the number killed in the Second World War) and creating seventeen million refugees, fleeing their homes to escape combat, imprisonment, hunger, and political persecution.

Genocide, torture, the trampling of human rights, and terrorism have become almost commonplace on all continents. Assassinations and mysterious deaths of national leaders and international statesmen have punctuated the postwar era in a macabre fashion. In India, the Mahatma Gandhi and Prime Minister Indira Gandhi (no kin) were murdered by fanatics almost forty years apart, emphasizing that fanaticism in our age tends to grow rather than vanish. Jordan's King Abdullah, Saudi Arabia's King Faisal, Egypt's President Anwar el-Sadat, and Lebanese Presidents Pierre Gemayel and René Moawad were gunned down by Middle Eastern fanatics. Dictator Rafael Trujillo in the Dominican Republic was shot down by victims of his oppression, and the Nicaraguan dictator Anastasio Somoza was killed in Paraguayan exile after his ouster by the Sandinista Revolution. In the United States President John Kennedy, Robert F. Kennedy, and Martin Luther King, Jr., were assassinated during the sixties for no discernible motive. Sweden's Prime Minister Olof Palme was similarly killed in the eighties. Count Folke Bernadotte of Sweden, the UN mediator, was killed in Palestine on the eve of the establishment of the state of Israel. UN Secretary-General Dag Hammarskjöld, also a Swede, died in an unexplained plane crash in Africa. Pakistan's President Mohammad Zia ul-Haq was killed aboard an exploding aircraft in 1988.

In terms of satisfying basic human needs everywhere, obstacles kept rising. Most important, the world's population more than doubled from two and a half to five and a half billion in the last fifty years, the fastest population increase in a comparable time span, and it goes on growing at an alarming pace amid starvation, disease, homelessness, unemployment, and deprivation. Twenty percent of the global population lives in what is officially defined as absolute poverty—and there are no prospects of amelioration.

Moreover, we have inflicted upon ourselves ecological disasters unknown in the simpler days before the war—presumably the price the world pays for progress. Lethal radiation escapes from nuclear power plants, and the coastal waters of both oceans are polluted by enormous oil spills and the dumping of chemical wastes. Vast forests and jungles from Brazil to Indonesia are burned to make room for new settlers. The air is poisoned by emissions from internal-combustion engines and industrial chimneys in the advanced nations and by coal and wood stoves in Third World cities and villages. And young people everywhere are polluted by the scourge of narcotics.

All in all, an inverse ratio has developed in our civilization between the scientific, material, and intellectual wealth we have accumulated and human behavior. While this wealth rises spectacularly from day to day, humankind's attitudes and actions grow more and more destructive and suicidal—even reverting to religion-motivated assassinations in Asia and the Middle East. It took a Marxist economist, József Bognár of Hungary, to conclude that "contradictions" between technology and society are so intense internationally that they influence "the way . . . countries and regions shape their economic and political priorities."

So, at the half century mark after the Second World War inaugurated humanity's new era, historians must begin to balance the ledger for this astonishing sweep of events. The first conclusion is bound to be that there has never been such a time in history.

II

The previous half century spanned the years between 1889 and 1939, constituting the prelude to our modern epoch. That period, however, has to be divided into two parts: from 1889 to the start of World War I in 1914 and from that date to the eruption of World War II, exactly twenty-five years later. The Great War was naturally a significant dividing line during the first half of the twentieth century though it did not generate the enormous changes the next global war ushered in. Four empires disappeared as a result of the First World War, but except in Russia, basic political and economic structures were not radically affected.

In order to comprehend the sequence of history that flowed from Hitler's invasion of Poland and is continuing to this day, it is useful to look back on its nineteenth-century origins—the one hundred years between 1889 and 1989. Some historians prefer other measurements to examine the unfolding of the patterns of the past. One approach, for example, is to regard the 1914–45 period as a "second" Thirty Years War in the sense that the basic tensions leading to World War I were not resolved at the Paris Peace Conference, producing, instead, World War II. Such measurements, however, tend to be artificial because they overlook the dynamics that already existed a century ago. By the same token, the ever-accelerating process of change did not halt with the Allied victory in 1945.

Many postwar events, in fact, had their roots in the history of the nineteenth century, notably in the multiple dimensions of nationalism and its explosive potential. Thus it should not have come as a surprise that first the Vietminh and then the Vietcong fought so successfully against the French and the Americans despite all conventional military odds and that soon after the Indochina victories, communism everywhere started its final ideological and political decline. This phenomenon had its own historical logic, but the West could never distinguish clearly between nationalism and Marxism-Leninism in both Europe and the Third World. By the same token, it stood to reason that Mikhail Gorbachev captured power in the Soviet Union in 1985. The Russian state had to overcome the ravages of seven decades of orthodox communism, and *perestroika* loomed as the only possible solution.

And it should not have surprised historians and policymakers that the shah of Iran was overthrown by a coalition of middle-class intellectuals, university students, and Islamic fundamentalists (who, unexpectedly, had mastered political technology to the point of flooding the country with cassettes with the inspirational voice of the still-exiled Ayatollah Khomeini). It also made sense historically that in the late eighties Palestinians succeeded in mounting a powerful challenge to Israel in the Occupied Territories. There was underlying logic in all these situations—as there was a half century and a century ago—but virtually nobody in authority in the West was prepared to think in those terms (or to listen to journalists who were on the scene and, seeing all the signs of onrushing change, were not as often trapped by conventional wisdom).

Then the West was astonished by the outburst of nationalist sentiment in the Soviet republics seventy years after the October Revolution (and forty-odd years after the forced incorporation of some of them into the Soviet Union as a consequence of World War II). Nationalism soared in Latvia, Estonia, and Lithuania, and in Armenia, Georgia, Azerbaijan, Uzbekistan, Kazakhstan, Tadzikstan, and Moldavia, and it was on the verge of exploding in the Ukraine as well. The ethnic hostility between Armenians and Azerbaijanis, neighbors in the Soviet Union's south, erupted in such hatred and bloodshed that Soviet officials in Moscow began to compare this conflict to the horrifying civil war in Lebanon. There are 3.4 million Armenians and 6.8 million Azerbaijanis, the latter mostly Muslim. In the predominantly Muslim-populated Soviet republics, religious resurgence was a factor. Relaxation under Gorbachev's *perestroika* liberalization policies has unleashed these forces, but the significance of these situations was that in spite of decades of Russification and repression, national identity, language, culture, and religion in each region have survived and, indeed, grown stronger— silently and even subconsciously—in the new generations. As I saw in the Soviet Union in 1988, the leaders of these nationalist movements were young and highly educated people, not their grandparents, who represented ancient traditions, not today's realities. Still, the roots were old and deep.

In 1889 the world, which then meant principally—and in that order— Europe and the United States, was reasonably stable after the violence and upheavals that had characterized three quarters of the nineteenth century. Much of that upheaval had resulted from surges of nationalism across Europe.

In Britain Queen Victoria reigned over her prosperous islands, consolidated and expanded the British Empire (planting the seeds of nationalist stirrings in the future), and ensured that Britannia ruled the waves. The Industrial Revolution, the colonies, and control of the bulk of overseas trade made Britain a great power.

In Germany Prince Otto von Bismarck, who had unified the country and turned it into a powerful European empire after defeating Austria and France, would retire the following year in his full glory as the "Iron Chancellor." Karl Marx, the German socialist and philosopher, had died in 1883 in fair oblivion; the *Communist Manifesto* he coauthored with Friedrich Engels and *Das Kapital* would not really be discovered for another generation or so. Marx was vindicated only three decades later, when the Russian Revolution came in 1917 (in 1889 Vladimir I. Lenin, who was to capture that revolution, was nineteen years old and a budding plotter, having already been involved in an assassination attempt against his sovereign, Czar Alexander III). Adolf Hitler and Charles Chaplin (who played Hitler in *The Great Dictator* at the outset of the Second World War) both were born in 1889. Irving Berlin, the composer who wrote "God Bless America," was one year old. He died in 1989 at the age of one hundred and one.

France was recovering from the 1870–71 debacle of the Franco-Prussian War and was riding an impressive wave of creativity with a new generation of poets, novelists, historians, composers, and painters. In 1889 France entered the limelight of modernity with the erection in Paris of the iron Eiffel Tower as the centerpiece of that year's Universal Exposition. The hot-air balloons invented by the Montgolfier brothers were flown during the Prussian siege of Paris more than a decade earlier, thereby inaugurating the age of military aviation. Curiously, then, as now, the world somehow could not associate the image of romantic, heroic, and self-indulgent France with its immense scientific and technological gifts and achievements. Even today most Americans find it hard to realize that the French are helping lead the great technological revolution (after producing Lavoisier, Pasteur, Joliot-Curie, and a host of other famous scientists).

In Vienna Francis Joseph ruled over the Austro-Hungarian Empire, a far-flung conglomeration of polyglot national territories, including Austria, Hungary, southern Poland (partitioned by Austria, Prussia, and Russia in 1795 and disappearing as a nation for 123 years), Bohemia, Moravia, big swatches of the Balkans, and northern Italy. In 1889 Francis Joseph had been emperor for forty-one years, and the dual monarchy functioned reasonably smoothly. There was nothing to suggest that the seeds of the Great War had already been sown in the Balkan soil and that Austria would be the first power to be drawn into it. But the Hapsburgs were not very well attuned to the tensions in and around their empire. Like the Bourbons, they had no sense of history.

The Russian Empire under Alexander III appeared solid, though the first rumblings of social and political discontent could be detected, especially if attention was paid to intellectuals and writers as well as to socialists and anarchists. But the St. Petersburg court was immune to such ideas. The czarist police did not think in political and ideological terms; to them, all opposition was simply criminal, a notion absorbed subsequently by Lenin and Stalin. Still, Alexander was an important voice in the European concert of nations.

The Ottoman Empire, stretching from Macedonia and Albania to European and Asian Turkey and clear across the Middle East to the fringes of North Africa, seemed safe in 1889 in the hands of reform-minded Sultan Abd al-Hamid II. The Sublime Porte, as the Ottoman government was known, controlled twenty-two separate nationalities, but it, too, could not correctly interpret rising inner pressures. Like the German, Austro-Hungarian, and Russian empires, the sprawling Ottoman Empire had no inkling that it would be liquidated within less than a generation.

The internal pressures in the lands that formed these four empires a century ago remain alive today, perhaps even more acutely. They are the nationalisms in Eastern Europe and the Soviet Union, in the Balkans (where the Yugoslav federation is torn apart by the conflicting interests of its component republics and autonomous regions), and, above all, in the Middle East, atomized by endemic disputes and conflicts among the Arab states, between Israelis and Palestinians, Muslims and Christians, Shiite and Sunni Muslims, Orthodox and Reformed Jews, and Levantine religious sects, family tribes, and militias.

None of the increasing nationalist problems and tensions much concerned the European courts (the Sublime Porte in Constantinople astride the Bosphorus thought of itself as European) or the elegant government of France's Second Republic. Toward the end of the nineteenth century these countries maintained the balance of power in Europe, and they did not believe that the status quo might be threatened. Nobody listened to the thinkers and the Cassandras, not to Charles Dickens, not to Emile Zola and

Anatole France, not to Tolstoy, Gogol and Dostoyevsky, and certainly not to Marx and Engels. But future generations of rulers throughout the twentieth century would not listen either, and they still refuse to listen to disturbing ideas.

The United States, barely a quarter century out of the crushing Civil War, was wholly remote from European problems, though the steady growth of the American population was fed by streams of European immigrants (five million arrived between 1880 and 1890, the record for a decade). Benjamin Harrison, a Republican, was elected President in 1888, and in 1890 the Congress passed the McKinley Tariff Act, designed to protect the nascent American industry from European competition.

Preparing to fulfill its own Manifest Destiny, the United States preferred to keep Europe at an arm's length, minding its own business, opening its West, and constructing railroads. This type of isolationism was to recur in American history in a much more accentuated form, and its subsequent manifestations should not have astonished the Europeans if they had observed moods and attitudes in the United States as Tocqueville had done in his time. After all, it was George Washington who first warned against foreign entanglements, and Americans followed his advice for a very long time. They may do so again.

III

A quarter century after the pleasant interlude of 1889, the First World War broke out in August 1914 as the first truly modern war and the first one to engage armies far from Europe. Australians and Canadians came to fight as members of the British Empire, and Gurkha and Sikh regiments were brought from India as imperial subjects. The French had colonial spahis and Zouaves. And the Yanks sailed "over there" in 1917 as Britain's and France's new allies in the war against the Central Powers.

It is possible to argue that the Great War need not have happened if all the rulers had kept their wits about them and their greed in check. Many respected historians take this view, enjoying the benefits of hindsight and access to most of the official archives.

British historian A. J. P. Taylor writes that both sides in World War I "found it difficult to define their war aims," conceding, however, that the answer to the question "What was the war about?" is: "to decide how Europe should be remade" and "to decide whether this remade Europe should continue." In retrospect, such vagueness by the contemporary rulers hardly justifies the four-year carnage of millions of combatants and civilians. There was no ideology of any kind at stake, and in Taylor's words, it was a war without heroes and without villains, fought mainly to determine "who's to be master." As such, the First World War inevitably had to lead to the Second World War.

As great wars go World War I lacked emotion, commitment, and purpose. Unlike the situation in World War II, when there were clearly defined moral causes to be defended by the Allies, no deep principles were involved in the 1914–18 affray.

The original Thirty Years War in the seventeenth century was over power, but it loomed primarily as a religious conflict between Catholic and Protestant kings and princes in the aftermath of the Reformation that shook Europe of that day. As another British historian put it, that religious war "was waged with the bitterness characteristic of such wars."

It is striking that religious wars and religion-related conflicts on a large and sustained scale have returned for the first time in three centuries to plague the world in the second half of the twentieth century. Today we find them in the Indian subcontinent (with terrifying clashes involving Hindus, Muslims, Buddhists, Sikhs, and Untouchables) as well as in Iran, Iraq, Afghanistan, much of the Middle East (Jews and Muslims in Israel and the Occupied Territories, Christians and Shiites in Lebanon, and Islamic sects among themselves), the Soviet Union (Christian Armenians and Muslim Azerbaijanis), and Indonesia and the Philippines (with Muslims facing Christians). In Northern Ireland the present phase of violence and death between Protestants and Catholics has gone on for twenty years, but the conflict's origins date back to the 1689 siege of Londonderry—three centuries ago—when Protestants successfully resisted King James II.

Likewise, religion—as represented by the deeply nationalistic Roman Catholic Church—has played a crucial and successful political role in the resistance against Marxism-Leninism in Poland. The Russian Orthodox Church reasserted itself in the Soviet Union under *perestroika*, seventy years after the atheistic Revolution, and one of the most startling sights I saw in Moscow in late 1988 was young people on Sundays filling the reopened churches, crossing themselves, praying on their knees, lighting candles, and joining in the singing of the beautiful, mystical hymns. In December 1989, Gorbachev called on Pope John Paul II at the Vatican.

It is, therefore, a major question for the nineties whether or not religion will help define the human condition in the technological age—perhaps as a reaction to excessive material progress and the erosion of faith. Islamic, Jewish, and Protestant fundamentalism has been markedly on the rise since the late sixties, and strict conservatism in Roman Catholic theology and observance of the dogma have been enforced by Pope John Paul II since his election in 1978. The church is already torn by increasing theological disputes and challenges to Vatican authority. The Kremlin fears a fundamentalist explosion among its huge Muslim populations, which never really accepted Marxism-Leninism. After the Soviet military defeat in Afghanistan the fundamentalism of the Muslim resistance fighters was rapidly spreading in that mountainous land situated between the Islamic influences in neighboring Iran and Pakistan. And Turkey, once the center of the Ottoman Empire, was witnessing a powerful Islamic revival. So was Egypt. Israel's President Chaim Herzog said to me late in 1989 that he was "horrified" by the attacks of Orthodox Jews—fundamentalists—on non-Jews. Both Muslim and Jewish fundamentalism, he believes, are frightful problems in the Middle East, not fully understood in the West.

Seventy-five years later it is still hard to understand why a world war broke out in 1914, even though it has been massively studied and analyzed by generations of historians.

These were the bare facts: Austrian Archduke Francis Ferdinand, the heir to the throne, and his morganatic wife, Sophie Chotek, were assassinated in Sarajevo in the Austro-Hungarian province of Bosnia on June 28, 1914, by a Serbian nationalist who supposedly belonged to a nationalist, anti-Hapsburg conspiracy. The assassination climaxed more than a half century of Balkan wars, resulting principally from the progressive loss of power in that region on the part of the Ottoman Empire and the rivalries among the newly created states there. The word "Balkanization," meaning the endless subdivisions of territories into smaller and smaller units, has its origin in these obscure wars. In 1914 Balkanization, quite insanely, plunged the rest of the world in a pointless war.

Vienna's reaction to the archduke's murder was to issue an ultimatum to the kingdom of Serbia, demanding apologies and amends. Serbia, an ancient nation that had only recently been liberated from Ottoman rule, deeply resented the Austro-Hungarian Empire's annexation of Bosnia and Herzegovina, an ex-Turkish province next door. Serbia was not about to humiliate itself before the Hapsburgs, and its reply to the ultimatum was not satisfactory to Vienna. The powerful empire had developed absolute paranoia over tiny Serbia, fearing that Serbian nationalist agitation endangered it in a fundamental fashion, and the Austrian-Hungarian response was to invade the Balkan kingdom late in July. Big powers tend to be paranoid about little countries that seem to defy them, as the United States has demonstrated in the Caribbean and Central America over most of the twentieth century, and the Soviet Union in Eastern Europe in the fifties and sixties.

When the Austrians invaded Serbia, all the European powers took leave of their senses in one of those extraordinary situations in which the rationality of statesmen becomes paralyzed and is replaced by blind opportunism. In Russia Czar Nicholas II mobilized his armies in support of Serbia, though he was not at all threatened. Germany's Kaiser William II reacted for his part by declaring war on Russia *and* France because a formal alliance existed between them (he ignored the fact that a decade earlier Nicholas had signed an alliance with him). The kaiser followed up his declaration by attacking neutral Belgium, an attack that in turn led Britain to declare war on the Germans. By August 4, 1914, the First World War was fully under way.

Though each of the powers had problems and aspirations in Europe and beyond—the early nineteenth century was a time of colonial appetites and overseas consolidations by the French, British, Germans, Italians, Belgians, and the Dutch—none even remotely justified a major war. In fact, Europe was quite peaceful at the outset of the twentieth century except for the Balkan wars of limited importance. A failed leftist revolution in Russia in 1905 and the czar's simultaneous defeat in a war with Japan were not perceived as *European* events that could affect the sacred balance of power.

The late Oscar Halecki, one of the outstanding specialists in Central European history, summed up quite accurately the origins of World War I when he wrote that the archduke's murder "necessarily provoked a dangerous diplomatic conflict, but a conflict which for both sides was rather a question of prestige than an issue of nationalism and which did not necessarily have to lead to a war and certainly not to a European or world war." But once everybody's prestige had become engaged in this absurd war, there was no stopping it until the conflict had run its military and political course. By then both the aims and the results of the 1914 folly had become dramatically altered in ways nobody could have possibly foreseen. Without this war the Russian Revolution probably would not have occurred when it did and in the manner it did (Leninist theologians cannot prove the contrary).

In any case, the start of the Great War provided an excellent demonstration of the fact that wars have a way of getting out of hand and that it is easier to get into a war than to get out. Unfortunately this verity was forgotten when the year 1939 rolled around and, again, in the postwar era, as America would discover in Vietnam and the Russians in Afghanistan.

Militarily the First World War brought great innovations—the foretaste of modern, mechanized combat—with the principal technological contributions supplied by the Germans and the British. The internal-combustion engine had been invented well before the end of the old century, and the first airplanes flew in the opening years of the new one. All these technical advances were promptly placed at the service of warfare—as had always happened in the past and would happen in the future.

At sea both Germany and Britain were equipped with submarines, a wholly new weapon in a new dimension of war, and they were used effectively against warships as well as against merchantmen. Naturally both nations had battleship fleets engaging in fierce encounters.

In the air the British, the French, the Germans, and then the Americans introduced the combat flying machine, an invention barely ten years old in the operational sense, and European battlefields hummed with the noise of the biplanes' engines overhead. The United States started late, with the National Advisory Committee for Aeronautics (NACA) and its first laboratory established at Langley Field in northern Virginia only in 1915, but it caught up quickly with friend and foe. Air combat also inaugurated a new romantic tradition in warfare: aces like Eddie Rickenbacker, Blue Max, the Red Baron, and so on. The Germans built dirigibles as the first long-range aerial weapons, and their zeppelins managed to bomb London several times. (My late mother, then in her teens, never forgot the fear of death coming down from the night sky during the family's wartime stay in England; a generation later, of course, London learned to live with the Nazi blitz.)

On the ground, in addition to various types of artillery fielded by all combatants (the Germans came up with Krupp's "Big Bertha," which hurled heavy projectiles farther than any existing cannon), armored vehicles that became known as tanks made their baptismal appearance on the European battlefields. Tanks were a British innovation, and interestingly it was Winston Churchill who became the principal advocate of tank development, though at the time he was first lord of the admiralty, not a War Office leader responsible for the army. The idea had been presented to him on October 14, 1914, and it remained Britain's greatest wartime secret until it first appeared in France on September 15, 1916. This marked the birth of Churchill's lifetime love affair with military technology, reaching the apex during his prime ministership in World War II. At the same time all the armies already had trucks, command cars, and automotive ambulances. Radio and the field telephone provided a new flexibility and speed in communications.

Technology, however, could not yet win a war alone. On the western front the kaiser was dealt the deathblow by the Allied armies fighting conventional land warfare—infantry and artillery—after millions on both sides were killed in the mass confrontations of the Marne, Verdun, and Ypres (where the Germans used poisonous gas for the first time in the history of war), the three battles of the Somme, and the slow agony of the trenches. On the eastern front the Germans beat the Russians in 1917, setting the stage for the Russian Revolution, and kept fighting in the West for another year until the capitulation on November 11, 1918.

Nevertheless, the Great War provided stimulus and funds for scientific research, inaugurating on both sides the concept of government-financed research in technology. And everything engineers and scientists learned from the performance of the biplanes and the dirigibles was rapidly applied to peacetime uses, accelerating very considerably the development of civil aviation in the world. The same happened with the automotive industry and radio and telephone communications; sadly wars were the great laboratories of human progress. And inevitably the same scientists and designers, especially in Germany, wasted no time in harnessing the lessons of the Great War to start arming for a still greater war.

* * *

Geographically and politically the map of the world was vastly transformed by the outcome of the First World War. Four empires—the German, the Austro-Hungarian, the Russian, and the Ottoman—simply disappeared. And the British Empire was weaker than at any time since Victoria had begun building it.

The defeated Germany turned into a chaotic, poverty-stricken republic. It lost permanently the territories it ruled in Poland since the 1795 partition as well as Alsace-Lorraine, which reverted to France (which had lost it in 1871). The coal-rich Saar and Rhineland were administered by the French as demilitarized areas. Germany also surrendered its African colonies.

From the ruins of the Austro-Hungarian Empire, there emerged the separate states of Austria and Hungary and the new nations of Poland, Czechoslovakia, and Yugoslavia (Serbia became part of Yugoslavia and remains in 1989 as much of a nationalist problem for its partners and neighbors as it was in 1914; now Serbian, Croatian and Slovene, and Serbian and Albanian nationalists are at each other's throats). Italy, which had been on the victorious side, reclaimed from Austria its northern lands, including the cities of Venice and Trieste. Russia lost the Polish territories it had dominated since the eighteenth century and the Baltic states of Latvia, Estonia, and Lithuania, which won independence. The Ottoman Empire shrank to the size of present-day Turkey; Britain took over most of its Middle East and Asian territories under an international mandate.

One school of historical thought maintains that the redesign of Europe at Paris—including the creation of Poland and Czechoslovakia demanded in President Woodrow Wilson's Fourteen Points and accepted by the European Allies, who might have been defeated without American assistance—was faulty and artificial, leading directly to the Second World War. However, this view is not at all convincing. Poland, Czechoslovakia, and Yugoslavia certainly made more sense as sovereign nations (although only Poland had been a full-fledged nation over long centuries before the partitions) than as appendages of obsolete empires or their successor states.

The truly grievous error at Paris was to invent the free city status for the port of Danzig (Gdańsk in Polish) on the Baltic and to place it under a high commissioner named by the League of Nations, the peacekeeping organization established by the Allies as the first experiment in international collective security. This was a preposterous compromise in lieu of granting the port city to either Poland or Germany, both of which claimed it.

A related absurdity was to give Poland access to the sea through a narrow Polish Corridor that divided Germany from East Prussia, a German province. Naturally Danzig and the corridor turned in time into proximate reasons for a new world war because such compromises never work. That this war happened at all in 1939, was, however, the result of the victorious Allies' inability to coordinate their policies over twenty years, in either domestic or international politics and actions.

* * *

The most significant single reality to face the world after the Great War was the 1917 Russian Revolution and the subsequent emergence of the Soviet Union as a completely unprecedented presence in international life. Sir Isaiah Berlin, the distinguished English philosopher, long regarded the Russian Revolution as the most important event of the twentieth century because of its vast consequences. The late eighties, of course, signaled the end of the Marxist-Leninist cycle.

Specifically, the first crucial moment in Soviet history came when Lenin and his Bolsheviks abolished the elected constituent assembly in 1918, launching the seven terrible decades of the "dictatorship of the proletariat." That was the Soviet Union's first and only free election until March 1989, when Mikhail Gorbachev presided over multicandidate balloting for the newly created 2,225-member Congress of People's Deputies. No longer a Leninist rubber stamp, the Congress instantly turned into a rousing political battlefield between Gorbachev and his conservative as well as radical critics. The 542-member Supreme Soviet, now the legislative upper chamber, asserted itself by rejecting many regime-proposed laws as unconstitutional.

Moreover, Lenin did not believe that the Communist Revolution should be confined to the Soviet Union. Marx had visualized a revolution based on the proletariat in industrial Central and Western Europe (this was the "scientific" cornerstone of his philosophy), and Lenin was determined to transport the "Flame of the Revolution" to war-ravaged Germany as soon as possible.

The new Poland, however, was in the way, and the Red Army that Lenin and Leon Trotsky had organized from the remnants of the czarist armies and from workers and peasants was dispatched to invade Polish territories early in 1919, the continuing civil war inside the Soviet Union and Western interventionist expeditions notwithstanding. Poland was a priority. But the seesawing 1918–20 conflict ended with the Soviet defeat at the gates of Warsaw (where the Poles were advised by American, French, and British officers, including Major Douglas MacArthur), and many European historians think that it was one of the decisive battles of the century in the sense that for the next 25 years communism was kept back behind Soviet frontiers.

Despite the Polish victory, this war played a fundamental role in fostering powerful anti-Communist sentiments in much of Europe. In general, the phenomenon of the Communist Soviet Union was one of the most fundamental elements in European politics between the world wars, as it was to be again after 1945. It inevitably affected both Western and Soviet decision making all the way up to the final days before September 1, 1939.

Only recently, under the *glasnost* practices instituted by President Gorbachev, historical materials that show whether Stalin's policies were designed to trigger or deter the Second World War and whether he, too, blundered into disaster are beginning to surface. Among these materials are the secret protocols of the 1939 Soviet-Nazi pact providing for the joint dismemberment of Poland and the incorporation of the Baltic states in the Soviet Union. The first secret protocol declared: "In the event of a territorial and political rearrangement of the areas belonging to the Polish state, the spheres of influence of Germany and the U.S.S.R. shall be bounded approximately by the line of the rivers Narew, Vistula and San." And Poland's "fourth partition" was exactly what happened when the Soviets invaded her on September 17, 1939.

IV

The summer of 1939 was one of the most gorgeous in memory. In Europe and the United States the weather was spectacular from late spring, and as vacation time came, hordes of pale city dwellers invaded seaside and mountain resorts and hideaways everywhere. The mood was singularly upbeat and almost celebratory, and people seemed determined to enjoy themselves hugely that summer—no matter what it took.

For those who lived it and later survived to be able to remember the vacations of 1939, it was an unforgettable interlude. For others, it was a magnificent farewell.

In Paris President Albert Lebrun (a political figurehead under the Third Republic), Premier Édouard Daladier (who was responsible for his nation's fate), and France's famous military chiefs—General Maurice Gamelin and General Maxime Weygand, who had learned their craft in the Great War and who doubted that concepts of the battlefield had changed all that much in twenty years—reviewed the Bastille Day parade along the Champs Élysées on July 14. For hours metropolitan infantry and artillery regiments, the tough Foreign Legion, and spahi horsemen from the African colonies excited the crowds along the broad avenue with their martial bearing and the beat of their bands. (As a thirteen-year-old boy I watched the parade with my mother, and a half century later I still remember it with a frisson; it was inconceivable that this fantastic army could disintegrate overnight.)

Absent from the celebrations, however, was Colonel Charles de Gaulle, the forty-nine-year-old commander of an armored regiment who was already famous as "Colonel Motor" because of the obsessive advocacy of tank warfare he first outlined in his book *The Advent of the Mechanical Force*. The top generals, like Gamelin and Weygand, ridiculed De Gaulle's theories, though they were happy to let him command one of France's few armored units. There was no need, however, to invite him to the Paris parade.

In Cannes, the jewel of the French Riviera, the summer of 1939 was a glorious season. *Everybody* was there. Private yachts were anchored in front of the Carlton Hotel on La Croisette, and men donned white dinner jackets to accompany their wives or mistresses to the exclusive Palm Beach Casino. The popular Sir Alfred Duff Cooper, who had resigned the previous autumn as first lord of the admiralty in protest against Prime Minister Neville Chamberlain's appeasement policies toward Hitler, and his supremely elegant wife, Lady Diana, ruled over Cannes's social set. From most European capitals, Hispano-Suiza, Bentley, Mercedes-Benz, Fiat, and Bugatti sports cars converged on Monte Carlo nearby for the annual Automotive Star Rally.

In Rolle, on the shore of Lake Geneva in Switzerland, the school year was ending at Le Rosey, the School of Kings, as it was called, with a sports festival for the 120 departing boys and their families, among them Rainier, the future prince of Monaco; the Hohenlohe twins of the Liechtenstein ruling family; the youngest sons of Persia's shah-in-shah (the eldest son, Reza Pahlavi, who would soon become emperor, had graduated earlier from the school); the sons of Middle Eastern potentates, British peers, and American millionaires. At the regal Beau-Rivage Hotel on the lakeside in Lausanne, even thirteen-year-old boys had to dress in black tie at dinner when they spent the night there with their parents en route home from Le Rosey. They saw no dark clouds on the horizon either.

In London those were happy days. Harold Nicolson, one of Britain's most outstanding diplomats and at the time a member of Parliament, described in his diary late in June the visit by King George VI and Queen Elizabeth to Parliament Square: "We lost all our dignity and yelled and yelled. The King wore a happy schoolboy grin. The Queen was superb . . . she is in truth one of the most amazing Queens since Cleopatra."

In July Nicolson went to the Soviet Embassy to have tea "and find a strange collection of leftwing enthusiasts sitting around the Winter Garden with a huge tea table spread with delicious cakes and caviar sandwiches, plus a samovar." Nicolson presumably did not know then that a number of young men among his close social acquaintances were secret members of the Communist party and already operated as spies for the Soviet Union. Harold Adrian Russell "Kim" Philby, who later rose to the top ranks of the British Secret Intelligence Service and finally fled to Moscow, had been spying since 1934, along with his friends Guy Burgess, Donald Maclean, and Anthony Blunt. They were idealists who believed that communism was the only answer to appeasement and to the social ills of the British system. Then, in August, Nicolson sailed for France, exclaiming in his diary, "How gay and happy we were!" And Noel Coward was completing a new play. The only depressing note was the news of the death of William Butler Yeats, one of the greatest English-language poets of the century, at his home at Cap-Martin in the south of France.

In Warsaw there was still no fear of war, notwithstanding Hitler's growing power and his daily threats to seize Danzig and the Polish Corridor in order to "protect" German populations there (as he had done in Austria and Czechoslovakia). Poland's regime had lulled itself into a false and foolish sense of security, choosing to believe that the Nazis would respect their 1934 nonaggression pact (the Germans had allowed the Poles to help themselves to a slice of Czech territory when they liquidated Czechoslovakia) and thereby leading the people into insouciance during the glorious summer of 1939. Incredibly Poland went on selling its excellent Loś (Deer) light bombers in foreign markets, including faraway Brazil, instead of keeping them at home for defense. (My father, then a Polish government official, was in charge of the bomber sales to Brazil.) Warsaw's elite vacationed at the Polish Baltic resort of Jurata or at mountain chalets around Zakopane in the Tatras. To the peasant families in their miserable huts in the Polesie swamps in eastern Poland, the summer meant simply the onset of harvest. But nobody was afraid of the Nazis; the peasants had barely heard of them in that Polish countryside preradio age of illiteracy.

In Moscow Russians were beginning to recover from the shock of the savage purges that Stalin had carried out between 1936 and 1938, when most of the old Bolshevik leaders were executed on trumped-up treason charges—as was Marshal Mikhail Tukhachevsky, the army chief of staff—and millions of citizens were rounded up and deported to Siberia. What made the Soviet summer of 1939 especially pleasant was essentially the end of the terror; the shortages and low living standards were facts of life the people had learned to accept in the twenty years since the October Revolution. Although the Soviet Union had become the world's second industrial power, the blessings of modernization were not reaching the citizenry; steel plants, dams, and cannons, not consumer goods, were the priority. And in these waning months of peace only Stalin knew where he was taking the Soviet Union; he was plotting in the shadows.

In Berlin, naturally, it was a euphoric summer. The Western powers had dared not interfere with the Führer's grand scheme of European expansion in past years, and now Hitler stood at the apex of his glory. He seemed unstoppable. And for the Germans, life had never been better. Unemployment, which stood at seven million when Hitler was named chancellor in 1933 by the senile President Paul von Hindenburg (Hitler did not capture power, as is widely believed, but received it legally because he commanded a parliamentary majority), was virtually zero in 1939. Hundreds of thousands of young German boys and girls from the Hitler Jugend bronzed themselves in summer camps from the North Sea to Bavaria. If Germans knew about the other camps, the concentration camps filled with Jews and other supposed enemies of the Reich, they were not talking about them. Fear of the black-uniformed SS men and the sinister civilians working for the Gestapo pervaded the country, and Germans just minded their business—and enjoyed the summer of 1939.

In the United States the nation was finally beginning to emerge from the drama of the Great Depression. The wave of the new American optimism was symbolized by the New York World's Fair—"The World of Tomorrow"—which had opened in March and had greeted twenty million people by late summer. The fair was the foretaste of the future ("I Have Seen the Future," the fair's lapel buttons proclaimed), displaying a RCA television set (the first TV signal in the United States was transmitted in 1936, but commercial broadcasting did not start until July 1941), a Westinghouse electric dishwasher (that was to go on sale the following year), and primitive robots. "Futurama" was the most popular exhibit, showing visitors a vision of what America would be in the faraway 1960's. It also was a golden year for Hollywood with the premieres of *Gone with the Wind* and *The Wizard of Oz*. At Saratoga Springs there were splendid Saturday parties during the racing season. And John Steinbeck, who later won the Nobel Prize for literature, published *The Grapes of Wrath*, a counterpoint to the prevailing national mood of renascent happiness.

So Americans were not eager to hear about European quarrels and politics—and certainly not about the possibility of a war into which they might be drawn as they had been in 1917. Isolationism was strong in the United States, and President Franklin D. Roosevelt, who understood perfectly the dangers posed by Hitler, failed in July to persuade the Senate that time had come to repeal or amend the Neutrality Act, which forbade military assistance to foreign countries at war. The act was to prevent the United States from helping France and Britain when the conflict broke out fewer than two months later.

Senator William E. Borah declared that "there will be no war this year," and even a summer visit to Washington by King George and Queen Elizabeth could not instill a sense of urgency in Americans about the fate of Europe. Joseph P. Kennedy, the isolationist-minded American ambassador in London, appealed to Hollywood moviemakers (many of them Jewish) to stop producing anti-Nazi films because they irritated Hitler and could turn him against possible peace negotiations with the West.

V

But Hitler was not interested in negotiations. He chose war—or perhaps he blundered into it—rather than a peaceful settlement for the latest crisis he had created that conceivably could have been ironed out through international diplomacy. We still do not really know why he took this decision.

By ordering the blitzkrieg against Poland on that first day of September 1939, Hitler compounded his catastrophic errors of judgment by assuming that Britain and France would fail to honor their commitments to the Poles. When they did fulfill their pledge forty-eight hours later by declaring war on Germany, he found himself with a world conflict on his hands, one for which he was not really militarily prepared at that moment. It appears entirely possible, in hindsight, that the Second World War was avoidable, just as was the First World War, and an understanding of the events leading to its outbreak is extremely relevant in terms of interpreting history after 1945 and preventing a third world war.

A.J.P. Taylor, the Oxford historian, was correct in affirming that "the Second World War grew out of the victories in the first, and out of the way in which these victories were used." Although the Germans claimed that their aggressiveness after Hitler's rise to power in 1933 was revenge for the harsh terms imposed on them in the Versailles Peace Treaty—especially the amount of reparations their defeated country was to pay the victors—in the end the Western powers were responsible for making this resurgent militarism possible. And from the very outset the Soviet Union helped the Germans to get back on their feet after Versailles—to fight it and the West another day. Indeed, the Soviet role between the wars is immensely fascinating.

Allied Great War victories were appallingly misused when it came to assuring a lasting peace because no sooner was the Versailles Treaty signed than the Western powers went their separate ways. In Washington the Senate vetoed American membership in the newly created League of Nations despite President Wilson's insistence that having decisively participated in the war in Europe, the United States should remain in Europe to aid in guaranteeing peace. This was the birth of American isolationism, which characterized the interwar years. The Pact for the Renunciation of War, signed by Secretary of State Frank B. Kellogg and French Foreign Minister Aristide Briand in 1928, was no more than a pious exhortation for peace, with no American commitment to enforce its observance.

At the same time U.S. business interests contributed to the reconstruction of Germany and its rearmament. The so-called Dawes Plan of 1924 greatly reduced German reparations payments and supplied public and private loans. The Young Plan in 1929 further diminished German payments, and the subsequent Lausanne Agreement canceled 95 percent of the debt. Alleviating German economic—and human—suffering naturally made sense, especially after the failed Communist revolution in November 1918, but the tragedy was that in economic as well as political matters the Allies had pulled apart.

Washington was proceeding unilaterally on the debt. France and Britain were supposed to be the "trustees" for Europe, in the word of a contemporary commentator, but they quickly became rivals for European political dominance, thereby inviting both Germany and the Soviet Union to take advantage of the situation. As Harold Nicolson put it, the subsequent disasters were "the harvest of weakness" of the Allied powers.

As Europe's pariahs, Germany and the Soviet Union concluded that misery loves company, and their foreign ministers signed on Easter Sunday 1922 a pact of friendship at Rapallo, Italy. Until Hitler ended it in 1933, Germany and the Soviets enjoyed an enormously profitable secret military relationship, incredible as it may seem in retrospect. In violation of Versailles Treaty provisions against rearmament, German officers trained in armor warfare and aviation in the Soviet Union while other German specialists assisted the Russians in building a defense industry. For a decade the two armies conducted joint war games and staff exercises, which prepared them to fight each other in the 1940's. Unbelievably the West was either unaware of these activities or unwilling to interfere.

Overall the Western penchant was to look the other way as Hitler—as well as his Italian Fascist partner, Benito Mussolini, and the distant imperial Japan—did as they pleased in Europe and Asia.

Actually it was Japan, about which the West thought precious little in those days, that moved first in the direction of war, invading Manchuria, a part of China, in September 1931 and following it up with a full-fledged invasion of the Chinese territory in 1937. Hitler, who evidently had more vision than the Western leaders, invented the Anti-Comintern Pact and had Japan sign it with him in 1936. It was simply a declaration against communism, providing for no action by either side, but it was widely interpreted as a solid anti-Soviet alliance. That same year Hitler and Mussolini formalized *their* alliance by creating the Berlin-Rome Axis. The West maintained a decorous silence on all these subjects although the world's militaristic bullies were organizing themselves for acts of defiance that would succeed each other until the final blunder in 1939.

Hitler took his first aggressive step as early as January 1935, obtaining a plebiscite to determine the future of the Saar, the rich territory administered by France since Versailles. Ninety percent of the population voted in free elections to be reunited with Germany, and Hitler took it as a signal to proceed with his carefully elaborated plan for the "Thousand-Year Reich."

In October 1935 Mussolini invaded Abyssinia (the ancient African kingdom now known as Ethiopia) to expand the Italian colonial empire and, probably much more important, to enhance the international importance of his dictatorial state. There was no particular reason for Italy to go to war in Africa at that exact moment, but Il Duce was determined to have action. By May 1, 1936, he had achieved victory over the tribal armies of Emperor Haile Selassie, surely the most pathetic figure of his time. The emperor's terrible disenchantment and sadness were that the civilized world did not really care much, the rhetoric notwithstanding, about powerful nations invading weak ones—a state of affairs that remained essentially unchanged a half century later.

The year 1936 marked the end of the postwar period and the start of the prewar period.

With the West's inability, or unwillingness, to use the fifty-two-member League of Nations as an instrument to force Italy to halt the invasion of Abyssinia—the League had not decided anything beyond a cutoff of oil supplies to Mussolini—the system of collective security simply collapsed. Hilter, who had already taken Germany out of the League, took advantage of the disarray by occupying, on March 7, the Rhineland region, demilitarized by the Allies in 1919. If France had reacted militarily against this move, the Germans most likely would have been beaten because their armed forces were far from ready for war.

But Hitler gambled successfully that the decadent West would not resist, and this spelled the farewell to Versailles. It also did away with the cherished illusion that the Western "great powers" had a real say in the destinies of the world. They had no say when civil war erupted in Spain on July 18, 1936, and both Italy and Germany dispatched troops and aircraft to fight on the side of Francisco Franco's Nationalists against the leftist Republican government. Pablo Picasso conveyed the new horror of Nazi precision air bombardment in his "Guernica" mural, one of the great symbols of war in our time.

The Soviet Union provided military equipment to the Republicans and helped organize the International Brigades, composed of left-leaning volunteers from Europe and the United States. In this sense the Spanish Civil War became the prelude to the approaching world war, militarily as well as ideologically and emotionally. And it brought sharply to the fore in the West acute anti-Bolshevik sentiments that dated back to the Russian Revolution and would help mold the Cold War after 1945.

Now Hitler knew he had the upper hand in Europe. He was certain the West would not challenge him, and he became convinced that combining patience with bluff, he would attain his objectives of making Germany the leading power in continental Europe and of wielding worldwide influence. In the meantime, the Nazis' first priority was to achieve invincible armed might, and by 1938, 17 percent of Germany's total industrial production was war-related (compared with 7 percent in France and Britain).

On March 12, 1938, German troops entered Austria to incorporate it into the Reich. That was the Anschluss, a word that has ominously entered history, and Hitler carried it out as the climax of intricate political maneuvers designed to abolish Austrian independence. Hitler's motivation was German nationalism—though he was born in Austria, he always thought in terms of "Greater Germany"—and his desire to expand the borders of the Reich, east and west, to "bring home" all German-speaking populations. Additional considerations included the lengthening of the German frontier with Czechoslovakia (German troops now stood along the old Czech-Austrian border) to facilitate the next step Hitler was preparing to take in Europe and the creation of a common border between Germany and Italy at the Brenner Pass in southern Austria. (Hitler never fully trusted Mussolini.)

Hitler was cheered by millions of deliriously happy Austrians (the Anschluss was not resisted by a single patriot), raising the subtle question of whether Austria was Germany's first victim, first ally, or both. It is a question that has not been answered to everybody's full satisfaction to this day. The whole painful issue was reopened in the eighties, when Kurt Waldheim, the former secretary-general of the United Nations, was elected president of Austria despite disclosures at that time that he had served with Nazi military intelligence units as an officer during the campaign against Yugoslav partisans (a fact Waldheim had long concealed). In any event, Vienna ceased in 1938 being a traditional cultural, artistic, and scientific center in Europe (it had been the home of Sigmund Freud and a brilliant generation of psychiatrists, psychoanalysts, writers, and composers), shrinking to the status of a German provincial city.

One of the Nazis' first undertakings in Vienna was to arrest, deport, and often murder the overwhelming majority of Jews living in the capital who were unable to flee in time. Vienna's Jewish population in 1938 was 182,000; in 1988 it was 6,400. Even so, anti-Semitism survives in Vienna today (a famous Israeli actress, returning there for the first time since she escaped as a little girl with her family and going to the building where she was born, was asked by the elderly woman janitor, "So, how did you escape the furnace?"). Imperial nostalgia survives, too. The coffin of Empress Zita, the widow of Karl, the last Hapsburg emperor, was carried ceremoniously on a hearse drawn by six black horses after she died in 1989 at the age of ninety-six.

Six months after the Anschluss, Hitler was again on the offensive and the Western democracies again on the defensive. This time the issue was the large German minority in the Sudeten region of Czechoslovakia that Hitler believed should be part of "Greater Germany." Though Czechoslovakia had an alliance with France and the Soviet Union (and the French expected British backing in case of war), in reality it had nothing to count on. France was frankly hesitant about its obligations while Britain openly sided with the Germans on the Sudetenland. Besides, Prime Minister Chamberlain, an old-fashioned and strikingly naive person, was convinced that Hitler would not be a threat to European peace if he had his way on the Sudeten; the Führer had impressed Chamberlain with his sincerity in the course of several visits the Englishman paid during September as the crisis escalated. In short, Paris and London prayed for a Czechoslovak capitulation.

Men are entitled to believe what they wish, but in Chamberlain's case it was a matter of disposing cavalierly of another nation's fate. He was easily able to persuade French Premier Édouard Daladier, likewise a weak man (of whom Harold Nicolson wrote, "he looks like a drunken peasant"), to participate in this exercise in appeasement, and the die was cast. Mussolini suddenly surfaced as a mediator, and on September 30 the three men met with Hitler in Munich to sign away Czechoslovakia's sovereignty. Chamberlain flew home to deliver—proudly—one of the most humiliating and misleading lines in modern times: "I believe it is peace for our time." And "Munich" is a word that, too, lives in infamy.

In the spring of 1939 the Axis was once more leading the assault on peace. On March 15 the Nazis occupied Prague, dismembering Czechoslovakia altogether and putting an end to its twenty-year existence as the only true democracy in Central and Eastern Europe. On March 23 Hitler struck in the northeast, annexing the port of Memel on the Baltic; it belonged to Lithuania but was conveniently adjacent to Germany's East Prussia lands. On March 28 Madrid fell to the Nationalists, and the Republican armies surrendered on April 2, writing finis to the Spanish Civil War. On April 7 Mussolini attacked and captured Albania, the small mountain kingdom on the eastern shores of the Adriatic.

By late spring and early summer, as Europe lapsed into the somnolence of the vacation months, Hitler turned his full attention to Poland. Despite their nonaggression pact and the Polish semifascist regime's care not to criticize Nazi aggressions all around Poland, the Germans now demanded Danzig and the Polish Corridor, making it clear that they would tolerate no opposition.

Hitler further strengthened his position with the signature in Moscow on August 23 of the nonaggression pact between Germany and the Soviet Union, one of the most stunning diplomatic feats between the wars. The pact neutralized the Soviets in the event of a war between Germany and Poland—Warsaw now knew it could not count on Soviet aid if Poland were attacked—and it virtually assured that with a little extra patience Hitler would gain his Polish goals without recourse to arms. At that stage France and Britain could no longer seriously interfere with Nazi plotting. The British guarantee to Poland, which resulted in Britain and France jointly declaring war on Germany forty-eight hours after the September 1 invasion, evidently was not taken seriously by the Führer.

Thus the mystery persists a half century later over his decision to invade Poland and risk a world war instead of waiting, as he had in the past, for one more easy triumph. In fact, Hitler broke off negotiations pushed by the West that looked most promising for him. Did he blunder into the war?

It is pointless, of course, to hypothetize over the course history might have taken if Hitler had committed no blunders and had not started the Second World War. It is most illuminating, however, to take a fresh look at the patterns of Soviet decision making in the years preceding the war because they throw significant light on *Russian* interests and attitudes in general and are therefore pertinent to the future in the nineties and beyond.

What is remarkable about Russian history and policies is their essential consistency over the centuries. Since the advent of *glasnost* in the Soviet Union under Gorbachev, enough new historical material has appeared to confirm the notion that regardless of system and ideology, Moscow is always first and foremost concerned with Russian security vis-à-vis the outside world. In this sense the Russians tend to act defensively—unlike Germany since Frederick the Great—even if their postures occasionally acquire the most extraordinary and contradictory aspects.

Signing the pact with Hitler was not that much of a historical departure for the Russians, sensational as a deal between Nazis and Communists, long-sworn enemies, may have loomed at the moment. The Russians were allied with the Germans in the eighteenth century (to partition Poland), in the nineteenth century (to resist the European wave of liberalism), and immediately after Versailles, at Rapallo, to help each other rebuild militarily after their respective Great War defeats. In August 1939 Stalin was prepared to sacrifice temporarily his Marxist-Leninist ideological purity (such as it was) in order to create a buffer between Russia and Germany by annexing the eastern half of Poland in the third week of the war under the clauses of the new pact.

The Ribbentrop-Molotov pact included a secret additional protocol outlining the proposed division of Poland and the Baltic states; three supplementary protocols were signed over the next two years. The original secret protocol established that "in the event of a territorial and political transformation in the territories belonging to the Baltic States (Finland, Estonia, Latvia, Lithuania), the northern frontier of Lithuania shall represent the frontier of the spheres of interest both of Germany and the U.S.S.R." A glance at the map indicates that Lithuania's northern border is also Latvia's *southern* border; thus both sides had agreed that Latvia, Estonia, and Finland would be absorbed by the Soviets. The ultimate fate of Lithuania was left open in the first secret protocol, as was the question of whether "the maintenance of an independent Polish state" would be "desirable." In the meantime, the protocol drew the dividing line in Poland between the German and Soviet "spheres of interest." Finally, the Soviets expressed their "interest" in Bessarabia (the Romanian province annexed by Moscow after the war and renamed Moldavia), and the Germans said they had none there.

A secret supplementary protocol was signed in Moscow on September 28, 1939, almost a month after the start of the war and after the grab by the Germans and the Soviets of western and eastern Poland, placing Lithuania in the Soviet "sphere of interest." In exchange, the Germans kept the Lublin district of eastern Poland. An additional secret protocol on October 4, 1939, defined precisely the Soviet-German border in Poland. Finally, a secret protocol, signed on January 10, 1941, six months before the Nazi invasion of the Soviet Union, declared Germany's renunciation of claims over Lithuania in exchange for a Soviet payment of 7.5 million gold dollars.

In 1939 the Soviets invaded Finland in the Winter War, and in 1940 Soviet armies occupied Estonia, Latvia, and Lithuania. John C. Wiley, my late uncle who then served as American minister to Estonia and Latvia, remembered bidding farewell at the Riga railroad station to the president of Latvia, Karlis Ulmanis, and his top aides as they boarded a train for Moscow, supposedly for Kremlin conferences. They were never again seen alive. Shortly thereafter the Soviets began deporting hundreds of thousands of Baltic states citizens and replacing them with Russian families. This was colonizing the Baltic nations as part of the Soviets' long-range defense preparations.

Stalin presumably realized that sooner or later the Nazis would attack the Soviet Union simply because they could not coexist in a Europe where there was room for only one preeminent power. He must have reasoned that the Russians could defend themselves more effectively if eastern Poland, the Baltic states, and eastern Finland were a barrier Nazi forces would have to traverse to reach Soviet territory.

Stalin went about erecting the bulwarks with his usual, limitless brutality. Millions of Lithuanians, Latvians, and Estonians were deported to Soviet Asia to serve as slave labor and, often, to die there because he did not wish to have anti-Communist populations undermining Soviet security in the new buffer areas. The term "genocide," meaning the deliberate destruction of a race or a nation, was first applied to the eradication of the Baltic nations, then to the Jewish Holocaust at the hands of the Nazis. Yet these Baltic nations were not really eradicated. In spite of the mass deportations and the transfer of Russian populations to their territories, Estonian, Latvian, and Lithuanian identities, languages, and culture survived in an astonishing fashion to demand a half century later virtual autonomy within the Soviet system—if not outright independence.

Stalin applied similar methods to the Poles, more than a million of whom were deported to Central Asia and Siberia. This included Wojciech Jaruzelski, whose parents died in a Soviet labor camp and who fifty years later entered history as the first Communist leader to share power voluntarily with the democratic opposition. Jaruzelski does not hide his parents' fate, allowing one to speculate what impelled him to take his historic course. In the forests of Katyń, a village near Smolensk in Byelorussia, nearly fifteen thousand Polish Army officers, captured in September 1939 and deported east, were executed by Soviet security units because they were thought to be anti-Communist. For forty-five years Soviet and Polish Communist regimes insisted that the mass murders were committed by the Nazis after they invaded Russia and that the charges against the Soviets were hostile Western propaganda. Only in 1989, under Gorbachev's *glasnost*, did the Kremlin admit that the Polish officers were assassinated on Stalin's orders.

Documents newly released in Moscow also disclosed—and there is no reason to doubt their authenticity—that the Soviet Union was ready to go to war with Germany in defense of Czechoslovakia in both 1938 and 1939 if the French and the British had lived up to their guarantees and if Poland had agreed to let Soviet troops cross its territory (the Poles refused even to discuss the topic).

During the 1939 Polish crisis, Soviet historians now say, Stalin was still prepared to move against Hitler in concert with the Western powers. However, when military talks between Moscow and London and Paris collapsed on August 17, and when Poland refused a military alliance with the Soviet Union, Stalin evidently concluded that his only remaining option was a pact with the Nazis. This version is generally consistent with the findings by Western historians in recent years.

The Germans, who closely watched Western contacts with the Russians, had simultaneously decided that *their* needs would best be met by a tactical arrangement with the Kremlin. That same week they sent their first secret message to Stalin to emphasize that "there exist no real conflicts of interests between Germany and Russia." Hitler's move obviously stemmed from the decision he had already taken to go to war against Poland and from his calculation that the Soviets would choose not to oppose him. With such convergences of interests, the Soviet-Nazi pact was signed on August 23, six days after the end of military discussions between the Russians and the Western Allies.

The Second World War erupted eight days later. Having taken out his Soviet insurance policy, Hitler felt free to fight rather than negotiate. Still, we do not know why he chose war.

VI

Germany invaded Poland on September 1, 1939, and France and Britain declared war on Hitler on September 3, finally realizing that appeasement had become suicidal. Now we know, however, that none of the parties was actually ready for war militarily, and this was the reason for the extraordinary effort launched on all sides to create whole new technologies in order to triumph in the conflict that nobody had needed.

Though France and Britain spent limited funds on defense during the 1930's—their governments faced controversial choices between expenditures on social programs and military modernization—they were not weaker than Germany in armed strength. A.J.P. Taylor writes that "even in 1939 the German army was not equipped for a prolonged war; and in 1940 the German land forces were inferior to the French in everything except leadership." He adds that in 1940 "the Germans won a decisive victory without great superiority in either manpower or equipment" and that "the French campaign proved nothing except that even armies adequately prepared for defense can be destroyed if they are led badly enough."

(The United States relearned the lesson about leadership in Vietnam more than three decades later, as the Soviet Union did in Afghanistan in the eighties, and, even more ironically, as the Vietnamese did during *their* ten-year war against Cambodia, following the 1979 invasion of their Communist Indochina neighbor. All three had to pull out: the United States in 1973, the Soviets and the Vietnamese in 1989).

In Europe, as it turned out, equality of arms was not relevant when World War II erupted. The French were content to hide behind the fortifications of their Maginot Line during the "phony war" of the opening months, but their armed forces were liquidated in just four weeks after Nazi armor struck in May 1940 across neutral Belgium, whose border was not protected by the famous line. In technology the West lagged far behind Germany until the British and the Americans began to catch up on a crash basis.

At that juncture in French history the only figure with real leadership qualities was Charles de Gaulle. Forty-nine years old and now a brigadier general, he had been named deputy defense minister in the latest French Cabinet on June 9, as France was collapsing under the Nazi panzer onslaught. By June 16 this Cabinet had fled southwest from Paris to Bordeaux. The next day De Gaulle flew to London aboard a small aircraft Winston Churchill had sent for him (after proposing in vain a British-French union to the paralyzed French government). On June 17 De Gaulle listened in London to the radio announcement by Marshal Henri Philippe Pétain, the new premier, that "Combat must cease. I have contacted tonight the adversary. . . ."

On June 18 De Gaulle went before BBC microphones to deliver his fervent appeal to the people of France: "Is defeat definitive? No! . . . Believe me that nothing is lost for France. . . . Because France is not alone. She is not alone. . . . Whatever happens, the flame of the French resistance must not be extinguished and it will not be extinguished. Tomorrow, like today, I shall speak on the London radio. . . ."

A teenager, I heard the general's BBC speech in a refugee-crowded café in Biarritz, the border resort town, from which my mother and I were trying to flee to Spain after the German invasion, having left my mother's house in Cannes. There are speeches one never forgets, boy or man. De Gaulle's speech that evening was such a speech.

As it was becoming evident that only America could stem Hitler's advances in the long run, the United States already led the world in overall industrial production in 1940, accounting for one third of the global output. It produced twice as much as Germany and ten times as much as Japan. But very little was being accomplished in defense-related research, still a novel concept at the time. In 1939 only $26.4 million in federal funds were earmarked for defense research and development (it was second to agriculture, which received $29.1 million). In 1989 the United States was spending about $120 *billion* on research and development in all technological fields, with defense accounting for the lion's share.

By and large, most significant research in the prewar years was conducted in Europe. When the war created the urgent need for such work, European refugee scientists contributed massively to the American effort; during the 1930's the Rockefeller Foundation helped hundreds of Jewish scientists flee Germany and be given opportunities in the United States, a private effort that paid off magnificently.

In Berlin, in the meantime, German scientists Otto Hahn and Franz Strassmann succeeded in splitting the atomic nucleus—they achieved nuclear fission by bombarding uranium by slow neutrons—as early as 1938. But there is nothing to suggest on the basis of postwar knowledge that Hitler was aware of this breakthrough or that he planned at that point to develop an atomic bomb. Nevertheless, the Nazis forbade the export of uranium ore from Czechoslovakia after they occupied the country in 1939, leading numerous refugee scientists in the United States to fear that the Germans might be working on the A-bomb after all.

Albert Einstein, the great German physicist whose discovery of the theory of relativity early in the century paved the way for nuclear physics, was among those who worried about it. Einstein, who emigrated to the United States in 1933, establishing himself at Princeton University, was never engaged in actual atomic research work, but he was kept posted on the research in this field by his scientific friends. He was instantly informed of the Hahn-Strassmann success in splitting the atom.

When Einstein learned that the Germans had stopped uranium exports from Czechoslovakia, he became alarmed. In July 1939 he wrote his friend Queen Elisabeth of Belgium, urging her to prevent Germany from obtaining uranium from the Belgian Congo, one of the world's principal sources of this ore, and to make it available to the United States (Belgium was conquered by the Nazis the following year, but they never gained control of the Congo).

On August 2, 1939, Einstein took it upon himself to call the attention of President Roosevelt to the possibility of achieving nuclear chain reactions in large masses of uranium and thus acquiring a weapon of unprecedented power. He wrote Roosevelt that "a single bomb of this type, carried by boat or exploded in a port, might very well destroy the whole port together with some of the surrounding territory. . . . [However,] such bombs might very well prove to be too heavy for transportation by air." He proposed that experimental work on nuclear fission be sped up in the United States and funds for research made available.

Einstein's letter unquestionably marks the birth of the atomic age. In his reply Roosevelt advised him that he had found "this data of such import that I have convened a board . . . to thoroughly investigate the possibilities of your suggestion regarding the element of uranium." The next step was the launching of the top secret Manhattan Project; six years later the United States was able to test the atomic bomb in New Mexico.

What the United States and Britain had underestimated, on the other hand, was the extent of advances in German research and engineering in rocketry. Nazi scientists at the laboratories in Peenemünde concentrated on the new weapons, the unmanned V-1 rocket and the V-2 "flying bomb," which Hitler hoped would allow him to escape defeat in the war. And Nazi scientists unveiled in that last year of the war the Messerschmitt Comet, the first rocket-engine operational fighter in the world, a spectacular break-through. The principal rocket geniuses were Carl Bosch, who had worked for three years before the war at a British research center, and the subse-quently famous Wernher von Braun, both of whom helped father American rocket and space programs after 1945. The British knew enough through their scientific intelligence about Peenemünde's potential importance, if not about its specific work, to have the Royal Air Force bomb it, starting in August 1943. But this did not prevent the Germans from firing 8,617 rock-ets and flying bombs at London in mid-1944, with 2,340 of them actually hitting the British capital in a devastating way.

In the end, however, it was Western technology that won the Second World War—not masses of men pitted against each other, as in the Great War. The Maginot Line, a relic of earlier wars, could not save France from the debacle of 1940. In the battle of the laboratories and the industries it was the West that prevailed over Hitler—and then over the Japanese Empire—despite the flying bombs and synthetic fuels and rubber and many other German inventions.

From nuclear energy to radar and to medicine, American and British science provided the edge of victory and built the bridge to the technological revolution of the second half of the century.

Exiled European scientists, such as Leo Szilard, Edward Teller, and En-rico Fermi, joined forces with their American colleagues to bring about the nuclear era. But the scientific community was split over the wisdom and morality of using the atomic bomb against Japan. Twelve leading scientists, including Szilard, Robert A. Millikan, and Eugene Wigner, sent a petition to President Harry Truman on July 17, 1945, requesting him "to rule that the United States shall not resort to the use of atomic bombs in this war unless the terms which will be imposed upon Japan have been made public in detail and Japan knowing these terms has refused to surrender." Truman chose to disregard the petition (which was classified a "secret" document by the government and declassified only in 1989) and ordered the atomic strikes on Hiroshima and Nagasaki, forcing Japan's capitulation.

The second-highest wartime priority in the United States after the atomic bomb was the production of penicillin, starting in 1943, and millions of Allied soldiers and civilians had their lives saved by it. Without this first antibiotic, developed by British scientists Alexander Fleming, Howard W. Florey, and Ernst Boris Chain, they might have died from battlefield infections. Tens of thousands of American lives in the Pacific were saved by the new antimalarial drug chloroquine. And Royal Air Force surgeons devised amazing techniques in reconstructive surgery in treating burn cases of aircrews that had been shot down. And the nuclear age soon brought nuclear medicine: radioactive isotopes and iodine and tracers.

Wartime research provided new stimulus to earlier theoretical work on what became the computer, and in this field, too, exiled scientists joined the Americans in opening new paths. Polish-born Jan Aleksander Rajchman, along with other mathematicians, pioneered in the mid-1930's the development of high-speed computer memory systems in the United States; he was an unsung hero of the new information society, one of the fathers of minicomputers and microcomputers that are making the technology revolution possible.

A study of that period by the National Science Board notes that during the war "the scientists in the United States found the process exhilarating and intellectually exciting." Steven Muller, the former president of Johns Hopkins University, writes that "with the outbreak of World War II, inevitably the mobilization of the whole nation also included the universities" and "technology played an unprecedented role in the war effort." Muller recalls that "not only were university specialists called to work on technologically sophisticated projects, but universities were requested to sponsor new laboratories to do research for military purposes." This scientific mobilization continued after 1945, and as Muller puts it, it lasted through the Cold War, the Korean War, and "until the closing of the Vietnam War."

R. V. Jones, a key member of the British scientific intelligence staff who worked closely with Winston Churchill throughout the war, writes in his memoirs that "we were remarkably fortunate in our opportunity . . . the very development in science and technology that led to everyday radio in the 1920s also led to the radar and radio navigational systems of World War II." Jones adds: "Further, there was leadership. In Churchill we had a Prime Minister with a genuine and strong interest in the possibilities opened up by science. . . . This interest, for example, made him anxious to be flown—even at some discomfort—in experimental aircraft to see for himself the state of airborne radar."

The Allied victory in 1945—over Germany in May and over Japan in August—represented the end of one long historical period and the dawn of another crucial period. Indeed, the year 1945 divided the twentieth century into two markedly distinct halves.

Prior to the Second World War, it still was the old order of great colonial empires and European rivalries and internal and external tensions and convulsions. The Russian Revolution and its aftermath were the only fundamentally novel—and disturbing—reality to surge forth from the Great War of 1914–18, followed by the awesome perils for humanity that Hitler posed.

From 1945 on a new world has come into being. Quite aptly that year was called Year Zero, the transition from war to a form of peace—and the advent of the age of contradiction. It was the start of what was thought to be the American Century. It was the exploding era of the Third World. It was the high technology revolution. It was the ascent and the demise of Marxism-Leninism, the demise occurring very abruptly at the end of the 1980's.

BOOK TWO

YEAR ZERO

The evil that men do lives after them;
The good is oft interred with their
   bones.

—WILLIAM SHAKESPEARE
Julius Caesar

I

*T*he year 1945 was the year of peace—the end of the Second World War—but this peace began to fall apart even before the fighting was concluded either in Europe or in Asia. As after the Great War victory twenty-seven years earlier, the victorious Allies instantly lost their cohesion. The Cold War between the United States and Britain on one side and the Soviet Union on the other erupted in a very real sense during the opening months of Year Zero although the hot war was still very much in progress with Germany and Japan. And to compound matters, important differences—with great impact on the postwar era—developed very quickly between Washington and London as well as between the Anglo-Saxons and the French, represented by the ever-inflexible figure of Charles de Gaulle.

The Cold War in multifarious forms was to be the central dimension of international politics for the next forty-five years. It was to spawn regional wars, swell beyond reason the size of national budgets, accelerate more and more defense-related research and, with it, the incredible scientific progress of the last half century as well as the resulting new high technology and biological revolutions. Only with the advent of the Gorbachev regime in the Soviet Union and accompanying profound changes in Soviet foreign policies in the late 1980's did the realization start dawning on the West that this Cold War was finally over and that a fresh and different epoch lay ahead for humanity. Progress would be possible peacefully.

Not surprisingly the demise of the Cold War coincided with the collapse of Marxism-Leninism as one of the two dominant ideologies and systems in the postwar decades; modern capitalism with a free-market economy and with representative government as its political hallmark was, of course, the other system. The West's overwhelming technological superiority in fashioning reasonably content modern societies—including the miraculous recovery and postwar economic achievements of Germany and Japan—while assuring political freedoms was crucial in forcing the recognition that Marxism-Leninism was not a viable model in the late twentieth century and beyond. By the end of the 1980's people in Eastern European Communist countries themselves had reached that conclusion and rose to become rid of the system.

This latest historical turning point in world relationships was being reached around 1990, coming as a long-overdue moment after the decades of turbulence, violence, conflict, and all the fundamental human and material changes that followed World War II.

As the war drew to a close in Europe, gigantic human, political, and economic problems faced the Allies. They affected the fate and shape of nations and the survival and life conditions of tens of millions of human beings. The problems overlapped and continuously generated new ones. But there were no formal or even tentative guidelines in Allied policies on how to deal with unanticipated situations stemming from the windup of the war. In the end many crucial decisions that defined the future of generations to come had to be improvised or taken in the field for purely military reasons of immediate concern to top commanders. This, too, contributed importantly to the onset of the Cold War.

Basic postwar political arrangements were ironed out by Roosevelt and Churchill at their meetings with Stalin first in Teheran in November 1943 and then in Yalta, in the Soviet Crimea, in February 1945. At least Roosevelt and Churchill *thought* they had reached firm agreements with Stalin, notwithstanding their quarrels and misunderstandings in the course of the war. Deep mistrust dominated this relationship.

The Soviet Union had joined the great alliance when Hitler attacked at 3:00 A.M. on Sunday, June 22, 1941, just two months short of the second anniversary of his nonaggression pact with Stalin. Code-named Barbarossa, the invasion of the Soviet Union was the latest colossal blunder committed by Hitler, against the advice of his military chiefs, one of those events that alter the direction of history.

Hitler's explanation at the time was that the assault on Russia was "not a case of conquering people, but of conquering agriculturally useful space." He may have believed it himself, but it turned out to be a suicidal move, one that was not necessary for Germany. Fresh material from Soviet archives confirms that Stalin had never contemplated initiating war against the Nazis—certainly not in 1941—and that on the contrary, he was a trusting business partner. Five months before Barbarossa, the Soviets signed a treaty providing for shipments of commodities to Germany in exchange for industrial goods, and during the period preceding the invasion, they delivered 1.5 million tons of grain, 2 million tons of petroleum products, and 1.5 million tons of timber to their Nazi clients.

It is obviously impossible to guess what Stalin would have done if Hitler had not struck at all. He might have remained neutral, letting the Western democracies and the Nazis bleed each other white, and then marched on Europe. Or he might have attacked Germany to deprive Hitler of a possible victory over the Allies, realizing that the Soviet Union would become inevitably the next target and could be destroyed by the Nazi power.

Two things, however, are certain. The first one is that by drawing the Soviets into the war in 1941 (and totally miscalculating the military equation), Hitler brought disaster upon himself. He could not sustain a two-front war, especially with the bolstering of Soviet forces by massive American industrial aid. The second result of Hitler's folly was the transformation of the Soviet Union into a world power as it captured Eastern Europe and Germany as far as Berlin and the Elbe in pursuit of the defeated Nazi troops. This was unquestionably the most important single political fact to emerge from the Second World War, the fact that determined postwar history in the next half century.

As the war went on, suspicions grew between the Americans and the British on one side and the Soviets on the other. Both the West and the East were thinking ahead to the new international order after victory over Hitler, and clearly their aims differed totally. To put it simply, Stalin was determined to consolidate the Soviet sway over as much of Eastern, Central, and Southern Europe as he could, and the Western Allies were just as determined to prevent it. Frictions and tensions over the future of Eastern European nations mounted as victory approached. The Soviets insisted that they needed a protective belt of "friendly" nations west of their borders (as well as permanent territorial gains) while the West saw in the demand the prelude to a Communist thrust for world hegemony.

Still, the parameters of peace had to be defined in some manner. The first steps to devise economic mechanisms for the postwar world and to construct peacekeeping machinery were taken during 1944. In July forty-five governments sent ranking representatives to the Bretton Woods resort in New Hampshire to draft and sign conventions setting up the International Monetary Fund and the International Bank for Reconstruction and Development. No such organs had ever existed, and the United States and the Soviet Union were among the signatories. Between August and October 1944 American, British, Soviet, and Chinese foreign ministers conferred at the Dumbarton Oaks estate in the Georgetown section of Washington, D.C., to produce what they called Proposals for the General International Organization, the blueprint for the creation of the United Nations.

The situation during the winter of 1944–45, with Paris already liberated by the Allies in the West and Warsaw taken by the Soviet armies in the East, made it imperative for the leaders of the three principal Allied powers to convene as soon as possible to lay the cornerstones for peace. Yalta was the chosen site, and a desperately ill Franklin Roosevelt made the supreme effort to fly there to meet his two wartime colleagues.

The conference, held between February 4 and 11, produced the Yalta Declaration of 1945. It surely is the most controversial international document since the Treaty of Versailles, and to many European and American political leaders and observers at the time—and subsequently to historians—it represented a de facto division of Europe into Soviet and Western zones of influence. To many others, "Yalta" is a word of opprobrium that stands for betrayal and capitulation much as "Munich" stands for the same notion in the context of appeasing Hitler over Czechoslovakia seven years earlier.

This time appeasement was over the fate of Poland, which since its first partition, in 1772, has been a problem continuously haunting Europe. It haunted the wartime alliance with the West supporting the London-based Polish government-in-exile and the Soviets manipulating Moscow-based Polish Communists into position as the future regime in Warsaw. Consequently, the Yalta Conference agreed on establishing "a strong, free, independent and democratic Poland" and on the creation of a provisional government of national unity composed of "democratic leaders from Poland itself and from Poles abroad." Such a government was believed by the West to be a workable compromise, and Roosevelt and Churchill accepted the Soviet pledge that free elections would be held in Poland as soon as possible. Moreover, the Western leaders agreed to cede the eastern provinces of Poland to the Soviet Union in exchange for "substantial" territories in the north and west to be carved out of Germany. Poland's map was redrawn, but Moscow quickly blocked the promise of democracy.

The Yalta Declaration called for the founding conference of the United Nations to be held in April and dealt with the establishment of Allied occupation zones in Germany. It issued a Declaration on Liberated Europe, a vague promise of joint action in solving the problems of the liberated countries "in accordance with democratic principles." What Yalta failed to accomplish, however, was to provide solid guidelines on how the war should be terminated militarily and politically, allowing the Russians to grab territory and power in Eastern Europe. This failure set the stage for new problems and for the advent of the Cold War. When, by midyear, Stalin chose to default on his commitment on democracy in Poland (to the extreme of imprisoning in Moscow sixteen Polish non-Communist leaders from the underground), the East-West confrontation acquired unstoppable dynamics.

The United States, too, was disoriented politically during the closing weeks of the war in Europe. President Roosevelt, who had returned from Yalta on February 12, died exactly two months later from a brain hemorrhage in Warm Springs, Georgia, where he had gone to rest. Death came on the eighty-third day of his fourth presidential term; he was only sixty-three years old (a year older than Stalin and eight years younger than Churchill). His last public appearance was an address to Congress on Yalta on March 1, when he spoke sitting down in the well of the House of Representatives and apologized for this unusual posture: "I know that you will realize it makes it a lot easier for me in not having to carry about ten pounds of steel on the bottom of my legs, and also because of the fact that I have just completed a 14,000-mile trip."

Instantly Vice President Harry S. Truman inherited all the responsibilities of governing the nation and bringing the wars in Europe and the Pacific to a victorious climax with a minimal loss of American lives. His initial and immense disadvantage was that he had not participated in the massive wartime correspondence with Churchill and then with Stalin (Roosevelt had not shared it with Truman), that he knew the British prime minister only slightly and Stalin not at all, that he was barely aware of the political-military decision-making process involving America and its allies, and, finally, that he had not been present at Yalta. The new President was fully and immediately briefed by Roosevelt's top aides, but this was an urgent and critical period with no time to absorb all the sensitive and secret mass of information being presented to him before making decisions that could not wait.

On April 12, the day Truman became President, the U.S. Ninth Army's vanguard units had reached the outskirts of Potsdam, fifty miles from Berlin, and General George S. Patton's Third Army was near the border of Czechoslovakia in the south. But powerful Soviet armies, moving west, were crossing the Oder River and approaching Berlin as well, while other Soviet forces were entering Czechoslovakia from the northeast.

The following day, the thirteenth, the Russians captured Vienna as they advanced from Slovakia and Hungary, and this conquest triggered a passionate argument within the Allied camp concerning the political aspect of the military operations. The issue was how far east the fast-striking American troops would be allowed to go before meeting the Russians and, even more important, whether the Soviets would be permitted to take Berlin and Prague.

Churchill took the view that the Americans should advance as far as possible, even within the previously delineated Soviet occupation zone, and to occupy the two capitals in order to hold better cards in future disputes with the Kremlin that the prime minister fully anticipated. General Dwight D. Eisenhower, Allied supreme commander in Europe, believed, on the other hand, that Berlin and western Czechoslovakia were low priorities militarily, and he feared that American efforts to control them could antagonize the Soviet Union and endanger the peace settlement.

The problem was further complicated by the absence of any Allied decisions (at Yalta or elsewhere) regarding the nationalities of armies that would occupy Nazi-held European capitals. Eisenhower himself "had no specific guidance" on any of these subjects, according to the account of the European war by his grandson, David Eisenhower. His own plan to halt the American advance on the Elbe River—and not to try to beat the Soviets to Berlin—was approved by Truman within days of the assumption of the presidency, as was Eisenhower's decision to forbid Patton to advance beyond Pilsen and Karlsbad in Czechoslovakia. Truman wrote later: "I agreed with Churchill that it would be desirable to hold the great cities of Berlin, Prague, and Vienna, but the fact was that, like the countries of eastern Europe, these cities were under Russian control or about to fall under her [sic] control."

Thus Eisenhower's views prevailed. On April 26 American and Soviet units met at Torgau on the Elbe, and on May 2 the Soviets stormed Berlin from the east. Hitler had committed suicide in his Reich Chancellery bunker two days earlier, shooting himself in the right temple with a 7.65 mm pistol. He had just turned fifty-six. Germany's formal surrender came on May 8, and Eisenhower accepted it at a ceremony at Rheims in the presence of British, French, and Soviet representatives.

On May 9 Soviet forces occupied Prague, following several days of hard fighting with retreating Nazi divisions and an uprising in the capital by the Czech underground. On that same day Truman, who was becoming increasingly disturbed by the consolidation of Soviet power in Eastern Europe, cabled Churchill to propose that they meet with Stalin soon to review the postwar situation. This was the Potsdam Conference two months later.

It has been said that the United States and Britain won the war in Europe but failed to achieve in the East the kind of democratic peace for which they had fought. It has also been charged that American naiveté, from the agreements signed by Roosevelt at Yalta to Truman's acquiescence in the Soviet capture of Berlin and Prague, had sold out Eastern Europe to Stalin. And it has been suggested that inasmuch as the Cold War already loomed inevitably during the final phase of the battle of Germany, the West should have ceded nothing to the Russians in Eastern Europe.

That Stalin was determined to rule that region—and to freeze relations with the West to the absolute minimum—is beyond discussion. So is the fact that the West responded with its own brand of hostility and that the two sides, in effect, joined forces to launch the Cold War. Until the Gorbachev era, the unwavering Soviet propaganda line, accepted to some degree among Western revisionist historians, was that the West alone was responsible for the Cold War because of its rigid anticommunism and its inability to comprehend the security requirements of the Soviet Union after the loss of twenty million citizens in the Second World War. Early in 1989, however, a leading Soviet historian stunningly admitted in print that the Kremlin was equally guilty and that Western public opinion was justified in regarding Stalin's Russia and Hitler's Germany as two "totalitarian colossi."

All Soviet spokesmen do not necessarily share this view, but wholly new ground was broken when Nikolai Popov, a member of the Moscow Institute for Sociological Research, wrote in *Literaturnaya Gazeta* that "we must try to see our country through the eyes of the rest of the world, both half a century ago and today, to understand the sources of the policy of the western states toward us." And in a number of private conversations I had in Moscow in 1988 with senior Soviet officials who specialized in foreign policy, even stronger condemnations were expressed on the subject of Stalin's postwar behavior.

In this sense, then, it is reasonable to conclude that Roosevelt at Yalta and Truman afterward had virtually no options in dealing with an expansionist Soviet Union. At that point there were twelve million Soviet troops in Europe, and as Truman writes in his *Memoirs*, "The Russians were in a strong position, and they knew it." The reality the President faced when the Reich collapsed was the presence of Soviet armies in the Baltic states, Poland, the eastern part of Germany, Romania, Hungary, Bulgaria, and Czechoslovakia. Short of an armed conflict with Moscow, a contingency Eisenhower refused to risk, the West had no leverage in terms of forcing it to honor the Yalta agreements on democracy in Poland and elections in the other liberated nations in the Soviet orbit. The atomic bomb had not yet been tested at that stage, and the United States feared that the war against Japan would be long and bloody.

Eisenhower and Truman had to bear in mind that Stalin had made a secret pledge at Yalta to engage the Soviet Union in war against Japan within three months of Germany's capitulation, and in light of the existing situation in the Pacific, a Japanese second front was vital. This, then, was another reason to keep the Russians politically pacified in Europe.

Furthermore, it was necessary for the United States to start transferring troops from Europe to the Far East as rapidly as possible to keep tightening the noose around the Japanese islands. B-17 and B-29 bombers were pounding Tokyo and other cities in Japan, the Army and the Marines were waging bloody battles as they hopped across the Pacific toward their ultimate objective, and the Navy—especially after the 1942 Midway victory—had won the control of the ocean. Still, Washington knew, more and more troops were needed. This calculation inevitably affected American political and military decisions in the European theater.

One of them, of course, was to let the Soviets take Berlin. As it turned out, the Germans fought so fiercely that it cost the Soviets a hundred thousand killed to win this prize. Marshal Georgi K. Zhukov, the top Soviet commander, described the battle for Berlin as the toughest of the war as his artillery mercilessly pounded the city at close range for days; the Russians, he remarked later, were doing to German cities what the Nazis had done to *their* cities when the Soviet Union was invaded. Eisenhower, naturally, would not have accepted such American losses for the sake of Berlin, and this was among his considerations in deciding to stay out of the war's climactic battle.

It is entirely possible that the Germans would not have resisted the Americans in any serious fashion. Their armies had been fleeing west from the Russian front to surrender to the British and the Americans rather than to the Russians, and they might have simply delivered Berlin to Eisenhower. But he could not take chances in Berlin—or in Czechoslovakia, where nearly one million Soviet troops were attacking one million retreating Nazis. Military realities defined the postwar political outcome.

In mid-May 1945, a week or so after the Soviet entry, Captain Zoltan Havas, a Czechoslovak-born intelligence officer in the U.S. Army, drove alone in his jeep to Prague from Pilsen, where Patton's army had its advance headquarters. Havas was the first American officer in uniform to appear in the capital—his official mission was to reopen the U.S. Embassy after the war years—and his arrival created a sensation. As Havas recalls it, his jeep was surrounded by crowds of Czechs cheering and embracing him—and asking, "But where are the tanks?" Rumors had spread that the Americans had decided to move into Prague after all, and the young captain was mistaken for a pathfinder for Patton's armor. There were tears of disenchantment when the Czechs learned the truth.

The Havas story illustrates the mood in Eastern Europe at the end of the war against Hitler. Although young idealists in all those countries thought they saw the dawn of social justice and equality in the political systems implanted under the shadow of Communist armies and security services, the faith would not last long and resistance would soon rise. It would be more than four decades until the next dawn.

The decisions taken in 1945—to divide, in effect, Europe as well as Germany politically between the East and the West—formed the basis for the entire postwar European order. For the next forty-five years, all the policies in the East and the West reposed on the assumption that this division would continue indefinitely. The Cold War stemmed from this assumption and so would the formation, soon, of North Atlantic Treaty Organization (NATO) and Warsaw Pact alliances. Therefore, when this reality changed abruptly with the Communist collapse in Eastern Europe in 1989, nobody in the East or the West really knew how to deal with the new Europe; to some people on both sides of the divide the idea of a reunified Germany was a nightmare, after all the years of piously urging a unified Germany.

II

In the meantime, Europe was awakening from the six-year night of horror. Adolf Hitler had died in his bunker, but he left behind a cemetery. Warsaw, Coventry, Rotterdam, Leningrad, Stalingrad, Berlin, Dresden, Essen, and lesser cities had been turned into ruins. London and Vienna were shattered. From Normandy to the Ukraine fields lay fallow.

Then there was the human destruction.

Apart from millions of soldiers killed and maimed in combat and millions of civilians killed in aerial bombardments, artillery shellings, and other armed encounters, at least six million were murdered in Nazi concentration camps in Germany, Austria, Poland, and Czechoslovakia. The majority of those who were gassed, burned in furnaces, and shot and hanged during the

Holocaust were Jews; Poland's prewar Jewish population of three million, for example, was reduced to less than a hundred thousand. Another million Eastern Europeans were killed or allowed to die in the Soviet Union, where they were deported as slave laborers after the 1939 annexation of sections of their countries.

When the battlefields of Europe fell silent in May 1945, the Western Allies suddenly found themselves with the responsibility of caring for the war's survivors. On the other side of the East-West dividing line—it became a hermetically sealed frontier as soon as the Allied and Soviet armies met at the limits of their respective occupation zones—the Russians could not or would not look adequately after the masses of uprooted civilians and war prisoners under their control. Moscow-installed or -backed regimes across Central and Eastern Europe were hardly able to keep life going at all in their utterly ravaged countries.

Western Germany and Austria were the immediate priorities. In the areas that came under their control there during the spring, American, British, and French armies liberated roughly eight million foreigners who became known as displaced persons, the pathetic DPs of the long war. Among them were the barely alive survivors of the Nazi death camps—Ohrdruf, Nordhausen, Buchenwald, Bergen-Belsen, Mauthausen, and scores of others—most of whom were Jewish. Prisoners in Auschwitz (Oświęcim), Majdanek, and other camps in Poland and Theresienstaat (Terezín) in Czechoslovakia had been liberated by the Russians. Then there were slave laborers from Eastern and Western Europe, employed by the Nazis in the war industries, and 1.5 million Soviet war prisoners captured by the Germans after 1941. Finally, the Western Allies had on their hands close to 5 million *German* war prisoners who had surrendered in April and May.

There probably were another eight million DPs in the Soviet-controlled zones, and additional millions of German prisoners of war (three hundred thousand were seized during the Battle of Berlin alone).

The Allies thus had to feed thirteen or fourteen million DPs and POW's in the Western occupation zones, provide minimal medical care and shelter for them (during the first year millions remained in wartime camps simply because they had no place to go), and try to decide their future. The Allies also had to organize the supply of bare-subsistence rations to forty million German civilians, a large percentage being refugees from their homes in different parts of the smashed Reich, because the entire machinery of the national economy had broken down. Eisenhower estimated that 175,000 tons of wheat and flour monthly were required to keep the DPs and the Germans from starving.

(In one of the most shameful episodes of sacrificing decency for political advantage, the Western Allies turned over to the Soviet authorities an estimated two million Soviet prisoners of war held in German camps who did not wish repatriation as well as other Soviet anticommunist exiles, among them thousands of surviving czarist émigrés. Along with Yalta territorial concessions, this gesture was supposed to gain Stalin's gratitude; the other excuse was that these two million reduced the numbers of displaced persons to be fed. Naturally, these men and women have vanished into Soviet prisons and labor camps, and Stalin was not in the habit of reciprocating gestures.)

The destitute millions across Europe represented the human detritus of war. And once the fighting ended, one of the greatest migrations in European history was under way. Several million deportees from the Soviet Union, including two hundred thousand Polish Jews interned in the Tashkent region in Central Asia, were seeking to make their way home in Eastern Europe, usually finding neither homes nor relatives. Other millions of Poles from the eastern lands around Lwów and Wilno, ceded at Yalta to the Soviet Union, had been moved west to be resettled in Germany's easternmost territories, which had been given to Poland, while the Germans from the cities and farms there had been pushed still farther west. The Soviet POWs were being returned home by the Allies, and Allied POWs from Germany were sent back to *their* countries, east and west. Then it was discovered that Jewish returnees from the Soviet Union, fearing anti-Semitism and pogroms in Poland, were moving into DP camps in West Germany, hoping to emigrate to Palestine or the United States. And throughout Europe men were being demobilized from their armies to go back home and start new lives.

That new lives could be indeed started so rapidly is a tribute to human courage, resilience, imagination, and hope. For what people found upon their returns home was fantasmagoric, seemingly unmanageable, and profoundly depressing. To put it simply, the entire continent had broken down. Railroads and highways had been disrupted by aerial bombing and ground combat. In the worst-hit cities there was no electricity, no heat, no running water, no telephones. No food had been grown, produced, or distributed in much of Europe since the previous year, and hunger, as Eisenhower instantly understood, was a real threat. The winters of 1944–45 and 1945–46, some of the coldest on record, were paralyzing to millions from London to Paris, Berlin, Warsaw, Belgrade, and Moscow. There was no fuel and no warm clothing.

Warsaw was sheer horror. After Nazi tanks, artillery, and dive bombers put down the great uprising in the latter part of 1944, German troopers dynamited the remaining standing buildings to turn the ancient capital into a silent ruin. Uprising survivors were forcibly removed to nearby towns, and Warsaw became an empty shell. Only when Soviet troops crossed the Vistula River in January 1945 to seize the city did people begin to return—little by little, then quicker and quicker, to start rebuilding and living again. Amid the rubble of what had been the historic Old Town Square, the first inhabitant to go back was an elderly woman, who proceeded to feed the pigeons that had stayed behind; today her memory is honored by an Old

Town restored house named The Dovecot. Warsawians wasted no time creating a new capital—everybody worked in clearing the rubble, from soldiers to schoolchildren and elderly folk—but for a year or more tens of thousands of families lived in the ruins.

It appears that Warsaw need not have been so utterly destroyed, however, if Stalin had not wished it. Historical materials now available show that the Soviets kept their armies on the right bank of the Vistula for months, refusing to cross and take the capital until the Nazis had destroyed the London-directed underground forces that had risen in August 1944. Their destruction removed the principal obstacle to the establishment of a Communist regime in Poland that Stalin had planned all along. In the new climate of liberalization that developed in 1988, government censors allowed dissident writers to start telling in newspapers and magazines the truth about the Soviet deed at Warsaw along with the truth about Katyń, where the Russians had executed fifteen thousand Polish Army officers at the outset of the war. In the past such mentions of Warsaw and Katyń had been taboo. But I saw in 1989 an article in a Polish weekly publication proclaiming that the true symbols of the Second World War and Polish martyrology were Oświęcim and Kolyma, the first being the terrible Nazi death camp in southern Poland that the West knows by its German name of Auschwitz, and the second being the Soviet Siberian prison center where Poles were deported to work in the mines. To understand Poland today—and its surge toward liberal rule—one must know about Oświęcim and Kolyma.

Germany was to be battled into unconditional surrender by the Allies under their coordinated policies, and American, British, and Soviet armed might concentrated on forcing the Nazis into accepting it. Total military power was Eisenhower's mandate, and every effort was made to smash the Reich into submission. The Morgenthau Plan to turn postwar Germany into an agricultural state (it was devised by Henry Morgenthau, Jr., Roosevelt's secretary of the treasury) had been abandoned by the Allies as too extreme, but the devastation was so great that the country might have become a vast farm if reconstruction had not progressed with astounding speed and determination—and with massive American aid.

This is how Hermann J. Abs, Germany's leading banker, remembers the hour of defeat: "The situation in May 1945 was a catastrophe. Germany was grappling with physical devastation and political turmoil. Only a very few cities had escaped complete destruction. . . . Cologne's population alone had been reduced from 800,000 to 40,000 during the war. Concerning the degree of destruction, there was a certain betting going on [over] which city had been more destroyed, the neighboring city or oneself's; this is a very cynical but genuine remark of that period."

Abs notes that as a result of the East-West partition and the loss of territories to Poland, almost ten million expellees or refugees had come from eastern Germany to West Germany by 1951; "that meant one out of five [inhabitants] was an expellee or a refugee from the East." To feed this population, Abs said, the United States spent $1.6 billion and Britain $700 million in the immediate postwar period.

Moreover, Abs recounts, "at that time the German currency had no purchasing power; the unit you paid to get a man to work for you for one hour or two was an American cigarette; the price was about two cigarettes an hour." Naturally the black market became the principal force in the German economy, and for cigarettes, liquor, or stockings, Western occupiers could buy everything from work to sex. Edmund Jan Osmańczyk, a Polish war correspondent who covered occupied Germany at the time, wrote that there was a saying among young women: "Better a man atop my belly than a bomb atop my house. . . ."

Paris, an open city, escaped destruction, but not the cold, hunger, and deprivation. German-born surrealist painter Max Ernst summed up the horror of the war in his canvas "Europe After the Rain II," which he painted in exile in the United States after the fall of France in 1940 and which was exhibited in Paris immediately after the liberation. Ernst's vision is of reddish and greenish ruins and rubble, grotesquely twisted shapes, and faceless, lifeless human figures. But the sky overhead is blue with light white clouds. Is it a promise of rebirth?

At this moment of transition between Europe's past and future, another activity was under way in Germany, the search by both the American and the Soviets for Nazidom's best scientific brains; it was a prelude to the Cold War, too. American and British intelligence teams hunted in both the Western and the Soviet occupation zones, looking for weapons laboratories and testing sites and concentrating on German research in both rocketry and atomic developments. Office of Strategic Services (OSS) agents were ordered by Allen Dulles, their European theater chief, to locate scientists and installations, while Soviet scientific intelligence was engaged in identical pursuits. Before long, groups of top Nazi scientists, precious war booty, wound up in the United States as well as in Russia, boosting preparedness for the Cold War. The OSS even arranged test firings of the German V-2 rockets at Nordhausen, putting the scientists to work for the West even before they were flown to the United States. The V-2's were the weapon that sowed destruction over London in the closing months of the war, but Dulles claimed later that his Nordhausen tests were crucial in triggering American rocketry advances.

And as early as the autumn of 1944 U.S. Army intelligence units, acting on top secret orders, began probing into the structure and capabilities of the Soviet armed forces. Special questionnaires were sent out through G-2 (intelligence) channels to officers assigned to the interrogation of German prisoners who had served on the Russian front to try to learn everything possible about the composition and tactics of Soviet forces they had fought. G-2 wanted to know all about armaments and especially about underwater bridges used by the Red Army. These bridges were used for crossing rivers, and they were partially submerged to escape detection from aircraft overhead. American experts had never seen such bridges, and they were anxious for detailed descriptions. Escapees from Soviet units were likewise interrogated by American intelligence. Quite possibly, Soviet intelligence was studying U.S. armed forces in the field in the same fashion; professionals on both sides were beginning to face the possibility of their switching from allies to potential enemies.

The liberation of the Nazi death camps and their zombielike survivors by Allied troops in the spring of 1945 produced an explosion of astonishment, shame, and rage in the supposedly civilized Western democracies fighting Hitler in the name of freedom. It also raised the immensely embarrassing questions of how much Allied governments had known about these camps before the invasion of Germany and of why nothing had really been done about them. The question of German guilt, destined to haunt old and new German generations for the next half century, emerged publicly for the first time. Finally, as we now know, the Holocaust played an overwhelming role in persuading all the big powers to create the state of Israel three years later. The world had to face great morality issues.

On April 12 (the day Roosevelt died), Eisenhower visited Ohrdruf, a relatively small concentration camp, the first one he had ever seen, meeting the emaciated inmates and attempting to gain some sense and understanding of what had occurred there over the years. There had been detailed press reports on the liberation of Oświęcim and other camps in Eastern Europe—these were tales of pure horror—but the discoveries in the West were essentially new, at least to the American public, and this led to the painful question of who knew what.

David Eisenhower writes of his grandfather that "Eisenhower and his colleagues in the high command . . . knew that the mass killings and work-torture deaths had reached a peak in the winter of 1944–45." He adds: "To an extent, the debates over strategy in the summer of 1945 had been debates ahead of time over the responsibility for prolonging these horrors, though postwar accounts of the principals—Eisenhower, [Field Marshal Bernard] Montgomery, [General Omar] Bradley, Churchill and [General Alan] Brooke—would grow vague or remain silent on the subject. Had enough been done? Was enough being done?"

Actually both the extent of the killing of Jews in Europe and Hitler's plans for a "Final Solution" were beginning to be known in the United States in the latter part of 1942—with the United States already at war with the Axis following the Japanese attack on Pearl Harbor the previous December—but the government in Washington was inexplicably reluctant to make all this information public. For equally inexplicable reasons, the State Department made every possible effort to conceal the truth about the annihilation of Jews.

The American Jewish community therefore resolved to act. On December 2, 1942, Rabbi Stephen S. Wise, president of the American Jewish

Congress, wrote his old friend Franklin Roosevelt that "the most over-whelming disaster of Jewish history has befallen Jews in the form of the Hitler mass-massacres . . . it is indisputable that as many as two million civilian Jews have been slain." In a private letter (which the National Archives made public only in 1989), Wise urged the President to "speak a word which may bring solace and hope to millions of Jews who mourn, and be an expression of the conscience of the American people." He also asked Roosevelt to receive a small delegation of American Jewish leaders to discuss the problem.

Roosevelt received Wise and his colleagues a week later and authorized them to state publicly that he was "profoundly shocked to learn that two million Jews had perished as a result of Nazi rule and crimes." It remains unclear why the President did "learn" of these massacres only when Wise called his attention to it. The State Department and private American groups had been receiving for long months a flood of reports on the subject, and it is hard to believe that Roosevelt remained in total ignorance. In any event, he assured the Wise delegation that "the American people will hold the perpetrators of these crimes to strict accountability in a day of reckoning which will surely come."

Again, this was sidestepping the immediate and lethally urgent question. The promise of future retribution evidently did not impress the Nazis (who, in 1942, were riding the crest of a victorious wave), and the fact that the Allies would indeed try Hitler's associates years later for war crimes had no bearing on the situation that Wise described so dramatically in his letter to the White House. In fact, the rabbi soon thereafter expressed deep disappointment over the American administration's basically passive role in rescuing Holocaust victims.

Stopping the "Final Solution" was not, of course, a simple matter, but there is little to suggest that much thought had been given to it in Washington or, for that matter, in London. It is known, however, that proposals to bomb rail lines leading to the huge death camp complex at Oświęcim in southern Poland had been vetoed by the American command on the ground that the aircraft were needed for more urgent missions for achieving victory. Inasmuch as virtually all the prisoners were transported to Oświęcim by rail, bombing might have reduced or slowed down the deliveries to these human slaughterhouses. Air raids in 1944 and 1945, when Eisenhower already knew that the mass killings were at a peak, might also have had psychological effects on the Nazis, especially those in charge of the death camps. Yet nothing was attempted, and the commanders in Europe were supported by the War Department in Washington in their refusal to interfere with the "death transports."

Perhaps when Eisenhower saw his first concentration camp, he realized that after all, he should have ordered bombings—or something—to arrest this tragedy. His biographer David Eisenhower acknowledges that "what went through Eisenhower's mind is unknown" after he inspected Ohrdruf, but he also says that the general issued orders for all men, women, and children of Gotha, the town next door, "to be turned out at bayonet point to parade through the camp and form work parties to bury the dead." Then Eisenhower is said to have turned to a U.S. Army guard at the camp to ask, "Still having trouble hating them?" Subsequently all American soldiers were ordered to visit liberated concentration camps.

III

The war had ended, but nobody knew what to do with the captive survivors. One could recognize concentration camp inmates by blue serial numbers tattooed on their forearms and show them sympathy.

Among the millions of DPs in Germany at the moment of victory, roughly a hundred thousand were Jews and their families, most of whom preferred to emigrate to Palestine rather than return home in Eastern Europe. They were the so-called nonrepatriables, and their numbers kept growing as other Jews fled the turbulence and renascent anti-Semitism of Eastern Europe for the Allied-protected DP camps in Germany.

However, the obstacle to the Jews' transfer to Palestine was Britain's absolute opposition to the idea. Part of the Ottoman Empire prior to the First World War, Palestine came under British administration as a League of Nations mandate in 1922, and during the 1920's and 1930's a certain level of Jewish emigration—chiefly Zionists from Eastern Europe—was allowed although there were ups and downs in visa-granting policies. In 1924, for example, nearly thirty-four thousand Jews entered Palestine to become settlers in what they saw as their biblical Promised Land.

But Palestine's population was predominantly Arab, and soon clashes, including killings on both sides, developed in the territory and the British curtailed Zionist arrivals. Anti-Semitic persecutions in Germany and, increasingly, in Poland led Britain to relax restrictions; sixty-two thousand Jews arrived in 1935. A major Arab rebellion erupted in April 1936, and the following year only ten thousand Jews were let into the country. Contrary to generalized belief, the problem was not religious—the Jewish and Islamic faiths coexisted peacefully and in mutual respect—but essentially economic and emotional. As immigrant Jews, often financed from abroad, built new cities and established farm kibbutz communities, the Palestinian Arabs felt more and more diminished in economic and political power though demographically they were in the heavy majority. All these elements were just as alive in the Arab-Israeli confrontation in the late eighties as they had been more than a half century earlier. In the midst of spreading religious wars, this conflict remains untouched by religious zeal. History is usually consistent.

The approach of the Second World War in 1939 served to stiffen the British resolve to limit Jewish emigration to Palestine. Nazi intelligence and political agents were infiltrating the Middle East, attempting to turn Arab populations against the British all over the region and against the British and the Jews in Palestine. The grand mufti of Jerusalem, Haj Amin al-Husseini, was profoundly anti-British and anti-Jewish, and his religious and political influence were so great that London could not afford to antagonize him. The mufti being the principal spokesman for the cause of barring Jewish emigration, the British moved to appease him and his allies by issuing a White Paper on Palestine on May 17, 1939. It proclaimed that the Palestine mandate would be maintained for another decade, when a binational Arab-Jewish state would be created. For the first five years of this period, Jewish emigration would be kept down to approximately fifteen thousand annually; thereafter the Arabs could decide whether more Jews should be allowed into Palestine.

This limitation triggered illegal immigration to Palestine by Jews fleeing Europe that British authorities fought with all the means at their disposal. They did not change their minds when the grand mufti went to live in Berlin in 1941, to become an adviser to Hitler (and to befriend a ranking SS officer named Adolf Eichmann). They did not change their minds three years later, when Hitler's "Final Solution" was nearing completion and when it appeared possible to save some of the two hundred thousand Jews remaining in Hungary from imminent deportation to Oświęcim. This was part of an immensely complex deal worked out by Hungary's regent Miklós Horthy, secret Jewish emissaries—and Adolf Eichmann. Eichmann was supposedly willing to let the Hungarian Jews go in exchange for trucks, other equipment, and large sums of money. The Jewish organizers of the scheme had to come up with a destination for the about-to-be-saved Jews, and naturally they selected Palestine.

The International Red Cross informed the British government that the arrangement had been worked out and it was awaiting visas and clearances for the Jews. But Foreign Secretary Anthony Eden, presumably on Churchill's instructions, summed up Britain's response in this manner: ". . . the first contingent of a total number of 40,000 Jews are to start leaving Hungary for Palestine in ten days. . . . Palestine cannot accept at the moment anything like so many immigrants." Though Palestine-recruited Jews—the Jewish Brigade—fought alongside the British in the Middle East against the Nazi Afrika Korps, this battlefield alliance did not extend to the acceptance of fresh Jewish immigrants in the mandate territory—even if it meant their death, which it did.

In mid-1945, when the death camps were liberated and DP camps were swelling with Jewish survivors, Allied authorities had no solution of their own for roughly a quarter million under their control in Germany. American visa regulations kept down the number of those eligible for emigration to the United States; moreover, a large percentage was not acceptable for health reasons. British occupation authorities for their part devoted extraordinary efforts in Germany, Austria, and Eastern Europe to track down illegal Jewish emigration routes to Palestine. British intelligence operatives hunted Jewish organizers with more dedication than they sought Nazi war criminals or Soviet secret agents.

A great tragedy, then, was in the making in the immediate aftermath of V-E Day, and it was not entirely confined to Jews. There were Poles and Czechs and Yugoslavs who wished not to return to live under communism in their homelands; to them the havens were the United States, Australia, Canada, and even Latin America, but everywhere governments were parsimonious with immigration visas. It was one thing to risk and sacrifice lives for the freedom of oppressed Europeans, and it was another to welcome surviving Europeans in the new worlds, where they could become job competitors.

To be sure, Roosevelt and Truman pressed Congress to increase visa quotas for Europeans, Jewish or not, but so soon after the Great Depression, Americans seemed less than keen to encourage massive emigration to their shores. Besides, many in Congress thought, Europeans should be rebuilding Europe, and Americans were prepared to foot the bill for it. Meanwhile, hundreds of thousands of Europeans the length and the breadth of the Continent lived through the excruciating drama of visa applications, the acceptances and the rejections. In the end, four hundred thousand DPs settled in the United States.

In a very frightening fashion Gian Carlo Menotti tells the story of the visa drama in his three-act opera *The Consul*, which was presented for the first time to hushed New York audiences in 1950, when all of it was still happening in real life. The action takes place in what Menotti describes in the libretto as "a small, shabby apartment in a large European city" and "the waiting room of the Consulate, a cheerless, coldly-lit room, furnished with the usual benches and wall desks." Though it is never identified, the consulate is clearly American. The Consul himself, the man who holds the power of life and death over visa applicants, is never seen; the visa seekers deal only with a character named the Secretary, obviously an American woman whose task is to keep callers away from the Consul, preside over file cabinets, and ask applicants, "Did you bring your birth certificate? . . . Your health certificate? . . . And your vaccination? . . . And your affidavit? . . . And the statement from the bank? . . . Your passport? . . . Three photographs? . . ."

The Consul is the story of a young couple in what evidently is an Eastern European capital already under Communist rule, their small child, and the wife's mother, who desperately want to flee—to the United States and safety—but first need visas. The man, a member of the underground, had been wounded in a raid, and the secret police keeps visiting the apartment where he is hiding; it is his wife who makes the humiliating pilgrimages to the consulate. In the end they are refused visas because of red tape, and the wife in hopeless resignation turns on the gas in the apartment and dies while the husband is taken away by the secret police.

Menotti's opera was pretty powerful stuff when I first saw it nearly forty years ago—I had instantly recognized the consulate and its furniture and its secretary from my own wartime childhood in Europe—and it was still pretty powerful when I went to see it at the Kennedy Center in Washington in 1988, in a new production supervised by Menotti himself. Because in the eighties a whole new generation of desperate foreigners, from Moscow and Bucharest to Bangkok, Hong Kong, Mexico, and San Salvador, were begging and praying for American visas just as their predecessors had done in the forties, *The Consul*, I thought, was as wrenchingly relevant now as it was at its premiere then. Some things never seem to change.

Most shocking, in contrast, was the knowledge we acquired much later concerning American visas and other forms of protection given Nazi intelligence experts, including war criminals, by U.S. military intelligence, the OSS, and its successor, the Central Intelligence Agency, in the immediate aftermath of V-E Day and in subsequent years.

While American scientific intelligence officers confronted their Soviet counterparts in the quest for Nazi scientists to advance their countries' respective military capabilities, espionage experts on both sides were after Nazi spies and counterintelligence agents. In reconstructing the history of the Cold War from its inception even before the end of World War II, it is ironic to realize that while the U.S. rocketry and space programs were immensely aided by at least 117 German specialists hauled over to America late in 1945, the Soviet Union most likely owes much of its development of the atomic bomb to German scientists shanghaied to Russia (as well as to such wartime German refugees in Britain as Klaus Fuchs, who voluntarily absconded to Moscow with priceless nuclear secrets).

In the conquest of space there is little doubt that today's American and Soviet programs owe a huge debt to the pioneering work of the Germans engaged in them since the late forties. The Soviet *Sputnik I* probe that, in effect, inaugurated the space age in 1957, was designed with German advice. So were the subsequent U.S. suborbital flights, leading to the first American manned landing on the moon in 1969 and, twenty years later, to the firing of the *Magellan* spacecraft from a space shuttle in orbit for a detailed mapping of the surface of the planet Venus; fifteen months were allotted for *Magellan* to reach Venus. The Soviets scored well with their manned space programs since the 1960's, when both countries began to unravel the mysteries of the solar system, and went the Americans one better by maintaining the *Mir* station in orbit for several years, with crew changes twice or three times annually. Unmanned surveillance and communications satellites quickly became commonplace.

American and Soviet space *and* nuclear enterprises, both born in World War II, were meshed together in the eighties with the developments of spatial nuclear attack and defense systems. Among the escalating satellite and antisatellite programs was President Ronald Reagan's multibillion-dollar Strategic Defense Initiative ("Star Wars") and the thirty-five Soviet spy satellites powered by nuclear reactors launched since the late 1960's (the United States had only one nuclear-powered satellite in space).

It is virtually impossible to determine the Soviet intelligence "take" in terms of SS, Gestapo, and military intelligence agents or of their importance and usefulness. Only in the fifties and subsequently did it become known that a certain number of key West German intelligence officers, working closely with the U.S. and North Atlantic Treaty Organization intelligence organizations were Soviet "moles," who for years had been passing on Western secrets to the KGB and the GRU, the Soviet military intelligence body. This was learned when such persons defected openly or clandestinely to the Soviet Union or were arrested in West Germany.

We now know, however, that from the very outset top-level decisions were made in Washington to recruit Nazis for service with the American intelligence against the Soviets. The rationale was that these Nazi officers had spent their prewar and wartime careers studying and penetrating the Soviet establishment to the extent Americans never had the opportunity to do and that this expertise should be acquired by the United States even in advance of a serious split with Moscow. A professional case can probably be built for the American use of such Nazi assets, including the fact that they were sheltered from denazification procedures after the war and, in certain cases, for punishment for war crimes. There is no room for ethics or sentimentality in big-power intelligence wars.

Indefensible, on the other hand, was the practice by top chiefs of American intelligence of assisting Nazi officers who had rendered useful services to U.S. operatives in Germany to leave the country with new identities or expurged wartime records and with U.S. financing. Thus they were aided in escaping punishment for war crimes—some of them were concentration camp commanders or SS executioners—by being supplied by American agents with visas for the United States and Latin American countries. Adolf Eichmann, Klaus Barbie, and Dr. Josef Mengele, the chief doctor at Oświęcim who conducted lethal research on inmates, may not have made it to South America without some form of American help. Eichmann, for example, was held for some time at a U.S. camp for detained Nazis in Austria before mysteriously making his way first to Italy and then to Argentina.

Simon Wiesenthal, the famous Nazi hunter, writes in his book *The Murderers Among Us* that "leading SS and Gestapo criminals" had fled west in the hopes of more lenient treatment by the Western Allies, and "their hope was fulfilled." He also noted that "the British authorities in Austria were more concerned about the illegal transports to Palestine than about Nazi war criminals in their zone." Joseph Wechsberg, an American writer deeply familiar with the postwar situation, says in a chapter in the Wiesenthal book that after the start of the Cold War power politics "became more important than the need for moral retribution." When I met Wiesenthal in Vienna almost twenty years later, he was still immensely exercised and angry over the comparative treatment Jews and Nazis were receiving from the Allies in the aftermath of the victory.

"All Nazis became good Nazis," Wechsberg remarks, "provided they were prepared to resist the new enemy, communism." And this was true in reverse as well inasmuch as former Nazis in Communist East Germany enlisted to fight the West. The East German regime has never admitted it, but in the case of the United States, documents declassified only in 1982 show that two wartime Nazi murderers were never called before the Nuremberg war crimes tribunal because they had supplied American intelligence with in-depth information about the Soviet Union. They were SS Major Friedrich Buchardt, who supervised the liquidation of the Jewish ghetto in Vitebsk in Byelorussia in 1943, and SS Brigadier General Franz Alfred Six, who was in charge of destroying the Smolensk ghetto (Six also had orders from Gestapo chief Heinrich Himmler to capture personally top Soviet leaders if the Germans succeeded in taking Moscow). CIA documents at the National Archives in Washington describe Buchardt and Six as "guilty of mass executions and atrocities during World War II," adding that incredible as it may appear, both were university professors in civilian life. Never tried, they simply vanished from sight.

Published reports in 1982 also disclosed that as many as thirty former Nazi officers served as instructors during the Korean War at the U.S. Army's Intelligence School, then located at Fort Holabird in Maryland. Also in 1982, Joseph Loftus, a former Justice Department prosecutor, revealed publicly that American intelligence had tampered with files of ex-Nazis to make them eligible for U.S. visas. In other instances, Loftus claimed, former Nazis entered the country through lightly patrolled Canadian and Mexican borders, and still others were routed via Argentina and other friendly Latin American dictatorships.

Loftus also charged that the State Department's Office of Policy Coordination, a covert operation that predated the CIA's clandestine branch, had smuggled into the United States "hundreds" of Byelorussians believed to have committed wartime atrocities. These were Soviet citizens who collaborated with the Nazis after the 1941 invasion, and a number of them were charged with mass murders of Jews. They were secretly brought to the United States to work as intelligence advisers in covert operations against the Soviet Union; some of them were employed by Radio Free Europe and Radio Liberty, anti-Communist broadcasting organizations financed at the time by the CIA.

Subsequently it developed that there were known Nazi war criminals among the German scientists and technicians rushed to the United States in 1945 to work on rocketry and space projects. Documents published in the *Bulletin of Atomic Scientists* in 1985 showed that American intelligence officials had concealed the Nazi wartime records of hundreds of German scientists and technicians hired for research in the United States although such procedures specifically violated a presidential order. Several of them had been charged with war crimes at the Nuremberg trials, and one, Dr. Hermann Becker-Freysing, former director of aeromedical research for the German air force, had been convicted and sentenced to twenty years in prison for participating in concentration camp experiments with inmates who died after drinking seawater to test its potability. Under programs known as Overcast and Paperclip, dossiers were altered, among others, for Becker-Freysing and Walter Schreiber, a scientist who was flown to the United States through Argentina in 1952 although he had been linked in U.S. documents to Nazi euthanasia programs.

But there was poetic justice in the fact that Justice Department investigators had been gradually spotting these Nazis, often succeeding in forcing their departure or deportation. The most famous case involved Arthur Louis Hugo Rudolph, the German scientist who developed the *Saturn* V rocket that boosted the American spacecraft on its voyage to the moon landing. (Another German scientist deeply involved in the Saturn moon project was Konrad K. Dannenberg. In Germany he helped develop the V-2 flying bomb. In the United States Dannenberg was head of the Saturn rocket systems engineering.) When he first came to the United States, Rudolph was named director of the U.S. Army's Redstone and Pershing missile programs (working with Von Braun), then manager of the *Saturn* V project for the National Aeronautics and Space Administration. He retired in 1969, immediately after the moon landing.

The Justice Department found out subsequently that during the war Rudolph had persecuted prisoners at the underground rocket plant near the Dora concentration camp in the Harz Mountains. The Dora prisoners worked at the Nordhausen test center where the V-2 was developed late in 1944. Investigators also discovered that Rudolph had been originally classified by U.S. authorities in Germany as an "ardent Nazi . . . 100 per cent Nazi, dangerous type, security threat. . . . Suggest internment." Though this file had been doctored in his favor by the CIA, Rudolph decided in 1984 to renounce his acquired American citizenship and return to Germany rather than contest Justice Department charges against him.

And in 1987, forty-two years after the war's end, a master list of 36,800 files on alleged Nazi war criminals, originally compiled by the United Nations War Commission but kept secret during all that time, was located in a U.S. Army archive in Maryland. Apart from such names as Hitler and Eichmann, the list provides material—never acted upon—against men and women who in a variety of ways had been active in the Nazi war machine. The UN files had remained closed until it was learned that they included the name of Kurt Waldheim, who was elected UN secretary-general in 1971 and served for ten years. The charge against him was murder and taking of hostages; he has forcefully denied it.

The total of persons accused of war crimes by the West German government in lists drawn up in 1958 stood at 160,000, and some 70,000 were sentenced by German courts by 1964, when legal procedures ended for all practical purposes.

In the light of present knowledge, it is probably fair to conclude that a half century after the fact as much punishment as possible has been dispensed to Nazi war criminals although obviously there is no perfect standard of justice. Hitler and Hermann Göring committed suicide. Eichmann was captured by the Israelis, tried in Jerusalem in 1961, and executed. Klaus Barbie, the "Butcher of Lyons," languishes in a French prison. The seventy thousand or so "small fry" of Nazidom were given sentences, usually light. Perhaps a dozen Nazi war criminals were deported from the United States, when their true identities were discovered, to stand trial in Europe.

Yet so many of the important war criminals, such as the scientists, eluded punishment, often because the United States had saved them. They lead, or have led, the kinds of prosperous lives that Gian Carlo Menotti's "Consul" denies the young couple in that "large European city." This is a nagging thought that does not go away. It is part of the memories of 1945. From Buchenwald and Oświęcim survivors to the slave laborers in the DP camps, and from Nazi scientists and spies to the millions of war prisoners, expellees, refugees, and wanderers, this was the tableau of the human condition in the heart of Europe when Adolf Hitler's fury of conquest had finally run its course.

That human condition and the whole horrible history of the past six years of war—and in many instances of the years that preceded it—naturally inflicted deep, raw wounds in the European psyche. Hatreds, guilts, and unforgiveness born from wartime have not vanished altogether after a half century, and they remain significant and sensitive political and emotional issues. In a structural sense, Western Europe has achieved an extraordinary degree of unity and cooperation in the postwar years. On other levels, however, questions of morality, ethics, and interpretations of patriotism versus treason or betrayal continue to plague old and new generations alike, for European memories are very long. Judgments are still applied to the dead and the living, and new arguments and controversies are emerging among historians and philosophers.

In West Germany and Austria, for example, there is a sense among citizens of varying backgrounds and generations that as losers they are inevitably subject to injustices and external impositions on their national lives. There is a school of thought that denies that the Holocaust actually occurred and that consequently Germans need not experience national or collective guilt. Inevitably these attitudes are reflected in contemporary politics and reactions to the outside world. In Russia and Eastern Europe, hatreds, guilts, and resentments exist as well, playing a central role in the great political and ideological changes in that part of Europe in the eighties. The prospect of a reunified Germany in 1990 has brought back all the terrible memories among her neighbors, and reopened old wounds and debates.

Each society has dealt differently with the problems inherited from the war, notably with what was regarded as fundamental violations of morality and patriotism. Of course, there have been glaring failures of omission and commission, and no nation believes it has resolved perfectly the matter of the sins against it.

In France the provisional government under General de Gaulle wasted no time placing on trial the ninety-year-old Marshal Henri Philippe Pétain, who served as head of the German-controlled regime in Vichy between 1940 and 1944, and his premier, Pierre Laval. It was a grim and painful affair, for Pétain was the hero of the First World War, one of France's most respected figures, and De Gaulle's mentor in military arts as the young officer rose to prominence from captaincy in 1924. Pétain had been removed from Vichy to Germany by the Nazis in 1944, then allowed to flee to Switzerland, but he made a point of crossing the border into France and surrendering to the general commanding a Free French army division. De Gaulle and his government remained totally removed from the trial, but he made no secret of his refusal to forgive the ancient marshal for signing the armistice with Hitler in 1940, establishing the traitorous Vichy regime, and promulgating racial laws that cost uncounted thousands of Jewish lives. Pétain was sentenced to prison, where he died at the age of ninety-five. Laval, a widely despised politician, was executed.

Elsewhere in France, those who had collaborated with the Nazis were shunned, and women who had befriended Germans had their heads shaved in public. Entertainers like the singer Maurice Chevalier and the actor Sacha Guitry were boycotted for a time for having performed for the occupiers, but they were not punished. The great cinema director Marcel Carné produced numerous pictures during the Vichy rule. He was criticized for ambiguities in his behavior, but *Port of Shadows*, which he completed just before the end of the occupation, was subsequently named by France's Academy of Cinema Arts and Techniques as the best French talking film ever. Truth, of course, is always exceedingly hard to establish in such nebulous circumstances as the Nazi occupation, and it will probably never be known, for instance, who betrayed to the Gestapo the resistance leaders Jean Moulin and Georges Mandel. When Klaus Barbie, the Nazi gauleiter in Lyons, was tried in 1987 for mass murders of Jews, his lawyers hinted darkly that he could exact revenge by revealing betrayals within the resistance, but no such information existed. That most of France was a maquis monolith is known to be a myth, but it is a pleasant one; the French Communist party and one or more conservative Cabinet ministers in the postwar period benefited from it by winning elections on the strength of alleged wartime resistance records.

In West Germany the Nuremberg trials and Allied denazification policies punished thousands of war criminals, but not all of them (at Oświęcim, for example, six thousand guards had served there during the war, and most escaped retribution). Although the statute of limitation for war crimes was extended by the parliament until 1969, quite a few former Nazis rose to high positions in the West German government (just as Kurt Waldheim was elected president of Austria in 1987). Later some of them quit under fire. Herbert von Karajan, one of the great orchestra conductors of the century and perhaps the outstanding Beethoven interpreter, had joined the Nazi party in 1933, possibly helping his career at its outset. In 1945 the Allies barred him from conducting for two years under denazification policy, and Von Karajan, who died in 1989 at the age of eighty-one, never forgot the slight.

Clearly the hardest of all is to judge (if one has the right to judge in the abstract) whether the wartime crimes were national or individual traits in the case of Germans or inexplicable aberrations at that place and at that time. To be sure, the Japanese were guilty of grievous atrocities in China in the thirties and in World War II, and Americans' hands were not wholly pristine in Vietnam either (nor the hands of the Vietnamese or Cambodians). Still, in the kind of world in which we live, these are not historical or theoretical discussions, and they require constant attention.

A disturbing judgment was made to me by Professor I. S. Kulcsar, who had repeatedly interviewed Eichmann psychologically in the Jerusalem prison before the 1961 trial. Kulcsar was director of the psychiatry department at a Tel Aviv hospital, and when we discussed Eichmann many years later, the professor said that contrary to general belief, the SS officer was not a blindly obedient conformist who was just "following orders." Instead, Dr. Kulcsar insisted, Eichmann was an individual of "good average intelligence" who knew exactly what he was doing. The Israeli psychiatrist's terrifying conclusion was that "in contemporary societies, modern man—wanting and being allowed to kill—would do it in the same manner as Eichmann did." And he added, "If you scratch long and deep enough, you will remove the veneer of civilization from any human being and Eichmann will come out."

I presume that this applies, at least, to professional jailers, and examples of executions and tortures abound all over the world. But there is a danger in generalizing. Simon Wiesenthal has cited examples of SS troopers punished for refusing to torture or kill Jews and of other Nazis' helping him survive. He said that "a man could come back from the war wearing a white vest, if he wanted to," explaining that in German weisse Weste is the symbol of innocence. Wiesenthal goes on to say that "unfortunately, for each man with a white vest there were many who didn't have to commit crimes but volunteered for executions and torture. . . . The victims were not always innocent either. I once talked with a Jewish concentration camp trusty who had saved his life by taking part in the execution of a fellow Jew . . . it was either he or the other man."

In Yugoslavia Marshal Tito, the Communist partisan chief, executed General Draža Mihajlović, a royalist who had risen against the Germans before Tito, on dubious charges of secret collaboration with the invaders. Mihajlović's death remains a point of contention among Yugoslavs decades later; they too have long memories. But there was wide approval when Tito smashed the Croat militias of Ante Pavelić, who worked for the Nazis and the Italians (some of Pavelić's cohorts found their way to the United States after the war). By the same token, Norway's Vidkun Quisling, whose name became synonymous with "treason" in all the languages, and Belgium's Léon Degrelle, a fellow traitor, were mourned by nobody.

And in the West what was one to make of Ezra Pound, the poet of genius and wartime advocate of Mussolini's fascism in Rome? Is there an absolute standard of judgment of fellowmen?

In the Soviet Union under Mikhail Gorbachev the public outcry is not only over crimes committed by Stalin and his henchmen against individuals of note, such as Leon Trotsky or Nikolai Bukharin, and millions of supposedly political prisoners but over the wartime destruction of national groups. Reading a February 1989 issue of *Moscow News*, I came upon a lengthy article describing how Stalin during the war had smashed Crimean Tatars by deporting more than 150,000 of them to Uzbekistan for no discernible reason (except that he distrusted all non-Russians despite being a Georgian himself). Some 40,000 Tatars starved to death in the process. Stalin had also uprooted 200,000 Koreans in the Soviet Far East, then ethnic Germans, Kalmyks, Chechens, Ingushes, Karachais, and Balkars from their homes throughout the Soviet Union.

So, again, practices from a half century ago become the new realities of today. The Ferment in the non-Russian republics in the Soviet Union since the advent of *perestroika* is not entirely due, I believe, to regional nationalisms but also to the resentments against the terrors of the Stalinist rule continued by his successors. With domination over 104 national groups, the Soviet Union was the world's last colonial empire. The Tatars were the first to demonstrate publicly in Moscow in the mid-1980's. With the advent of Gorbachev in 1985 came the mass manifestations by Latvians, Estonians, and Lithuanians, who were forcibly incorporated into the Soviet Union in 1940 (and were subject to severe denationalizing policies), and Armenians, Azerbaijanis, and Georgians, who suffered for seventy years under the *Russian* Communist yoke. In 1989, more than 49 percent of the Soviet Union's 287 million inhabitants were non-Russian.

The wounds of the war remain real and raw across the continent of Europe in the minds and souls of millions. They were slashed open by maddened dictators, torturers and executioners, traitors and opportunists. These injuries came to the fore when the European war ended in 1945. But no sooner were they inflicted than the world's new rulers moved to plunge much of humanity into a fresh epoch of drama, with the outcome still a question mark nearly a half century later.

IV

Year Zero, 1945, achieved two totally contradictory results as all sides strove for advantage in seeking to settle postwar problems. On one hand, the victorious big powers constructed the foundations for global peace that were maintained for forty-five years. On the other hand, the victors set in motion new forces whose nature they did not comprehend and created very fundamental conflicts and divisions that led to enormous tensions and regional wars throughout the second half of the twentieth century.

Big-power interests merged with those of national movements seeking liberation and decolonization, continuously attempted to co-opt them for their own aims, and often became hostage to their commitments to the nascent Third World. On a number of occasions, the East and the West came to the brink of nuclear war over such issues—from Korea and Indochina to Cuba—as rival ideologies and strategic objectives overwhelmed the decolonization process and as the East and the West competed for the new countries' allegiances. The birth of the Third World was not really anticipated in this fashion by any of the colonial empires—not the European, the American, and the Soviet—and it rapidly turned into an overwhelming postwar phenomenon. A half century later the Third World reality is still overwhelming and unmanageable.

For its part, the United States contributed halfway through Year Zero to the development of the atomic weapon, first in its July test in New Mexico, then in the aerial attacks on Hiroshima and Nagasaki in August. Scientifically, militarily, and politically, the atomic bomb marked the start of the most dramatic era in history, with all its potential implications, risks, dangers, and promises. It was inevitable that the Soviet Union would follow suit by acquiring *its* atomic weapon four years later, and the resulting mutual deterrence (plus nuclear weapons subsequently built by Britain, France and China) became both a guarantee of world peace and the basic dimension of the Cold War.

A half century after the Second World War produced the nuclear gift, the peaceful uses of atomic energy are a vital part of the high technology revolution. Yet the growing spread of nuclear weapons to Third World nations, each devoted to its special causes and interests, is an immense threat to peace; once a country uses the weapon, there is no way of predicting what will happen next.

None of these perils—not nuclear weapons, not Third World explosiveness—were on the minds of the peace builders of Year Zero. At the San Francisco Conference, where the Charter of the United Nations was drafted and signed (it was Roosevelt who proposed in 1941 the name of United Nations for the new organization), these topics were not mentioned. To be sure, the conference met between April 25 and June 26, ending exactly one month *before* the secret Los Alamos test of the 18.6-kiloton atomic bomb—nobody had the slightest idea the United States was on the verge of a breakthrough.

Although numerous underdeveloped nations (most of them from Latin America), later to be classified under the Third World heading, attended the San Francisco Conference, decolonization and new-nation building were not UN themes, either, at that point. The Charter created a Trusteeship Council under the new structure to prepare so-called trust territories for self-government or independence, "as may be appropriate," but this affected only prewar League of Nations mandates or areas "detached from enemy states as a result of the Second World War." It was not saying very much about the approaching explosion of decolonization albeit powerful nationalist stirrings were already evident in India, French Indochina, most of the Middle East, and North Africa. The insights of the great statesmen of the time definitely belonged to the prewar years. Franklin Roosevelt, an early proponent of independence for India and the Indochina states (and who had promised freedom to the Philippines even before Pearl Harbor to end what was to be more than fifty years of American rule), had died two weeks before San Francisco, and Truman was much less sanguine about such idealisms.

Foreign ministers at San Francisco were already adept at Cold War skirmishes. The United States agreed to UN membership for the Ukraine and Byelorussia, accepting the Stalinist fiction that they were "autonomous" republics within the Soviet Union, and the Russians let the Americans bring in Argentina, whose governments during the war were virtual Axis allies. An agreement was worked out on the veto power of the five permanent members of the UN Security Council, essentially meeting the demands of Moscow, which knew it could be otherwise outvoted by the United States, Britain, France, and China (the Soviets used the veto while they were in a minority in the eleven-member Council, and the Americans did likewise when the situation changed adversely in the 1970's with the entry of Third World countries as nonpermanent members but with full voting rights). Then the West pilloried the Russians for violating the Yalta commitments

on implanting democracy in Poland, bowing in the end to Stalin's determination to do things his way. That V-E Day came during the San Francisco conclave was simply an occasion for more speeches and champagne.

The Potsdam Conference in July and August, which brought together
Stalin, Churchill, and Truman (at the latter's suggestion in May), produced
much foolish mischief and precious little serious peace building. Probably
its towering accomplishment was to legitimize the role of the Soviet Union
as a fully recognized world power now that the war in Europe was won and
the fruits of victory could be savored by those who were the quickest about
it. One of them was obviously Stalin, whose voice had been essentially
irrelevant internationally before 1939 and who even at Yalta had tended to
be regarded with certain condescension by Churchill and Roosevelt (although there, behind Roosevelt's back, Churchill was willing to swap British
influence in Greece for Soviet dominance in Romania, Hungary, and Bulgaria).

In a practical sense, Potsdam was a disaster for the Anglo-Saxons, who
also made the mistake of not inviting General de Gaulle, already president
of the French provisional government in Paris, which administered one of
the Allied occupation zones in Germany and Austria. De Gaulle was an
overdignified and quarrelsome fellow; but he was a tough pragmatist with
extraordinary political and historical instincts, and the Westerners could
have used his presence during the two weeks at Cecilienhof Palace near
Potsdam. As it happened, the inexperienced Truman believed he could establish a profitable personal relationship with the smiling Marshal Stalin.
Churchill had to stop smiling the second week of the conference when his
Conservative party was stunningly defeated in the general election; he had to
be replaced at the Potsdam table on July 28, by the Labour party's Clement
R. Attlee, the new prime minister, and the equally unprepared new foreign
secretary, Ernest Bevin. Truman writes in his *Memoirs* that the British
change of guard at Potsdam "was a dramatic demonstration of the stable and
peaceful way" in which democracies alternate their governments and that
the Allied position remained intact. I suspect this was courtesy rather than
reality.

In terms of formal accomplishments, the Potsdam meeting is not memorable. It established the legal basis for four-power control over Germany
(and over the Berlin and Vienna enclaves within Soviet zones) to last until
Germans would be able "in due course to take their place among the free
and peaceful peoples of the world." The expression "in due course" provided the vagueness and flexibility that the Big Three wished to preserve in
dealing with Germany's political future. That the real but unstated decision
of the conference was to keep Germany indefinitely divided between the
East and the West—neither side in the accelerating Cold War wished to see
a unified Germany—was emphasized by the fact that the Potsdam Agreement did not provide for the preparation of a German peace treaty. The

agreement called for peace treaties for Italy, Romania, Bulgaria, Hungary, and Finland as defeated powers; on Germany, it simply stated that a peace settlement would be prepared when a German government "adequate for the purpose" had been established.

To put it simply, the division of Germany was sanctified at Potsdam primarily because no other acceptable solution existed at the time; for that matter, it still did not exist a half century later, following the demise of East German communism in November 1989, when the Berlin Wall ceased to divide the former capital into two German worlds. The 1949 West German constitution establishes reunification as a national goal, but in the weeks and months following the end of the Communist rule in East Germany— and therefore with the removal of the ideological and geopolitical reasons for the existence of the Soviet-organized German Democratic Republic— the West and East Germans could not quite agree how and when to go about it. In a very insightful essay published in 1989, but before the dramatic events of November, George F. Kennan remarked that while it would be an exaggeration to say that after forty years of separation from the rest of Germany the East Germans had developed a new sense of nationality, "these long years . . . unquestionably have affected them in many ways—in their habits, their outlooks, and their tastes and preferences." While they may envy the West Germans their living conditions, Kennan noted, "there are other aspects of West German life that they would not find entirely congenial and where they would prefer to preserve habits, outlooks, and, in some instances, even institutions to which they have grown accustomed." Indeed, the earlier conventional wisdom that the East Germans overwhelmingly wished instant reunification was overturned almost immediately when the Berlin Wall and other impediments to East-West travel were removed, confirming Kennan's assessment. Though millions of East Germans crossed to the West on weekends, virtually all of them returned home to work afterward; by the end of 1989, it was clear that even prodemocracy East German groups were wary of unification commitments. After the euphoria and the emotion of the first moments of the memorable November, the West Germans too began to rethink their positions, aware of the immense economic cost of in effect absorbing East Germany. Early in 1990, between three and four thousand East Germans daily were fleeing to the West, exhausting West German resources.

At the same time, the "German Question" became even more complicated in 1990 than it had been before the fall of communism. The European Community had obvious reservations over the weight and power of a reunified Germany in the context of the single market planned for January 1, 1993. Eastern Europe and the Soviet Union were, not unnaturally, rediscovering security fears of a half century ago. Enmity between Poland and East Germany over the postwar borders favoring the Poles was a rising factor in the Central European equation.

* * *

The "Polish Question" inevitably surfaced at Potsdam as well—in continuation of the Yalta and San Francisco quarrels. Actually Stalin had made concessions (which turned out to be tactical) by allowing a number of key members of the exiled London government to join the Polish provisional government formed in the eastern city of Lublin. The most notable of these was the highly respected Stanisław Mikołajczyk, the leader of the Peasant party, who had served as premier in London and now was named second deputy premier and agriculture minister. He agreed to join the Communist-directed postwar regime even though sixteen of his opposition colleagues were still on trial in Moscow because of his belief that the presence of a democratic faction might somehow arrest Poland's slide toward Communist totalitarianism. When Mikołajczyk decided to participate in the provisional government, Truman concluded that the Yalta commitment had been fulfilled. He pushed Churchill to recognize the Polish regime, and Britain and the United States did so on July 5, still during the conference.

The Potsdam Agreement hailed the Polish settlement, and again, Stalin offered the tactical concession in signing with the others an exhortation for the free elections promised at Yalta. Truman and Attlee were underestimating Stalin (Churchill, according to his biographer Martin Gilbert, said at the time to Anthony Eden, the outgoing foreign secretary, that "the Bolsheviks are crocodiles"). Polish history was to go full circle with the legalization of the free trade union Solidarity in 1989, the first free postwar elections that same year, and the naming of Solidarity's Tadeusz Mazowiecki as prime minister in August, before democracy became possible. In the end it was Stalin who underestimated the Poles and the power of democracy; Mazowiecki was among those imprisoned eight years earlier when the Warsaw Communist regime attempted to bury Solidarity. In the autumn of 1989, Mazowiecki was received with full honors by Mikhail Gorbachev at the Kremlin.

The most important events at Potsdam occurred away from the Cecilienhof Palace table. The first was the successful atomic blast at Los Alamos, New Mexico, on July 16, and as Truman writes in his *Memoirs*, "this news reached me at Potsdam the day after I had arrived for the conference of the Big Three," which opened on the seventeenth. The new President noted that "we were now in possession of a weapon that would not only revolutionize war but could alter the course of history and civilization."

What followed at Potsdam was the most extraordinary diplomatic minuet, one that Truman failed to understand at the time and that remains unclear to this day in terms of Stalin's behavior. Naturally no public announcement was made of the Los Alamos test—it was still America's best-kept secret—but Truman decided to inform immediately Churchill (who was aware of the Manhattan Project, though not of the imminence of the New Mexico experiment) and then, about eight days later, Stalin, still at Potsdam.

Truman describes it as follows: "On July 24 I casually mentioned to Stalin that we had a new weapon of unusual destructive force. All he said was that he was glad to hear it and hoped we would make 'good use of it against the Japanese.'"

It is inconceivable that Stalin did not understand what Truman had told him or that he underestimated the tremendous importance of the American achievement. While the Soviets were also working on nuclear weapons, they were far from building them in mid-1945. Nevertheless, they possessed sufficient technical and strategic knowledge to be able to conclude instantly that the world military balance had been fundamentally altered on July 16 and, specifically, that the prospects for winding down the Japanese war had changed just as dramatically. Surely these views reached Stalin.

In truth, the new situation was as delicate for Stalin as it was for Truman, requiring superb gamesmanship. At Yalta, before the United States knew whether it would actually have a workable atomic bomb, Roosevelt and Churchill had persuaded Stalin to commit himself to declare war on Japan within three months of the German surrender. His only condition was that the Chinese Nationalist government of Generalissimo Chiang Kai-shek sign a treaty with the Soviet Union, granting certain territorial concessions on the Pacific. Stalin, of course, supported the Chinese Communist armies of Mao Zedong in the civil war against Chiang, so the Russians were in something of a bind.

As for Truman, he was so anxious to have the Soviets engage the huge Japanese army in Manchuria and prevent it from defending the home islands from an American invasion that one of his principal reasons for desiring to meet Stalin was to hear him reaffirm the Yalta promise. General George Marshall had warned Truman that an invasion of Japan might cost a half million American lives. Apprising Stalin of the Los Alamos burst, the President evidently hoped for a reaction indicating the Soviet plans and whether they would change in the light of the atomic bomb's advent on the scene.

What Stalin ignored, however, was that Truman had already decided to use the atomic bomb against the Japanese, which might have explained his ambiguous response to the President's "casual" remark. In fact, on the day of their conversation—July 24—orders were sent by the acting chief of staff of the U.S. Army, General Thomas T. Handy, to General Carl Spaatz, the commanding general of the Strategic Air Forces, to "deliver its first special bomb as soon as weather will permit visual bombing after about 3 August 1945 on one of the targets: Hiroshima, Kokura, Niigata and Nagasaki." Truman does not say so in his *Memoirs*, but at that point he may have hoped that Stalin would abandon the idea of war with Japan; the United States no longer needed the Russians in the Far East though the Soviets might not see it that way.

Most likely both to avoid the need to drop atomic bombs on Japan and to clarify Soviet intentions, Truman and the British drafted on July 25 an

ultimatum to Japan demanding unconditional surrender and future democratization. China added its signature (by cable from Chiang) to the ultimatum issued in Potsdam; Stalin did not, and his reasons were not
explained. On July 28 Radio Tokyo announced that Japan would continue
to fight. It did not mention the ultimatum, but Truman later wrote: "There
was no alternative now. The bomb was scheduled to be dropped after August 3 unless Japan surrendered before that day." Both Stalin and Truman
left for their respective homes on August 2, and there is no known record of
any further exchanges about Japan or the bomb. But once home, Stalin
began negotiating with Chinese Nationalist envoys and with the Japanese.

The bomb on Hiroshima was dropped on the evening of August 5, local
time, and the death toll by the end of 1945 (including casualties from radiation and related causes) stood at 140,000. Nagasaki was hit three days later,
and 70,000 inhabitants had died by year's end.

Stalin may have been taken aback by the American atomic bombing, but
he did not alter his strategy or at least the impression that he was living up to
his Yalta pledge. Thus, on August 8, hours after the Nagasaki explosion, the
Kremlin announced that it would be at war with Japan the following day;
this would be exactly three months after the German surrender. While
Truman writes that "our dropping of the atomic bomb on Japan had forced
Russia to reconsider her position in the Far East," this may have been a
hasty and uninformed conclusion. Subsequently the emergence of archival
materials has led to revisionist discussions on whether the United States
really needed to use atomic bombs against Japan. This argument is based on
the views expressed in 1946 in at least one War Department study that the
Soviet Union's entry into the war against Japan would have forced Tokyo's
surrender, obviating the strikes at Hiroshima and Nagasaki. It is a matter of
judgment that cannot be disproved. On the other hand, it will never be
known if the Russians would have declared war on August 9 if the nuclear
weapons had not been employed.

With the European war behind him, Stalin was free to turn his attention
to the Far East, an area of historical Soviet interest (where Russia lost to
Japan in their 1904–05 conflict), and the atomic bombs may have merely
quickened his decision. He wanted to be in for the kill before it was too late,
and his immediate move was to subscribe belatedly to the Potsdam ultimatum. Stalin declared the war on Japan just in time because Tokyo accepted the Allied ultimatum on August 10. General Douglas MacArthur,
the supreme commander for the Allied powers in the Pacific, received the
Japanese surrender aboard the battleship USS *Missouri* in Tokyo Bay on
September 2, the date Truman proclaimed as V-J Day.

When we reconstruct the political history of the last half century, the first
conclusion is that the Soviet and Communist influence in Asia—from
China and Korea to Indochina—may be traced back, at least in part, to
Stalin's perspicacious decision to go to war with Japan, an inexpensive move
under the circumstances. It legitimized the Soviet military presence in

northern Asia, possibly helping in the establishment of a Communist regime in North Korea and in the Communist victory in China and playing an indubitable role in the Korean and Vietnamese wars. For a start, the Soviets occupied most of Manchuria, dispatching a half million captured Japanese troops to Siberian work camps. Then Stalin landed forces on southern Sakhalin and Kuril islands, which were Japanese home islands, claiming (without real American contradiction) that Roosevelt had promised them to Russia at Yalta. Fifty years later the Soviets still held the islands—without signing a peace treaty with Japan. Finally, Moscow gained membership on the Council of Allies in Tokyo and on the Far East Commission in Washington. These bodies had no effective political power, but what Stalin wanted was diplomatic presence.

As for the West, notably the United States, which bore the brunt of the Pacific war, it wound up in positions of weakness and inferiority, most of the time because of its own inattention and folly. It all goes back to 1945, Year Zero.

The foolishness began at Potsdam. Having first secured with the Soviets the permanent division of Germany, the Western Allies proceeded to divide Vietnam in a shoddy and inexcusable manner.

As they raced through their bilateral agenda (sandwiched between sessions with Stalin), President Truman and Prime Minister Attlee realized that no provisions had been made for the Japanese surrender in Indochina. On the eve of the planned atomic bombings of Japan, they knew that its armies in Southeast Asia would capitulate very quickly and that someone should take over. Staffs were instructed to come up with a solution, and they came up with the bizarre idea of dividing Vietnam along the sixteenth parallel. The plan was for Chinese Nationalists to disarm the Japanese in the North in the region of Hanoi, and for the British in the South, around Saigon. It was absolutely insane, but nobody in authority acted to halt this idiocy.

Many years later, after the French and American wars in Indochina, Lord Louis Mountbatten, who had served as the supreme Allied commander in Southeast Asia, described the Potsdam decision to let the Chinese disarm the Japanese in the war as "a crime of the great powers." Mountbatten said that if he had been made responsible for the liquidation of all the Japanese armies in Vietnam, he would have negotiated an accord with Ho Chi Minh, the Communist Vietnamese leader, and the Indochina Wars might have been averted. France, to be sure, might have taken a dim view of a British mediation in its former colonies. But had General de Gaulle been invited to Potsdam, all these catastrophes probably would not have happened. If nothing else, De Gaulle knew the subject.

Actually the Americans and the British stepped into the Indochina nightmare just at a moment when De Gaulle himself may have been near a solution in terms of Ho's demands for autonomy and independence. Ho, like so many other Vietnamese, had been educated in Paris and, according to many accounts, wished for an accommodation with France under the concept of *doc lap*, a form of independence. Ho was ideologically a Communist, but he also was a Vietnamese nationalist, a distinction that only a few Frenchmen and virtually no Americans ever understood. As early as March 1945 De Gaulle himself proposed the creation of a federal state of the five Indochinese states (Annam, Tonkin, Cochin China, Cambodia, and Laos) that constituted the prewar colony as part of the French Union. This was his idea of a French commonwealth.

Ho and his associates rejected the commonwealth plan, and on September 2, two weeks after Japan's surrender, Vietnamese independence was proclaimed in Hanoi. Emperor Bao Dai, named by the French and on the throne throughout the Japanese occupation, abdicated the same day. De Gaulle turned to a two-track strategy: He let a trusted diplomatic team continue talking with Ho in Hanoi while he sent Admiral Georges Thierry d'Argenlieu and General Philippe Leclerc, a war hero, to Saigon to build French military power before embarking on major negotiations with the Vietnamese.

Interestingly Leclerc quickly emerged as an advocate of Vietnamese independence. Perhaps as a military man he could foresee the horrors of trapping a European land army on the Asian mainland. And Leclerc may have sold De Gaulle the next solution: It was to bring back Prince Vinh San (the former emperor Duy Ton) from Réunion Island in the Indian Ocean, where he had lived since 1917, when he was deposed by the French from his imperial throne in Saigon) to make him the head of an independent federation of Vietnam, Laos, and Cambodia. De Gaulle received the prince in Paris on December 14 and promised to accompany him to Indochina for Vinh San's inauguration. It is a moot point whether Ho would have accepted the princely solution; Vinh San's aircraft disappeared over Africa ten days later, as he was returning from Paris, never to be found.

Alain de Boissieu, De Gaulle's confidential aide and son-in-law, subsequently told the general's biographer Jean Lacouture that this collapse of the secret plan for Indochina was among the principal reasons for the resignation in January 1946 of the chief of the French provisional government. The other reason, perhaps the overwhelming one, was that in the October 21, 1945, elections for the Constituent Assembly (the first postwar elections in France) the electorate rejected De Gaulle—as the British had rejected their war hero, Winston Churchill. The rejection came in a 50.7 percent vote received by the Communist and socialist parties (the Communists came in first), while De Gaulle's Popular Republican Movement (MPR), a right-of-center party, won only 25.6 percent.

De Gaulle was not a power-sharing statesman, and interpreting the vote as a personal defeat, he chose to walk away from his presidency (legally he could have stayed on). Clearly, however, he expected to be called back soon, and he privately informed his Indochina emissaries that his absence from power was temporary and that nothing should be done in Vietnam until his return. Of course, he was wrong (he came back only twelve years later), and events could not wait for him forever. Actually the new government should have pursued the talks with the Vietnamese because no doors had been closed to a rational settlement. However, Félix Gouin, the new provisional president, and his foreign minister, Georges Bidault, ended the contacts with Hanoi though Ho visited Paris for talks in May 1946. The First Indochina War erupted late in 1946, with Ho and his movement now totally identified with communism.

Jean de Lipkowski, one of the last surviving top aides to De Gaulle, told me in Paris in 1987 that if the general had stayed in power, or had returned at once, he would have produced a settlement preventing the war. De Lipkowski also offered a fascinating insight into De Gaulle's thinking: When he handed the general in Paris the flash announcing the explosion of the Hiroshima bomb, the provisional president reacted with horror, predicting that a new and awesome arms race would develop among the superpowers for nuclear weapons. De Gaulle remarked to his aide that this was "the worst piece of news of the whole war," and in a sense he was absolutely right.

It is unlikely, in retrospect, that the United States could have played a stabilizing role in Vietnam after having proposed its partition in Potsdam. And the little America did before and after V-J Day was, at best, ambiguous. Stanley Karnow writes in *Vietnam*, his detailed account of the war, that Roosevelt promised De Gaulle in 1942 the return to France of all its overseas dominions. "The next year," Karnow says, "he told his son Elliott that he would work 'with all my might and main' against any plan to 'further France's imperialistic ambitions.' A year after that, he proposed an international trusteeship for postwar Indochina. . . . He amended that idea later, suggesting that the French could repossess the territory by pledging its eventual independence. And in 1945, he offered Indochina to Generalissimo Chiang Kai-shek."

Both the French and the Vietnamese, who, not surprisingly, were confused by American policy shifts, emerged with varying interpretations of what Washington desired. Lacouture reports that when De Gaulle visited Washington in August 1945, right after the atomic bombing of Japan, Truman told him that the United States was "*not* opposed to the return of the French authority and army" to Vietnam. Lacouture's comment is that "this was a deep innovation in relation to the positions taken earlier by Roosevelt . . . who had at first favored the expansion of the Viet-minh." Michel Jobert, who served as foreign minister in the seventies, writes in his book *The Americans* that France's "conscience and pride" were jolted when Roosevelt and his successors kept "liberating" Indochina from "French colonialism," but between 1954 and 1976 the Americans "found themselves implicated in an enterprise which they knew not how to justify."

Ho himself was anxious for American support, and Karnow writes that the United States "might have plausibly emulated Marshal Tito, the

Yugoslav Communist leader who was soon to defy Moscow." But Vietnam in the mid-forties was entirely irrelevant to American policymakers in a prelude to the coming lost wars. The errors of Potsdam were being compounded. Early in 1945 a team from the Office of Strategic Services parachuted into Ho's jungle camp to train and arm the Vietnamese guerrillas against the Japanese. This was a short-lived experience despite the efforts by Ho, who had once visited the United States, to develop a permanent relationship—with an eye on the postwar world. Perhaps this would have changed history. But, as Karnow writes, "the OSS era has been either effaced by Vietnamese Communist historians unwilling to concede that Ho sought the help of U.S. 'imperialists' or inflated by French colonial apologists who submit that the United States conspired to deprive France of Indochina."

Korea was another instance of American folly in the Far East. Inasmuch as Korea's postwar fate had not been discussed at Yalta or Potsdam, the Japanese collapse in August and the Soviet Union's entry into the Pacific war forced the Truman administration to make some decision concerning the Korean situation. Korea had been part of Japan since 1910, when it was annexed by Tokyo and the ruling Yi dynasty disappeared after six centuries on the Korean throne. The country had played no role in the Second World War, and basically, Americans knew nothing about it or its problems.

The only international commitment was the 1943 Cairo Declaration by the United States, Britain, and China that Korea would become free and independent "in due course," and at some point Washington toyed with the idea of a Korean trusteeship. But only on August 10, 1945, two days after the Nagasaki bomb, did the United States decide to participate in the occupation of Korea. Staff officers (including Dean Rusk, the future secretary of state) had no guidelines on how to proceed with it, including how far north to go. In the absence of a better idea, the officers drew a line on a map across Korea, establishing the thirty-eighth parallel as the division between zones where the Americans and the Russians would respectively disarm the Japanese forces.

Whether the staff officers realized that they had actually partitioned a country—it was the third that month, following the divisions of Germany and Vietnam—is unknown. But that was precisely what happened, and this action, too, set the stage for a war. Immediately Soviet forces poured into northern Korea (Stalin saw nothing wrong with this method of partitioning countries so long as he was a beneficiary), installing as the chief of their puppet Communist regime in Pyongyang a thirty-three-year-old party member named Kim Il Sung. Precious little is known about him except that he was an active guerrilla leader against the Japanese from the mid-1930's, a nationalist, and a Communist and that he was forced to spend most of the world war in the Soviet Far East. Fifty years later he remains a figure of mystery (as is his son and designated successor, Kim Jung Il). Local propaganda calls him "the supreme leader of the entire working people of the world," but he has not been seen outside Korea (except for rare visits to Moscow and Beijing). Stalin naturally had a plan for Korea in the broader Far East context, but the Americans had none.

When units of the U.S. Army's XXIV Corps began landing in Inchon late in August, their mission was entirely vague. General John R. Hodge, the American commander in Korea, was simply instructed to "create a government in harmony with U.S. policies," but he had no clue to what that meant. Moreover, he had no Korean speakers on his staff and could find no Koreans who spoke English. Consequently the Americans began dealing with former Japanese officials, much as they did with ex-Nazis in Germany, because it was easier to run the country through them. Max Hastings, a historian of the Korean War, concludes that "General Hodge and his colleagues found it much more comfortable to deal with the impeccable correctness of fellow soldiers, albeit recent enemies, than with the anarchic rivalries of the Koreans." (About the same time MacArthur's occupation forces in Japan also began doing business with former military and intelligence officers and war criminals.)

In the end the United States installed as Korea's political leader in the South a seventy-year-old conservative politician named Syngman Rhee, who had lived much of his life in exile. Korean liberals who had fought the Japanese at home and often paid with prison sentences were not included in the new government. It never occurred to Washington that the elderly Dr. Rhee would be called upon to symbolize democracy in contest with the Soviet-backed Kim Il Sung. Nor did the United States ever caution Stalin or Kim against adventures in the South. Therefore, they did embark on a very bloody adventure before much more time elapsed.

China was another American quagmire in Asia that nobody in Washington knew how to confront. After the Japanese surrender and the Soviet occupation of Manchuria, the Chinese reality was the recrudescence of the civil war for the control of the country between the Nationalists and the Communists. Throughout World War II the United States supported, trained, armed, and advised the Nationalists in the struggle against Japan though cooperation with Chiang Kai-shek was an excruciating experience for all the top Americans who had to deal with him. The generalissimo and his corrupt regime and armed forces simply demanded to have his way on every subject.

Now the United States faced a situation in which Mao Zedong's Communists were receiving very substantial military and economic support from the Soviet Union, and China was rapidly entering the East-West Cold War dimension (though the war between the rival Chinese bands could be very hot at times). Obviously Washington could not support the Communists, but supporting the Nationalists in an unrestrained fashion would expand and lengthen the civil war that at least some State Department experts considered unwinnable by the generalissimo. The quandary, therefore, was how to help end the Chinese internecine conflict without a catastrophe that would result from a clear Mao victory.

To try to resolve the quandary—mediating, in effect, in the civil war—President Truman named in November 1945 General George C. Marshall, the retiring wartime Army chief of staff and one of the most imposing figures in Washington, to head a special mission to China. American military and intelligence officers had had extensive contact with the Communists during the Japanese war, as had several State Department specialists, and a presidential envoy had had unfettered access to Mao's headquarters. Ideas concerning a possible Nationalist-Communist coalition had been floating, but Truman wanted the opinions and recommendations of the man he trusted most.

Marshall arrived in China on December 20, to launch unquestionably the most complex and intractable postwar mission. He knew that China's survival and viability as well as its place in the East-West conflict were at stake, and he understood that a Communist China, hostile to the United States, could radically alter the postwar balance of power in Asia. The continent was already in turmoil everywhere as liberalization and decolonization pressures mounted uncontrollably, and China was at the epicenter of these huge historical processes.

He may not have known, on the other hand, how much China would become part of American domestic politics and that these political realities would render absolutely impossible the mission he was now undertaking. China instantly became the greatest postwar challenge to the United States as the leader of democracy in the world.

At the end of 1945 the wartime alliance had disintegrated both in purpose and in the majesty of its leaders.

A fundamental ideological divide now separated the East and the West, their power interests diverged dramatically, and the Cold War had been set in motion—with all the attendant dangers for humanity.

In the West the giants were gone. Franklin Roosevelt died in April, Winston Churchill was defeated and removed from the political scene in July, and Charles de Gaulle announced in December that he was leaving the French presidency. Only Joseph Stalin in Moscow represented continuity and singleness of purpose.

BOOK THREE

THE FORTIES

America is faced with a solemn obligation. Long ago
we promised to do our full part. Now we cannot
ignore the cry of hungry children. Surely we will not
turn our backs on the millions of human beings
begging for just a crust of bread.

—HARRY TRUMAN,
radio address, April 19, 1946

I

With the return of peace the United States had everything going for it: a powerful industry, agriculture that would be able to produce more food than Americans could consume, a fine system of education, social and political stability, unmatched military might, and boundless optimism.

The rest of the world had nothing going for it—except extraordinary American generosity and the courage and the determination of its people to rebuild from the tremendous ravages of war and, in the case of the nascent Third World, to build where little or nothing had existed before. For Europe alone, this generosity ranged from saving it from starvation immediately after V-E Day to the massive Marshall Plan, launched in 1947.

As the war ended, the United States was the dominant power on the planet, an economic giant and the center of all hope. It accounted for 40 percent of all production in the world. And as never before, Americans held the lead in technology, from atomic energy to electronics and medicine. They would quickly spawn the great technological revolution of the second half of the twentieth century, and soon the whole world would miraculously change with it. Indeed, the postwar period loomed as the "American Century."

In contrast, Europe and Japan were in ruins. The Soviet Union was exhausted by the four years of savage combat on its territory; it had lost between twenty and forty million citizens in the war (even in 1989 Soviet historians remained uncertain about the figure), and its great cities, like Leningrad and Stalingrad, were flattened by prolonged sieges. The rest of the globe lived amid immense problems and tensions as hundreds of millions on three continents strove for independence from colonial rule. China was foundering in civil war.

America's transition to peace was easier than expected. Sixteen million returning veterans, discharged as rapidly as the military machinery could handle it ("Bring the boys home!" was the cry in Congress), were being quickly absorbed into the economy as it shifted gears from wartime to peacetime consumer production. And the victorious World War II veterans were welcomed and greeted with love, pride, and admiration. The homecoming fighters marched in parades under rains of confetti, the bands blared, and everything was red, white, and blue. They had won the most popular war abroad in American history.

The nation was eager to show its gratitude. The best jobs went to the veterans (often they had been kept open for the duration), and a fine war record could be rewarded with a political career. Under the GI Bill of Rights, which was perhaps the single most important societal idea to emerge from the war, millions of veterans had access to first-rate free education, from vocational schools to university doctoral programs.

Americans had the chance of becoming the best-educated generation ever, and this is why it was such a shattering discovery in the mid-eighties, just forty years later, to find that education in the United States was "stagnant," that thirty-six hundred students dropped out of school on an average school day (an official report called it "a national tragedy"), and that illiteracy in the country was a shocking 27 percent. Steven Muller, the former president of Johns Hopkins University, noted that "in the quarter century between 1945 and 1970, American higher education more than tripled in size and capacity." This pattern vanished in the eighties for reasons that are suggestive of how easily a society can slip into complacency.

In 1946, however, all was upbeat. In addition to the GI Bill of Rights, veterans could enjoy a pleasant transition to civilian life with the "52-20" payments from the government: twenty-dollars a week for fifty-two weeks, and in those days this was *not* a pittance. A seventy-five-dollar-a-week salary was adequate even for a married man. Besides, a great many GIs came home with wads of U. S. currency in their pockets; if anything, there was more money to go around than things to buy as the postwar conversion still was in its first stages. Wartime rationing of virtually everything, including sugar, coffee, cigarettes, meat, gasoline, and nylons, was gradually ending, and Americans were impatient for shopping sprees.

The American love of the automobile was the most unrequited. Both Ford and General Motors had produced their last passenger cars in February 1942, two months after the Japanese attack on Pearl Harbor, and turned entirely to the manufacture of trucks, jeeps, tanks, and aircraft (in that last month Ford built only 19,483 automobiles). The .GIs fresh from the war had to settle at first for used 1942 models, and Alfred H. Edelson, a young advertising executive arriving home after Army Air Forces service in Italy, was happy to pay twelve hundred dollars for a black 1942 Packard sedan; it was a lot of cash, he recalled to me four decades later, but it was worth it. Ford produced 359 cars in July 1945, as it resumed civilian production, and they were snapped up overnight. General Motors unveiled its 1946 Pontiac, the first postwar car, on September 29, 1945.

It was almost impossible to buy a man's white shirt until mid-1946, but the first frozen foods, developed for the troops during the war, began appearing and marked the start of the food revolution in the United States (and soon thereafter elsewhere in the world). They were followed by an endless variety of quick foods, born from soldiers' canned rations, that seem to have affected forever American eating habits, making meals easier and quicker to prepare (and making consumers increasingly unhealthy).

The mood of the time, the period that became known as the Truman years, was perfectly captured in Sam Goldwyn's prizewinning film *The Best Years of Our Lives*, screened in New York in November 1946 to a wildly enthusiastic reception. Directed in black and white by William Wyler and starring an amputee named Harold Russell in a peerless performance, along with Myrna Loy, Fredric March, Dana Andrews, and Teresa Wright, it was an emotional story of returning veterans and the rediscovery of the real world after the dream and nightmare of the war. Robert Sherwood wrote the screenplay, and *Best Years* was a cinematic jewel, exactly what Americans wanted to see (it grossed ten million dollars in its first year). And Miles Davis, Dizzy Gillespie, and Charlie Parker produced the bebop breakthrough in jazz.

Americans had considerably more than cinema to entertain and edify them in 1946. Leonard Bernstein, a versatile American musical genius, could be heard (and very much seen in his theatricality) conducting the New York Philharmonic Symphony Orchestra at Carnegie Hall. Three years earlier, when he was twenty-five, he became its assistant director under Demitri Mitropoulos, and Bernstein's musical *On the Town* had been running on Broadway for two years. He was an instant musical sensation and a member of the new generation who helped place an American stamp on universal music, in the words of the critic Henry Raymont. William Kapell, the pianist who died in his thirties in an airplane crash, was a member of that generation, along with violinists Isaac Stern, then twenty-six (he was born in Russia but came to the United States as an infant) and already famous, and Brooklyn-born thirty-year-old Yehudi Menuhin. Artur Rubinstein and Vladimir Horowitz, both hailing from Eastern Europe but regarding themselves as Americans, played concerts for standing-room-only audiences across the country. Arturo Toscanini conducted his great opera performances. And the American Ballet Theater, born just before the war, was becoming, under Lucia Chase and Oliver Smith, the world-class dance company it is nowadays. The choreographer Martha Graham had presented her *Night Journey*. Serge Koussevitsky was inspiring young American musicians and composers at Tanglewood, and Aaron Copland had just written *Appalachian Spring* (in 1958 the twenty-three-year-old Texan Van Cliburn would stun the musical world by winning, as the first American, the Tchaikovsky Piano Competition in Moscow).

All of a sudden New York and America had soared as world centers of art and culture—and fountainhead of talent—in place of sad and suffering Europe. For the first time America was seen artistically as more than the land of the industry that produced tanks and warships and the atom bomb and more than the haven of millionaires and immigrants. America's artistic coming of age was one more consequence of the war, coinciding with the emergence of native American talent. Musicians like Leonard Bernstein and Isaac Stern, as

I knew them then and now, always thought of themselves as part of the American ethos, not looking across the ocean for approval or inspiration.

Yet there were clouds on this happy horizon. At home the reconversion to peacetime production and the veterans' return were causing deepening labor problems that before long led to major strikes. In addition, in a fundamental way, democracy's triumph overseas failed to be matched in the United States by the implantation of racial equality. The victorious armed forces remained segregated (there were all-black infantry battalions, an all-black air fighter squadron, and blacks in the Navy were confined to mess-steward duty). My first visit to Washington, which was beginning to be called the capital of the free world, was late in 1946, and I remember my shock at seeing Whites Only or Colored signs at rest rooms at Union Station and elsewhere in that still very provincial and very southern city.

Although the war against Hitler was designed to end racial and religious prejudices—the "Final Solution" for Europe's Jews being the overwhelming example—America's "dirty secret" was the perpetuation of quiet anti-Semitism in higher education, access to certain types of employment, and housing and social acceptance. anti-Semitism in America was generally a taboo subject until Darryl F. Zanuck (one of the very few major non-Jewish Hollywood producers) had the courage to shatter it in 1947 with *Gentleman's Agreement*, a shocker of a motion picture based on a novel by Laura Z. Hobson, starring Gregory Peck and John Garfield (who was Jewish). That the problem did not really go away was illustrated by the release in *1988* of *Scandal in a Small Town* in which Raquel Welch plays a cocktail waitress ostracized for challenging her daughter's high school teacher's anti-Semitism. In this picture, among other statements, the teacher blames the Jews for America's failure to win the Vietnam War. And during the eighties there was a marked rise in anti-Semitic incidents—and antiblack incidents— across the United States. In the 1940's, just as four decades later, Americans had trouble dealing with basic societal issues at home.

Abroad the clouds were turning quite dark. Polarization between the United States and the Soviet Union was growing at an alarming rate, and the Cold War was steadily acquiring momentum. The key to postwar history was the immense disparity in the strength and resources between the two powers. The contrast between the affluence of capitalism as represented by the United States and the backwardness of Soviet socialism was instantly translated into mutual suspicions, reinforced by the basic ideological differences.

As seen from Washington, Stalin was engaged in promoting Communist expansion everywhere by consolidating Soviet power in Eastern Europe, attempting to maintain a foothold in oil-rich and very strategic Iran, and directing subversion in Western Europe through strong local Communist parties. As seen from Moscow, the United States was determined to push its hegemony and "imperialism" everywhere in the world, to keep old military bases overseas and establish new ones to control vital areas, and to surround and threaten the Soviet Union. Often perceptions were more important than realities.

The most significant reality was that in 1946 the United States retained the atomic monopoly, regarding it as a guarantee of its preeminence. The American assumption was that the Soviets would not develop a nuclear weapon in fewer than ten years, if then, and this colossal error in estimating Soviet capabilities stemmed from the pitiful condition of American scientific intelligence. Nobody in Washington suspected that the Soviet atomic bomb was only three years away. Still, the United States had every intention of staying ahead in perfecting nuclear weapons.

In April 1946 Dr. Edward Teller, the Hungarian-born physicist who from the outset had played a central role in developing the atomic bomb, presided in Los Alamos over a secret conference to determine how quickly and efficiently a thermonuclear bomb could be built. This was the hydrogen bomb, or the "Super," which with an explosive force up to ten megatons was to dwarf the 1945 atomic bomb, becoming the nearest thing to an ultimate weapon. At that point the American arsenal consisted of only nine atomic bombs, but two were exploded in tests at the Bikini atoll in the Pacific in July 1946 (after the American authorities evacuated its inhabitants in a most irresponsible and damaging fashion, exposing them to radioactivity at a relocation site too close), in order to accelerate research.

Although the United States believed that its atomic monopoly assured that neither the Soviet Union nor—certainly—a lesser nation would challenge it anywhere, it is clear in retrospect that this monopoly was actually destabilizing in political terms. For one thing, the Soviets were fully aware of American nuclear advances; not only could they monitor the Bikini tests and measure the fallout, but Dr. Klaus Fuchs, the German-born British scientist who had operated as a Soviet agent since 1942, had attended the Los Alamos conference and alerted Moscow that before long the United States would have the "Super." (An article in the January 1990 issue of the *Bulletin of the Atomic Scientists* stated that the Soviets had learned more about the hydrogen bomb from monitoring U.S. tests in the Pacific than from Dr. Fuchs, who had given them nothing more than "false assumptions.") Inevitably this knowledge affected all Soviet strategy, apart from forcing even more the pace of the work on the atomic bomb.

In a series of maneuvers that the United States did not anticipate and did not fully understand at the time, Stalin decided to keep challenging America to gain maximum advantage before the hydrogen bomb became operational and proceeded on this course until the monopoly ended. It appears from recently obtained materials concerning Stalin's foreign policy that he gambled that Truman would not use the atomic bomb over such crises as Iran, Poland, Czechoslovakia, or even the Berlin blockade the Soviets imposed in 1948. However, Stalin knew he had to back down when the situation turned dangerous, and in the end he did so, notably in Eastern Europe.

Naturally these Soviet actions led to increasingly angry American responses, and the Cold War hardened from month to month. As early as January 5, 1946, Truman had written Secretary of State James F. Byrnes, "I'm tired of babying the Soviets," and, in effect, invited him to resign for supposedly being too soft on the Russians. On September 20, 1946, the President fired Commerce Secretary Henry Wallace (who had served as Vice President under Franklin Roosevelt in the latter's third term) for advocating in public more conciliatory policies toward the Kremlin.

Inevitably the entire process of postwar life was poisoned by Soviet-American hostility. Looking back at the formative period of the Cold War, one is struck by the degree of the fears that existed on both sides, defining the formulation of policies. As John Kenneth Galbraith observed many years later, it would be a mistake "to make light of these differences and these fears in their time." He added that "they, especially the fears, were very real" and that "it was inevitable that they would become the foundation of foreign and military policy in both the great powers." For decades these great powers remained distracted by their rivalry and their fears, often blundering toward the edge of disaster.

In the meantime, much of the world needed urgent help to survive and to start reconstruction. But even in this endeavor the United States and the Soviet Union, always wary, always afraid of each other, could not see eye to eye.

The American decision to embark on a massive program of recovery overseas stemmed from both humanitarian sentiment and pragmatic self-interest. Truman, his top advisers, and congressional leaders realized that a highly affluent America in the midst of an impoverished world was an economic and social absurdity, and foreign aid became one of their principal priorities. That the United States needed export markets for its goods—and therefore had to rebuild overseas economies to enable them to buy from America—was a very secondary consideration at that stage; the charge that U.S. assistance was a form of "economic imperialism" represented cheap propaganda on the part of foreign ideological critics at a time of real hunger and deprivation.

The first gesture was toward Britain. Though victorious in the war, the British Empire was already seeing the sun set over it, and the British had no illusions about their place in the new world order. Britain would, of course, retain its special relationship with the United States, but as a junior member of this association of English-speaking people. In fact, it had been so frightfully damaged in its economy after six years of war that vast transfers of funds to the British treasury became imperative. On December 6, 1945, Truman authorized a credit line of $3.75 billion—an extraordinary amount at that time—plus $650 million in fresh Lend-Lease funds repayable by the year 2000. The British loan was only the beginning of the role America proposed to play in the changing world.

The specter of famine rose over Europe immediately after V-E Day. Judge Samuel I. Rosenman, long one of Roosevelt's most trusted advisers, undertook an inspection of Western Europe and reported to President

Truman that the prospects were bleak for food supply in Britain, France, Belgium, and Norway. On the Continent, land mines and explosives in the fields prevented farmers from returning to till the land, and the U.S. Department of Agriculture estimated that food production in Europe for 1946 would be even below 1945 levels, the lowest since prewar days. Transportation networks were shattered, and there was virtually no fuel. Agriculture Department experts told Truman that continental Europe alone would need twelve million tons of food during 1946 to prevent large-scale starvation.

As Truman emphasizes in his *Memoirs*, American farm yields happened to be the lowest since prewar days, and the supply of meat in the United States in the spring of 1945 had become extremely "tight." But he believed Americans had to help. In a post-victory radio speech to the nation the President said: "Europe today is hungry. . . . As the winter comes on, the distress will increase. Unless we do what we can do to help, we may lose next winter what we won at such terrible costs last spring. . . . If we let Europe go cold and hungry, we may lose some of the foundations of order on which the hope for worldwide peace must rest."

Because American military forces in Europe were being reduced after Germany's surrender, the United States had military-surplus food stocks on the Continent. Truman decided, however, that these stocks could not be turned over to civilian populations because of the need to feed "the huge numbers of German prisoners who had fallen into our hands." Instead, he ordered fifty million pounds of meat shipped to France and Belgium from domestic stocks despite the shortages. Britain was able to resume prewar meat imports from Argentina. International organizations also started providing aid. The UN Relief and Rehabilitation Administration— UNRRA—was active in Greece. In October 1945 the UN created a permanent agency to deal with international food problems, the Food and Agriculture Organization (FAO). The United States was the principal source of support for both agencies.

Early in 1946 the threat of famine "became almost global," in Truman's words. Disruptions of war combined with extreme droughts in much of the world to create a food crisis that the President was told could be the worst in modern times. Wheat crops in Europe and North Africa and rice crops in Asia were far below expectations. World food production per capita was 12 percent below the prewar years; it was 25 percent below normal in Europe and Japan. The United States had to ship sugar to the Philippines, normally a sugar exporter. Data presented to Truman showed that while Americans lived on a diet of about thirty-three hundred calories daily, more than 125 million Europeans survived on fewer than two thousand calories, and large groups subsisted on one thousand calories.

In the first half of 1946 the world wheat deficit was estimated at seven million tons and the rice deficit at two million tons. Truman writes that Prime Minister Attlee cabled him on January 4, 1946, that unless these shortages were met, widespread famine faced Europe and Asia in the next few months. And the problem was not only obtaining food but finding shipping and land transport to deliver it to the hungry populations.

Truman was so preoccupied with the world food crisis that on February 6, 1946, he announced a nine-point emergency program intended to avoid starvation. Americans were told to conserve food, particularly bread, as part of "a vigorous campaign" to save the maximum for overseas deliveries. Bakers and retailers were instructed to cooperate to reduce waste. The government calculated that 20 million bushels of grain would be saved for food by the end of June through the banning of the use of wheat in the production of beer and alcohol and the limiting of the use of other grains. And Truman ordered the export of 1.6 *billion* pounds of meat during 1946, plus cheese and evaporated milk.

Still, the situation continued to worsen everywhere. India, which had a population of four hundred million, suffered a tremendous crop failure because of monsoons, requiring imports of more than four million tons of wheat and rice to maintain even minimal rations. Britain halted issuing rice to the civilian population and had to return to the wartime practice of baking darker bread to save flour and to reduce the weekly fat ration to levels below those of any time during the war.

In Washington Truman established in April the Famine Emergency Committee, but he soon discovered that Americans were not conserving food and that a postwar black market was diverting resources. Furious, he addressed the nation again by radio on April 19: "America is faced with a solemn obligation. Long ago we promised to do our full part. Now we cannot ignore the cry of hungry children. Surely we will not turn our backs on the millions of human beings begging for just a crust of bread."

This time Americans responded, and Truman was able to announce at the end of June that the United States had exported six million tons of bread grains during the first six months of 1946. And in the course of the year millions of tons of American coal were shipped to Europe to start the economy moving.

Americans probably were not aware of the magnitude of their generosity through wartime economic assistance to the Allies as part of the overall effort to beat the Axis. It had added up to a staggering $46 billion between 1941 and 1945, with $11 billion going to the Soviet Union (including $1.6 million worth of buttons, Truman noted). It was over the question of continued American aid—and postwar credits—that Soviet-American relations plunged to the lowest level in the history of the alliance.

Acting on the advice of the State Department—especially on recommendations from W. Averell Harriman, the American ambassador in Moscow, and his deputy, George F. Kennan—President Truman ended lend-lease assistance to the Soviet Union on May 11, 1945, three days after V-E Day. When Harry Hopkins, the presidential adviser Truman inherited from Roosevelt, visited Moscow on May 27, Stalin complained that this action had been "unfortunate and even brutal."

Truman was accused, then and subsequently, of cutting off the aid for political reasons, mainly to gain more leverage with the Russians over Eastern Europe. His decision, the critics said, was not justified because the Soviets had not done anything to suggest that they were cheating on their Yalta commitments, and the Potsdam Conference had not yet been held. The President was charged with being the original "cold warrior," and some commentators intimated that through his policies the United States pushed Stalin into hostile acts (earlier Roosevelt was accused of trying to win Stalin's cooperation through various concessions).

The matter, however, was much more complicated. It involved broader economic relationships among the wartime Allies in the years to come, the sharing of international responsibilities, and the extremely difficult moral question of whether a democracy like the United States should be helping regimes that deny democratic rights to their own people. On the latter point, the argument can easily be made that no such help should be offered, but unfortunately the United States destroyed its credibility by aiding rightist dictatorships elsewhere in the world in the years that followed.

What many American policymakers found highly irritating about the Soviets was that they were not participating in the American effort to save much of Europe from starvation—let alone in the efforts to assist in postwar reconstruction—but were insisting on the right to go on drawing on the largesse of the United States. The Soviet Union had been crippled by the war; but it remained a viable state with a formidable military establishment, and the Truman administration thought it should behave accordingly.

George Kennan, a thoughtful student of Soviet conditions, put it this way in a memorandum he drafted late in 1945:

> I know of no justification, either economic or political, for any further granting of Lend-Lease aid to Russia, for any agreement on our part that Russia, not being a contributor to UNRRA aid, should receive any substantial amount of UNRRA aid, or for any extension of U.S. government credit to Russia without equivalent political advantage to our people. . . . The Russians have no great need for foreign aid unless they insist on straining their economy by maintaining a military strength far beyond the demands of their own security. Their resources and productive powers, agricultural and industrial, are sufficient to assure fairly rapid recovery without outside aid.

Kennan, whose views during that period served to shape American policy toward Moscow for decades, also felt that it would be wrong and imprudent from a political and moral stance to assist "a ruthless authoritarian regime." His judgment was that it was as impossible to help people without helping the regime in such a country as it was to harm the regime without harming people. Under the circumstances, Kennan wrote, it was better "neither to help nor to harm, but to leave people alone."

Naturally, all this was written before Stalin's death and the subsequent revelations of Stalinist crimes against his own people, and U.S. policies were criticized by those who went on believing that the contemporary Soviet Union was a deserving ally. It should come as no surprise, however, that Kennan's views are fully vindicated by the findings of the new generation of Soviet historians who see Stalin as a Cold War culprit. And as I discovered in my Moscow conversations late in 1988, there is an almost masochistic tendency to berate the Soviet Union's postwar behavior.

On another level, the United States had to deal with the expressed Soviet interest for sizable credits after the war. Actually Washington was equally interested in a loan that the Russians would use to purchase American industrial equipment. Even before the war's end Foreign Minister V. M. Molotov had raised the question of a $6 *billion* loan (equivalent to more than one half of the total Lend-Lease aid received by the Soviet Union) at a 2.5 percent interest rate. There is nothing to indicate that Stalin had mentioned the matter of a loan at either Yalta or Potsdam, but conversations on this topic went on desultorily for nearly two years. Kennan wrote that after learning in early 1946 of a Washington proposal for a $3.5 billion loan, he and two other embassy colleagues cabled the State Department that they would regard $2 billion as a maximum. In Washington the Congress in July approved a bill authorizing a $1 billion loan.

By then, however, Stalin had evidently lost all interest in any form of intimate economic relations with the United States. For reasons that may have been aggressive or defensive (both were possible in his mind), he decided to go it alone in the postwar world. In February 1946 the Soviet Union made known its unwillingness to join the International Monetary Fund and the World Bank (although it was among the cofounders at Bretton Woods and was offered 13 percent of voting shares, the largest block after the United States and Britain), and the American loan was never brought up again. (Forty-three years later, President Bush would offer at the Malta summit United States economic support to the Soviets and Gorbachev would gratefully accept it.)

In retrospect, it appears that Stalin had defined Soviet postwar policies, foreign and domestic, early in 1946, just as Truman was defining American policies, both men being remarkably firm in their attitudes. Stalin unveiled his plans in a speech he delivered on February 9, at the Bolshoi Theater on the eve of a Supreme Soviet election with a single list of candidates. It was one of his extremely rare public speeches, and the sixty-seven-year-old Stalin told the four thousand Communist party and Red Army leaders in the audience that victory in World War II meant that "our Soviet system has won."

This was a powerful reaffirmation of the Marxist-Leninist ideology and, in effect, the rejection of any internal or external compromises. The Soviet Union, backed by its invincible army, Stalin made it clear, would take on any comers to defend its faith. He announced a postwar five-year plan of economic development and remarked in an intriguing fashion that if Soviet

scientists are given the necessary help, "they will be able in the near future
. . . to surpass the achievements of science beyond the boundaries of our
nation." American experts reading the speech in Washington the next day
thought that Stalin was hinting that he would soon have the atomic bomb.

In Moscow George Kennan, acting as the American chargé d'affaires, sat
down on February 22, two weeks after Stalin's speech, to dictate an eight-
thousand-word telegraphic message to the State Department to describe his
conclusions about emerging postwar Soviet policies and to recommend
American responses. Known as the Long Telegram and published the following year in the quarterly *Foreign Affairs* as an article titled "The Cold
War" and signed by "X," the Kennan message has become perhaps the most
famous document in the annals of modern American diplomacy for its content and the influence it wielded.

Kennan's central conclusion in his analysis of postwar Soviet Union is
that "we have here a political force committed fanatically to the belief that
with US there can be no permanent modus vivendi, that it is desirable and
necessary that the internal harmony of our society be disrupted, our traditional way of life be destroyed, the international authority of our state be
broken, if Soviet power is to be secure." He notes at the same time that
unlike Hitler's Germans, the Soviets are not "adventuristic" and do not take
"unnecessary risks."

Having thus diagnosed the Soviet Union as pursuing an expansionist policy (though without using the word "expansionism"), Kennan goes on to
argue that this Soviet problem is within America's power to solve—"and
that without recourse to any general military conflict." He proposed a series
of political measures for the United States to take, starting with firmness in
resisting Soviet inroads and initiatives, and this became known as containment though Kennan never used the expression. Unhappily the least
noticed among Kennan's recommendations is his notion that "the greatest
danger that can befall us in coping with this problem of Soviet communism
is that we shall allow ourselves to become like those with whom we are
coping." His insights must have told him that something like witch-hunts,
McCarthyism, and a loss of American national equilibrium lay ahead as an
expression of the fears Americans were developing—unnecessarily but painfully, as it turned out—in the face of the Soviet threat.

Almost forty years later Mikhail Gorbachev publicly complimented Kennan on his penetrating understanding of the Soviet—and the Russian—
problem. As he was launching his *perestroika* to transform his nation and
tear it away from the Stalinist past, Gorbachev's conclusions evidently differed little from Kennan's. For his part, George Kennan at the age of eighty-
five, a still-outspoken and revered American elder statesman, was able to tell
the Senate Foreign Relations Committee in April 1989 that "whatever reasons there may once have been for regarding the Soviet Union primarily as
a possible, if not probable, military opponent, the time for that sort of thing
has clearly passed." The Soviet Union, he added, "should now be regarded

essentially as another great power, like other great powers—one, that is, whose aspirations and policies are conditioned outstandingly by its own geographic situation, history and tradition, and are therefore not identical with our own but are also not so seriously in conflict with ours as to justify any assumption that the outstanding differences could not be adjusted by the normal means of compromise and accommodation."

For Kennan, and many other students of history, the Cold War had finally run its course in the late eighties—forty years after he had signaled its advent. He was the last of the great diplomatists of our time to see that historical phenomena come and go. And public opinion showed clearly that Americans no longer had that fear of the Russians characterizing the postwar decades.

But in 1946 the Cold War was accelerating day by day. In late winter (when Kennan was drafting his telegram in Moscow), the growing concern in Washington was the Soviet Union's failure to withdraw its troops from Iran by March 2, as previously agreed on. Not only did Moscow insist on keeping its forces there past the Allied withdrawal deadline (Soviet and British troops had entered the country under a wartime accord, and Britain evacuated its army on time), but it also demanded that Iran grant autonomy to the Soviet-backed insurgent provinces of Azerbaijan and Kurdistan and, for good measure, that oil concessions be assigned to the Soviets on Iranian territory. The Iran issue became so important to Truman in terms of forcing the Soviets to keep their commitments that on March 6 the American Embassy delivered to Foreign Minister Molotov in Moscow the most tough-worded note ever addressed by the United States to the Soviet Union.

The day before, as it happened, Winston Churchill, out of power for nearly a year but an immensely influential voice in world affairs, traveled to the small town of Fulton, Missouri, where Westminster College wished to give him an honorary degree. Truman, of course, was from Missouri, and he asked Churchill to accept the invitation, promising that he would come along for the ceremony. On March 5 Churchill spoke in Fulton in what is still remembered as one of the most famous among his many very famous speeches. It was a speech that had impact on world policies, and on history, as few politicians' addresses do.

The best-remembered phrase is Churchill's warning that "an iron curtain" had descended across Europe from Stettin on the Baltic to Trieste on the Adriatic, representing the dividing line between communism and democracy. Although Churchill himself spoke earlier of the iron curtain and it is unclear where this expression really originated, it is now identified forever with him. Moreover, it quickly became one of the most commonly used symbols of the Cold War in the West. In a sense, the iron curtain speech looms as the West's formal recognition of the existence of the Cold War, and it is amazing that it was accomplished by a private citizen—even if he was Winston Churchill. The fact that Truman subsequently avoided publicly endorsing the address, which also called for a de facto Anglo-American alliance against Soviet expansionism, did not diminish the impression it caused on public opinion everywhere. Charles de Gaulle, himself a private citizen since January, told associates he fully agreed with Churchill (with whom he had very frequently disagreed during the war) that a conflict between communism and the West was inevitable. In Moscow the Soviet press published accounts of the Churchill speech under the rubric of Western "war propaganda"; he could be attacked but not ignored. Stalin compared his wartime partner with Hitler.

But just as George Kennan had predicted, the Russians did not look for confrontation for its own sake and tended to pull back when resistance developed to their probes. This was true of the Iran crisis. After the stiff American protest and the placing of the topic by the Iranian government before the UN Security Council, the Soviet Union withdrew its troops in the course of April. It is not inconceivable that Churchill's speech had influenced Stalin's decision; he may not have wished to escalate the Cold War too far too soon.

Total Communist (and therefore Soviet) domination of Eastern Europe was an overwhelming Western concern even before Yalta. It was assumed that this was Stalin's ultimate objective, but during 1946 he was moving in that direction with caution and deliberate speed. He preferred *faits accomplis* when the political situation in those countries had been sufficiently consolidated to premature confrontations with the West when local anti-Communist explosions could occur, inviting Western help. He knew the United States would not go to war to displace a Communist regime already implanted in Warsaw or Budapest or Prague, and therefore, patience was his guideline.

Thus, in 1946, there were coalition governments in Poland, Czechoslovakia, Hungary, Romania, and Bulgaria even though powerful pressures were building up against the non-Communists. Yugoslavia's Marshal Tito, the victorious Communist guerrilla chief, had accepted a coalition after the 1945 elections, as did the Communists in neighboring Albania. East Germany, of course, was under Soviet military occupation. It was a matter of time before the iron curtain would fully descend over Eastern Europe, but in the meantime, Western influences were still reaching the region. Poland and Hungary, for example, were recipients of UNRRA assistance. And unlike the Soviet Union, most of the Eastern European countries had joined the International Monetary Fund and the World Bank.

II

The rise of the Marxist tide in Eastern Europe—and to an important extent in Western Europe as well as in China and then in the Third World— represented a historical movement that emerged as one of the principal political consequences of the Second World War. Yet this phenomenon was much more complex and fundamental than the force of Soviet armies' bayonets or Communist conspiracies and manipulations. Before the war the Communist system was confined to a single country, the Soviet Union, and the great change taking place after the fall of Nazi Germany lay in communism's ability to break out beyond Soviet borders. The question that has not yet been completely answered, even several generations later, concerns the appeal of this ideology at the outset of the postwar period in Europe and elsewhere.

In March 1989 the Polish Roman Catholic opposition periodical *Tygodnik Powszechny* published a sarcastic front-page editorial about Marxism (an article that censorship would have never cleared even a year earlier), describing Karl Marx as "one of the most antipathetic and sinister figures of the nineteenth century." It goes on to propose that "intellectuals of the world, in the name of their honor, and without awaiting the verdict at the Last Judgment, indict Marx for permanently misleading the people" about the present and the future. The article equates Marx with Satan, arguing that Marx's reputation for "meaning well" actually condemns him "because Satan likes to use that kind of man, and the saying that the road to hell is paved with good intentions was not created in vain." The author concludes that while "socialism" is simply a system under which all would be well for the people, "in order to avoid misunderstandings, I would propose an alternative and less loaded term: PARADISE LOST!"

That such views could be expressed openly in a country where the Communist party was still formally in power signified that for all practical purposes, Marxism-Leninism, and with it the Soviet practice of communism, ceased to be relevant to the national reality and that it was no longer taken seriously. This, of course, marked the end of the postwar Marxist period. After forty years the Marxist tide had receded in 1989—it had happened not only in Poland, Hungary, East Germany, Bulgaria and Czechoslovakia, but also under Gorbachev in the Soviet Union and in China under tremendous pressures from below—and the cycle of the rise and fall of Marxism was complete. Nevertheless, the writer of the Polish article was historically and emotionally correct in calling that period, in bitterness, the Paradise Lost.

As a reporter I have had the opportunity of observing the evolutions and convulsions in Eastern Europe since the late 1960's—I witnessed the Prague Spring and the Soviet invasion that smashed it—until the present time, and I carry in my memory and my notebooks the essence of uncounted conversations about the motivations and experiences of men and women who once upon a time believed in the Marxist ideology and its promises. They are the ones who lost the paradise or, rather, who never saw it come, because the masses had little faith in it from the outset. The leaders and the true believers were those Marx had led astray, and it must be remembered that *they* then led the liberalizing protests, challenges, and reforms.

Ideology, politics, and emotions often blend under great pressures of life—such as war, occupation, prison, or concentration camp—and this is particularly true among young people (of course, mature people can also be captivated by this spirit). This was the situation in the countries of Eastern Europe as World War II drew near its end, the hated Nazis fleeing in defeat. For those who fought in partisan bands in the countryside and in urban undergrounds as well as for prison and camp survivors the immediate question was, What next?, in terms of new societies that would rise from the ashes of the prewar systems and the destruction of war.

The young people anxiously asking the question were patriotic and idealistic—almost by definition—and they craved faith and belief. They were romantic (in a terrible fashion the war had a romantic dimension), and they searched for mysticism and even messianism. To many among them Marxism—or communism—provided the vision they needed, easy answers to difficult questions, and the nearest thing to a secular religion. They trusted communism to eradicate prewar poverty and social injustices, to do away with the power of the elites of the *ancien régime* (about which they heard and read though had been too young to know) and the rigidities of the old-fashioned Roman Catholic Church, and to lead their nations into the triumphal sunshine of economic growth and prosperity for all.

It should be said at once that the majority of this group of early young believers came from family backgrounds of education and learning; they were often children of intellectuals becoming youthful intellectuals themselves. And perhaps most of them belonged to traditional affluence. The degree of idealism and politicization was considerably more limited among the urban working class and the peasantry. *Their* centennial traditions were of vast and permanent cynicism about any political or social system; it had really never touched them in the past, and they were happy to remain political illiterates so long as they had barely enough to eat.

Why was the promised Marxist paradise lost for the young Communists as the years wore on? The simplest and briefest answer is that this experiment could never live up to expectations because it was too filled with internal contradictions (ironically, Marx based *his* philosophy on the concept that capitalism is the victim of its own contradictions). The principal contradiction resided in humanity's eternal quandary of whether and how social justice and political freedom can be reconciled, and the ardent young Communists in Eastern Europe very quickly realized that the new system offered no answers.

Everywhere the system was held together, more and more, by the apparatus of security forces and the secret police, there was an absolute denial of all normal democratic liberties, there were imprisonments and sometimes executions of those who demanded these liberties, and politically Eastern Europe under Soviet and local Communist sway was seized with rigor mortis.

In terms of social justice, initially there were reasons for hope. Free education and health care were provided by the state, an unprecedented condition, theoretically giving every citizen an equal chance at the start of life. But in reality these chances were extremely limited because the Stalinist insistence on state ownership of all resources and a centralized command economy soon pushed most of Eastern Europe into stagnation. Even allowing for traditional economic differences, Western Europe was recovering from the war at a pace embarrassingly quicker than the "camp of peace," as Moscow liked to call Eastern Europe.

It is arguable that the Marxist approach may have been useful at the outset to establish bases for new industry and to guide to some degree the process of economic development (this argument was the most convincing in the opening years of Communist rule in China), but this justification vanished in the early 1950's. The economies became increasingly paralyzed, new housing was tragically inadequate, foodstuffs were in permanent shortage, and consumer goods were a dream. The deepening corruption within the Communist parties on all levels rendered matters totally unmanageable.

At that stage Marxism was hoisted with its own petard; because for a time education was successful, young people began to ask the very basic questions, *Why* isn't the system working? Why the shabbiness, shortages, and hopelessness? Why the corruption in the name of the "dictatorship of the proletariat"? Why not even a scintilla of political freedom? This questioning of the fundamental premises of the existing system led first to disenchantment, then to revolt, and finally to the dying stages of Marxism-Leninism in that part of the world.

The most cogent and honest explanation and description I know of the process of the attraction exercised by Marxism and communism on Eastern Europe's educated postwar generations was provided by Leszek Kołakowski, the famous Polish philosopher who once belonged to the Communist party, then was expelled, and finally exiled himself in the West. Kołakowski, the author of the authoritative three-volume *Main Currents of Marxism*, divides his time between professorships at Oxford and Chicago universities, but he revisited Poland for the first time in twenty years in 1988 and freely discussed the past in a wide-ranging interview published in the Polish press without a single word having been censored. What is the most striking about

Kołakowski's interview is that it does not exculpate, justify, or rationalize his and his companions' actions four decades earlier; as a philosopher he simply explains the phenomenon.

The attraction to Marxism, he said, was both purely intellectual and political, and these strains were inseparable. He went on:

> Marxism attracted me, as it attracted many people, because it appeared to offer a rational—not sentimental—vision of history, in which everything was clarified, everything became understandable (clearly in appearance), and in which not only the past was explainable, but the future was transparent. Marxism attracted one with its purely humanistic—that is anthropocentric—philosophy. [Jean-Paul] Sartre said once that Marxists are lazy in the sense that Marxism—especially in its simplified, primitivized form, in which it acted during long years as a political ideology—was easy to accept, gave the comfortable feeling that one had the mastery of the entire historical knowledge, without any necessity of studying history for that purpose. Moreover, it gave a clear perspective of the future as well as the conviction that one was on the right side in social conflicts, on the side of the exploited, persecuted, et cetera. All of this was, of course, based on cruel falsehood. Nevertheless it functioned for long years with a certain effectiveness.

But, Kołakowski recalled, there were other motives:

> Like many of my colleagues and friends who traveled the same road, I reacted rather sharply against certain Polish tradition, which I disliked—a clerical-bigoted-nationalistic, anti-semitic and fascistic tradition, which seemed to me to be culturally malevolent and repelled me personally. Communism, as I imagined it, was a certain continuation of a tradition, which was closer to me, as a rationalistic and cosmopolitan tradition of free thinking. When you say these things today, they sound laughable, considering the real circumstances under which this communism has functioned.

Kołakowski continued:

> I have no intention of justifying these illusions, and I only wish to say that if we analyze the attraction to communism that a part of Polish intelligentsia accepted during the war years or in the postwar years, I would oppose bringing it down to the level of stupidity or morally despicable motivations. . . . The question should be to ponder how this communism manifested itself

as the negation of certain currents in the Polish culture that, especially in the last prewar years, was incredibly irritating and hostile to the leftist intelligentsia. We had reacted to an important degree against this side of the Polish tradition, which I still dislike. . . . I still dislike the fascistoid tradition, Polish chauvinism, clericalism—although the meaning of this tradition has changed in the meantime. . . . This tradition is alien to me albeit Marxism long ago ceased to be the intellectual place where one could escape from that tradition.

Just as the attraction to Marxism for people like him was political and intellectual, Kołakowski said, its abandonment had the same two aspects. In a first phase, starting in 1955, he and some of his colleagues believed that Marxism could be "regenerated" or reformed without surrendering its fundamental principles. His group was therefore accused of "revisionism," but soon these Communist intellectuals realized, Kołakowski emphasized, that their hopes were in vain although this attempt "contributed to the decomposition of the dominant ideology."

With all due respect for the integrity of Kołakowski and his generation, one is tempted to wonder why it took men and women of such high intelligence and integrity so long to realize that they had been "misled" by Marx and that they lived in the Paradise Lost. After all, Stalin had died in 1953, and the horror of Stalinism was revealed in January 1956 in Premier Nikita Khrushchev's "secret speech," which became immediately available to Polish Communists. In October of the same year Soviet tanks on Khrushchev's orders had crushed the rebellion in Hungary and were on the verge of invading Poland. Polish and other Eastern European Communist intellectuals long had private access to such tales of Stalinist destruction of men's souls as Arthur Koestler's *Darkness at Noon* and such visions of totalitarian future as George Orwell's *1984*, first published in 1945.

It is naturally heartrending for honest believers to admit that they have been profoundly wrong in their faith and sacrifices, and it must be immensely difficult to break with one's church even if it has become rotten and corrupt. That must have been Martin Luther's dilemma at Augsburg four centuries earlier. I did not know Leszek Kołakowski in his Communist days (we met much later, when he had already achieved fame for his critiques of Marxism), but I think I can understand his acknowledgment in the 1988 interview that he and many of his friends remained Communist party members for a number of years afterward "not for ideological reasons, but judging, rightly or wrongly, that in such conditions of intellectual repression and restriction imposed on the freedom of the speech, the party was still a forum where one could fight for some changes."

In retrospect, Kołakowski may have been right concerning the strategy of fighting from inside, rather than voluntarily opting out. Though the party expelled him in 1966, he has exercised a huge influence on the evolution of

Polish Communists toward the extraordinary liberalization of the late eighties; he was the vindicated honored guest when he visited back in 1988. Most of the key intellectual advisers to the Polish Solidarity free trade union, legalized in 1989 after brutal disbanding by Warsaw's Communist military regime in 1981, are former party members.

Bronisław Geremek, the bearded medieval historian who is the closest political mentor of Solidarity chief Lech Wałęsa, and the philosopher Adam Michnik, who is the conscience of the opposition movement (both were elected in June 1989 to be deputies in parliament, Geremek becoming Solidarity's majority leader in the lower house) make no bones about their Communist past. We often discussed it during long Warsaw evenings when freedom had not yet quite reappeared in Poland. The same is true of the leading Polish novelist Tadeusz Konwicki. And Mieczysław Rakowski, who became prime minister to lead the Communist party to the legalization of Solidarity, an unthinkable thought only a few years earlier, also chose to do his battling within the ruling establishment (after Solidarity's Mazowiecki replaced him as Poland's first postwar non-Communist prime minister, Rakowski agreed to serve as the Communist party's first secretary, to preside over a gradual disappearance of the party itself). When I first met him in the 1960's during his tenure as editor of the party's weekly publication *Polityka*, Rakowski was ostracized by the hard-liners for being a liberal.

In Czechoslovakia the 1968 experiment of "Marxism with a Human Face" was born among Communist intellectuals, writers, and journalists as well as senior party leaders. And in the Soviet Union, of course, Mikhail Gorbachev launched the watershed *perestroika* revolution after rising to the position of general secretary of the Communist party in 1985. Not surprisingly, as I realized in Moscow late in 1988, much resistance to his reforms comes from honest Communists who cannot bear the idea, as a newspaper editor told me one evening, that "I have lived a lie all my life, and now I'm supposed to admit . . . It's tough, you know. . . ."

Clearly the rise and fall of Marxism after World War II cannot be judged by a single standard. Most of the Eastern European countries lived the drama of their intellectuals sincerely embracing the ideology, then plummeting in disenchantment. But there were other dimensions.

The men and women who implanted communism in Eastern Europe under the protection of the Soviet army and security services after 1945 were for the most part "old Communists," who had spent many prewar years in prisons in their own countries. During the war they were in Moscow, or in anti-Nazi miliary or partisan units, or in concentration camps. They equated Stalinism with Marxism-Leninism (many actually believed it; others accepted it as opportunists), and no means were too brutal to impose the Communist rule and destroy the opposition. In Poland, Romania, and Hungary they smashed their original coalition partners through massive arrests and electoral fraud (notably in Poland in 1946 and 1947), and in the end these Moscow-manipulated leaders destroyed each other through kangaroo-court show trials and executions. Many were still Communist believers as they faced the hangman or the execution squad; some of the worst Communist tragedies in Eastern Europe were self-inflicted through rivalries for power and the Kremlin's favor.

Because so much romanticism and mysticism formed part, naively or not, of the Eastern European Marxist *via crucis*, it is important to bear in mind that among the most interesting Communist leaders in the postwar years—and the men who espoused liberalizing reforms within their parties—were veterans of the International Brigades that fought in the Spanish Civil War. The Yugoslavs, Czechs, Poles, Hungarians, and Romanians who, as young Communists (or sympathizers) in the mid-1930's, rushed to Spain to defend the republic from the fascists, belonged to a very special romantic fraternity.

The Spanish Civil War was Europe's greatest trauma before the Second World War, and the loyalties and friendships of the battles of the Ebro and Barcelona and Madrid never really died. The veterans were the supreme idealists, and when I met many of them after the war in their Eastern European capitals, where they initially held much power, the talk touched on the famous names of their fellow fighters from abroad: Orwell, André Malraux, and the future British prime minister Clement Attlee. It made sense for them to become postwar Communist liberals at home—Spain was a war for democracy, not communism—and many paid with their lives for their Spanish pasts (Stalin was rightly suspicious of them). At the same time, as I discovered in conversations, quite a few of the veterans retained the Communist allegiance because the victorious Western allies had not disposed of the dictatorships of Francisco Franco in Spain and Antônio de Oliveira Salazar in Portugal.

In Western Europe the Communist strength in the postwar decades stemmed from old political traditions as well as from the Second World War. In the French maquis, for example, disciplined Communists played an important role in the anti-Nazi resistance, bringing workers and intellectuals together. In Greece the pro-Communist EAM was one of the main anti-Nazi movements. In Italy some of the most effective *partiggiani* were Communists, and immediately after the war the Communist party became a major force in national politics. A remarkable group of French intellectuals were Communists or pro-Communists: the poets Paul Éluard and André Breton and the philosopher Jean-Paul Sartre.

To be sure, Moscow guided and financed communism in Western Europe in the postwar years, but its influence waned gradually. The powerful Italian party openly broke with the Soviets after the 1968 invasion of Czechoslovakia. The French party had shrunk to less than 10 percent of the electoral vote in the eighties. The Spanish and Portuguese Communist parties flowered in the seventies, then eroded away. The fear of "Eurocommunism" that developed in the ever-nervous United States in the seventies—the horrifying notion that Communists could win power through elections—evaporated when the Communist parties themselves discovered that they were boring the new electorates to death.

In a most astounding fashion Soviet *glasnost* pioneers soon demanded the settling of accounts with Western intellectuals who so long and so blindly defended and justified Stalin's tyranny. Writing in *Novi Mir*, the organ of the Soviet writers union, the reviewer of the new Soviet edition of Arthur Koestler's *Darkness at Noon* used the occasion to ask about these intellectuals: "What darkness at noon blinded them?"

M. Zlobina, the reviewer, took after Theodore Dreiser for refusing to intervene in favor of his persecuted Trotskyite friends; after George Bernard Shaw, Lion Feuchtwanger, Louis Aragon, and Romain Roland for attempting to defend "the indefensible"; after Jean-Paul Sartre for demanding the suppression of information about the gulag in order not to "depress" the French proletariat; after Sidney and Beatrice Webb for writing that there was total freedom of speech in the Soviet Union; and after Harold Laski for believing that the Moscow show trials were conducted according to the rule of law. The Western intellectuals, Mrs. Zlobina writes, "betrayed not only themselves, but also us; they were disloyal . . . to that principal duty which made Émile Zola write *J'accuse* and which motivates every intellectual, upon seeing an injustice, to grab a pen and ring the alarm bell."

Western liberals still owe a mea culpa to the Soviet people and to themselves, it seems to me, even if it means humble acceptance of what the conservatives (and right-wing intellectual thugs) were saying all along. It is a spiritual debt.

Marxism, however, had a second life—in the end equally disappointing—in the new nations awakening from European colonial rule. The West helped bring it about, along with all the accompanying confrontations, because of its incurable shortsightedness.

III

From a political, human, and demographic standpoint, the most fundamental and far-reaching consequences of the Second World War was the process of decolonization. It was often frighteningly bloody and savage, costing millions of lives on all sides, and it went on for all the postwar decades. It had not run its course even by the end of the eighties, with additional national and ethnic groups across the globe awaiting and demanding sovereignty and independence.

Decolonization and the wars of national liberation, as they were called by their leaders (and by Communist governments seeking to co-opt these movements), drastically changed the map of the world. The colonial empires have virtually vanished, after fighting mightily to survive, not comprehending that the forces of history were arrayed against them. As a result, there were more than three times as many independent nations in 1989 as on V-E Day. When the Charter was signed in San Francisco in 1945, 51 countries were United Nations members, and there were 159 UN members forty-five years later.

The demographic phenomenon accompanying decolonization was the population explosion. The number of people in the world soared from about 2.5 billion in 1945 to 5.5 billion by 1990. This more than doubled the world's population in forty-five years as birthrates accelerated breathlessly; in the early part of the century it took thirty years to add 1 billion to the global total. Demographers do not have a precise scientific explanation of the link between the creation of new nations and the immense population increases, all of them occurring in the impoverished Third World (in both countries independent before the war and those becoming free after 1945); but a link must exist, and the growth of the human mass is the greatest challenge and problem for all their governments. None of them can cope with the extreme poverty, unemployment, hunger, and disease affecting hundreds and hundreds of millions in the Third World.

Finally, decolonization has added a completely unexpected new dimension to the fabric of international relations. In their unceasing efforts, as part of their overall rivalries, to control as much as possible the new and old nations of the Third World, the nuclear superpowers—ironically—have become chattels of their weak and poor client states. In the most dramatic example of such distorted relationships, the United States and the Soviet Union came to the brink of nuclear war in a dispute over Cuba in 1962. Striving for regional ascendancy, the Soviets launched the Korean and Afghanistan wars (one by proxy, one directly), and the United States followed France in bogging down in the losing Indochina Wars, then involved itself in the Central American quagmire.

It was the United States that led the West in voluntarily decolonizing its overseas possessions. It did so by granting independence to the Philippines on July 4, 1946, in fulfillment of a pledge made by President Roosevelt in 1935. At that time the Filipino archipelago was awarded internal autonomy with full independence to come within ten years (the Pacific war and the reconquest of the Philippines from Japanese occupation delayed it by one year). The United States had formally annexed the islands in 1899, following its victorious war with Spain, which had erupted the previous year over

Cuba (for nearly a century American history kept being affected by Cuba in one way or another) and that also raised the Stars and Stripes over Puerto Rico in the Caribbean and Guam in the Pacific.

Although the United States lacked a colonialist vocation in the European sense, it was not about to surrender what it had won in the entirely unnecessary Spanish-American war. This truth was soon discovered by Emilio Aguinaldo y Famy, a young Filipino who thought that if the United States challenged Spain supposedly to free Cuba, the same principle should apply to his country as an ex-Spanish colony. When it turned out that President William McKinley had other ideas and decided to keep the rich islands, Aguinaldo proclaimed independence and formed a guerrilla army. An American-Filipino war erupted soon thereafter. Two years later American armed power prevailed, and Aguinaldo's "insurrection" was over. Immense savagery was exercised by the victors, some two hundred thousand Filipino civilians having been killed in the conflict. It almost foreshadowed Vietnam more than a half century later, the two events together illustrating how little changes in the behavior of powerful nations. In his book *In Our Image: America's Empire in the Philippines*, Stanley Karnow calls this carnage "one of the forgotten wars of American history."

The next forty years were a period of fairly benevolent American rule under which powerful families and companies in both countries did extremely well for themselves, but little was done to develop the Philippines economically beyond plantation status and to set solid bases for subsequent development. The islands also were fine training grounds for the American military, and both Douglas MacArthur and Dwight Eisenhower served there over extended periods. After the Philippines became a commonwealth in 1935, MacArthur was asked by its president, Manuel Luis Quezon y Molina, to form and command the national army. MacArthur was there when Japan invaded the archipelago after Pearl Harbor, and he fled Corregidor before it fell, vowing to return.

Return he did, on January 9, 1945, landing on a Leyte beach. Manila, a city in ruins, was recaptured in March. MacArthur was in Tokyo, presiding over the occupation and the start of reconstruction of Japan, when Filipino independence was proclaimed on the Fourth of July 1946. His protégé, Manuel Roxas, was the first president of an independent Philippines, elected with a comfortable margin over another politician of old-family background and moderately conservative views.

Naturally there were nationalists in the Philippines who regarded this road to independence as continuation of American rule in disguise; they were identified with the Hukbalahap movement, a pronouncedly leftist faction that soon embarked on guerrilla warfare against the new government. Ensuing Filipino history was rich in violence and conflict. Yet the fact remains that the United States lived up to its word, and independence was transferred to the Filipinos willingly, without a drop of blood being shed.

Six years later Puerto Rico was given commonwealth status and internal autonomy, partly on the Filipino model, and Puerto Ricans were given the choice of voting for a continued commonwealth, statehood, or independence. After nearly four decades they opted to retain the commonwealth arrangement. Interestingly, America's greatest problems in the second half of the century were not with its former possessions or territories but with nationalisms of various types in countries with which it never had real ties.

European colonial empires were less lucky in dealing with the new trends of history set in motion by the war. Perhaps they lacked wisdom or perspective; perhaps they were overburdened by imperial tradition and the habit of economic greed (especially after the destruction in the metropolises of the empires); perhaps their rulers really believed that Asians and Africans would happily return to *status quo ante bellum*, welcoming back their prewar rulers under more cosmetically pleasing forms of enlightened colonialism. The Europeans seemed to believe that euphemisms would be acceptable in lieu of reality, ignoring that now they had to deal with new generations of nationalist-minded politicians, most of whom had learned the rhetoric of freedom in Paris, London, or Brussels and took it in all seriousness, especially after hearing for six years that the war had been fought for liberty and democracy.

In any case, neither the French nor the British, Dutch, Belgian, Portuguese, and Spanish empires were prepared to contribute to their own dissolution, in most cases preferring to fight than to let go of the past. Only Italy was deprived of its empire as a loser in the war. Winston Churchill had proclaimed in the first year of the war that he had not become prime minister to preside over the liquidation of the British Empire, which dated back nearly three centuries to the Revolution of 1688, and he meant it absolutely. Most Britons always cherished the idea that the sun never set over their empire, and they wished to keep it that way. Among the other wartime Allies who once held colonies a certain ambiguity existed about retaining them, but by and large, the old mentality prevailed. Portugal, a fascist dictatorship that remained neutral during the war, did not even consider abandoning its vast African empire and Asian enclaves, and it had the distinction of fighting the last great traditional colonial war before going down in defeat when the 1974 revolution imposed both peace in Africa and democracy at home.

France faced the worst problems and dilemmas. First, there was Indochina, where for all practical purposes, the French were engaged since late 1946 in a neocolonial war against the Vietminh combination of nationalists and Communists demanding independence. Then General de Gaulle's provisional government was challenged the length of North Africa in the protectorates of Algeria, Tunisia, and Morocco, where immediate independence was the central theme. Finally, France was pressed to grant independence to Lebanon and Syria, which it had administered as League of Nations mandates since 1919, after the defeat of the Ottoman Empire in the

First World War. Colonies in black Africa were quiescent for the moment, but it was only a matter of time before the decolonization fever reached them, too. Madagascar, the big island in the Indian Ocean, wanted freedom soon. It is astounding, in retrospect, how the French, including De Gaulle, misread so incredibly all the signs and portents.

France's war to retain Indochina, which lasted nearly eight awful years, was to an important degree the result of political confusion and divisions in Paris as well as of mounting radical pressures on the Vietminh side, and it might have been avoided altogether if all the players had tried hard enough.

In retrospect, it appears, perhaps surprisingly, that the man who may have made the greatest effort to find a peaceful solution was Ho Chi Minh. Despite on-and-off fighting between French and Vietminh units early in 1946, Ho decided to fly to Paris for what he hoped would be serious negotiations. He remained there for four months—from the start of June until the end of September—participating in desultory discussions with French officials who were not quite sure what they were seeking to accomplish.

Georges Bidault, who became a coalition prime minister about the time Ho reached Paris, was a right-of-center Gaullist Christian Democrat who had no intention of compromising with the natives in Indochina. Admiral Georges Thierry d'Argenlieu, the French high commissioner in Saigon, named by De Gaulle, was even more opposed to concessions. The only ranking French officials who hoped to strike a reasonable deal were General Leclerc, the top military commander (also sent by De Gaulle), and Jean Sainteny, a banker and an "old Indochina hand," who was negotiating with the Vietminh in Hanoi, likewise on De Gaulle's behalf.

As had happened on innumerable other occasions, De Gaulle could be astoundingly ambiguous in his positions. Before resigning early in 1946, he was represented in Indochina by two sets of powerful emissaries with opposite viewpoints. It is known that while still in office, he worked hard on a compromise solution, then shifted gears and, as an influential private citizen, urged toughness late in the year when the war was exploding. Jacques Chaban-Delmas, a close associate of De Gaulle's who served as prime minister from 1969 to 1972, told me in Washington late in the eighties that "Ho wouldn't have gone home with empty hands from Paris if the general had been in power at that time," but this is only a supposition.

What Ho gained during his four months in Paris was an interim agreement that, in effect, let the French keep South Vietnam while the Vietminh held the North. Returning to Hanoi in October, Ho found himself criticized for his concessions by the most militant Vietminh; but his authority was not questioned, and he continued to lead the movement as full-fledged war developed. Leclerc had been replaced as military chief by General Étienne Valluy, a hard-liner, and it became too late to salvage peace.

In mid-November the French and the Vietminh fought in the port city of Haiphong in preliminary skirmishes though Valluy used tanks to smash enemy barricades in the streets. On November 23 the French gave Ho an ultimatum to remove his forces from Haiphong, then attacked with tanks, air bombardment, and shelling from a cruiser in the harbor. French commanders said that around six thousand Vietnamese were killed, while the Vietminh claimed the casualties numbered twenty thousand. The French could be very effective militarily against ex-colonials.

Ho, still hoping for a settlement, pressed the French National Assembly to help halt the war. Instead, the National Assembly acted in the middle of December to confirm Léon Blum as the latest prime minister. Blum, an old-line Socialist, had been French premier during the Popular Front in 1936, and Ho assumed that with a Socialist back in power, the Indochina dispute could be amicably settled. Ho and Blum exchanged heartwarming messages, but they had no control over the events. A few days later the Vietminh guerrillas set fire to Hanoi's power plant and murdered French civilians in their homes. The French Army struck back, and now Hanoi became a combat area. When Paul Ramadier, another Socialist, replaced Blum as prime minister early in 1947, supported by his Communist party associate Maurice Thorez, he confirmed orders to fight the Vietminh uprising to the bitter end.

Strangely, it took French Socialists and Communists to commit their nation to nearly a decade of war in Indochina to preserve the prestige and image of France in the emerging new world. The French Communist party was totally subservient to Moscow, but Soviet calculations at the time attached greater importance to communism's influence in France than to the destiny of Asian jungle fighters. And Charles de Gaulle, too, now stood for the grandeur of France.

Being something of a legendary figure in France, General de Gaulle has escaped, by and large, history's criticism for some of his actions that at the least raise some disturbing questions about his ethics and sense of responsibility. His shifts over Indochina were matched by his shifts over Algeria, that other terrible French tragedy, and although it was the general who in the end found a solution for the Algerian colonial war, he must share the blame for much disgrace at the outset of the conflict.

Algiers was De Gaulle's headquarters as president of the provisional government until the reconquest of France from the Nazis, and the general could not have been unaware of the powerful independence stirrings in Algeria as well as in Tunisia and Morocco. North African troops had fought the Germans under the Free French tricolor in Italy and Germany, and it was evident that the three protectorates expected independence when the Allies won the war for democracy. Independence movements in the North African territories dated back to the mid-1930's, and the French governments at the time dealt with them by imprisoning or exiling the leaders (just as the British were doing in India in the happy prewar years of unquestioned colonialism).

Inevitably the war quickened the independence impulse and, North African leaders thought, rendered them more acceptable and legitimate. Thus, in February 1943, Ferhat Abbas, who became a key figure in the independence war, launched a "freedom manifesto," urging an Algerian republic federated with France. But the Free French authorities were as hostile to these ideas as their prewar predecessors, and they presumably included De Gaulle. The only gesture toward the Algerians was the ordinance in March 1944 granting French citizenship to several tens of thousands of Algerian Muslims, an idea so insulting that it was bitterly denounced by Islam's leaders.

The Algerian War, in a real sense, may have started on August 14, 1944. That was the day Charles de Gaulle triumphantly flew from Algiers to liberated Paris to be anointed in the capital of France with legitimacy as provisional president. Before his departure De Gaulle told the French commander in chief in Algeria that "it must be assured that North Africa does not slip through our fingers while we are liberating France." This directive set the stage for all the tragedies that followed.

On May 1, 1945, nationalist riots erupted in Algiers and Oran; the police fired, killing four Algerians. On May 8, during V-E Day celebrations, nationalists rioted again, and during the night and the next day armed fellahin (proindependence guerrillas) murdered nearly a hundred French civilians, including women and children, in their homes in the Sétif region. Retaliation by the French forces was instant and terrible: Artillery and aircraft bombed all the villages in the area, destroying them completely, while the French Army's units of black troops swept through, killing and raping and pillaging the homes of the Arab Muslims. Algerians also claimed that French commanders drafted Italian and Nazi war prisoners still in Africa to help in the massacres. In the course of forty-eight hours as many as fifteen thousand Algerians may have been killed; the French rightist journalist Henry Bénazet described the repression as "inhuman." This was the pattern of wholesale French military operations against nationalists that was repeated later that year in Indocina.

It is wholly implausible that as obsessive a disciplinarian as General de Gaulle would have tolerated actions of such magnitude without his personal approval. And if he gave it, how does it define him in terms of history, even if ultimately he opened the door to Algerian independence? Jean Lacouture, the very sympathetic biographer of the general, notes that De Gaulle disposed of this bloody episode in only three lines in his memoirs, calling it the "start of an insurrection." Lacouture, recalling the general's directive on his departure from Algiers, concludes that he was "the engine of the terrible repression rather than an obstacle."

Coinciding with the drama of Algeria was a clash between De Gaulle and Churchill over Syria and Lebanon when the hypersensitive general convinced himself that the British planned to replace the French as rulers of the two mandates. He took the view that France's responsibility toward Syria and Lebanon would be transferred to the United Nations—to move toward independence—but without a phase of British control.

This 1945 dispute was typical of the surviving colonial mentalities and all the picayune concerns of the vanishing empires that seemed unable to discern the new realities. In fact, all of the Middle East was in postwar turmoil. Jews in British-mandated Palestine, many of whom had served in the British army, were agitating for the creation of the state of Israel and for unrestricted Jewish immigration. The Jewish Agency for Palestine was operating as a shadow government under Chaim Weizmann and David Ben-Gurion, a secret army and terrorist commandos were being organized, and the British should have known that they could not block change indefinitely.

Palestinian Arabs were conspiring to create *their* state in Palestine, and often Jews and Arabs clashed. Still, Britain's idea was to cling to the mandate by encouraging local national rivalries. In Cairo, the capital of theoretically independent Egypt, a sixteen-year-old Palestinian student named Yassir Arafat helped smuggle arms to fellow Arabs in his homeland and conspired with Egyptian nationalists to end British influences. When, in 1989, I met Arafat in Tunis in his capacity of chairman of the Palestine Liberation Organization, he reminisced at length about those early years, telling me that his experiences against the British had turned him into a lifelong revolutionary.

Another event the West underestimated was the creation of the Arab League in Cairo in March 1945. This was the first time Arabs from the wide arc stretching from North Africa to the Persian Gulf were uniting for political purposes, but the British and the French noted it with condescension, if at all.

At midnight on August 15, 1947, two new nations were born in southern Asia from the flesh of the British raj that had ruled the subcontinent for nearly three and a half centuries. They were India and Pakistan, and they were being given their independence, at long last, by King George, represented at the great ceremonies by the last viceroy, Louis Francis Albert Victor Nicholas Mountbatten, the viscount of Burma and a great-grandson of Queen Victoria.

Independence for India and Pakistan represented the first act of *voluntary* postwar decolonization by a European empire. "Voluntary," however, was a relative term, for Britain had decided to let go of the subcontinent chiefly because that huge landmass was being swamped by blood and violence, and Prime Minister Clement Attlee's Labour government had concluded that the situation was beyond control. Two years earlier he had replaced Winston Churchill, who had sworn he would not liquidate the empire and who still opposed freedom for India.

Britain had been pressed for independence by Indian political leaders and intellectuals—Hindus as well as Muslims—since the 1930's. The onset of the war in 1939 infused added passions into the demands. India had sacrificed hundreds of thousands of troops under the Union Jack in the two world wars, and now the rising sentiment was that anticipated victory of the democracies required the recognition of Indian identity—or identities. Throughout much of the war the British would not hear about independence or negotiate it. Jawaharlal Nehru, the leader of the Congress party, had been repeatedly jailed by the British, most recently in 1943. Nationalist manifestations were put down violently by the British forces. A huge explosion was a matter of time.

But a special dimension of religion compounded the problem: India was composed of three hundred million Hindus and one hundred million Muslims—the principal population groups—and they had a history of hatred and communal hostility and violence. The Muslims, led by the Muslim League's chief, Mohammed Ali Jinnah, refused to join with the Hindus in an independent India. If the British tried to force the Hindus on the Muslims, Jinnah warned repeatedly, a frightful civil war would break out—and nobody doubted his word.

To find a solution, Prime Minister Attlee named Mountbatten in January 1947 to serve as viceroy with the specific task of resolving the religious quandary. Attlee's choice was inspired. The forty-six-year-old Mountbatten, who had served until recently as Supreme Allied Commander, Southeast Asia, was familiar with India and acquainted with its key personalities. Also, he believed in the need to grant independence to the people of the subcontinent without triggering a tragedy of extraordinary magnitude; this was the heart of his assignment. Mountbatten was given virtually plenipotentiary authority by Attlee, and he decided that the independence process must be completed within six months.

Consulting continuously with Nehru, Jinnah, and Mahatma Gandhi, the beloved "passive resistance" symbol of Indian emancipation, Mountbatten realized that the raj had to be partitioned into two nations between the Hindus and Muslims. He understood it was a disastrous solution (especially placing Muslim-inhabited East Pakistan on the other side of India from West Pakistan), but he also understood that it would be even more disastrous not to do it. Because millions of Muslims lived in India and millions of Hindus in Pakistan, partition meant transfers of populations on a colossal scale.

Communal slaughter followed. Hindus and Muslims were killing each other—the final death toll was in the millions—and Sikhs from the Punjab were murdering Muslims. It all was done in the name of religion or religious fanaticisms, and people were asking whether God really existed if such tragedies were perpetrated in his name (people went on asking in the decades that followed how God could permit unspeakable cruelty among humans as they did before in the Nazi concentration camps and in the Soviet gulag). Gandhi went on a hunger strike to force a halt to the violence, and his spiritual influence was so immense that the subcontinent began to calm down. On January 30, 1948, a fanatic young Hindu named Nathuram Godse shot Bapuji Gandhi to death as he worked at his spinning wheel in the garden of a house in New Delhi where he was recovering from his hunger strike.

Later that year, 1948, the British granted independence to Burma (where the nationalist leader U Aung San had also been assassinated) and to Ceylon (now known as Sri Lanka). In 1971 the population of East Pakistan rose against the central Pakistani government in a secession movement. India and Pakistan, whose unabating hostility had already led to three full-fledged wars, fought over the territory in another armed conflict, with the Indians supporting the rebels. Secession triumphed, and Bangladesh as a sovereign nation took the place of East Pakistan. Sri Lanka was torn during the eighties by savage ethnic conflicts, and India dispatched troops as a peacekeeping force. But also in the eighties, in the Punjab the Sikhs found themselves in deadly struggle—based on religion—with Muslims and Hindus. Prime Minister Indira Gandhi, the daughter of Jawaharlal Nehru, was assassinated by her Sikh bodyguards, and another cycle of violence hit India.

During visits to India and Pakistan during the 1980's I was astounded by the sustained high level of violence and death in the subcontinent. Daily, I saw, the front pages of the newspapers reported the machine gunning or knifing or burning of Sikh, Muslim, Hindu, or Untouchable families in the Punjab; battles between Muslims and Buddhists in Kashmir; attacks by the Gurkha Liberation Front commandos in northeastern India; lethal violence by separatists in Assam; massacres of Tamils, Sinhalese, and Muslims in Sri Lanka; and murders of Untouchables in India by unknowns. I remember remarking to Indira Gandhi in New Delhi in 1982 how staggering religious and political violence appeared to be in her part of the world. "Oh," she said, "it's a phase in our very complicated history. . . . In time it will go away. . . ." She was killed two years later.

Israel, too, was born in blood, strife, and violence in 1948, as part of an immensely intricate process in which universal conscience, the needs of millions, and the phenomenon of decolonization all had roles. There was ample precedent, certainly since the First World War, for successor states to be carved out from territories of other nations—usually empires disintegrated in conflict. New countries were created by peace conferences, impositions of power on bordering states, or voluntary or forced decolonization.

Israel, however, is the only state to have been, in effect, *created* by an international body, the United Nations. Moreover, this action had the support of both the United States and the Soviet Union, one of the very few occasions when the two superpowers agreed on a major issue in those Cold War days. Britain had also voted for the resolution in the UN General Assembly on November 29, 1947, that provided for a partition of Palestine between Jews and Arabs.

But when the Arab states opposed the establishment of *any* Jewish state, the British simply washed their hands of the whole affair and announced that they were giving up the Palestine mandate and withdrawing all their forces by May 14, 1948. It was a bitter and pathetic end of nearly thirty years of Britain's rule over Palestine, a period characterized until almost the last moment by its iron determination to limit Jewish immigration to avoid displeasing the Arabs (and by just as unforgiving a campaign of Jewish terrorism against the British). President Truman sums up in his *Memoirs* the horror of the British crackdown on illegal Jewish immigrants: "People who were still wearing their concentration-camp uniforms were being turned back as they tried to land in Palestine without certificates."

On the day the British departed, May 14, 1948, the state of Israel was proclaimed in Tel Aviv in a technically unilateral action based on the previous November's United Nations resolution reserving roughly one half of Palestine for the Jews. Not only did Palestinian Arabs lack sufficient organization to set up their state in the other half of the mandate, but overall Arab policy was to reject partition and go for the whole country. Truman writes that early in 1948 "the military forces of the Arab states that adjoin Palestine more and more openly began to enter that country" and that "On February 13 it was reported to me . . . that the Arabs were expected to start full-scale military operations in late March."

The Arab League, whose creation three years earlier had been ignored by the West, had taken charge of the anti-Israeli campaign following the UN vote, but Arab armies were not really prepared to attack before the Jews actually proclaimed independence. Truman, however, had been forewarned of the date and exact hour of the planned proclamation, and he was determined to protect the new state. Eleven minutes after the state of Israel was officially born at midnight, the White House issued the announcement of the *de facto* recognition of the provisional government in Tel Aviv.

The Arabs did move on May 15 "to restore order" in Palestine, but Israel already had one powerful friend. During the yearlong independence war the Israelis were able to obtain military equipment in the United States for their nascent armed forces (though shipping arms abroad was supposedly illegal). Interestingly, their other major source of arms was Czechoslovakia, where the Communist coup d'état had succeeded in February, and it was there that the first pilots of the Israeli Air Force learned to fly. At that juncture Moscow and its satellites were hedging their bets between the Arabs and Israel. National elections were held in January 1949, and a week later the United States gave Israel *de jure* recognition.

The 1948 war was exceedingly savage, and Arabs and Israelis alike were guilty of inexcusable atrocities, proving again that no nation and no people anywhere in the world are free of inhuman practices if the pressures on the individuals are powerful enough. Within three years of the end of the most terrible war in human history, the French had brutalized Vietnamese and Algerians, the British had done it to Indians prior to partition, then the

Hindus and the Muslims went after each other, the Dutch were slaughtering Indonesians fighting for independence, and now the Jews and the Arabs were perpetrating murders of civilians. Of course, the Vietminh and Algerians massacred French colons. Across the world in China the Nationalists and the Communists were deep in civil war slaughter.

The first Israeli-Arab War ended in 1949, with UN-mediated armistices, but Palestinian Arabs fled their homes, never to forget the defeat and humiliation. There were to be three more full-fledged Arab-Israeli wars in the ensuing four decades, endless border conflicts, an Israeli invasion of Lebanon, and the Arab irredentist terrorist warfare against Israel by Palestine "liberation" groups. Israel was given a chance at independence because to a great extent, the world conscience was jolted by the Jewish Holocaust at the hands of the Nazis. The only conceivable compensation for genocide, if such a concept is even possible, was to grant Jews a homeland for the first time in two millennia. And it followed, logically and morally, that Israel open its arms to all the Jews through ingathering. That one act of universal expiation produced other acts of violence and suffering, and new war was—evidently—part of the human condition in our time.

But there was so much hope. At the end of 1948 Truman wrote his friend Chaim Weizmann, then the president of Israel, "What you have received at the hands of the world has been far less than was your due. But you have more than made the most of what you have received, and I admire you for it."

One of the most overwhelming arguments for creating Israel as the home for wandering Jews was the future of the survivors in European DP camps and those in Eastern Europe who feared communism and wanted to flee. Then there were the fear-ridden Jews in the Arab countries. In all, one million Jews wanted to emigrate to the Holy Land. The settling of Jewish refugees in Israel unfortunately but inevitably spawned the Arab exodus and the Arab refugee problem.

I saw Palestinian refugee camps on the West Bank, in the Gaza Strip, in Jordan, and in Lebanon in the late sixties, and they were a hell of inhumanly overcrowded hopelessness that international agencies could not remedy; the third generation of refugees, millions of people, was festering in the camps. By the end of the 1980's the fourth and fifth generations were wasting away in the camps that were becoming centers of Palestinian irredentism and therefore targets for Israeli military reprisals. At the outset Arab governments failed in their duty to help the refugees find a future; their miserable existence in the camps represented a political asset for the Arab cause. Later it was beyond any government's capacity to deal with the Palestinian problem. It was a vicious circle of human degradation—and the breeding ground for the great Palestinian uprising in Israeli-occupied territories, the *intifada*, that surged forth in the late eighties. Arab youths hurled stones at the Israelis and killed collaborators. The Israeli Army shot demonstrators, and Israeli crowds chanted, "Death to the Arabs!"

The first postwar wave of decolonization ran its course during the forties with the births of India, Pakistan, Burma, Sri Lanka, and Israel. In every case the politics and realities of decolonization gave life to new refugee dramas on a vast scale. The second wave of decolonization was to crest, with even greater ferocity, in the next decade.

The unbounded cruelty of human beings toward other human beings seemed to characterize the birth of new nations as it did the practices of ancient states in Europe and elsewhere during the Second World War and afterward. Now, in peacetime, dictatorships of the left and the right proliferated, and there appeared to be nothing in international law to denounce and halt colossal violations of human rights.

Cynics argued that compassion cannot be codified and that no government would listen to voices telling it how to run its internal affairs. But the other opinion was that respect for human rights must become law, no matter how long it takes for it to be enforced. Otherwise, what was the point of fighting the war against Hitler other than to deprive him of his conquests?

The United Nations loomed as the only international forum where human rights could be addressed—there was no real precedent in the old League of Nations—and finally the persuasion paid off. With Eleanor Roosevelt, the President's widow and U.S. delegate to the United Nations, and the French philosopher René Cassin leading the effort, the General Assembly approved on December 10, 1948, the Universal Declaration of Human Rights, a document that in ensuing decades increasingly paved the way for treaties and conventions designed to protect human rights.

Among them was the Anti-Genocide Convention, the brainchild of a Polish-born lawyer named Rafael Lemkin, who survived Nazi concentration camps to push through his idea. I remember him in those days at Lake Success, where he UN first convened, then in New York City, a frail, stooped figure, stubbornly buttonholing delegates, pleading and exhorting. Lemkin died many years ago; he should not be forgotten now that the anti-Genocide Convention is part of the body of international law; he did it single-handedly.

In the meantime, there was still the drama of China in its postwar convulsions.

In China the contest was over ultimate power and domination, involving Chiang Kai-shek's Nationalists and Mao Zedong's Communists (known in American government and journalistic jargon as Chinats and Chicoms). This vast country was caught up in a civil war between two indigenous forces, and quite rapidly the Nationalist-Communist conflict entered the parameters of the broader East-West division in the world. In view of China's great importance in Asia, the outcome was expected to have a perhaps decisive impact on Asian nations coming to life through decolonization.

The hope of a peaceful internal settlement in China after Japan's defeat was maintained for the duration of the yearlong mission there by Truman's personal emissary, General George Marshall. Remaining in China from December 1945 to January 1947 the unbelievably patient Marshall believed for much of his mission that a coalition government formed by Nationalists and Communists was possible after the integration of their warring armies so that the Chinese could concentrate their energies on rebuilding the country after generations (if not centuries) of warlord battles and the decade-long Japanese occupation.

Marshall's mission failed in the end principally because the Generalissimo, as Marshall's reports to Truman indicated at the time, had military superiority in 1946 and therefore no intention of sharing power in any way with the hated Communists. In one of his final reports Marshall said that "the Generalissimo stated that he felt that it was necessary to destroy the Communist military forces . . . [that] if that were done there would be no great difficulty in handling the Communist question. . . . he was confident that the Communist forces could be eliminated in 8 to 12 months." Marshall's reply to Chiang was that the Nationalists could not ignore a group as large as the Communists and that the destruction of communism could not be achieved without plunging China into complete economic collapse.

In retrospect, it appears that a historical error was committed when subsequently the United States accepted Chiang Kai-shek's judgment that the Chinese Communists were under the total influence of the Soviet Union. Chiang had self-serving reasons for insisting on this point, as did his conservative allies in the Kuomintang ruling political party, but the Americans had much evidence that the Chinese situation was vastly more complex. Chiang and Mao, for example, had been battling each other for nearly twenty-eight years when Marshall arrived on the scene, for motives that had much more to do with Chinese domestic problems than with the Soviet Union. Moreover, the Soviet Union had been far from being a world power when the Nationalists and the Communists began fighting over China's fate, and prewar relations between the two Communist parties had been far from cordial.

Forrest C. Pogue, Marshall's superb biographer, emphasizes that George Kennan, then stationed in Moscow, wrote an absorbing analysis of the Soviet-Chinese relationship in the aftermath of the Second World War, concluding that it could not be proved that the Chinese Communists were acting on the Kremlin's orders—much as the Russians may have desired such a state of affairs. Kennan, who had been right all along on all aspects of Soviet politics, remarked in his telegram to the State Department that the Chinese had little reason to be grateful to the Soviets after they had removed practically the entire industry from Manchuria as war booty (after being at war with Japan for less than a week). He argued that the Chinese had their own brand of Marxism and their own mature Communist party, hardened by the Long March in the thirties and subsequent years of warfare. The Chinese Communists, Kennan added, had their own vested interests and their own form of nationalism.

All this leads one to reflect whether it was really foreordained for the Chinese and the Soviets to come together for a time after Mao's victory in 1949 and whether Communist China might not have developed into an independent force in Asia—not necessarily anti-American. Pogue also writes that Marshall had reported to Truman that on January 10, 1945, Mao and Zhou Enlai (Mao's chief aide, later prime minister) had proposed to the American Embassy in Chongqing (Chunking) that they travel to Washington to explain Chinese problems to President Roosevelt. For obscure reasons, General Patrick J. Hurley, then U.S. ambassador, chose not to forward this offer, and Roosevelt never knew of it.

Throughout the war Chinese Communist leaders maintained close contacts with American diplomats, military and intelligence officers, and journalists both in the wartime capital in Chungking and at Mao's headquarters in Yenan (the two Chinese rival bands had joined forces against the Japanese before resuming their own struggles in 1945). For these and other reasons, including new historical material recently coming out of China (I saw some of it in Beijing in 1985), it is certainly plausible that the Communists were interested in a long-term relationship with the United States—very much as Ho Chi Minh sought one simultaneously in Vietnam. During his year in China Marshall was permanently in touch with the French-educated Zhou, the official Communist negotiator, for whom he developed considerable respect. He met Mao at least once.

Marshall's influence with the Communists vanished when Chiang kept pressing his military offensives against his foes in total disregard of the American envoy's advice; at that stage Marshall decided to leave. Now Communist propaganda began targeting the United States—and even Marshall—for aiding and abetting Chiang's appetite for conquest, and the American effort to settle the Chinese Civil War thus came to an end.

Two and a half years later, in the autumn of 1949, the Chinese Communists won that war militarily, forcing Chiang and the remnants of his armies to flee to Taiwan. The People's Republic of China was proclaimed in Beijing on October 1, 1949, when Mao Zedong climbed atop the Gate of Heavenly Peace to announce that "from this moment, the Chinese people have stood up." While an aberrant political debate broke out in the United States over "Who lost China?" as part of the rising Cold War hysteria, little serious thought was given to the proposition that perhaps China need not have been lost if America had acted with greater wisdom and insight (also listening to its own experts) as well as with more patience.

Domestic political rages, however, overshadowed historical perspective and clearheaded analysis of the Kennan brand. It did not seem to occur to policymakers that over the centuries (really since Peter the Great) the Chinese had hated and despised the Russians for their imperialist impulses. In the postwar years Stalin invariably treated the proud Chinese as junior partners and Communist "little brothers," hardly conducive to a warm ideological partnership. Above all, it should be remembered that a full year *before* Mao's victory, Yugoslavia's Marshal Tito broke with Stalin over the Soviet practice of draining white the Yugoslav economy for the USSR's benefit while expecting Belgrade to remain an obedient client state. With ill-concealed joy, Washington applauded this surprise development while Yugoslavia moved ahead with Titoism, a politically and ideologically independent form of communism.

Not only did the United States not mind such independent communism, but it offered Yugoslavia economic aid, which was an automatic American gesture toward all challengers of the Kremlin. There is nothing to suggest, however, that anybody in Washington had the imagination (or courage) to restore contacts with the Chinese Communists as they clearly neared victory to offer them an alternative to a Soviet alliance; just conceivably, Maoism might have become ideologically synonymous with Titoism, and, actually Kennan said in October 1948 that he was "almost certain" that Titoism "is going to spread in Asia."

But political imagination was not in abundant supply in Washington in the late 1940's as the Cold War increasingly imposed rigidity and fear and therefore stereotypical thinking. Kennan was ignored. The "loss" of China (and possibly Indochina later) showed American inability to take advantage creatively of extraordinary opportunities that occasionally present themselves.

Hard as it may be to imagine today, many serious policymakers and political analysts in Washington refused to believe for years that a Soviet-Chinese split actually occurred in 1959, following Premier Nikita Khrushchev's almost desperate visit to Mao in Beijing. Mao, whose first postwar visit to Moscow was as late as 1954 (five years after his victory and a year after Stalin's death), broke with the Kremlin for reasons that closely resembled Tito's: the Soviets' compulsive need to control everything in every sphere of an ally's national life. Chinese-Russian history, to say nothing of the Tito example in 1948, should have explained the split; the *serious* thinkers in the United States remained long convinced that it was an incredibly adroit feint and conspiracy to mislead Americans and lull them into a false sense of security.

History's sequences are marvelous in the American-Soviet-Chinese postwar triangle. China's domestic Thirty Years War ended in 1949 with the Communist triumph. In 1950 China and the United States fought in Korea. In 1959 China and the Soviets ruptured their ties, and ten years later their troops fought border skirmishes. The CIA said the Soviets had considered a nuclear strike at China. In 1972 the United States and China dialogue finally came alive when Richard Nixon flew to meet Mao in Beijing (in the midst of the Vietnamese War), then flew to meet Leonid Brezhnev in Moscow. In 1988 Mikhail Gorbachev went to the United States to meet once more with President Ronald Reagan, the man who had called the Soviet Union the "evil empire" when he first assumed office. Then Reagan went to see Gorbachev in Moscow, the two men grinning together on Red Square, in front of onion-domed St. Basil's Cathedral. In February 1989 President George Bush visited Beijing and China's octogenarian reform leader, Deng Xiaoping. In May Gorbachev, the Soviet reformist, arrived in Beijing to confer with Deng—thirty years after Khrushchev had last conferred with Mao.

Stunning Deng as well as Gorbachev, Chinese students filled Beijing's Tienanmen Square to display their prodemocracy sentiments for the Soviet leader's benefit but managed to embarrass him at the same time by preventing, with their sheer mass, his entry into the Great Hall of the People, fronting on the square. Shortly after Gorbachev's departure, Deng ordered the carnage of students, setting back the Chinese reform movement by many years. The Beijing episode emphasized the difference between the Soviets and the Chinese in approaching the basic reforms in Marxism-Leninism. While Gorbachev accepted from the outset of his *perestroika* experiment the concept that political reform must precede and accompany economic reform, Deng and Chinese Communist hard-liners have dug their heels in opposing political liberalization.

In the course of private conversations with a group of top Chinese newspaper and radio editors in Beijing in 1986, when prodemocracy movements were first openly emerging there, I found consensus that the economic change would fail in the long run without a Chinese version of *glasnost*. Still, superpower reaction to the Tienanmen massacre underscored tensions at the time of the profound changes in the Communist world: In Moscow Soviet news media covered the Beijing events fully, but without comment, and in Washington the Bush administration refused to condemn flatly the Deng policies (it sent, instead a top-level delegation in total secrecy to see Deng). Caution was the instinctive response in the superpower capitals.

In Latin America decolonization meant nationalism. The only colonies on the South American continent were the British, French, and Dutch Guianas in the northern jungles. The Caribbean at war's end was the domain of British island colonies (and the Belize enclave in Central America). There was also a smattering of French and Dutch territories and possessions plus Puerto Rico and the U.S. Virgin Islands under the Stars and Stripes. They all produced sun, sugar, and rum.

Latin American nationalism, and a degree of anti-Yankeeism, predated the Second World War with the Mexican Revolution of 1910 and the expropriation of American oil concessions in 1938. In Brazil Getúlio Vargas, a benign dictator with a strong social sense, invented the slogan "This land has an owner" and gave foreign investors a hard time. Elsewhere nationalism was an intellectual exercise.

The Second World War, with all the political and social implications of the victorious cause, provided new and major dimensions for Latin American nationalisms. Their leading spokesman at the time was Colonel Juan Domingo Perón of Argentina, a populist who admired Benito Mussolini and invented a social-political "philosophy" he called *justicialismo*, a word derived from "justice." Perón, a marvelously gifted public speaker, first gained power through military coups in 1946, then was elected to the presidency by millions of Peronista workers, to whom he had pledged social justice and dignity. He was at loggerheads with the United States, which he regarded as "imperialistic," and he nationalized British railroads and American telephone companies. Later he ruined Argentina economically with the full support of his equally beloved first wife, Evita.

Juan Perón was already a world celebrity when a twenty-one-year-old Cuban law student named Fidel Castro Ruz found himself in the midst of a revolutionary explosion in Bogotá, the capital of Colombia, in April 1948. Castro was a member of a three-man delegation from the University of Havana chosen to attend a radical conference of Latin American students (financed by Perón's regime) to coincide with a conference of foreign ministers from Latin America and the United States. The idea was to demonstrate the contempt of the new Latin American generation for their governments—and the Yankees.

The assassination of a popular Colombian political leader threw Bogotá into revolutionary uproar. Castro, who thought of himself as a revolutionary figure even as a student, joined the protests and riots with immense joy and dedication. The Cuban Embassy had to arrange to free him from arrest by the police and fly him home to Havana, but for Fidel, Bogotá was an extraordinary experience. Almost forty years later, as we talked about his youthful memories, Castro told me, "That was my revolutionary baptism."

IV

A different revolution was shaping up clear across the world in Paris as if to demonstrate that the exhaustion with the war demanded radical changes in every realm of human life and activity. This revolution, as spontaneous as all revolutions, suggested as well that the new ideas and concepts rising in the immediate postwar period could not be confined to politics and ideologies. It was just as important to a great many people how one looked, not only how one thought and spoke. Frivolous or not, the message was that people do not live by ideas alone or, as a French critic remarked at the time, "you do not have to dress badly in order to think well."

This particular new revolution became known as *Le New Look*. It was conceived, designed, and launched by a timid, slightly paunchy Parisian named Christian Dior who realized, even before the war was over, that women in France were desperate for new clothes—specifically, for beautiful and original new clothes—after the deprivations and suffering of the war. Dior also knew that women elsewhere in the world shared this desire and that their men would pay for it.

To launch *Le New Look* in the midst of the poverty of the first years in postwar Paris and against the background of ruins and refugee camps throughout Europe was not at all, as it turned out, in poor moral taste. Dior understood that it is human nature to look up to things of beauty even in the shabbiest and saddest surroundings and that after the war's grimness there was a hankering for aesthetic excitement.

Events proved Dior right. *Le New Look* was an instant sensation, conquering New York as rapidly as it did Paris. That most women could not afford Dior originals or even copies was irrelevant; fashion magazines and newspapers acquainted the world with the new designs, and they could be copied at home everywhere. Wartime fabric shortages were ending in most countries, and one of Dior's concepts was to restore long hemlines on skirts and dresses as a sign of new elegance. *Le New Look* was a psychological triumph for Dior, but also a tremendous boost for French haute couture, and it quickly led to the rise of the modern ready-to-wear industry with less expensive versions of famous-label designs.

Actually Dior had designed his first classical *tailleur* when he still worked for the Lucien Lelong house of prewar fame in the winter of 1943–44. Opening his Maison Dior, on February 12, 1947, he contracted a young designer named Yves Saint Laurent. At Dior's death in 1957 Saint Laurent created his own label and his own great fame. But the Dior name has never died, quite apart from chic apparel and accessories produced around the world under its franchise.

In 1987 the Louvre's Museum of Fashion Arts exhibited Dior's designs—154 of them—during a six-month retrospective show to commemorate the fortieth anniversary of *Le New Look*, an honor never before accorded a fashion designer. Visiting the exhibit, I was surprised by the crowds filling the museum's five levels and by the predominance of very young people. Evidently it was not a nostalgia event but curiosity and interest in an era that already was sliding into history.

The Second World War opened the sluice gates of new literature flowing from the experiences still as fresh as if they had happened that same day and written with astounding speed as if the authors could not wait another moment to tell their tales.

Ernest Hemingway and John Steinbeck were the great stars in America—both soon received Nobel Prizes for literature for the work of a lifetime—but it was the new generation of immensely talented, though still unknown, authors that surged forth. Norman Mailer's *The Naked and the Dead* was published in 1948, when he was twenty-five. James Jones was completing *From Here to Eternity*. In France Albert Camus burst onto the literary horizon. In Germany it was Günter Grass. Older names acquired freshness. In the Soviet Union it was Ilya Ehrenburg (and, in and out of the gulag, Aleksandr Solzhenitsyn). In Italy it was Ignacio Silone. The new philosophers were Sartre and Camus; in Italy, Luigi Einaudi, and in Germany, Richard von Weizsäcker.

Holocaust literature followed rapidly from Israel, the United States, and Europe; it was urgent to bear witness lest it be forgotten. American novelist John Hersey wrote *The Wall*, a story of the Warsaw ghetto, in 1950; Hersey's first novel, *A Bell for Adano*, published in 1944, dealt with American GIs in an Italian town, and in 1946 *Hiroshima* was fabulous reportage in the *New Yorker* that depicted what the atomic bomb had wrought.

Superb cinema appeared instantly in Europe, narrating the postwar life. Vittorio de Sica produced *Bicycle Thieves* with Lamberto Maggiorani and Enzio Staiola in 1949; Federico Fellini wrote the scripts for Robert Rossellini's *Open City* and *Paisan*, then produced his own *La Strada* and *La Dolce Vita*. All these films became classics. The French *nouvelle vague* and *cinéma réalité* emerged as admired postwar innovative contributions to moviemaking.

The war did not curtail human creativity. On the contrary, it inspired fabulous creation and the postwar golden age of culture. The cultural rebirth went hand in hand with the overall recovery of Europe.

The engine and centerpiece of European recovery was the Marshall Plan, under which the United States committed itself in the European Recovery Act to provide $13.6 billion over four years to assist in the revival of Europe. President Truman, the plan's most fervent advocate, tells the story:

> Never before in history has one nation faced so vast an undertaking as that confronting the United States of repairing and salvaging the victors as well as the vanquished. . . . Nations, if not continents, had to be raised from the wreckage. Unless the economic life of these nations could be restored, peace in the world could not be re-established. In the first two years that followed V-J Day the United States provided more than *fifteen billion dollars* in loans and grants for the relief of the victims of war. We did everything humanly possible to prevent starvation, disease, and suffering. . . . We helped rebuild wrecked economic systems in one major country after another. For the first time in the history of the world a victor was willing to restore the vanquished as well as to help its allies.

George Marshall, named by Truman to be secretary of state after his China mission, unveiled the plan in a commencement speech at Harvard on June 5, 1947. The basic concept was that the Europeans themselves should draw up a recovery plan that the United States would finance, and a sixteen-nation conference convened in Paris in July to prepare it. But

European needs were so urgent that Congress agreed to provide $580 million as a stopgap measure. On April 3, 1948, Truman signed the European Recovery Act.

The European Recovery Program (ERP) shored up Western Europe economically and politically at a moment of intense crisis, but even more important, it provided the foundations for future European prosperity and for European unity under the Common Market, which came into being a decade later. The Marshall Plan also pioneered international economic cooperation on a vast scale, and in terms of American domestic politics it demonstrated that bipartisanship is possible in foreign policy in the Congress if the cause is valid and it is properly presented by the executive branch.

In the short run the Marshall Plan may have helped to bring about Communist defeats in 1948 elections in Italy and France. Communist victories in Western Europe loomed as a nightmare to the United States, and Truman really feared that Soviet influence would spread to the Atlantic if that were to occur. Former French Foreign Minister Michel Jobert, not an admirer of the United States, writes that the Marshall Plan was based on a simple principle: "If credits, meaning dollars, were not distributed, the United States would have been isolated in its prosperity in a world ravaged by war and poverty. . . . The gesture was well calculated. It was better to have tomorrow a prosperous and competitive Europe than today a desperate Europe with no purchasing power in America."

Less cynically, Hermann Abs, the former chairman of the Deutsche Bank, has remarked that the Marshall Plan was "of essential importance for the rehabilitation and the reconstruction of Germany." Without Marshall Plan aid, Abs adds, "a European Economic Community, a European Coal and Steel Community would not have been possible."

The Marshall Plan was, of course, the result of a political decision to rebuild Europe. On the level of private American generosity, however, there was the long-forgotten Friendship Train organized by newspaper columnist Drew Pearson, which crossed the nation, halting at stations and whistle-stops to collect food and clothing for Europe brought to the railroad by thousands upon thousands of individual American families. As a young reporter at the time I thought that this train said more about America than the billions—always an abstraction—voted on Capitol Hill.

As far as Stalin was concerned, the Marshall Plan was an American trap for the Soviets. Inasmuch as the United States invited *all* the European nations to participate, the Russians faced the dilemma of accepting "capitalist" solutions or challenging them as a matter of principle. Soviet Foreign Minister V. M. Molotov briefly attended the Paris conference, mainly to inform himself about the American idea, then went home denouncing it. Poland, still under a coalition regime, indicated its interest in joining the Marshall Plan, but Moscow told it to forget it. Czechoslovakia's Foreign Minister Jan Masaryk, backed by President Eduard Beneš, had actually informed Washington of its acceptance. The Kremlin forced the Czechs to forgo what might have developed into an alliance with the West (the Czechs were not yet under total Communist domination, but they knew they could not defy the Russians). Many historians believe that the Marshall Plan had convinced Stalin with utter finality that the Cold War was the only possible policy toward the United States and the West.

As far as America was concerned, the Cold War had been in existence all along, virtually since Potsdam. First, the Truman administration battled Stalin over the failure to allow democracy in Poland and elsewhere in Eastern Europe, as agreed at Yalta, and over his refusal to remove Soviet troops from Iran.

The next episode was the crisis over Turkey and Greece, which helped to create the political climate for the Marshall Plan. It opened with a Soviet proposal to Turkey to confine the international control of the Dardanelles Strait to Black Sea powers: Turkey, the Soviet Union, Bulgaria, and Romania. The Dardanelles were to be defended jointly by the Soviet Union and Turkey. To Truman, this was a dangerous Soviet move to grab the control of the eastern Mediterranean, and he encouraged the Turks to resist it. Simultaneously the British informed the White House that they could no longer afford to keep troops in Greece, where a civil war raged between Communist and anti-Communist factions, and requested the United States accept the Greek responsibility as well.

The American response was what became known as the Truman Doctrine, spelled out by the President in a speech before a joint session of Congress on March 12, 1947: "I believe that it must be the policy of the United States to support free peoples who are resisting attempted subjugation by armed minorities or by outside pressures." The Congress responded by voting $250 million in aid to Greece and $150 million to Turkey, as requested by Truman, with military assistance included in the package. The Truman Doctrine has remained over the decades the cornerstone of American foreign policy, reaffirmed in various forms by Presidents from John Kennedy to Ronald Reagan. The Marshall Plan, unveiled less than three months later, completed the shaping of United States Cold War positions.

Cold War tensions propelled Truman to tighten up White House foreign policy operations and to create a professional full-fledged intelligence agency, a body the U.S. government had never possessed. Truman writes that "on becoming President, I found that the needed intelligence information was not co-ordinated at any one place." Consequently, he established in 1946 the Central Intelligence Group to replace the wartime Office of Strategic Services and, the following year, the Central Intelligence Agency (CIA) to be the permanent organization.

The CIA was set up under the 1947 National Security Act, which also gave the President the National Security Council to advise him on major foreign policy decisions. This system remained basically intact for the next four decades although the intelligence community (which grew to include the National Security Agency, specializing in technical intelligence, and the military intelligence agencies) has expanded into a colossal institutional network. Most covert and paramilitary operations in the postwar decades were carried out by the CIA—some of them extremely useful and still secret, others absurd fiascos.

To be sure, neither the new CIA nor the Federal Bureau of Investigation (FBI) knew at the time that Western intelligence had been penetrated by the Soviets in the persons of at least four key British agents, including Kim Philby, who since 1945 had served as chief of counterespionage and intelligence gathering for the British Secret Intelligence Service (SIS). Since the CIA and the SIS exchanged a great deal of information, chances are that Philby could keep Moscow abreast of American thinking and plans under the Truman Doctrine and otherwise (though Truman's concern with security was so great that he subjected federal employees to a loyalty oath, the real subversives were never caught).

With his new foreign policy tools, the President moved swiftly to implement his doctrine in the eastern Mediterranean, and the results pleased him greatly. Truman saw that when challenged, Stalin drew back: Turkey was left alone, and outside help to Greek Communists soon stopped. They lost the civil war.

But the following year, 1948, Soviet defiance of the West resumed. On February 25 a Soviet-engineered coup d'état in Czechoslovakia installed the Communist party in absolute power, leading Beneš to resign the presidency while Foreign Minister Masaryk was killed, mysteriously falling out of the window of his Prague apartment. Now that the Soviet control of Eastern Europe was complete, Stalin decided to test the West again.

This time the chosen Cold War battleground was Berlin. Though the city was deep inside the Soviet occupation zone of Germany, American, British, and French forces were present there under an arrangement for Berlin's quadripartite rule; the former capital had been divided into four zones. As of April 1, however, the Soviets announced they would immediately start inspecting all U.S. freight shipments and military personnel crossing the Russian occupation zone in Germany en route to Berlin. Washington refused the inspection demand on the ground of standing Soviet assurances of free access, and Stalin then moved to seal off Berlin by highway, railway, and river traffic. In other words, Berlin was blockaded.

It was military brinksmanship. An armed clash could easily occur, and for the first time since V-E Day there was imminent danger of war between the Soviets and the Western allies. Yet the real reasons for the Berlin blockade remain unclear, as do so many other of Stalin's moves. Numerous historians believe, as Truman did, that this was the Soviet retaliation for the Marshall Plan, but it is not entirely plausible because the risks outweighed propaganda advantages—or simple bloody-mindedness. Several Soviet historians I met in Moscow in 1988 tended to think that Stalin tried to score political points to prevent the establishment of a West German government the Allies were then quietly preparing. He may have been looking for a *quid pro quo* deal: no German government, no Berlin blockade. I find this interpretation more credible; but the Berlin confrontation was an example of how superpowers can blunder into a world war, and it was only the first example.

In the end Stalin was beaten by American imagination and technology. To break through the blockade, the United States launched an around-the-clock airlift that for more than a year kept Berlin supplied in everything from food to coal. At the airlift's peak, American and British aircraft were delivering five thousand tons of supplies daily, the Berliners' spirits were high, and it was Stalin who was increasingly looking silly as the United States placed the issue before the UN Security Council. On May 12, 1949, the Berlin blockade was lifted.

The Berlin experience encouraged the United States to strengthen its defenses. Elected the previous November in his own right for a full term, President Truman considered he had the mandate to pursue containment foreign policies toward the Soviets and help rebuild war-smashed countries. On April 4, 1949, Truman watched Dean Acheson, his new secretary of state, sign the North Atlantic Treaty Organization's charter at a Washington ceremony. Under the NATO banner, the United States was joined by Canada, Britain, France, and six other Western European countries in an alliance designed to prevent Soviet advances in Europe. As Truman noted, NATO was "the first peacetime military alliance concluded by the United States since the adoption of the Constitution," and he named General Eisenhower to be NATO's supreme commander.

The same year the Western allies ended military government over West Germany, recognizing the sovereignty of the new Federal Republic of Germany even in the absence of a peace treaty. A half million Western allied troops remained there, however, as protection against the Soviet Union (forty years later they were still stationed in West Germany for the same reason; although with the end of the Cold War, the United States and the Soviets were in 1990 negotiating mutual withdrawal of their conventional forces from Central Europe). The right-of-center Christian Democratic Union won the elections, and Konrad Adenauer, the seventy-three-year-old mayor of Cologne, was chosen chancellor. In office for fourteen years, Adenauer was among the most imposing postwar figures in Europe. He led his defeated nation to reconstruction and democracy, joined Charles de Gaulle in cementing French-German friendship after nearly a century of hostility, and was a powerful voice in unifying Western Europe. In my experience as a reporter, no other West German leader has come close to *Der Alte* (the Old One) as a statesman.

The birth of the Federal Republic and the proclamation of its 1949 constitution did not do away with the "German Question." The weight of historical guilts was too great to be erased overnight in the minds of the Germans and those who had been victims of the Germans. Principal Nazi leaders were tried at Nuremberg in 1946—it was the precedent-setting trial on charges of "crimes against humanity"—and a number of them were sentenced to death and executed (Hermann Göring committed suicide by swallowing a poison pill in the dock rather than face hanging). The denazification process resulted in prison for other war criminals and dismissals from jobs of others. The German government has paid out hundreds of millions of dollars in reparations to Nazi victims around the world. Morally was it sufficient?

Thoughtful Germans do not wish to escape history. Richard von Weizsäcker, the philosopher who was elected president of West Germany in 1984, affirmed it in an essay in 1988 on disputes among historians about the truth in the German past. He writes: "The German nation . . . cannot make others responsible for what it and its neighbors endured under National Socialism. It was led by criminals and allowed itself to be led by them. It knows that it is true, especially where it would prefer not to know this. . . . Yet genuine liberation is achieved by freely facing the truth, by allowing oneself to be overwhelmed by it. . . . And what, after all, would it mean for us if Auschwitz could be compared with the ruthless extermination of other people? Auschwitz remains unique. It was perpetrated by Germans in the name of Germany. This truth is immutable and will not be fogotten."

From the days of Adenauer, West Germany has been a believer in the unity of Europe—as much as anything else because this makes it finally belong to Europe. And just as Adenauer was taking office in Bonn across the Rhine, another great voice was heard in Strasbourg, the ancient Alsatian city over which the French and the Germans had fought for so long. This gravelly voice belonged to Winston Churchill, British private citizen, who came to French Strasbourg on August 12, 1949, to speak of the new Europe. The occasion was the first session of the European Assembly, the forerunner of the European Parliament, and Churchill decided to emphasize his Europeanism by his choice of language. "Be on guard!" he exclaimed. "I shall speak in French," and he proceeded to do it in an English accent as atrocious as his command of the French language was formidable. Churchill told the crowd:

> For my part I am not the enemy of any race or any nation in the world. It is not against a race, it is not against any nation that we have assembled here. It is against tyranny in all its forms, ancient or modern, that we rise resolutely. Tyranny always remains the same, whatever her false promises, whatever the name she adopts, whatever the disguises her servants wear. . . . We must rise above the passions that have ravaged Europe and put her in ruins. We must end our ancient quarrels. We must renounce territorial ambitions. . . . In our long history, we have triumphed over the dangers of religious wars and dynastic wars;

after thirty years of struggles, I trust that we have reached the
end of nationalistic wars. . . . There is no reason not to succeed
in achieving this goal and establishing the structure of a United
Europe. . . .

V

The postwar balance of power in the world was altered forever at 4:00 A.M.
on August 29, 1949, when the Soviet Union successfully tested an atomic
bomb over its Central Asian landmass. This ended the four years of the
American nuclear monopoly and, in effect, created the existing basic superpower stalemate. Pax Americana turned into an illusion. From that moment
on the world strategic equation reposed on qualitative and (for a long time)
quantitative nuclear competition.

Although the Russians exploded their bomb late in August, nearly a
month elapsed before the rest of the world (probably including the entire
Soviet population except for a tiny leadership and scientific elite) learned
about this feat, and it was President Truman who announced it on September 23. He said in a formal statement: "We have evidence that within
recent weeks an atomic explosion occurred in the U.S.S.R. Ever since
atomic energy was first released by man, the eventual development of this
new force by other nations was to be expected. . . . This recent development emphasizes once again, if indeed such emphasis were needed, the
necessity for that truly effective enforceable international control of atomic
energy which this government and the large majority of the United Nations
support."

To be sure, the United States did not announce the 1945 Los Alamos test
until it was good and ready, and the Soviets seemed to follow the secrecy
principle to the point of never having publicly stated on what date their
explosion took place or what was the device's kilotonnage.

The United States learned of the Soviet breakthrough through the U.S.
Air Force's Long Range Detection System, which had been secretly developed after 1945 precisely to avoid being surprised by a Soviet test. While
Truman acknowledged that no American "intelligence experts" had anticipated a Soviet detonation before at least 1952 (the conventional wisdom in

Washington was that the Russians lagged far back scientifically and industrially), the Air Force had the foresight to assign a number of its B-29 Superfortress bombers to fly special missions around the globe to collect random air samples that then were analyzed for radioactivity.

On September 3, 1949, a B-29 picked up a suspicious sample over the North Pacific, and the Royal Air Force collected others off Britain. Top American physicists were immediately summoned to study the data, and Truman was informed on September 21 that indeed, the Soviets had broken the monopoly. The detonation of "Joe I," as the Soviet bomb was called, had the public effect of renewed American demands for international controls along the lines of the President's statement. But behind the scenes the reaction was to escalate the nuclear race, and Truman wrote later that "one of the positive effects of this development was to spur our laboratories and our great scientists to make haste on hydrogen bomb research." In fact, he said, the research on the superbomb was already so advanced when "Joe I" exploded that "we were almost ready to put our theories into practice."

The reality, of course, was that the scientific-military progress resulting from the immense research and development efforts of the Second World War opened the way to a nuclear arms race that threatened a third world war. This was instantly understood by both sides, and for more than a decade the atomic weapon was a dangerously destabilizing factor in international relations. Before and after the 1949 Soviet test the United States toyed with the idea of using the bomb against the Soviets, the Chinese, and even the Vietnamese—and subtly threatened to do it. Considering the Western perceptions of Soviet intentions, the very fact that the Kremlin possessed the bomb was equivalent to an imminent threat.

At the outset of the Berlin blockade in 1948, for example, Truman dispatched forty-five Superfortresses to bases in Britain to make Stalin think the United States was poised for an atomic strike. Whether or not the B-29's actually carried nuclear weapons, this was the kind of perilous brinksmanship punctuating the postwar decades. In any event the Soviets always knew that the development of the atomic bomb was their first priority if they were ever to break out of their military inferiority status vis-à-vis the United States, and they proceeded accordingly.

Nuclear research on the laboratory level started in 1939, but wartime pressures and the forced evacuation of scientific centers by German advances delayed it considerably for three or four years. Scientific principles of atomic fission were not a secret, but what the Soviets needed was expertise in actual weapon construction and an industrial establishment to produce the bombs. Thus there is no question that captured Nazi scientists were crucial in the nuclear program (as it was with the rocketry needed for atomic delivery vehicles).

A highly classified and never published study on the Soviet program— "How Russia Became a Nuclear Power: The Untold Story of the Soviet

Atomic Bomb," assembled by the Central Intelligence Agency—concludes that its success did not depend on the "theft" of American secrets. Apart from conventional industrial espionage in the West, the Russians built their bombs by harnessing native talent (considerable), captured Nazi scientists, slave labor on a colossal scale for the industrial infrastructure, and the full resources of the KGB's security forces. The CIA study suggests that the Soviets might have exploded an atomic device even sooner had Stalin not purged Jewish scientists from the program in 1947; this was the beginning of his anti-Semitic paranoia that lasted until his death.

Interestingly the Soviets had created a Commission on Uranium in 1939, a year before President Roosevelt approved the Uranium Committee, the forerunner of the Manhattan Project. As early as 1938 the Leningrad Radium Institute had completed a study showing that only a few kilograms of U-235, the isotope required to build a bomb, were needed for a nuclear explosion through a sustained chain reaction. Unfortunately the United States was unaware of this history until 1983, when the CIA drafted its "untold story" of the Soviet program.

It is a fascinating story. Thus Igor Vasilyevich Kurchatov, known as the father of the Soviet atomic bomb, attempted in 1940 to buy a kilogram of refined uranium from the Germans. Under the previous year's nonaggression pact, Moscow and Berlin conducted voluminous economic exchanges, and Kurchatov, who was aware of Nazi nuclear research, tried to take advantage of this situation. It is unknown whether he was successful, but Kurchatov, then only thirty-six years old, and three of his associates simultaneously presented to the Uranium Commission a plan providing for "crash development" of the atomic industry.

After World War II broke out, nuclear research became direct responsibility of Lavrenti Beria, and NKVD security chief, with the bearded Kurchatov and S. Semyonow, a member of the Academy of Sciences, acting as the principal scientific advisers. A major search for uranium was launched, and as the CIA comments, "it may be said that this was the modest beginning of the Russian atomic project." In 1942, the CIA says, Stalin learned of the existence of the Manhattan Project through spies in the United States, and he "summoned leading experts" to inquire "about the possibility of making a Russian atomic bomb, and whether it would be possible to make it fast."

The Nazi invasion slowed down the program, but Stalin ordered a supreme effort to accelerate the research at all costs. In October 1942 Kurchatov was named scientific manager of the "uranium program," the basic Soviet operation. Six government ministries provided support for the new nuclear production infrastructure. One of the main Soviet breakthroughs was the discovery of uranium ore deposits in the Altai and Turkestan regions of Soviet Central Asia, but the United States did not learn about it until the 1949 test explosion. In fact, American postwar policy was based on the wrong assumption that the Russians lacked uranium and therefore would be unable to produce atomic weapons for a decade or more.

According to the CIA, the next step was to organize the extraction of the ore and the construction of uranium concentrate mills. Labor was provided by convicts from Central Asian and Siberian prisoner camps. Without this slave manpower, the Soviets would probably not have achieved their atomic objective by 1949. Eight processing facilities were established in the area of Novosibirsk, and much of the ore was extracted "with wooden tools and shovels." Soviet scientists themselves refer to this period as neanderthalism. More modern methods were used in the production of metallic uranium, which was the next industrial step in the process, at a special atomic center in the Chelyabinsk-Zlatoust region in the southern Ural Mountains, where weapons-quality plutonium was later produced and where the worst peace-time nuclear disaster occurred in 1957 (but was revealed only twenty-two years later).

The atomic center is described by the CIA as "a gigantic conglomerate of mines, plants, proving grounds, airfields, towns and depots, spread over hundreds of square kilometers and kept under special wartime security." This center's existence was kept secret even in the Soviet Union for forty years—the CIA's study of 1983 was an American intelligence secret—and it became public knowledge only in 1989, when Gorbachev invited foreign journalists to see it.

When Nazi armies began retreating in 1943, Kurchatov moved his head-quarters back to Moscow, and it was then that because of a uranium short-age, the Soviets decided to use plutonium as the bomb's principal fissionable material. In 1944, we now know, the first Soviet cyclotron was activated to produce plutonium for laboratory tests, and late that year the first batch of plutonium was manufactured by Kurchatov's brother, Boris, a chemist. Early in 1945 Igor Kurchatov completed his laboratory experiments and proceeded to build a uranium pile designed to produce weapons-grade fissionable materials. As Soviet troops invaded Czechoslovakia and East Germany, uranium ore shipments to the Soviet Union became a top pri-ority from Czech mines in Příbram and Jáchymov and East German mines in Saxony. It was the repetition of what the Nazis had done in 1939 for their atomic program.

The capture of German scientists became the next move. Special Soviet security units succeeded in catching Manfred von Ardenne, who headed the Nazi nuclear project, and sent him to work on the Soviets' electromagnetic uranium separation, as well as Gustav Herz, the developer of the gaseous diffusion technology, and the physicists Hans Barwich, Friedrich Walter, and Max Volmer. This was on the eve of the American nuclear test in New Mexico, but the United States had no idea what the Soviets had already achieved in their program. Stalin's lack of visible excitement when President Truman told him in Potsdam that the United States had developed a new powerful weapon may have stemmed from his familiarity with the Manhat-tan Project and his awareness of how far his scientists had progressed.

The war's end had liberated sufficient economic resources for the nuclear program, and hundreds of thousands of slave laborers were available in the gulag for mining and processing uranium. Stalin renamed the nuclear project Borodino, the site of the great 1812 battle between the Russians and Napoleon, and Beria was put in command. Kurchatov was the top scientist, and Boris Lvovich Fogt was appointed technical director. By 1946 Borodino functioned as a superministry, with the entire Soviet industrial and military structure supporting it. Late in 1946 Stalin decreed at a closed conference at Sochi on the Black Sea that "atomic bombs were the cheapest means of war," and deadlines were set for missile tests in 1947. In Washington Brigadier General Leslie R. Groves, the head of the Manhattan Project, predicted that it would take the Russians from ten to twenty years to build the bomb by "normal effort."

In October 1947 the Russians successfully tested ballistic missiles in Kazakhstan; American intelligence failed to monitor them. Simultaneously Kurchatov set up a new network of laboratories in Central Asia, known as Zone V, including the crucial installation at Obninsk, where atomic critical masses studies were conducted. The German scientists worked in a complex of Moscow villas, near Kurchatov's own laboratory. Also in 1947, thirty-two new large uranium-mining compounds were inaugurated in Central Asia, and five industrial facilities were established near Moscow, among them the Podol'sk plant near Moscow. It was a "carbon copy" of the K-25 uranium-separation plant in Oak Ridge, Tennessee. The assumption is that this was the result of Soviet industrial espionage—not secrets, but equipment.

By 1948 Stalin had six industrial power reactors in which uranium isotopes could be reprocessed into weapons-grade plutonium. They were called *sharik* (little ball) in Russian. They were the industrial base for the nuclear bomb. In the spring of 1949 Kurchatov had enough plutonium on hand to build his first atomic device. He called it *Tykwa*, Russian for "pumpkin." Two bombs were assembled for the test blast, initially scheduled for June 1949, at the Moskva proving ground, near the village of Karaul in the Semipalatinsk region of Kazakhstan. The command post was at Ust-Kamenogorsk.

There were additional technical delays, but the *Tykwa* was exploded at 4:00 A.M. on August 29, 1949, in the presence of Beria and Kurchatov. The test's code name was Pervaya Molniya (First Lighting). The Soviets made no announcements, and the United States first learned of the test on September 9. Moscow confirmed it on September 25, after Truman had disclosed that a Soviet blast had occurred. But neither the Soviets nor the CIA ever told publicly the story of the development of Stalin's atomic weapon.

Though Truman has reported that Stalin's reaction in Potsdam to his news of the new powerful weapon was muted, it is known that as soon as the American President was out of sight, the Soviet leader informed his top aides that Russian efforts to build the bomb now really had to be accelerated. Other historians believe that American tests on Bikini in 1946 were regarded by Stalin as additional provocation, but it must be obvious that since his conversation with Truman in Potsdam, he knew he could not afford much longer to be at the mercy of the Americans. Curiously, however, intelligence analysts in Washington never took these political aspects into consideration when they estimated Soviet atomic capabilities and the urgency of the Soviet program. Continuously complacency and a mistaken sense of superiority in all realms were the hallmark of American attitudes in the postwar era.

By the same token, the United States should not have been surprised when, in 1946, the Soviets blocked the passage of an American resolution in the United Nations providing for international controls of atomic energy. It was a propaganda loss, but Moscow clearly was not about to subject itself to any constraints as it raced to reach nuclear status, a fact that was lost on American diplomats unaware of the Soviet progress in the field. Besides, the Russians made up in propaganda before long with their Stockholm Peace Appeal.

What seemed to be missing from all the public debates about the nuclear age was the dimension of morality, certainly as far as the governments were concerned, in the use of the bomb. Truman explains in his *Memoirs* that he chose to bomb Hiroshima and Nagasaki to shorten the war and save American lives on a grand scale. From the start of the atomic era both superpowers have been competing in portraying the horrors of nuclear war, but world leaders have said precious little on the theme of the underlying immorality of considering the use of the bomb. Witness Truman's choice of words when he wrote that the Soviet blast was a "positive" development in spurring the construction of the American hydrogen weapon—the "Super."

Technology, it appeared, was running ahead of humanity, a problem that grew at a spectacular speed as the inventions of war defined the quality of life in peace.

The high technology revolution of the eighties, born largely of the mobilization of brainpower and resources in the Second World War, has already given us the science fiction marvels of space travel, nuclear energy, microchips, giant computers, the new information society, and medical discoveries. In the fifth postwar decade, however, research continues subordinated to military requirements to an immensely disturbing degree. But it is almost certain that much of this research in the United States may be paralyzed if peace really comes to humankind in lieu of the postwar armed truce—unless the private sector stops depending so greatly on Federal funds.

Marek Thee, a leading international authority on military technology, sums up this situation in a 1988 essay by stating that "the expansion of military R&D [research and development] into almost all fields of basic and applied research means that today the military holds a controlling position in almost all contemporary R&D endeavors." Professor Thee adds that "a new order of magnitude in harnessing modern science and technology for the arms race has come into existence."

World War II was the turning point in modern technology, and as Thee points out, afterward military research and development "expanded rapidly in the wake of the emergence of nuclear weapons and the explosion of modern military technology." According to the *Bulletin of the Atomic Scientists*, military needs in the United States accounted in 1986 for more than 70 percent of all government spending on research. Thee also found that about 40 percent of all scientists and engineers in the United States are on military research and development payrolls and that "on a global scale, military R&D employs today approximately 750,000 to one million of the best-qualified engineers and scientists, with a budget of about $100-billion annually."

And Steven Muller, former Johns Hopkins president, writes that "as defense technology kept widening to include space, chemical and biological warfare, electronics, and virtually all materials, the concept of the national interest irresistibly expanded to include the whole range of science and technology within the university." Dr. Muller found that ever-expanding government needs beyond weapons systems and into space and communications technology have forced American industry to create its own elaborate research establishments along with government and university laboratories.

The great technological revolution now under way started in America in 1945 with the appearance of ENIAC, the huge first computer, built with U.S. Army funds. It continued in an industrial laboratory in the United States in 1947, with the invention of the transistor. The transistor was the crucial follow-up to wartime research, and as Frank Press, the president of the U.S. National Academy of Sciences, puts it, "that single invention began the information revolution, the joining of computers and telecommunications to transform how we communicate, to create whole new industries, and to organize services electronically."

The transistor is a small electronic device manufactured from a wafer of germanium or silicon (the reason why the center of high technology industry in California is known as Silicon Valley) that basically acts as an amplifier but has a magical range of other applications. Because it is tiny and light, the transistor has supplanted the vacuum tube in radio and television. It has made possible the development of highly functional computers; several thousand transistors can fit in a single computer without taking up much space.

Invented by Bell Telephone Laboratories scientists John Bardeen and Walter H. Brattain and subsequently improved by their associate William Shockley (the three shared the 1956 Nobel Prize for physics), the transistor is the basis of portable radios and hand calculators as well as of computer memory, logic and switching circuits, minicomputers, medical electronic devices, and industrial automatic control systems.

Because transistors are made from semiconductor material, they can be joined with other integrated circuit parts on semiconductor chips (commonly known in the past as printed circuits). Integrated circuits, which are electronic chips, were designed in the late 1950's under military contracts. A single integrated circuit chip measures about one-half-inch square, and it may contain hundreds of transistors, resistors, :nd capacitors. Dr. Press of the National Academy of Sciences has observed that the "age of the transistor," based on condensed matter physics, has led to the modern age of micro-electronics, the semiconductor laser, and optical fibers. Lasers and optical fibers are the keystone of state-of-the-art telephone and computer circuits—there is virtually no limit on the volume of conversations and transmissions these circuits can carry—and have launched the information revolution.

Bardeen, Brattain, and Shockley, who should be household names around the world for inventing the transistor, built on the prewar and wartime work of scientists like Jan Aleksander Rajchman, one of the pioneers of high-speed computer memory systems, and the Hungarian-born mathematician John von Neumann, who was the mind behind the postwar computer revolution. Scientists who were children when the transistor was invented were opening still new horizons of supertechnology in the late eighties in a quickening chain of discoveries. Thus the X-ray laser, first triggered by a nuclear bomb explosion in 1979 to serve as an antimissile beam, was applied ten years later to the development of a microscope for the study of the tiniest details inside living cells. Acting as visible light, the X-ray laser allows scientists to observe organisms smaller than a chromosome. Another new microscope can pick out individual atoms, which may be the ultimate limit for microscopes.

In terms of the industry and the consumer response, wartime research produced breakthroughs with plastics. The first synthetic plastic, celluloid, was discovered around 1870. Bakelite (produced from the linkage of the chains of molecules of phenol and formaldehyde) appeared in 1909. In the ensuing years, plastics for everyday uses were made from acrylics, ureas, cellulosics, vinyls, polyesters, and so forth. Nylon and nylon stockings appeared before the Second World War.

The war pushed plastics into a whole new dimension, ranging from parachutes to optical lenses, artificial eyes, acrylic dentures, machine gears, fabric coatings, wall surfacing, and plastic lamination. Famous trademarks emerged from the plastics revolution: Plexiglas, Lucite, and Polaroid, among thousands of others. Modern plastics produce safety glass, electrical equipment, fabrics, insulators, building panels, musical instruments, records, automotive parts, and costume jewelry. Plastics and fiber glass—light and tough—form the bodies of aircraft, cars, and boats. It is virtually impossible, in fact, to visualize modern life without plastics; it may be a notion of derision to snobs and traditionalists, but they, too, must use plastics.

And there is no limit to the future of plastics in the context of the high technology revolution. Reinforced plastics and hard ceramics are tougher than steel—and lighter. Supersonic fighters' fuselages in titanium diboride and jet engines in heat-resistant ceramics are the last word in aircraft design. The U.S. Army has discovered that armored vehicles built from a polymer composite are superior to those using aluminum alloys, and cheaper, and that ceramics work fine in tank armor.

German wartime research on metals also helped British industry decades later. When a British manufacturer of steel casings was faced in the mid-1980's with the tripling of the price of nickel he needed for increasing his products' tolerance to heat, he discovered that in the closing months of the war the Luftwaffe had come up with nitrogen-alloyed steel. The Germans were running out of nickel required for exhaust valves, and nitrogen became the solution. Wartime technical records led the British manufacturer to the German invention.

The biological revolution—biotechnology stemming from genetics and permitting the transfer of genes from any living organism to another—is the latest frontier of science being traversed. But biotechnology had its beginnings when Dr. Linus Pauling (another Nobel Prize winner) identified the blood flaw in sickle-cell anemia, a killer disease, in 1949 as a result of his wartime work on cell pathology. Thus genetic screening had its origins nearly a half century ago.

The transistor revolution has already played a spectacular role in postwar political revolutions and in education. The transistor radio has eliminated illiteracy in the Third World and in rural Eastern Europe as a barrier to political consciousness and participation. In violence-torn mountain villages of Colombia and in the Amazonian jungle in Brazil, I saw illiterate voters preparing themselves for the trek to polling stations by listening to candidates' propaganda on transistor radios. I also saw in Brazil, Mexico, and India the use of transistor radios in schools, where pupils could listen to educational programs. Roman Catholic and Protestant missionaries in Latin America and Africa depend on their broadcasting stations—and transistor radios—to spread the gospel and catechism.

In Iran Ayatollah Khomeini won his Islamic Revolution in 1979 in part thanks to his messages recorded on audiocassettes (which use transistors) that were smuggled to his followers from exile in France. In Poland, after the Communist military regime smashed the Solidarity trade union movement in 1981, Lech Wałęsa and other workers' leaders started communicating with their underground as soon as they were released from imprisonment; they employed video and audiocassettes. And when anti-Communist revolts broke out across Eastern Europe in the autumn of 1989, it was national television in each country—in the hands of prodemocracy groups—that carried them live to the rest of the population, acting as a crucial factor in the ultimate cave-in of the regimes. In Beijing in May and June 1989 prodemocracy students and workers facing the Chinese Army assault stayed informed by communicating among themselves by walkie-talkies and listening on their transistor radios to the Voice of America, the BBC, and Australian and Japanese broadcasts.

The 1940's were the decade of war and liberation, death and suffering and hope, and recovery and revolution. It was the time of the birth of the nuclear era and of the greatest transformations in the twentieth century. The forties were an end and a beginning, the night and the dawn and the new day.

In terms of history the 1940's were, then, the bridge to the second half of our century and to the changes that the fifties imposed on the world.

BOOK FOUR

THE FIFTIES

There is always an element of moral ambiguity in
historic responsibilities. . . . Our survival as a
civilization depends upon our ability to do what
seems right from day to day . . . without alternate
moments of illusion and despair.

—REINHOLD NIEBUHR,
cited by Dean Acheson, 1969

I

*T*he 1950's were the most dangerous period since the end of the Second World War, reflecting as they did the ever-growing tensions between the superpowers, each of them now armed with atomic weapons. The first half of the decade was especially fraught with peril—virtual war hysteria seemed to reign in Washington as well as in Moscow—before the pressures receded in what became a cyclical pattern of confrontation and détente in East-West relations. With the relaxation, the industrial nations could concentrate on postwar reconstruction, institution building, and peacetime progress.

For the United States the 1950's were the start of a golden age of affluence and complacency notwithstanding the foreign threats. America dominated the world economy, Americans were discovering the joys of suburbia and inventing a whole suburban culture. Nearly one million moved during 1950 alone into houses in instant villages pioneered by Levittown on Long Island, less than one hour from jobs in New York City, and the work ethic of young families was the assumption that *their* children would have even better lives. It was the age of optimism and unlimited expectations.

It also was the time when poverty in America acquired a form of permanence that Michael Harrington, the American Socialist thinker, described in his 1963 book *The Other America*. The poverty aspect of America, less visible than the middle-class affluence of the fifties, was never to vanish, turning instead into the continuously expanding underclass of the homeless, life on welfare, school dropout drama, and the drugs and crime of the eighties.

In the Third World the birth pangs mounted throughout the 1950's, with decolonization battles and wars of national liberation alongside terrible internal turmoil of societal, economic, and religious adjustments. The new phenomenon was that the big nuclear powers were, in effect, becoming hostage to their underdeveloped client states while attempting to use them for their own policy ends.

Indeed, the world was playing with fire, including nuclear fire, in the first part of the fifties—and mostly in the Third World. The nuclear stalemate became a fact of life, but there was still brinksmanship and the risk of blunders like the Soviet invasion of Hungary to preserve communism.

Two major and long wars were fought simultaneously on the Asian mainland: the American-supported French war in Indochina against Ho Chi Minh's indigenous Communists and nationalists and the American war in Korea against the Soviet- and Chinese-supported Communist North Korean regime. In the context of these parallel wars, the United States considered the use of nuclear weapons on at least three occasions.

Naturally this early American involvement in the Asian conflicts following the "loss" of China to communism in 1949 was the prelude to the United States' own great Vietnam War. In retrospect, it appears that nobody in Washington in those years seriously analyzed the future. The Americans (like the French) simply could not visualize that Third World guerrillas would be able to paralyze and defeat the white man's armies with their heavy and sophisticated weapons systems and communications and total mastery of the air. Mao Zedong in China had beaten the Nationalists in what essentially was a conventional war (although he had perfected the concept of modern guerrilla warfare), and Korea was likewise a traditional encounter of massed bodies of troops.

A short but full-fledged war exploded between Britain, France, and Israel on one side and Egypt on the other over the control of the Suez Canal in the mid-fifties—the second of the four big wars involving Israel and the Arabs in the forty years of Israeli statehood. Egyptian nationalism was at the root of the tripartite attack in 1956, which was designed to wrest back the canal, just nationalized by Egypt's new military leadership.

France, more than any of the other Western powers, refused both politically and intellectually to comprehend the surge of nationalism in the Third World, unwilling to compromise until the bitter and bloody end. Curiously the French experience as a colonial empire for a century should have led to insights into the thinking of the people of the colonies. Ironically it was France that bestowed superb education on the top nationalist leaders from the colonies (the Sorbonne and other major schools were opened to the eager young students from Indochina, North Africa, and black Africa), and it was in French cadences that they learned about the Revolution of 1789, about "liberty, equality, and fraternity," and about the rights of man. Yet when the new leaders sought to apply these hallowed French principles to their native lands, France repressed them with unbelievable brutality.

Blind to reality, successive French governments, starting with Charles de Gaulle as provisional president, convinced themselves that the colonial status quo could be preserved through fictional notions like "autonomy" within a French Union. When these offers were rejected, France responded with the force of arms, still oblivious of the fact that the neocolonial wars were unwinnable. Though the Indochina War had sapped the energies and funds that France should have channeled into postwar reconstruction at home (one third of American Marshall Plan aid went into the financing of the Indochinese nightmare) and led to ultimate and humiliating defeat, the French still insisted on colonialist formulas. Refusing to consider independence for Morocco and Tunisia, they thought even less of Algeria's aspirations despite the massacres of the mid-forties. The Indochina War had barely ended in 1954 before France allowed the Algerian Independence War to break out in all its fury; it was to be eight years of tragedy and shame. And with the Algerian War rising in crescendo, Paris decided to help launch the Suez clash in 1956.

To be sure, France was not alone in refusing to let its colonies go. The Netherlands, seeking to apply the same neocolonial formulas to Indonesia, fought a losing war on the vast archipelago, finally recognizing Indonesian independence in 1949. The British, who had had the sense to leave India in 1947, chose to fight for ten more years in Malaya, granting it sovereignty only in 1957.

From the outset the Soviet Union proclaimed itself the champion of decolonization, nationalism, and all the wars of national liberation. This was a logical move for Moscow, placing itself squarely on the side of the oppressed in the Third World and supplying them with arms and advice. Though Karl Marx had predicted that colonialism would collapse someday (if nothing else, Marx had a sense of history and the political imagination to accompany it), the Russians obviously were not acting out of ideological missionary impulses. There were so many strategic spots in the Third World that it stood to reason that the spread of Communist and Soviet influences in these regions both challenged and weakened the West.

Above all, it pushed the United States into the role of the defender of neocolonialism as practiced by its Western European allies, which, the Russians reasoned, would make Americans conveniently unpopular or, worse, help tilt the East-West balance toward the Kremlin. Washington, on the other hand, found itself in a dilemma it did not understand. The Rooseveltian wartime opposition to colonialism having been erased in postwar practice, American policymakers (with rare but outstanding exceptions, such as George Kennan and the State Department's China experts, to whom nobody listened anymore) settled for the facile conclusion that if the Soviets supported nationalism around the world, all nationalism had to be suspected of being at the service of what was called in those days international communism. This, of course, suited the Kremlin fine because it forced the Americans into impossible situations.

Some of those situations were grotesque. The State Department, for example, decided in the early 1950's that the United States had to support the French war in Indochina to the hilt for "European reasons," the notion being that failure to do so would turn patriotic Frenchmen against America and democracy—and make them vote at home for the powerful Communist party. The Soviets recognized the Ho Chi Minh regime in January 1950, but the French Communist party was playing it both ways: supporting France's position in Indochina (it did not want to lose votes on patriotic grounds among its electors) while simultaneously paying homage to the courage of the Indochinese people. Cartesian-minded Frenchmen could reconcile intellectually the two positions; the State Department could not. And the governments of the French Fourth Republic strongly encouraged Washington to invest in the Indochina War to the tune of four hundred million dollars annually (the average figure in the early 1950's) in the name of anticommunism. This consumed much of the Marshall Plan allocation for France, slowing reconstruction efforts at home.

Much as the Soviet Union backed nationalism in the Third World, it had immense and insurmountable difficulties in accepting it in Eastern Europe, where it had completed the consolidation of Communist power (and allegiance to Moscow) by the end of the forties. To provide international coordination of this power, Stalin established in 1947 the Cominform, which stood for Communist Information Bureau, sounding less menacing than the Comintern (Communist International) he had abolished during the war to please the Western Allies, who hated the word "Comintern." Of all places for the Cominform's headquarters, Stalin chose Belgrade.

Marshal Tito's defection from the ranks of Soviet satellites in 1948 was followed by Yugoslavia's expulsion from the Cominform, which was moved to Bucharest, but this organization simply vanished in the ensuing years because it irritated foreign Communist parties that preferred a semblance of independence from Moscow. The Tito defiance shook the Kremlin, setting it firmly against *that* kind of nationalism. To Stalin, Titoism was equivalent to Trotskyite treason. Subsequently Soviet force was applied during the fifties to discourage the Eastern European brand of nationalism when uprisings erupted in East Germany, Poland, and Hungary, and it was again applied in Czechoslovakia in 1968.

II

As the fifties opened, Washington and Moscow were mirror images of each other in Cold War strategic planning aimed at deterring World War III and at fighting it victoriously (which was thought to be possible) in the event it happened. In both cases this was translated into an enormous secret escalation in warmaking potential, basic conclusions about the presumed intentions of the adversary, and an effort to strengthen the alliances behind each superpower.

Sufficient historical material is now available to reconstruct with reasonable accuracy the thinking and planning in the United States under the Truman and Eisenhower administrations. Virtually no similar materials are obtainable for the same period in Soviet policy-making by Stalin and his successors. But with *glasnost* reigning in Moscow, Soviet historians themselves are beginning the labor of reconstruction, and the first results suggest that in 1950 both powers were on the same wavelength in analyzing the international situation from their respective viewpoints.

The great remaining gaps concern Stalin's decision-making processes in the years immediately preceding his death, and it is unknown whether his actions in many instances were aberrational or part of policies he had carefully devised and put into effect. Naturally, American experts had no way of reading his mind or even correctly projecting or anticipating his behavior.

The problem of predicting Soviet policies, however, was not confined to Stalin and his paranoias; it went on jolting Western analysts under Nikita Khrushchev and Leonid Brezhnev, and it still does in different ways under Mikhail Gorbachev. The orderly and pragmatic Western minds seem stymied in coping with the unpredictable among, say, the Russians or the Chinese, and they have difficulties with the abstractions that often underlie their decision-making processes.

Under the circumstances, therefore, the United States had to rely on visible patterns of Soviet attitudes and moves and draw its conclusions from what it had been observing since the end of World War II. By the end of the forties three sets of occurrences had persuaded the Truman administration that the Soviet Union was proceeding in a fashion that posed basic threats to the United States and its allies. They were, sequentially, the transformation of Eastern Europe into a bulwark of Soviet power and Communist sway in violation of the Yalta agreements, the Berlin blockade, and the Russians' acquisition of the nuclear weapon.

Whether the Soviets were acting out of fear of the West, especially after the United States had exploded atomic bombs over Japan, or whether they held their own aggressive designs was really a moot point; what counted was Soviet behavior and the size and quality of its arsenals. It is entirely possible that Soviet experts were asking themselves similar mirror-image questions, but they, too, had to accept "worst case" interpretation. This was the way Cold War dynamics were inexorably pushing the two powers toward confrontation, and it is truly extraordinary that the ultimate face-off never came.

In the case of the United States, all the events related to the Soviet Union plus the Communist takeover of China led to the resolution that a complete new strategy had to be designed for the Cold War four years after the end of the 1939–45 conflict. In-depth studies were undertaken in Washington, and one by one, President Truman made decisions of the gravest import to be carried out in the 1950's.

On October 10, 1949, the Special Committee of the National Security Council on the Proposed Acceleration of the Atomic Energy Program recommended to Truman that the production of atomic bombs be increased at once. The Joint Chiefs of Staff and the State Department concurred in this view, and the President ordered a buildup of the American nuclear arsenal; at that moment the United States had about two hundred atomic bombs. This was presumably enough to deal a lethal blow to the Soviet Union, which had tested its first bomb six weeks earlier, but the arms race mentality with its overkill emphasis had overwhelmed the whole strategic planning process; it was to control it for decades.

And almost overnight Truman had to make another decision concerning nuclear arms: whether to go ahead with the construction of the hydrogen bomb, the Superweapon that would be one thousand times more powerful than the Hiroshima bomb. The theoretical possibilities of constructing such a fusion bomb (in which energy is released by joining together of hydrogen isotopes instead of the splitting of uranium and plutonium as in a fission atomic bomb) had been known by American physicists since 1942, but the issues facing the President were both the necessity and the morality of producing such a monster.

The scientific community and senior administration officials were divided over the hydrogen bomb though the Pentagon was urging an affirmative decision to assure that the United States develop the "Super" before the Soviets did so. Having the atomic bomb, they surely had the knowledge required for the hydrogen weapon. On November 10, 1949, Truman named a commission composed of Secretary of State Dean Acheson, Secretary of Defense Louis Johnson, and Atomic Energy Commission Chairman David Lilienthal to make formal recommendations to him. On January 5, 1950, the three men recommended the construction of the hydrogen bomb (although Lilienthal initially sought to delay it). Acheson wrote later that he believed that the Soviets would not delay hydrogen bomb research even if the United States delayed it and that "the American people simply would not tolerate a policy of delaying nuclear research in so vital a matter while we sought for further ways of reaching accommodation with the Russians after the experiences of the years since the war."

On January 31, 1950, the President announced his decision, adding that he was instructing the secretaries of state and defense "to undertake a reexamination of our objectives in peace and war and of the effect of these objectives on our strategic plans, in the light of the probable fission bomb capability and possible thermonuclear bomb capability of the Soviet Union." As historian John Lewis Gaddis notes in his book The Long Peace, Truman's decision "was made on political grounds: deterrence could not be expected to work if the United States was perceived to be falling behind in any major category of weapons system, whether or not that system would be of any use in fighting a war." At that point, in fact, the Pentagon had not yet even developed plans on how to use a hydrogen bomb in wartime.

In any event, another Rubicon was crossed as the result of the sheer political dynamics of the Cold War. Almost two years later, on November 1, 1952, the United States exploded its first hydrogen bomb—a device named "Mike" that yielded the TNT equivalent of 10.4 million tons—in a secret test on Eniwetok islet in the Pacific. Official observers watching from forty miles away saw seawater turn into steam and reef being pulverized. Because "Mike" weighed sixty-five tons, it was not a weapon that could be delivered against an enemy anywhere, and the designers went back to work.

The Soviets were not far behind. They exploded in August 1953, a small hydrogen bomb, designed by their famous physicist Andrei Sakharov (who later became even more famous as a Soviet human rights dissident and died in December 1989, as the liberal leader in the new Soviet parliament.) The test, of course, vindicated Acheson's judgment; it had taken the Russians more than four years to catch up with America in building an atomic bomb, but only nine months to catch up with the hydrogen weapon. In 1954 the United States tested in the Pacific a fifteen-megaton bomb (half again as powerful as "Mike") that was small enough to be transported in an aircraft. In November 1955 the Soviets matched the feat by dropping a hydrogen weapon from a plane.

By then France was already well advanced on its secret project to build an atomic bomb, its decision to proceed already having been taken in 1952 by associates of General de Gaulle. The general himself was out of power, but as former Premier Jacques Chaban-Delmas told me many years later, he and other Gaullists with quiet influence in the government and the French armed forces launched the nuclear project on their own—with De Gaulle's private blessing. The funds, Chaban-Delmas said, were "out of budget"— that is, they were made secretly available by the Defense Ministry from unvouchered secret monies. This story has never been told publicly. Most Frenchmen believed fervently that without their own atomic weapon, they courted another humiliation like the defeat at the hands of the Nazis in 1940 should a new war ever come. As De Gaulle said, "Never again," France was to explode its bomb in 1960.

It subsequently became an important nuclear power in Europe (in 1989 France had ninety-six multiple-warhead nuclear missiles on six submarines, eighteen ballistic missiles programmed to hit the Soviet Union from ground silos, and a Hadès missile tactical atomic force aimed eastward). Under a secret arrangement approved by President Richard Nixon in 1973, the United States assisted the French in expanding and refining their nuclear program in such areas as the miniaturizing of their warheads. Though De Gaulle had previously removed France from centralized peacetime NATO commands and the assistance to the French program was technically in violation of a 1958 amendment to the Atomic Energy Act on limiting help to foreign nuclear projects (except for Britain), the Ford, Carter, and Reagan administrations maintained this help.

Britain detonated its first bomb off the coast of Australia in October 1952, becoming the world's third atomic power. France was the fourth, and China was to become the fifth in 1964. The world was entering the age of the thermonuclear bomb—by the early 1970's all five nations possessed the hydrogen weapon—with limitless explosive power.

The Truman decisions on the nuclear arsenal represented the purely military aspect of changing American strategies. Now new fundamental political postures had to be adopted to deal with the political threat the administration believed was posed by the Soviet Union as well as China. In fact, Washington was reaching the conclusion that the Russians and the Chinese formed a hostile Communist monolith, with the Kremlin issuing orders that the junior partner unquestioningly implemented. This may have reflected the quintessential ignorance of the real nature and nuances of the Soviet-Chinese relationship, but American policymakers were impressed by Mao Zedong's visit to Stalin in Moscow in December 1949 and the signing on February 14, 1950, of the treaty of friendship they had negotiated. Communist China's seizure of autonomous Tibet and the bloody repression of Tibetans during 1950 added to the concerns about Mao's policies.

The new American strategy took shape through the President's acceptance of recommendations contained in top secret government studies that he ordered as well as through a barrage of public speeches, announcements, and pronouncements in the opening months of 1950. While the public posture had the twin purpose of reassuring Americans that their safety was virtually guaranteed by such measures as the decision to build the H-bomb and preparing them for overseas reverses like the possible loss of Taiwan (still called Formosa in those days) to Communist China, much confusion and contradiction were being sown by careless statements delivered by top officials.

Moreover, it was not always clear that the administration really had the means of enforcing its strategic projects. Policy toward Eastern Europe, for example, was enunciated in December 1949 in NSC-58/2, a top secret National Security Council decision document (all NSC study and decision memorandums and documents have high classifications at the time they are issued; many of them are later declassified). NSC-58/2 propounded the thesis that the situation was "ripe" to "consider whether we cannot do more to cause the elimination or at least a reduction of predominant Soviet influence in the satellite states of Eastern Europe."

It was questionable even at the time that this could be accomplished in light of overwhelming Soviet power in the region, and covert CIA operations launched in Albania and Poland presumably to create armed local resistance to the Communist regimes were doomed to failure even before they were betrayed by Soviet moles in Western intelligence services.

In the Albanian case it was Kim Philby, the high-ranking mole in the British MI 6 service, who alerted the Russians to the infiltration of subversive agents whom he had personally organized for the mission and, in effect, sent to their deaths.

In Poland the CIA invested in the moribund Kedyw (Diversion Directorate) branch of the anti-Communist Home Army (known as AK) which had orchestrated the 1944 Warsaw uprising against the Nazis. The Kedyw was left behind as a guerrilla force harassing the new Communist authorities; but General August Emil Fieldorf, its chief, had surrendered in 1948 (he was executed in 1953), and the remaining units were liquidated by 1951.

What had not been understood in Washington was that the satellites could be pried away from the Soviets only by their own Communist regimes—as in the case of Tito's Yugoslavia in 1948—or by spontaneous uprisings by the populations that did not occur in Eastern Europe until much later. The efforts to organize guerrillas from the outside were criminal nonsense because they inevitably cost lives, producing no results.

Far Eastern policy was also badly muddled and may have dangerously confused the Soviets and the Chinese in addition to the Congress and the American public opinion. Thus, on January 5, 1950, Truman issued a statement declaring that the United States "has no predatory designs on Formosa . . . nor does it have any intention of utilizing its armed forces to interfere in the present situation." He added that "the United States Government will not pursue a course which will lead to involvement in the civil conflict in China" and "will not provide military aid or advice to Chinese forces in Formosa."

Though Truman's declaration was mainly intended to prepare Americans for the fall of the Chinese Nationalists' island bastion, it also could be read in Beijing as an invitation to invade it. It is arresting to see how often drafters of top-level policy pronouncements fail to anticipate how they will be interpreted by friend and foe.

Confusion increased when Secretary of State Acheson addressed himself to the question of China in a speech a week later. His intent was to explain rationally why the Communists had triumphed in the Chinese Civil War the previous year, but Acheson's January 12 speech at Washington's National Press Club was to be remembered for a careless omission. Discussing military security in the Pacific, he described America's "defensive perimeter" as running "along the Aleutians to Japan" and including "the Ryukyu Islands under Japanese rule and the Philippines." Not having specifically listed Korea as part of that "defensive perimeter," Acheson was later accused of having thereby encouraged the Communist invasion of South Korea.

When Yakov Malik, the chief Soviet delegate to the United Nations, walked out of the Security Council on January 17, in protest against the presence of Nationalist China on that body—he said he would not return until Communist China was seated—it seemed to confirm even more convincingly that Moscow and Beijing worked hand in hand. But history has its own ways of perversity as the Communists discovered before long.

The document that became the American charter in the Cold War was NSC-68, the National Security Council secret directive issued on April 14, 1950, after months of concentrated study. Drafted principally by Paul Nitze, then the State Department's Policy Planning Staff director, NSC-68 expanded the ideas of containment expressed by the 1947 Truman Doctrine on aid to Greece and Turkey, and it became the intellectual and strategic guide for American foreign policy for the next four decades. Significantly Mikhail Gorbachev's conciliatory policies opened a debate in the United States in the late eighties on whether the Cold War had finally ended and, consequently, the principles of NSC-68 should be discarded. An octogenarian Paul Nitze led the American delegation that negotiated with the Soviet Union the pact on the mutual removal of intermediate-range nuclear weapons from Europe, the most tangible sign that the Cold War was indeed winding down.

NSC-68 had concluded that the Soviet threat was worldwide although "piecemeal" aggression by the Kremlin's satellites was the most immediate danger, and it urged a major jump in American defense expenditures in both nuclear and conventional forces (Truman had already authorized the construction of the hydrogen bomb). Acheson writes that the study analyzed the threat posed by the combination of "the ideology of communist doctrine and the power of the Russian state" in contrast with "the American aim" of "an environment in which free societies could exist and flourish."

But, he adds, "the purpose of NSC-68 was to so bludgeon the mass mind of 'top government' that not only could the President make a decision but that the decision would be carried out." Even so, Acheson observes, "it is doubtful whether anything like what happened in the next few years could have been done had not the Russians been stupid enough to have instigated the attack against South Korea and opened the 'hate America' campaign."

NSC-68, as Paul Nitze may proudly recall, was prophetic in asserting that there would be "no lasting abatement" in East-West tensions "unless and until a change occurs in the nature of the Soviet system." Similarly the study urged the United States to allow time for internal Soviet contradictions to come to the fore so that natural tensions within the Communist system could be exploited.

It was probably inevitable that the external threats and such public decisions as Truman's green light for developing the hydrogen bomb would help create a domestic political climate in the United States that made it difficult for our free society to flourish as fully as most Americans wished, or said they did.

The combination of fear of war, fear of the Soviet Union, and deeply rooted anticommunism produced something akin to hysteria in the United States on a variety of levels. On one level, pressures were rising to "get it over with" as far as the Soviet Union was concerned by using at once our nuclear weapons, and this included personages who should have known better, at least in terms of the consequences of a nuclear holocaust. Thus Secretary of the Navy Francis P. Matthews delivered a speech in Boston in August 1950 proposing a preventive war against the Russians, and General Orville Anderson, commandant of the Air War College, announced publicly that the U.S. Air Force awaited orders to bomb Moscow. Truman had the good sense to remove both of them from their posts.

At the same time plans were drawn for the construction of shelters for the population and the designation of basements in big buildings as sites for protection from radioactivity. In New York City the subway system was regarded as the place to survive. The government joined all the radio and television stations into the emergency broadcast system (which was still being tested daily forty years later), and urban evacuation plans were made although nobody had the slightest idea what would happen if a Soviet nuclear missile hit an American city.

Enterprising builders and store owners offered individual steel and concrete shelters for suburbia and the countryside, complete with canned food supplies, bottled water, and flashlights—and the business boomed. Shelter owners also bought weapons, including submachine guns, to protect themselves and their families from postexplosion attacks by starved or maimed survivors. It was national folly. I lived in New York at the time, and I remember a physicist friend of mine, George T. Senseney, who had been present at the Bikini and Eniwetok tests, telling me, "I would rather die in my living room with a martini in my hand than in a crowded subway among people to whom I haven't even been introduced. . . . You don't survive anything even approaching a direct hit" (George died peacefully in his Connecticut country house a quarter century later, probably with a drink in hand).

The early fifties were also the time of extreme political intolerance, suspicion, and anti-Communist witch-hunts. On January 21, 1950, Alger Hiss, formerly a ranking State Department official and then the president of the Carnegie Endowment for International Peace, was convicted for perjury. This was because his testimony responding to charges brought by Whittaker Chambers, a journalist once belonging to the American Communist party, that Hiss had passed secret U.S. government secrets to the Russians was said to have been false. The Hiss case was a cause célèbre, dividing public opinion in an emotional fashion, and Dean Acheson himself never lived down his remark that "I do not intend to turn my back on Alger Hiss," who was a friend. A young California congressman named Richard M. Nixon, who helped win Hiss's conviction, built his political career on it.

On February 9, 1950, the forty-one-year-old junior senator from Wisconsin, Joseph R. McCarthy, delivered a speech in Wheeling, West Virginia, charging that he had the names of eighty-one persons with Communist leanings who served or had served in the State Department and that fifty-seven card-carrying Communists were still employed there. McCarthy terrorized the State Department, the rest of the government, politicians, and other public figures for nearly five years—until the Senate censored him for insulting his own peers—but the term "McCarthyism" has survived him in English and scores of foreign languages as a derogatory noun meaning "unfair and dishonest accusations."

Apart from the harm McCarthy caused the conduct of American foreign policy through wild charges of treason against key State Department and other government officials, the phenomenon of McCarthyism poisoned for years the mood of America. Just on the strength of suspicions or whispers, highly experienced specialists were removed from sensitive posts—with no appeal. This alone destroyed the cadres of the State Department's China experts, the "old China hands," who were pushed into premature retirement. In the private sector, journalists and broadcasters and cinema writers, actors, and directors were refused work if they refused to name before congressional committees their friends and colleagues who belonged or had belonged to the Communist party.

One of the most egregious cases of injustice involved Owen Lattimore, a distinguished Asian scholar who was accused by McCarthy of being "the top Soviet espionage agent" in the United States. Lattimore, who died in 1989, describes his chilling experiences in *Ordeal by Slander*, a book published in 1950, while the attack on him was still in progress. He makes the terrifying point that "it is important for as many people as possible to learn soon that 'it can happen here.'" It took several years for Lattimore to be vindicated as *his case* included indictments for alleged perjury that were subsequently squashed, FBI reports that there was no case against him, and finally a Supreme Court split decision that led the government to drop the prosecution and the persecution. Nevertheless, Lattimore never fully recovered from his ordeal, and the United States lost one of its best experts on China and Central Asia.

At the other end of the spectrum of its irrational Cold War practices, the government barred Charlie Chaplin from reentering the United States in 1952, presumably because he held controversial political views (the technicality was that the British-born Chaplin had refused to become an American citizen). He was allowed to enter twenty years later to receive an honorary Oscar from Hollywood.

That the United States had the right to protect itself from subversion was widely recognized. President Truman's 1947 executive order had set up departmental loyalty boards in government agencies and a national Loyalty Review Board to ensure fairness, but by 1949 the Congress had begun to grant department heads the right to fire employees on security grounds without the right of appeal. This was the start of the witch-hunt, and the eminently fair Harry Truman rose against it. As he says in his *Memoirs*, "some reports showed that people were being fired on false evidence." He adds that "these reports were distressing to me, as I was very anxious that no injustice be done to any individual and that no individual be deprived of his rights."

He proposed new legislation to avoid such injustices, remarking that "I am determined that the United States shall be secure. . . . I am equally determined that we shall keep our historic liberties." But on September 23, 1950, the Internal Security Act was passed by the Congress in what Truman describes as "an atmosphere of emotion and excitement" in which legislators "chose to go along with the advocates of extreme measures." Truman's veto was overridden, and the President commented that "it is one of the tragedies of our time that the security program of the United States has been wickedly used by demagogues and sensational newspapers in an attempt to frighten and mislead the American people."

It took courage in those purge days to speak out publicly against this wave of witch-hunting. One of the voices of courage was the playwright Arthur Miller whose *The Crucible* premièred on Broadway in 1953. His play told the story of the Salem witch trials in the seventeenth century to emphasize that while there are people who accept tyranny and become part of its infamous machine by denouncing their neighbors to the authorities, others will sacrifice themselves for freedom, and the law in the end will be on their side. Naturally, it also took Broadway courage to stage *The Crucible*, with the producers risking a McCarthyite witch-hunt. Another such courageous voice was that of Edward R. Murrow, the most famous television commentator of his time, who denounced McCarthy in a prime-time special and in subsequent on-the-air pronouncements. Morrow's immensely controversial broadcasts also made the subtle point that there are times in life—and in history—when journalists must speak out as a matter of conscience on great issues of justice and decency rather than adhere blindly to mindless objectivity.

Curiously the American people reacted against McCarthyism and Senator McCarthy himself when they were given the opportunity to see them in action. This was made possible by live television, which entered active politics through the coverage of the hearings on organized crime held by Senator Estes Kefauver of Tennessee in New York in 1951, dramatically affecting American attitudes on public life. Audiences that in those days were treated to the new comedy stardom of Lucille Ball in *I Love Lucy* and George Burns and Gracie Allen and primitive news programs were suddenly faced on their home screens with brutal reality.

When McCarthy took on the U.S. Army over loyalty issues in 1954, Americans saw him for what he really represented as the televised hearings turned into a daily drama witnessed by millions. My newspaper assignment at the time was writing the advance obit of the Wisconsin senator (this is a routine practice, not a desire to see a public figure die), and I watched the hearings gavel to gavel. The most unforgettable moment came when Joseph Welch, the bow-tied, pixie-looking Boston lawyer for the Army, asked McCarthy, "Have you no sense of decency, sir, at long last?" That question instantly ended McCarthy's career in American politics.

Still in 1953, Julius and Ethel Rosenberg were convicted of atomic espionage for the Soviets and put to death in the electric chair in an upstate New York prison. Along with the Hiss case and McCarthyism, the Rosenbergs' fate became one of the great political and emotional controversies of the decade. Were they really guilty, or were they victimized by the prevailing mood in the country? Had Moscow's secret nuclear development program truly needed the Rosenbergs? The CIA's classified study of the Soviet bomb project seems to negate it.

III

The North Korean invasion of South Korea on June 25, 1950, confirmed the worst fears and suspicions of Americans about communism in general and the Soviet Union in particular. While there is no question that this invasion was sanctioned, if not actually ordered, by Moscow, *why* the Russians had desired it remains a mystery, along with the parallel question of whether it did not, in fact, constitute one of Stalin's most dangerous blunders. Stalin could not have predicted what his Korean folly would bring, but Dean Acheson acknowledged that late in 1950 "we were closer than we had yet been to a wider war."

When North Korean armor and infantry crossed the thirty-eighth parallel just before dawn of that June Sunday and swooped down on the South Korean capital of Seoul right below the dividing line, it may have appeared to the United States that it was facing the final move in a perfectly orchestrated Communist expansionist operation in Asia. This was why President Truman acted instantly to commit the limited American forces in the Far East to the defense of South Korea (raising for the first time the still-unanswered question of presidential war powers) and secured the support of the United Nations for the huge "police action," as the war quickly became known.

The American reaction to the Korean invasion was justified in terms of interpreting the Communist thrust as a basic defiance rather than as a local situation. All the other pieces seemed to be in place: China was threatening to grab Taiwan and destroy the remnants of Chiang Kai-shek's fugitive Nationalist army while Vietnamese Communists had been battling the French in Southeast Asia for more than three years. Now North Korea, a creature of the Soviet Union, was attempting to unify the peninsula by force after having signed a friendship pact with the Russians on March 17, 1949.

Mao and Ho were bound to Moscow by friendship treaties signed early in 1950. Thus everything pointed to a beautifully choreographed enterprise under the aegis of a triumphantly smiling Marshal Stalin.

Because Americans tend to think geostrategically as well as demonologically, such a scenario was unfolding in their minds. By 1949 the Soviets had completed strangleholding Eastern Europe and acquiring the atomic bomb. The Berlin blockade ploy having failed the previous year (when the Soviets still lacked the bomb), the next logical place to defy the United States was Asia, especially in the light of the Communist victory in China. After all, NSC-68 had established the expansionist character of the Soviet Union, having even predicted that the Russians would move piecemeal and use proxies, and indeed, this was a neat Communist strategic scenario—as perceived in Washington.

The only trouble with it, we now know, was that the entire premise was wrong. Washington was wildly overestimating the degree of orchestration the Kremlin was capable of imposing in Asia, even if it wished to do it, and it blissfully ignored the very real, if hidden, differences between the Russians and Asian Communists as well as within the latter. The quality of Western political intelligence in that part of the world was woefully inadequate, and the analysis was inevitably of inferior caliber. The peril implicit in such erroneous geostrategic judgments was that they could lead to catastrophic responses, including, as they almost did on three occasions, the use of nuclear weapons.

As one looks back at the Korean War forty years later, it is still hard to discern the reasons that impelled Stalin to encourage or allow Kim Il Sung, the North Korean leader he had installed in power in 1945, to launch the invasion. That Kim, then only thirty-eight years old, but already a mystical megalomaniac on a grand scale, yearned for the control of the South was understandable. His guerrillas had been fighting the South Koreans in the border hills since the end of the war. But this was no reason for the Soviets to equip him militarily for such an adventure with tanks and Yak and Ilyushin jet fighter-bomber aircraft and to keep the North Koreans going for the three years, one month, and two days that this wholly pointless conflict lasted.

The war cost the United States and its allies more than 170,000 killed and wounded, the bulk of them Americans, and the South Korean losses were around 850,000 soldiers. The estimate of North Korean and Chinese casualties is 1.5 million men. But even if no Russian lives were sacrificed (Stalin sagely kept his soldiers home, not even sending "volunteers), it is now clear that the Soviet dictator and the Soviet Union gained nothing in the end from unleashing the mad Kim. It was a miscalculation from every conceivable viewpoint, and paradoxically, if anyone benefited from the war, it was Kim Il Sung. The Chinese saved him from being crushed by the Americans in the first six months of the conflict, and the Soviets incurred obligations to him in the form of vast economic aid for reconstruction in recognition of his eager willingness to be unleashed.

Over the years North Korea built its Communist prison state efficiently and without Soviet interference, becoming by choice one of the most isolated nations in the world. Kim Il Sung constructed an unparalleled personality cult for himself (dwarfing even Stalin's cult), being officially hailed as "the nation's sun" and "the genius of the revolution." Rarely seen in public, the octogenarian Kim still reigned in 1990 over his sad land. He has held power longer than any Communist leader in history.

It must be asked, of course, whether the aging and paranoia-seized Stalin was capable of acting rationally in 1950, when he triggered the Korean War. The conquest of South Korea had little to offer the Russians economically or militarily, and simply awarding it to the North Koreans could not have been a serious Soviet priority. From a security standpoint there was no direct threat to the Soviets in Asia in 1950. The USSR had incorporated Outer Mongolia from China (later making it into a fictitious "independent" state) and, after disarming the Japanese, denuded Manchuria of all movable industrial equipment and rolling stock as war "reparations." It held the northern Japanese islands, and the American occupation forces in Japan obviously did not menace it.

Thus the Korean adventure was a huge miscalculation or several miscalculations. The first was what might be called an American miscalculation. Boris Notkin, a Moscow University historian of the *glasnost* persuasion, told me in 1989 that there were indications that Stalin simply wanted a triumph over the Americans "on the cheap" for its own sake or, possibly, as revenge for the Marshall Plan and the Berlin airlift—not very rational foreign policy motivations. Stalin must have concluded, Notkin suggested, that the Americans, who had evacuated all their combat troops from South Korean in 1949, leaving behind only five hundred military advisers, would not return to fight—just as they let Chiang Kai-shek be beaten in China. Truman's announcement in January 1950 that the United States would not defend Taiwan may have reinforced Stalin's assessment, as may have been the case with Acheson's careless omission of South Korea from his definition of the American defensive perimeter in the Pacific.

The second mistake may have been the Chinese miscalculation. Consistent with Stalin's duplicity and his biological inability to tolerate even minor rivals, it is the most convincing explanation for the Korean War. The key to this operation is the fact that contrary to belief in the West, Stalin was far from enchanted with Mao Zedong's total victory over the Nationalists and his consequent mastery of all China. To Stalin, *this* was a short- and long-range threat to Soviet interests because he feared that a united China with its huge population could not be controlled and manipulated from Moscow.

Milovan Djilas, one of Tito's closest associates in the Yugoslav Communist leadership during and immediately after the war, had visited Stalin on numerous occasions before the Soviet-Yugoslav split in 1948, and he has written about these experiences in his *Conversations with Stalin.* Concerning China, Djilas concludes that it cannot be excluded that Stalin "anticipated future danger to his own work and to his own empire from the new Communist great power, especially since there were no prospects of subordinating it internally." Djilas adds most insightfully that "he [Stalin] knew that every revolution, simply by virtue of being new, also becomes a separate epicenter and shapes its own government and state, and this was what he feared in the Chinese case, all the more since the phenomenon was involved that was as significant and momentous as the October Revolution."

Djilas cites Stalin's comment in a conversation in January 1948 to the effect that "when the war with Japan ended, we invited the Chinese comrades to reach an agreement as to how a *modus vivendi* with Chiang Kai-shek might be found." Stalin went on to say that "they agreed with us in word, but in deed they did it their own way when they got home: they mustered their forces and struck." It is a matter of record that the Soviet military aid to Mao's forces after 1945 was confined to captured Japanese arms, and many historians suspect that Stalin had hoped for a very protracted Chinese civil war that he also hoped might attract American troops to Asia and thereby weaken Western Europe.

It is also known that the negotiations between Mao and Stalin in Moscow between December 1949 and February 1950, when their treaty of friendship was finally signed, were extremely difficult and unpleasant although they were careful to preserve the appearance of comradely friendship. The Soviet locustlike passage through Manchuria and the fate of Mongolia were serious issues between the two men, and the resentments lived on until the 1959 Sino-Soviet split. Stalin's concept after the Mao visit was to debilitate China as much as possible by creating an Asian conflict into which the Chinese would inevitably be drawn—and injured in the process.

In his biography of Stalin Adam B. Ulam writes that "it is doubtful that Mao had been forewarned of the Korean gambit, most unlikely that he could have wished for the North Korean attack, although the Americans thought he was to blame." Ulam comments accurately that "the Chinese, not to mention the North Koreans, had to foot the bill for Stalin's miscalculations." This was so because when the American forces (which Stalin did not think would be in the war at all) approached the Chinese border at the Yalu River, Mao, concerned about *his* security, ordered his armies into action against the United States. Afterward China wanted a rapid settlement, but as Ulam notes, only after Stalin's death in 1953 "did the Kremlin heed the Chinese pleas, and then the Korean armistice was signed."

Prior to the armistice, the United States had been strongly tempted to use atomic weapons in Korea, which might have engulfed everybody, including the Russians, in a wide war. Simultaneously Truman decided to shift policy and to dispatch the Seventh Fleet to protect Taiwan from a Chinese attack, further complicating the Far Eastern picture.

Notwithstanding the cost in lives, China rose to the rank of a major world power as the result of the Korean involvement, not exactly what Stalin had in mind, and it went on developing according to its own lights. And as far as Soviet security in that region of Asia is concerned, Korea remains divided, with forty-three thousand American combat troops still stationed in the

South in 1990, where there were none when Stalin hit upon the idea of the invasion. Finally it was the Korean War that marked the start of Japan's recovery; the war helped it to get rich and, in time, to emerge as an economic empire.

These origins of the Korean War provide the opportunity to pause in the examination of the 1950's to look at the personalities of Joseph Stalin and Harry Truman, the two men who held in their hands the fate of the world at the start of the decade, when the Cold War acquired ominous momentum and both superpowers had growing arsenals of atomic weapons.

In 1950 Stalin was seventy years old. He was a despot, unchallenged during the twenty-six years in power he captured after contriving to succeed the dying Lenin, but he was rapidly deteriorating in multiple ways. Stalin's condition at the outset of the fifties is best described in the title of one of the final chapters of Adam Ulam's biography, "The Aging God." Stalin's megalomania (apart from his murderous manner of governing) was at the apex, yet his sense of insecurity was overwhelming him. As Ulam puts it, "the vision of himself coming to Lenin's end—incapacitated, surrounded by sorrowful lieutenants who from solicitude would keep him out of things—was now very much on Stalin's mind. . . . He no longer could keep abreast of everything happening in the Party and the state, and from his point of view this meant that more than ever he must not only be feared and worshipped but appear mysterious and unfathomable."

Djilas was the only foreigner who had been given extraordinary access to Stalin, often as a guest at all-night supper and drinking bouts at the old man's villa near Moscow, and his accounts are frightening. Djilas visited Stalin as Tito's emissary over a four-year period, the last time in 1948, shortly before the Berlin blockade and two years before the Korean War, and his portrayal of the marshal makes one wonder whether Soviet foreign policy at that juncture was the product of a sane mind. Djilas himself fell from grace in Yugoslavia and was forced to resign from the Communist party in 1954 for opposing the corruption and ideological rigor in Belgrade.

His gradual conversion from an unquestioning associate of Tito's to a cynic appears to have been greatly influenced by his exposure to Stalin and the inner workings of the Soviet system—he did not wish to see it repeated in Yugoslavia—and Djilas was among the first Marxist thinkers to predict the ultimate collapse of the orthodox system, as we saw it in the late eighties. He paid with nine years of prison sentences for publishing his views abroad, for he was unable to publish at home.

In his *Unperfect Society*, published in 1969 (a year after Soviet armies had destroyed the Czechoslovak experiment in liberal Marxism), he writes: "Communism in Eastern Europe can no longer change conceptually. Nor can it, without great difficulty, rejuvenate any of the features of its administration, despite the fact that Communists spontaneously and consciously take refuge in deceiving themselves and others by proposing 'far reaching' measures 'based on principle.'"

I met Djilas about the time *Unperfect Society* was published in New York. I visited him in his sunless apartment behind the National Assembly's building in Belgrade, and he told me in the interview that the Prague events of 1968 had been only the first step in a historical process and that he was optimistic about the future of freedom in Eastern Europe. He lived to see his prophecies confirmed in 1989. Djilas also gave me a copy of *Conversations with Stalin*, the publication of which abroad in 1962 had been punished with a new prison term ordered by Tito. Djilas refused in those days to discuss Tito, but when I had the opportunity that same week to converse with the Yugoslav chief, resplendent in his white marshal's uniform, I think I detected what Djilas may have seen in his old guerrilla boss: imperial absolutism and corruption of power, perhaps reminiscent of Stalin.

At their first meeting in 1944, with the war still raging, Djilas found out how Stalin felt about his Western allies: "Churchill is the kind who, if you don't watch him, will slip a kopeck out of your pocket. Yes, a kopeck out of your pocket! By God, a kopeck out of your pocket! And Roosevelt? Roosevelt is not like that. He dips in his hand only for bigger coins. But Churchill? Churchill—even for a kopeck." Pointing to a wall map where the Soviet Union was colored in red, Stalin exclaimed to Djilas as he continued his denunciations of the British and the Americans: "They will never accept the idea that so great a space should be red, never, never!"

Djilas writes that Stalin's dinners with the leadership, lasting from ten at night until five o'clock in the morning, were characterized by an "enormous" variety of food and drink with "hard liquor predominating." He observes that "it was at these dinners that the destiny of the vast Russian land, of the newly acquired territories, and, to a considerable degree, of the human race was decided."

The picture Djilas draws of Stalin from personal knowledge could not be matched by the most fervent Western anti-Communist: "His country was in ruins, hungry, exhausted. But his armies and marshals, heavy with fat and medals and drunk with vodka and victory, had already trampled half of Europe under foot, and he was convinced they would trample over the other half in the next round. . . . His conscience was troubled by nothing, despite the millions who had been destroyed in his name and by his order, despite the thousands of his closest collaborators whom he had murdered as traitors because they doubted that he was leading the country and people into happiness, equality and liberty."

Describing Stalin at a dinner in 1948, Djilas remarks that "there was something both tragic and ugly in his senility . . . the ugly kept cropping up all the time. Though he had always enjoyed eating well, Stalin now exhibited gluttony, as though he feared that there would not be enough of the desired food left for him. . . . His intellect was in even more apparent decline. . . . In one thing, though, he was still the Stalin of old: stubborn, sharp, suspicious whenever anyone disagreed with him."

Adam Ulam stresses in his biography that in the last five years of his life, which included the launching of the Korean War, Stalin's behavior was, in effect, clinically insane. Returning to the tradition of the great purges of the 1930's, when he liquidated his closest associates, Stalin staged a secret trial to climax what was known as the Leningrad Affair. Early in 1949 the secret police arrested on charges that were never publicly explained in any elucidating detail three senior officials whose political base had been Leningrad. They were Nikolai Voznesensky, a leading economist, the chairman of Gosplan (the economic planning agency), and a Politburo member; Aleksis Kuznetsov, a Leningrad party leader and a secretary of the Central Committee of the Communist party; and Mikhail Rodionov, the prime minister of the Russian SSR.

Investigations and the trial lasted for more than a year. In September 1950, with the Korean War already under way, these three men and numerous associates were executed for unspecified treason. Actually Stalin did not appear to be particularly interested in the war once it was launched. Ulam writes that the moment the war erupted and the United States intervened, the general expectation was that Stalin would publicly address himself to the international crisis he had sprung, but instead, he published a long essay on linguistics. It dealt with obscure relationships involving Marxism, nationalism, and language that virtually nobody understood in the Soviet Union; to Stalin, however, it was a tool of ideological struggle and an opportunity to show himself in his final years as a theoretician and philosopher in the literary and intellectual footsteps of Lenin.

Stalin's article appeared in *Pravda* just as the first American troops were landing in South Korea; but the Soviet press was seized with his linguistics debate, and as Ulam writes, the news from Korea was confined to a few paragraphs. If Stalin was jolted by the obviously unexpected American decision to fight, he did not show it. But immediately he began rebuilding the Soviet armed forces to the point where they doubled in four years (the process continued after his death). He, of course, had no inkling that the United States was contemplating using the atomic bomb in Korea and China, but he must have doubted it because he made no early effort to halt the war. And Stalin, whose own nuclear weapon had been tested for the first time only a year earlier, was in no position to start an atomic war himself; it would have been suicide, and even he must have known it.

In 1951, with the war still undecided, Stalin turned again to alleged plots and conspiracies against him. A number of officials were executed. Then he ordered show trials in Czechoslovakia against top party officials, including Rudolf Slánský, the general secretary of the Communist party. Stalin's obsessions were blending into one vast paranoia as the trials were aimed at Trotskyites, Titoists, Jews in general, and Zionists in particular (Slánský was Jewish). Slánský and ten colleagues were executed in November 1952.

At that stage Stalin was losing what was left of his sense of reality. Again feeling the need to leave behind him a major intellectual work, he concentrated on writing an enormous essay on the economic problems of socialism in the USSR. He craved still more adulation, so in early October he convoked the Nineteenth Congress of the Soviet Communist party. There he heard Georgi Malenkov, his second-in-command, proclaim that Stalin's "discoveries in the field of theory have world-historic importance."

Stalin's farewell contribution to his country and the world was the "Kremlin Doctors' Plot," which his security services produced on January 13, 1953. The accusation was that "a terrorist group of doctors," mainly Jewish, had caused the premature death of a number of top Soviet leaders. Among the doctors who were arrested was Stalin's personal physician, Dr. V. N. Vinogradov. It is entirely plausible that in his final delusions Stalin had convinced himself that plotters were trying to kill him. He died six weeks later—on March 5, 1953—of a stroke at his villa at Kuntsevo, thereby saving the lives of the "terrorist doctors," who were freed at once.

He was seventy-three years old. Though he lived only eight years of the postwar era, his influence on world affairs had been immense, and in a sense, it continued from beyond the grave—until Mikhail Gorbachev entered the scene thirty-two years later. Mao Zedong did not attend Stalin's funeral.

Harry Truman was a secure, self-confident, unhesitating, and totally courageous figure. He knew when to act and when to be restrained. He listened to the best available advice, then made up his mind. He chose to drop atomic bombs on Hiroshima and Nagasaki—a decision that he always defended and that history will someday judge—and he resolved not to go nuclear over Korea. He did not tolerate provocation and wasted no time in responding to it with adequate force, as he did over Greece and Turkey, Berlin, and finally Korea. He fired Douglas MacArthur for what he saw as megalomaniac insubordination, and he publicly chastised a music critic who disliked the voice of Truman's daughter, Margaret. He had astonishing historical vision; his great legacy to the war-ravaged world was the Marshall Plan, which he persuaded the Congress to authorize in one of the great American gestures of the twentieth century.

From June 25, 1950, through the end of his term on January 20, 1953, the hot Korea War, the Cold War, and all their domestic and international ramifications constituted Truman's principal concerns. In every aspect of foreign policies, the President relied greatly on the talents and personality of his secretary of state, Dean Gooderham Acheson. No two men could have been more dissimilar in appearance and background than Truman and Acheson, yet they complemented each other in an extraordinary fashion with limitless loyalty on both sides.

Acheson, a Harvard Law School graduate, was Roosevelt's undersecretary of the treasury when the New Deal was launched in 1933. He served in top State Department positions during World War II and the advent of the Cold War, then was named by Truman to be secretary of state in 1949, replacing George Marshall. Fifty-seven years old when the Korean War came, the tall, elegant Acheson with his stylish mustache towered over the bow-tied President, who was sixty-five at the time (and privately called "the mad haberdasher" by Stalin), but together they looked like the formidable and steely team they formed. Acheson was the most creative and professional secretary of state in the postwar half century (only Henry Kissinger was of comparable intellectual caliber), and Truman was immensely lucky to have him at his side during that exceedingly complex and perilous period of American history. For a young reporter to attend a briefing by Acheson was tantamount to a graduate seminar on international relations, for Acheson tended to be informative, trenchant, cutting, or sarcastic among journalists, depending on the questions. His mustache bristled when he was annoyed or impatient, and we saw this quite frequently when Acheson visited the temporary headquarters of the United Nations at Lake Success, New York, during the summer and autumn of 1950 to coordinate allied actions in Korea.

From the moment word reached Washington that the North Koreans had crossed the thirty-eighth parallel early on Sunday, Acheson started planning the American response, first telephoning Truman at his home in Independence, Missouri, where the President was spending the weekend, to inform him of what was happening (it was Saturday night in the United States, and Acheson himself was at his Maryland farm). In *Present at the Creation*, Acheson provides a very detailed account of the invasion and all that followed, but most surprisingly, he omits to explain why the United States was so totally unprepared for the Communist attack.

Acheson mentions that in 1947 the United Nations approved a resolution calling for "an independent, united Korean government," then drops the subject of preinvasion events, remarking that "the American Government was not willing to commit its forces to the task of creating an independent and united Korea against any and all opposition." This single sentence disposes of the fact that the United States had pulled out its combat troops from South Korea in 1949 while the Soviets were building up the North Korean Army (an easily observable fact for American intelligence agencies proliferating in the region).

According to Max Hastings, a CIA report on March 10 said that the invasion would occur in June. The American ambassador in Seoul, John J. Muccio, testified before a congressional committee early in June that Communist forces poised above the parallel posed an imminent menace and requested urgent new aid for South Korea. But Hastings writes that General MacArthur in Tokyo "repeatedly declared his disbelief in the imminence of war" and paid absolutely no attention to the combat training of American divisions under his command in Japan.

Inattention to Korea may have been a major American blunder early in the fifties, and it certainly was not Acheson's finest hour in anticipating the moves of the adversary. Still, he reacted instantly, advising the President to act against the invasion. In his *Memoirs* Truman comments that "Communism was acting in Korea just as Hitler, Mussolini and the Japanese had acted ten, fifteen, and twenty years earlier" and that "I felt certain that if South Korea was allowed to fall Communist leaders would be emboldened to override nations closer to our own shores. . . . If this was allowed to go unchallenged it would mean a third world war, just as similar incidents had brought on the second world war."

Forty years later Korea has become a forgotten war and the first one ever the United States failed to win. Though American losses were tremendous, the Korean War seems to be real only to those watching television reruns of the vastly popular *M*A*S*H* program about an Army hospital just behind the front lines. (Only in 1989 did the Congress authorize a Korean Memorial in Washington near the Vietnam Memorial in the shade of the Lincoln Memorial; a South Korean company exporting cars to the United States will pay for it.)

Few, if any, objective historians question today the wisdom of Truman's decision to send troops to Korea, but in the first weeks and months it was a desperate gamble. Unprepared and ill trained, the troops of the South Korean regime of President Syngman Rhee (the first in the postwar generation of catastrophic Asian leaders the United States chose to support in its primitive anti-Communist approach) were being crushed by Communist tanks and artillery. Sunday afternoon the UN Security Council approved by a vote of nine to zero (Communist Yugoslavia abstained) a resolution declaring the invasion to be "a breach of peace" and urging North Korean withdrawal behind the thirty-eighth parallel. The resolution paved the way for the armed UN "police action" that followed; it could be passed only because the Soviets were still boycotting Security Council meetings over the issue of Chinese representation and were not there to cast the anticipated veto.

Acheson thought this was a basic diplomatic victory, but the next day he had to inform Truman that "the situation in Korea was becoming . . . desperate." On June 27 the President announced that he had ordered American air and sea forces to support the South Koreans although he knew this was wholly inadequate. Because the administration still had the idea that the Korean invasion was part of a vast Communist enterprise in Asia, Truman added that a Chinese attack on Taiwan would be "a direct threat to the security of the Pacific area and to United States forces." He said the Seventh Fleet was being dispatched to keep the Communists from assaulting Taiwan and the Nationalists from operations against the mainland. Suddenly the United States was militarily engaged in Asia.

The military history of the Korean War is well known. By the end of June Truman had authorized MacArthur to dispatch two American combat divisions to South Korea while refusing a Chinese Nationalist offer of thirty-three thousand troops to fight on the peninsula if the United States transported and supplied them. Merging the Korean War with the Chinese Civil War was not what the United States needed at that point.

By mid-July the South Koreans and the Americans had lost the whole country to the invaders, except for a coastal perimeter around Pusan. An American Army general was captured. On Acheson's advice, Truman asked the Congress for authority to send more American troops to Korea and to embark on a substantial increase in U.S. armed forces. Thus the first consequence of this "nasty little war" was the tripling of the U.S. defense budget, a decision to rearm West Germany, and the start of preparations for a peace treaty with Japan. The Soviets naturally began to rearm, too, at a quickened rate. The summer of 1950 was a watershed in the Cold War.

It also was the beginning of the MacArthur problem for the U.S. government. The general, whom Acheson and his associates regarded as a loose cannon, had been in Tokyo for five years in charge of the occupation of Japan and of all the reforms he had decided to bestow on the defeated empire. His proconsular role has become over the decades the source of much revisionist controversy, with historians claiming that MacArthur took unjustified credit for the transformation of Japan by American and Japanese experts in the postwar period and that he did not have the slightest understanding of Asian psychology. Presumably the Japanese constitution renouncing war and basic measures like the land reform were encouraged by MacArthur, who also favored retaining Emperor Hirohito on the throne after the defeat, but younger scholars dispute the view that real democracy exists today in Japan albeit the general was convinced that he had implanted it. In fact, he told George Kennan that his mission was "to plant the seeds of democracy and Christianity among a billion of these Oriental peoples on the shores of the Pacific."

In 1950, however, Washington was not assessing MacArthur's value as a social scientist but worrying about his penchant for self-aggrandizement at the expense of government policy. In August, for example, he proclaimed in a message to the Veterans of Foreign Wars that Taiwan was "an unsinkable aircraft carrier" and that "nothing could be more fallacious than the threadbare argument by those who advocate appeasement and defeatism in the Pacific that if we defend Formosa [Taiwan] we alienate continental Asia. . . . They do not grant that it is in the pattern of Oriental psychology to respect and follow aggressive, resolute and dynamic leadership—to quickly turn on a leadership characterized by timidity or vacillation. . . ." To Truman and Acheson, this was "effrontery" and "insubordination" inasmuch as it contradicted the new policy of neutrality over Taiwan and suggested that the United States had broader designs on the big island. That was when Truman first thought of firing MacArthur.

With the arrival of fresh American troops, MacArthur stabilized the front around Pusan in the south and, in September, carried out with panache surprise landings at Inchon on the coast, just west of Seoul. He was on the offensive, and as it turned out, nothing would stop him—short of a new defeat. Seoul was retaken, and the North Koreans fled back across the thirty-eighth parallel. Now the question became whether MacArthur should pursue them into North Korea or halt at the parallel, having accomplished the United Nations mandate to free South Korea. Policymakers were divided over this issue, but MacArthur moved to help them solve the dilemma by proposing that he march north to capture Kim Il Sung's capital of Pyongyang and establish a solid line across the peninsula on the other side of the parallel. As Acheson recounts it, he recommended that Truman accept the general's plan, and MacArthur cabled back, "Unless and until the enemy capitulates, I regard all Korea as open for our military operations."

Thus all parties were to blame for the disaster that befell the United States within weeks; military and political greed were not MacArthur's monopoly. And in this greed the administration abandoned its caution. After the Inchon landings Chinese Foreign Minister Zhou Enlai informed the Indian ambassador in Beijing that if the Americans crossed the parallel, China would enter the war; the message was immediately passed on to Washington (what the Indians were not told was that Mao Zedong had begun organizing "volunteers" for Korea). At the United Nations the Soviets called for a Korean cease-fire and a coalition government for all Korea, but Washington decided not to take these signs seriously.

After the UN General Assembly passed, on October 7, a resolution urging a "unified, independent and democratic" government in Korea, MacArthur chose to read it as orders to impose such a government and issued an ultimatum to North Korea to surrender or face "such military action as may be necessary to enforce the decrees of the United Nations." At that juncture Truman decided to have a talk with the general, summoning him to a meeting on Wake Island in the Pacific on October 15, but he failed to dampen MacArthur's conquering enthusiasm. Instead, he was assured that the Chinese would not intervene, and if they did, no more than sixty thousand would cross the Yalu River, the border between China and North Korea. The MacArthur story is, of course, a textbook example of how nations can blunder into great wars because of failure fully to understand the situation. That was what Stalin had done six months earlier.

Now, without consulting Washington, MacArthur sent his forces to the Yalu River, which they reached on October 25. Unknown to him, large concentrations of Chinese forces had already crossed the Yalu to the south, and they began decimating American and South Korean units. On November 1 Chinese MiG jet fighters appeared over the battlefield. An American division was thrown back from the Yalu by overwhelming Chinese military superiority, but MacArthur resolved to launch a counteroffensive while his aircraft were bombing Yalu River bridges. Clearly the United States had lost control over the situation.

This was the first time American and Communist troops had fought each other anywhere in the world, and fear that a new war was in the offing swept Western capitals. Now the administration began considering what to do if the Soviets, too, entered the fray. Acheson wrote later: "Here . . . the Government missed its last chance to halt the march to disaster in Korea. All the President's advisers in the matter, civilian and military, knew that something was badly wrong, though what it was, how to find out, and what to do about it they muffed." The tragedy, however, was even greater: When

America became involved in Vietnam a decade or so later, all the lessons of Korea had been forgotten.

With the defeat in Korea deepening every day, Truman, who was not as careful as he should have been that day, compounded the world tension by acknowledging at his news conference on November 30 that the use of the atomic bomb in Korea had always been under "active consideration." Then he really stunned the audience by remarking that the "military commander in the field" would decide when to employ the nuclear weapon. This, naturally, meant MacArthur, and now panic really hit around the globe. British Prime Minister Attlee demanded to be received by Truman in Washington.

Whether the United States had seriously planned at any point to use atomic weapons in Korea remains unclear forty years later. According to John Lewis Gaddis, the historian, the Joint Chiefs of Staff did raise this question with MacArthur after China had entered the war—probably with tactical weapons in mind—but there is controversy over what the general recommended. He is known to have talked about laying a belt of radioactive waste across North Korea—whatever that meant. Paul Nitze at the State Department argued that the use of the bomb might provoke a Soviet intervention, which would result in a global conflict.

In February 1953, weeks after being inaugurated, President Eisenhower told the National Security Council "that we should consider the use of tactical atomic weapons" in Korea. Professor Gaddis has written that Eisenhower "was not at all reluctant to give the *impression*" that atomic weapons could be used to end the military stalemate in Korea. Eisenhower's first secretary of state, John Foster Dulles, said after the 1953 armistice that "we had already sent the means to the theater for delivering atomic weapons," and the plan was to use them against China. Having served as a news correspondent in Taiwan in the fifties, I happen to be acquainted with at least one former Air Force officer, a specialist in arming nuclear weapons, who was sent out with a bombing crew to the island in readiness for a possible strike. This may have added up to psychological warfare—Dulles said he did not mind that the Chinese learned about the nuclear preparations—but it was playing with fire. As McGeorge Bundy writes in *Danger and Survival*, "there were threads of nuclear danger in the Korean war."

From the time Truman alluded to the atomic bomb in November 1950 to the armistice in Korea, two and a half years were to elapse in blind pursuance of this aimless war. In March 1951 MacArthur was finally able to hit back at the Chinese and the North Koreans, retaking Seoul for the second time and again crossing the thirty-eighth parallel. But that was the end of his martial career.

Determined to march north once more and being held back by Washington, MacArthur wrote early in April a letter to Representative Joseph W. Martin, the Massachusetts Republican who served as the minority leader of the House of Representatives (and thus as one of Truman's chief political opponents), that "if we lose this war to Communism in Asia the fall of Europe is inevitable. . . . We must win. There is no substitute for victory." Then a British newspaper published an interview with the general, who charged that "United Nations forces were circumscribed by a web of artificial conditions. . . . The situation would be ludicrous if men's lives were not involved."

To Truman, the general was no longer tolerable. He wrote later that "the kind of victory MacArthur had in mind—victory by the bombing of Chinese cities, victory by expanding the conflict to all of China—would have been the wrong kind of victory." The President added: "The time had come to draw the line. MacArthur's letter to Congressman Martin showed that the general was not only in disagreement with the policy of the government but was challenging this policy in open insubordination to his Commander in Chief."

At one o'clock in the morning of April 11 the White House announced that General of the Army Douglas MacArthur had been relieved of all his military commands and his post of Supreme Commander, Allied Powers, in Tokyo, because he "is unable to give his wholehearted support to the policies of the United States Government and of the United Nations in matters pertaining to his official duties." Truman named Lieutenant General Matthew B. Ridgway, commander of the Eighth Army and hero of the Battle of Bastogne in World War II, to replace MacArthur in all the commands.

Returning home in May, MacArthur received a hero's reception. In a speech to Congress he said defiantly and pathetically that "old soldiers never die; they just fade away." And fade away MacArthur did very quickly in this nation, where heroes or supposed heroes are rapidly discarded.

In Korea offensives and counteroffensives rolled up and down the peninsula—with staggering bloodbaths on both sides—through most of 1951. Though armistice talks opened in July, fighting went on. It continued during the following year with heavy American air raids against Yalu power plants and Pyongyang to encourage the Communists to negotiate; this diplomatic practice was applied in Vietnam twenty years later to secure "peace with honor." On November 4, 1952, Dwight Eisenhower defeated Adlai Stevenson for the presidency of the United States to inherit Korea, China, and Indochina—and all the other preoccupations of limited hot wars and the overarching Cold War.

The Asian wars in the opening years of the fifties failed to distract the world from the tasks of reconstruction, building great new institutions, and binding the wounds of the Second World War. This was the permanent contradiction of the postwar era: destroying and creating, all at the same time.

In Western Europe, where the Marshall Plan had laid solid foundations for restoring the economies, the event of vast historical significance was the signing in Paris on April 18, 1951, of the treaty creating the European Coal and Steel Community. The brainchild of France's Robert Schuman and Jean Monnet, the treaty was the forerunner of what would be the six-member Common Market in 1957 and the twelve-nation integrated Common Market to start on January 1, 1993. It was the first time in history that nations of Europe were joining in a common endeavor, each forsaking a measure of their sovereignty for the sake of unity and a more prosperous common future.

Schuman and Monnet came up early in 1950 with the idea of the Coal and Steel Plan under which the entire French-German production of coal and steel would be placed under a joint authority. The French government's statement explained that "the gathering together of the nations of Europe requires the elimination of the age-old opposition of France and Germany." The concept of pooling coal and steel production would be open to other European nations, and the initial conference of representatives of France, Germany, Italy, Belgium, the Netherlands, and Luxembourg opened on June 20, 1950, in Paris. The French had invited Britain to join as well, but it had decided in May to stay out—a grave error because afterward the unforgiving General de Gaulle kept the British out of unified Europe until the late 1960's. In just under one year the six finished negotiating and signed the treaty, an incredibly speedy procedure in European terms.

The Council of Europe, a political body without much power but plenty of important symbolism, had already begun functioning. The United States was careful to keep its distance from the European Community and the European Council to avoid any suspicion of interference in the renascent economies of Europe, but Secretary of State Acheson fought for years for a European Defense Community that was to include a rearmed West Germany and serve as a European army within NATO. That was too rich for the blood of the Europeans—they were not ready for their own military integration—and the notion fell by the wayside (to be revived by the French and the Germans in the 1980's).

The Anglo-American "special relationship" was powerfully revived when Winston Churchill was returned to power in October 1951. Relations had been less than perfect under the Labour government, especially over the atomic bomb in Korea scare, and Truman was delighted to greet the restored prime minister in Washington in the new year. In January 1952 Churchill addressed for the third time a joint session of Congress, the only foreign visitor to rate such honor (later the Congress voted to make him an honorary American citizen, an act without precedent). The prime minister then spent a few days in New York, on his way to Canada, and I had the privilege of attending the news conference he held in his bed, covered with newspapers and official dispatches, in his suite at the Waldorf Towers. He was seventy-eight years old, and I remember being surprised by his absolute lucidity—and by a much thinner voice than I had expected.

As the West went on reorganizing itself, Greece and Turkey joined NATO at a ministerial conference in Ottawa in September 1951, legitimizing, in effect, the Truman Doctrine of 1947. It followed the signing in San Francisco two weeks earlier of the peace treaty with Japan, principally drafted by the United States and Britain and signed by fifty governments. To general surprise, Soviet Foreign Minister Andrei Gromyko accepted the invitation to San Francisco, but he walked out with his delegation and all the Eastern European delegations when he was prevented from amending the treaty from the floor. Forty years later Japan and the Soviet Union still had not joined in a peace pact. And because Germany was divided into two states, the wartime Allies had never contemplated a German peace treaty.

The Truman years included a bad scare. On November 1, 1950, several Puerto Rican nationalists attempted to break into Blair House, their guns blazing, to assassinate the President. The Truman family had moved to Blair House across Pennsylvania Avenue from the White House, which was undergoing structural repairs, and they were vulnerable there. In the shooting one of the Puerto Ricans and a White House policeman were killed; simultaneously other Puerto Ricans fired weapons inside the House of Representatives.

Americans were beginning to learn about political violence at home.

IV

The election of Dwight D. Eisenhower to the presidency brought America a sense of contentment, perhaps superficial because the world's problems would not go away but nevertheless noticeable. Much of it had to do with the new President and the impressions he projected.

Eisenhower was sixty-three when he was inaugurated on January 20, 1953, and he was by far the most popular figure in the land. He won the election under the slogan "I like Ike," and Americans really did like him. Everybody called him Ike. He was the product of the Second World War and the subsequent Cold War as the victor in North Africa and Europe; the Supreme Commander, Allied Powers, Europe, heading NATO and hammering together the postwar alliance against the Soviet threat; and the President-elect who rushed to Korea within a month of the balloting in fulfillment of a campaign pledge.

The Korean armistice was signed on July 27, 1953, most likely as a result of the general exhaustion of the combatants as well as of Stalin's death six weeks after Ike's swearing-in ceremony. Eisenhower's contribution to the end of the Korean War was at best marginal (the enemy did not know that Ike considered using the atomic weapon to break the battlefield stalemate), including his most publicized visit to the front, but Americans were perfectly content to let him have the credit for peace and for bringing the boys home. Now Eisenhower was expected to lead the nation in the Cold War in the nuclear age as an experienced military chief, a world-class diplomat (being NATO commander was being more diplomat reconciling differences among alliance members than pure soldier), and an educator (because of his postwar tenure as president of New York's Columbia University).

In short, Eisenhower inspired confidence, and he was a father figure to millions. His bright smile communicated optimism to people. Never before active in politics, he chose to run as a Republican (after Truman had invited him to run as a Democrat) probably as a result of his mildly conservative social and economic views and his belief that 1952 was a Republican year. Eisenhower was the man to whom the company of big-business executives on the golf course was more congenial than were profound chats with intellectuals and liberal ideologues, but he represented the moderate wing of the Republican party over the strongly rightist faction led by Senator Robert Taft.

The reason he so easily beat Adlai Stevenson, his Democratic opponent, was that Americans trusted Eisenhower's reassuring image of solidity more than the sophisticated humor and liberal social and international views of the "egghead" candidate from Illinois. That Stevenson, formerly governor of Illinois, was constantly referred to as an "egghead" in a contemptuous fashion reflects the mood of that time in America. Americans wanted their President to protect them from communism, and they had no use for liberal preachings.

They even went along with Ike's decision to keep Richard Nixon (of the Alger Hiss fame) as his running mate notwithstanding something of a disturbing controversy over the Californian's campaign funds. When Nixon went on nationwide television to defend himself—and to introduce the family dog, Checkers—the voters accepted him. This still was the age of American political innocence, and Nixon's powerful anti-Communist stance did him no harm. Finally, Ike's and Nixon's campaign marked the birth of the TV age in national politics. They used television often and well, reaching tens of millions, and presidential races were never the same again. New technology had scored one more milestone point.

Ike and his smile formed the paternalistic aspect of the presidency. But basically Eisenhower was tough and consistent in his attitudes (he was elected for that reason), and he could be cold and even unpleasant in private (that was none of the public's business). He could be hard and even threatening over Korea, China, Indochina, and later Berlin, but he produced highly innovative proposals for international nuclear arms control measures and gladly went into summits with the Soviet leadership. When he thought America's allies were at fault, he acted accordingly, as he did to prevail on Britain, France, and Israel to halt the Suez War they started in 1956. But he preserved his old friendship with Anthony Eden, who was British prime minister and an author of Suez, as he did with Winston Churchill, his wartime comrade. Churchill was prime minister during part of Eisenhower's first term.

And Ike was much more insightful about the affairs of the Third World than foreign policy observers realized at the time. His tours of South America and South Asia were significant contributions to the formulation of American attitudes toward the emerging nations.

One of the most significant events in American history occurred during the Eisenhower presidency, and his own behavior was exemplary. It was the famous Supreme Court decision on May 17, 1954, to forbid racial discrimination in public schools, handed down in an opinion in the case of *Brown et al.* v. *Board of Education of Topeka*. This decision became the cornerstone of all future civil rights legislation and, in effect, marked the proclamation of the end of all racial discrimination in the United States. Volumes have been written about the *Brown* decision and the continuing problems and dramas of desegregation, but what must be recorded here is that Eisenhower never hesitated to enforce the Court ruling. Thus, in September 1957, he dispatched armed federalized National Guard troops to Little Rock, Arkansas, to guarantee that black children would be free to attend Central High School in the face of opposition by Governor Orval Faubus. Eisenhower lost some conservative support, especially in the South, but the issue was to protect constitutional principles. He also realized that American policies in the Third World would be torn to shreds if the government allowed the Supreme Court rulings, particularly in the racial area, to be ignored. Racial discrimination in the United States was always a major theme of Communist propaganda worldwide. It was on Eisenhower's watch that civil rights protests on a national scale erupted in the United States. On December 1, 1955, Rosa L. Parks, a forty-two-year-old seamstress, took a seat in the front of a bus in Montgomery, Alabama, in violation of antiblack segregation practices, pronouncing the historic words "No, I won't move back. . . ." She was arrested and fined fourteen dollars for "overlooking" bus segregation rules, but her defiance triggered the famous Montgomery bus boycott, lasting 381 days, during which forty thousand city blacks walked rather than rode. A twenty-six-year-old clergyman, the Reverend Martin Luther King, Jr., was arrested for inciting citizens to boycott the buses; it was his first prominent public act. The boycott ended when the U.S. Supreme Court upheld the legality of Rosa Parks's gesture.

The Eisenhower years acquired a reputation of boredom, vulgarity, and fascistoid propensions in the eyes of European intellectuals and domestic cultural snobs, a reputation rich in stereotypes and clichés. As Robert Hughes remarks in a 1989 review of the book *America* by the French sociology professor Jean Baudrillard, this was left-wing "bigotry" about the United States. To be sure, the fifties had produced McCarthyism, Cold War attitudes (which prevailed everywhere under different guises), the development of nuclear weapons (to which a half dozen powers were likewise dedicated, talking less about it publicly), and new cultural strains, which were peculiarly American and before too long were transmitted to the critical outside world. That, of course, was when Albert Camus was denouncing his own French society in *The Plague* and Günter Grass was doing it with *The Tin Drum* in West Germany.

It was in the 1950's that rock 'n' roll exploded in America, and vulgar or not, it conquered the globe. It all started with the release of Bill Haley and the Comets' release of "Rock Around the Clock" on April 12, 1954, and it never stopped. Elvis Presley and his companions were tearing up and down American highways in his pink Cadillac, starting the same year to do one-night stands, bringing the new music to small towns. By 1955 Presley was already known as the "King of Rock," and his first motion picture, *Love Me Tender*, premiered in 1956. (He died in 1977 at the age of forty-two, an American idol even a decade after his death, with one million visitors touring his Tennessee estate of Graceland in 1988.)

Rock 'n' roll obviously was a revolution in American tastes and mores though it fitted well into the age of contentment, which was not necessarily an age of conformity and boredom. It was the young people's first postwar assertion of identity. James Dean, the car-racing cinema actor, was already a cult hero when he died in an accident at the age of twenty-four in 1955; he was perceived by his contemporaries as a heroic rebel, and his last movie, *Giant*, released a year after his death, has become a classic of sorts. John Steinbeck had published *East of Eden* in 1952, certainly not a boring work of conformity. And the June 1956 marriage of playwright Arthur Miller (whose *Death of a Salesman* and *The Crucible* were powerful theater) and Marilyn Monroe was a national event. When Philadelphia-born actress Grace Kelly, then immensely popular, married Monaco's Prince Rainier that same year, it was an international event on a magnificent scale, the "wedding of the century" as society pages put it (she died in 1982, having abandoned her cinema career after she became princess). Jackson Pollock's death the same year was a tragedy for American modern art; Pollock surely was not conventional. How short are memories.

The contentment years included golf courses and dancing to the musical strains of Glenn Miller's orchestra and other big bands. Americans increasingly watched television (and color was arriving) that fitted their relaxed mood: series (now known as sitcoms) like *Father Knows Best* and the *George Burns and Gracie Allen Show*, which appeared every week from 1950 to 1958 (Gracie died, but George Burns was still on television and in night-clubs with his cigars in 1989). Lucille Ball's *I Love Lucy* ran between 1951 and 1957, single-handedly doubling the number of television viewers. Cole Porter updated in 1956 his "You're the Top" tune from the *Anything Goes* show of twenty years earlier to add "You're Mahatma Gandhi. . . . You're Napoleon brandy. . . ." Americans did feel they were "the top."

This was the nature and the climate of the nation that Eisenhower was chosen to lead through most of the fifties. It was not boring by a long shot. It was contradictory, irritating, rich in justice and injustice, glorious in its talent, and very American. New scholarship in the mid-eighties, based on the study of long-classified White House materials, began to produce a new image of Eisenhower: as a highly informed and activist President who had chosen to practice what Fred I. Greenstein, professor of politics at Princeton University, has called "hidden-hand leadership." He exercised this leadership at home, but neither the country nor Eisenhower ever lost—or was allowed to lose—its or his paramount concerns with the outside world.

After Stalin's death and the Korean armistice, the Soviet Union remained relatively quiescent in terms of the Cold War for the balance of the fifties. To be sure, Moscow, along with Washington, was continuing the military buildup and the testing of bigger and better nuclear weapons, and the USSR increased efforts to win influence and friends in the Third World as decolonization proceeded apace. At home the Soviet leadership was preoccupied with the power struggles in the aftermath of the vanishing of Stalin. Abroad its concerns were stability in Communist Eastern Europe and—to an extent not appreciated at the time in the West—relations with China.

The only Soviet move that could be construed as hostile to the West during Eisenhower's first term was the constitution of a formal European Communist military alliance through the signing of the Warsaw Pact on May 14, 1955. This was responsive to the creation of NATO six years earlier—and, more immediately, to West Germany's admission to NATO on May 6—and all it accomplished was to legitimize the existence of a Soviet forward command in the guise of Warsaw Pact headquarters in the Polish capital, free movements of Soviet forces throughout Eastern Europe (except for Czechoslovakia and Romania, where at the time no Soviet troops were permanently stationed), and better-integrated training of satellite armies.

In the economic sphere the Soviets sought to integrate regional economies through the Council for Mutual Economic Assistance (better known as Comecon) established in Moscow in 1949, probably as a reaction to the Marshall Plan. Although Comecon is often described as the Communist Common Market, it also coordinates overall economic planning in the region, including production quotas and the "division of labor" among member states with some concentrating mostly on agriculture and others on heavier industry. For a long time, Comecon assigned economic tasks to different countries in response to specific Soviet needs. The Western European Common Market came into being only with the signing of the Treaty of Rome by the six original members on March 25, 1957 (with Britain still out), but of course, the United States was not a participant—unlike the Russians in Comecon.

Immediately after Stalin's death, the shadowy men in and around the Kremlin had to decide who would replace him and to what extent. Foreign policy had to wait. Naturally Stalin could not be replaced politically because none of the leaders had the necessary stature; besides, Stalin, who may have believed in immortality, had never named a successor. The question, therefore, was how day-to-day power in the Soviet Union would be allocated and who, if anybody, would be *primus inter pares*. Conspiracies for succession had burgeoned even before the old man died; such was the Kremlin tradition.

The Soviet historian Roy Medvedev writes in *Khrushchev* that after Stalin's first brain hemorrhage on the night of March 1–2, four men who aspired to power formed a temporary alliance to keep the other hungry buzzards away. They were moon-faced Georgi M. Malenkov, the most powerful figure in the Communist party Secretariat who had delivered the political report of the Central Committee in Stalin's place at the Nineteenth Congress of the Communist party on October 6; the blunt Nikita Khrushchev, the former Ukrainian party boss and a member of the party Secretariat in Moscow since 1950; white-goateed Marshal Nikolai Bulganin, who had served as defense minister until 1949; and Lavrenti P. Beria, the balding, bespectacled deputy prime minister in charge of security and the most sinister man of the lot.

The foursome had kept a vigil at Stalin's bedside since his first stroke, each setting his private plot in motion. Khrushchev, who feared that Beria would grab power because of his control of the security forces, made a deal with Bulganin to prevent the policeman from holding the Ministry of State Security (the MGB, the forerunner of the KGB) after Stalin's death. Beria, suspecting Khrushchev and Bulganin, made *his* deal with Malenkov, and the moment Stalin died on March 5, he was able to take over the MGB, which had the secret police as well as its own armor-backed army. It was intrigue straight from the times of Ivan the Terrible and Peter the Great, but the leadership group was so divided, despite Beria's control of the security forces (the armed forces' views had to be taken into account as well), that they all realized that a compromise was necessary.

While Stalin's body lay in state in the Palace of the Soviets, about twenty of the key men met in the Kremlin to settle the immediate future of the Soviet Union. Inevitably their decisions would affect for a long time not only their own country but the rest of the world as well. Under the March compromise, Malenkov was chosen chairman of the Council of Ministers (prime minister), the most powerful position in the country because Stalin had abolished the post of the first secretary of the Communist party. In practice, the prime minister was simultaneously the party chief. It was Beria who nominated his ally Malenkov. The new prime minister repaid the gesture by putting Beria in charge of both the Ministry of Internal Affairs and the Ministry of State Security and making him a deputy prime minister. Bulganin became again defense minister, and Vyacheslav Molotov returned to the post of foreign minister. As for Khrushchev, he was elevated to the Politburo while retaining the key assignment of Secretariat member. Malenkov, Beria, Bulganin, and Molotov were also on the Politburo. But Leonid Brezhnev, an upcoming Stalin protégé, was dropped as an alternate from the Politburo, having to start his career all over again; it was good for him that he was a man of patience.

As a result of this first go-around, the first collective leadership consisted of Malenkov, Beria, and Khrushchev. Malenkov tended to enjoy his chairmanship, but Khrushchev and Beria circled each other for the kill; they were the real rivals. This time Khrushchev jumped first. He convinced Bulganin and his deputy, Marshal Georgi Zhukov, that Beria must be liquidated; this brought the Red Army to the side of the plotters. Then Khrushchev persuaded Malenkov that Beria should be arrested and tried. They agreed to do it at a joint meeting of the Council of Ministers and the Politburo in mid-July, having obtained an arrest warrant signed by K. Y. Voroshilov, chairman of the Presidium of the Supreme Soviet and thus nominal chief of state.

The deed was done in a classical czarist family coup fashion, complete with secret troop movements as a contingency against civil war. At stake were no principles, no ideology, no discussions about the fate of the people under this "dictatorship of the proletariat"—only sheer power appetite. In Khrushchev's version, used in Medvedev's reconstruction of the events of that July day, soldiers led by General Zhukov waited in a room adjoining the conference hall where the leaders were to meet. When Malenkov pressed a button on his desk there, a bell was to ring in the antechamber and Zhukov was to rush into the hall with the armed guards. Khrushchev arrived with a gun in his pocket and took his seat at the table. Beria brought along a briefcase, which he placed on a windowsill. Malenkov gave the floor to Khrushchev, who in a lengthy speech accused Beria, of all things, of having been in 1918 in the pay of the British intelligence service and anti-Communist Azerbaijani nationalists.

Beria now was the target of the kinds of improbable accusations that he had hurled at thousands of his victims to please Stalin when he was security chief. Automatonlike, Molotov, Bulganin, and several other "Old Bolsheviks" rose to repeat the charges against Beria. Malenkov thereupon rang the bell for Zhukov, whose soldiers seized Beria and placed him under arrest in a nearby room. With two Red Army tank divisions outside the Kremlin to neutralize any attempt by Beria's security units to rescue him, the dethroned minister was driven to the Moscow Military District headquarters and confined to an underground air-raid shelter. He was kept there under heavy guard for several days and nights.

Then the Politburo convened to decide that Beria must be executed but that an investigation and a trial were needed first. Naval frontier guards flown to Moscow that day replaced the security guards at the Kremlin. All the commanders of Internal Affairs Ministry military units were arrested, as were all the top security chiefs throughout the Soviet Union. The entire operation was conducted so smoothly that neither Moscow inhabitants nor Western observers—diplomats and journalists—were aware of the coup against Beria and the security apparatus. Roy Medvedev sums up the events in these words: "[The] Ministry of Internal Affairs had already ceased to be the all-powerful organization that had once subjugated Party and Government. The credit for the success of this difficult and dangerous assignment belonged to Khrushchev, though he had been ably assisted by Bulganin, Malenkov and Zhukov, under whose supervision the Army had played, for the first time, a decisive role in a crisis at the summit of political power."

The second post-Stalin ruling group was formed by Malenkov, Bulganin, and Khrushchev, but this was not the end of the Kremlin struggle. In his testimony during the investigations, Beria smeared Malenkov's reputation with charges that were true or false (it did not really matter), and Bulganin quickly withdrew into a purely nominal role. This left Khrushchev in real political command, and in September 1953 he was elected by the Communist party's Central Committee to be first secretary through the restoration of the title Stalin had abolished.

On December 17, 1953, the prosecutor general announced that Beria and a group of associates had been found guilty of conspiring to seize power in the Soviet Union, of having links with foreign intelligence services, and of ordering terrorist murders. They were subsequently tried by a special tribunal chaired by Marshal Ivan S. Konev, a war hero, and composed of other generals (the military were squaring their accounts with the security services, from which they had suffered for decades). The proceedings of the six-day trial were never published (not even under *glasnost*) because much of Beria's dirty work would have embarrassed the new leadership. He was sentenced to death, as planned, and executed forthwith. This marked the end of the first post-Stalin phase.

The Soviet system does not tolerate power sharing, and before long Nikita Khrushchev was ready to do away with the whole idea of collective leadership. When the Central Committee met in February 1955, Malenkov admitted responsibility for failures in managing agriculture and heavy industry (the ever-reliable Molotov was there to suggest that, indeed, it was so) and resigned as prime minister. As Medvedev puts it charmingly, "his resignation was accepted without hesitation." Khrushchev proposed the figurehead Bulganin to replace Malenkov, who was relegated to be deputy premier and minister of electric power stations. Marshal Zhukov, Khrushchev's friend, became defense minister. As the party's first secretary Khrushchev was *de facto* ruler of the Soviet Union.

* * *

As the middle of the decade approached, thoughtful planners on both sides in the Cold War started thinking that the time might be ripe for a big power summit. The last one had been held at Potsdam ten years before, still in the prenuclear age, and the international tensions were abating sufficiently to warrant a conference of chiefs of state. And this time France would be represented (unlike at Yalta and Potsdam) as an influential member of the new Western Europe.

The Korean armistice had been in force for two years. The French colonial war in Indochina had ended in 1954, with the final defeat of France at Dien Bien Phu and the subsequent conference in Geneva, where the foreign ministers of the combatant powers, plus the United States, Britain, the Soviet Union, and China, divided Vietnam into two states, setting the stage for a new war in Southeast Asia. But in the meantime, no serious attempt had been made to look into the future of the world, notably in controlling nuclear weapons, and there was clear interest in the principal world capitals for a big power summit.

President Eisenhower had come forth as early as December 8, 1953, with a proposal before the General Assembly of the United Nations for joint efforts to harness nuclear energy to peaceful uses. This was his Atoms for Peace concept providing for contributions from the nuclear powers' stockpiles of uranium and fissionable materials to an international atomic energy agency. The idea was that everything from the generation of power for electricity to the production of medical isotopes could be channeled away from the warlike potential of the nuclear arsenals, and Eisenhower pledged the United States "to help solve the fearful atomic dilemma—to devote its entire heart and mind to find the way by which the miraculous inventiveness of man shall not be dedicated to his death, but consecrated to his life."

Eisenhower, the general and the statesman, was telling the world that the inventions of war should be placed at the service of peace, but because technology had progressed so vastly in the years since Los Alamos, this was not mere rhetoric. Indeed, science and industry were already perfectly capable of assimilating nuclear knowledge and resources to limitless purposes, and all that they needed was a modicum of international cooperation to spread the new wealth and hope around the world.

Eisenhower's notion was to combine Atoms for Peace with a nuclear arms control package. This in the end proved impossible, but when the suggestions were made the following year and early in 1955 for a meeting with Nikita Khrushchev to discuss the whole atomic agenda, Ike was willing. He was disturbed by the rising rivalry in thermonuclear weapons between the United States and the Soviets, and he was probing for solutions, even though at the same time, with another part of his mind, he was seriously considering the use of nuclear weapons against China over the Taiwan crisis.

Still, nothing is ever lost. Eisenhower's Atoms for Peace did not die with the speech or subsequent difficulties, and it became a major international program of scientific, medical, and industrial exchanges among nations, with the United States playing the positive role the President had promised. It was a felicitous by-product of the Cold War, especially for Third World countries that otherwise would have limited access to the technology and the resources. In 1989, for example, four hundred nuclear power reactors were operating in thirty-one countries. Sadly, however, atoms for peace resources were used illegally in countries like India, Pakistan, Israel, Argentina, Brazil, and perhaps others to start clandestine research and work on atomic bombs. The first three nations named above have the nuclear weapon, and their acquisition of it may have stemmed from Atoms for Peace.

For his part, Nikita Khrushchev, too, was ready for personal international diplomacy. Now that he felt politically secure at home, he plunged irrepressibly into the outside world. In September 1954 Khrushchev flew to Beijing to meet Mao and discuss the situation after the Korean and Indochina wars and the bilateral ties between China and the Soviets. Additional economic aid was promised to Mao, but serious frictions had developed between the two leaders. In May 1955 Khrushchev went to Belgrade to determine whether Soviet-Yugoslav relations could be improved (Tito had broken away from the Kremlin seven years earlier). There was no spectacular breakthrough, but gradually a more civilized relationship developed. At the same time Moscow agreed to settle the question of Austria, joining the Western powers in a state treaty that ended the quadripartite occupation and made the little republic into a neutral, sovereign nation.

On July 18, 1955, Eisenhower met in Geneva with Khrushchev, British Prime Minister Anthony Eden (who succeeded Churchill on the old warrior's retirement earlier that year) and French Prime Minister Edgar Faure. On the third day Eisenhower unveiled his Open Skies proposal as the next major step in the control of nuclear weapons. According to McGeorge Bundy, the decision to proceed with it was made only the day before the speech because Secretary of State John Foster Dulles, not a risk taker, and the chairman of the Joint Chiefs of Staff, Admiral Arthur Radford, had to be convinced that it was a good idea.

Open Skies called for each country—meaning the United States and the Soviet Union—to give the other "a complete blueprint of our military establishments, from beginning to end." The next step was for each to offer the other "ample facilities for aerial reconnaissance." Unbeknown to friend and foe, however, this was one of the two tracks Eisenhower was pursuing to obtain maximal information concerning Soviet military dispositions and research and construction centers for nuclear weapons. The other track—secret—was the decision to build a photoreconnaissance aircraft, capable of flying the highest altitudes ever, to look down at the Soviet territory. This was to be the famous U-2 spy plane, and the idea came from the Technological Capabilities Panel that Eisenhower created early in 1954, chaired by James R. Killian, the president of the Massachusetts Institute of Technology. It was before the advent of globe-circling satellites, and the U-2 represented the acme of existing spy-in-the-sky technology, still another result of wartime research in high-flying planes.

The Open Skies proposal was fashioned by a group headed by Nelson Rockefeller, then an assistant to the President, but he was never told about the Killian panel's U-2 recommendations. One must assume that Eisenhower deliberately kept Rockefeller in the dark to make him concentrate on Open Skies, as he might not have done had he known that the U-2 would, in effect, make a mockery of the voluntary cooperation Eisenhower was championing at Geneva over Dulles's and Radford's reservations for the benefit of the Russians and world public opinion.

In any event, Khrushchev settled the matter by rejecting Open Skies on the ground it would give the United States considerable intelligence advantages. From his viewpoint, he was right. Dulles and Radford were delighted privately at the rejection because they disliked the notion of Soviet aircrafts monitoring the American territory; they preferred to engage in arms control measures only after all the other Cold War issues were resolved. Khrushchev discovered five years later—when a U-2 was shot down over the Soviet Union—how right he had been in Geneva. In retrospect, it is unclear why Eisenhower came up with Open Skies at all when the U-2 was already in the prototype stage—unless it was for public relations. In 1989, for reasons that were even more mystifying, President George Bush resurrected Open Skies even though the skies were by then full of everybody's spy satellites.

Not long after the Geneva summit, West German Chancellor Konrad Adenauer visited Khrushchev in Moscow, and the two men agreed to establish diplomatic relations between their countries. This was a postwar milestone.

Inasmuch as both sides realized that a formal peace treaty with divided Germany was out of the question, they concluded that trade relations and other forms of exchange between Bonn and Moscow would be extremely beneficial.

For the Soviets, German industrial exports and technology were essential, and for the Germans an independent relationship with the Russians tended to diminish their utter political dependence on the West. Adenauer's trip opened the way to subsequent *Ostpolitik* by West Germany, which increasingly turned its energies toward the East, and the trend, established in 1955, resurged with immense force in the late eighties, when Bonn was anxious for a full-fledged political deal with Gorbachev's Soviet Union. It is useful to recall again the long history of German-Russian collaboration and alliances, going back to the early nineteenth century and the 1939 nonaggression pact; the idea that they may be the most natural partners in Europe seems to be dawning on the two countries. The United States may have to come to terms with this reality and its implications for NATO and all the other European postwar arrangements, especially in the presence of a reunified Germany.

*   *   *

Few events in the history of communism have been as decisive and dramatic as Nikita Khrushchev's so-called secret speech before a closed session of the party's Twentieth Congress on February 25, 1956, just short of the third anniversary of Stalin's death. The speech, which stopped being secret very soon because of its dissemination by word of mouth at home and abroad, was a savage denunciation of Stalinism and Stalin's crimes. By extension, of course, it was an indictment of the Communist party itself for having connived with Stalin in the purges, imprisonments in the gulag camps, murders, and executions that affected untold millions of people. Men like Malenkov and Molotov tried to dissuade Khrushchev from such a frontal attack on Stalin and his cult of personality, and the first secretary had to hide from them his decision to go ahead with it.

Communism was never the same again after Khrushchev's address. Deep doubts about the system, not just about Stalin, emerged from the new knowledge of the savagery perpetrated for so many decades in the name of the people. Khrushchev himself encouraged a relative liberalization in the Soviet Union, starting a thaw in the rigid relations between the rulers and the ruled. In June the Central Committee passed a resolution "On overcoming the cult of personality and its consequences," and Khrushchev himself gained credibility by admitting that he had known about many Stalinist crimes but had been afraid to protest. More to the point, the government ordered the instant liberation of masses of political prisoners (there are no figures) as well as the review of all the cases of those who died in camps and prisons between 1935 and 1955. In most instances, they were rehabilitated posthumously.

In culture the relaxation was also visible. Ilya Ehrenburg, who always knew where the wind was blowing, published a short novel, *The Thaw*. Writers who could not be published in the past suddenly found themselves in print. Yvgeny Yevtushenko, the poet with an acute sense of political patterns, became one of the spokesmen for literature under Khrushchev's thaw. But there were very clear limits how far this thaw could go. Boris Pasternak was refused permission to publish *Dr. Zhivago*, a novel about a man who could not decide where he stood toward the Great Revolution, and he sent it to Italy. It became a best seller in scores of foreign countries, but the Soviet press was allowed to mention Pasternak only when he received the Nobel Prize in 1958.

It is a matter of controversy why Khrushchev's liberalization attempts failed in the end. More relevant is the fact that in his own way, he prepared the climate and the terrain for Gorbachev's *perestroika* nearly thirty years later. This makes the twin point that communism cannot survive without basic reforms (if it can survive at all) and that in the Soviet Union before Gorbachev events moved with glacier speed.

Much more rapidly the impact of the secret speech was felt in Eastern Europe, with the uprisings in Poland and Hungary and revolts against orthodox communism in the region over the next three decades. Even in China Mao Zedong was impelled to proclaim, "Let one hundred flowers bloom, let one hundred schools of thought contend." Mao feigned liberalization, if this was what it meant, presumably to appear for the time being in step with Khrushchev. But he cut those flowers at the root the moment they bloomed, imprisoning the intellectual and ideological "gardeners." In the end Mao split with the Soviets as much over Marxist-Leninist ideology and its interpretations as over the issues of power and economic management. In communism, after all, nothing is inseparable.

The first open challenge to communism in Eastern Europe erupted in East Berlin, of all places, on June 17, 1953. This was more than three months after Stalin's death, but almost three years *before* Khrushchev's anti-Stalin pronouncement. The event was a sudden riot by East German students, briefly supported by workers, and it was a spontaneous revolt by young East Germans against the Soviet occupation and communism as the wave of *their* future. It did not last long. Communist East German police and Soviet tanks put the rebellion down that same day with an unreported number of casualties.

This was the first and only time prior to 1989 that East Germans rose against their Communist state or the Soviet presence. In their Prussian pragmatism they saw no purpose in defiance and much promise for economic well-being in accepting the new conformism of ruling Marxism-Leninism. Even in 1981, the last time I visited East Germany, East Berlin and the other cities as well as the rural areas seemed affluent by Central European standards and content to accept the status quo. Only the Evangelical Church and a handful of intellectuals like the writer Stefan Heym were the voices in opposition against the paralyzing system the Soviet Union and its East German accolytes were imposing on their country after the Allied victory over nazism.

Political dynamics are unpredictable. In the autumn of 1989 tens of thousands of East Germans began fleeing west through Hungary, Czechoslovakia, and Austria in an extraordinary display of defiance and rejection of their ossified and repressive regime. Following the year's events in Poland and Hungary, it was the latest crisis of European communism. In 1989, over 350,000 East Germans out of a population of 16 million, had fled to the West, legally and illegally, when it became clear that their affluence was fiction.

Mass demonstrations in East German cities, catching the outside world by surprise, erupted in October, the first such defiance since 1953. On November 9, the Berlin Wall, erected by the Communists in 1961 to keep the East Germans from escaping to the West (2.8 million had left between 1949 and 1961), was open to free passage by the Communist authorities. The entire ruling regime headed by Erich Honecker was forced to resign, and soon thereafter he and his colleagues were charged with corruption, illegal transactions, and luxurious living. Honecker was arrested. The secret police were disbanded and political prisoners released. The Communist party agreed to abandon its power monoploy and free elections were set for 1990.

It is extremely difficult to understand and explain what makes groups of people or nations rise against what they perceive as oppression, injustice, or the violation of their sense of national identity. Each case is different from the other, and there are no scientific formulas (nothwithstanding the claim that Marxism is scientific) to provide easy answers. But rebellion in Eastern Europe against the existing order was what already faced Nikita Khrushchev in the autumn of 1956. That was the moment of truth when Khrushchev had to choose between his own experiments in liberalizing Marxism and the overriding national interest of the Soviet state. The accepted wisdom is that Khrushchev's secret speech (which, by the way, the CIA obtained from Polish Communist party contacts and the State Department distributed in English to the press on June 4) was directly responsible for the explosions in Poland and Hungary. In truth, the Polish and the Hungarian revolts erupted late in 1956 simply because the societies in those countries were politically and biologically ready.

Poland was the first to challenge in a sustained fashion the orthodoxy, the police oppression, the economic disaster, and the stultifying national boredom that communism had bestowed on it. Unlike most of Eastern Europe, Poland had a long tradition of ties with the West, particularly with France and Italy, and the imposition of narrow-minded Stalinist doctrines went against the grain of its sense as a nation. As far back as 1948 Polish Communist leaders conveyed to the Russians and other Eastern European Communists the message that Poland would find its own "way to socialism" and did not feel bound to follow blindly the example of Soviet experiences. For openers, the Poles announced that they had no intention of enforcing land collectivization after the Soviet model because they did not think it would work, certainly in terms of assuring decent farm production.

By 1956, with the economy plummeting and political repression rising, Communist and non-Communist liberals—or, more precisely, the thinking people of the country—had concluded that something had to be done to restore Poland to Western civilization. Antoni Słonimski, Poland's greatest living poet and the owner of the greatest sense of humor of his Polish generation, had returned from London exile to participate in what he had hoped would be a Polish cultural renaissance. Already in August 1955 the young poet Adam Ważyk began publishing verses of protest. Writers belonging to the Communist party or not launched their protest publication *po prostu*, meaning "simply." The atmosphere was happily tense, awaiting the confrontation with Stalinism (which had not died with Stalin) that everybody knew and hoped would soon come. Polish romanticism was ready to burst into deeds and songs of patriotism—and into sacrifices.

It happened on June 28, a warm day in the western industrial city of

Poznań, where some sixteen thousand workers from the Zispo metal plant marched to the downtown Freedom Square with banners demanding bread and freedom. They were joined in their march by as many as a hundred thousand Poznań citizens. Then the crowd stormed the secret police headquarters to the shouts of "Out with the Russians!" The explosion came because the workers had been demanding pay rises, but management would not listen to them. A delegation had traveled to Warsaw earlier in the week to press its case with the government and to warn it of a general strike on June 28 if the authorities remained unresponsive. The workers were informed that strikes were not tolerated under socialism and that tanks would meet the strikers in the streets. It was typical of Communist authorities to ignore workers and their demands and to try to deal with them by force, and this attitude helped unravel over ensuing years the whole political fabric of Eastern Europe's "socialist" states. Communist leaders were more and more like the Bourbons: They learned nothing; they forgave nothing.

The Poznań crowd attacked the secret police building because of reports that the workers' delegation in Warsaw had been imprisoned, perfectly credible in the Polish People's Republic. Policemen began firing on the people on the square, but elsewhere workers and young people captured stores of weapons of the People's Militia to be ready for real combat. They built barricades from overturned streetcars and trucks. Another crowd released inmates from city prisons and burned secret police files. Communist party authorities turned to the army for help, but soldiers from the Poznań garrison refused to shoot people. The situation was utterly out of control; nothing of the kind had ever happened under communism.

At sundown special security units were flown from Warsaw, followed by tanks and artillery. For the next two days the troops battled the people of Poznań. Fifty-four were killed, and more than two hundred injured. Instantly the Poznań events became part of a larger process of protest against the system. The fairly free press of that period reported that the rebellion stemmed from just demands of the workers. In Moscow an official statement attributed the riots to "provocateurs and diversionists paid by foreign agents," a classical response by Communists to situations they could not understand or control, and even Tito in Yugoslavia joined the denunciation (he may have broken with the Kremlin, but not with the notion that no challenge to authority can be tolerated).

During most of July Communist party factions fought over power and the direction that should be taken to calm the nation. In desperation they all turned to Władysław Gomułka, the Socialist party leader who had orchestrated its merger with the Communists and brought Communist rule to Poland in 1945. Having argued for the "Polish way to socialism" and having opposed forced land collectivization, he had been demoted, expelled from the party, and placed under house arrest. Now it was becoming clear that only Gomułka could unite the country—he was regarded as the chief of the liberal faction—and on October 18 the Politburo named him the party's first secretary.

At this point Khrushchev entered the affray. Prospects of a liberal Communist leadership in neighboring Poland were too much for the Russians, and on the morning of October 19 Khrushchev landed at the Warsaw airport with all the top Soviet politicians and military commanders in his retinue to try to get rid of Gomułka. Simultaneously Soviet forces began converging on Warsaw from all directions. At an unbearably tense meeting Gomułka told Khrushchev that Polish security troops were now under the command of General Wacław Komar, a friend of the liberals who had spent years in prison for having fought in the Spanish Civil War, and would use their weapons to stop the Soviets. Moreover, he said, he would not continue negotiating under the gun and would go on radio and television to apprise the people of the Soviet intervention. There would be war, he warned.

Workers and students lined up behind the party leadership even if they were not Communists; the confrontation had become a national issue. In the evening General Komar blocked Soviet tanks sixty miles east of Warsaw. At dawn of October 20 Khrushchev accepted defeat. He agreed to withdraw Soviet forces from Poland and stay out of Polish internal politics if Gomułka committed himself to keeping the country in the Warsaw Pact and allowed limited numbers of Soviet military units to continue to be stationed in the countryside. The Soviets' concern was to protect communication lines through Poland between the Soviet Union and the massed Soviet armies in East Germany; the Poles were willing to agree to Khrushchev's request. That night Gomułka told the nation where he was guiding it: "The road of democratization is the only road leading to the construction of the best model of socialism in our conditions. . . . Our Party is taking its place at the head of the process of democratization. . . ."

Almost exactly thirty years later, Mikhail Gorbachev uttered virtually the same words in Moscow. In Poland, unfortunately, Gomułka rapidly lost his dedication to liberalism and democratization, liquidating with growing brutality the experience of the Polish October. But nothing is lost in history. When I was in Poland in 1981, to see the rise of the Solidarity free trade union movement—the intellectuals were unanimous in reminding the workers' leadership that the roots of Solidarity were in 1956, that first moment of hope. Bronisław Geremek, one of the original advisers, said to me in Warsaw as we discussed the latest crisis, "You realize, of course, that Solidarity was born in the Polish October."

At the end of the eighties Hungary was achieving a pluralistic political society though the renamed Communist party remained in power. The Hungarian road to democracy had also begun in 1956, in the Budapest October, but differing from Poland, this democracy was born in blood.

In the immediate sense, the Hungarian events were precipitated by those in Poland. Hungary's rebellion erupted on October 23, 1956, a day after the Poles had won their confrontation with Khrushchev, in order to take advantage of the momentum created in Poland. But the Hungarian pot had begun boiling at least two years earlier when Mátyás Rákosi, the hard-line head of the Communist party, and his more liberal premier, Imre Nagy, decided to release from prison János Kádár, a Communist leader who had been imprisoned since 1951 on charges of espionage, treason, and Titoism and had been subjected to terrible torture. Kádár was a victim of Stalin's rages, and his release came principally because Stalin had died and stirrings of change were appearing among Hungarian Communists. It was still before Khrushchev's secret speech, but Rákosi and Nagy were becoming quite tolerant of cultural dissent and general aspirations for a touch less rigor. Writers Gyula Háy and Tibor Déry spoke out publicly against the Soviet doctrine of submission of literature to communism.

In the seesaw manner of Communist politics, Nagy was dismissed as premier in 1955, when Kádár was already free but still a "nonperson," because Rákosi did not wish to go too far with liberalization. Nevertheless, three hundred "baselessly convited" persons were released from prisons, and Hungarian writers and the press were acquiring more and more freedom. In the spring of 1956 demands came from all directions for Nagy's return to the premiership. When the Polish crisis broke out in June, the Hungarian press reported it in exquisite detail, and word of Khrushchev's capitulation in Warsaw fueled the eagerness for confrontation.

On October 23 thousands of students attended a rally in Budapest, producing a long list of demands, including the withdrawal of Soviet troops permanently stationed in Hungary. The following day a crowd of three hundred thousand people engaged in a spontaneous and joyous demonstration of support for Poland and for the demands of the Hungarian students. By evening a huge mass of people had converged on the parliament building to chant pro-Nagy slogans. Nagy, brought to parliament by a delegation of writers, addressed the crowd and asked it to disperse; he feared bloodshed. Across town a huge statue of Stalin was brought down and smashed in the street by a crowd shouting, "Russians, go home!" At the Budapest radio station security troops shot and killed three students when a crowd of young people insisted that their demands be broadcast.

By midnight it was full-blown revolution. The army was summoned, but it refused to fire on the crowds. Instead, soldiers gave arms to factory workers, who commandeered trucks to rush them to Radio Budapest. Security troops fired again, but this time armed workers shot back and burned police vehicles. On the morning of October 24 the rebels, who still lacked leaders or organization, took over police stations in Budapest, obtaining more weapons.

It was at that moment that the Soviet government ordered its tanks and infantry into Budapest to battle the crowds. It was never determined whether Ernö Gerö, a sinister figure in the European Communist cast who had replaced Rákosi the previous year and was regarded as Moscow's agent, had asked for the Soviet intervention or whether it was Khrushchev's initiative. Still on October 24, the official radio announced that Imre Nagy was appointed premier and that the government had "applied for help to Soviet formations stationed in Hungary." It is obviously implausible that Nagy would ask for Soviet assistance, especially when he was being propelled into the leadership of the revolution.

Throughout Hungary "Revolutionary and Workers' Councils" assumed the functions of government from the collapsing Communist party. Hungarian army units joined the rebels in fighting Soviet tanks, and only the Hungarian security forces, the AVH, sided with the Russians. On October 25 Nagy was arrested at the Communist party headquarters while Soviet tanks fired point-blank on a crowd of some twenty-five thousand people, including women and children, killing perhaps as many as eight hundred. It was total confusion: Gerö fled to Soviet-controlled areas, and Nagy was set free. He returned to his office in the parliament building and formed a new government on October 27, inviting Communists and non-Communists to become ministers. The Soviet tanks were unable to liquidate the Hungarian "freedom fighters"—a mix of civilians and Hungarian army soldiers—and Nagy proposed a cease-fire, thinking the liberals had won.

Then Nagy proceeded to abolish the AVH and formally ended the one-party system in Hungary. János Kádár was named first secretary of the Communist party, and he agreed that it no longer would try to exercise the dominant role in order "to avoid further bloodshed." With a Cabinet composed of representatives of most political parties, Hungary seemed to be back at the happy postwar coalition days of 1945. Soviet forces began to depart from Budapest, and normal life was resuming.

But the Russians were not giving up that easily. On November 3 Nagy heard that fresh Soviet troops were entering Hungary under a plan worked out secretly by Kádár and the Soviet ambassador, Yuri V. Andropov (who rose to be the head of the KGB and the general secretary of the Soviet Communist party after Leonid Brezhnev's death in 1984). Because the Russians ignored Nagy's requests to send home their troops, the premier informed Andropov that Hungary was leaving the Warsaw Pact and becoming neutral in the East-West contest. This was one thing the Soviets would never tolerate in Eastern Europe; to them the Warsaw Pact was sacrosanct.

On November 4 the Soviets acted. At dawn their troops struck again, capturing the capital. Nagy fled to asylum in the Yugoslav Embassy, and Kádár announced the formation of the Hungarian Revolutionary Worker-Peasant Government. Eighteen days after he sought refuge at the Yugoslav Embassy, Nagy left in a Soviet vehicle, accompanied by Yugoslav diplomats, supposedly on his way home under an agreement worked out with Kádár. But the vehicle stopped at the Soviet military headquarters, and the diplomats were asked to leave. The car took Nagy to an unknown destination. Two years later the Soviet and Hungarian governments admitted that a secret trial had been held: Nagy and his defense minister, General Pal Maléter, were executed. Jozsef Cardinal Mindszenty, the head of the Roman Catholic Church in Hungary, received asylum in the American Legation, where he would reside for nearly twenty years.

The Hungarian experience illustrates how tortuous and unpredictable are the actions and lives of Communist leaders. Kádár had been imprisoned for three years by Moscow-line Hungarian Communists for alleged liberal penchants. When the Revolution erupted, he was chosen to be first secretary as a Communist liberal. But within days he had shifted his allegiance to the Russians and the domestic hard-liners, causing the collapse of the Nagy government and sharing with the Soviets the blame for Nagy's murder. In the decades that followed, Kádár shifted gears once more, this time presiding over a quiet but effective economic reform along liberal lines.

Visiting Budapest on the twentieth anniversary of the Revolution, I found with some amazement that Kádár was not a hated figure to most Hungarians, who were benefiting from the relative affluence of their country. Still, in 1988, after thirty-two years in power, the aging Kádár was unceremoniously ousted from leadership for not being sufficiently liberal and the events of 1956 were officially recognized as patriotic acts; the old charge of "counterrevolution" was dropped. Kádár, of course, was not harmed, and he was free to ponder about a life of being both a hero and a villain several times over. Kádár died at the age of seventy-seven in 1989, an unlamented person at that stage. His death coincided with Nagy's formal reburial, with full honors, attended by the top leadership of the Communist party. Nagy was declared to have been a national hero; Kádár, who had ridden a trajectory from hero to villain to Communist hero, again fell into oblivion. The 1956 uprising was no longer officially regarded as a "counterrevolution." The Communist party's monopoly on political power was ended through a change in the Constitution voted by parliament, and Hungary was declared to be a multi-party republic. Reformist Communist leaders changed their Party's name to "Socialist," hoping to do well in elections slated for 1990. It took thirty-three years for the real revolution to triumph peacefully.

In the United States the Hungarian drama was overshadowed by presidential elections in November: Eisenhower was reelected for a second term, again defeating Stevenson. Americans evidently trusted Ike.

V

For Nikita Khrushchev, the mid-fifties were an extremely difficult and dangerous period. He capitulated in Warsaw but triumphed in Budapest's bloodbath. His biographer Roy Medvedev believes that Khrushchev had no alternative but to apply force to neutralize the growing opposition to him in the Soviet Politburo by those "who linked the political crises in Poland and Hungary with his 'secret' speech at the Twentieth Congress." True or false, Khrushchev was very much in trouble when 1957 rolled around.

He was being criticized for his foreign and domestic policies, and there was rising pressure to remove him from power. It may have been part of his counteroffensive to make the incredible statement that within three or four years the Soviet Union would catch up with the United States in its production of meat, milk, and butter per capita in the population. Since most Russians had no idea how much the Americans were producing on their farms, it may have sounded credible to them. As far as his Politburo enemies were concerned, Khrushchev was acting foolishly, and something had to be done about it.

On June 18, 1957, the Politburo voted to dismiss him as first secretary. Even his friend and partner Premier Bulganin voted against Khrushchev. But the first secretary was not about to bow to the group's will. He demanded a plenum meeting of the Central Committee to be convoked to decide his fate, and when the Politburo refused, Khrushchev turned to his network of political friends. Hundreds of Central Committee members streamed into Moscow in an operation coordinated by Defense Minister Zhukov and key men in the security services, and the plenum held between June 22 and 29 Khrushchev won hands down. The first thing he did was to fire Molotov and Malenkov from the Politburo (replacing them with Zhukov and Brezhnev, who was starting his comeback). Malenkov was also fired as deputy premier and made manager of an electric power station. He lasted for four years after Stalin's death, then became a "nonperson."

Nikita Khrushchev's great vindication and victory came on October 4, 1957. On that day the Soviet Union successfully launched the artificial satellite *Sputnik*, placing it in orbit and thereby inaugurating both the space age and the space race.

Sputnik's ninety-two-day orbital flight (it burned out, as planned, when it reentered the atmosphere) was the first time anyone was able to place an object in space, and it represented the greatest postwar technological breakthrough. Though *Sputnik I* (there were nine more) was a ball of aluminum alloy weighing only 184 pounds, the fact that the Russians had launched a satellite first served to force a reconsideration of scientific, technological, military and educational assumptions in the United States. Needless to say, *Sputnik I* came as a tremendous shock to Americans, who simply never expected to be outpaced by the Russians.

McGeorge Bundy writes in *Danger and Survival* that "*Sputnik* signaled high Soviet achievement" because "it showed the existence of a powerful ballistic missile, because nothing less could have placed in orbit so large an object." He cites MIT's James Killian (about to become Eisenhower's science adviser as a result of *Sputnik*, having completed his work on the U-2) as saying about the Soviet accomplishment that "what I felt most keenly was

the affront to my national pride . . . this did violence to a belief so fundamental that it was almost heresy to question it: a belief I shared that the
United States was so far advanced in its technological capacity that it had in
fact no serious rival."

Apart from space exploration aspects of *Sputnik*, its appearance raised the
fundamental question whether, as Bundy notes, the Soviets had more effective ballistic missiles than the United States. The issue was whether the
Soviets had surpassed the United States in intercontinental ballistic missiles,
which, with nuclear warheads, constituted the most lethal weapon poised at
the United States. At the end of August, about six weeks before *Sputnik*, the
Soviets reported publicly major tests of atomic and hydrogen bombs on their
territory, and Moscow was puzzled that the United States seemingly paid no
attention to the tests. They were timed, of course, to produce a double effect
with the *Sputnik* announcement to convince the Americans that Moscow
had both a hydrogen weapon in good shape and new means of delivering it.

The satellite was a technological marvel. A four-antenna radio broadcasting unit was installed inside the ball, and *Sputnik*'s two transmitters sent
signals heard everywhere because the satellite was in an orbit slanting toward
the equator, providing full coverage. On November 3 the Russians
launched *Sputnik II*, weighing seven times more than *Sputnik I* and carrying a dog, Laika. It remained in space for 161 days, and Russian scientists
acquired a mass of invaluable data on life in space from the instruments
attached to Laika and broadcast down to earth. The shock in America was
even greater than in October.

To the Soviets, *Sputnik* meant that they now had the capacity not only of
firing nuclear weapons aboard intercontinental missiles but also of using the
missiles to intercept high-flying American aircraft, as was to happen before
too long. Finally, Soviet planners were beginning to play with the idea of
using satellites for offensive or defensive warfare in space, the "Star Wars" of
the next generation. A completely new and unpredictable era began that day
in October, and three decades later all work on space and missiles dates back
to the first *Sputnik*.

To be sure, *Sputnik* was a direct result of wartime missile research, especially by German scientists. The Soviets had watched with immense interest
the V-1 and V-2 missiles launched at London toward the end of the war,
and they instantly understood that they needed missilery and experts to design it. It was the same concept they had applied to the construction of the
atomic bomb. The decision to recruit or capture German scientists taken
long months before the war's end had paid off in both realms although
Soviet scientists S. P. Korolev, M. Keldysh, V. P. Glushko, N. A. Pilygin,
V. P. Barmin, and M. K. Yangel—almost completely unknown in the
United States at the time—made enormous contributions to the final designs. It was also in 1957 that the Soviets built their first cyclotron and
launched the first nuclear-powered vessel, *Lenin*.

Killian's surprise over the Soviet feat and Soviet technological advances illustrated the incredibly patronizing attitudes Americans had (and still have) toward the Russians. The conventional wisdom had been all along that the Soviets were so far behind in so many areas of daily life, to say nothing of technology, that they could not be expected to catch up with the United States for years or decades. Notwithstanding the lessons of the Soviet atomic and hydrogen bombs and *Sputnik*, that same conventional wisdom convinced American policymakers in the early 1970's that the Russians were long years away from MIRV, the multiwarhead missile in nuclear strategic forces; that error was responsible for faulty negotiating positions on the part of the United States in the 1972 negotiations of SALT I (Strategic Arms Limitations Talks) Treaty with the Soviets.

Overlooked in our democratic society was that an authoritarian system like the Soviets can assign priorities and harness the resources for programs the regime considers vital, even at the cost of totally disregarding consumer needs and desires, without public outcry. That Moscow had computer technology when it built *Sputnik* in 1957 was a source of amazement to American specialists; in the late eighties the tendency was still to dismiss Soviet advances in computers and to believe that the Russians are wholly dependent on technology they can buy or steal from the United States. Those are costly as well as foolish misjudgments.

As far as the Soviets were concerned, they were delighted to see the Americans lulled into a false sense of technological security. Khrushchev personally had devoted much time and attention to the needs of Soviet scientists and engineers in nuclear and rocket sciences, and he could break logjams and accelerate progress without bureaucratic interference. He said nothing when Americans laughed about his claim that the Soviet Union would overtake America in per capita farm production in a few years; there was no laughter on October 4, 1957. Naturally Khrushchev took massive personal credit for the Soviet technological achievements, and they helped him survive politically for another seven years. (What Khrushchev did not disclose was that late in September 1957, just a few days before *Sputnik* was launched into space, the Soviet Union suffered what was probably the world's worst nuclear disaster. This was the explosion of radioactive nitrate salts and acetate from nuclear wastes collected at the Kyshtym atomic center in the southern Urals where the Soviets first developed their bomb. Soviet biologist Zhores Medvedev, who now lives in London, believes that the Kyshtym blast released more radioactive strontium 90 than the accident at the Chernobyl power reactor in 1986, thereby becoming the worst nuclear disaster ever. Medvedev claims that hundreds may have died from the radiation effects while the Soviet government, confirming in 1989 that such an accident did occur, offers no casualty figures. It did acknowledge, however, that some ten thousand citizens were urgently evacuated from the Kyshtym-Chelyabinsk area and that about seventy square miles were declared unfit for human habitation after approximately two million curies of radioactive materials were swept up by winds after the explosion. It took Gorbachev's *glasnost* for the truth to be told thirty-two years after the fact.)

* * *

The first American artificial satellite was launched on January 31, 1958, after several failures. It set the United States on an urgent track of improving its rocketry and space capabilities, and of course, it did catch up with the Russians. In the meantime, the Soviets kept up their space spectaculars. On July 3, 1959, another *Sputnik* took two dogs and a rabbit into space, teaching Soviet scientists even more about spatial biology and medicine. On September 13 the Soviet unmanned probe *Lunik* landed on the surface of the moon, causing another acute embarrassment for the United States.

In America, where spirits soar to limitless optimism as easily as they sink into depression, *Sputnik* had the effect of opening a major debate on the "missile gap" with the Soviet Union that lasted well into the sixties. The debate, affecting foreign policy, military budgets, and electoral politics, was very quickly distorted by advocates of various viewpoints. It did not help the national interest; it confused it in the end and led to major defense production decisions that may not have been wise.

The other impact was on education. *Sputnik* released a virtual hysteria about the state of American education, particularly in the sciences and engineering. Charges were made that American children and college students were not taught enough and well enough. In customary American fashion, education crash programs were launched, new money was found for university and industrial research, and in time the United States recovered. In that sense *Sputnik* may have been the best thing to happen to shake American complacency and the tendency to patronize others. After *Sputnik*, Eisenhower remarked that the Russians "have in fact done us a good turn, unintentionally, in establishing the concept of freedom of international space."

Following the *Sputnik* jolt, American-Soviet relations for the balance of the decade moved in a pattern that seemed to change continuously from good to bad and vice versa, largely because of Khrushchev's moodiness. But the United States, too, had a way of raising the international temperature. And in all cases nuclear threats punctuated the crises.

Unlike Truman, President Eisenhower and Secretary of State Dulles believed that the United States should state unequivocally that it was prepared to use nuclear weapons if warranted by the circumstances. As early as October 1953 a National Security Council document on "Basic National Security Policy" (NSC-162/2) stated: "In specific situations where a warning appears desirable and feasible as an added deterrent, the United States should make it clear to the USSR and Communist China . . . its intention to react with military force against any aggression by Soviet bloc armed forces. . . . In the event of hostilities, the United States will consider nuclear weapons to be as available for use as other munitions." To this, Dulles soon added his own doctrine of massive retaliation—meaning nuclear—for any attack.

Khrushchev would not be left behind in this brinksmanship game, which was essentially psychological and political but inevitably always carried the danger of getting out of hand. When the Chinese Communists started bombarding the Nationalist-held Quemoy and Matsu offshore islands in the latest crisis in that area in September 1958, the Eisenhower administration made it clear that nuclear weapons would not be ruled out if the confrontation continued. Now in the post-*Sputnik* age and after the test of his big hydrogen bombs, Khrushchev sent Eisenhower on September 20 a message of warning: "Those who harbor plans of an atomic attack on the People's Republic of China should not forget that the other side too has atomic and hydrogen weapons and the appropriate means to deliver them. . . . To touch off war against People's China means to doom to certain death sons of the American people and to spark off the conflagration of a world war."

This was spelling out mutual nuclear deterrence in the clearest possible language. The China coastal crisis dissolved without confrontation, but within two months the Soviets had touched off another dispute, this time over Berlin. Coming out of the blue, Moscow informed the United States, Britain, and France in formal notes on November 27, 1958, that a peace treaty must be signed with Germany so that the status of West Berlin could be redefined. Since 1945 the divided city had been under quadripartite rule, and the West saw no reason to change the arrangements. But the Soviets warned that if a peace treaty were not accepted within six months, Moscow would make a separate peace with Communist-run East Germany (the German Democratic Republic) and West Berlin would no longer be politically part of West Germany. Khrushchev's contribution to the diplomatic note was that "only madmen can go to the length of unleashing another world war over the preservation of privileges of occupiers in West Berlin."

It is hard to say why Khrushchev suddenly resolved to challenge the West or to bluff. Not surprisingly the Western allies turned down the idea. By mid-1959 Khrushchev was no longer pressing over the German peace treaty, shifting now to the warm friendship route with the Americans. As an American diplomat who worked on Soviet affairs remarked one day between crises, "the beauty of it is that you never know in which direction Nikita will turn next . . . you see, consistency is a bourgeois trait he despises. . . ."

In July 1959 an American trade exhibit opened in Sokolniki Park in Moscow as a follow-up to a Soviet exhibit in New York the previous month. With presidential elections just over a year away, Vice President Nixon appeared in Moscow to inaugurate the show and gain precampaign publicity. He was the candidate to replace Eisenhower for the term starting in 1961. Khrushchev was on hand to greet Nixon, and the two men found themselves in a mock-up one-family house in the American exhibit. Khrushchev did not care for the house, he said, because it was not substantial, and a vivid discussion ensued in the kitchen of the exhibit house; it became known in American politics as the kitchen debate. Nixon delivered a speech about the American way of life, and Khrushchev personally ordered the full text to be published in the Soviet press. The next day the two men walked among sunbathers on the banks of the Moskva River, and Khrushchev asked Nixon, "Do these people seem to you like slaves of communism?"

Also during July the two governments announced that Khrushchev would visit the United States in the autumn as Eisenhower's guest. Again tensions seemed to have vanished. The Soviet leader arrived in the United States on September 15, 1959, which happened to be two days after *Lunik* landed on the moon and planted a Soviet pennant on the surface. Khrushchev obviously could not resist the temptation of teasing his host, but the two-week visit was largely a success. Eisenhower took him to his weekend retreat near Washington known as Camp David (named after his grandson) for lengthy discussions, free of hostility. There was no argument about Berlin, for example, and the new relationship entered history as "the spirit of Camp David."

Americans were fascinated by Khrushchev, his folksy manner, and his decidedly nonmartial appearance. They followed him on television from Washington to New York, then San Francisco, Los Angeles, Hollywood (but he was denied for mysterious reasons the visit to Disneyland he had requested), Des Moines, and a private farm in Iowa. Khrushchev made a fine peace-loving impression in the United States, and the assumption was that "the spirit of Camp David" would last forever. Among important American personalities Khrushchev met during his Washington stay was a forty-one-year-old senator from Massachusetts, John F. Kennedy. There is no record of what they said to each other or how they impressed each other. They were to meet again before too long under vastly different circumstances.

VI

From the United States Nikita Khrushchev traveled to Beijing for an encounter with Mao Zedong. It is not known what they said to each other (both men have long been dead, and minutes of their talks probably do not exist), but Khrushchev's visit marked with absolute finality the end of the Soviet-Chinese Communist alliance, such as it was, and the advent of the profound rift between the two parties and governments that has never fully healed.

The precise reasons for the split, kept secret by the two sides, remain an enigma a generation later. Though there clearly were ideological differences between the Soviet and Chinese leaderships (the Chinese never endorsed Khrushchev's denunciation of Stalin and his crimes), the problems dividing them were pragmatic. And in retrospect, it appears that China acted as the aggrieved party and precipitated the break.

Foremost, Mao Zedong resented having his young people's republic being treated with superior airs first by Stalin, then by his successors. The Russians had done little to help the Chinese Communists win the civil war in 1949, having earlier denuded Manchuria of its industrial infrastructure as the spoils (undeserved, in Mao's mind) of victory over Japan. In the ensuing decade, the Chinese believed, Moscow used them for its own aims while keeping them on a short leash. Thus Mao was deeply resentful that China had had to bear the military brunt of the Korean War, started by Stalin and Kim Il Sung during the first year of the people's republic's existence, and that only after Stalin's death in 1953 did the Russians agree to the armistice that Beijing had wanted all along.

Then, in Mao's estimate, the Soviets had not done enough to assist Ho Chi Minh in Indochina in his independence war against France (compounding it by urging the French Communist party to join other French political parties in defending the metropolitan colonial interests so that the Communists would not lose their patriotic cachet at home).

Next, China took the view that the Soviets had failed to assist it in developing an atomic bomb by withholding technical support and weapons-grade fissionable materials. It is now clear that the Russians abhorred the idea of a Chinese bomb—they simply feared a militarily independent China—and therefore, Mao was not able to develop one with his own resources until 1964 (five years later the Soviets seriously contemplated a preemptive nuclear strike to destroy this infant arsenal). Finally, the Chinese were furious that Moscow showed niggardly attitudes toward their Great Leap Forward in 1958, which was Mao's grandiose scheme to industrialize China on a crash basis.

The West, especially the United States, seemed to have no inkling of this colossal Communist schism. The conventional wisdom was that "international communism," was absolutely monolithic and that Mao, Ho, and all the Eastern Europeans simply obeyed Moscow's orders. The few analysts who suspected that separate Communist identities could be encouraged in Beijing and Hanoi (on the Tito model in Yugoslavia) were regarded as mad romantics. Though neither the Soviets nor the Chinese were keen on publicizing their split—the monolith idea was still useful—American policymakers were obviously remiss in failing to meditate on the long history of Russian and Chinese relations and their traditional differences and to draw more perceptive conclusions from what they were observing. They might have spared America immense grief if they had possessed adequate political and historical sense.

As late as 1965, when the United States was already deeply enmeshed in Vietnam, attempting to reverse history, even Secretary of State Dean Rusk remained convinced that the Soviet Union and China were in cahoots, repeating at every opportunity that America would go on fighting until

Hanoi and Moscow and Beijing halted their "aggression" against South Vietnam. Rusk, possibly the most simpleminded American postwar secretary of state, was among the officers who had arbitrarily split Korea in 1945 along the thirty-eighth parallel, and he went on misunderstanding Asian situations until the end of his tenure, following President Lyndon Johnson along the disastrous course of Vietnam escalations.

The late James Jesus Angleton, who served as head of the CIA's Counter Intelligence Staff from 1954 to 1974 and exercised immense influence on the thinking of the entire intelligence community in Washington, went even farther than Rusk. He was convinced, and said so in both public and private, that the Sino-Soviet split was a "brilliant" grand deception (and disinformation) cooked up by Moscow and Beijing to lull the United States into a false sense of security. Angleton was obsessed with deceptions and enemy intelligence penetrations (the reason for his ultimate dismissal was this paranoia), but he was not alone among important analysts to insist that the rift was a feint.

Even in terms of Indochina, American policy thinkers shied away from history in interpreting current events. Not many of them appeared to know that China and Vietnam had been sworn enemies since the early Middle Ages and that profound ethnic hatreds traditionally existed between the Vietnamese and the Khmers of Cambodia. In the late seventies, for example, there was astonishment in Washington when Communist Vietnam invaded Communist Cambodia three years after winning the war against the United States and its South Vietnamese client and when the Communist Vietnamese fought a border war with Communist China (apparently triumphantly). It is hard to understand, indeed, why the notion of widening splits within the body of "international communism" was contemplated as heresy among the West's leading anti-Communists.

In any event, top Soviet and Chinese leaders were not to meet again for thirty years after Khrushchev's departure from Beijing in 1959. And when Mikhail Gorbachev flew there in May 1989, the fate of communism in the two countries had reached the stage of dramatic and irreversible crisis.

It is important to bear in mind that the Soviet-Chinese split represented for Moscow, above all else, a classical Third World conflict though neither its nature nor the phrase ("Third World") were recognized as such. China was in every sense an underdeveloped Third World country and made a point of identifying itself with the new nonaligned countries. To Moscow's great annoyance, Beijing was making a pitch for Third World leadership— therefore becoming a rival in Soviet eyes—and Premier Zhou Enlai demonstrated it by joining India's Prime Minister Nehru and Egypt's strongman Gamal Abdel Nasser at the neutralist Afro-Asian Solidarity Conference in Bandung, Indonesia, in April 1955. Regardless of ideology, the overwhelming fact of life was that the Russians were the Second World as a Communist superpower (the United States and Western Europe saw themselves as

the industrially mature First World) and the Chinese were the wholly under-
privileged Third World with backyard steel furnaces, "barefoot doctors," and
an economy based on manual labor.

The emerging Sino-Soviet rift was in synchrony with Third World conflicts arising around the globe during the fifties to challenge in different but
fundamental ways the West and the Soviet Union. As a geopolitical and
heartbreakingly human reality, the Third World came into its own during
that decade through bloody wars and revolutions and the ever-mounting
suffering and despair of its billions, and it has not ceased to grow in magnitude for the balance of the century.

In its many guises and dimensions (including as a trigger in superpower
confrontations and basic economic realignments), the Third World became
the central reality of the second half of the twentieth century and certainly
of the 1950's. As such, it helped spawn the era of American overt and covert
interventions around the world to defend weak regimes it liked and to try to
destroy the ones it disliked.

Naturally, no master plan existed under the Truman and Eisenhower administrations to intervene from Asia to the Middle East and Latin America.
There was, however, a fundamental national policy of blocking Communist
expansion everywhere, combined with an often exaggerated tendency of
seeing or suspecting the hand of communism (Soviet and/or Chinese) in
situations escaping American control. Moreover, many of these situations
were frequently misunderstood or misinterpreted by senior U.S. foreign policy and intelligence officials, leading to actions that were precipitate and
unwarranted by the events. Then there was the constant confusion between
Third World nationalism and communism, fear of Communist inroads in
processes of nationalism, and the extraordinarily naive belief (as we now
know) that the Soviet Union and China actually had *their* master plan to
conquer the Third World in some fashion and then deal the ultimate blow
to the United States and the West.

That the Soviets continuously attempted to capitalize on Third World
turmoil to expand their international influence is unquestionable. The
United States devoted vast efforts and resources to achieve the same aims as
part of the postwar superpower rivalry. Inevitably the Cold War between
Washington and Moscow spilled over into Third World conflicts. Korea was
the best example of such spillovers, providing proof that indeed, the Russians were behind all the challenges in the Third World. Unfortunately the
United States failed to see the difference between the Communist aggression
in Korea—an unjustified Soviet power play—and the Vietnamese Independence War against France. Because the two wars ran on parallel tracks in
the early fifties, the American assumption was that both formed part of a
larger and highly orchestrated phenomenon, and the U.S. response was
essentially the same in both cases: military engagement to stem communism.

This approach ruled out subtleties and nuances in policy-making, undermining the American position in the end. It also allowed the Soviets and the Chinese to espouse popular causes such as Third World independence wars against the old colonial powers while the United States found itself defending the status quo and shoring up hated and corrupt regimes in the name of anticommunism. Inevitably, nationalist leaders across the Third World turned toward radicalism and communism because America afforded them no acceptable alternative.

Under the circumstances, it is truly astounding how much goodwill the United States and Americans continue to enjoy throughout the world, including countries where some of the most brutal and thoughtless policies have been carried out. The only plausible explanation is that in the minds of generation after generation on every continent the United States stands for values that transcend negative official American actions. Having worked as a journalist since the end of World War II in scores of countries—from Cuba to the Soviet Union and from Vietnam to the Dominican Republic—I am persuaded that anti-Americanism is a superficial phenomenon, more often than not fed by deliberate hostile propaganda. This is a journalistic fact that academic prophets of the American decline may wish to ponder, perhaps through exposure to people in all these foreign lands.

In the fifties (as in the sixties), however, the obsessive fear of communism robbed the United States of superb diplomatic and political opportunities that might have changed the course of history. China is a textbook example. After the Korean War and the French defeat in Indochina, Beijing evidently concluded that it should repair its relations with the United States, probably realizing already that a split with Moscow was inevitable.

Consequently, Premier Zhou Enlai decided to take advantage of the Indochina Peace Conference in Geneva in July 1954 (which followed the French defeat at Dien Bien Phu in May) to establish contact with Secretary of State John Foster Dulles. In a famous incident Dulles scowled at the smiling Zhou, refusing his proffered handshake because the Chinese had killed Americans in Korea. Many years later I was told by Huang Hua, then Zhou's adviser (and later himself foreign minister), that the Chinese premier was ready to submit a series of concrete proposals to Dulles but could not bring himself to pursue his initiative and invite another public rebuff.

Dulles, for his part, also chose to disregard the helpful role Zhou had played at the conference. While the North Vietnamese and the Russians insisted that Vietnam be partitioned between the Communist north and the anti-Communist south at the sixteenth parallel, awarding Ho more territory and population, the Chinese quietly sided with France and the United States to draw the line at the seventeenth parallel. This was the final decision at Geneva, and it may have been the first manifestation of the nascent Soviet-Chinese differences. And China, unlike the Soviet Union, was not making an issue of the fact that Washington had supplied the French with modern arms, both covertly and openly, from the very outset of the Indochina War (which for two years, between 1947 and 1949, paralleled the Chinese Civil War, in which the Americans were arming the Nationalists against the Communists).

Nine months later, in April 1955, Zhou stopped in Rangoon, the capital of Burma, en route to the Bandung conference. I was at the airport to cover the story for my newspaper, and Krishna Menon, at the time India's chief delegate to the United Nations, introduced me to Zhou as an American reporter and friend. Having established quickly that we shared French as a language (Zhou was educated in France), the premier invited me to tea at the Chinese Embassy, where he informed me that his government had decided to release sixteen crewmen of a B-29 bomber shot down over China in **the** waning days of the Korean War. This, he said, was meant as a friendly gesture toward the United States. It was an exclusive story, but its publication the next morning in *The New York Times* produced no American response.

In Bandung Zhou proclaimed China's "Five Principles" of proposed peaceful relations—a move addressed directly to the United States—but again, Dulles and Eisenhower showed no interest. They concentrated, instead, on forming the Southeast Asia Treaty Organization (SEATO) as another instrument against communism in the region. When President Nixon went to China seventeen years later, the new relationship was based on Zhou's principles, and the premier had the satisfaction of negotiating the final text personally with Nixon and Henry Kissinger.

The first major American involvement in Asia after China went Communist in 1949 was the dispatch of troops to South Korea following the North Korean invasion in June 1950. The Korean War lasted three years, but from the first day it created a mind-set in Washington concerning the Communist challenge in Asia that survived for a quarter of a century—until the ultimate U.S. departure from Indochina in 1975.

In the context of the American strategic presence in Southeast Asia at the time of Korea, nothing was more important than the Philippines and the twenty-three military bases and installations, including the naval base at Subic Bay and Clark Air Base, leased to the United States for ninety-nine years in 1947. By 1950, however, Americans had begun to discern bad trouble in the archipelago in the form of the Communist-led Hukbalahap (or simply Huk) peasant rebellion. The Huks, whom Stanley Karnow describes in *In Our Image* as consisting overwhelmingly "of poor peasants fighting for reform rather than revolution"—not, as American intelligence analysts at the time put it, seeking "to further the objectives of world communism"—were a powerful force of some fifteen thousand guerrillas and possibly as many as one million sympathizers. They derived much of their strength from the corruption of the wealthy elites ruling the Philippines in the aftermath of independence, wasting American economic aid and doing nothing to improve the lot of the impoverished masses. It was a classical postcolonial situation, and because the Huk leadership was increasingly Communist-oriented, the Truman administration (with the Eisenhower team following its lead) decided it had to act.

For once the democratic cause lucked out, at least for a while. Under American pressure, Ramón Magsaysay, a military provincial governor who had impressed U.S. commanders when he led anti-Japanese guerrillas during the war, was named secretary of defense. To advise him, the CIA's top secret Office of Policy Coordination, specializing in clandestine activities, assigned an Air Force intelligence officer named Edward Geary Lansdale who had a prewar advertising background, knew the Philippines, and was destined to grow into something of an American secret-works legend in the ensuring years. Magsaysay and Lansdale did everything right from the intelligence and military standpoint. They disposed of a half million dollars in U.S. arms and economic aid and had the sense to treat Filipinos throughout the country like people instead of chattels. By 1952 the Huks were no longer a threat, and Magsaysay was elected president the following year (with enthusiastic CIA support).

In postcolonial Asia, wholly bereft of credible democratic leaders, Magsaysay stood out as a paragon of virtue and vision. When I interviewed him at the Malcañang Palace in Manila in mid-1955, he talked at length about land reform plans, rural housing, and the eradication of official corruption—none of which was easy to achieve in the Philippines—and as I saw subsequently, he was actually doing something about it. Unlike other new Asian rulers, Magsaysay was totally accessible to the people, even at the palace. But the Filipino luck did not last long: Magsaysay died in a plane crash in March 1957. The next thirty years witnessed his nation's ever-quickening slide into new and greater corruption, social injustice, political turmoil, murder, and, finally, a new Communist uprising and the gangster dictatorship of Ferdinand E. Marcos.

Common sense would suggest that successful lessons be learned well and quickly. In the case of Ramón Magsaysay and the Philippines, the larger tragedy was that the United States, as protector of Asian freedom, absorbed nothing from this experience and example except for the notion that well-financed anti-communism will work in the Third World under adequate CIA management. This was the idea that Colonel Lansdale carried to his next assignment, the American intervention in Vietnam.

In a sense, this involvement, destined to last twenty-one years, began with Lansdale's arrival in Saigon on June 1, 1954. The Ho Chi Minh forces had destroyed the French militarily at the siege of Dien Bien Phu only three weeks earlier and the Geneva Conference to resolve the political fate of Vietnam had not yet constructed its compromises; but the United States was determined not to waste a second in setting up its own regime in the South.

The Eisenhower administration had decided from the outset to do everything possible to avert France's humiliation in its former colonial empire, and the President even considered proposals for smashing the Communists at Dien Bien Phu with three tactical atomic weapons or, at least, authorizing air strikes by American warplanes with conventional ordnance. In the end, Eisenhower's instincts of military and political caution prevailed, and the French were left to capitulate. The only direct aid to besieged Dien Bien Phu were several resupply flights by unmarked American transport planes flown by CIA pilots, including "Earthquake" Murphy, a huge wartime flier whom I knew briefly at the time (unhappily his real first name escapes me).

But as soon as it was all over, the Americans stepped into the South Vietnam vacuum. When the fighting was still in progress, Secretary of State Dulles told Lansdale to be ready to go to Saigon to "do what you did in the Philippines," according to Neil Sheehan's account in A *Bright Shining Lie* (which is the best chronicle extant of the American war in Vietnam). The Geneva Conference had decided on July 21 to partition Vietnam between the Vietminh in the North and the non-Communists in the South along the seventeenth parallel, thus inviting a new war by repeating the Potsdam error of dividing the country, and to make Laos and Cambodia (which had belonged to France as well) independent states. Lansdale's task, therefore, was to set up an American-controlled government in Saigon and to arm it as well as possible while doing everything in his power to sabotage North Vietnam.

That close to a million soldiers and civilians on both sides died in the course of the largely American-financed French colonial war (never openly opposed at home by the French Communists) was not a factor in dissuading the United States from setting the stage for an inevitable new war—with more millions to die. The calculation by the Dulles brothers—John Foster at the State Department and Allen at the head of the CIA—was that the Communists now in power in Hanoi could be annihilated by the American client regime in Saigon at the proper time, and Lansdale was in charge of the complex scenario designed to attain this objective. It never occurred to Eisenhower and the Dulles brothers that American troops would ever be required in Vietnam. Having helped end the Korean War less than a year earlier, Ike had no intention of again bogging down U.S. forces in the quagmire of an Asian land conflict. And Lansdale's success in the Philippines seemed to guarantee that the same methods could work in Vietnam.

This was a catastrophic error in judgment, the kind of error the United States and its intelligence agency smugly repeated far across the world in the next decade, and it was based on both arrogance and ignorance. In the first place, it was absurd to compare the Vietminh with the Huks; they, unlike the Filipino guerrillas, held territory and had a full-fledged government and a large, conventional army. In the second place, the Americans had no Ramón Magsaysay in Saigon; they had an uninspired and uninspiring puppet named Ngo Dinh Diem, whom Lansdale brought from exile and made prime minister under Emperor Bao Dai, another puppet restored to office. Though within a year Lansdale removed Bao Dai through a "plebiscite" and elevated Diem to the presidency of South Vietnam, it is hard to imagine whatever led him to think that his protégé could be a tenable chief of state. To be sure, the CIA colonel knew virtually nothing about Vietnam, its history and politics.

The Geneva Conference provided for free elections to be held in 1956 to decide whether a unified Vietnam would be governed by Hanoi Communists or Saigon anti-Communists guided by France. But the French had neither the stomach nor resources to remain in Vietnam, and they gave the Americans free rein to do what they pleased in Saigon. The first thing the United States was anxious to avoid was such an election because, as Neil Sheehan points out, "Eisenhower acknowledged in 1954 that if a free election should . . . be held in North and South Vietnam, Ho Chi Minh would win 80 per cent of the vote as the father of the country in the eyes of most Vietnamese." Inasmuch as the United States was not prepared to tolerate a Communist Vietnam, the decision was taken—automatically—to turn South Vietnam into an impregnable anti-Communist bastion, leaving the North to Ho's cohorts.

Ho Chi Minh, naturally, had every intention of reunifying Vietnam under his banner, but he was in no rush to do so. He understood that there would be no Geneva-mandated election to award him the prize, and his strategy was gradually to build up nationalist and Communist power in South Vietnam so that sooner or later the Saigon regime would collapse. What he did not expect, however, was that the bellicosity of the Diem government and army toward their own citizens would create a climate for a spontaneous revolt in the South that Hanoi had to support, even if it thought it premature. Americans in the mid-fifties could not possibly imagine that the seeds were being sown for the most terrible and unnecessary war in their history. Unnoticed, a 650-man American military training mission was already in South Vietnam, and by the end of the Eisenhower presidency, $1.5 billion was spent on Diem and his army.

The Eisenhower administration's preoccupations in Korea, the Philippines, and Indochina did not preclude it from engaging almost simultaneously in covert operations of considerable significance in such diverse spots as Iran and Guatemala. It was the worldwide watch against Communist inroads, and while these operations were successful in the short term in dislodging governments Washington tended to detest or fear geopolitically, they subsequently did the United States much lasting damage.

Again, it was arrogance and ignorance that molded the decisions by the small group of policy and intelligence executives running a secret White House committee known to initiates as 5412 (after the number of the presidential order that set it up) to which Eisenhower had, in effect, delegated total operational power to protect him under the bizarre doctrine of plausible deniability, invented in his first term. The idea was that if the United States were caught red-handed in an illegal or embarrassing international situation, the government could claim that it was an unauthorized "rogue" operation of which Dwight Eisenhower had no previous knowledge. For all practical purposes, the covert enterprises were handled by the Dulles brothers, the corporate lawyers, in what was an extraordinarily dangerous and irresponsible way of running foreign policy. That was in the happy days before the advent of congressional intelligence oversight committees and at least partial CIA accountability.

The 1953 "countercoup" in Iran was the first great covert intelligence operation apart from the political-military engagements in the Far East. It was a smashing success though it could be argued that the United States paid a terrible price for it twenty-five years later, such being the ironies of history. Code-named Ajax and executed almost single-handedly by the CIA on behalf of American and British political interests in the oil-rich region, this operation was launched to oust the nationalist regime of Premier Mohammad Mossadegh and to restore the Peacock Throne to His Imperial Majesty Mohammad Reza Shah Pahlavi, who had chosen to flee his country rather than deal himself with the radicals.

The official justification for Ajax was that Mossadegh was increasingly allying himself with the Tudeh (Communist) party and that Iran would slide under Soviet influence as it almost had in 1946, when Stalin refused to remove his troops stationed there during the war. The truth was much more complicated and less sinister.

For one thing, Iran (known earlier as Persia) was not a typical postcolonial situation. The Persian Empire went back 2,500 years to Cyrus, who welded warring tribes into a single nation around 550 B.C., making it "the foremost people in the world" in the words of an English nineteenth-century historian. Over the long centuries, however, Persia had shrunk considerably and lost most of its influence, losing territory to Russia and the Ottoman Empire. In the nineteenth century Russia and Britain competed for control of this already strategic area astride Middle Eastern military and trade routes. After World War I an army colonel named Reza Shah captured power; the parliament elected him shah in 1925 as the founder of the Pahlavi dynasty.

The old shah was a formidable personage, but political judgment was not his strong suit. I remember the awe and the hush that descended over Le Rosey, the boys' prep school in Rolle on the Lake of Geneva attended by his sons, including the future emperor, in the mid-1930's when the shah arrived in his huge Rolls-Royce for an annual visit amid the pomp displayed by his traveling court. Coming from a poor family, the shah was determined to give his heirs a first-rate Western education, and Le Rosey in Switzerland was certainly a step in the right direction (ironically, another Rosey student was Richard Helms, who served as CIA director and ambassador to Iran when the postwar crises plagued the ancient empire).

During the war the old shah played it all wrong. Betting on the defeat of the Allies, he allowed Nazi agents to consolidate in Iran. A German coup d'état that could have affected the course of the whole war by making oil and crucial territory available to Hitler was prevented when British and Soviet troops invaded the country in August 1941, forcing Reza Shah to resign in favor of his son, twenty-year-old Mohammad Reza. After the war (and the ultimate departure of the Soviet forces), Britain was clearly the dominant power in Iran, and the British-controlled Anglo-Iranian Oil Company (AIOC) dictated, in effect, British policy there. That was when the crunch came.

In 1947 the Majlis, the Iranian parliament, requested a renegotiation of a 1933 treaty with AIOC under which Iran had virtually no voice in the running of its oil industry. This was not a "radical" defiance of the Crown but a demand for a long-overdue improvement in the share of oil earnings granted Iran. Moreover, Iran needed revenues to start modernizing its economy. AIOC, however, refused to negotiate a new agreement, offering instead—two years later—an increase in oil royalties' payments to Iran plus a flat payment of twenty-three million pounds sterling. ($5.2 million). It was a ridiculous response, especially so because Labour, not the Tories, was in power in London, and inevitably it led to disaster. Dean Acheson, who was the Anglophile secretary of state when the drama was unfolding, writes in his memoirs that the British government and AIOC acted with "unusual and persistent stupidity" and, paraphrasing his friend Winston Churchill, that "never had so few lost so much so stupidly and so fast."

While pressures were building up in Iran, the British not only refused to budge (ignoring Truman's and Acheson's advice) but provoked Iranian nationalists even more by dispatching warships to the Persian Gulf in a revival of old-fashioned gunboat diplomacy. Among the most outspoken of these nationalists was the elderly Dr. Mossadegh, who had served in the Majlis for thirty years and, contrary to general belief, was not a fiery radical but a traditional Iranian patriot. As Acheson remarks in *Present at the Creation*, the West never understood him: "We were, perhaps, slow in realizing that he was essentially a rich, reactionary, feudal-minded Persian inspired by a fanatical hatred of the British and a desire to expel them and all their works from the country regardless of the cost."

By then the shah himself became convinced that Iranian pride made imperative the nationalization of AIOC, about the only thing on which he and Mossadegh agreed. Consequently, Mossadegh was appointed prime minister on April 28, 1951, and AIOC's nationalization was proclaimed on May 2. What is often forgotten in the long history of Iranian crises is that the nationalization was as much the doing of the shah as of his histrionic prime minister.

That autumn Mossadegh came to New York to argue the nationalization case before the UN Security Council, turning instantly into the first international political television celebrity and displaying astounding thespian talents. He ranted, wept real tears, threatened, cajoled—and, in the end, had his way when a British condemnatory resolution was defeated. As a reporter covering the United Nations I attended news conferences Mossadegh held in his New York hospital room, usually wearing a camel hair bathrobe over his pajamas, and I fully concur with Acheson's conclusion that conversing with the seventy-year-old prime minister "was like walking in a maze and every so often finding oneself at the beginning again." I never knew how to write a story about what he *really* said.

Churchill and the Conservatives returned to power late in 1951, but on Iran their policy remained the same as under the Labour party: no compromise. They accepted the *principle* of nationalization but not its *implementation*, which was Iran's occupation of AIOC's refineries and other facilities. But Mossadegh could no longer be stopped; in September 1952 he broke diplomatic relations with Britain and expelled all British citizens, including all AIOC personnel, from Iran.

Two months later Eisenhower was elected to the presidency in the United States, and the British, in fair despair, turned to the Americans for aid in overthrowing Mossadegh. The Dulles brothers (and presumably Eisenhower) agreed to accept the responsibility for Iran (the United States remained responsible for it over the next twenty-five years), and the CIA was ordered to execute the plot. To supervise this undertaking, it drafted Kermit Roosevelt (Theodore's grandson and Franklin's cousin), who had a wartime intelligence background, knew the Middle East well, and had personal friends in Iran. So long as America was to intervene in Iranian affairs, Roosevelt was easily the best choice, being knowledgeable, disciplined, and politically honest. As his memoirs (*Countercoup: The Struggle for the Control of Iran*) make clear, he shared the administration's reasoning that Mossadegh had to be removed to assure stability in the British Empire and prevent the Soviets from becoming the dominant player in the Persian Gulf.

Roosevelt arrived in Iran in July 1953 to organize the coup *in loco* while CIA resources to support him were set in place in Rome, Beirut, Baghdad, and Damascus. It was the most complex international covert operation the CIA had run until then (Lansdale had not materialized in Vietnam, where the French were still fighting), and Roosevelt conducted it with imagination and panache. To replace Mossadegh, he had selected General Fazlollah Zahedi, a conservative career officer whom the British had imprisoned during the war for his Nazi sympathies but now were willing to adopt because of his utter loyalty to the shah. At that point, in fact, Zahedi was in hiding because Mossadegh had issued orders for his arrest.

Meeting clandestinely with the shah in a car driving at night around the palace garden, Roosevelt completed his planning. They had agreed that most of the armed forces would support the shah in a showdown and that Zahedi was the right man to become prime minister. Roosevelt, as he tells it in his memoirs, also informed the shah that he had about one million dollars in cash on hand to finance the coup.

The plan called for the shah to sign firmans (decrees) firing Mossadegh and naming Zahedi to his post, and he did so early in August 1953 after reaching a hideout on the Caspian Sea where he was to await the coup. Roosevelt's problem was to have these firmans delivered; but a young officer betrayed the conspiracy, and loyal units saved Mossadegh from being dismissed. The prime minister went on the radio to announce that the plot had failed and that he was "obliged" to assume all powers in Iran. The shah fled from the Caspian coast to Baghdad, then to Switzerland.

But Roosevelt and his network saved the day for him. They were able to bring major armed forces commanders to the side of the pro-shah conspiracy and, with the help of Teheran crowds, to force out and arrest Mossadegh. On August 22 the shah returned in triumph to his capital. The following evening he and Roosevelt celebrated over "tiny glasses of vodka and caviar canapés." The new government and Britain worked out an oil agreement under which an international consortium replaced AIOC.

The successful American intervention kept the shah on the throne for another quarter century. In time the United States trained his secret police, the SAVAK, and turned Iran into the principal military power in the Persian Gulf region—a surrogate power. Unhappily, however, the shah never regained contact with the realities of his society. The roots of the 1979 Revolution that established the Islamic Republic can be traced back to the events of 1953 and the American involvement.

To be sure, as Acheson observes, the British could have struck a better Iran deal without a confrontation five years earlier, but colonialist instincts died hard in London. (During the 1950's, for example, Britain granted independence only to Ghana and the Sudan among its colonies, the 1940's having marked freedom for the Indian subcontinent.)

Three years after Iran, in 1956, British colonialist blindness persisted. The day after Nasser, now Egypt's president, had nationalized the Suez Canal Company on July 27, the British government headed by Prime Minister Anthony Eden (who had replaced Churchill) approved in principle the use of force against the Egyptians. Secretly, Eden and his Cabinet produced the scenario for the top-secret "Musketeer" operation, which provided for Israel to attack Egypt's Sinai Peninsula and for Britain and France to land there, supposedly to separate the two sides, but really to oust Nasser and regain control over the canal. Eden easily persuaded the Israelis (who should have known better but were greedy) to participate in this mad charade. France, which was convinced that Nasser was behind the Algerian independence revolt, was happy to go along with any plan that would get rid of him.

The attack by the Israelis and then British and French aviation and airborne troops was launched in October, and at the outset, the advance by Israel's forces in the Sinai progressed well. But Eden had chosen not to inform his American allies of the true purpose of "Musketeer," and as soon as Eisenhower realized that Nasser's demise was the concealed British goal, he moved to halt the war on the grounds it was risking inflaming all the

Middle East. He accomplished his aim simply by withdrawing dollar support for the pound sterling, and Britain caved in at once. The Suez enterprise, with all its secrecy and blunders, would later be called "the British Watergate," and in the meantime, it forced Eden to resign. More seriously, it marked the end of Britain's influence in the Middle East—making room for growing American as well as Soviet presence.

VII

Just as the Eisenhower administration and the CIA had concluded following Colonel Lansdale's success in the Philippines that this could be repeated in Vietnam, it now decided that Kermit Roosevelt could replay Iran in Guatemala, the next milestone along the road of American interventions. Roosevelt was offered what he called the "command" of the Guatemalan operation planned to overthrow a leftist regime, but he had the sense to decline it. As he wrote in *Countercoup*, he later resigned from the CIA—"before the Bay of Pigs disaster underlined the validity of my warnings that such operations tend to backfire." Guatemala would succeed in the short run even without Kermit Roosevelt though in the end it was the prelude to a catastrophe.

The ostensible reason the Dulles brothers resolved to engage the CIA in Guatemala was the fact that its elected president, Jacobo Arbenz Guzmán, was a leftist whom the administration suspected of Communist sympathies and secret planning with the Russians for the spread of their influence in the Western Hemisphere. There is no question that Arbenz, a former army officer, was a politician of a very leftist persuasion (Guatemala had a strong leftist tradition), but there was no evidence that he was a Soviet front. The real reason for the intervention was that he had nationalized the lands of an American agribusiness company, and Washington would not let him get away with it.

The U.S. government in the 1950's regarded nationalism, to say nothing of nationalizations, as evil and subversive. And when it came to Latin America—"our backyard," in the patronizing rhetoric of the time—nothing could be worse than revolution. Its very mention triggered the imagery of Mao Zedong and Ho Chi Minh and Communist treacheries. There was no place for revolutions in the Western Hemisphere if Eisenhower and the Dulles brothers had anything to say about it.

The Truman administration had tolerated a leftist revolution in Bolivia in 1952, mainly because its leader, Victor Paz Estenssoro, was not an anti-American radical and confined nationalizations to Bolivian-owned tin mines. (As a Social Democrat, he would serve an elected term thirty years later.) The Eisenhower administration was barely five months in office when the young Cuban revolutionary Fidel Castro attempted to storm the Moncada army barracks in Santiago on July 26, 1953, to start a national uprising against the military dictatorship of General Fulgencio Batista, and wound up in prison instead. There is no reason to believe that anyone of consequence in Washington paid the slightest attention to Castro and his adventure.

It was noticed, however, in Guatemala, which was becoming a haven for potential Latin American revolutionaries since Arbenz's 1950 election to the presidency. One of them was Dr. Ernesto "Che" Guevara, a youthful Argentine physician who was in search of a revolution and was able to meet in Guatemala several survivors of Castro's Moncada attack. The fiery young Latin Americans talked revolution day and night, but neither they nor the Arbenz regime appeared to pose much danger to the United States or hemispheric stability. As early as 1952 the Truman administration toyed with the idea of having the CIA do away with Arbenz as a matter of principle, but both Acheson and his undersecretary of state, David Bruce, talked the President out of it. In those innocent days they saw this kind of intervention as illegal.

What sentenced Arbenz to political extinction was the nationalization of the United Fruit Company's lands. The Boston-based corporation was the largest economic entity in Guatemala, growing bananas (as it did elsewhere in Central America, whose countries consequently were known derisively as banana republics) as well as rice, running its own railway transportation system, operating as the biggest single employer of labor, and historically playing a key covert role in national politics. United Fruit failed, however, first to prevent Colonel Arbenz's election and later to dissuade him from nationalizing its holdings. Arbenz believed that the time had come for a radical land reform to benefit the largely destitute Indian-descended peasant population, and United Fruit in 1953 became the principal victim.

Just as Britain could not contest the principle of oil nationalization in Iran—international law does not bar sovereign nations from nationalizing their resources—the United States did not contest Guatemala's right to confiscate United Fruit's lands. But it demanded compensations on a scale Guatemala could not meet, and Arbenz committed the error of refusing to submit the dispute to the International Court in The Hague. That was all the Dulles brothers needed to mount, with Eisenhower's approval, Operation Success against Arbenz.

Political foundations for the intervention were laid in March 1954, when

John Foster Dulles persuaded a conference of foreign ministers of the inter-American system meeting in Caracas, Venezuela, to denounce Guatemala for its behavior. Then the CIA selected an anti-Arbenz officer, Colonel Carlos Castillo Armas, to lead an armed movement to oust the regime. The agency installed a "Voice of Liberation" radio station in neighboring El Salvador to urge the Guatemalan masses to rise with Castillo Armas in the name of freedom. Then, most fortuitously, the CIA discovered that a Swedish freighter was approaching the Guatemalan port of Puerto Barrios with a load of Czechoslovak-manufactured arms (which Arbenz had ordered in Prague, on credit, because he could not procure weapons elsewhere and he knew that an American-organized attack was in the offing). It was a marvelous self-fulfilling prophecy, and now the United States was free to hit Arbenz.

The operation was coordinated in Washington by Frank Wisner, the agency's chief of clandestine services, and fully supported by the top-level leadership in the State Department (opposition from Latin American specialists being ignored). American ambassadors in Guatemala City and San Salvador were part of the political-military planning. So was the United Fruit Company.

The Castillo Armas enterprise was portrayed as a spontaneous Guatemalan uprising against communism, but even the principal players made no effort to maintain this pretense. Writing the Guatemala story for *The New York Times* in New York to supplement the newspaper's reporting from the field, I received every afternoon a complete military briefing on the rebels' progress in Guatemala from a friend who was in charge of United Fruit's public relations and made no bones about what was really happening.

Because Castillo Armas's army was having problems winning this little civil war, the administration decided in mid-June to assign unmarked fighter aircraft, P-51 Mustangs, flown by American pilots to help him out with air strikes. In the evening of June 18, Guatemalan Foreign Minister Guillermo "Willy" Torriello in Guatemala and I in New York were discussing the situation over the telephone when he suddenly shouted, "We are being bombed. . . !" and my connection with the presidential palace went dead. Inasmuch as Arbenz had no planes to counter the Mustangs, he and his loyalist military units surrendered a few days later.

The CIA's Guatemala victory coincided almost exactly with Colonel Lansdale's arrival in Saigon to launch the latest American covert operation, and the men in charge of American intelligence in Washington were flushed with success and hope for additional achievements. In Guatemala Castillo Armas installed a traditional military regime and hastened to return the nationalized lands to United Fruit. He was assassinated four years later to be replaced by another hard-line military chief, General Miguel Ydígoras Fuentes, who made the 1961 Bay of Pigs invasion possible by allowing the CIA to train Cuban exiles on Guatemalan territory (the embittered Arbenz went to live in Havana after Fidel Castro won his revolution in 1959).

Guatemala had the extra bonus of convincing the CIA (and the Dulles brothers) that after the Philippines, Iran, and Guatemala the United States could not fail at covert operations to rearrange the world according to its wishes. This was a most dangerous conclusion, creating an illusory "can-do" psychology in the government that before long led to a series of major American foreign policy disasters.

The agency's inability during the late 1950's to dislodge Cheddi Jagan, a dentist of East Indian descent who was the elected Marxist chief minister of British Guiana (then still a crown colony), and the failure to overthrow President Sukarno and his Communist allies in Indonesia in 1958 with a plot that involved a passel of local army colonels and a number of American CIA aircraft pilots did not dampen the agency's high spirits during the decade. Jagan was thrown out a few years later in elections in which his opponent was funded by a CIA labor front. Sukarno was ousted in the mid-1960's in a bloody military revolution in which the CIA performed crucial organizing functions.

America's principal political and intellectual problem in the Western Hemisphere was that it was taking the Latin Americans for granted and therefore treated them with inattention and often contempt. President Truman visited Brazil in 1947 (rejecting calls for a Marshall Plan for Latin America,) but Eisenhower went to South America only at the end of his second term, in February 1960. He was received warmly in Brazil (in Rio de Janeiro crowds thought it apt to chant a line from that year's leading carnival song, "Hey, you there. . . . Give me some money there! . . .") as well as in Argentina and Chile. Belated as it was, the trip was a good idea, a display of friendly interest. When I first arrived in Brazil late in 1955 as *The New York Times* correspondent for South America, Oswaldo Aranha, then foreign minister and throughout his long diplomatic career one of the most thoughtful Latin Americans, put it this way to me: "You Americans must treat us Latin Americans the way a man treats a woman he courts: Show a little attention, a little love, whisper endearing words, and occasionally bring a bouquet of roses. . . . We are not demanding a Marshall Plan, just a touch of affection."

The other aspect of the broad problem was Washington's proclivity under both Truman and Eisenhower administrations to maintain extremely cordial relations with dictatorial regimes in Latin America so long as they were anti-Communist. By the same token, it opposed nationalism in all its forms, and the principal reason the United States turned against Juan Perón in Argentina was that he nationalized the American-owned telephone company (along with British railways) and criticized Washington's "imperialism" as part of his populist rhetoric.

Similarly—and almost as a reflex—the United States discouraged and undermined Latin American initiatives in social and economic realms. It criticized the United Nations Economic Commission for Latin America

(ECLA), which pioneered comprehensive economic research in the region, for advocating national development planning and a Latin American common market because (as I was told at the time by senior American diplomats) it smacked of "socialism" and threatened free enterprise and foreign capital. When Juscelino Kubitschek, Brazil's visionary president and nation builder (including the city of Brasília), proposed in 1958 a plan for U.S.-Latin American cooperation for economic development under the name of the Pan-American Operation, the Eisenhower administration simply ignored him. Kubitschek's ideas predated Castro's social revolution in Cuba, but President Kennedy's Alliance for Progress in 1961, which was an alarmed response to Castro, was a carbon copy of the Brazilian concept. This is why, subsequently, signs proclaiming GRACIAS, FIDEL! appeared alongside schools, hospitals, and other projects financed by the Alliance for Progress.

Moreover, the United States could not make up its mind how to treat the phenomenon of collapsing military dictatorships in the mid- and late 1950's, with which it had immensely friendly relations and which it freely supplied with arms. It welcomed Perón's ouster in a military revolution in September 1955 principally because his *justicialismo* populist doctrine was increasingly anti-American (Perón always was Fidel Castro's hero even though he was a military ruler), and the generals who succeeded him were both conservative and pro-American. I was with General Eduardo Lonardi, the leader of the anti-Perón uprising, as we flew together from his provincial headquarters in Córdoba to assume power in Buenos Aires, and his first remark to me was "I hope the United States will support our democratic revolution." It did support it because there was no other alternative, but Perón, whom I visited several days later aboard a Paraguayan gunboat in Buenos Aires Harbor, where he lived in temporary asylum, complained that "you Americans were behind this imperialist coup. . . ."

Until they were overthrown by younger military officers responding to civilian pressures, the dictatorial regimes in Peru, Colombia, and Venezuela were cherished by Washington. When Batista seized power in Cuba in a military coup in 1952, the Truman administration accepted it without protest. The Eisenhower administration was probably unaware that Fidel Castro, freed from prison by Batista and exiled in Mexico in 1955, had landed with a small band of followers in eastern Cuba in December 1956 to launch his guerrilla war. When the Castro rebellion turned into a serious matter, the United States kept supplying Batista with arms almost until the end.

The American penchant for dictatorships (which often were guilty of political imprisonments, tortures, and murders) combined with the wave of nationalism increasingly sweeping the region in the late fifties created what turned out to be an unhealthy climate for a South American tour in May 1958 by Vice President Richard Nixon. The trip was meant to alter Latin American perceptions of the northern power in the aftermath of the fall of Colombian dictator Gustavo Rojas Pinilla in 1957 and Venezuelan dictator

Marcos Pérez Jiménez in January 1958, and it opened with a stop in Buenos Aires for the inauguration of Arturo Frondizi, a left-of-center civilian elected to the presidency in the first post-Perón elections.

Fidel Castro had not yet emerged on the hemisphere scene as the catalyzer of anti-American sentiments, but Nixon encountered the first resentments against the United States in the course of the Buenos Aires stay. I had been assigned by *The New York Times* to travel with him and realized very quickly that this would be more than a routine vice presidential journey. In La Paz, Bolivia, Nixon found himself booed, but the real explosion came the next day in Lima, Peru. We could feel the hostility as the motorcade drove through the city, and when Nixon went to visit San Marcos University (against the advice of the Peruvian police), we were attacked with stones, bricks, garbage, and spit in an explosion of youthful wrath no American statesman had ever encountered abroad.

The next stop was Quito, Ecuador, where no violence occurred, but where Nixon was exposed to a lesson in what does and what does not make the United States liked in foreign countries. As it happened, the New York Philharmonic-Symphony Orchestra with Dmitri Mitropoulos and the spectacular young conductor Leonard Bernstein was traveling in South America at the same time Nixon was, moving counterclockwise on its concert dates while we flew clockwise. The Philharmonic had scored tremendous successes playing in Caracas and Bogotá as an admirable institution while the Nixon party was being attacked by mobs as something less than an admirable American presence.

The two groups arrived in Quito on the same day and shared a gala dinner at the American Embassy. Later in the evening several reporters had a nightcap with Lenny Bernstein, comparing our divergent travel experiences. Bernstein was ecstatic over the reception for the orchestra in Latin American concert halls, but he complained that it was impossible to raise adequate money from the U.S. government to finance overseas tours by American musical and cultural groups. "Imagine," he said, "what we could show the world about the American culture if we just had the means. Why, do you realize that the cost of our entire South American tour is less than that of a wing of a B-52 jet bomber?"

Later that week Nixon was mobbed in Bogotá and was nearly killed in Caracas when wrathful mobs attacked his motorcade en route from the airport to the city. This was five months after American-backed dictator Pérez Jiménez had been ousted, and Venezuelans vented their fury against the United States (though there is no question that the attack was organized by extreme leftist groups in Caracas). As for the Philharmonic, it continued its musical tour of South America, eliciting more and more applause—almost in an inverse ratio to the assaults against Nixon. In Rio de Janeiro, for example, Bernstein conducted a concert for eighteen thousand Brazilians who filled every seat at a huge indoor basketball court at the local stadium, and the Philharmonic had to play the Brazilian national anthem to restore calm so that the players could get away to catch their plane at the airport. Otherwise, as Bernstein said later, "we would have been there all night, playing encore after encore."

The Philharmonic's South American tour was an unusually dramatic example—and contrast—of the impact of the United States on the rest of the world. Almost invariably, American musical presentations, theater troupes, writers and artists, and art exhibits have met in the postwar years with extraordinary appreciation abroad—in sophisticated Western Europe, subjugated Eastern Europe, and the emerging Third World countries. Intellectuals everywhere are familiar with William Faulkner, William Styron, and Saul Bellow. Much of the goodwill for America in the world, I think, stems from this artistic impact.

Unquestionably, American jazz is one of the greatest triumphs of native American culture abroad. World tours by such great jazz and blues musicians as Louis "Satchmo" Armstrong, going back to the mid-1930's, and Duke Ellington have attracted millions of admiring fans. Jazz was an instrument of success in the Cold War as well. Because jazz was regarded as decadent—and therefore forbidden—during the Stalinist era, veritable jazz-players' undergrounds came into being in the Soviet Union, Poland, and Czechoslovakia. Apart from American jazz musicians, their great hero was Willis Connover, the jazz disc jockey of the Voice of America, who probably had more impact in the Communist countries than any other single American. But because the law forbids the broadcast of Voice of America programs at home, Connover was completely unknown in America.

Another American jazz hero was a U.S. diplomat of my acquaintance who was a first-rate clarinetist and who during his assignment to the embassy in Prague in the early fifties devoted his free evenings to secret jam sessions with Czech students. Immediately after the war even sophisticated Paris was proud of Le Hot Jazz Club de France, which included several expatriate American musicians.

U.S. Army bands and visiting artists who entertained American occupation troops after the surrender introduced jazz to the new Japanese generations in a most surprising and spontaneous act of cultural penetration, and in the eighties Japan was totally jazz-crazy. The Japanese music publication *Shosha* says in a 1988 article that "in a closed circle of a defeated and disheartened society, suspicious of its own traditions of conformity, jazz blew like a fresh, clean wind of promise, individualism and explosive intellectual creativity." At least 150 jazz titles were pressed monthly on compact digital disks in the late 1980's (the Japanese instantly applying their newest technology to their favorite imported music), and cornetist Terumasa Hino, alto saxophonist Sadao Watanabe, and pianists Toshiko Akiyoshi and Makoto Ozone became quite well known in the United States.

Now that jazz has won acceptance in the Soviet Union, I saw it sanctioned on the highest level when I spotted Raisa Gorbachev a few seats away at the premiere of a Soviet-American production of Duke Ellington's

Sophisticated Lady at the most prestigious Moscow concert hall in September 1988. That happened to be the day her husband was formally elected president of the Soviet Union (following a deft coup d'état in the Politburo twenty-four hours earlier), but this did not distract her from applauding "Take the 'A' Train" and all the other great Ellington tunes. Spending a night at the royal palace in Paro in the Himalayan kingdom of Bhutan in October 1989, I tuned in my short-wave radio to a fabulous program of Basin Street jazz—to find out it was being broadcast in the international service of Radio Moscow (the next day, palace servants told me they often listen to jazz: Voice of America or Moscow, whichever they can find on the dial).

East and West, Hollywood pictures have mesmerized the world since the thirties, and a half century later they continue to convey a magic, if often distorted, image of America, to ignite intellectual debates and to turn American actors into celebrities from Cannes to Warsaw and from Caracas to Beijing. Taken together, then, the surge and attraction of American culture, however it is defined, remain a foundation for a unique relationship between the United States and all the other worlds.

It would be misleading to suggest that the United States was wholly unaware of the needs and travails of the nascent Third World in the wake of the Second World War. In fact, American support for the economies and societies of the Third World, especially in the 1940's and 1950's, may have been crucial in their survival.

Thus, as early as June 1949, Truman requested Congress to provide funds for technical assistance to underdeveloped nations under what was known as his Point Four legislation (because it was the fourth point in his message on foreign assistance). In his 1950 State of the Union message, he said that "if the ideas of freedom and representative government are to prevail in these areas," it was essential that "their people experience in their own lives the benefits of scientific and economic advantage."

The first Point Four appropriation was $34.5 million, not an insignificant amount in those days, and by 1951, 350 American technicians were working on more than a hundred technical cooperation projects in twenty-seven countries. In the next four decades tens of billions of dollars went into worldwide foreign assistance. India alone, critical as it often was of American policies, received $12.1 billion in American economic development assistance between 1951 and 1985, nearly the amount spent on the Marshall Plan for all of Western Europe. This included 2 million tons of wheat to avert famine in the face of crop shortages in the 1950's (two thirds of its rupees sale value was given outright to India for economic development projects). In part because of American aid, India was able to increase food grain production from 50 million tons in 1947 to 150 million in 1987, becoming self-sufficient in food though the population doubled during the same period.

Writing about American responses to decolonization and the awesome problems of the new nations, Dean Acheson sums it up in these words: "Attacking a multiplicity of problems with large appropriations of our resources and almost missionary fervor, we threw ourselves into providing, directly and through international organizations, capital, education and technological instruction. Again we learned the immensity of the task and the strength of the four horsemen of the enemy—human fecundity, human ignorance, human pugnacity, and human stubbornness. Foreign aid remains both a noble aim and a dirty word. Here we must be content with hoping that we gave a lead and a sample of what the best might be."

Forty years after Harry Truman inaugurated America's economic assistance to impoverished lands, considerable perspective has been gained on the function and results of foreign aid, including the realization that it will never be enough because Third World ever-mounting needs simply cannot be satisfied in our time. It was Richard Nixon who, rather sadly, made that point to me. Early in 1989 we happened to meet aboard an airliner between New York and Washington, and I mentioned to him that—incredibly— *thirty-one years* had elapsed since our Lima and Caracas adventures. "Yes," Nixon said, "It *was* such a long time ago, but don't you find that the same problems that plagued Latin America when you and I went there are still plaguing the Latins?"

But not only the United States was being challenged by the Third World in the fifties. In Africa, Asia, the Middle East, and Latin America demands rose for freedom and self-assertion from the colonial powers. The instability of the Third World was endemic and rising, and it was threatening the stability of Western Europe as well.

In 1958, as a result of an unbelievable chain of events, Third World defiance brought France, the immensely civilized cradle of revolutionary liberty, to the brink of a right-wing military dictatorship and a civil war. Notwithstanding its Indochina defeat in May 1954, France was unwilling to consider independence—or even "equality"—for its three North African possessions: Algeria, Morocco, and Tunisia.

In the case of Algeria in particular, France seemed to prefer a new war to concessions to the National Liberation Front, and in November 1954 the French intransigence triggered the explosion of the awesomely bloody Algerian insurrection. Curiously, it was the Radical Socialist government of Premier Pierre Mendès-France, the man who earlier that year had extricated his country from the Indochinese War after the fall of Dien Bien Phu, that took the uncompromising hard line. Addressing a National Assembly commission, Interior Minister François Mitterrand (who became the Third World's leading advocate after he was elected president of France in 1981) flatly rejected any idea of negotiating with the "rebels," assuring the deputies that if "war" were imposed on France, the challenge would be met without the slightest hesitation.

The war came instantly, and for the next three years it was an unspeakably savage contest of wills between the colonized and the colonizers, rich in cruelty, torture, and murder practiced by both bands in addition to continuous military encounters. Winning the terrible Battle of Algiers and liquidating much of the National Liberation Front leadership, the French remained unable to put down the rebellion, which by 1958 had turned into an overarching political crisis in Algeria as well as in the metropolis. For the large French colonial population of Algeria, the non-Arab *pieds-noirs* (black feet), the destruction of the rebellion was a matter of economic survival. For the French armed forces, it was a matter of honor to vanquish the Algerians; it was intolerable that a half million of the best troops, including the elite Foreign Legion, could not put down twenty-five thousand urban and rural guerrillas. Following the debacles of World War II and then Indochina and Suez, a defeat in North Africa was simply unacceptable.

In its fourth year, however, the Algerian War was dividing France as it had not been divided since 1940, when Charles de Gaulle escaped to London to pursue the war and Marshal Pétain remained behind in Vichy to collaborate with the Nazis. The Mendès-France government had fallen in 1956, and succeeding Cabinets of the collapsing Fourth Republic, born at the liberation in 1945, with De Gaulle at its head, could no longer control the situation. And now it was again Charles de Gaulle, absent from power for eleven years, who was emerging as the central personage of the new French tragedy. It was a bit more than a coincidence.

The great crisis took shape during April 1958. The Algeria-based French Army, fearful that civilians at home would seek an armistice with the rebels and reduce military appropriations, demanded more resources and a free hand to destroy the enemy. In mid-April Premier Félix Gaillard was ousted by the National Assembly as a result of a complex manuever by a group of traditional Gaullists, to be replaced by René Pleven, who had been De Gaulle's finance minister and whose first move was to encourage the generals in Algiers to exact a commitment from the government that Algeria would never cease to be "an integral part of France." Simultaneously committees were formed demanding that De Gaulle assume power, though the general himself remained silent at his village retreat at Colombey.

On May 9 the military commanders in Algiers concluded that France required a government of "national salvation" on the model of the French Revolution to purify its political structure—and, of course, to keep Algeria under its banner. To do so, they drafted a secret plan for an armed coup to overthrow by force the Cabinet in Paris and, possibly, set up a military junta, an unprecedented event in contemporary Western Europe. They sent a virtual ultimatum to President René Coty (whose powers under the Fourth Republic were largely confined to the choice of prime ministers) to protect the interests of the army and Algerian populations or face "desperate" consequences. At Colombey De Gaulle was kept posted of the developments hour by hour.

The next step in this political intrigue was to force out the Pleven Cabinet and to push President Coty to turn to Pierre Pflimlin, who had just publicly called for a cease-fire in Algeria, to form a new government. As Mitterrand remarked at the time, this was the "suicide" of the Fourth Republic. The great crisis entered its final phase on May 12, when General Raoul Salan, the commander in chief in Algeria, issued a warning that "disorders" would occur unless De Gaulle were recalled to power as the only man who could guarantee that Algeria would remain French. On May 13 hundreds of thousands of French *pieds-noirs* demonstrated in Algiers for De Gaulle's return. But the sixty-seven-year-old general continued his silence.

On May 14 the generals in Algiers formed their own National Salvation Committee, no longer recognizing the authority of the government in Paris and still waiting for De Gaulle to accept power. They set May 28 as the date for landing troops in Paris in the event that parliament refused to name De Gaulle to be prime minister, or that De Gaulle, as prime minister, needed military support to remain in power, or that a Communist coup, endangering the republic, required military intervention.

Code-named Operation Resurrection, the generals' plan provided for dropping on Paris two paratroop regiments from Algeria and two paratroop regiments from bases in the southwest of France. The *paras* would then occupy all the strategic centers in the capital as well as parliament, the office of the prime minister, and the Eiffel Tower—and De Gaulle would assume power. Still, the generals desired a formal approval for Operation Resurrection from De Gaulle, and they delayed the attack. On May 29 an emissary of the Algiers generals was informed by De Gaulle's representatives in Paris that "you can launch the operation."

Clearly the general was a master of brinksmanship. In the afternoon of May 30 the first six aircraft with the paratroopers took off for Paris from the southwest, but they were ordered to turn back when the military chiefs were informed that President Coty would receive De Gaulle in the evening to offer him the government. To avert what appeared as imminent civil war— all Frenchmen were unlikely to accept passively a military coup—Coty and the leaders of the political parties accepted the general's conditions that he could exercise "full powers" for six months, governing without parliament.

On June 2, 1958, he was again the prime minister of France with powers that parliament had refused him eleven years earlier, pushing him into political self-exile. More than a decade later, when he was again out of politics, Charles de Gaulle wrote in his memoirs that he had realized in May that an explosion was imminent, that it was clear that France faced subversion with the arrival of paratroopers in Paris to establish "a military dictatorship," and that a civil war would ensue unless "a national authority" could take the country in hand. He added: "This authority could only be mine."

Historians may debate whether Charles de Gaulle had contrived the military crisis in order to regain power. It is probable that he did so to arrest what he perceived as a decomposition of France's body politic as a result of the Algerian War. But it is certain that his ultimate objective—naturally unrevealed in May 1958—was to end the conflict with a grant of independence to Algeria when the time was ripe; De Gaulle understood the forces of history. Indeed, he gave the Algerians their freedom in fewer than five years, risking but preempting another civil war.

France and De Gaulle had weathered in the spring of 1958 one of Europe's most serious postwar crises, a crisis resulting from a Third World challenge and endangering the whole concept of orderliness that the big powers sought to maintain globally. Still, neither France nor its allies, notably the United States, were able to develop intellectual, political, and economic mechanisms to deal with the Third World's quintessential threat to that orderliness. Their instinct was to think, as they had always done, in terms of broad geopolitics and most particularly of the basic East-West rivalry. As the fifties were drawing to an end, the West still could not comprehend that the realities of the Third World were inseparable from the totality of international life.

Barely two months after the Algerian crisis, the Third World demonstrated anew its potential for creating trouble for the West. This time the locus was the Middle East. On July 14 (as France celebrated Bastille Day), leftist officers ousted the royal government in Iraq, the oil-rich nation that was little more than a British protectorate. The Baghad coup alarmed the British and the Americans to an extraordinary degree because it appeared to be part of an expanding pattern of hostility to the West and capitalism in the Middle East. In Egypt Colonel Nasser had inaugurated "Arab socialism" after nationalizing the Suez Canal and surviving the Anglo-French-Israeli invasion—ironically, thanks to the United States. Syria, also proclaiming adherence to "Arab socialism," had merged with Egypt to form the United Arab Republic. Now with Iraq in this camp, much of the Middle East seemed to have gone over to the enemy.

In Anglo-American perceptions this enemy was the Soviet Union, increasingly busy making friends and gaining influence in the region. After John Foster Dulles had changed his mind about American financing for the Aswan High Dam on the Nile—a top-priority Egyptian development project—for wholly mysterious reasons, the Russians stepped in to help Nasser build it. To complicate matters even more, a political-religious conflict erupted in Lebanon, a former French territory adjacent to Syria. This incipient civil war pitted conservative Christians led by President Camille Chamoun against pro-Nasser and leftist Muslims, and instantly fears arose in Washington that Syrian leftists supported by the Egyptians and the Iraqis would grab Lebanon in an action presumably orchestrated by Moscow.

Because Washington had no grasp of Levantine politics and did not have the sense to consult the French, who knew well their former client states (the British were providing advice that was both bad and nervous), it allowed

itself to be stampeded into a foolish reaction. This was the decision by
Eisenhower on the recommendation of Secretary of State Dulles to intervene militarily in Lebanon, the start of a thirty-year American drama on
those beaches.

Thus ten thousand marines landed in Beirut in mid-August in an operation rendered even more bizarre by the spectacle of American Ambassador
Robert McClintock, a veteran career officer, greeting the troops from his
limousine as they came ashore. His little dog sat next to the driver in the
front seat. The British, not to be left out of the Middle East rescue enterprise, dispatched three thousand paratroopers to Amman to assure that Jordan's King Hussein, a client of Britain, came to no harm from his leftist
neighbors in Iraq. Jordan, too, was to live in perpetual turbulence as regional and big power interests clashed and intersected in the sands of the
Middle East.

The Marines accomplished nothing useful in Lebanon (except for inspiring Nikita Khrushchev in Moscow to engage in vague threats of using the
atom bomb against the Americans over the Beirut affray) and departed before too long. The U.S. Marine Corps was to return there a quarter century
later to be trapped in a tragedy that was as unnecessary as its inconclusive
intervention in 1958. By 1990 Lebanese Christians and Muslims continued
to slaughter each other, pulverizing the once-beautiful city of Beirut in the
process. The West's Third World misunderstandings never seemed to end.

Within months of the intervention in Lebanon, the United States had to
face another Third World dilemma, this time once more in the Western
Hemisphere. On New Year's Eve 1958 General Batista fled Cuba for the
Dominican Republic as his army and government collapsed in the face of
the rebellion led by Fidel Castro in the forests of the Sierra Maestra and in
the Cuban cities where his 26th of July Movement had been fighting for two
years.

The bearded thirty-two-year-old lawyer and guerrilla chief soon assumed
full political power in Havana, setting in motion a profound social revolution and affecting to a vast degree the political equilibrium in Latin America. The Eisenhower administration, a faithful supporter of the Batista
regime, was taken by surprise by Castro's victory, principally because American intelligence in Cuba was shockingly inefficient, never capable of conveying an accurate picture of what had been happening on the island since
the rebels landed there two years earlier. Newsmen in Cuba were better
informed than the CIA, a shortcoming that the agency never knew how to
correct.

Once Castro had won, the United States did not know how to handle
him. When he visited Washington in April 1959 in a private capacity,
Eisenhower chose to go out of town to play golf. Nixon, however, received
Castro for a long conversation from which the two men emerged with a
considerable dislike of each other. During that first year the United States

had no coherent policy toward revolutionary Cuba though Castro knew exactly where he was going with his nationalizations of American property. By the end of 1959 relations had deteriorated to the point where the CIA began planning his overthrow. Iran and Guatemala had worked so well; why not Cuba?

As for Eisenhower, South Asia was giving him the kind of welcome an American President deserved. Visiting India in December, he helped restore the warm ties that had existed before the disputes over Korea and Indochina, and the tour was something of a Third World honeymoon for Ike. An estimated one million Indians greeted him in New Delhi, Prime Minister Nehru displayed his immense charm, and the President had the opportunity of pledging that the United States would pursue a "worldwide war against hunger." He told an immense crowd that "we can eliminate the hunger that emaciates the bodies of children; that scars the souls of their parents; that stirs the passions of those who toil endlessly and earn only scraps."

The 1950's was a decade of fundamental transition for the entire world from the aftershocks of World War II to a new era of totally altered relationships among nations and peoples and to a precarious and fragile peace. Fabulous advances were made in the sciences, health care, and education in the course of this evolution from wartime to peacetime, and new horizons of fantastic discovery loomed ahead.

Then the wild sixties rolled around, and nothing would be the same again.

BOOK FIVE

THE SIXTIES

I have a dream. . . .
—MARTIN LUTHER KING, JR., 1963

I

*T*he decade of the 1960's was one of marvelous dreams.
It also was a decade of frightful nightmares.

The 1960's burst forth with the hope and promise of a brave, innovative, and humane age. The Second World War and its aftermath receded into history, and now it was the time of joy and flowers, song and music and dance—before being overshadowed by tragedy upon tragedy.

In the United States John Fitzgerald Kennedy, at forty-three the youngest American President—and the first Roman Catholic to be elected to the presidency as religious prejudices finally began to crumble—captured imaginations with his sense of vision, his New Frontier, and his engagingly youthful looks. His impact was even greater abroad than it was at home (a Brazilian newspaper columnist wrote of Kennedy's narrow-margin election that "if Brazilians could have voted, he would have won by seventy million votes . . .").

Kennedy inspired American blacks to pursue their dream of equality with his commitment to an aggressive observance of constitutionally guaranteed civil rights, and he inspired the poor to believe that poverty in America must end (he kept repeating that every night seven million Americans went to sleep hungry). He launched the United States on the conquest of space, charting the course of the astronauts to the moon, and achieved the first nuclear arms control accord with the Soviets. He created the Peace Corps, drawing on the idealism of young Americans keen to help the Third World.

In Rome John XXIII, indisputably the most extraordinary twentieth-century pontiff, brought the ancient church into modernity, restoring its often forgotten dedication to universal compassion, with the three years of the labors of the Second Vatican Council. "Papa Giovanni," as he was lovingly called, was a powerful intellectual as well as spiritual force in his time of papacy, short as it was, a statesman on a world scale, and an ardent believer in ecumenism and limitless religious tolerance.

In Prague "Marxism with a Human Face" emerged in 1968 to challenge Stalinist orthodox communism in a revival of the Polish and Hungarian gestures of democratic assertion of the past decade. This Prague Spring for the brief period of its life was a warm and emotional glow of freedom as Czechoslovaks, young and old and from medieval Charles University to the steel mills of the sooty suburbs, debated the past and the future and listened to great musicians, who converged on the banks of Vltava River for the spring festival among the golden spires of the Bohemian capital. These were intoxicating days for the people of Prague and for foreign journalists who strove to comprehend the phenomenon of "human Marxism" and to convey it to the world beyond. It was a magnificent dream.

The counterpoint to the dreams of the sixties were the nightmares.

The worst of them were the wars, old and new. For Americans the entire decade was darkened by the Vietnam War, which seemed never to end, tearing asunder the fabric of the national life, dividing the country as it had not been divided since the Civil War a century earlier, spawning riots and hatreds, and transforming the society in multiple deep ways. The American instinct for intervention, not dampened by Kennedy, also led to the Bay of Pigs in Cuba and the invasion of the Dominican Republic.

France suffered the Algerian War and its violent consequences in the first half of the decade, once more threatened by civil war. Liberation wars in Portugal's African colonies broke out in 1961, to last thirteen years. Israel fought the victorious Six-Day War against its hostile Arab neighbors, but real peace went on eluding it. Saudi Arabia and Egypt conducted a proxy war in Yemen. India battled China and Pakistan in separate armed conflicts. In western Africa the province of Biafra lost the secession war with Nigeria, and mass starvation of civilian populations became the new weapon in Third World conflicts. There was an Algerian-Moroccan war as soon as the two North African states became free of France.

Revolutions, most of them born of the convulsions of liberation from colonialism, raged from the Congo (later renamed Zaire) to Indonesia, with the United States playing a more or less covert role in them. Democracy fared ill in Latin America, where military coups ousted elected civilian governments in Argentina, Brazil, the Dominican Republic, and Peru.

And the threat of nuclear East-West confrontations arose when the East German regime, supported by the Kremlin, erected the wall between East and West Berlin and when, the following year, Nikita Khrushchev deployed atomic weapons in Cuba to defy the United States. The Soviet invasion of Czechoslovakia, designed to liquidate "Marxism with a Human Face," posed no such menace (the West was not about to defend Czechoslovak freedoms in 1968, any more than it had in 1938 and 1948), but it froze superpower relations for a time.

On another level, unprecedented youth rebellions—total challenges to the status quo—swept the United States, France, West Germany, Italy, and Mexico. In each instance these revolts were triggered against specific policies of the governments (like the antiwar movement in the United States), but the protesting new generations were basically questioning the existing social order (borrowing language from the left, their militants were venting their resentments on the "bourgeoisie"), and there is no question that the uprisings of the sixties left a permanent mark.

In the United States racial tensions and "long hot summer" explosions in the ghettos from Newark, New Jersey, to Detroit and Washington, D.C., punctuated the course of the civil rights campaigns, as did the killings of black and white activists in the struggle for racial equality. Endemic poverty in the inner cities combined with the constraints imposed by segregation (Atlanta, for example, did not integrate its public schools until 1961) to raise pressures in the American society.

The seemingly unsolvable contradiction of expanding poverty in the world's most affluent nation was analyzed for the first time in an in-depth fashion by the late Michael Harrington, the old-line American Socialist, in his 1962 book *The Other America: Poverty in the United States*. In this classic study Harrington informed his fellow citizens that existing in this country was an "underclass" of tens of millions, people living below the poverty line, even if employed, and neglected by the rest of the society. In the nearly three decades that followed Harrington's alarm bell, successive administrations claimed they waged "wars against poverty" (like Lyndon Johnson's Great Society), but by the end of the eighties there were more Americans below the poverty line than ever (in absolute and relative terms), and the phenomenon of the homeless was a new scourge on rich America.

What ultimately did away with American innocence were the stunning assassinations in the sixties: John F. Kennedy in 1963, his brother Robert F. Kennedy in 1968, and the Reverend Martin Luther King, Jr., that same year. At the end of the eighties the motives for the three killings were still a mystery. We continue ignorant of the dark forces that were at work in those years that so deeply wounded the soul of this nation.

II

The Vietnam War tortured the American soul as no foreign war had ever done before.

For all practical purposes, this war began under Kennedy late in 1961, though Americans did not realize for several years that the United States had trapped itself in another land war in Asia.

It lasted the entire decade, spilling well over into the seventies. In the sixties, it was roughly divided in three stages: the Kennedy period of gradual escalation until his death in November 1963; the Lyndon Johnson period from 1964 to 1968, when the administration was convinced that victory over

Vietnamese Communists was possible through massive aerial bombings and the buildup of American troops on the ground to a level in excess of a half million; and the final phase, starting with the triumphant Communist Tet offensive in 1968 when the United States and its Saigon ally clearly began to lose the war, and peace negotiations opened in Paris. The Nixon period, which began with his inauguration in 1969, was to lead within four more years to the "peace with honor" American withdrawal from Vietnam.

In one sense, it is difficult to understand Kennedy's decision to commit the United States to a war in Vietnam though it could be argued that he never contemplated a full-fledged engagement and that his policies during his fewer than three years in the White House were a limited operation aimed simply at training, advising, and shoring up the South Vietnamese Army. But of course, events have a way of getting out of hand and acquiring a life of their own—especially when they are handled in a secretive fashion vis-à-vis domestic public opinion.

Kennedy, running against Richard Nixon, was perceived as a "liberal" candidate, a modern statesman who understood the changing postwar world, and a man of peace, who would seek compromise and agreement rather than confrontation in world affairs. This, in fact, was one aspect of Kennedy's personality, and there was every reason to assume that his empathy with the Third World would move him toward a settlement in the renascent Vietnamese Civil War. With the French gone, the situation developing in Vietnam in the late fifties and the start of the sixties was a fratricidal conflict, and it probably should have been left that way.

The new President's background predisposed him against what might have been called American neocolonialism represented by the intervention in Vietnam. Arthur M. Schlesinger, Jr., a close friend and adviser, writes in A Thousand Days that as a senator in the mid-fifties Kennedy "had begun to see in Algeria the same pattern of colonial decay he had already inspected in Southeast Asia; and he feared that French intransigence would have the same outcome of uniting the nationalists with the communists." In a Senate speech in 1957 (this was before General de Gaulle's return to power), Kennedy accused the French government of repeating in Algeria the errors of the past, notably in refusing to accept the reality of nationalism.

What, then, pushed Kennedy to disregard his own opinions four years later and, like the French in Indochina and Algeria, refuse to accept this reality of nationalism? In hindsight, probably the best answer is that the President concluded that with communism on the offensive everywhere (or so it seemed in Washington) and with the United States saddled with major failures during his first six months in office, he had no choice but to stand behind the Ngo Dinh Diem regime in Vietnam. Kennedy inherited the commitment to the Diem regime from Eisenhower—as he inherited the Cuban exile force trained to overthrow Fidel Castro—and in both situations he chose to honor these inheritances rather than seek alternatives.

In short, Kennedy was embracing firm anti-Communist policies because he thought that his and America's credibility were at stake if he acted in any other fashion but also because he genuinely believed that the Soviet Union and its allies had become an imminent danger to the security of the United States.

The President had foreshadowed his world policies in his inaugural address though perhaps he was not adequately understood. In one of the most memorable passages of the speech, he said, "Let every nation know, whether it wishes us well or ill, that we shall pay any price, bear any burden, meet any hardship, support any friend, oppose any foe to assure the survival and the success of liberty."

All of it was more easily said than done in a world that Kennedy said in another context was "not fair." He was to learn very soon how hard it was to pay a price and bear a burden to achieve these noble American objectives and how complex it was to define liberty, let alone its survival and success.

Thus, in mid-April 1961, Castro's forces decimated the exiles' brigade, trained by the CIA in Guatemala and landed by CIA-chartered ships on the beaches of southern Cuba, and clearly this was a painful defeat for American prestige. Kennedy, of course, had had the power to cancel the invasion—since his election, when he was first apprised of the Bay of Pigs plan, he had agonized over it—but all his advisers (except for Senator William Fulbright of Arkansas, who had a mind of his own) urged him to let the exiles attack. Interestingly, all the liberals in the Kennedy entourage pushed for it; it was a harbinger of the attitudes that were developing toward the Vietnam dilemma.

This problem had been festering since following the French debacle and the Geneva Conference in 1954, the United States had assumed, for all practical purposes, the responsibility for the survival of a non-Communist South Vietnam. In the aftermath of Geneva, Eisenhower had written Ngo Dinh Diem, then the new prime minister, assuring him of American support "in developing and maintaining a strong viable state, capable of resisting attempted subversion or aggression through military means." General Lansdale had rushed to Saigon at the same time to start putting a South Vietnamese government and military structure in place, and by 1957 General Samuel T. Williams, who headed the new U.S. Military Advisory Group there, already had 342 American trainers at his disposal. At the end of Eisenhower's term this number had risen to 685 Americans, the limit imposed by the Geneva Conference.

Still on Eisenhower's watch, in March 1960 Vietnamese Communists in the South unveiled their National Liberation Front, marking the start of open warfare against Saigon. Post-Vietnam Communist accounts made available in Hanoi indicate that Ho Chi Minh had not planned a concerted offensive that early in South Vietnam (he wanted to consolidate better the 1954 victory), but he had to back his southern comrades, and North Vietnam became formally committed to the new war in September 1960.

Eisenhower's final contribution to what the United States hoped would be a relatively easy solution in Vietnam was to instruct the Pentagon to develop a counterinsurgency program, which strangely, the American armed forces had never had. Even with the examples of Indochina, Algeria, Indonesia, Cuba, and Malaya facing them as examples of a new dimension of warfare, U.S. military chiefs continued to think in terms of conventional wars and firepower superiority.

When Kennedy entered office, he had no real awareness of how the situation in South Vietnam had deteriorated. What concerned him to an enormous extent was the fate of Laos, the small kingdom in western Indochina, and, according to Arthur Schlesinger, "in the first two months of his administration he probably spent more time on Laos than on anything else." Though the Geneva agreement had provided for the Communist Pathet Lao guerrillas, who had also fought the French, to join a new Laotian "national community," the Eisenhower administration decided that Laos should become "a bulwark against communism," very much the same as South Vietnam. Over a five-year period the United States invested some three hundred million dollars in that chaotic country of two million inhabitants, but it turned out to be wholly counterproductive.

The Pathet Lao went back on the warpath, forcing the American-backed government to accept the guerrillas in a coalition government. The United States responded by having the CIA organize a rightist government under a Laotian career army officer who had fought with the French in the Indochina War, and now the kingdom had two governments. Late in 1960 the Soviet Union began to airlift food, oil, and arms to the coalition regime, and Kennedy had a ready-made foreign policy crisis the moment he moved into the Oval Office.

In a broader sense, the President was discovering the extent of torment the Third World was imposing on the United States and the West from Asia and Africa to the Caribbean. Soon he would also realize the Western propensity to shoot itself in the foot in trying to cope with this new wave of defiance, a propensity that the passage of ensuing decades did not arrest. Early in 1960, for instance, Fidel Castro and the Soviet Union entered into their first agreement (Eisenhower's planning for the Bay of Pigs started a month later). In September, Castro and Khrushchev met and embraced at a dilapidated hotel in New York's Harlem, where the Cuban premier was staying during the session of the United Nations General Assembly (Khrushchev resided at the elegant East Side compound of the Soviet Mission to the UN), sealing their alliance. Then Khrushchev delivered a milestone speech pledging Soviet support to all wars of national liberation, which Kennedy read as a confirmation of his suspicion that it was principally Soviet hegemony appetites that the United States had to face in Laos and Vietnam as well as in Cuba and the Congo.

But as the Eisenhower administration had done, the Kennedy White House tended to concentrate more on the "international communism" aspects of Third World crises than on the fundamental phenomenon of nationalism, a state of affairs from which the Soviet Union was increasingly benefiting. Except for Cuba, where Khrushchev knew he had a potential strategic advantage of vast proportions, the Russians were running their Third World policies at a small cost—the liberation wars were fought by the locals, not by Soviet soldiers—and they enjoyed the spectacle of the Americans becoming directly trapped all over the world.

Late in March 1961, in fact, some of Kennedy's top advisers proposed that the United States dispatch a limited military force to the Mekong River valley to demonstrate the American resolve to save Southeast Asia from communism. Military chiefs told the President it had to be a major enterprise—tens of thousands of troops backed by tactical nuclear weapons or nothing—and the compromise was to land five hundred helicopter-borne marines on the Thailand side of the Mekong River.

In April, Cuba and Laos converged in Kennedy's mind as related challenges. The same day that it became obvious that the Bay of Pigs had failed, April 20, he authorized American military advisers in Laos to start wearing their uniforms (up to then they had gone around in sports shirts in a feeble attempt at deception) and to accompany Laotian troops into combat. This move—and the threat of others—did work because the Soviets tended to draw back when challenged though the United States had not yet grasped their on-the-cheap approach to crises. On May 11, as a result of Moscow's advice, the Pathet Lao accepted a cease-fire and the fighting in Laos ended.

Success in Laos and what Kennedy perceived as continued Soviet attempts to "test" him served to convince him that the United States could not evade its responsibilities in Vietnam. He knew that would inevitably mean some form of American military presence there, and once he had reached that decision with his small circle of intimate advisers, he could not be dissuaded from it. During his meetings with President de Gaulle in Paris early in June as part of a visit that turned out to be a spectacular public success for Kennedy and his wife, Jacqueline, the subject of Southeast Asia came up repeatedly because both men realized the importance of that region to Western strategy. De Gaulle cautioned him against engaging ground forces in Vietnam or Laos because, in his opinion, it would not be tenable either militarily or politically, but Kennedy did not agree with his host.

For one thing, the President had developed the notion that the United States could act successfully to checkmate Communist advances in Vietnam if it possessed a counterinsurgency capability sufficient to match the unconventional warfare of the guerrillas. He also thought that the Communist insurgency had to be countered with political and social-economic measures that would win "the hearts and the minds" of the Vietnamese peasants. Kennedy then applied the "hearts and minds" concept to the grandiose plan of the Alliance for Progress development program for Latin America that he had announced in March, just a month before the Bay of Pigs invasion.

Theoretically, as is now clear, the President was absolutely right on both counts. He naiveté lay in the reality that the national leaders in the countries facing Communist threats—not the United States—had to do the winning of "hearts and minds" of their own people, that counterinsurgency techniques were workable only where the military had the support of the people.

Impressed by the fact that Colonel Lansdale and President Magsaysay in the Philippines were able to defeat the Huks by applying unconventional warfare tactics, and, at the other end of the spectrum, by Fidel Castro's revolutionary victory in Cuba, Kennedy made counterinsurgency his personal top-priority project. The Army's Special Warfare Center at Fort Bragg, North Carolina (the home of the Eighty-second Airborne Division, America's premier elite unit), was given the task of expanding the Special Forces to be able to respond to emergencies everywhere in the world, and a Counter-Insurgency Committee was established under General Maxwell Taylor, who was Kennedy's personal military adviser at the White House. Having heard about *On Guerrilla Warfare*, the manual written by Ernesto "Che" Guevara, the Argentine physician who was Castro's companion in the Sierra Maestra, the President ordered it translated from Spanish into English for the benefit of the Special Forces and Foreign Service officials, who were likewise instructed to learn about counterinsurgency and "hearts and minds." He also made them read Sun-tzu, the Chinese military genius of 500 B.C. and the father of spies. Even foreign correspondents with Third World experience were drafted to lecture on these subjects, often improvising as they went along (as I had to do when addressing a class at the National War College and prospective military attachés at the Defense Intelligence Agency). And a new American military romance was born with the Green Berets.

Kennedy's view that South Vietnam had to be saved was further reinforced by Vice President Lyndon Johnson, who undertook a fact-finding tour of Asia for Kennedy in May, just before Kennedy was to meet De Gaulle. In language that reflected the patronizing way in which Americans generally regarded the Third World, Johnson recommended streamlined military aid to Saigon (but no American combat troops) and social and economic policies Diem should be made to adopt if he were to win any hearts. This is how Johnson put it: "It would be useful to enunciate more clearly than we have—for the guidance of these young and unsophisticated nations—what we expect or require of them."

Kennedy's own foreign travel that late spring took him from Paris to Vienna for meetings with Khrushchev. The result bordered on disaster as the two men disagreed on Berlin (Khrushchev still wanted the Allies out of the divided city), nuclear test ban treaties (Kennedy was for them, Khrushchev against), Laos, and just about everything else. Kennedy believed that the Bay of Pigs defeat had placed him at a disadvantage with Khrushchev, and his impression was correct: The Russian thought that the young President was indecisive, and Khrushchev's future actions stemmed from this judgment. Roy Medvedev sums it up this way in his Khrushchev biography: "It is clear that Khrushchev and Kennedy did not understand each other very well. Each man underestimated his opponent. They became acquainted not through polite discussions in Vienna but through two international crises—the Berlin crisis of 1961 and the Cuban crisis of 1962."

New historical materials that became available in Moscow in the late 1980's showed that Khrushchev made the fatal mistake of concluding that Kennedy's failure to order American warplanes to support and save the Cuban exiles at the Bay of Pigs was due to weakness or irresolution, not to a firm political decision not to involve the United States directly in a war with Cuba.

This misapprehension presumably led Khrushchev to trigger the latest Berlin crisis on August 13, 1961, when East Germany closed all the crossing points between the eastern and western sectors of the city by ordering troops and the police to set up roadblocks. Four days later the East Germans began erecting the Berlin Wall that would keep the city physically divided until November 9, 1989. Whether the Berlin move came because of the massive flight of East Germans to West Germany or because Khrushchev made it part of his continuing pressure to change the city's postwar status quo (or both), the administration interpreted it as the most serious crisis facing the United States since 1945. It could not be ruled out that the Russians were preparing for a nuclear confrontation (though Kennedy personally did not believe it), and there was consensus that an energetic response had to be given Moscow. Consequently, Vice President Johnson flew to Berlin to offer assurances that Berlin would be defended, and fifteen hundred American troops moved in convoy from West Germany across East Germany to Berlin. Again the Soviets relaxed their diplomatic pressures on Berlin, and the crisis ended—although the wall stood for over twenty-eight years.

Vietnam, however, would not go away. Reports from the field left no doubt that the Saigon regime could not stem the Vietcong insurgency (Vietcong was the name given by the Americans to the Vietnamese Communists in the South to distinguish them from the regular North Vietnamese Army), and Kennedy resolved that action was required. In October he dispatched General Taylor and Walt W. Rostow, who was deputy special assistant to the President for national security affairs (he was an economist with counterinsurgency as an avocation), to take a hard look at South Vietnam and to make recommendations. In a way Kennedy was organizing a self-fulfilling prophecy: Taylor and Rostow were hard-liners on Vietnam, and the only question was the dimension of U.S. intervention they would propose. Secretary of State Rusk and his department were left out of this exercise, suggesting that the President now saw Vietnam as chiefly a military equation.

Taylor and Rostow urged Kennedy to increase substantially the American direct involvement in what was still categorized as a civil war—perhaps the assignment of as many as ten thousand men for self-defense combat duties in the context of training and advising the South Vietnamese—but the President had a residue of doubt. Schlesinger quotes him as saying, "They want a force of American troops . . . they say it's necessary to restore confidence and maintain morale. But it will be just like Berlin. The troops will march in; the bands will play; the crowds will cheer; and in four days everyone will have forgotten. Then we will be told we have to send in more troops. It's like taking a drink. The effect wears off, and you have to take another." Schlesinger's own interpretation was that Taylor and Rostow had recommended "a shift from arm's-length advice to limited partnership."

In December Kennedy acted to set in motion what was to be the decade-long American war in Vietnam. He named General Paul Harkins, a Taylor protégé and an officer with conventional views and background, to assume the command of U.S. forces in the country, instructing him to work hand in hand with the American ambassador in Saigon, Frederick Nolting, a career Foreign Service officer with ideas that differed little from the general's. It remained American policy until the end to maintain the impression that the general and the ambassador were equals so that the total effort would appear to be both military and political (in practice it depended on the opinions of the general and the ambassador at a given time who was more equal than the other).

On the last day of 1961 there were 3,200 American advisers in Vietnam, and openly so. The United States no longer felt bound by the Geneva Conference's restrictions on the number of foreign military personnel in South Vietnam inasmuch as tens of thousands of North Vietnamese troops were streaming down from the North in support of the Vietcong. In February 1962 Harkins formally inaugurated the U.S. Military Assistance Command, Vietnam, which became known by the abbreviation MACV. It continued to be called the Assistance Command even when it commanded upward of a half million Americans. By Christmas 1962 Harkins's command consisted of 11,300 American officers, noncommissioned officers, and enlisted men. American military pilots flew warplanes and helicopters into combat. This was more than Taylor and Rostow had proposed a year earlier, but the situation was worsening steadily. In addition to MACV, the CIA was building a vast operation devoted to intelligence gathering, political manipulation, and paramilitary enterprises. Now the die was cast. The United States was trapped in Vietnam.

Yet this fact did not seem to be noticed in America in any particularly disturbing fashion. The United States had more than three hundred thousand men in Western Europe, some forty thousand in South Korea, so why would the eleven thousand or so in faraway Vietnam matter to the average newspaper reader or television viewer (although the quality of TV coverage, both journalistically and technically, was improving impressively in the early sixties and beginning to bring the Vietnam War to American homes)?

No Americans were dying in combat in Asia, as far as anyone knew, and there were no serious stirrings in the Congress over this imperceptible but real involvement in the life-or-death affairs of South Vietnam.

The few American journalists assigned full-time to Vietnam—there were few of them because this was not yet a great story—tried very hard to convey the gravity of the Vietnamese situation to the American public and discovered that not many people outside Washington really cared. Reporters like Neil Sheehan, then of United Press International, and David Halberstam of *The New York Times* wrote dispatches early in 1963, to warn that the corruption, dishonesty, and cowardice of most South Vietnamese commanders were handing the victory over to the Communists regardless of the efforts of American advisers attached to their units and the availability of military technology made in America. They described how the guerrillas shot down American helicopters ferrying ARVN (Army of the Republic of Vietnam) soldiers into combat, with the loss of American pilots' lives, because both South Vietnamese and U.S. intelligence was unable to track accurately enemy movements and presence. Sheehan wrote vividly how the guerrillas were able to neutralize American-supplied M-113 armored vehicles because South Vietnamese officers and crews dared not fight the Communists, even from behind the shelter of their armor.

The Saigon reporters also told of the "harvest of American weapons" by the Vietcong and North Vietnamese regulars from the ARVN and provincial forces. As in the Chinese Civil War, U.S. arms sent to its client armies were rapidly captured by the Communists, greatly simplifying their logistics and helping them match the South Vietnamese firepower. Though the point these journalists sought to make with all their detailed accounts was that urgent measures were required to make the Diem regime and its commanders act responsibly and professionally, they succeeded primarily in antagonizing the U.S. establishment in Saigon and the bureaucratic hierarchy in Washington. ARVN officers in the field filed dishonest reports to cover up their failures, Diem and his top commanders covered up for the field officers (they all shared the sense of discomfort with military action, always hoping that in a crunch Americans would bail them out), and General Harkins and most of *his* officers covered up for the South Vietnamese to protect themselves.

In Washington the official conclusion was that the reporters in Vietnam were either dishonest or incompetent—or unpatriotic. I worked in the capital at the time, covering the State Department for *The New York Times*, and I heard continuously the complaints against our Saigon colleagues. Soon, in fact, any criticism or even any questioning of the official line began to be regarded as downright subversive. I remember the occasion when Secretary of State Rusk, who used to meet with a group of newsmen for relaxed drinks in his office almost every Friday afternoon, lashed out at a television correspondent who questioned some aspect of Vietnam policy. Reddening in the face, Rusk hissed: "Are you with us, or are you against us?"

* * *

So much was happening in these opening years of the sixties that indeed, little attention was paid to Vietnam. First, there were the Kennedys themselves, the captivating clan from Hyannis Port whom many Americans tended to regard as the royal family: the President and his wife, Jackie, his brother Robert, who served as attorney general, and all the other relatives and countless children. After the sober Eisenhower era it now was the spirit of the chic at the White House and in Washington and beyond: the youth, the glamour, the clothes, the humor, the music and songs, the welcome to artists and writers, the optimism, the bravado, and that charming arrogance of power. Apart from Pennsylvania Avenue, home to the Kennedys was Hyannis Port and Palm Beach, Florida, with their sense of casual wealth and elegance. A new style had come to America, and the country did not wish to be distracted by the grim news from Vietnam or Laos.

Wherever the Kennedys went abroad together—Paris, Vienna, Latin America—they seemed to conquer. Charles de Gaulle was taken with Mrs. Kennedy, who spoke reasonably fluent French. The President did just as superbly alone. In West Berlin, he cried, *"Ich bin ein Berliner!"*; in Ireland he spoke of remote ancestry and charmed the Irish; in London he reminisced with the British over their glorious wartime years. And in Caracas, Venezuela, where fewer than four years earlier Richard Nixon was nearly stoned to death, the crowds were ecstatic over Kennedy, cheering wildly as he spoke of the legacy of Simón Bolívar, "the Liberator," democracy and social justice. It was the same reaction in Bogotá and Mexico City. In March 1963 the President flew to San José, Costa Rica, to meet with Central American presidents in furtherance of the Alliance for Progress. As usual the White House press plane landed first, and we stood on the tarmac for ten or fifteen minutes awaiting Air Force One when I suddenly realized that my sunglasses were covered with what appeared to be soot. My clothes and everybody else's at the airport were similarly covered, and we were told that the nearby Irazú volcano had erupted that morning for the first time in many years. Someone else told me it was an ill omen when Irazú's ashes hid the sun. I instantly forgot about it when Kennedy landed, and the rest of the day was spent in joyous amity with Costa Rican university students and crowds. I remembered it eight months later, when I heard about the shots in Dallas; I also learned that the 1963 Irazú eruption was one of the greatest calamities to hit Costa Rica in this century.

The world, meanwhile, was fascinating in its triumphs and tragedy—and frivolity. Russians and Americans flew into space, the first manned flights in history.

But Dag Hammarskjöld, the greatly admired Swedish diplomat who was the second secretary-general of the United Nations, was killed in September 1961 in a mysterious aircraft crash in the Congo, where he went to try to prevent the secession of Katanga Province and to stop a savage civil war. His was the first mysterious death of the 1960's. But his sacrifice was not wholly in vain. It was in the Congo that Hammarskjöld set in motion the first United Nations peacekeeping operation with the use of the Blue Helmets, UN forces drawn from national military contingents of the member states. In the end the Blue Helmets saved the Congo/Zaire from being slashed in two by the secession war, and without them the civil conflict would surely have been vastly more savage. For the next thirty years UN peacekeeping forces were sent to dozens of war situations—mainly in the Middle East and Africa—and if they did not necessarily bring peace, they often helped avert catastrophes. The Nobel Prize in 1988 went to the UN peacekeepers.

In Washington President Kennedy judged that the economy was strong enough to justify cuts in personal and corporate taxes; he could not have even imagined the fiscal ravages the Vietnam War would bring. And America's cultural image was enhanced when John Steinbeck won the Nobel Prize for literature in 1962 (eight years after Ernest Hemingway). The Beatles had invaded America in 1964 from their Liverpool, England, home, and Beatlemania spread and spread—and lasted for decades to come. The generation of the 1960's becomes dew-eyed when it hears "Yesterday." The twist, the first disco dance, was born at the Peppermint Lounge in New York and, overnight, reborn at the Peppermint Lounge in Palm Beach, not far from where the Kennedys stayed.

The world of cinema was struck as if by lightning by the French new wave with directors like Jean-Luc Goddard, François Truffaut, and Louis Malle almost reinventing the art. Britain's great contributions in the early 1960's were *Lawrence of Arabia* and *Tom Jones*, both Oscar winners.

And Marilyn Monroe, the blond American idol and symbol of sex, committed suicide in 1962, shocking millions who adored her on the screen. She had been married to baseball's great hero Joe DiMaggio and to playwright Arthur Miller and was said to have had affairs with John Kennedy and Robert Kennedy. A quarter century after her death Marilyn Monroe was an American cult figure.

Cassius Clay, still another American hero, won the world heavyweight boxing championship before he was twenty-two; then, in 1964, rich and famous, he joined the Nation of Islam, changing his name to Muhammad Ali.

In March 1962 President de Gaulle finally achieved a cease-fire in the Algerian liberation war, weathering a generals' putsch in Algiers and ugly riots in Paris. In September the independent Algerian republic was proclaimed. It took immense courage on De Gaulle's part to abandon the commitment to *Algérie Française* after eight years of merciless war and so much blood spilled on both sides. The generals' revolt against him had failed, but something akin to a civil war developed, with the French armed forces splitting over the Algeria issue. The Algiers commanders—including such great generals as Raoul Salan and Edmond Jouhaud—and legendary Free French leaders like Georges Bidault, who had served as De Gaulle's foreign minister and was one of his closest wartime and postwar advisers, formed the Secret Army Organization (OAS) to seek the president's ouster and the resumption of the Algerian War.

Attempts to assassinate De Gaulle and other spectacular acts of terrorism were traced to the OAS, and for a time it was touch and go whether he would survive the rebellion. There was the threat of OAS-led paratroopers to jump on Paris. Arthur Schlesinger writes in A *Thousand Days* that "Kennedy promptly offered de Gaulle his assistance," a tantalizing and unexplained bit of information. What would Kennedy have done? In the end De Gaulle's government was saved by French troops based in West Germany who sided with him against the OAS. Salan was imprisoned, an army colonel who planned the assassination plot was executed, and Bidault lived in exile until 1968. Nothing of the sort had happened in modern French history. And it was the Third World's defiance that had precipitated this terrible convulsion in France.

De Gaulle did what Kennedy had urged the French to do five years earlier. He let go of the colonial past and acknowledged the force and the right of nationalism. De Gaulle, of course, knew all along that this was the path he would follow because his sense of history and reality dictated it.

But at that very time Kennedy was beginning to sink America in Vietnam in a replay of the French experience of Indochina and Algeria in the preceding decade. The astonishing thing about the direction the President was taking was that he, too, was a student of history, as were many of his closest advisers; even General Taylor was considered a military intellectual. This proved, if anything, that politicians can manipulate history and reality if such manipulation suits their requirements—ideological or otherwise. It also proved how easy it is to plunge headlong blindly into absolute disaster when a ruler is guided by dogma, not reason.

Naturally, manipulation feeds on itself, acquires its own life and momentum. This is what happened in Vietnam. When Kennedy belatedly realized in mid-1963 that President Diem and his family were, in effect, pushing South Vietnam into national suicide through their refusal to move ahead with any reforms while antagonizing most of the population and losing the war, he went along with recommendations for a coup against them. The weightiest recommendation to get rid of Diem came from Kennedy's new ambassador in Saigon, Henry Cabot Lodge, after the regime turned its violence on Buddhist monks. To be sure, the Americans were not contemplating the assassination of Diem and his brother Ngo Dinh Nhu. But the embassy, MACV, and the CIA let Diem's military foes know that they would see with favor Diem's ouster, and the South Vietnamese commanders obliged with a vengeance. A rebel officer shot the brothers after they were arrested by the plotters on November 2, 1963. Afterward there was no soul-searching or recrimination among the commanders now in power. Wars are savage after all.

As for Kennedy, he was "somber and shaken" when he learned of the killings, in Schlesinger's words. He adds: "I had not seen him so depressed since the Bay of Pigs. No doubt he realized that Vietnam was his great failure in foreign policy, and that he had never really given it his full attention." At that stage there were 17,000 American servicemen in Vietnam; approximately 120 had already been killed.

Twenty days later, on November 22, 1963, John F. Kennedy was assassinated in Dallas by Lee Harvey Oswald for reasons unknown. This date, among so many other meanings for America, marked the end of the first phase of the American war in Vietnam.

III

It is impossible to say whether or not Kennedy had given Vietnam the attention it merited. It is true, however, that there were so many other urgent demands on his time and concentration in terms of foreign policy—plus all the domestic concerns ranging from the economy to civil rights—that Kennedy probably could not have dealt adequately with Southeast Asia even if he had so desired. Under the circumstances, much of the decision making had to be left, in effect, to his principal advisers. With the multitude of interests and responsibilities in a nuclear world that the United States had to face in the sixties, this was probably inevitable. In fact, this state of affairs has grown geometrically more alarming since the Kennedy presidency; as the eighties drew to an end, it was almost axiomatic that the President of the United States could not handle more than one or two major crises at a time without nearly total intellectual dependence on his advisers.

In Kennedy's case, the central foreign preoccupations of his time in office were first and foremost the Soviet Union, as the Cold War continued unabated, and Fidel Castro's Cuba. These two concerns became intertwined in a most dramatic manner, underlining again the theme of the impact of the Third World on the nuclear superpowers and their relations. Vietnam and Laos were also part of the East-West contest—they belonged to the anti-Communist crusade—but in Kennedy's day, they lacked the overwhelming importance they soon acquired.

Coming to power, Kennedy had to deal instantly with two issues, one real and the other one imaginary, touching on the technology of the Cold War that Eisenhower had left for him to resolve. The real problem resulted from the downing by Soviet rocketry over Soviet territory of the CIA's U-2 spy plane on May 1, 1960. The U-2 was a single-seat unarmed jet aircraft capable of flying at over eighty thousand feet (and thus supposedly hard to detect) that was developed in great secrecy by Lockheed in the late 1950's to provide the United States with a capability of observing and photographing Soviet and other Communist nuclear ballistic deployments, troop movements, and so forth.

This was the most exciting quantum leap toward the creation of a high technology dimension in sophisticated intelligence gathering; the best human agents (HUMINT, as "human intelligence" is called in professional jargon) could never report as precisely and rapidly on installations and deployments as the U-2. The Russians had no such plane. In fact, this super aircraft was vitally necessary because U.S. human intelligence collection was alarmingly deficient in the Soviet Union, a closed society that was exceedingly hard to penetrate with spies. Because its function was to gather intelligence, the U-2 was operated by the CIA, which recruited and trained its own pilots (most of whom came from the military services), and was flown from U.S. Air Force bases or air bases in friendly countries.

In 1960 the U-2 was especially crucial in view of a bizarre argument that plagued the U.S. government and its military and intelligence services over the relative American and Soviet nuclear capabilities and delivery vehicles—that is, intercontinental missiles. This was the dispute over the "missile gap" between the two superpowers, with the advent of the myth, resulting from faulty intelligence or inexcusable domestic political games (or both), that the Soviets had successfully opened such a gap and held the United States at its mercy. Having lost the atomic monopoly in 1949, Americans, who have masochistic tendencies, became hysterically convinced that the Russians had caught up with them and were now far ahead in the nuclear arms race. That the Soviets most likely lacked the industrial base to open such a gap in such a relatively short time was not taken into account by the most senior and serious officials, all of whom should have known better. Even as expert a witness as General Thomas Power, the commander of the Strategic Air Command, had no hesitation in informing a Senate committee that the Russians "could virtually wipe out our entire nuclear strike capability within a span of thirty minutes." Few people were prepared to question the word of the SAC commander.

This is where the U-2 entered the picture, virtually as arbiter. Prior to its flights the CIA and the military intelligence services based their estimates on murky sources (chiefly HUMINT and guesswork), often disagreeing among themselves and in-house in the individual agencies about what the data meant and how it should be interpreted and presented to policymakers. Because intelligence and policy-making intersect when they reach White House level, there has always been a tendency on the part of both intelligence producers and consumers to manipulate the information and its meaning to achieve policy decisions each side judges the most suitable.

With the public missile gap controversy, the so-called net assessments of American and Soviet strength turned into a nightmare and a maze. There no longer was any objective truth. But the U-2 came to the rescue, and as a result of spy-in-the-sky photography in the early months of 1960, "all the intelligence services sharply reduced their earlier estimates of what the Soviets would deploy, and when"—in the words of McGeorge Bundy.

Eisenhower, who personally authorized every U-2 flight, was anxious not only to end the missile gap but also to learn more about Soviet nuclear capabilities in preparation for discussions with Khrushchev at the summit they had scheduled for Paris in May on a limited test ban treaty the President favored. Thus he agreed in April to a CIA request to authorize one more U-2 flight before the summit to obtain up-to-date information on Soviet missiles sites. The plane, with an ex-Air Force pilot named Francis Gary Powers at the controls, took off from a base in Pakistan on a flight plan that would take it to a landing in Bodø, Norway, after overflying the western Soviet Union—including the Tyuratam missile-testing center—on a roughly south-north trajectory. But the Soviets, who were aware of the U-2's existence (and had privately protested the overflights, preferring not to admit publicly their inferiority in spy planes), succeeded in shooting Powers down over Sverdlovsk with an antiaircraft missile. The pilot bailed out, was captured unharmed on the ground by the Russians, and placed on trial after the Eisenhower administration had wasted precious days of American credibility in absurd denials that it knew anything about the U-2. Powers's confession clinched the Soviet case, but Khrushchev had already canceled the summit although both he and Eisenhower were already in Paris.

The epilogue of the missile gap argument and the U-2 fiasco was Eisenhower's warning in his farewell address against the dangers posed in the United States by the "military-industrial complex." It was a surprising remark from a military man who, during his presidency, had built up considerably American armed power and was believed to have contemplated the use of tactical atomic bombs against China in the event it invaded the offshore islands between the mainland and Taiwan. It appears that Eisenhower may have finally concluded that the pressures to keep arming the United States—of which the missile gap may have been an example—were the handiwork of greedy defense contractors in tandem with trusting and concerned military chiefs. The events in the ensuing three decades confirmed Eisenhower's fears as the U.S. defense budget skyrocketed year after year.

What Kennedy found, therefore, upon assuming office eight months after the U-2 incident was Soviet-American relations at their lowest point since the advent of the Cold War. Khrushchev had revived the Berlin crisis, he was causing mischief in Laos, he gave Kennedy a hard time at their Vienna encounter in June 1961, and as 1962 rolled around, he was preparing a whole set of new perils in Cuba. Unpredictable, opportunistic, a loose cannon, Khrushchev had to be taken with the utmost seriousness by the Kennedy administration.

Cuba was the place he selected for his next confrontation with the United States. It was over Fidel Castro's island that the nuclear superpowers committed in succession some of their most dangerous errors in judgment, each having developed its own Cuban obsession. The story of the triangular drama engaging the United States, the Soviet Union, and Cuba opened early in 1960, when the Russians began to gain influence in Havana and the Americans to lose theirs very rapidly. Whether or not Castro had informed visiting Soviet Deputy Premier Anastas I. Mikoyan in February that he had decided to align his revolution with the Marxist-Leninist ideology and to seek a Soviet alliance—publicly the Cuban leader was still careful not to characterize so precisely the nature and the plans of his regime—the Russians were more than anxious to strike a deal with him. It would give them the first beachhead ever in the Western Hemisphere.

The agreement signed by Castro and Mikoyan provided basically for purchases of surplus Cuban sugar at favorable prices and for limited economic assistance; that was the official portion of the deal. Secretly the Soviets agreed to start shipping modern arms to Cuba (which was already buying light Czechoslovak war materiel) and to provide advisers, the first step toward their deep involvement in Cuba's fate. Ironically, it coincided with the Eisenhower administration's decision to increase substantially the American military commitment in South Vietnam; there seems to have been a spontaneous symmetry in superpower behavior around the globe.

While the Soviets accepted, in effect, the role of defending Cuba, the United States almost simultaneously made the first formal move toward the goal of destroying the Castro revolution, a goal that had begun to take shape among American policy planners almost immediately after its victory the previous year. This was Eisenhower's approval on March 17, 1960, of a basic operational paper prepared by the CIA and the White House Special Group (which was in charge of major secret operations), titled "A Program of Covert Action Against the Castro Regime." Vice President Nixon became the White House overseer of this program. There is nothing to suggest that Eisenhower's authorization was a direct consequence of the secret Soviet-Cuban arms arrangement; chances are the United States was wholly unaware of it. History simply was taking its course.

Governments often embrace demonology to interpret events unfolding before them. The administration in Washington thought it saw a link between Khrushchev's cancellation of the Paris summit and Moscow's decision to establish formal diplomatic relations with Cuba. It saw a new Communist offensive along all fronts. When Castro seized American-owned oil refineries and began importing crude from the Soviet Union, the United States responded by halting its sugar imports from Cuba, thereby undermining the Cuban economy (though the refineries incident was really an excuse for the sugar move, planned beforehand as a blow at the revolutionaries). Again, the Soviets confirmed American fears by coming to Castro's rescue. On July 9, two days after the Washington announcement on sugar, Khrushchev announced that not only would the Soviets buy the Cuban production that would have gone to the United States, but it would protect the island's integrity. "The Soviet Union is raising its voice and extending a helpful hand to the people of Cuba," he said in a speech, "[and] in a figurative sense, if it becomes necessary, the Soviet military can support the Cuban people with rocket weapons. . . ." It is impossible to say whether Khrushchev was already toying with the idea of deploying nuclear missiles in Cuba, but naturally, his speech was greeted with alarm.

Later that month Castro celebrated the revolutionary holiday of the Twenty-sixth of July (the anniversary of his 1953 attack on the Moncada army barracks), and in Havana it was pure euphoria. The Revolution still commanded almost total support among Cubans, and the regime brought tens of thousands of straw-hatted *guajiros* from the countryside, their peasants' machetes glinting in the sun, to participate in the feast. Standing not far from Castro on the rostrum beneath the monument to José Martí, Cuba's independence hero, on Revolution Plaza, I watched the sea of humanity cheering and cheering the new national hero. Castro's response in his speech, lasting well into the summer twilight, was that by cheering and applauding, the *pueblo* had "elected" the revolutionary regime, and therefore, old-fashioned Western-type elections were no longer necessary. A veritable club of the Latin American left had assembled around Castro that afternoon: Guatemala's deposed President Jacobo Arbenz, former Mexican President and legendary revolutionary leader General Lázaro Cárdenas, British Guiana's Marxist chief minister Cheddi Jagan, and an obscure Chilean physician named Salvador Allende Gossens, who a decade later was the first Marxist elected to his country's presidency. Washington policy planners now had no doubt that Castro was a danger not only in Cuba but elsewhere in the hemisphere as well. Planning for the exiles' attack on Cuba was accelerated.

Khrushchev's and Castro's embraces in New York in September coincided with the first intelligence reports that Cuban pilots were being trained in Czechoslovakia and the Soviet Union to fly MiG jet aircraft. I remember the CIA's station chief in Havana mentioning these reports to me (presumably to encourage me to have them published in my newspaper) and warning that "something must be done" before the pilots returned to Cuba—with the MiGs—and made it invulnerable to external pressure. As it turned out later, this was among the principal arguments adduced by the CIA to convince Kennedy to go ahead with the invasion.

The Eisenhower administration's final foreign policy act in January 1961 was to break off diplomatic relations with Cuba, opening the way for military action. Subsequently a reluctant Kennedy approved the operation, and the exiles' brigade landed at the Bay of Pigs on April 17 (which happened to be Khrushchev's birthday). The next day, while combat was still in progress,

Khrushchev dispatched a note addressed personally to Kennedy, warning: "We shall render the Cuban people and their government all necessary assistance in beating back the armed attack on Cuba." This was no longer figurative; modern Czech and Soviet weapons were crucial in assuring Castro's victory against the tank-equipped exiles. The weapons had arrived just weeks before the attack.

In the immediate aftermath of the Bay of Pigs, all sides made preparations for the next chapter in the Cuban drama. The United States remained determined to liquidate Castro one way or another, the Cubans were just as determined to defend their revolution, and the Soviets stood more than ready to assist their new Caribbean allies to the hilt.

American planning began in great secrecy within weeks of the debacle, right after Kennedy publicly accepted the blame for the invasion and its failure. CIA Director Allen Dulles was encouraged to resign, particularly when a board of inquiry headed by General Taylor (who dealt with all military emergencies for the President) concluded that the intelligence planners had completely underestimated Castro and his defensive doctrine.

New brains undertook the new planning, and the stage was set for the next disaster. Basically the policy was spelled out in the top-secret Taylor study, submitted to Kennedy in mid-June. It stated that "there can be no long-term living with Castro as a neighbor" and recommended that under a reappraisal of the whole Cuban situation, "new guidance be provided for political, military, economic and propaganda action against Castro." The approach the administration's finest brains were taking was three-pronged: destabilization of Cuba through intelligence, economic, propaganda, and paramilitary operations that would lead to Castro's internal collapse; the assassination of Fidel Castro; and a full-fledged invasion by American forces.

The first track that even then could not have represented more than wishful thinking was the responsibility of the CIA, except for economic warfare measures that were coordinated by the State, Treasury, and Commerce departments. The second one—Castro's assassination—was intended to be undertaken simultaneously with the first track.

That the United States had been involved in the killing of foreign leaders has been established firmly in subsequent Senate hearings on intelligence operations; it was a concept spawned for the first time in American history in the 1960's. There were attempts in 1960 to murder the Congo's leftist leader Patrice Lumumba, in which the CIA had a hand, and he was finally killed early in 1961, shortly after Kennedy took office, by parties unknown. Rafael Leonidas Trujillo Molina, the bloodthirsty dictator of the Dominican Republic for three decades, was assassinated on May 30, 1961, by civilian plotters who were determined to end the tyranny by any possible means. There are convincing reasons to believe, according to what I learned in the Dominican Republic later that year, that the CIA had at least advance knowledge of the conspiracy, that it favored it, and that it supplied the weapons for the deed. Interestingly, the first information concerning Trujillo's death came from the entourage of President Kennedy, who was then visiting Paris. If, indeed, the United States approved (or abetted) this assassination, the explanation would be that members of administration reasoned that it would be evenhanded, so to speak, to have both leftist and rightist dictators in the Caribbean dead (a ministerial conference of the Organization of American States in mid-1960 had condemned both regimes in resolutions supported by the United States).

The unanswered historical question is whether President Kennedy knew about the Trujillo and Castro assassination plans and whether he authorized them. My personal experience is a meeting I had with the President in the Oval Office in November 1961 to discuss the Cuban situation in the light of my conversations with Castro both before and after the Bay of Pigs, which were part of my reporting for *The New York Times*. I was invited in a personal capacity, not as a reporter, on the recommendation of Attorney General Robert Kennedy and presidential assistant Richard N. Goodwin, with whom I had chatted about Cuba earlier that autumn. In the course of my White House visit, the President stunned me by asking, "What would you think if I ordered Castro to be assassinated?" I answered that I felt the United States should not be involved in political assassinations, and Kennedy told me, "I agree with you completely," adding that he was under pressure from advisers he did not identify to authorize the killing of Castro. Goodwin, who was the only witness to our conversation, testified before a Senate committee in 1975 that several days later Kennedy alluded to it, saying, "We can't get into that kind of thing, or we would all be targets." Nevertheless, Castro assassination plans and attempts did occur starting in 1962, and it is known that Bobby Kennedy, in charge of overall Cuban policies, was fully informed of them. Could he have acted behind his brother's back?

On November 30, about two weeks after I met with the President, the National Security Council staff and the CIA presented Kennedy with a blueprint for action against Castro. Kennedy then advised Secretary of State Rusk that he had decided to "use our available assets . . . to help Cuba overthrow the Communist regime." Castro invited even greater American fury when he announced in a speech on December 1, 1961, that he had always been a Marxist-Leninist and that Cubans must accept that "to be a communist is a merit." Shortly thereafter the operational control of the anti-Castro enterprise was handed to Brigadier General Lansdale, who had just returned from Vietnam and received his first star; with his Philippines and Vietnam experience, he was the best the administration thought it had in sophisticated counterinsurgency and subversion. Lansdale's operation was code-named Mongoose.

The most crucial of the anti-Castro tracks was that of an American invasion, if all else failed. It is also a textbook example of how perceptions—or misunderstandings—can determine the course of decision making and determine history. Despite the passage of time and the emergence of new materials on the subject of the 1962 Cuban missile crisis—notably contributions made since 1988 under *glasnost* by Soviet historians and participants in Kremlin decision-making—it still is not entirely clear what happened and, most important, why it happened.

In the first place, it has not been established with certainty that the American invasion idea had gone beyond the stage of contingency planning and entered actual military preparations with proposed deadlines. In itself contingency planning is meaningless; the Pentagon has contingency plans for everything imaginable simply because it has the responsibility for drafting them. What does matter, however, is whether the other side (in this case Cuba and the Soviet Union) really believed that an invasion was in the offing and that Khrushchev decided to deploy nuclear missiles in Cuba as a deterrent against such an attack.

General Taylor's recommendations to Kennedy included "military" action among steps he proposed to overthrow Castro, but the declassified portions of this document do not explain what exactly he had in mind. A top secret memorandum titled "The Cuba Project" and distributed by Lansdale on February 20, 1962, outlines detailed plans "for a revolt which can take place in Cuba by October 1962" and urges the administration to come up with a "military support plan." In it, this question is raised by Lansdale: "If conditions and assets permitting a revolt are achieved in Cuba, and if U.S. help is required to sustain this condition, will the U.S. respond promptly with military force to aid the Cuban revolt?" On March 14 a top secret memorandum on "Guidelines for Operation Mongoose" was circulated by the National Security Council staff, stating that "political, economic and covert actions will be undertaken short of those reasonably calculated to inspire a revolt within the target area, or other development which would require U.S. armed intervention." It would appear that at least at that stage the White House was *not* contemplating an invasion, and the Kennedy administration never addressed itself publicly to the question of its intention before the October missile crisis.

Extraordinary attention to the whole decision-making process during that crisis—when the United States discovered that the Russians installed missiles on the island—was paid to this episode at the time of its twenty-fifth anniversary in 1987 and subsequently, taking advantage of *glasnost*. A group of American policymakers who played key roles in 1962, told much, if not all, of it at a conference at Hawk's Cay, Florida, in March 1987. In October 1987 American and Soviet scholars and policy specialists gathered at Harvard, with the Soviets for the first time telling their side of the story. In January 1989 this exercise continued in Moscow.

What I found disconcerting in the accounts of these meetings was the relatively limited discussion of what prompted Khrushchev to challenge Kennedy with the missiles and especially of the possibility that Soviet concern over an invasion of Cuba might have been the central motivation.

Moreover, the Cuban version of these events, obviously of great significance, was totally absent from the discussions. Curiously, what the Americans were most interested in discussing was the defusing of the crisis—not its genesis—which suggests a somewhat distorted approach to history. The bulk of the time was devoted to analyzing Kennedy's actions in assembling military forces to counter the Soviet threat and the way he and Khrushchev finally hit on a solution.

Possibly the full truth will never be known. Two of three principals in that crisis are dead, and it is unknown whether or where complete records exist in Washington, Moscow, and Havana. It is useful, however, to note that Fidel Castro's version, which I recorded in a series of interviews with him in 1984 and 1985, emphasizes that the Soviet proposal for deploying medium-range missiles with nuclear warheads—forty-two of them—was made in response to his request for military protection from an American invasion he feared. In view of the rising scope of Mongoose operations around Cuba, it is not astonishing that Castro convinced himself that indeed, he was in mortal danger. And in view of the Soviets' own paranoia, it is perfectly credible that Khrushchev believed him.

The likelihood of an American assault against Cuba was cited by Khrushchev in a speech before the Supreme Soviet in December 1962 as the reason for his attempt secretly to ship the missiles to Cuba and place before Kennedy a fait accompli. This may have been self-serving as well as true. Sergo Mikoyan, who was an aide to his father, Deputy Premier Anastas Mikoyan, during the crisis, told both the Harvard and Moscow scholars' conferences that he accepts Khrushchev's explanation. He expanded on it in great detail in conversations in Washington with me in 1989. Aleksandr Alekseyev, the first Soviet ambassador to Cuba, writes in his memoirs, published in 1988 in the Soviet magazine *Planetary Echo*, that Khrushchev's key motivation was the danger to Castro. The Soviet leader's belief was that Soviet credibility both among Marxists and in the Third World would be catastrophically damaged if the Cuban Revolution were allowed to be smashed.

Unquestionably Khrushchev took advantage of the Castro request to improve the Soviet military position in the world by placing nuclear missiles ninety miles from American shores. The bald, stocky Ukrainian was a political gambler and risk taker on a grand scale, but by all accounts he was not irrational to the point of triggering gratuitously a nuclear face-off, stationing more than forty thousand Soviet combat troops in Cuba, and inviting a war with the much more powerful United States.

Fidel and Raúl Castro presented their version of the crisis in secret speeches before the Central Committee of the Cuban Communist party in 1968, repeating their earlier accusations that Khrushchev in the end betrayed Cuba by removing the missiles from the island as part of a compromise with Kennedy without consulting the Castro brothers beforehand. Fidel Castro also disclosed that he had asked Khrushchev to sign a formal military alliance with Cuba before sending the missiles but that the Soviets refused.

The Kennedy-Khrushchev settlement, which included the removal of obsolescent American Jupiter missiles from Turkey and a guarantee that Cuba would not be invaded, ended the confrontation, which was as near as the world has ever come to nuclear war. Great lessons about nuclear crisis management were obviously learned during these "thirteen days in October." But it is not certain that the most important lesson was really comprehended: that among nations perceptions are as vital as palpable realities. The Cuban episode might have never arisen if the Cubans and the Soviets had not chosen to believe that an invasion was imminent. And such a misperception might not have developed if the United States had not let psychological warfare under Operation Mongoose get out of hand. Moreover, the Soviet *Cosmos* 9 reconnaissance satellite, then covering the Caribbean, carried no cameras to photograph American preparations—if there were any.

In hindsight, McGeorge Bundy, who was Kennedy's principal foreign policy adviser, has recognized that the White House had not given enough thought to how the anti-Castro operations would be read in Moscow. He writes in *Danger and Survival* that Khrushchev "certainly knew of our program of covert action against Cuba, and he could hardly be expected to understand that to us this program was not a prelude to stronger action but a substitute for it." Obviously the United States should have clarified its intentions—thus quite possibly averting the confrontation—and the Soviet Union should have done likewise. Bluff is a lethal game in the nuclear age, as Kennedy and Khrushchev demonstrated in 1962.

My own recollection of the Cuban crisis is arriving home in Washington at dawn on Sunday, October 28, after long hours of helping to cover the story in *The New York Times* bureau. Our last edition had gone to bed some hours after an American U-2 high-flying reconnaissance plane was shot down over Cuba by Soviet SAM-2 rocket batteries, and war appeared imminent. I told my wife and children, "Well, this may be *it*—and let's get some sleep." But Kennedy had decided not to order an air strike on Cuba—yet—and within hours he received Khrushchev's conciliatory message that paved the way to the settlement.

Several weeks later I was sent to the United States naval base at Guantánamo in Cuba (an enclave Castro has never tried to wrest back) to report on the removal of the Soviet missiles. The mission was to fly aboard a Navy aircraft whose pilots were inspecting Soviet freighters sailing out of Cuban ports with the big missiles lined on decks under tarps. As our jet came down screaming over the first freighter, the spectacular sight before my eyes during that fraction of a second was of a shapely young Russian woman in a yellow bathing suit, sunning herself atop a medium-range missile.

* * *

During 1962 Vietnam, Cuba, and Berlin occupied most of Kennedy's foreign policy time, but other urgent obligations were clamoring for his attention as well. The United States was now so deeply engaged in world affairs on every continent in the Cold War rivalry with the Soviet Union that nothing could be overlooked or left to chance.

In Asia, apart from Vietnam, the Laotian civil war was festering while at a conference in Geneva, Averell Harriman, the most versatile of American diplomatic statesmen, was endeavoring to find a solution in negotiations with Laotian parties (rightist, Communist, and neutralist), North and South Vietnam, the Soviet Union, China, France, and Britain. It took Harriman well over a year to hammer out the Declaration on the Neutrality of Laos, signed on July 23, 1962, as fighting in neighboring Vietnam kept rising in fury. The neutrality never really happened because the Soviets kept supplying the Communist Pathet Lao while Ho Chi Minh used Laotian jungle trails to infiltrate men and equipment from North to South Vietnam. In the end Laos blurred into Vietnam as part of the widening American Indochina war, but Geneva was a good try—at least establishing the principle of neutrality there.

Incredibly, just as Kennedy was in the midst of the Cuban missile crisis, war broke out in the Himalayas between China and India. With its growing interests in Asia, the United States could not ignore this newest conflict, especially because China appeared to be the aggressor. Though the Kennedy administration was satisfied that the Soviet-Chinese split was a reality, it could not discount the possibility that Beijing was taking advantage of the Caribbean affray to advance its own cause against the democracies. Thus time was found to make the decision to rush military equipment for the Indian Army fighting on two fronts in the high Himalayas along mountain passes that rise to fifteen thousand feet. Up to then American military aid had gone only to Pakistan, which was a member of the pro-Western Central Treaty Organization (CENTO), which John Foster Dulles had invented in the fifties, but the Pakistanis also had been at odds with India since the 1947 partition.

To be sure, nobody in Washington had the slightest idea what was occurring on the roof of the world. The dispute was arcane, arising from old British demarcation lines between Tibet and India, but the administration concluded that this was a great opportunity to cement the generally rocky relationship with New Delhi, where Prime Minister Nehru and his associates were inclined to preach to the United States over Korea, Vietnam, Laos, and a variety of other themes. Nehru was a leader of the nonaligned movement, which more and more assumed a stance hostile to the United States. The American ambassador to India was John Kenneth Galbraith, the gangling Harvard economist and philosopher, whose appointment was among Kennedy's most felicitous, and he was instrumental in improving the climate—especially when American arms began to arrive. (In 1965, India used these arms in the war with Pakistan). Nonalignment, as the United States discovered on this occasion, was a relative concept. Contrary to Washington's concerns, China had no intention of sending its armies down the Himalayas to the Indian plains, and the conflict fizzled out; it remains unclear who really was at fault.

Then there were the Latin American concerns. The Charter of Punta del Este, the cornerstone of Kennedy's Alliance for Progress, had been signed at a conference at the Uruguayan resort in August 1961. Cuba's Che Guevara had attended the meeting, attracting more attention than any other delegate, but he had refused to sign the charter. Now, in January 1962, another inter-American conference in Punta del Este expelled Cuba from the OAS; this was part of the broad anti-Castro campaign designed to isolate him in the hemisphere. In June Kennedy flew to Mexico to extol the Alliance for Progress—and mend fences with the Mexicans, who, familiar as they were at home with the history of American interventions, opposed the anti-Castro campaign. And militarism returned to Latin American with the ouster of the democratically elected President Frondizi in a coup that marked the start of two more decades of dictatorship and Argentine self-destruction.

In the roller-coaster pattern of Soviet-American relations, the nuclear confrontation dissipated so rapidly that within months, by spring 1963, the administration concluded that the time had come for a thaw, certainly not for rubbing it in that Khrushchev had been defeated over Cuba. The logic of the October events suggested that the thaw could best be found in the nuclear realm, and on June 10 Kennedy announced in a commencement speech at American University in Washington that the United States, Britain, and the Soviet Union would start negotiating a treaty to ban nuclear testing. Averell Harriman, who had served as wartime ambassador to the Soviet Union, led the American delegation to the Moscow talks, and before the end of July the treaty had been initialed. This was a record time for a complex agreement with the Russians, showing how self-interest, when it coincides among negotiators, becomes the magic formula for success.

IV

Success had also blessed the United States in a field of rivalry with the Soviet Union that was as emotional as it was technological. It was the conquest of space, one of the great postwar American dreams that at first seemed to elude the nation.

Control of space and the perfecting of rocketry required to allow humans to soar beyond the Earth were transformed as a result of Second World War research and development from Jules Vernesque science fiction and comic strips into an attainable reality. Naturally, space and rockets had evident military and intelligence-gathering applications, but at the outset of the sixties, when the space age was born, national prestige and pride were principally at stake.

From the very beginning the Soviet-American space race was both in man-made satellites and in manned flight. But because immensely powerful propulsion rockets are necessary to launch space vehicles, the Soviet Union as well as the United States was developing them for the parallel purpose of creating arsenals of missiles capable of delivering nuclear warheads across the world. The same rocket engine that propelled a satellite or a space capsule, scientists on both sides realized, would propel an intercontinental ballistic missile (ICBM). In the sixties defense planners paid scant attention to immediate and practical military uses of space; this came two decades later with "Star Wars" concepts when technology rendered them feasible.

For the United States, the space race opened with humiliations. In October 1957 the Russians launched the 184-pound *Sputnik I* and a month later the 1,120-pound *Sputnik II* with a dog aboard, the first man-made satellites in space. The Americans' first satellite was the tiny 3-pound *Vanguard I*, and it was not launched from the Cape Canaveral, Florida, space center until March 1958. It was described as a "scientific satellite." The Soviets raised the ante even more impressively later that year with the 3,000-pound *Sputnik III*, whereas *Vanguard II*, weighing only 22 pounds, was not placed in orbit until February 1959. The Sputniks added to Soviet glory by producing photographs of the previously unseen far side of the moon.

The Soviet space program clearly favored size and weight of its satellites—*Sputnik VI*, launched in February 1961, weighed an unbelievable 14,292 pounds—suggesting that it aimed at manned flight and space stations before too long. Its accomplishments coincided with Soviet reports of record missiles flights over Soviet territory and the Pacific. The Russians were unquestionably preeminent in rocket boosters and seemingly uncatchable in space and ICBM programs.

But while the Soviets concentrated on space spectaculars, the United States devoted its resources to the development of specialized reconnaissance (spy-in-the-sky), communications, navigational and weather satellites. This choice paid off in the long run, ultimately providing the United States with versatility in space the Soviets could not or would not match. *Courier* and *Echo I* were the first communications satellites, launched in 1960, but the Discoverer intelligence satellites were sent up as early as February 1959, from Vandenberg Air Force Base in California.

Twenty-six Discoverer "birds" flew over the Soviet Union and China over the next three years as part of a top secret reconnaissance program, and twenty-three of them carried photographic film capsules that were ejected on radio command and recovered in midair over the Pacific by Air Force planes or on the ground in the United States. The photography was superb; from an altitude of three hundred miles, it provided the resolution of approximately twenty feet on Earth. The Discoverers complemented the photography from U-2 flights that began late in 1956, but they were also equipped to measure infrared radiation from ballistic missiles in flight and from launch countdowns on the ground.

While Discoverer satellites were still flying, new technology led to the launching of the even more secret SAMOS (Satellite-Missile Observation System) vehicles in January 1961. SAMOS constituted a crucial breakthrough because it could transmit pictures by radio, obviating the need for the recovery of film capsules from earlier satellites. SAMOS inaugurated a new era in technological espionage, and the Soviet Cosmos birds were left far behind in this aspect of space competition.

The other aspect, of course, was manned flight. Again, the Soviets were off to a lightning start, but the United States more than made up for it in a relatively short time. Both space programs depended initially and almost completely on captured German scientists who had designed and built the Nazi V-2 rockets. Philip J. Klass, an American journalist specializing in space and aviation, put it perfectly when he wrote in his *Secret Sentries in Space* in 1971 that "almost no one in the West had the vision during the early post-World War II years to foresee that the progeny of the German V-2 ballistic missiles would reshape strategic warfare and threaten the international balance of power."

The United States, however, appears to have leaned more than the Russians on German brainpower. More than four hundred German scientists and engineers from the V-2 project—including Wernher von Braun and Walter Dornberger, who deserve credit for shepherding the American program from its infancy to the moon landings—were brought to the United States. Then German V-2 rockets were tested between 1946 and 1951 on New Mexico proving grounds. As far as it is known, fewer German specialists were in Soviet hands, and most of them were repatriated after several years. All the great Soviet achievements were subsequently made by native talent, but the Russians have not said much publicly about their space work, not even under *glasnost.*

The Eisenhower administration had no way of knowing what the Russians had in mind regarding manned flight. Nevertheless, it authorized the National Aeronautics and Space Administration (NASA) in 1958 to initiate Project Mercury, intended to launch American astronauts (the Soviets call their space fliers cosmonauts) on short orbital flights in the early sixties. The Pentagon, which supplied candidates for the first seven Mercury astronauts from among the best military pilots, had intense interest in the project because defense uses of space were attracting increasing attention among more sophisticated thinkers.

But the Mercury astronauts were not ready for outer space conquest. On April 12, 1961, Yuri Alekseyevich Gagarin, a twenty-seven-year-old Soviet Air Force pilot and cosmonaut, became the first man in history to orbit in space. His five-ton spacecraft *Vostok* (East) circled the earth once, reaching the maximum altitude of 188 miles. The flight lasted one hour, twenty-nine minutes, and one second, but all *Vostok* controls were operated by radio from the ground while Gagarin's physical and mental reactions and conditions were monitored by the controllers as well. Gagarin's capsule floated down to the ground on a parachute after atmospheric reentry.

The news of Gagarin's accomplishment was a jolt to the United States, though not quite on the scale of *Sputnik*, which shattered the space barrier. The young officer became an instant world celebrity as the Kremlin pulled all the stops to celebrate this Soviet achievement. To President Kennedy in Washington, the Gagarin flight was the start of a run of bad luck within short months of his inauguration. The following week Kennedy watched the drama of the collapse of the Bay of Pigs invasion, further undermining America's international prestige.

In his search for a response to the new Soviet primacy in space, the President turned, among others, to Vice President Lyndon Johnson, whose responsibilities included nonmilitary spatial programs; it was one of those make-work assignments often given Vice Presidents of the United States to keep them busy and out of the way. At NASA headquarters the Steering Committee for Manned Space Flight had proposed in 1959 a moon landing enterprise costing thirty-eight billion dollars over a decade (it would have been ten times as much in 1990 dollars), but Eisenhower had turned it down flatly. Johnson revived the idea, telling Kennedy that a lunar landing would "symbolize the technological power and organizing capacity of a nation . . . part of the battle along the fluid front of the Cold War." Kennedy bought the moon concept at once. The competition with the Russians was so powerfully embedded in the minds of America's top leaders that sky was really the limit in outdoing the Soviet Union in the eyes of the world.

As it happened, NASA and Project Mercury made it easier for Kennedy to convince Americans to join the manned spaceflight race. On May 5, 1961, Navy Commander Alan B. Shepard, Jr., thirty-eight years old, an engineer and a test pilot, soared into orbit aboard *Freedom 7*, the Mercury spacecraft propelled by a Redstone rocket developed at the Army's Redstone Arsenal in Huntsville, Alabama, by a team headed by Wernher von Braun. It was a much shorter flight than Gagarin's—302 miles at a maximal altitude of 116.5 miles and lasting only fifteen minutes—but America watched it excitedly and gratefully. Unlike in the Soviet Union, the spaceflight in the United States was a public event, and tens of thousands of Americans gathered on Florida's Cocoa Beach to watch the liftoff from Cape Canaveral and to cheer when *Freedom 7* blasted into the sky and flew gracefully in an arc toward the splashdown point east of the Great Abaco Island in the Bahamas. It was American romance and American adventure.

Von Braun, too, was on hand to watch the dawn of the American space age, the supreme moment of his career. He and the ten thousand other individuals involved in Project Mercury were certain that the eighty-three-foot-long *Freedom 7* would fly (in January a Mercury Redstone had carried a chimpanzee named Ham 414 miles over the Atlantic to a safe landing), but it had to be seen to be believed—in person or via television. Describing the experience in a subsequent article, Shepard notes, "I encountered no problem in respiration, observation, and reporting to the ground," and naturally these were the reactions NASA experts watched the most carefully. Weightlessness was another unprecedented human experience, and Shepard writes that during the five minutes it lasted during his flight, "Movements, speech, and breathing are unimpaired, and the entire sensation is most analogous to floating."

With Project Mercury still aglow from its triumph, on May 25 Kennedy sent a message to Congress on "Urgent National Needs" with this extraordinary appeal: "Now is the time to take longer strides. . . . I believe that this nation should commit itself to achieving the goal, before this decade is out, of landing a man on the moon and returning him safely to earth."

Carl Sagan, the astronomer, later put Kennedy's proposal into perspective, writing that its "scope and audacity . . . dazzled me." He goes on: "We would use rockets not yet designed and alloys not yet conceived, navigation and docking schemes not yet devised, in order to send a man to a world not yet explored, not even in a preliminary way, with robots—and we would bring him safely back, and we would do it before the decade was over. This confident pronouncement was made before any American even achieved Earth orbit." Sagan and others have argued over the years that Kennedy's moon landing project—240,000 miles away from Earth—was not primarily about science or even space but about ideological confrontation and nuclear war.

This is, of course, a subjective judgment, and it is essentially academic because man—American man—*has* reached the moon. But Sagan himself also acknowledges that if it had not been for Kennedy's "political purpose," the "historic American expeditions of exploration and discovery throughout the solar system would not have occurred" and that "something similar is true for the pioneering Soviet efforts in solar-system exploration, including the first landings of robot spacecraft on another planet. . . . What began in deadly competition has led us to see that global cooperation is the essential precondition for our survival."

What counted when Kennedy issued his challenge to America was the nation's ability to accomplish the lunar landing within the decade, considering the incredible technological obstacles and the immense cost it exacted. The United States, however, already had the tradition of the Manhattan Project and the building of the atomic bomb, human and material resources existed, and scientific research was more advanced than ever before in the country's history. Lyndon Baines Johnson, now the President, evidently would not turn against his own original idea—notwithstanding the mounting costs of the Vietnam War and of the Great Society he desired to construct at home—and the Congress knew that public opinion strongly favored Project Apollo. Thus America embarked on lunar exploration.

Inevitably there were setbacks and tragedies. On August 6–7, 1961, three months after Kennedy announced the moon enterprise, Gherman Titov, another Soviet cosmonaut, became the second man to fly in space, spending a full day in orbit. Khrushchev chose to be bellicose about it. On August 9 he informed American visitors at the Kremlin: "If you want to threaten us from a position of strength, we will show you our strength. You do not have 50 and 100 megaton bombs. We have stronger than 100 megaton. We placed Gagarin and Titov in space, and we can replace them with other loads that can be directed to any place on earth." And on October 30 the Soviets exploded a fifty-eight-megaton hydrogen weapon in the Arctic. To translate such megatonnage into comprehensive measurements, suffice it to say that the Pentagon estimated that a single weapon of this size would create total destruction over 250 square miles. Khrushchev seemed to bear out Sagan's opinion that space was really about nuclear war and ideological confrontation.

On the more encouraging side of the ledger, Americans overcame the Russians in space on February 20, 1962, when John H. Glenn, Jr., a forty-year-old Air Force colonel, circled the Earth three times in a Mercury vehicle. The first American in space orbit, Glenn flew 81,000 miles at 17,545 miles per hour, reaching an altitude of 187.75 miles. He remained four hours and fifty-six minutes in space between Cape Canaveral blastoff to a landing off the Bahamas. His achievement and his poetic description of what he observed from the spacecraft windows earned him national fame; this balding colonel went on to serve as U.S. senator from Ohio and to become the Senate's leading expert on nuclear weapons verification procedures and strategic intelligence.

In the mid-sixties the Mercury program was succeeded by first the Gemini and then the Apollo space programs. In January 1967 Apollo astronauts Edward White, Roger Chaffee, and Virgil "Gus" Grissom died horribly when their spacecraft exploded and burned on a Cape Kennedy launching pad. New problems appeared daily, but the project moved inexorably ahead.

(In 1989 the Russians informed the world of their space-related tragedies. In 1960 an ICBM rocket had exploded at the Baikonur space center, killing Field Marshal Mitrofan Nedelin, the chief of the Soviet missile forces, and fifty-three others. On March 18, 1980, a Vostok rocket blew up at the Plesetsk Space Center during fueling on the launch pad; fifty Soviet soldiers died, burned to death.)

Then it happened. On July 16, 1969—eight years after John Kennedy's promise—*Apollo 11* lifted from its Florida pad atop a Saturn V rocket for the flight to the moon. The spacecraft hovered over the moon in the afternoon of July 20 (eastern daylight time) as the lunar module *Eagle* with pilot Neil Armstrong and copilot Edwin E. "Buzz" Aldrin, Jr., separated from the command module *Columbia*, flown by Michael Collins, to begin the careful descent to the lunar surface. Finally, Armstrong and Aldrin stood on the moon, fulfilling thousands of years of humankind's dreams.

They remained on the moon for an hour and forty-five minutes, exploring the area of the Sea of Tranquility, where the *Eagle* squatted, they planted the Stars and Stripes on the surface, and they unveiled a plaque proclaiming: "Here men from the planet Earth first set foot on the moon, July 1969 AD. We came in peace for all mankind." With forty-six pounds of moon rocks and particles, Armstrong and Aldrin returned to the *Eagle* and ascended up to the *Columbia*, rejoining Collins. The *Eagle* was left behind. The *Columbia* splashed down in the Pacific on July 24, and the three astronauts were taken aboard the aircraft carrier *Hornet* to be welcomed "back to Earth" by President Richard Nixon.

Nixon told them that "over 100 foreign governments, emperors, presidents, prime ministers, and kings have sent the most warm messages that we have ever received . . . they represent over two billion people on this earth, all of them who have had the opportunity, through television, to see what you have done." Actually at least six hundred million people across the globe had watched the moon landing, broadcast live from the lunar surface down to the Earth and television networks everywhere. If all John Kennedy had had in mind was to win recognition and admiration for the United States, he had certainly achieved it. In the Communist world, for example, television in Yugoslavia and Romania (but not the Soviet Union) carried the entire broadcast live. I was watching it with my family in the dining room of a small restaurant near the Yugoslav town of Rijeka on the Adriatic; the manager had placed a tiny American flag on our table, and when Armstrong and Aldrin stepped down on the moon, the Yugoslavs in the room cheered, and many came over to congratulate us—the only Americans in sight.

It is probably inevitable that revisionism will touch and question every historical event of consequence. And so it was with the American lunar program on the twentieth anniversary of the *Apollo 11* mission, in 1989, when books, articles, and editorials appeared massively to weigh the pros and cons of the moon enterprise. There were five more American Apollo missions to the moon before the program was terminated in 1972, apparently for fiscal reasons, and NASA manned flights have been entirely shifted to the space shuttles. The anniversary discussions of the first lunar descent were addressed largely to what has been gained from it.

Reasonable scientists like Carl Sagan take the view that the Apollo voyages opened the way for the exploration of the solar system by Americans, Russians, and others. President George Bush used the anniversary to urge a new program that would aim at a manned spacecraft landing on the planet Mars in the first or second decade of the next century from a base on the moon. Apollo having cost twenty-five billion dollars, clearly the investment should not be abandoned; Kennedy's lunar concept reaffirmed the truth that humankind will go on striving to discover more and more, that it will go to Mars simply because "it is there." A month after the Apollo landing's twentieth anniversary, the unmanned *Voyager 2* reached the planet Neptune after a twelve-year flight of 4.4 billion miles.

Critics claim that the 841 pounds of lunar samples brought back by moon expeditions have added nothing to our knowledge of the universe. That may be so, but obviously Apollo was not designed for collecting rocks. More to the point, it seems, would be an assessment of technological lessons learned from manned spaceflight and of the program's practical spin-offs. To try to calculate whether the twenty-five billion dollars spent on the Apollo program has brought a decent commercial return is absurd because the gains are too dispersed and long-range to be quantified in terms of a bottom line; this was never the idea.

Aside from the fact that space technology was first and foremost an inheritance of World War II, the interesting questions concern the degree to which the moon program has stimulated research and production. While, for example, the program did not lead to basic developments in microelectronics (because they already existed), NASA and military contracts for space vehicles and guidance systems served to stimulate the microcircuit industry to think faster and better.

Miniaturization of on-board computers required by the Apollo spacecraft encouraged the design of small personal computers for commercial use. ENIAC, the world's first electronic digital computer, was built at the University of Pennsylvania in 1945, as a thirty-ton monster. During the ensuing four decades, when both space and nuclear technologies were demanding more manageable and efficient computer hardware, the point was reached where ten *billion* bits of information could be stored on a single videodisc.

The space program has created the vast networks of communications and weather satellites that have revolutionized lives since the early eighties, creating the new information society. Not only do telephone and television circuits based on satellites have a limitless capacity (especially with the conversion to fiber optics, lasers, and digital systems), but the latest navigation satellites allow an aircraft or a ship to determine instantly its position within thirty-one feet anywhere in the world—in the air and on the sea. This is a significant contribution to safety in transportation.

Weightlessness in space has opened new vistas for the production of better and cheaper pharmaceutical compounds. Along with surgical instruments stemming from space experiments, they may become the technological equivalent of nuclear medicine. This is turning into the next extraordinary heritage from the 1939–45 war that killed millions; is it poetic or divine justice? Unquestionably, more should be spent at this stage on space-derived biological breakthroughs and life-support systems. But these are decisions that society must make as it goes along; space programs have provided the scientific base.

In the sixties scientific, technical, and medical progress was already taken for granted to such a great extent that disasters resulting from new technology were received with disbelief, fear, and anger. The most serious dangers emanated from the advent of the nuclear age, in both its military and its industrial applications. The superpowers were steadily building up their nuclear arsenals and expanding nuclear defense and offense systems. And the growth of nuclear power plants had a peril potential as well.

I shall never forget the absolute sense of terror—the paralyzing fear of the unknown—that possessed the people of Palomares when four hydrogen bombs tumbled out of the sky onto their village in southern Spain on the morning of January 17, 1966. A U.S. Air Force B-52 strategic jet bomber had collided with an Air Force jet tanker refueling it in midair, and the deadly thermonuclear cargo came crashing down from 30,500 feet.

Three of the 1.5-megaton plutonium-uranium weapons (the destructive power of each was seventy-five times that of the atomic bombs that blasted Hiroshima and Nagasaki) hit the ground at Palomares. The fourth bomb fell in deep Mediterranean waters five and a half miles offshore, to be recovered only three months later. The B-52 was flying over Spain en route home to the United States after a night on its secret airborne alert station not far from the Turkish-Soviet border. Such missions were flown around the clock all along Soviet frontiers by nuclear-armed B-52's, ready to go into action the moment war erupted, and their presence there gave the United States the advantage of permanent proximity to key targets. The practice was for the B-52's heading for the Turkish station to be refueled over Spain and again on their way back by aerial tankers stationed at the Spanish Air Force Base of Morón. This was what the two aircraft were doing that morning high over the Spanish coast.

Arriving in Palomares (the name means "dovecotes" in Spanish) two days after the midair collision—when it was already public knowledge that the four bombs were *nuclear*, not conventional, devices—I realized that the overwhelming concern on the part of American experts already on the spot was over radioactive contamination from particles of plutonium scattered by the wind over the village and its fields. And the experts' concern was instantly permuted into the fear gripping the 250 families inhabiting Palomares, mainly poor tomato growers. Of the three bombs that landed there, one remained intact, posing no danger. But in the two others the impact had caused the explosion of TNT trigger charges inside the plutonium-uranium warheads, releasing alpha radiation into the air. There was no actual nuclear explosion because the hydrogen bombs were not armed for attack— the TNT trigger alone is not sufficient to start a critical reaction—and there were no emissions of lethal beta and gamma radiation. Still, there *was* intense radiation from the warheads' plutonium particles.

Plutonium has a biological half-life of two hundred years, and its particles may cause cancer if inhaled, as was presumably happening to the people of Palomares. This was the first time since Hiroshima and Nagasaki that a civilian population had been exposed directly to radioactive contamination from nuclear weapons, and there was extraordinary uncertainty both among the American scientists in Palomares and among the villagers over possible future consequences. (The Soviet accident at Kyshtym in 1957 involved nuclear wastes.)

At the time—in 1966—it was not yet known that cancer damage would affect Pacific islanders from the Bikini and Eniwetok atolls, where America's atomic bombs and the first hydrogen weapons were tested between 1946 and 1963 (testing in the atmosphere ended in the latter year, when Washington and Moscow signed the nuclear test ban treaty). The islanders had been evacuated from their homes prior to the explosions, but radioactivity drifted toward their resettlement areas. A crewman aboard a Japanese fishing vessel reached by radioactive ash from the Bikini blast was known to have died, but there was no experience with nuclear weapons accidents resulting in contamination.

Both the United States and the Soviet Union exposed their soldiers to extravagant—and now we realize irresponsible—risks to assess the psychological effects of nuclear explosions on the troops and to test protective gear; troops were used massively as atomic age guinea pigs.

These experiments were conducted in secret, but the U.S. Defense Department acknowledged decades later that between 250,000 and 500,000 American troops participated in exercises linked to atmospheric nuclear explosions in the Pacific and in Nevada between 1946 and 1963. In Operation Crossroads in June 1946, 42,000 American servicemen were aboard ships on station near Bikini during three atomic detonations, and the vessels became contaminated by radioactivity. After 1952 soldiers were deployed in trenches within four miles from explosion sites in Nevada (there also were sheep there), and units were then ordered to ground zero. Nevada inhabitants have been petitioning Congress for compensation for damages to their health; almost nothing is known of what happened to the troops.

In September 1989 the Soviet Union admitted that in 1954 it had dropped an atomic bomb in the open air fifteen hundred feet over the heads of troops in the southern Ural Mountains to see if men could fight amid radiation. In reporting the exercise, the Soviet army newspaper *Krasnaya Zvezda* says that "after the atomic strike, there were not only no landmarks left on the terrain, but the area itself became unrecognizable." It writes that there were no injuries, but "long-term effects of the radiation were never taken into account," adding that "only nine years after a war that had taken 20 million of our compatriots' lives, it never even occurred to us to question any measures meant to bolster the army's battle worthiness and the country's defense capabilities."

The blast's heat melted tanks, and "soon everything was covered with stones, dirt and dead animals." One soldier, the newspaper says, avoided blindness from the "scarlet flames" by throwing himself facefirst into a trench; other young soldiers were terrified, hiding where they could.

On both sides this was the secret criminality of the Cold War.

In a sense, Palomares was lucky. There might have been additional radiation emissions from the other bombs fallen over the village, and if winds had been weaker or blowing in another direction, great volumes of plutonium particles would have clung to the tomato vines. Nevertheless, that chapter has not yet been closed because as long as thirty years may elapse before cancer affects a person who has been exposed to radioactive particles. Twenty-four years after the accident no such case has been reported. But the frightening lesson of Palomares was that in our postwar nuclear world no city, no village, and no person are safe from death—not to say, obliteration—from mishaps with calamitous weapons designed to assure peace.

V

After John Kennedy's assassination in November 1963, peace became more elusive than ever in Vietnam. It has been alleged by his associates that Kennedy planned to start reducing the American military presence there after Christmas in order to avoid the appearance of a warmonger candidate during the 1964 presidential campaign; he had every intention of running for a second term. In retrospect, it is clear that Kennedy could not have removed the advisers and the MACV structure without forcing a prompt collapse of the South Vietnamese regime. The war was going from bad to worse, and after Diem's death the government in Saigon kept changing hands, from military coup to military coup. At least Kennedy was spared the agonizing decision of what to do about Vietnam and the probability of presiding indefinitely over a very large Asian war with vast numbers of American soldiers fighting and dying for Vietnam's cause.

As for Lyndon Johnson, four days after having been sworn in as President aboard Air Force One at the Dallas airport within hours of the assassination, he moved to continue the Vietnam War the Kennedy way. In fact, he authorized its escalation. In a National Security Action memorandum issued on November 26, Johnson committed himself to maintain the policies designed to help Saigon to win the "contest against the externally directed and supported Communist conspiracy." When Henry Cabot Lodge called on him during a brief consultations trip from his Saigon embassy, the new President promised that he would "not lose Vietnam" though he clearly did not realize how exceedingly difficult it would be to save it.

In this vein Johnson obligingly authorized the military and the CIA to launch clandestine operations against North Vietnam on a scale never before attempted. This plan was devised by Major General Victor Krulak, a Marine Corps hero of World War II and Korea who was General Taylor's deputy at the White House and later a special assistant for counterinsurgency to Defense Secretary Robert McNamara and the Joint Chiefs of Staff. A Kennedy favorite, Krulak was regarded as a "modern" and imaginative officer with insights into all the newfangled thinking about irregular and psychological warfare, destabilizing the enemy's infrastructure behind his own lines, and winning the "hearts and minds." He had a powerful ally in Walt Rostow, the economics professor turned foreign policy adviser to Kennedy at the White House (and soon thereafter chairman of the State Department's Policy Planning Staff), who was an ardent believer in covert operations. On at least one occasion Rostow told me in an off-the-record conversation that Hanoi would be forced to abandon the war in the South if American power could be applied in a sophisticated fashion against targets in North Vietnam. I, of course, had no idea that such operations had already begun.

The Krulak-Rostow blueprint provided for commando teams of South Vietnamese and Asian mercenaries recruited by the CIA to be landed by sea or parachuted into North Vietnam to destroy communications and transportation centers. Another wrinkle proposed by Krulak was to dispatch Navy PT boats to shell coastal radar and other defensive installations. He described his overall plan as "destructive undertakings" that in time would be extended to North Vietnamese industry and other economic centers. Krulak and his allies (and possibly even Lyndon Johnson) may not have imagined when they proceeded with this clandestine warfare offensive that it would result in a colossal escalation of the whole Indochina War.

The disconcerting thing about the new directions the conduct of the war in Vietnam was taking late in 1963 and in 1964 was that it proposed to apply guerrilla methods to an enemy (North Vietnam) that was master of guerrilla warfare while fielding conventional armies against Communist guerrillas in South Vietnam who were directed and supplied from the North. When North Vietnam later decided to send *its* conventional forces to fight in South Vietnam, American and ARVN commanders faced a situation that made absolutely no sense. Among strategic planning faults was the notion that doctrines can be transposed from war to war, country to country, and decade to decade; in other words, Krulak and Rostow with their World War II backgrounds assumed that commando actions that had proved effective against the Nazis in Europe would work in North Vietnam and that conventional forces could stabilize South Vietnam against the guerrillas.

In the unreal world of the Vietnam War, Johnson apparently felt justified in approving the clandestine operations scenario even more when McNamara informed him after a quick trip to Saigon in December that the military situation "has in fact been deteriorating in the countryside since July to a far greater extent than we realized." This was the first time that a ranking American official had reported to the President of the United States (but in private, of course) that the war, in effect, was being lost. Johnson's reaction was to do everything in the power of the United States to win that war, and he moved to seize control of the entire enterprise after authorizing Krulak's covert missions.

Johnson concentrated during most of 1964 on reorganizing American military, political, and diplomatic structures in Vietnam as he began devoting more and more time to the presidential campaign. He was determined to be elected in November in his own right, and his instinct was to preserve the status quo in Vietnam, at least as far as public opinion was concerned. He did not want war headlines or Americans in Vietnam shown on television. Johnson's strategy was to present himself as a pro-peace candidate, promising to keep American soldiers out of Vietnam, while making Senator Barry Goldwater of Arizona, his Republican opponent, appear a demented hawk who would unleash a nuclear conflict over Indochina. The conservative Goldwater was much more honest when he responded in his acceptance speech at the Republican convention, "Extremism in the defense of liberty is no vice." Still, as the election approached, neither Johnson nor Goldwater really knew how to cope with the Vietnam quandary.

Changes in the Saigon American command structure started with the arrival in January 1964 of Lieutenant General William C. Westmoreland, a forty-nine-year-old West Point graduate, who was named deputy to General Harkins and replaced him as chief of MACV in June. Harkins had become discredited in the eyes of Washington for failing to whip the South Vietnamese into shape and win the war, but the reason for replacing him with Westmoreland was kept quiet to avoid embarrassing the military establishment. Still, the choice of Westmoreland was extremely puzzling if the United States indeed planned to conduct an imaginative campaign to wrest the initiative away from the Communists. Stanley Karnow has described him as "a corporation executive in uniform, a diligent, disciplined organization man who would obey orders . . . he saw the war as essentially an exercise in management."

Just as Westmoreland took over MACV, Lodge resigned as ambassador to South Vietnam when it occurred to him that he had a chance for the Republican presidential nomination (this was shortly before the convention chose Goldwater). Top officials volunteered for Lodge's job because the Vietnam War was now becoming something of a moral crusade to the Johnson administration though the President still wished to avoid public warlike acts damaging to his candidacy. On July 2 Congress had passed the

Civil Rights Act, the first civil rights legislation since 1866, and Johnson wanted to make sure that foreign disasters did not detract from his domestic accomplishments. To curry favor with Johnson, at least three Cabinet officers—Secretary of State Rusk, Defense Secretary McNamara, and Attorney General Kennedy (who had not yet developed antiwar sentiments)—as well as McGeorge Bundy, the presidential special assistant for national security affairs, bid for Saigon. However, the appointment to the Saigon embassy had to be a sure bet, and the President picked General Taylor (known as "Max") for it. Taylor had been promoted by Kennedy to be Chairman of the Joint Chiefs of Staff after his stint as White House military adviser, but he did not consider the ambassadorship to be a demotion.

With Taylor and Westmoreland in Saigon (the former had proposed the latter for MACV), the military ran the entire South Vietnam show. They were not really listening to civilian experts from the Agency for International Development (AID), which in theory was in charge of rural "pacification" programs; the United States Information Agency (USIA), which tried to keep tabs on the South Vietnamese population's moods by conducting secret public opinion polls; and even the CIA, which naturally had very good contacts in the country and was more clear-eyed about the war than the generals.

This was too bad because the principal problem in South Vietnam was that *its* generals were unable to decide who should be top dog. Diem had been replaced in power by a four-man military junta headed by Major General Duong Van Minh (known as Big Minh) who had served as military adviser at the presidential palace, where mad plotting was more comfortable. Besides, he was a fine tennis player, a fact that endeared him to top American officials. The junta was incapable of directing military operations that would interfere seriously with a major offensive the Communists launched late in November 1963 throughout the Mekong River delta and in the region north of Saigon, allowing the Vietcong to score their greatest successes to date. At the end of January 1964 the junta was overthrown (with quiet American blessings) by the ARVN, and Lieutenant General Nguyen Khanh, a thirty-six-year-old French-trained paratrooper, was made chief of the government. Khanh lasted in power just over a year, during which the Communists made vast advances. He was replaced in April 1965 by Air Vice-Marshal Nguyen Cao Ky, a flamboyant nonentity. His deputy was Brigadier General Nguyen Van Thieu, the man destined to become tragically famous in Vietnamese history.

As the elections approached (and Johnson's fans across the United States sang "Hello, Lyndon!" to the tune of the smash hit "Hello, Dolly!"), the President continued to avoid any actions in Vietnam that would alarm the voters. Clandestine operations against North Vietnam, including naval raids and shelling, were naturally kept from the American public because they were classified top secret (though not from the North Vietnamese, who knew they were being attacked). The number of American advisers in South Vietnam was slightly in excess of twenty thousand early in 1964, not enough to cause Johnson political problems. The cost of Vietnam was only five hundred million dollars for 1963. The President, however, was always ready to seize an opportunity when it beckoned.

And it beckoned on August 2, 1964. Three days earlier the destroyer *Maddox* had sailed into the Gulf of Tonkin, which bathes North Vietnamese and Chinese coasts in the South China Sea, on a secret intelligence mission intended to locate radar installations in North Vietnam. The *Maddox* had been outfitted as an ELINT ship (ELINT is "electronic intelligence" in professional parlance) and was one of a number of vessels with similar capabilities patrolling Soviet, North Korean, and Chinese coasts (USS *Pueblo* would be captured in 1968, off North Korea, and its crew put on trial, then released).

The specific reason the *Maddox* was dispatched to the Tonkin Gulf related to equally secret plans of the Johnson administration to begin heavy bombings of North Vietnam after the elections. It was part of the broader concept of bringing the war to enemy territory on a very large scale, but in order to select targets, Pentagon planners needed to know the location and frequencies of North Vietnamese radar, which guided antiaircraft missile batteries. South Vietnamese commandos, active under the clandestine operations program devised by Krulak and Rostow, were landed at spots where radar stations were believed to have been installed in order to provoke their crews into turning them on and for ELINT ships to be able to detect them. These missions were code-named DeSoto. Actually all this added up to military provocation of the highest order.

Six commando teams had raided North Vietnamese offshore islands to trigger the radar stations there on July 30, and the *Maddox* cruised nearby, monitoring the radar signatures. The destroyer was within the twelve-mile limit of territorial waters claimed after World War II by North Vietnam and most other countries in the world, but because the traditional three-mile limit was still ensconced in international law, the United States was technically correct in its view that the *Maddox* was in international waters. In any case, the administration was not greatly preoccupied with legal niceties at that point. Remaining in the gulf, the *Maddox* intercepted early on August 2 North Vietnamese radio transmissions concerning unspecified "military operations," but the Navy's Seventh Fleet command ordered the vessel to stay in the area.

Shortly after noon the *Maddox* was attacked with torpedoes by North Vietnamese patrol boats as it sailed some ten miles off the estuary of the Red River. The torpedoes did no damage, and the destroyer's guns and jets summoned from an aircraft carrier on station not far away sank one patrol boat and hit two others. Johnson was immediately informed of the incident, but he held back from reacting. Instead, he sent a message to Khrushchev in Moscow to express his concern over North Vietnamese attacks on American warships in international waters and a warning to Hanoi that it faced "grave consequences" if it interfered again with them on the high seas. The *Maddox* and another destroyer, the *C. Turner Joy*, were ordered back toward the North Vietnamese coast—to see what responses would follow. With Johnson kept abreast of every operational detail, the American scenario was unfolding to the White House's enormous satisfaction.

During the night of August 3–4 the two destroyers, steaming in the dark to test American "legitimate rights in international waters" (as Navy orders to their captains put it), suddenly gained the impression that they might be under North Vietnamese assault. Neither the ships nor carrier jets overhead could see anything, but their instruments registered what appeared to be the sound of patrol boats and signatures of radar locking in on the destroyers. The *Maddox* and the *C. Turner Joy* started firing their guns toward what they thought were enemy craft. If any torpedoes were fired at them from anywhere, they did not strike the ships. When the dawn rose on August 4, the two skippers had no idea what had actually happened during the night, and they so reported to the Seventh Fleet.

In Washington, however, President Johnson decided that something *had* happened, specifically that the destroyers had been attacked. Still, on August 4 he informed the congressional leadership that he would order retaliation. He also mentioned that he would ask the Congress for a resolution supporting whatever action he took, but he failed to tell the congressmen that the White House and the State Department had drafted a resolution of this type months earlier and that the planning for the bombing of North Vietnam had been completed after many months of studies. In the evening the President went on national television to announce that American warships had been attacked *twice* by the North Vietnamese in a deliberate fashion and that the United States was responding even as he spoke. In what was the first American air strike at North Vietnam, carrier jets hit patrol boat bases and fuel storage tanks along the coast. And the first two American aircraft to be shot down over North Vietnam went down that night.

The next day Johnson sent up to Capitol Hill the resolution he wished the Congress to approve to give him a free hand in Southeast Asia. So absolute was the nation's faith in the veracity of the reports on the Tonkin Gulf attacks that American public opinion rallied massively behind Johnson and both houses of Congress voted on the resolution exactly the way he wanted it (unanimity in the House of Representatives and only two opposing votes in the Senate). Just as important, the legislation was shepherded through the Senate by the highly respected chairman of the Senate Foreign Relations Committee, J. William Fulbright of Arkansas, a leading liberal.

When the truth—that there never was a *second* attack on an American warship and that the administration had been planning all along to bomb North Vietnam—came out in Senate hearings several years later, Fulbright felt betrayed. He never forgave Johnson. The resolution was repealed in 1970.

*   *   *

At the end of 1964, however, President Johnson interpreted the Tonkin Gulf resolution as the equivalent of a declaration of war, equipping him with full powers to conduct the war as he saw fit. The last time the Congress had formally declared war was in 1941, after the Japanese strike at Pearl Harbor, and Johnson did not believe that it was necessary to deal with Vietnam any differently from the Korean "police action." Nevertheless, the resolution was the turning point in the American war in Indochina.

Lyndon Johnson was elected overwhelmingly on November 3, with Hubert Humphrey of Minnesota as Vice President, and the victory strengthened Johnson's mandate in all realms. Though Goldwater lost badly, the twenty-four million votes he did garner represented, as it subsequently developed, the birth of ideological conservatism in the United States that matured with Ronald Reagan sixteen years later. And in a transference of loyalties, great numbers of Goldwater voters shifted to Johnson's side when he escalated America's involvement in Vietnam while his original liberal supporters felt orphaned and moved into bitter opposition to his administration.

President of the United States in his own right, Johnson had a new super-power opposite number in the Soviet Union, forcing him and his administration to face the possibility that different and unpredictable policies might emerge in the Kremlin. On October 13 the Politburo had removed Nikita Khrushchev from power in a move that came as a complete surprise to American Kremlinologists—and to Khrushchev himself. The new first secretary of the Soviet Communist party was fifty-eight-year-old Leonid I. Brezhnev, a professional apparat functionary who had worked his way to the top from prewar apprenticeship under Stalin, entering the Politburo in 1957, three years after Khrushchev had become the party boss. He was twelve years younger than Khrushchev, but he lacked Khrushchev's flamboyance, élan, and imagination—perhaps the main reason his coconspirators chose him to replace the leader they were removing after his turbulent ten years in office.

Khrushchev may have been his own worst enemy in the sense that increasingly he was becoming too authoritarian to suit the rest of the Politburo. This was the main theme in the fifteen-point bill of particulars brought against him at that fateful meeting when he was, in effect, invited to resign. Interestingly, however, Khrushchev's 1962 Cuba fiasco was not among the charges. That in post-Stalinist Soviet Union excess of authoritarian behavior was no longer tolerable was an illustration of how the country and its politics had changed in the eleven years since Stalin's death. The party seemed to prefer a collective dictatorship. Ironically, Khrushchev had set this evolution in motion with his speech denouncing Stalinist crimes, and he then paid for his own penchant toward one-man rule and a personality cult (he was not guilty, of course, of Stalinist criminality). Another major change in the Soviet way of conducting politics was that with Khrushchev's fall the Politburo passed a resolution separating the functions of first secretary of the Communist party and of the premier, both of which he had exercised simultaneously. Aleksei N. Kosygin, an engineer by training and long a party faithful, was named premier when Brezhnev was chosen first secretary. Finally, there was no real power struggle at the end. No revenge was invoked against Khrushchev, who simply turned into a nonperson, ignored by the official establishment but free to write his memoirs (rich in opinions), which soon found their way into print in the West.

The main concern about Brezhnev in Washington was that he appeared to be ignorant about foreign affairs, clearly a problem in the midst of the continuing Cold War and the escalating Vietnam conflict. Khrushchev, on the other hand, was superbly traveled and had met everybody: Eisenhower and Kennedy, Mao and Zhou Enlai, Tito and De Gaulle, Churchill, Nehru, Ho Chi Minh, Adenauer, Nasser, Sukarno, Castro, just about every leader who counted in the world. Brezhnev was and remained a bumpkin. To be sure, Johnson's personal experience was limited, too, but this was not his view of himself; LBJ was not a man of modesty.

Great leaders were disappearing one by one, in one fashion or another. Kennedy was killed in 1963, Nehru died early in 1964, Khrushchev was ousted later that year, and Winston Churchill died at the age of ninety in January 1965, five days after Johnson's inauguration. Churchill had been out of power for many years, but he was an extraordinary world presence until the end: He won the Nobel Prize for literature, he became the first foreigner in history to be made honorary citizen of the United States by act of Congress, and he could have been a duke if he had not refused the queen's offer to raise him to peerage. And his opinions were always strong; he referred to John Foster Dulles, for example, as "that slab-faced bastard."

The last of the great leaders still in power was Charles de Gaulle, majestically exercising the presidency of France at the Élysée Palace (but discreetly finding recreation in viewing motion pictures that starred Steve McQueen, his favorite American actor, and in reading James Bond spy novels in French). De Gaulle, however, was no help to Johnson. He had already warned Kennedy in 1961 that Vietnam ("this rotten country") would become "a bottomless military and political swamp" for the United States. In 1963 he urged "a neutral Vietnam," and in 1966 he was to denounce in a speech in Pnom Penh, the Cambodian capital, the risks of the American intervention in Indochina. In fact, De Gaulle seemed determined to annoy the United States at every opportunity: In January 1964 he granted full diplomatic recognition to Communist China (the British had done it much earlier, also annoying Washington); in March 1966 he wrote Johnson to inform him that he was removing French armed forces from NATO command (he had already removed in 1963 the French Atlantic fleet from joint allied command); and he went on to denounce the "hegemony of the dollar" in still another display of the French go-it-alone approach to the world.

In Vietnam the United States under Johnson was very much alone, too, but not by choice. The President had to depend on his own instincts and on the opinions of those surrounding him, practically all of them men who had eased John Kennedy into Vietnam.

* * *

Lyndon Johnson's entire term—from January 1965 to January 1969—was overwhelmed by the unrelenting savagery and mounting magnitude of the Indochina War. It became Johnson's War, overshadowed his efforts to build his Great Society at home and ameliorate race relations through additional civil rights legislation, and, finally, discouraged him from seeking a second elected term.

From the outset he faced an awesome dilemma. Large-scale Communist attacks launched late in 1964, and gaining in intensity during 1965, left no doubt that Hanoi and the Vietcong were determined to win the war truly at any cost, no matter what the Americans did. Johnson knew, as he was inaugurated on January 20, that the South Vietnamese alone stood no chance whatsoever of resisting the Communist onslaught. Only unrestricted use of American military power could save Saigon and, in the opinion of the administration, the rest of Southeast Asia. Washington geopoliticians invented the domino theory, convincing themselves that if the South Vietnam "domino" fell, so would Laos, Cambodia, Thailand, Malaysia, Indonesia, and even the Philippines. Again, Americans were ascribing to "international communism" power and unity it never possessed.

Having made this judgment on Vietnam's importance to the United States, Johnson proceeded to build up the American presence there, increment by increment, until it became the largest anywhere overseas since World War II. Still, it was never enough, bearing out Kennedy's prediction four years earlier that "we will be told we have to send more troops . . . it's like taking a drink. . . . The effect wears off, and you have to take another."

Armed with the Tonkin Gulf resolution, Johnson opened a new phase of the war in February 1965 with a heavy air strike by carrier jets on a North Vietnamese army camp (in December he had authorized Operation Barrel Roll, which consisted of secret raids on Communist infiltration routes in Laos). The February raid, code-named Flaming Dart, was the prologue to three and a half years of sustained bombing of North Vietnam, known as the Rolling Thunder campaign. It started on March 2, with an attack on an ammunition dump by more than a hundred aircraft. Subsequently Johnson (who personally approved individual targets and missions) added "carpet bombing" of the countryside by the huge B-52 jet bombers as well as the use of napalm and fragmentation bombs against troop concentrations in the South and the North and often against villages and civilians.

The recommendation by the Air Force chief of staff, General Curtis LeMay, to bomb North Vietnam "back into the Stone Age" was not followed by Johnson, who, with exceptions, left Hanoi and other cities pretty much alone. Under Rolling Thunder, which ended in November 1968 643,000 tons of bombs were dropped on Vietnam. The total for the entire Indochina War, ending in 1972, was 6.3 million tons, three times the volume of bombs dropped by the Allies over three continents in the six years of World War II. Inasmuch as the United States failed to win the war, this massive bombing had no decisive impact on the military situation. Mark Clodfelter, an Air Force major and historian at the Air Force Academy, writes in his book *The Limits of Air Power,* that American political and military leaders continued to think of Vietnam in terms of wartime Europe, disregarding the fact that the B-52's could not liquidate guerrillas in the jungles and that North Vietnam, lacking a major industrial infrastructure, would not be brought to its knees by bombings around Hanoi and Haiphong, which Nixon started later. Even strikes at railway lines from China made virtually no difference. And the cost in aircraft and American crews' lives was extremely high.

The next step in escalation was inevitable. Within days of the start of Rolling Thunder, two Marine Corps battalions landed at Da Nang, the port city on the South Vietnamese coast northeast of Saigon, to protect an air base being completed there for new raids on the North. Almost instantly the marines entered into combat with Vietcong guerrillas, and direct American intervention in the Vietnam War was an accomplished fact.

In Saigon the game of musical chairs continued. Nguyen Van Thieu, the general who was Marshal Ky's number two, became president of South Vietnam as a result of arcane plots and maneuvers by ARVN commanders. He held that post until "peace with honor" liquidated the war and sent him away in exile a decade later. In July 1965 General Max Taylor went home and Henry Cabot Lodge returned as ambassador for the second time. And General Lansdale was back in South Vietnam in September to plan and run clandestine operations. The anti-Castro Operation Mongoose had run its course, and although it had produced no results whatsoever, Lansdale's talents were still in demand among his military friends in Saigon.

Now American troops with tanks, artillery, and helicopters streamed into Vietnam. By July Westmoreland had 50,000 Americans in uniform under his command, and Johnson had told him privately that he could have a total of 200,000 men to finish off the Communists. A whole U.S. Army corps was organized in the Mekong Delta area to handle the Vietcong there, but the Communists went on eluding defeat. Now Westmoreland concluded that he would need 400,000 American soldiers by the end of 1966; the ARVN totaled around 670,000 troops, but they were largely useless, and the United States, at the rate the war was going, would nearly match South Vietnamese totals. At Christmas 1965 Westmoreland demanded a total of 460,000 men to stem Communist advances and conduct "search-and-destroy" operations, his contribution to the doctrine of American soldiers fighting a ground war in Asia.

Now, all told, well over one million men on both sides were engaged in this unending battle. The United States was unprepared for a conflict of this type and size so far away, and commanders simply improvised as they went along. Though American casualties were rising (they exceeded five hundred killed weekly at the end of 1966), uncounted thousands of lives were saved by military medicine as a result of vital lessons learned in the Second World

War and in Korea. Curiously, military doctors were learning fast while the top commanders still functioned in the past. World War II, Korea, and then the Vietnam War turned into gigantic laboratories for dramatic improvements in medicine in general under conditions that do not exist in peacetime. If there is such a thing, this was the only silver lining in the black clouds of wars.

The U.S. Army's Medical Department had the foresight to disseminate all this new knowledge by publishing an impressive history of its wartime experiences in forty-five volumes that cover every imaginable aspect of military medicine. Treatment of trauma in the wounded was among the great breakthroughs, but there was more. After the Army discovered that the traditional vaccine to prevent epidemic typhus had lost its potency, researchers at the Army Medical School were able to restore the vaccine's effectiveness; this was why American troops in World War II were untouched by typhus. It was very helpful in Vietnam as well.

Also during World War II, the Army set up the School of Military Neuropsychiatry to deal with mental and emotional disorders caused by battles and related tensions among the troops. The school believes that this wartime training of drafted physicians became the "nucleus" for the subsequent expansion of civilian psychiatry. The Army's Research Institute of Environmental Medicine provided the present scientific capability to design adequate clothing for combat in various climates and to define water requirements under different conditions; this was a lifesaver in the Indochinese jungles. No time was wasted by the Army in using penicillin (discovered by the British shortly before the war), its first mass application being the North African campaign in 1943. Again, this wartime experience led to generalized use of penicillin and other antibiotics in civilian medical practice afterward. Military malaria control teams began using DDT (first tested by the Army during a typhus epidemic in Naples in 1943) for mosquito control in the Pacific in 1944; it remains the primary insecticide for malaria control in tropical countries. Studies of battlefield shock led to the conclusion that whole blood rather than plasma should be used on the wounded in such cases. The Army Medical Department believes that "documentation of the need for large amounts of whole blood after acute trauma revolutionized the civilian practice of traumatic surgery" after the war. Then the Army came up with an unbreakable artificial eye from acrylic plastic, resembling the coloring of the human eye. Next, the Army's Epidemiological Board found that gamma globulin could prevent infectious hepatitis; it has been used worldwide ever since (it was tested on 107,803 soldiers in Korea).

During the Korean War Army researchers produced lightweight body armor for ground troops, which became a major factor in reducing mortality from wounds in first Korea and then Vietnam. The use of helicopters to evacuate the wounded was started in Korea (where 17,000 casualties had been thus evacuated), and at the time of the Vietnam War the UH-1 (Huey) chopper was adapted as an aerial ambulance, saving thousands of lives there. A team in Korea developed new methods for repairing vascular injury, greatly reducing the amputation rate. Korean-devised methods for resuscitation from shock reduced mortality after wounding by 50 percent. It was in Korea that the first artificial kidney was brought to a combat zone. Research in Korea also contributed new knowledge about septic shock. In 1958 the Army published *Emergency War Surgery* in conjunction with military physicians in every NATO country; the book became most valuable in Vietnam a few years later. Finally, field research in Korea led to the discovery that a "once-a-week" combination tablet of chloroquine diphosphate and primaquine suppresses malaria attacks and relapses. It was a godsend in Vietnam, and it remains the most effective protection against vivax malaria.

As American troops began pouring into Vietnam, the Army installed in 1966 the first portable field surgical hospital. It was an inflatable rubber shelter with electric power, air conditioning, heating, cold and hot water, and waste disposal, and it could be transported by cargo aircraft, helicopter, or truck.

The wars also advanced to an immense degree facial and dental surgery and dentistry. They served as the great laboratories for studies in these fields under real conditions. Facial surgery on burn cases was pioneered by Royal Air Force surgeons at the time of the Battle of Britain in 1940, opening the way for millionaire practitioners of plastic surgery—face-lifts and whatnot—by surgeons like Brazil's famed Ivo Pitanguy.

Men whose jaws and even whole faces were shattered in combat can be rebuilt in a growing number of instances with techniques learned in America's last three wars. Often complete reconstruction is done with titanium and plastics, which, in turn, are technological by-products of the Second World War. Titanium columns are also used in osseointegrations, the new art of tooth implants. New palladium-silver alloys form tooth crowns. However, there are limits to reconstructive surgery. Specialists say that there is a high suicide rate in military hospitals among patients whose faces were too destroyed to permit surgical relief; they prefer to die rather than live with monstrous disfigurations. Finally, wartime technology provided dentistry in the seventies with its greatest breakthrough: compressed-air handpiece drills that function at 480,000 rotations per minute, compared with only 15,000 RPMs in the past. Now dental work can be accomplished in a fraction of the time it required in the old days, and it is infinitely more accurate.

The Congress went on passing civil rights legislation in the mid-sixties, but racism at home was still so strong as to make the defense of democracy in Vietnam something of a mockery. While white and black American soldiers were dying in Indochina (the proportion of blacks was exceedingly high in terms of American populations), young civil rights militants (white and black) were being killed in ambushes in the American South, beaten, manhandled, and imprisoned.

Returning black servicemen were subject to segregation in the South after fighting for "freedom" in Vietnam. A young black Army lieutenant named Colin Luther Powell came home with a Purple Heart in 1963, to be refused service at restaurants in Birmingham, Alabama, and Columbus, Georgia. It was a memory that has never left him; when Powell, now a four-star general, became chairman of the Joint Chiefs of Staff in 1989 (the first black ever), he remembered the shock of that experience and mentioned it repeatedly. "All I wanted was a hamburger," he said, remarking that he was not even thinking of doing a sit-in. After the Civil Rights Act was passed the following year, Powell went back to get his hamburger.

By 1966 the nation was growing weary of the war. Casualties were running into tens of thousands. Americans were jolted more and more by television and magazine images of paratroopers and marines burning down Vietnamese village huts and of Vietnamese children horribly burned by American napalm. (In 1989 the horror of these 1966 actions was brutally portrayed in Brian De Palma's picture *Casualties of War.*) And there was no sign of a victory, no indication when this nightmare would be over. Young Americans began burning their draft cards or fleeing to Canada and Sweden. Antiwar demonstrators chanted, "Hey, hey, LBJ! How many kids did you kill today?" and the increasingly paranoia-dominated President instructed both the FBI and the CIA to determine whether opposition to the war was being fomented from abroad—presumably by Communists.

Not only were youngsters against the Vietnam involvement, but within the administration Defense Secretary McNamara began developing doubts about the wisdom of pursuing the war much longer under existing conditions. Clearly, neither the B-52's nor chopper-borne infantrymen were effective against the Vietcong and North Vietnamese "main force" regulars now entering the battle. Others had doubts, too, but few dared to challenge Johnson's conviction that the war was winnable; the President was pleased with Westmoreland's "body count" figures for the enemy and ready to keep authorizing ever-greater American investment in Southeast Asia.

Influential outside voices were being increasingly heard. Chairman Fulbright of the Senate Foreign Relations Committee opened hearings on Vietnam late in 1966—it was a direct defiance of LBJ—and perhaps the most damaging testimony came from George Kennan to the effect that Vietnam was not vital to American interests and the United States should withdraw from there as soon as possible. Coming from "Mr. X," the diplomat who had devised America's postwar policy of containment of communism, this was a powerful salvo. Still, Johnson would not relent. He shared Secretary of State Rusk's obsessive view that China was behind Ho Chi Minh's stubborn warmaking, and he saw the United States as the guarantor of non-Communist Southeast Asia. The administration simply would not accept the realities of Asia, which was why all the policies in the region were failing. A quarter century later a top Vietcong leader now living in Ho Chi Minh City (formerly Saigon) explained to an American journalist how the

Vietnamese Communists felt about China: "China was no model for me and other comrades in the South. . . . At that time we were really not interested in political systems and ideology but only in how to win this war." Unfortunately, however, American political intelligence in Asia was so deficient that the foreign policy of the United States was based on conventional wisdom (or conventional error) and clichés. Experts in Washington were barely aware that China was exploding internally with the Cultural Revolution launched by Mao Zedong in May 1966.

Interestingly the Soviet Union remained ambivalent about the American war in Vietnam. Naturally it supported Hanoi, but this did not prevent the Kremlin from friendly dealings with the United States, showing how large détente loomed in the Soviet thinking. Thus Premier Aleksei Kosygin flew to America in order to confer with President Johnson in Glassboro, New Jersey, on June 19, 1967; they agreed that a Johnson-Brezhnev summit would take place the following year.

The beginning of the end in Vietnam came on January 30, 1968, although the agony was to last seven more years. It was the nationwide offensive the Communists launched with seventy thousand troops on the lunar New Year, known as Tet. This was the famous Tet offensive, with the rebels penetrating for the first time Saigon and all other important cities and towns in South Vietnam. Ineffective as American and South Vietnamese intelligence was throughout the war, the Tet offensive came as a total surprise for which nobody was prepared. The Vietcong raiders even reached the American Embassy in midtown Saigon.

The intensity of the fighting was unprecedented in the war, as were the casualties. Military historians may differ on whether the Tet offensive was actually intended by Hanoi to score an overwhelming victory, force the collapse of the South Vietnamese government, and oblige the humiliated Americans to leave. This is unlikely because the Communists were too experienced and too realistic to expect such a result. Instead, it would appear, they wanted to emphasize how powerful they had become, that they could no longer be confined to the countryside, and that the war would be excruciatingly costly to the United States—especially in lives. Ho and his colleagues were very much aware of the importance of American public opinion and the coalescing antiwar movement, and the Tet offensive was for their benefit as well.

The pity of it was that General Westmoreland—and President Johnson— did not understand what was happening. Because the Communists suffered immense losses in the battles between the end of January and early March 1968—fifty thousand killed was the American count, and it turned out to be approximately correct—and failed to win the war then and there, the Johnson administration concluded that Tet had been a defeat for the enemy and therefore a victory for the United States and the South Vietnamese. It admitted that two thousand Americans and four thousand ARVN troops died during that period, a militarily acceptable casualty count. The misin-

terpretation was that the Communists would be crippled, perhaps defini-
tively, because of the losses and would be destroyed sooner or later.
Therefore, Westmoreland asked for still more American troops—to admin-
ister the coup de grace.

In March 1968, two months after Tet, the My Lai incident occurred in
South Vietnam, jolting America when the full truth was revealed. This was
the killing of between 175 and 400 civilians in the village of that name by a
U.S. Army unit commanded by Lieutenant William Calley, Jr.

At least in the state of New Hampshire, however, the voters took a different view of LBJ and his war policies. In the Democratic party presidential
primaries in February the President barely managed to win over Senator
Eugene McCarthy of Minnesota, his only challenger for the nomination.
McCarthy was not known nationally; but he was an antiwar militant, and
his performance in New Hampshire was quickly read by politicians as a
repudiation of the President and the war. On March 31 Johnson went on
television for a scheduled speech to discuss Vietnam, and he produced two
historical decisions.

The first was his announcement that bombings of North Vietnam would
be limited to the area below the twentieth parallel, meaning that American
raids would be restricted to the southernmost section of the country, and
that he would be prepared to enter peace negotiations with Hanoi. The
second was the bombshell that he would not seek reelection. To put it suc-
cinctly, the Tet offensive had brought it all about.

A week later North Vietnam agreed to negotiations. Averell Harriman was
again drafted by an American President, and on May 10 he met in Paris
with a North Vietnamese delegation. But no progress was made for months,
the two sides being in complete disagreement over everything, and the war
went on raging as November rolled around and Richard Nixon defeated
Hubert Humphrey for the presidency.

When Nixon assumed office on January 20, 1969, there were nearly
550,000 American troops in Vietnam, and 30,000 Americans had already
been killed. Nixon and Henry A. Kissinger, his national security adviser,
knew that a way must be found to extricate the United States from Vietnam,
but they insisted on "peace with honor," which provided for the survival of
the Saigon regime. The new policy was double-edged: to fight throughout
Indochina, if necessary, to prevent a Communist victory and to negotiate a
settlement at the same time. Nixon also made up his mind that he had to
start removing American troops from Vietnam, forcing the ARVN to take
on the brunt of the war under "Vietnamization."

In practice, Nixon authorized secret bombings of Cambodia to prevent
the Vietcong from using it as sanctuary (American intelligence believed that
the central Vietcong command was operating from inside Cambodia) while
maintaining the bombing halt over North Vietnam. Westmoreland went
home, being replaced by General Creighton Abrams, who was equally gung
ho and who had persuaded Nixon to bomb Cambodia. In August Kissinger

held the first secret meeting with the North Vietnamese in Paris. On September 2 Ho Chi Minh died in Hanoi.

The Indochina War, twenty-three years after Ho first defied the French for independence, had entered still another phase.

VI

Even apart from Indochina, the sixties were a decade of immense violence. There were full-fledged wars on four continents and countless bloody and savage revolutions. Both nuclear superpowers engaged in armed interventions in their respective zones of influence. Political assassinations again ravaged the souls of Americans. And in the affluent West the youth rose in rebellion against everything their elders seemed to represent to the sound of fierce speechmaking, the rhythm of rock, the whiff of drugs, and the whispers of love.

But there were magnificent dreams, too.

National security, desire for freedom, political ambition and greed, territorial disputes, religious and tribal hatreds, and personal hostility among rulers were the motivating forces behind the international wars that spanned the sixties in the Third World and its periphery. In most cases these wars produced no beneficial results for either party involved, simply causing military casualties, the slaughter of civilians, and great damage to the fragile economies of the warring countries. Unhappily the big powers overtly or covertly contributed to the hostilities through political support or the supply of arms. In fact, nobody ever had any trouble being armed for a conflict with a neighbor.

Inasmuch as all these wars were wholly unrelated to each other—there was no geographical or ideological pattern—chronology is the best way of recording them.

The first war of the decade (aside from Vietnam) was in the medieval kingdom of Yemen on the Red Sea. After the imam of Yemen died in September 1962, President Nasser of Egypt decided this was his opportunity to expand his "Arab socialism" in the south of the Arabian Peninsula, and he helped organize a military coup against the imam's successor. Saudi Arabia, the oil-rich conservative kingdom next door, moved its forces to save the royalists. Nasser sent troops from Egypt. The United States and Britain became involved diplomatically, Yemen being part of a strategic region in which both had political and economic interests. Ellsworth Bunker, a businessman turned diplomat and one of the best American negotiators, was dispatched to mediate the Egyptian-Saudi War in Yemen. It dragged on inconclusively for years until a settlement was ironed out—and Yemen lapsed back into oblivion. So did the victims of the conflict.

The next war, in the autumn of 1962, was that Himalayan Indian-Chinese affray in which Kennedy sent arms to India.

In 1965 Algeria and Morocco, both newly independent from France, fought a desert war, apparently over iron deposits along their border in the sandy Tindouf area. That Algeria was a socialist state (by its own description) and Morocco a conservative kingdom added an ideological dimension to the conflict. Fidel Castro, who had developed a friendship with Algerian President Ahmed Ben Bella, rushed artillery and tanks by ship from his Soviet-supplied arsenal to fellow revolutionaries in North Africa. The French were quietly helping the Moroccans. That was the time when Che Guevara was in Algiers teaching guerrilla tactics to Mozambique Frelimo rebels, who had risen against their Portuguese colonial masters and when the United States was saving Algerians from starvation with emergency food shipments. The Algerian-Moroccan War also had an inconclusive end, and the two countries were to fight a proxy conflict over the former Spanish Sahara more than a decade later. But socialist Algeria proved many times in the future its friendship for the United States.

Also in 1965, India and Pakistan fought two miniwars with no meaningful consequences. Bitter enemies since the 1947 partition of British India on religious lines (Hindus in India, Muslims in Pakistan) and unresolved territorial questions—most important the state of Kashmir and Jammu held by India but claimed by both—they went at each other in the spring and the autumn. Both sides had American warplanes. In April their armies battled in the Rann of Kutch, a region on the Arabian Sea. In September they fought for three weeks in Ladakh, an eastern Himalayan territory adjacent to Kashmir and likewise controlled by India. It seems that Pakistan wished to wrest it away from the Indians, and the men conducted excruciatingly difficult warfare at altitudes over fifteen thousand feet. Nothing changed, and the two miniwars are utterly forgotten (but India and Pakistan were not finished with wars).

By the mid-1960's all of Portuguese Africa was aflame in anticolonial wars. Nationalist rebels fought for independence in big, rich Angola and Mozambique as well as in small, impoverished Guinea-Bissau and on the Cabo Verde (Cape Verdes) and São Tomé islands off Africa's west coast. The colonial wars were to end in 1974, when young Portuguese officers overthrew the ancient dictatorship in Lisbon and gave the colonies their independence. But Angola turned into a major international conflict that involved the United States, the Soviet Union, South Africa, Zaire, and Cuba until the late 1980's.

*   *   *

The shortest, most spectacular, and potentially most dangerous war of the sixties was the Six-Day War in June 1967, pitting Israel against Egypt, Syria, and Jordan. It was the third Middle Eastern war since the birth of Israel in 1948 and the one that brought the most dramatic changes to the region and kept it in violence and savage turbulence twenty years later.

It was Israel that struck on June 5, but the Arabs and the Soviet Union had made it inevitable. Nasser, anxious to maintain and extend his influence in the Arab world, concluded in 1966 that a combination of diplomatic and military pressures on Israel might result in the collapse of the Jewish state though it is impossible to reconstruct what went through his mind to make him believe it. He found a willing partner in General Salah Djedid, the revolutionary leader of Syria (the only Arab country to refuse to sign an armistice agreement with Israel in 1948), and a more reluctant one in Jordan's King Hussein, who feared Nasser's "Arab socialist" subversion. The Soviet Union, which wanted a solid foothold in the Middle East after financing Egypt's Aswan High Dam, quietly offered military assistance. This was Leonid Brezhnev's first major undertaking in foreign affairs, but it was less of a risk than what Khrushchev had attempted in Cuba five years earlier.

The Israelis, who knew that the Arabs remained determined to liquidate their country, began to be concerned about new dangers when Nasser signed a federation pact with Syria and Iraq in 1963. It was not the federation itself that worried them—they did not take it seriously—but the fact that Nasser was building alliances around their territory. Shortly thereafter Israeli Prime Minister David Ben-Gurion visited President de Gaulle in Paris for what may have been one of the most historic meetings of the decade. It is not known what exactly was said, but it is a matter of record that the deliveries of the most sophisticated French weapons to Israel—additional Mirage III jet fighter-bombers, AMX tanks, and Alouette helicopters—increased rapidly after Ben-Gurion's and De Gaulle's conversation. And Israel was promised the brand new Mirage V jet and a flotilla of supermodern patrol boats.

Most important of all, it was then that De Gaulle agreed to accelerate secret French assistance to the development of Israel's nuclear weapons. Israel has never admitted that it has nuclear arms, but every government in the world takes it for granted that Israel is a nuclear state. France's original commitment to aid Israel with the bomb came after the unsuccessful Suez War against Egypt, which the French, the Israelis, and the British launched together (and Eisenhower halted). This was before De Gaulle's return to power, and the French had just begun, also in secret, to develop their own nuclear arms; but they transferred technology as rapidly as they could. Israel, of course, had an adequate stable of its own scientists; what it needed from France was equipment and engineering experience.

With De Gaulle back at the Élysée, nuclear cooperation continued apace. Late in 1960 the CIA reported to Eisenhower that France had supplied Israel with a reactor that was installed in what was officially described as a textile plant near the town of Dimona in the Negev; the plant had extensive underground work areas. As a result of the De Gaulle–Ben-Gurion meeting, the French provided Israel in 1965 with a plutonium extraction facility in Dimona, by then a heavily guarded area. This installation was needed to obtain plutonium from uranium to produce weapons-grade fuel for this particular type of plutonium bomb.

Late in 1966 Israel had processed enough uranium at Dimona to build the first nuclear weapon. The French assistance was discontinued by De Gaulle after the 1967 war—he was angry with the Israelis for having started the conflict rather than await attack and defend themselves with French weapons—and the slack was picked up by a supersecret section within the CIA, quite possibly without the knowledge of CIA Director Richard Helms or President Johnson. This was the handiwork of the late James Jesus Angleton, the head of the virtually autonomous CIA counterintelligence (CI) staff, who had an intimate connection, bordering on the emotional, with Mossad, the Israeli intelligence service. There are reasons to believe that Angleton helped Israel to obtain illegally fissionable materials from the United States—including two hundred pounds of reprocessed uranium from a Pennsylvania plant—as well as the services of nuclear physicists he was able to control. One of them was a British scientist whom Angleton caught red-handed passing U.S. secrets to the Russians, and blackmailed into performing covert acts for him.

In any event, as the clouds of war began gathering in 1966, Israel knew it had a nuclear weapon it could use to assure its survival *in extremis*. The Mirage jets could deliver it, and the Israelis were busy developing a missile that could carry a nuclear warhead. Meanwhile, Arab pressures grew. On November 4 Nasser and Djedid signed a defense pact. Almost simultaneously the Soviets began delivering jet aircraft, tanks, and artillery to Egypt and Syria. And guerrillas of the Palestine Liberation Organization increased their cross-border raids into Israel from Syria, where they had started operating the previous year, after Nasser had expelled them from Egypt (he did not wish to invite Israeli retaliation at that point).

On April 7, 1967, Syrian MiGs invaded Israeli airspace, losing twenty-one planes in a succession of dogfights. At this point Levi Eshkol, who succeeded Ben-Gurion as prime minister, and his Cabinet decided in consultation with Israel's military chiefs to prepare a preemptive war against Egypt and Syria. On May 15 Nasser dispatched several additional army divisions to the Sinai desert. The following day Egypt requested United Nations peacekeeping units, stationed in the Sinai since 1957, to leave the peninsula. U Thant, the Burmese secretary-general of the United Nations, agreed at once, possibly bringing the war closer.

Now Nasser's pressure was inexorable; it is improbable that as alleged in some accounts, he was acting only to please his Arab allies. On May 20 Egyptian forces occupied Sharm el Sheikh on the Red Sea, replacing

United Nations detachments and assuming the control of the Straits of Tiran through which ships navigate to and from the Gulf of Aqaba and the Israeli port of Eilat. On May 22 Nasser announced the blockade of the gulf. Israeli Foreign Minister Golda Meir concluded this was provocation as well as *casus belli*. Now the war had to come, the Soviet Union having refused a big power conference to deal with the blockade.

On May 29 Nasser delivered a speech demanding that the 1948 Israeli "aggression" against Palestinians be erased, and on May 30 he persuaded his enemy King Hussein to sign a mutual defense pact with Egypt and place Jordanian troops under Egyptian command. With Jordanian troops, including the crack Arab Legion, deployed in West Jerusalem and on the West Bank of the Jordan, the threat to Israel rose sharply. On June 1 Eshkol formed a "national unity" Cabinet with Moshe Dayan as defense minister and Menahem Begin of the conservative opposition as one of the principal civilian ministers. Dayan, who had conquered the Sinai in 1956, belonged to Rafi, a small opposition group.

It was the military genius of Dayan, Chief of Staff Itzhak Rabin, and Air Force Commander Mordechai "Motti" Hod that gave Israel the lightning victory over infinitely more powerful Arab armies. First, Hod had his Mirages (Israel had no American aircraft at the time) fly at 8:30 A.M. on June 5 west over the Mediterranean, then turn sharply to the left and come over the principal Egyptian air bases. Because Nasser had expected a dawn strike, the alert at the Egyptian bases had been lifted for the day when the Israeli jets roared overhead. Other jets hit Syrian bases. By dusk three hundred Arab aircraft, including Soviet Tu-16 jet bombers, were smashed. Then Israeli armor moved into the Sinai and toward Syria. On June 6 Hussein decided to attack, probably the worst idea of his reign. The Israelis responded by destroying his small air force on the ground, then attacking the Jordanians on the Jerusalem front. The Jordanians fought the best of all the Arab armies, but it was not good enough.

Visiting Israel in 1989, I discovered that the story of the Six-Day War has not been fully told. Retired General Uzi Narkiss, who led Israeli troops to the Western Wall and was the hero of the Battle of Jerusalem, astounded me by affirming flatly that the army had had no contingency war plans (the air force had) and that "we improvised from hour to hour." He lacked troops and equipment in the central sector he commanded, Narkiss said, and the Jordanian attack was a disturbing surprise; the fight for the Old City could have gone either way—except that the Israelis were lucky and Narkiss evidently was a fine improvising commander.

In the course of their victorious advances the Israelis committed an unforgivable error, too. Their planes and patrol boats attacked the *Liberty*, a United States ELINT ship monitoring all intelligence traffic off the Israeli coasts, killing thirty-four American sailors. The *Liberty* perhaps should not have been that close (the ship never received a signal from Washington to move away), but Israeli commanders should have known better. (De

Gaulle, who had warned Ben-Gurion against starting a war, embargoed Mirage and patrol boats' deliveries just before the conflict erupted. But LEKEM, the Defense Ministry's secret scientific espionage division, was able to deliver almost instantly spare parts for the fifty Mirages the Israelis already had as well as blueprints for a more advanced version of the Mirage. Other Israeli intelligence operatives commandeered the impounded patrol boats in Cherbourg and sailed them from the Atlantic to the eastern Mediterranean under the noses of the French navy and air force).

On June 10 the war was over. Israel took all of the Sinai, West Jerusalem and the West Bank region in Jordan, and the Golan Heights in Syria. A cease-fire went into effect at 6:00 P.M. On November 22 the UN Security Council approved the famous Resolution 242, providing for a "just and lasting peace" and "secure and recognized boundaries" for Israel, which, in exchange, would withdraw "from occupied territories." This language did not say "all" or "the" territories in deference to Israeli and American insistence; in any event, the resolution had not been implemented by 1990. As Abba Eban, then Israeli foreign minister writes in his autobiography, if the resolution were ignored and the Arabs refused to make peace, "there would be international justification for maintaining our position on the cease-fire lines."

As for Leonid Brezhnev, his first venture in world politics was short of great success. The Soviets' military clients were soundly defeated, their equipment destroyed or captured by Israelis, and Soviet diplomats were unable to influence the outcome in the Security Council. Moscow had threatened intervention in the closing hours of the war, but its only noticeable gesture was to break diplomatic relations with Israel. All the Communist countries except Romania followed the Soviet example. The cost was great in arms, money, and prestige, but the Russians did not quite win a toehold in the Middle East.

(Only in 1989, under *glasnost*, did the Soviet Union and Poland reopen contacts with Israel—the Poles and the Israelis established ambassadorial "interests sections" in each other's capitals—while Hungary restored full diplomatic relations.)

The sixties ended, as they began, with wars on all the continents except Europe.

In Indochina America was still trapped in its doomed quest for "peace with honor." To the north, China and the Soviet Union engaged in 1969 in a dangerous war, doing away once and for all with Western suspicions that their split was a myth. Even with the improvement in their relations in the late 1980's and the emergence of some historical materials, it is still extremely difficult to determine why they reached the stage of armed clashes.

That China became a nuclear power in October 1964 (just as Khrushchev was fired) certainly affected the two countries' attitude toward each other. China was no longer wholly vulnerable to Soviet attack. By 1969 the two

Communist countries had assembled armies of millions of men facing each other across their long border, and late in the year they fought skirmishes on islands in the Ussuri River and along the Amur River. As McGeorge Bundy points out, it was "the only case on record in which nuclear-weapon states have engaged in ground fighting with each other" with each being "certainly aware of latent nuclear danger." The Soviets actually persuaded the Nixon administration that they were contemplating a preemptive nuclear strike at China though this probably was a war of nerves. The fighting ended in October.

In the Middle East, Israel and Egypt engaged in 1969 in a war of attrition, firing artillery barrages at each other across the Suez Canal. In Africa the liberation wars against Portugal kept gaining in intensity, beginning to ruin Lisbon economically. Nigeria was slowly but surely smashing the Biafra secession war, with horrible casualties among civilians and the mass starvation of children. The most bizarre of all the wars of the sixties broke out in July 1969 between Honduras and El Salvador as the result of violence at a soccer match between their national teams in what a diplomat described as "the first instance of continuation of a soccer game by other means." The Organization of American States forced the return of peace and stationed observers along the jungle frontiers.

Nuclear superpowers have learned to practice restraint in their dealings with each other. But as was again demonstrated during the sixties, such restraint does not apply to small nations within their zones of influence that dare to defy them. Under one pretext or another they feel free to intervene militarily. Thus the "Johnson Doctrine" and the "Brezhnev Doctrine" were born to dress up naked acts of brutal intervention.

The Johnson intervention was in the Dominican Republic in April 1965, a month after the first battalions of marines were landed in South Vietnam and American bombs began falling on North Vietnam. It must have been Johnson's mind-set about Communist perils that pushed him into simultaneous armed interventions at opposite ends of the world.

After the dictator Trujillo had been assassinated in 1961, a civilian provisional government gave Dominicans one of their first tastes of political freedom since Columbus discovered the island of Hispaniola in 1492. In December 1962 Juan Bosch, a white-haired poet, novelist, and political intellectual of the left-of-center Latin American tradition, was chosen president in a free election. He was a charming but wholly incompetent chief executive who antagonized the military and the business community with his social reformist ideas and who distracted his own aides with his impracticality. The Roman Catholic Church was furious because the new constitution passed by the Bosch-influenced Congress had instituted divorce. During the summer of 1963 Bosch conceived the notion of invading Haiti, the neighbor republic on Hispaniola, to oust President François "Doc" Duvalier, a cruel and unstable dictator who practiced voodoo. An alarmed American ambassador dissuaded Bosch in time from starting a war.

On September 25, 1963, the army overthrew Bosch, an act that deeply saddened John Kennedy, who had hoped that the Dominican Republic would become a democratic showcase of the Alliance for Progress. He severed diplomatic relations rather than recognize the military regime. After his assassination two month later Lyndon Johnson, who as Vice President had attended Bosch's inauguration, made the recognition of the army regime his first action in the field of Latin American affairs. A civilian, Donald Reid Cabral, served as the chief of the military government, but soon the officers, mostly Trujillo-appointed commanders, began plotting against him. For one thing, Reid Cabral was doing away with the corruption in the armed forces.

On April 24, 1965, the military moved to remove him, but, simultaneously a group of young officers launched a revolt of their own to restore Juan Bosch to the presidency. They called themselves constitutionalists, and they had the support of university students, intellectuals, and the leftist political spectrum.

What was happening in Santo Domingo added up to a civil war between two military factions. The pro-Bosch rebels captured the downtown section of the capital, entrenching themselves there and arming civilians. The right-wing military had tanks and planes, and its plan was to dislodge its rivals from the old city. To the American Embassy in Santo Domingo, the leftist movement, headed by a young colonel named Francisco Caamaño Deñó, represented the threat of a Communist takeover. Bosch, they thought, would establish communism in six months. The second conclusion was that U.S. armed forces were required to put down the Caamaño movement. These ideas were contained in telegrams the embassy was sending to the State Department these first days of the civil war.

While the administration pondered these reports in an atmosphere in which nothing seemed worse than a "second Cuba" (Fidel Castro had formally proclaimed during the year that his island would be a full-fledged Marxist-Leninst state), the slaughter went on in Santo Domingo as armor assaulted the old city and P-51 Mustangs bombed and strafed it. The rebels took the pilots' families as hostages to stop the raids. On April 27 President Johnson, who was reading all the reporting from the Dominican Republic, decided to land Marines in the capital to organize the evacuation of several thousand Americans who lived there. He was also contemplating a military intervention against the pro-Bosch forces.

The six-ship Caribbean Amphibious Task Force led by USS *Boxer*, a helicopter carrier, was already off the Dominican Republic. The fifteen hundred marines aboard the ships, which also carried tanks, armored vehicles, and artillery, were ready to go ashore. A Marine brigade at Camp Lejeune and the Eighty-second Airborne Division at Fort Bragg, both in North Carolina, were alerted. On the morning of April 27 the operation began.

Four Marine helicopters flew to the polo grounds of Hotel Embajador, which overlooked the Caribbean and where American civilians were being assembled for evacuation. Two ships moored at the nearby Haina port. Both sides in the civil war promised not to interfere with the evacuation. At the Embajador a band of armed civilians burst in to look for "counterrevolutionaries" and in the process lined up a group of Americans against the wall and fired their weapons into the ceiling. This became the pretext for the large-scale intervention although 1,172 Americans had already been evacuated.

On April 28 Colonel Pedro Bartolomé Benoit, who had just been named head of the right-wing military junta, informed the embassy that he could no longer guarantee the safety of Americans still in the city because the rebels had not been defeated. He requested U.S. military assistance although no American had been threatened or touched. The embassy cabled the request to Washington, where it was delivered immediately to Johnson. The American ambassador, W. Tapley Bennett, Jr., then spoke to the President by telephone; Johnson could hear gunfire in the background. A few minutes later Johnson ordered Secretary of Defense McNamara to begin landing the Marines.

The first 520 marines, landed by helicopter on the morning of April 29, found nobody to oppose them. A few hours later reporters, who had been transported to the *Boxer* the previous evening aboard a Navy LST (Landing Ship Tanks)—I was one of them, representing *The New York Times*—were also flown ashore. By the next day there were 1,700 Marines in the city, and two battalions of the airborne division were on their way to the Caribbean.

Now the administration stated officially that the American troops, soon to total twenty-two thousand, were in the Dominican Republic to save it from communism. Though most of the fighting continued to be between the two Dominican military factions, paratroopers and Marines helped keep the rebels confined inside the old city. One column of the Eighty-second Airborne Division marched through the old city, firing bazookas at buildings where snipers might have been hiding.

Soon the American-supported military junta ended the rebellion. From my daily observations, I firmly believe that the junta would probably not have triumphed without U.S. troops providing backup to its forces, delivering equipment, ammunition, and even food. Then it took almost three months for the American diplomatic team headed by the ambassador to the Organization of American States, the seventy-one-year-old Ellsworth Bunker, who had just completed mediation missions in Yemen and Indonesia, to put together a provisional government for the Dominican Republic that enjoyed reasonable national support. Héctor García-Godoy, a respected diplomat, became provisional president on September 3; American forces were withdrawn, a smaller Latin American peacekeeping contingent replacing them.

The Dominican intervention damaged President Johnson politically at home just as he was launching the huge escalation in Vietnam. He was denounced by Senator Fulbright and he lost much of the liberal support he needed badly for his domestic and foreign policy. It is at best debatable whether the intervention stemmed communism in the Dominican Republic; there never was any proof that such a danger really existed. In Latin America anti-Yankee sentiment surged again, greatly pleasing Fidel Castro in Havana with the memories of past U.S. Marine Corps landings in Mexico, Cuba, the Dominican Republic, Nicaragua, and Haiti. As for Lyndon Johnson, he was convinced that he had been right and that the American press had twisted the truth about his achievement against communism.

Three years later it was the turn of the other superpower to intervene in its backyard—this time to *save* communism. It was the invasion of Czechoslovakia on the night of August 20, 1968, by nearly two hundred thousand Soviet troops accompanied by small Warsaw Pact contingents from Poland, East Germany, Hungary, and Bulgaria. It was carried out as part of what became known as the Brezhnev Doctrine, which stipulated that the Soviet Union would not tolerate any attempt to weaken Communist party rule in Eastern Europe or to experiment with liberal forms of Marxism. It was the same doctrine that had led Khrushchev to dispatch tanks to Budapest in 1956 to crush the Hungarian rebellion and that Brezhnev applied to Poland when the Solidarity movement burst forth in 1980. Historically the invasion of Czechoslovakia did extraordinary harm to the Soviet and Communist causes, reinforcing rather than destroying the yearning for liberalization in Eastern Europe.

I was fortunate that my *New York Times* assignments had taken me to that part of Europe in 1968, allowing me to observe the amazing experiment in "Marxism with a Human Face," the ideological centerpiece of the Prague Spring, and the poignant drama of its destruction by Brezhnev's soldiers. As it happened, I could witness an American intervention and a Soviet intervention in the affairs of small states, both forming part of the basic East-West conflict still very much alive in 1968. And both interventions were against the backdrop of the unending Indochina War.

In the case of Czechoslovakia, the liberalizing movement *within* the ruling Communist party posed a new dilemma for the Kremlin. The Hungarian rebellion, though also led at the outset by party figures, had rapidly turned into a violent anti-Communist and anti-Soviet uprising. In Prague, in January 1968, a liberal-minded majority in the Politburo handed the post of first secretary to Alexander Dubček, a party official from Slovakia, chiefly because he represented a compromise and could be persuaded to direct change. Profound opposition to Stalinist policies of the party had broken out at the writers' union annual conference the previous year, and soon intellectuals, Charles University professors, writers, journalists, and moviemakers were pressing for a wholly new approach to Marxism-Leninism—its humanization. Nothing of the kind had occurred before in Eastern Europe (apart from a brief period of relative liberty in Poland in 1956), and Moscow was not sure what to make of it.

By mid-spring the new leadership tolerated (if not encouraged) considerable freedom of expression even in the official press and on the government's radio and television networks. Politburo members raced around the country to explain "Marxism with a Human Face" to workers at big industrial plants, peasants at collective farms, and soldiers at their barracks. I accompanied several of them on a number of such sorties, and I developed the uneasy feeling that the liberal Communists' movement and program were essentially elitist, not really reaching politically or emotionally the masses in whose name the experiment was being conducted. It clearly was not the popular explosion of sentiment that I was to see with Solidarity in Poland in the early eighties, but at that time in Prague there were no comparative measurements.

At the beginning of the summer the reforms increasingly affected party structures, removing hard-line (and pro-Moscow) Communists from influence. There was talk of creating political clubs that would become de facto opposition political parties, and demands were rising for the reopening of the show trials of the 1950's, in which key party figures had been sentenced and executed to meet Soviet demands. Stalin was still alive when the purges began, and his suspicion of fellow Communist leaders everywhere had led to the trials with fabricated evidence (as had happened in Hungary, Bulgaria, and Romania).

Now Moscow was making no secret of its annoyance over the Prague Spring, and talk of an invasion grew among Czechoslovaks. Memories of Budapest were still very fresh, and more and more people were convinced that Brezhnev would not allow the liberalizing process to get out of hand altogether. In a show of force Soviet forces launched "maneuvers" in Czechoslovakia (where no Soviet troops were permanently stationed), crossing the borders freely from Poland, Hungary, and the Ukrainian provinces of the Soviet Union. One sunny day I drove out into the Bohemian countryside to see for myself what the Soviets were doing, and soon I encountered a long column of Soviet tanks advancing slowly along a highway, led by a Czechoslovak police car with flashing lights. I managed to make my way inside the column, driving my American-made convertible (with a big USA sign on the rear fender) between two Soviet tanks, but nobody seemed to mind. It was as improbable a scene as a reporter can imagine.

The Soviets, however, minded more and more what was happening in Prague. On July 28 Brezhnev and his Politburo met with Dubček and *his* Politburo, including President Ludvík Svoboda, in a luxury train parked at the railroad station of Čierna-nad-Tisou, the village where Czechoslovak, Soviet, and Hungarian borders meet. Brezhnev, who had called the meeting, now berated Dubček for betraying international socialism and serving the "imperialist" cause. Dubček rejected the charges, but on the fourth day of these unprecedented Politburo-to-Politburo negotiations, he either made concessions to the Soviets or appeared to make them. There is no record of the Čierna talks, and what really happened in those closely guarded trains is unknown; but the two sides parted with what they said was a general agreement. The Czechoslovaks had won a reprieve.

On August 3 Brezhnev presided over a meeting of all the Warsaw Pact leaders in Bratislava, the capital of Slovakia. Again, nothing is known of the private discussions, and the joint declaration mouthed platitudes about co-operation in "socialist construction," not even mentioning the Czechoslovak experiment. In retrospect, it appears that Brezhnev did not wish to carry alone the burden of ordering an invasion; that was why he gathered in the entire Politburo at Čierna and his Communist allies at Bratislava. He could claim that the liquidation of "Marxism with a Human Face" was a collective decision.

When Soviet tanks rolled into Czechoslovakia at 11:00 P.M. on August 20, and Soviet aircraft disgorged airborne troops at the Prague airport, the Kremlin announced with a straight face that the Warsaw Pact was engaging in an action of "fraternal assistance" requested by Czechoslovak "comrades." As the Americans did in Santo Domingo in 1965, the Soviets found local leaders in Prague in 1968 to "invite" the invasion. Superpowers are enamored of legalisms when they embark on dubious enterprises.

It is trite but true to say that what dictators fear the most is the power of ideas. Thus, when I drove out after midnight to inspect the situation in Prague, I discovered that the first objectives of the Soviet tanks and para-troopers were the headquarters of the Central Committee of the Czechoslovak Communist party overlooking the Vltava River, the command post of the Marxist liberals, and the headquarters of the writers' and journalists' unions. All three buildings were instantly occupied by the invading forces; this way, the Soviets reasoned, there would be nobody to speak out credibly against the "fraternal assistance." At the party headquarters Dubček and his liberal Communist colleagues were arrested, then flown in manacles to Moscow. Because the Czechoslovak Army offered no resistance, the Soviets did not get around until later to the occupation of military headquarters and installations. They missed, however, the Prague radio and TV, which stayed on the air for at least twelve hours, until Soviet tanks dispersed with machine-gun fire the crowds defending the broadcasting stations. Afterward broadcasts continued for weeks from secret locations, infuriating the Russians.

The most poignant moment, I thought, was the quiet warning by the Prague Radio announcer early in the morning of August 21 that when the station stopped playing Jan Smetana's My Country, which it played inter-mittently all night between communiqués, "it will mean we have been occupied." The soft strains of music then ended abruptly; my Czech secretary burst into tears, and I almost did, too.

Twenty-one years and three months after the liquidation of the Prague Spring, Czechoslovaks again challenged the Communists—and this time they triumphed, clearly for keeps. It was one more peaceful democratic revolution in Eastern Europe in the autumn of 1989—an autumn to be remembered in history—and it followed the year's similar revolts in Poland, Hungary, Bulgaria, and East Germany.

On November 24, after a week of street demonstrations by hundreds of thousands of people in Prague, the Czechoslovak Communist party's Politburo headed by Miloš Jakeš, one of the three hard-line Communists who "requested" the Warsaw Pact invasion in 1968, was forced to resign. On December 10, President Gustav Husák, who had ruled the country with an iron hand since the ouster of Alexander Dubček and his companions, resigned his post as well. That same day, the first government in forty-one years without a Communist majority assumed power though the premiership was still held by a Communist, an obscure *apparatchik* politician from Slovakia chosen to run the bureaucracy on a day-to-day basis.

Historically, two major elements caused the end of the lengthy period of suppression in Czechoslovakia. The first one, I believe, was the fact that the Prague Spring had not been forgotten by the older generation and that its spirit was transmitted to the new generation. The second element obviously was the advent of Gorbachev and *perestroika* in the Soviet Union, a guarantee that Soviet tanks would not roll into the country if it reached again for freedom. These two factors made the fall of Husak and Jakes inevitable, sooner or later, especially when the Communist dominoes began falling in Eastern Europe in the summer of 1989 with the Polish elections and the rise of Solidarity-backed Tadeusz Mazowiecki to the premiership.

And it was fitting for Mazowiecki, an anti-Communist, to represent Poland when the leaders of the Warsaw Pact gathered with Mikhail Gorbachev at the Kremlin on December 4 to jointly condemn as "illegal" the 1968 invasion of Czechoslovakia. Mazowiecki had to be present because the Pact leaders were meeting on the level of chiefs of government, and Polish forces had participated in the military action ordered by Leonid Brezhnev under his "doctrine" of protecting Communism in Eastern Europe with military force. Ironically, the only Warsaw Pact leaders to stay away from this expiatory occasion in Moscow were the Romanians who refused to take part in the invasion on the grounds of respecting principles of nonintervention— and who in 1989 were the last Eastern European holdouts of orthodox Communists and Gorbachev's unforgiving critics.

The Prague leadership, which opposed the Gorbachev reforms from the outset, along with East Germany and Romania, resisted the winds of change as long as it could: as late as November 17, the regime's police stormed demonstrators with extraordinary brutality, evidently believing that the old methods would still work. But this time there were no Brezhnev and no Soviet tanks—and the nation, encouraged by anti-Communist revolts all around, was ready for the ultimate face-off. This time, history was on the side of the democratic "people power," a phenomenon hard-line Communists had never expected to occur.

Watching from afar the Czechoslovak reconquest of liberty, I was reminded of that night in August 1968 in Prague when the Soviet tanks' chief objectives were the headquarters of the writers' and the journalists' unions, and I was delighted by the new symbolisms. The natural leader of the 1989 uprising was the playwright Vaclav Havel, one of the main activists of the Prague Spring, who for twenty-one years remained true to the democratic cause, enduring uncounted imprisonments and hardships. He was among the brave handful of men and women who founded the Charter '77 movement in 1977, to demand political and human rights for his fellow citizens, paying for it with prison terms—up to the very eve of the triumphant democracy surge. Havel, the candidate of the "people power," then became President of Czechoslovakia (Dubček was greeted as a hero wherever he went, but, as a Communist, he was not desired to lead the post-Communist Czechoslovakia). And Jiři Dienstbier, the journalist who played a key role in the Prague Spring and suffered prison for his Charter '77 activities, was the new foreign minister. It was almost surreal to hear him announce that the agreement under which Soviet troops were stationed in his country was illegal because it was reached under duress and that he had begun negotiating their departure with the Soviet government. On his first day in office, he received a courtesy call from the Soviet chargé d'affaires.

Czechoslovakia had come full circle from the tragedy of the 1960's.

VII

Parallel with international wars and superpower interventions, the sixties produced a surge of great revolutions and uprisings everywhere in the Third World. They followed no pattern, either, except for the killings and the suffering in the name of causes that most victims never understood.

In 1965 and 1966 a frightful revolution swept the archipelago of Indonesia. Dictatorial and repressive rule by President Sukarno, the father of his nation in the anticolonial struggle against the Dutch, accompanied by uncontrolled corruption and his close alliance with Indonesian Communists, led the army to a coup to topple him. The CIA, which had once before tried to get rid of Sukarno, helped the military plotters. Hundreds of thousands were killed in the revolution before it ran its course by 1967. Some were Communists and leftists in general; others were ethnic Chinese hounded by Indonesian Muslims in a sudden burst of religious prejudice.

General Suharto, who led the revolution, was elected president of Indonesia in 1968 by the People's Consultative Assembly, which he easily manipulated. Ever since Indonesia has been a quiet country living under highly authoritarian rule and battling to improve the living standards of the huge population. In 1976 the Suharto regime annexed East Timor, a former Portuguese territory in the Indonesian "sphere of influence," and tens of thousands died during and after the invasion mandated from Jakarta. At the end of the eighties there still was guerrilla warfare against the Indonesians in Timor.

The fiercest and bloodiest revolution the world has seen since World War II was launched by the aging Mao Zedong in China in October 1966. This Cultural Revolution, which cost at least one million lives, including his closest associates and the leading thinkers, destroyed a whole Chinese generation, and wrought havoc on the economy that lasted for a decade. Even at the end of the eighties it was not entirely certain that the flames of that inferno had been finally doused.

To the extent that the Cultural Revolution was understood as a political phenomenon (and this is not certain either), Mao undertook it to maintain ideological purity and presumably to revive the revolutionary fires in the breasts of the new generation. He decreed the Cultural Revolution a decade after his 1956 campaign to "Let one hundred flowers bloom, let one hundred schools contend" flushed out intellectuals, writers, and artists with their own opinions; the purge that ensued resulted in the killing, imprisonment, and torture of at least three hundred thousand of the most outstanding citizens of China. (Mao himself later admitted that seven hundred thousand Chinese "counterrevolutionaries" were killed during the post-1949 land redistribution and Communist consolidation campaigns. It is generally estimated that tens of millions died as a result of the catastrophic failure of his Great Leap Forward industrialization attempt and the simultaneous crop failures; mass starvation had resulted.) Mao's anti-intellectual bent can only be explained by that same fear of the power of ideas that caused the tragedies of Budapest and Prague when the Russians applied the same standard.

The Cultural Revolution formally ended with Mao's death in 1976. When I met with a group of leading editors in Beijing in 1985, I was assured that a new Cultural Revolution could never happen in China. Even the Communist party was too mature to allow it again, they said. But after the mass killings of the prodemocracy students in Tienanmen Square in June 1989 and the subsequent decision to force all Chinese students to spend one year on collective farms or industrial plants, it appeared that the Cultural Revolution was back in a more sophisticated form. Liberal-minded Communist newspaper and magazine editors have been fired, and the rigors of total censorship reimposed. The Chinese gulag began to fill up once more with intellectuals.

As the eighties ended, the Chinese economy had improved spectacularly in the aftermath of the reforms of the past decade. Per capita incomes in real terms were nearly ten times as high as at the outset of the Revolution in

1949, and life expectancy had doubled to sixty-nine years. Yet China was again turning into a political and intellectual graveyard.

In the jungle-covered mountains of Bolivia, army rangers assisted by the CIA and U.S. Army Special Forces advisers succeeded in October 1967 in tracking down a small guerrilla force and killing its leaders. This event would have gone unnoticed if the group's top leader had not been Ernesto "Che" Guevara, the Argentine doctor who was Fidel Castro's legendary associate in the Sierra Maestra. After the triumph of the Cuban Revolution, Guevara acquired an iconlike mystique for a whole generation of young people around the world—even for Roman Catholic priests attracted to the Christian ideas of social justice.

Almost a quarter century later it remains a mystery why Che had left Cuba and embarked on the wholly improbable Bolivian adventure in a countryside where he did not speak the local Indian languages and did not know his way around. There are theories that he was betrayed by pro-Moscow Bolivian Communists and that Castro himself was not displeased when Che disappeared.

After his death Che was deified by those who admired him in life. I have seen Che's portrait next to images of Jesus Christ in the homes of young priests in Spain and Latin America; in a very special way, I believe, Che Guevara will have left behind an even greater impact than Castro. He was a figure of romance, adventure, and worldwide daring, and he was not burdened with the responsibilities for the executions and imprisonments and economic failures that have characterized Castro's more than three decades in power. Having known him briefly but pleasantly in Havana and New York, I had the impression that Che had a richer and more interesting mind than Castro and that he was a kinder and gentler man.

Throughout the sixties Latin America was a political earthquake zone. Apart from the very special Bolivian episode involving Che Guevara, elected governments were falling one after another. Juan Bosch was thrown out by the military in 1962. In Brazil João Goulart, an incompetent and corrupt figure with leftist penchants who had been elected vice president in 1960 and became president in 1961, was ousted in an army coup in 1964, in which the United States played a major covert role. When Goulart replaced Jànio Quadros, the president who resigned after less than a year in office for unexplained reasons, he let Brazil shift to the left. Peasant organizations, demanding land reform and inspired by the Cuban Revolution, sprang up in the northeast of Brazil. The Johnson administration, obsessed by Communist dangers, pushed for a military coup. For the next twenty years Brazilians lived under a brutal dictatorship, operating with death squads and forsaking Brazil's great tradition of tolerance and gentleness.

In 1968 Peruvian generals and admirals favoring social change (but not communism) overthrew the president, Fernando Belaúnde Terry, an architect who had been elected on a platform of the country's economic development. The military were not despotic; they simply ruined what was left of Peru's economy. Social and economic pressures also loomed large in Panama when students and intellectuals rioted against the United States, demanding the return of the Panama Canal Zone. Johnson was able to negotiate an agreement with the strongman General Omar Torrijos, and tranquillity returned briefly to the little isthmian republic.

Then there were separatisms and nationalisms compounding the world's unrest in the 1960's. In the six counties of Northern Ireland, clashes between Roman Catholics and Protestants—the former as a majority demanding freedom to join the Republic of Ireland and the latter wishing to remain British—forced Britain in 1969 to deploy army troops to restore order. Ten thousand of them were still stationed there twenty years later, with no hope of a settlement in sight. The terrible sectarian violence over the two decades cost nearly three thousand lives, mostly civilians, and thirty thousand injured and wounded in indiscriminate firing and bomb explosions. In northern Spain, Basque extremists of the ETA secret organization fought to secede from the kingdom; thousands have been killed among ETA militants and the police and innocent bystanders.

Even North America, experienced separatism. In Canada the French-speaking citizens of Québec Province strove through the sixties and the seventies to gain at least autonomy in the overwhelmingly English-speaking nation. Even a National Liberation Front emerged in Québec, engaging in very mild terrorism. And Charles de Gaulle was no help when he shouted, "*Vive le Québec libre!* [Long live free Québec!]," as he was being greeted in front of the Montreal city hall. In the end this movement subsided.

Everywhere in the world people and nations demanded freedom, equality, justice, and happiness. They prayed, fought, and died for their hopes and beliefs. This was what made the 1960's so very special in our century.

VIII

"I still have a dream," the Reverend Martin Luther King, Jr., the thirty-four-year-old black minister from Atlanta said to a crowd of a quarter million Americans in front of the Lincoln Memorial in Washington, D.C., on the sweltering afternoon of August 28, 1963. "I have a dream that on the red hills of Georgia the sons of former slaves and the sons of former slave-owners will be able to sit together at the table of brotherhood. . . . I have a dream that one day every valley shall be exalted, every hill and mountain shall be made low, the rough places will be made plain, and the crooked places will be made straight, and the glory of the Lord shall be revealed and all flesh shall see it together. . . . I have a dream. . . !"

The masses of blacks and whites and old and young who had gathered there on the Potomac, coming from all corners of the United States for this March on Washington, were hearing one of the most memorable phrases in one of the most memorable speeches delivered in this country in this century. King's "I have a dream" phrase entered instantly into the American language, and it was as familiar to millions a quarter century later as it was to those who heard it in person or on radio or television.

When King finished, his arms raised high, the crowd broke into the Baptist hymn that in the years and decades to follow was sung from America to South Africa and Eastern Europe and every spot on earth where there was oppression and there was hope: "We shall overcome, we shall overcome/ We shall overcome, someday./ Oh, deep in my heart I do believe,/ We shall overcome some day. . . ."

The sixties were becoming the civil rights decade. Since the Supreme Court school desegregation decision in 1954 virtually nothing had been done in the land to advance racial equality. Blacks had been fighting and dying in World War II (when they belonged to segregated units like the famous Army Air Corps 99th Fighter Squadron and the 332d Fighter Group), in Korea, and now in Vietnam. But, as Roger Wilkins writes, in those days "[t]he entire culture was segregated. . . . White people did important things, but nothing of consequence happened to blacks. In movies, white people were handsome and beautiful and had romances and toppled nations; blacks were presented, when they appeared on screen at all, as ludicrous, bumbling clowns." (When General Powell became chairman of the Joint Chiefs of Staff in August 1989, he remarked that there were "four black regiments who went up San Juan Hill with Teddy Roosevelt" in Cuba during the Spanish-American War but that "we've never seen a picture of them.") And of course, public accommodations remained segregated, and in Wilkins's words, this drove "a lot of pain straight into the soul."

To Kennedy, who meant his presidency to open a new chapter in American life, the racial denial was intolerable, as it was to a whole generation of young Americans, white and black. One of the new President's top priorities was the passage of comprehensive civil rights legislation to end all segregation at this century mark after the start of the Civil War. He knew that failure to act could lead to frightful explosions among the blacks. But the going in Congress was tough; the burden of racial prejudice was still so heavy that Kennedy feared that there would be no votes to pass the bills.

The civil rights movement was born in the first years of the sixties. The March on Washington was its first great milestone, and the Reverend Dr. King's eloquence made it part of American history. Ironically, however, this very event created opposition to civil rights within the administration that was advocating the new legislation. Kenneth O'Reilly, the author of *Racial Matters: The FBI's Secret File on Black America, 1960–1972*, writes that after the 1963 March on Washington there was an "absolute commitment to bring the weight of Bureau resources against the black struggle for equality."

O'Reilly, who has examined declassified FBI and Justice Department files, believes that FBI Director J. Edgar Hoover had concluded that "blacks had gone too far with their protests and now posed an imminent threat to the established order." Though Robert Kennedy had been attorney general since January 1961, O'Reilly states that at that time an agreement was already in existence between Hoover and Justice Department officials "to limit somehow or direct the struggle for black equality." And it is a matter of record that Hoover, who believed that King was a Communist, had the FBI tap his telephone throughout the sixties; Hoover was especially interested in King's sexual life—for his files or possible blackmail.

Kennedy was assassinated fewer than three months after the March on Washington, but the civil rights movement was acquiring momentum. So was the determination of its foes to arrest progress toward racial equality. White students from northern colleges and universities drove south on freedom rides to help blacks register to vote and to organize politically. During 1964 children of our friends would spend the night at our Washington home en route to the South. On one occasion my wife and I discovered that a friend's daughter had been jailed in an Alabama town for "disturbing the peace" and had promptly gone on a hunger strike; we had to keep informed the parents, who were in Europe at the time, unfamiliar with the novel idea of having one's children arrested.

Others fared much worse. In an incident that captured the nation's attentions, two white civil rights workers from the North—Michael Schwerner and Andrew Goodman—and a black friend from Meridian, Mississippi, James Chaney, were shot in the countryside by Ku Klux Klan white supremacists on June 21, 1964; their bodies were bulldozed under tons of dirt. There were other murders and beatings. Journalists who had covered the Congo and Vietnam for their newspapers now feared more for their lives in Alabama and Mississippi. All summer Klan crosses burned fiercely across the South. And in northern cities, riots exploded in black neighborhoods; it was the "long, hot summer."

Lyndon Johnson concentrated on the Congress to win the passage of the civil rights legislation, neglecting his concerns in Vietnam. The Senate debated the bill for eighty-three days, then finally approved it. The President signed it on July 2, 1964. The balance of the sixties was the continuation of the national struggle for racial equality, with more and more success. In 1965 Johnson was able to sign the Voting Rights Act, allowing black Americans to participate fully in the democratic process.

On April 4, 1968, Martin Luther King, Jr., was shot dead by James Earl Ray, a white man, at a motel in Memphis, Tennessee. King, thirty-nine, was the undisputed leader of the civil rights movement in the United States. Ray was caught, but the motive for the killing was never uncovered.

King's death touched off terrible riots in Washington, D.C., and 125 American cities. The cities were truly on fire as blacks vented their grief, fury, and frustration. Johnson had to deploy sixty-five thousand federal and National Guard troops to restore peace; nothing like it had ever happened in the United States. Chicago, Baltimore, and Kansas City burned, and black smoke hung over Washington. The streets of the nation's capital were patrolled by Army jeeps with machine guns manned by soldiers. Twenty years later burned-out buildings still stood along the Fourteenth Street "corridor" in Washington's inner city as monuments to this violence. On June 5 Robert F. Kennedy was shot in a Los Angeles hotel after winning the California Democratic primary; he died the next day. The killer was a twenty-four-year-old Palestinian named Sirhan Bishara Sirhan. Motive: unknown.

King and the Kennedy brothers had worked for civil rights in the United States as hard as any Americans. After their assassinations the struggle proceeded. In the decades that followed, immense progress was made, but Americans also learned that human attitudes cannot be legislated; they must change from prejudice to acceptance gradually, sometimes very slowly. At the end of the eighties, fifty years after the start of the world war which was fought for freedom and democracy everywhere, race problems were still very much alive in the United States.

In Washington in August 1963 Martin Luther King, Jr., had put it this way: "Now is the time to rise from the dark and desolate valley of segregation to the sunlit path of racial justice. Now is the time to lift our nation from the quicksands of racial injustice to the solid rock of brotherhood." In 1964 King had been awarded the Nobel Peace Prize.

Not only racial justice defined the protest and the anger of younger Americans—and even of older ones. The sixties were turning into a time of soul-searching, questioning, defying authority in all forms, and demanding change in policies, ideas, behavior, human attitudes, sex, music, and styles. In a very broad sense a global revolution was under way. It broke out in California, New York, and Michigan—and in Nanterre, Paris, Warsaw, Prague, and Mexico City.

But it first found its voice in the United States, initially at American universities and colleges, usually among the children of the affluent and the privileged, and much fueled by the converging civil rights and antiwar movements. And of course, television became the trailblazer for these movements, spreading their gospel and imagery.

A quarter century or so later the sixties as a revolutionary era appears remote, even quaint, and not entirely understandable to the generation of the eighties. As a political movement oriented toward the left, the sixties have vanished without much of a trace. In a society that has no deep-rooted ideological leftist traditions in a Western European sense—the limited and quasi-elitist influence of the American Communist party in the thirties of the Great Depression and up to the war was really an exception—the leftism of the sixties looks in retrospect shallow and mainly rhetorical. It spawned sudden readership among middle-class students of the works of Engels, Marx, and Lenin (though less of Kropotkin and Bakunin) and, jumping stages, of Jean-Paul Sartre, Heinrich Böll, Albert Camus, and Frantz Fanon.

But how much of it was intellectually and ideologically absorbed is debatable inasmuch as the generation of the sixties in its overwhelming majority left this experience behind. No original post-Marxist philosophy or thought of lasting value appears to have emerged from the maelstrom of the decade in America (Michael Harrington, the serious leftist thinker, had been writing long before, and teachers like Herbert Marcuse have not added much to the Marxist treasure trove). The American bourgeois strain evidently was much more potent; at the end of the eighties there was no interesting center of leftist thought in the United States (again with a few honorable exceptions, like Washington's Institute for Policy Studies).

What the sixties produced in abundance was militant politicization. Young people read Mao Zedong's revolutionary aphorisms in the Little Red Book, venerated from afar North Vietnam's Uncle Ho and Cuba's Fidel Castro and Che Guevara. It was idealistic and romantic, but none of this inspiration was adaptable to the American experience, and it fell by the wayside once the Vietnam War—and the draft—were finished.

The Yippies' protest movement (following the hippies and the peaceniks) has sadly disappeared; now it was the affluent and ambitious yuppies of the eighties (BMW cars, stockbrokerage, elegant cocaine use). Of the Chicago Seven, the group that threw the 1968 Chicago Democratic Convention into riot and turmoil over the Vietnam War, Jerry Rubin became a stockbroker though predicting that the movement would someday be reborn "in coat and tie." Abbie Hoffman, one of the most famous of the Seven, committed suicide in April 1989. David Dellinger, the oldest of them, is a forgotten figure. On August 22, 1989, Huey P. Newton, the cofounder of the Black Panther party, was shot to death in his home neighborhood in Oakland, California (after he was imprisoned in 1967 in connection with the killing of a policeman, the cry on American campuses was "Free Huey," and these words were spray-painted on thousands and thousands of walls across the country).

Pete Seeger, one of the great voices of the sixties, sang softly at Hoffman's funeral. Bob Dylan, whose song about which way the wind blows—only the "weatherman" knows—inspired the radical, bomb-planting Weatherman faction of the Students for a Democratic Society (SDS), was making a living in the eighties at commercial concerts, still commanding big audiences. Of the great protest and cult singers of the rebel era, Janis Joplin and Jimi Hendrix died of drug overdoses in 1970, Keith Moon in 1978, and Paul Butterfield in 1987. Judy Garland, the star of *The Wizard of Oz* and a woman of little personal happiness, died from an inadvertent drug overdose in 1969. In the end the waste of enormous talent and idealism was shocking after their music had served as the cutting edge of the counterculture of the sixties. Rock was the language of the revolution, a defiance of the middle-class values of the parents, and it was a critique of the war overseas and poverty at home. It proclaimed: "Make love, not war!"

The critique was largely gone in the late eighties though rock remained as the quintessential American musical expression, conquering the world as jazz once had. The Beatles had long disappeared, but the Rolling Stones and the Beach Boys were still very much present. The twentieth anniversary of the Woodstock Music and Art Fair—the most fabulous extravaganza of the revolution of the sixties—held on a farm in Bethel, New York, in mid-August 1969, was celebrated with a spate of magazine articles, books, and television programs, a bit the way the Civil War is commemorated, like history. More than a half million young people had assembled there in 1969 for days and nights of singing and listening to Joplin and Hendrix and the Jefferson Airplane, making love, bathing in the nude, rolling in mud, smoking grass, and having a perfectly wonderful sense of absolute liberation. They were kids, and as one of the Woodstock chroniclers remarked, naturally they behaved like kids. Unhappily they were objects of commercial exploitation; sponsors, organizers, and producers of Woodstock motion pictures earned millions. In 1968 *Hair,* the first musical showing naked actors onstage, and part of the new culture, was produced on Broadway. It ran for twenty-one years (at home and abroad, including Belgrade, Yugoslavia, where I first saw it). The bourgeois greed fed on the protest idealism.

The sixties created—and left as heritage—much that was sublime and certainly useful and much that was ridiculous.

If this American social revolution can be dated, its beginning may well have been the Free Speech demonstration at the Berkeley campus of the University of California above Telegraph Hill on December 2, 1964. It was led by a nearly forgotten student named Mario Savio, and its ostensible purpose was to remove academic restrictions on the use of four-letter words. Inevitably the Free Speech movement went beyond that simple objective, blending with all other strains of youthful American protest. If nothing else, the Berkeley upheaval did away with much Victorian hypocrisy in American literature, academia, and entertainment, certainly a plus.

Students occupied colleges and universities in America (like New York's Columbia University), demanding the end of the Vietnam War in violent confrontations with the authorities (in May 1970 four students were shot dead by the National Guard at Kent State in Ohio), blowing up Reserve Officers Training Corps (ROTC) centers on the campuses, chasing away CIA recruiters, protesting against defense-related research by professors, and insisting on a "relevant" curriculum—however that was defined. They also clamored for open-admission policies at institutions of higher learning.

Educators and parents were immensely stunned by this explosion. They were probably too scared and too permissive. In retrospect, American education suffered considerable damage during the sixties; in the eighties (as after *Sputnik* in 1957) cries arose for rebuilding, improving, and modernizing education so that the United States is not left behind Asia and Europe. But the revolution forced the introduction of black and African studies into the universities, broadening the American cultural base and enhancing the racial respect the blacks so desperately sought and that Afros and dashikis alone could not produce. Blacks discovered that "black is beautiful." Unhappily these studies began to vanish in the eighties; this generation of young blacks seemed to lose interest. The sense of liberation was expressed in moviemaking; *Easy Rider* with Peter Fonda, for example, opened in 1969 new horizons to serious cinema. Afterward directors and producers could muster the courage to try to show on the screen what Vietnam really was for those who fought there—died or survived.

The sexual revolution presumably meant that men and women (and men and men and women and women) were free to practice sex without the moral or hypocritical constraints of the past. Did it lead to too many conceptions, too many abortions, and the constitutional battle over women's right to abortion? Nobody really knows. Has the sexual revolution contributed to the AIDS epidemic? Nobody knows that either. Could it be sex or shared-needle intravenous drug injections, or both?

Feminism (colloquially but inaccurately dismissed by many men as "women's lib") was shaped during the sixties as women acquired voice and courage of self-assertion. They could now deal better with social issues like abortion, equal access to work at equal pay, and men's attitudes toward women.

At the ridiculous end of the spectrum of the revolution of the sixties was everything from the topless craze in bars (it started in San Francisco) to the phase of radical chic practiced by the rich and famous. This took the form, for example, of entertaining antiwar activists and the Black Panthers at caviar-and-champagne parties and raising funds for them. It was pandering to the rebels, who naturally treated their hosts with contempt. Mysteriously, Leonard Bernstein, the ever-youthful composer and conductor, lent himself to the propagation of radical chic. But this was America.

In 1968 the youthful revolution crossed the ocean to France (just as the American Revolution of 1776 inspired the French Revolution of 1789). In mid-January the huge university at Nanterre, just outside Paris, declared itself on strike, coinciding with massive industrial walkouts throughout France. Toward the end of March the strikers formed a revolutionary movement (with a vague program) under the leadership of Daniel Cohn-Bendit, known as Danny the Red. On May 1 Cohn-Bendit was threatened with expulsion for organizing student occupations of Nanterre university buildings. President de Gaulle and his advisers hardly noticed this event, concerned as they were with foreign affairs; Vietnam peace talks were about to start in Paris and the French government carefully watched the Prague Spring.

The next day, May 2, the Nanterre revolt exploded in full. The Interior Ministry ordered the university closed; the students marched on Paris and, together with their colleagues there, occupied the Sorbonne on the evening of May 3, erecting street barricades in the spirit of 1789. During the night riot police took back the ancient university, arresting four students, who were then sentenced to two months in jail.

Still, the government went on underestimating what was happening. Prime Minister Georges Pompidou had left on May 1 on an official visit to Iran and Afghanistan, and De Gaulle continued to plan a trip to Romania later in the month. Around the Sorbonne the students put up more barricades, demanding freedom for their jailed companions and battling the police. Several hundred students and police were injured, but the government still failed to comprehend the situation: that French society was suddenly disintegrating.

By May 10 the revolt was spreading and deepening, with the government at a loss with whom to negotiate and what to negotiate. There was no central leadership and no clear goal in the uprisings. The Paris newspaper *Le Monde* summed it up in an editorial declaring, *"France is bored,"* and my other journalist friends told me not to worry about it: "It's not such a big story for America. . . ." But on May 11 more barricades went up in Paris, and the Communist-led General Labor Confederation (CTG) called a general strike.

When American and Vietnamese diplomats met on May 13 in a palace on Avenue Kléber to negotiate a peace settlement, Paris was still paralyzed by the general strike, and three hundred thousand demonstrators marched through midtown, chanting for De Gaulle's benefit, "Ten years is enough. . . ." Ignoring the protests, the general flew to Bucharest on the long-scheduled visit as soon as Pompidou returned from the Middle East. Now the general strike was paralyzing the entire country, and nobody really knew why. Walking past the Odéon Theatre one late afternoon, I came upon a large group of bearded young men sitting on the sidewalk. When I asked them who they were, the leader said smilingly, "We are the Katangese. . . . We want to secede from France," and everybody laughed happily.

De Gaulle did not find it all amusing. He broke off his Romanian tour on May 18, announcing on his return that "the recreation is over." Still, the strike and the riots continued. The impression spread that the government was about to fall, and on May 28, armored army units surrounded Paris; De Gaulle seemed ready to resign. But the old man was not through. On the morning of May 29 he flew secretly to Baden in West Germany, where the commander of the French Army stationed there, General Jacques Massu, assured him of the loyalty of his forces. De Gaulle was back at the Élysée

Palace before nightfall; as he drove into the city, a huge Communist demonstration filled the streets.

On May 30, now sure of the army, De Gaulle struck back. He went on national television to announce that he was dissolving the National Assembly—that is a presidential prerogative—and calling new parliamentary elections for June. At night a half million Parisians marched from the Place de la Concorde to L'Étoile, chanting, "De Gaulle is not alone. . . ." The revolt was over (the government having pacified the trade unions with a 35 percent pay rise), and De Gaulle had the satisfaction of being informed that on August 24 France had exploded its first hydrogen bomb in the Pacific. His joy did not last long: On April 27, 1969, the French rejected a wholly unnecessary referendum De Gaulle had called over the issue of a Senate reform. Incapable of not having his way, the seventy-nine-year-old president resigned, leaving French politics forever. His last official act was to travel to Washington on March 30 to be present at the funeral of Dwight Eisenhower. Now all the great figures of World War II were dead or retired.

I traveled in France in 1989, gathering material for articles on the 200th anniversary of the French Revolution, and in the course of conversations with historians and politicians, I found nearly a consensus on two related points. The first was that the 1968 rebellion was the "final spasm" of the great eighteenth-century revolution. The second was that it appeared twenty years later that the student and worker uprising of that May had not been at all in vain. May 1968, I was repeatedly told, jolted France out of a sense of empty self-satisfaction that had developed with the postwar prosperity and forced it to modernize in mores as well as in its approach to the world. It broadened French horizons, my interlocutors said, and placed the nation in a better position to deal with the outside world. "I was a 1968 rebel, and I'm proud of it," a young Cabinet minister remarked at the end of a long conversation about the new France.

Mexico, another nation with old revolutionary traditions, had its "1968" as well, but it was no source of pride. When tens of thousands of students rioted against the pseudodemocratic Mexican government and its high-handedness—and against the deepening poverty in the cities and the countryside—the army and the police fired bullets into the crowds. Scores were killed. Shortly thereafter the government proudly played host to the Summer Olympics. The fruit of 1968 ripened only in 1988; for the first time since the 1910 Revolution, the one-party government was challenged so powerfully by right-wing and left-wing opposition that it nearly lost presidential and congressional elections. It was a jolt tantamount to the earthquake that had devastated much of Mexico City three years earlier, and Mexico entered a new political era.

The Polish 1968 played itself out in March, quite tragically. With the Prague Spring taking shape next door, students in Warsaw poured out into the streets to demand that the Communist regime authorize performances of

a classical patriotic play by the poet Adam Mickiewicz, who had fled Poland
in the nineteenth century rather than live under Russian rule. The play's
message was explicitly anti-Russian, and the regime, headed by Władysław
Gomułka (the liberal hero of 1956), dispatched the police to beat students
with nightsticks and arrest their leaders.

For reasons he never explained, Gomułka used the occasion to launch an
anti-Semitic campaign, firing Jews from important positions and forcing
them into exile. It was as repulsive as it was absurd; after Hitler's concentration camps, Poland's Jewry was reduced from three million to approximately
thirty thousand. Months later Gomułka gladly agreed to send Polish Army
contingents to help the Soviets quell the Prague Spring, cynically telling
Warsaw editors, "I'd rather see Soviet tanks in Prague than in Warsaw." In
December still another Polish rebellion forced *him* to resign, setting in motion the chain of events that culminated in 1989 with the triumph of Solidarity.

Eras need symbols, and the sixties were rich in symbolisms. There were
the great dreams, the great tragedies, and the great gestures. But if that
decade was mainly about freedom, as I think it was, the Swedish Academy
expressed it best by awarding in 1967 the Nobel Prize for literature to the
Guatemalan poet, novelist, and diplomat Miguel Ángel Asturias, nearing
the end of his life at age sixty-eight. Nobel Prizes honor the full body of a
writer's work. This, naturally, held true for Asturias. But the judges remembered that his most important novel was titled simply *The Dictator*. It is a
tale of what dictatorships inflict on people and nations.

BOOK SIX

THE SEVENTIES

Today we have concluded an agreement to end the war and bring peace with honor in Vietnam and in Southeast Asia. . . .

—Richard Nixon
January 23, 1973

I

*D*ividing history into precise periods like decades is, of course, an arbitrary exercise; events do not follow calendars. Nevertheless, the postwar era does lend itself to a fairly defined chronological approach because basic trends and patterns have arranged themselves in an extremely convenient fashion for purposes of narration.

In the case of the seventies, this decade constituted a clear turn in most of the directions the world had been taking since the end of the 1939–45 conflict, politically as well as economically. The 1970's ushered in a completely new epoch.

Great postcolonial wars waged by the traditional powers in a largely ideological context (and in this sense the United States acted as a traditional power) ran their course with the American departure from Indochina and the Communist takeover in 1975. Portugal's African wars ceased after the collapse of the dictatorship in Lisbon the previous year.

Peace, however, did not bless the world. Old-type wars were replaced by the new regional wars in the Third World: the Indian-Pakistani War over Bangladesh, the Arab-Israeli War of 1973 (preceded by the Syrian-Jordanian War), the Ethiopia-Somalia War, the Libya-Chad War, the Yemens' War, the Polisario War over the western Sahara, rather incredibly the Vietnam-Cambodia and the Vietnam-China wars, and, finally, the Soviet invasion of Afghanistan. These conflicts produced new dimensions of nationalisms within the Third World, tending to paralyze its economic development and, as always, spawning more suffering by more millions.

Revolutions and civil wars and the emergence of still other passions and tensions were by-products of the new regionalisms and nationalisms. Occasionally the revolutions and civil wars merged into foreign wars, and at times it was hard to distinguish one from another. The Iranian Revolution was religious, nationalistic, and ideological. The Lebanon War, which erupted in 1975 and was to remain unresolved for fifteen years amid unceasing death and destruction, was religious and political in nature though it also involved the strategic interests of Syria, Iran, Iraq, Israel, France, and the United States, bringing all of them actively into the picture. In the process Lebanon virtually ceased to exist as a functioning sovereign nation. The Ethiopian civil wars, which also incorporated a foreign war, first broke out in 1961, to continue unabated twenty-nine years later, in 1990, as secessionists from Eritrea and Tigre Province fought the central government. The civil war in Zaire resulted in a French-American military intervention. Colombia had been torn by a succession of civil wars since 1948, compounded in the 1980's by the terror imposed by powerful cocaine cartels.

The elected Chilean Marxist government was overthrown by a military revolution in which the United States played at least an indirect role; it was part of the broader ideological warfare in the world. The civil wars that erupted in Central America toward the end of the decade were rapidly internationalized by the East and the West. Revolutions and bloody civil wars along with merciless repression swamped Argentina and Uruguay.

All these unleased passions brought forth the new phenomenon of internal and international terrorism on a grand scale: in the Middle East, Western Europe, and Latin America. It swept the world through the demented courage and sacrifice of its perpetrators and their passionate beliefs in their causes, through the cold-blooded hatreds displayed by so many and the availability of lethal state-of-the-art technology of death.

In the seventies the world's economic structures underwent a drastic transformation as a result of a combination of trends and events that were unavoidable in some instances and wholly unpredictable in others. America's unquestioned domination of the international economy came to an end as postwar reconstruction in Western Europe and Asia was completed (with vast American aid), and West Germany and Japan became economic powers in their own right. This was formalized, in effect, when the United State accepted in 1971 the reality that the dollar no longer was the *only* currency that really counted in world trade and agreed to free the price of gold for the first time in nearly forty years.

Then came a series of "petro-shocks," demonstrating the West's—and America's—immense dependence on Third World oil producers. First, Libya and Iran joined in imposing higher prices on foreign producers extracting crude oil from their territories under antiquated concessions agreements. Then the 1973 Middle East War triggered the Arab embargo on oil exports to the West, causing havoc in the industrialized countries. Americans learned about long lines and shortages at gas stations, belatedly realizing that in its complacency the United States had relied on cheap foreign imports for more than one half of its oil consumption (it did so again in 1990).

Before long petroleum prices leaped tenfold, with the Organization of Petroleum Exporting Countries (OPEC) suddenly becoming a household name and a much feared and detested institution with extraordinary power in its hands. From one third in 1960, OPEC's share of world production rose to one half in 1975. Now the key word in international economics was "petrodollars," nobody quite knowing what to do with the uncounted billions of dollars sloshing back and forth between Third World producers and the great Western banks. For the United States, the "golden" years ended.

*   *   *

For Americans, quite apart from the economic shocks, the decade was politically and emotionally wrenching. The remarkable thing is how well the American system has held up under incredible pressures.

The agony of the deeply divisive antiwar movement and of winding up the Indochina conflict was followed by the post-Vietnam syndrome, a sense that having for all practical purposes lost the war, the United States was what Richard Nixon had earlier warned against: a pitiful, helpless giant.

This, to be sure, was far from reality—and this was not the way friend and foe perceived the United States—but Americans do have a masochistic penchant. It was illustrated by the outpouring of articles and books about the decline of the American age and empire (a theme that was mindlessly resurrected in the eighties through an avalanche of best-selling doom books authored by hitherto obscure academics). President Jimmy Carter contributed to this mood by his diagnosis that "malaise," which he did not explain, prevailed in the land.

What had shaken America the most, overlapping the drama of the final years of Vietnam, was the Watergate scandal, which resulted in Nixon's resignation from the presidency in 1974. Vice President Spiro Agnew had resigned the previous year as he faced charges of malfeasance, and the Republic was living through the greatest crisis in its history as Congress prepared to impeach Nixon for alleged obstruction of justice in the Watergate affair. Having lost one President through assassination a decade earlier, the United States was now losing another one through resignation. Gerald Ford helped restore political sanity as he replaced Nixon in the Oval Office, but in the seventies the United States had three Presidents and four Vice Presidents.

The dangers to the nation were immense during that summer of 1974 though their extent may not have been realized at that moment. Two stark memories stand out in my mind about the dark days in Washington. The first was of a silent crowd massed before the White House on an August evening, awaiting word of Nixon's resignation. The second was of being told by Defense Secretary James R. Schlesinger on the day before the resignation (I had a long-standing appointment with Schlesinger, whose profile I was writing for a magazine) that he and General George Brown, the chairman of the Joint Chiefs of Staff, had just agreed to disregard and disobey any presidential orders to the armed forces that they would judge irresponsible. Schlesinger and Brown simply could not rule out, remote as it was, the possibility that Nixon, in despair and determined to cling to power, would order a military strike (even a nuclear one) somewhere in the world or call out the troops to surround the Capitol to prevent an impeachment vote. In retrospect, this sounds fictional, but it shows how seriously the top players were assessing the situation at that juncture.

It was a tribute to the strength of the American system and the courage of a number of leaders in the executive, legislative, and judicial branches of the government that in the end the nation took Watergate in stride. Amazing (and amusing) was that the whole Watergate crisis, including Nixon's resignation, was never understood abroad—not by the Soviets, not by the sophisticated Western Europeans, and not by the Latin Americans so tolerant of their own leaders' foibles. Why, it was asked over and over, was a botched break-in at the offices of the opposition political party and financial manipulations by the ruling party—or even the President's hiding the truth or telling lies—such a great scandal?

It was virtually impossible to explain the puritan American approach to politics and presidential ethics to people who thought it was both irrelevant and probably hypocritical. As for Nixon, he was received as a hero in Paris, Beijing, and Islamabad, among other capitals where his foreign policy had always been applauded—so much for differences between cultures— and he went on to write best-selling books and op ed page articles and to gain a measure of new respect.

The seventies brought breakthroughs and contradictions in the lives of nations. In the United States and France abortion on demand was legalized after bitter emotional battles. In Washington the Supreme Court ruled in the *Roe* v. *Wade* case in 1973; the right to abortion was protected under the Constitution. But at the end of the eighties, prolife and prochoice advocates went on fighting over the Court's soul—whether or not the opinion should be maintained.

In France, a predominantly Roman Catholic country, the abortion drama was played out in the National Assembly in 1974. Under a 1917 law, women who sought abortion were subject to a six-month prison sentence, but President Valéry Giscard d'Estaing had concluded that this was wrong. Giscard, a right-of-center president and a practicing Roman Catholic, was determined to modernize France, and he took the view that the time had come to change the law. He noted that affluent women could have legal abortions in Britain, Belgium, or Switzerland, while others "were reduced to clandestinity and to recourse to means that were degrading to their feminine dignity, [and] that often compromised their health."

Giscard writes in his memoirs, *Le Pouvoir et la Vie* (Power and Life): "We could not stay that way. Civil law had to be made compatible with real social conditions. It was not a question, as it had been said, of 'approving' abortion, but to transfer to personal responsibility a part of what until now was in the domain of collective law. Everyone should respect the demands of her conscience or faith, but would no longer decide for others."

To lead the struggle in parliament to abolish the ban on abortion, Giscard selected Health Minister Simone Weil. She is one of the most remarkable women I have ever met. As a young Jewish girl she was arrested during the German occupation and deported to Oświęcim concentration camp. She survived wartime horrors to return to France, complete her education, turn to social work and politics, and be named to the French Cabinet by

Giscard's prime minister, Jacques Chirac. I met Madame Weil in the early 1980's, when she served as one of the first presidents of the European Parliament, greatly strengthening this infant institution.

Giscard provides in his memoirs a description of how the abortion law was ultimately approved by the National Assembly. He writes that he watched the all-night debate on television, and "what moved me the most, and what I remember as if I still had it before my eyes, was the sight of Simone Weil, in her Chanel *tailleur*, sitting in the government benches at the end of a night session, and weeping in distress." He adds: "She had been grossly attacked in a debate that up to then did not lack in dignity. She cracked under fatigue, under the insult, and, perhaps, when the nerves weakened, under remembrances. This image shattered the public opinion. In the National Assembly as in the Senate, the law was passed by a majority." Giscard noted that under no succeeding French government or parliamentary majority was the question of abortion ever reopened.

In the seventies, the whole question of birth control and skyrocketing populations, especially in the Third World, was becoming acute. Governments and international organizations were aware of the growing emergency: Latin America, Asia, and Africa could not even begin to feed, house, clothe, educate, and employ the millions upon millions of new inhabitants—or provide them with medical care. There was consensus that disaster—starvation, disease, and social calamity—loomed ahead. Contraceptive measures—from the rhythm method to interuterine (IUD) devices—were universally known, but in the Roman Catholic countries of Latin America and in the Philippines the church opposed birth control as a matter of dogma.

Following the liberalizing Second Vatican Council in the sixties, some hope had arisen that the Holy See might relax its rigorous rejection of birth control, especially with growing numbers of young priests in the Third World urging a change. But the death of John XXIII put an end to these hopes. Paul VI, his successor, was absolutely against any form of change. As a newspaper correspondent I traveled with the pope to Turkey and the House of Mary near Ephesus in the summer of 1967, and because he was going to overpopulated Asia, the question of birth control was raised in a brief conversation with reporters when the pontiff visited the press section of the plane during the flight. We knew that the matter was under study by a special commission, but Paul VI shook his head, unwilling to talk about it.

The previous day in Istanbul the pope had demonstrated the church's increasing tolerance when he met at St. George's Church in the Phanar (the city's Greek district) with Athenagoras I, the patriarch of the Greek Orthodox Church, to celebrate with him in the new ecumenical spirit the end of a half millennium of spiritual separation after their schism. It was a glorious spectacle: the tall, powerful, bearded Athenagoras embracing the tiny, white-clad figure of the pope and exchanging kisses on the cheek with him. But the tolerance did not include birth control. Presently the special commission issued a report firmly rebuffing it.

When Karol Cardinal Wojtyła was elected to the papacy on October 16, 1978, as the first non-Italian pope (not counting the French pope of Avignon), hopes were sparked anew that there would be great changes. The Polish-born pope, who took the name of John Paul II, was widely regarded as a modern man and an outstanding intellectual. I had the privilege of meeting him when he was archbishop of Kraków in southern Poland in 1973, and he was an impressive presence. Our conversation concerned principally the problems of the church in a Communist state and his youth under Nazi occupation, and I never thought about touching on questions like birth control. Upon his surprise election, I remembered the Kraków discussion and wondered whether his unusual background would lead to new thinking in Rome.

John Paul II was not prepared, however, to depart from tradition, and he appeared to resent actions by Roman Catholics in what he saw as violations of dogma. Giscard d'Estaing writes in his memoirs that he made a point of explaining France's action on abortion to both Paul VI and John Paul II, with both expressing their "preoccupation," but the latter reacting with "reproval." Giscard says that he told him:

> I am a Catholic, but I am president of the Republic of a lay state. I must not impose my personal convictions on my fellow citizens, but I must see to it that the law corresponds to the real condition of the French society so that it will be respected and observed. I understand fully the view of the Catholic church and, as a Catholic, I share it. I judge it to be legitimate that the Church demand that those who practice its faith respect certain interdictions. But they may not be imposed through penal sanctions by civil law on the entirety of the social body. . . . I was not seeking to justify myself in [his] eyes, but to make [him] see the dilemma that was mine and that I had had to resolve in my conscience!

As for John Paul II, he was increasingly an enigma; whereas Vatican Council II under John XXIII, brought a vast amelioration of Catholic-Jewish relations, they seemed to deteriorate under the Polish pope.

New cracks began to appear during the 1970's in the facade and structure of the European Communist bloc. The 1968 invasion of Czechoslovakia had failed to dampen antiregime sentiments throughout Eastern Europe, and it was again Poland's turn to defy Communist rule.

When the government announced steep rises in food prices in December 1970 (quite thoughtlessly just before Christmas), workers rioted in the port city of Gdańsk in the worst outbreak of violence in the country since 1956.

Władysław Gomułka, who had been elevated to power as a Communist liberal as a result of that rebellion, responded fourteen years late as foolishly as his predecessors: He ordered soldiers and tanks to fire into the crowds, and again scores of workers were killed. What seemed to gall the bald Gomułka most was that the workers had burned down the provincial headquarters of the Communist party. Two years after dispatching Polish troops to Czechoslovakia to quell "Marxism with a Human Face," he showed even greater brutality at home.

Curiously, however, public opinion counted even under the Communist dictatorship. The revulsion against the Gdańsk killings was so enormous, and the threat of riots and strikes elsewhere in Poland could not be disregarded, that within days Gomułka's Politburo colleagues decided to fire him and to cancel the price hikes. Gomułka became a nonperson, relegated to a Warsaw apartment and promptly forgotten by the nation he had betrayed.

The Gdańsk episode, as it turned out, was the start of historic events that culminated in that same city in the birth of Solidarity a decade later and, at the end of 1989, in the virtual erosion of the Communist party. Gomułka was replaced as the party's first secretary by Edward Gierek, a younger-generation Communist leader who had spent much of his youth working as a coal miner in France and Belgium and therefore was familiar with the West, unlike other Eastern European Communist leaders.

Gierek, who relaxed considerably the straitjacket of Communist rule, was determined to modernize Poland's economy at almost any cost. His stand made him popular in the West (he visited Nixon in Washington, the first Eastern European leader to be invited to the United States), where he acquired a debt that ultimately soared to nearly forty-billion dollars. With the signing in December 1970 of a Polish-West German treaty which masked but could not erase extremely deep Polish-German resentments, Poland now looked like an exemplary political and economic partner for the West in Eastern Europe.

Then, in the spring of 1976, Gierek repeated Gomułka's error by raising food prices with no advance notice to the population. Strikes erupted in the huge Ursus truck plant on the outskirts of Warsaw, in other cities, and throughout the national railroad system. Gierek saved himself this time by canceling overnight the price increases and sacrificing his prime minister, whom he forced to resign. He had, however, the good sense or the humanity to forbid the army and the police to use arms against the protesting strikers. This self-restraint allowed him to stay in power, showing again that public opinion could not be ignored. Besides, Gierek was not generally despised by the nation as Gomułka had been.

Though there was no violence against the strikers in 1976, there were numerous arrests of workers' leaders, presumably because the regime could not simply pretend that nothing had happened; the arrests and firings of the leaders from their jobs were primarily a face-saving device. But they led to an extremely momentous event, the creation of a clandestine Committee for the Defense of the Workers (known as KOR after its Polish acronym). I was visiting Warsaw at the time on a magazine assignment, and I realized that I was witnessing an unprecedented phenomenon in a Communist country: the alliance of workers and intellectuals against the regime. KOR was virtually unknown abroad for several years, but KOR intellectuals— such as Tadeusz Mazowiecki (who became prime minister in August 1989), Bronisław Geremek, Adam Michnik, and Jacek Kuroń—became the principal political advisers to Lech Wałęsa and Solidarity at its birth four years later.

It was an amazing breakthrough. In 1956 the intellectuals (writers, philosophers, university professors, and the like) had failed to rise in support of the workers though they subsequently benefited from the Polish October. In 1968 the workers, perhaps remembering 1956, had looked the other way during the purge of intellectuals (Jewish and non-Jewish). In 1970 it was the intellectuals' turn to sit on their hands while Gdańsk rioters were being killed. But they joined forces—spontaneously—when the protests broke out on what happened to be the twentieth anniversary of the 1956 affray.

KOR's ostensible aim was to obtain the release of the workers from jails and the restoration of their jobs, and the Roman Catholic Church supported fully and publicly KOR's efforts. But as it was explained to me at secret meetings in Warsaw apartments with the new organization's leaders, KOR was meant to be a permanent institution dedicated to the protection of human rights in Poland and, to the extent it was feasible, to act as political opposition. While KOR lawyers defended workers in court (then defended fellow KOR members when they, too, were being arrested), others were publishing underground bulletins, mimeographed at first, then printed, and listing the editors with their real names in an added defiance of the regime. More and more leading citizens joined KOR, and the organization soon branched out into "flying universities," with classes held clandestinely in private apartments to teach students government-forbidden themes of history, philosophy, and politics. And secret contacts were steadily developing between KOR and workers' leaders in trade unions and at industrial plants.

Though the regime punished KOR members with short jail sentences (and occasional beatings by party thugs), it committed the colossal error of not taking KOR seriously, preferring to lessen tensions through a relatively lenient treatment of opposition activists; Gierek, for one thing, did not want to blacken his image in the West, where he kept borrowing more and more money for his grandiose projects. Only in 1980, when Solidarity entered the stage with advice from the intellectuals, did the regime understand KOR's immense importance.

While a certain relaxation came to Poland during the seventies, Brezhnev in the Soviet Union was busy imposing the type of repression that had not been experienced since Stalin's days. The KGB, the powerful secret police, was ordered to stamp out the growing movement of intellectual dissidents; there were massive arrests and show trials of writers and intellectuals and scientists who published underground literature (samizdat), spoke out against the regime when they met foreign journalists, or acted or were suspected of acting in a hostile fashion toward the government. More and more dissidents were placed by the KGB in psychiatric institutes, both to keep them isolated and to discredit them in the eyes of the public.

Aleksandr Solzhenitsyn, the novelist, was in prison when the Nobel Prize for literature was awarded to him for what the Swedish Academy called in the citation "the ethical force with which he has pursued the indispensable traditions of Russian literature." Solzhenitsyn naturally was not permitted to travel to Stockholm to receive the prize though he was allowed later to emigrate to the United States in exchange for a Soviet spy held in the West. Boris Pasternak, the author of *Dr. Zhivago*, had declined it in 1958, when Khrushchev refused to let him go to Sweden for the ceremony. Pasternak was regarded as an enemy of the regime, and his work (which the Swedish Academy described as being in the "great Russian epic tradition") was published in the Soviet Union only in the late eighties under Gorbachev's *glasnost*.

After the wild turbulence of the youth of the sixties, the new decade was somewhat more tranquil and reflective in the West—perhaps as a reaction—even though in the United States massive antiwar moratorium demonstrations went on until the peace accord was signed in 1973. Politics became more conservative in France and Britain with the election of right-of-center Giscard d'Estaing (in 1974) and Margaret Thatcher (in 1979). In the United States Jimmy Carter had conservative traits, and his presidency paved the way for Ronald Reagan's election in 1980. Men, even young men, began wearing three-piece suits as a mark of respectability.

Rock remained the dominant music genre of the seventies, but it was increasingly commercial. The decade produced three types of rock—reggae, disco, and funk—but none was memorable. The end of the "real" rock—vibrant and spontaneous and young as it was in the sixties—may have come with the assassination of the Beatles' John Lennon in 1980.

In literature the West began to discover the astoundingly rich vein of Latin American literature. The Chilean poet Pablo Neruda received the Nobel Prize for literature in 1970 for "a poetry that with the action of an elemental force brings alive a continent's destiny and dreams." This was the year after Salvador Allende Gossens, a Marxist, was elected Chile's president, and Neruda, himself a senator for the Communist party, was approaching death. Americans and Europeans also came to know Colombia's Gabriel García Márquez, whose *One Hundred Years of Solitude* was published in English in 1970 (*his* Nobel Prize came in 1982), Mexico's Carlos

Fuentes and Octavio Paz, Argentina's Julio Cortázar, and Brazil's Jorge Amado, and Peru's Mario Vargas Llosa.

The world's horizons were broadening.

II

There were 536,100 American servicemen in Vietnam when Richard Nixon took office in January 1969. At the start of 1970 the total was down to approximately 430,000. Under his policy of "Vietnamization," announced in Guam halfway through his first year in the presidency, the President was withdrawing Americans as rapidly as he prudently could without pulling the rug out from under the Saigon regime. Melvin Laird, his defense secretary, had convinced Nixon that it was politically untenable to keep hundreds of thousands of Americans indefinitely in Indochina; with periodic rotations of men, more than 3 million young Americans would have served in Vietnam under extremely inauspicious conditions, and this was increasingly disrupting the society at home. Laird argued that even with such high numbers the war would not be won anyway and that the nation would not stand much longer for hundreds of flag-draped coffins coming back every week.

In a milestone study *The Military and the Media*, published in 1989, the U.S. Army Center of Military History concludes that "what alienated the American public in both the Korean and Vietnam wars was not the news coverage but casualties. . . . Public support for each war dropped inexorably by 15 percentage points whenever total U.S. casualties increased by a factor of 10." Addressing itself to charges that the media had lost the war for the United States, the study says:

> The only viable option open to the United States was to con-
> vince the enemy that there was no hope for the communist
> cause. To do that, however, the administration had first to con-
> vince the American people that South Vietnam was either worth
> a prolonged war of attrition or that U.S. forces could win in the
> end without a major sacrifice of lives and treasure. Neither alter-
> native was possible. . . . President Johnson and his advisers put
> too much faith in public relations. They forgot at least two com-
> mon-sense rules of effective propaganda: that the truth has

greater ultimate power than the most pleasing of bromides, and that no amount of massaging will heal a broken limb or a fundamentally flawed strategy.

By 1970 Nixon knew that the best he could achieve would be to repatriate all the Americans during the next three years and to hope that with American matériel the South Vietnamese would survive. In what became known as the Nixon Doctrine, he said on Guam that concerning internal security and military defense, the United States "has a right to expect that this problem will be increasingly handled by, and the responsibility for it taken by, the Asian nations themselves." He remarked that "if the United States just continues down the road of responding to requests for assistance, of assuming the primary responsibility for defending these countries when they have internal problems or external problems, they are never going to take care of themselves."

Whether Nixon really believed that the South Vietnamese could hold their own after the American departure is dubious. He was much more realistic than Johnson, and he knew more about foreign policy. His principal adviser, Henry Kissinger, the German-born Harvard historian, was equally realistic with an additional Machiavellian touch. In retrospect, however, it does not appear that they had much choice but to go on fighting while gradually disengaging from the battlefield and, as Kissinger had already done in his secret meetings with the North Vietnamese in Paris that started in August 1969, to continue negotiating a settlement. An abrupt pullout and the then inevitable collapse of President Nguyen Van Thieu's fragile government in Saigon would have undermined American credibility internationally and, Nixon believed, encouraged the Soviets and Communists around the world to embark on fresh adventures at the expense of the United States.

Ironically the liberals—Kennedy and Johnson—had mired America in the Indochina swamp, and the right-winger—Richard Nixon—had to extricate it. It is, of course, a complex philosophical and historical question whether the preservation of American credibility justified three more years of war, the lives of ten thousand more Americans (in addition to the forty-eight thousand already killed in the previous decade), and tens of thousands of Vietnamese lives on both sides. Nixon's answer at the time was obviously in the affirmative; but now we know that the prestige of the United States did not suffer greatly when the Indochina War was lost in the end, and it could be argued in hindsight that matters would not have been very different if the President had taken the advice of the late Senator George Aiken of Vermont that America should simply announce, then and there, that "we have won and we're going home."

Another unanswered question is whether Nixon and Kissinger were being told the truth about the political and military situation in Vietnam in the early seventies. Publicly General Abrams, the new American commander in chief in Saigon, was effusively optimistic, and it is entirely possible that he

truly believed that the war was winnable. But if this assessment was transmitted as gospel truth up the Pentagon command chain all the way to the
Oval Office, then the President was being dangerously misled and a significant and dangerous fault existed in the system of governace.

My own impression is that Defense Secretary Laird was less euphoric
about an approaching victory than was Robert McNamara during the gung
ho sixties and that both the CIA and American Ambassador Ellsworth
Bunker (dispatched to Vietnam despite his advanced age by Nixon after
practicing his crisis diplomacy for Kennedy and Johnson from Yemen to the
Dominican Republic) had a much keener analytical sense and provided
truer and more valuable information to Washington.

Even in the field in Vietnam it was exceedingly difficult to nail down the
truth. When Nixon dispatched American troops into the Fishhook salient in
Cambodia, almost directly west of Saigon, on May 1, 1970, he presented it as a
thrust designed to capture the COSVN, the elusive Vietcong command
structure for Vietnam, supposedly operating from Cambodian sanctuaries, and
to save "neutral" Cambodia from being swept by North Vietnamese troops.
This was one of Nixon's most controversial decisions in the war (now "Nixon's
War"), resulting, among other tragedies, in the death of four protesting students
in a confrontation with the National Guard at Kent State University in Ohio.

The President coupled the Cambodia announcement with the promise
that 150,000 more men would be withdrawn from Vietnam by the spring of
1971, bringing the total down to 265,500 servicemen. In the meantime,
however, he had enlarged the war for no convincing reasons; there was
never any hard intelligence that COSVN was actually operating out of
Cambodia or that the North Vietnamese were about to capture Pnom Penh,
the Cambodian capital. Of course, Cambodia had been subjected to secret
American bombings since 1969, for similarly tenuous reasons. It is impossible to determine whether Nixon suspected that he was acting on the basis of
unreliable intelligence or whether he was gambling that an attack on Cambodia might force Hanoi into more forthcoming negotiations with Kissinger
in Paris (the Communists chose to suspend the talks for many months as a
result of the Cambodian incursion).

In July 1970 I had accompanied Secretary of State William Rogers on a
trip to the Pacific and Southeast Asia, and Vietnam was one of the stops.
From Saigon we were flown to a fortified village in the Mekong River delta
to receive a detailed military briefing from American and ARVN officers.
With the aid of maps and overlays, the officers outlined the progress
achieved in pacifying the area, emphasizing that highways in the delta were
now safe for travel even at night. I wandered off toward a shady spot under a
clump of trees where two U.S. Army captains, both advisers to the ARVN,
sat quietly, in their jeep, drinking beer. I introduced myself, mentioned the
highlights of the briefing, and asked how accurate it was. The captains
looked at each other and burst out laughing. "That's bullshit, man," one of
them said. "It's worse than ever. . . . I'd have to have my head examined
before I'd drive *anywhere* at night around here. . . ."

* * *

While America strove for Nixon's "peace with honor" in Indochina, new crises—and new waves of violence—swept the world in the early seventies, from Syria and Jordan to Chile and Cuba and from East Pakistan to Turkey.

In 1970 the most dangerous series of crises developed in the Middle East. To compound matters for the United States, the Soviets established for the first time a military presence in the region, challenging American supremacy in the Mediterranean as well as threatening Israel's security. The Russians had not mounted such a serious challenge since the 1962 Cuban missile crisis, and Nixon and Kissinger wondered whether they were trying to take advantage of the United States' concentration on Indochina to stake out a claim for influence in the Middle East. At the same time, however, negotiations aimed at a limitation of strategic arms—the SALT talks initiated in Helsinki in November 1969—were proceeding in a satisfactory, if slow, fashion. Never before had the two nuclear superpowers engaged in an effort to restrain the arms race, and the Nixon administration was encouraged by Soviet goodwill in this realm.

Still, Soviet behavior was disconcerting to Nixon and Kissinger. Whereas their intellectual inclination was to form a logical body of foreign policy and pursue linkages between its different strands, Moscow seemed to be often guided by a hit-or-miss approach. The American war against the Communists in Indochina was generally ignored by the Soviets (apart from rhetoric), who saw no reason that it should interfere with SALT and other affairs. Under the circumstances, then, it was mystifying why Brezhnev was risking a collision by dispatching fifteen thousand combat troops to Egypt, installing SAM-3 antiaircraft-missile batteries to deflect Israeli deep-penetration bombing raids from Egyptian territory, and assigning Soviet pilots to fly combat missions along the Suez Canal and Egypt's seacoast. The Soviet Mediterranean fleet was growing in size and power, an air and naval base was established in Alexandria, and aircraft from there shadowed American warships.

As Washington attempted to decipher long-range Soviet intentions in the Middle East (and prepared to start delivering new jets to Israel to assure its continuing mastery of the air), the kingdom of Jordan suddenly blew up. King Hussein, a moderate Arab leader despite his decision to join Nasser in fighting the 1967 war, came under vicious attacks by guerrillas of the Popular Front for the Liberation of Palestine (PFLP), and his survival was at stake. The guerrillas had established themselves in Jordan after 1967, using Jordanian territory for ground raids across the river into Israel, but Hussein moved to stop them because of hard-hitting Israeli retaliatory air strikes. The PFLP, therefore, undertook to overthrow the king, assaulting government buildings in Amman on June 9, as a prelude to the planned seizure of the entire capital. It was one more demonstration of Arab inability to maintain unity among themselves and their proclivity to slaughter each other.

Because more than five hundred Americans resided in Amman, the administration contemplated dropping Eighty-second Airborne Division paratroopers on the city to protect them and to ferry in marines aboard helicopters from aircraft carriers in the Mediterranean. After several days Hussein and the PFLP negotiated a settlement, but this Jordanian affray marked the start of what would be the Palestinian War in the region and would continue for twenty years and beyond. In August a cease-fire between Israel and Egypt in their air and artillery conflict went into effect as a result of an American-Soviet understanding; neither superpower wished to let the situation get out of hand.

The Middle East now seemed to be under control. Yet the unexpected always happened there. On September 6, 1970, PFLP guerrillas hijacked a TWA airliner and a Swiss airliner over Europe, and forced them to fly to an abandoned airfield in Jordan. An attempt the same day to hijack an Israeli airliner failed when security guards subdued three guerrillas, killing one and turning over to the British police, the other two, including the beautiful Leila Khaled, who became the latest international figure of revolutionary romance. The next day, however, the PFLP captured a British airliner, also forcing it to Jordan. In all, the guerrillas held 475 hostages on the sunbaked desert airstrip.

These September hijackings opened the era of lethal, large-scale international terrorism, a new horror that went on to haunt the world. Airliners were hijacked or blown up at airports and in the air, men and women who were specific political targets were assassinated in the streets of Western European and Middle Eastern cities, and scores of innocent men, women, and children were machine-gunned at airports or hit by bombs at railroad and bus stations. Arab terrorists worked with Japanese terrorists of the Red Army in the killings and hijackings. The Japanese killed twenty-eight and wounded seventy-six at Israel's Lod airport in 1972; the Palestinians murdered Israeli Olympic athletes in Munich. Terrorist organizations composed of young people from affluent families sprouted up in Italy (the Red Brigades who kidnapped and executed Prime Minister Aldo Moro in 1978), West Germany (the Red Army Faction and the Baader-Meinhof group), and France (Direct Action). In Latin America the Montoneros in Argentina and the Tupamaros in Uruguay specialized in the early seventies in kidnapping foreign diplomats and wealthy businessmen—though the Tupamaros also "executed" Dan Mitrione, an American police adviser to the Uruguayan government—and in wholesale guerrilla raids. The names of Carlos, the Venezuelan international terrorist, and Abu Nidal, of the radical Palestinian group, joined Leila Khaled in the rogues' gallery of terrorism. In 1985 there were terrorist acts in eighty-four countries.

But such is the contemporary mind-set that real-life incidents of terrorism provided great entertainment material. Motion pictures based on the Mitrione execution (directed by Costa Gavras) and the 1976 Israeli commando raid on Entebbe in Uganda to free hijacked airline passengers were box-office hits. So were fictionalized films, including tales of nuclear terrorism—still a theme of real fear on the part of governments everywhere.

In the case of the planes hijacked in Jordan in September 1970, the guerrillas demanded the freedom for all Palestinians in prisons in Israel (3,000 of them) and in Western Europe—including Leila Khaled—and threatened to blow up the airliners with the hostages if they were turned down. With Arab diplomats conducting negotiations, the hostages were freed in exchange for 450 Palestinians held in Israel—and for Khaled. In Amman that same week King Hussein decided to destroy the PFLP once and for all, nearly starting a full-fledged Middle East war.

Thus, on September 19, at least three hundred Syrian tanks crossed into Jordan in support of the guerrillas. Nixon placed the Mediterranean fleet and airborne troops in the United States and West Germany on high alert, and Israel mobilized its army. There was agreement that Jordan had to be saved from the Palestinians and Syria at all costs, and the Nixon administration could not rule out a confrontation with the Soviets now that they had become so deeply involved in the area.

Again, Third World conflicts were pushing the superpowers toward a face-off; the judgment in Washington was that Brezhnev was gambling on Jordan but did not wish a clash. As more Syrian tanks poured into Jordan, Hussein informed the United States that he would welcome Israeli air support—such being the reality of Arab politics—but in the end he was able to force back the Syrians with his own small air force. Curiously, General Hafez al-Assad, the Syrian Air Force commander, refused to send up his planes against the Jordanian jets. On September 24 the war was over, the Syrian regime fell, and General Assad became the new president, a post he still held twenty years later. On September 28 Egypt's President Nasser died of a heart attack at the age of fifty-two. Another phase in Middle Eastern affairs had opened.

Next, it was Latin America's turn to command crisis headlines, and once more the United States chose to play an active part. There was a Chilean crisis and a Cuban crisis, both in September 1970, and coinciding with severe diplomatic and military problems in Indochina as well as in the Middle East. To complicate matters, Nixon had chosen September to fly to Italy, Yugoslavia, Ireland, and Spain and to visit the aircraft carrier *Saratoga* in the Mediterranean. Kissinger vanished twice from view to hold secret meetings with the North Vietnamese in Paris.

The crisis in Chile was the election on September 4 of Salvador Allende Gossens, the physician of Marxist persuasion, to the presidency of his country. To the Nixon administration, fighting communism in Indochina and the Caribbean and worrying about it in the Middle East, this was a slap in the face, a threat to American security, and a defiance of the United States. A study issued by the CIA two months earlier had predicted that if elected, Allende "would proceed as rapidly as possible toward the establishment of a Marxist-Socialist state . . . a Chilean version of a Soviet-style East European Communist state." This was rank nonsense (State Department analysts disagreed with it), but Kissinger created a public controversy by declaring shortly after the elections that "we should not delude ourselves that an Allende takeover in Chile would not present massive problems for us, and for democratic forces and pro-U.S. forces in Latin America."

During the electoral campaign the CIA and the International Telephone and Telegraph Company (which feared the Chilean telephone company it owned would be nationalized) joined forces in a covert operation against Allende; well over one million dollars was spent by the CIA (authorized by the White House) and American businessmen to cause his defeat. Allende won by such a small margin over two opponents that under Chilean law a runoff election by the Congress was required to choose between him and the conservative candidate, Jorge Alessandri, who had come the closest. The parliamentary election was set for October 24, and the White House busied itself with plans to block a second Allende victory. Specifically Nixon instructed the CIA to organize a military coup to prevent Allende's accession to power.

This was the rerun of Indonesia, Iran, Guatemala, Cuba, and the Dominican Republic (U.S. interventions occurred impartially under Democratic and Republican administrations), but the operation failed. Among the scenarios designed by Chilean officers favorable to the coup was the abduction of General René Schneider, chief of staff of the army, who was known for his dedication to constitutional procedures (Chile, in fact, had a remarkable democratic tradition by Latin American standards). Two days before the vote in the Congress, Schneider was killed during the kidnapping attempt, and the public revulsion was so great that the plotters dropped their plans.

Allende took office, but he lasted fewer than three years in power. In September 1973 he was overthrown by a bloody military revolution led by General Augusto Pinochet Ugarte. He died, apparently by his own hand, as the presidential palace in Santiago was being attacked by the rebel army. Veritable terror followed the coup, with executions and imprisonments. Though the United States had used all its resources to undermine the Allende government economically and politically, there is no evidence that it actually helped organize the coup. A man of absolute honesty but great political naiveté, Allende allowed the extreme left wing of his Socialist party to ruin the national economy through irresponsible policies, turning public opinion against his government. During 1971 he endured a three-week visit from Fidel Castro, who toured Chile from one end to another, delivering speeches everywhere he went to sing praises of social revolutions.

In 1970 it was Cuba that produced the other Latin American headache for the Nixon administration, just a week after Allende's election in Chile. This was the suspicion in Washington that the Soviet Union was establishing a nuclear submarine base on the island and thereby violating the agreement under which the 1962 missile crisis had been resolved. Photography by U-2 spy aircraft showed that new barracks, communication towers, and antiaircraft sites were being constructed near the naval base of Cienfuegos in southern Cuba. The aerial pictures also pointed to a new soccer field in the area, and Kissinger, a soccer fan, concluded that it had to be for the Russians inasmuch as the game was not normally played in Cuba. Moreover, a Soviet submarine tender, a nuclear submarine, and two barges for storing radioactive wastes were spotted in the Atlantic, not far from Cuba.

When *The New York Times* published an account of these suspicions, Kissinger warned that a Soviet nuclear submarine base in Cuba would be regarded as a "hostile act." In mid-October the Soviet government announced that it had no plans to establish bases in Cuba, and the matter was dropped. It is impossible to determine whether this was another Brezhnev gamble, but American preemptive diplomacy stopped it in time. What the United States had ignored was that at Castro's request a three-thousand-man Soviet combat brigade had remained in Cuba after the 1962 crisis as a precaution; it is entirely possible that the soccer field was being built for these soldiers.

As for Castro, he had more serious concerns in 1970. Having decided initially that Cuba should end its "colonial" dependence on sugar and develop other resources, he changed his mind in the late sixties, committing the country to a record harvest of ten million tons in 1970 (it had never before exceeded seven million tons). Despite work around the clock by practically the entire population (plus American volunteers and visiting Soviet generals), the harvest fell considerably short of the goal, marking the beginning of a gradual decline in production that could not be remedied even in the late eighties.

Elsewhere in Latin America, political oppression by right-wing military regimes was the hallmark of the seventies. In Brazil and Uruguay the generals and admirals had been ruling their countries with institutional terror since the mid-sixties; no vestiges of democracy had remained.

In Argentina the military allowed free elections in 1973, and Hector Cámpora, a follower of Juan Perón, the dictator ousted eighteen years earlier, won the presidency. The aging Perón immediately returned from exile and was elected president in a new election five months later, Cámpora having conveniently resigned. It was extraordinary for the Perón myth to have survived so many years; Perón himself died a year later at the age of seventy-eight, to be replaced by his widow, Isabel. In March 1976, as guerrilla warfare mounted in the country, she was overthrown by the army, which launched the "Dirty War" that lasted for six years, with thousands of opponents killed; other thousands simply disappeared. (In 1989 a new-generation Perón follower, Carlos Saúl Menem, was elected Argentina's president, keeping *Peronismo* alive into the fifth decade.) Until Jimmy Carter entered the White House in 1977, the United States had no visible interest in encouraging democracy or protecting human rights in the hemisphere.

The early seventies lived through ever-rising violence on all the continents because of economic and social deprivation, nationalistic and religious hatreds, and personal power ambitions.

In West Africa the secessionists in Biafra surrendered at the start of 1970, with reunified Nigeria in the throes of disease, despair, and hunger. In September 1969, a young colonel named Muammar al-Qaddafi had thrown out King Idris in oil-rich Libya. In January 1971 a former Army sergeant and boxing champion named Idi Amin conquered power in Uganda in East Africa, launching a reign of medieval terror, murder, and torture and nearly two decades of civil war that went on long after *his* ouster. In March 1971 the military in Turkey carried out its second coup in a decade, again interrupting the democratic process and setting the stage for waves of great violence in the seventies and eighties.

A new war between India and Pakistan exploded on December 3, 1971, this time over the determination of East Pakistan to become the independent state of Bangladesh. East Pakistan was a disastrous consequence of the partition of British India in 1947, when a huge area of Bengal and its predominantly Muslim population were established as a province of Pakistan, separated from the western part of the country by hundreds of miles of Indian territory. The independence movement had started early in the year, but the Pakistani Army was able to stamp it out through sheer military force until India began supporting the Bengal guerrillas and finally entered the civil war on the side of Bangladesh.

It was another stunningly cruel Asian war, with five million Bengali refugees descending on Calcutta, swelling its population of ten million to an almost intolerable point. There was no food, no shelter, no medical care, no compassion under Calcutta's baking sun and then monsoon rains. Inevitably, this conflict, too, was caught up in superpower politics.

Because the Soviets had heavily armed India, the Nixon administration decided to "tilt" (in the expression of the day) in favor of Pakistan in spite of the savage repression of the Bengali uprising and the fact that the country was under a military dictatorship. The administration, however, believed it had sound reasons for taking the pro-Pakistani stance, and it dispatched a naval task force to the Indian Ocean to prevent the victorious Indian Army from attacking West Pakistan as well. It was brinksmanship once more and still another American involvement in a Third World conflict.

III

Richard Nixon's voyages to China and the Soviet Union in 1972—and the entire phenomenon of détente—served to illustrate most convincingly that long-range national interests override all other considerations in foreign policy. Although the American war in Indochina still raged, Vietnamese cities were open targets for American air raids, and American soldiers died every day in this crusade against communism, the President had no reservations about visiting the two great Communist capitals. By the same token, Mao Zedong in Beijing and Leonid Brezhnev in Moscow were delighted to welcome Nixon notwithstanding the war the United States was waging against their Communist allies—or clients—in Indochina.

For the three nuclear powers, the Indochina conflict had ceased to be relevant in terms of their relationships. All three were anxious for this war to end so that they could concentrate on truly important affairs in the world and lessen the drain on their resources resulting from their respective Indochina commitments. To put it bluntly, Nixon was as ready to let Saigon drift away as Mao and Brezhnev were ready to see the same happen with Hanoi. Sadly for them, neither Saigon nor Hanoi really understood superpower politics and interests; their Third World Marxist-Leninist comrades in Havana had learned their lesson the hard way during the 1962 missile crisis.

The Americans began thinking about détente almost from the time Nixon assumed office and he and Kissinger began sorting out the real national priorities. The dangers of an uncontrolled nuclear arms race with ever-improving technology had led Washington and Moscow to proceed with SALT, and after two years of patient negotiations, considerable progress had been achieved. In the case of China the courtship of Mao was initiated in the first months of the Nixon administration, and in the summer of 1971 Beijing had finally responded. Operating in absolute secrecy, Nixon and Kissinger were now moving along two parallel tracks: to China and to Russia.

In the meantime, the White House was transforming itself into what became known as the Imperial Presidency, with the top actors having a marvelous time of it. The President owned vacation homes at San Clemente, California, and Key Biscayne, Florida, and the official retreat at Camp David, near Washington, was available to him for weekends or quiet weekdays. Marine Corps helicopters shuttled the Nixons between the White House lawn and Camp David or Andrews Air Force Base outside the capital, where Air Force One was always in readiness. In his five and a half years in the presidency, Nixon flew 147,686 miles in international travel, each foreign trip a vast logistic operation that involved thousands in the planning, execution, and security.

Much as Nixon displayed his taste for crowds, pomp, and circumstance—at one point he had the White House police dress in *Student Prince* operettalike uniforms for formal occasions (he quickly canceled it when the masquerade invited public ridicule)—he was essentially a loner. Most of his great decisions were reached in the loneliness of the Lincoln Sitting Room in the White House family quarters or a small hideaway in the Executive Office Building next door. He made other decisions with a few close advisers aboard the presidential yacht *Sequoia* as they cruised up and down the

Potomac. When antiwar demonstrators paraded through Washington in moratorium protests in 1969, 1970, and 1971 (twelve thousand were arrested during the last mass manifestation), Nixon would be in San Clemente or watching football (his favorite sport) on television. Before and after the Cambodia incursion, the President drew inspiration from watching George C. Scott in *Patton* in the White House projection room.

Among Nixon's favorite pastimes was offering advice—with diagrams—to the Redskins football team in Washington (later he drew up an "enemies list" on a yellow pad). He shared in the capital's sorrow when the Washington Senators baseball team moved away to Texas in 1971. Kissinger, too, became a Redskins fan (it was an in thing), but his principal impact on Washington, apart from foreign policy planning, was social. A bachelor (he was divorced at the time), he dated beautiful and famous women, and great hostesses of the capital prayed for "Henry" to attend their dinners and parties. He also was the man who had authorized the FBI to tap the telephones of his closest aides and of several outstanding journalists in Washington to know whether his secrets were being leaked.

It was a curious dichotomy: The nation was at war, but (as Talleyrand had said on a similar subject a century and a half earlier) the court was amusing itself. Nixon had decided that a "silent majority" of Americans supported him, and Vietnam had been downgraded to a theme of interest to the poor (who made up the majority in American combat units) and to the young, who still protested the killing and the bombing. In the midst of its éclat and self-congratulatory mood about détente and economic affluence, Washington hardly paused to take note of the death of Harry Truman, a great American President, on December 26, 1972. He was eighty-eight.

The China breakthrough was accomplished on July 9, 1971, when Kissinger landed in Beijing after a secret flight from Rawalpindi over the Himalayas aboard a Pakistani airliner. His forty-eight-hour stay in the Chinese capital had been arranged so that in meetings with Premier Zhou Enlai he could create a formal relationship between the two countries—for the first time since the People's Republic had been founded twenty-three years earlier. This climaxed two years of exchanges through Chinese and American ambassadors in Warsaw and then through several intermediaries, among which Pakistan was the most important; China was finally ready to deal with the United States.

The invitation to Kissinger had come through Pakistan, and he stopped there, ostensibly en route from Saigon to Paris for a scheduled session with the North Vietnamese, then vanished from sight for two days (the official cover story was that he was resting at a government guesthouse in the hills). The special flight carried only Kissinger, three of his aides, a Navy stenographer, Secret Service agents, and four Chinese officials, who had come ahead to meet Kissinger in Rawalpindi. There were no leaks, and Kissinger once more succeeded in keeping his mission secret. There was subsequent speculation that it was in exchange for the Pakistanis' diplomatic assistance with China that the administration tilted toward them during the war with India over Bangladesh later that year. But this was never proved, and it is entirely possible that the decision was made in the light of the Chinese-Pakistani friendship, as opposed to latent Chinese-Indian hostility, dating back to their 1962 war.

In Beijing Kissinger met with Premier Zhou for eight hours immediately after his arrival, then twice more before flying back to Pakistan. Mao Zedong chose not to receive the American emissary—there was no diplomatic or protocolary need for it—but he was kept informed in detail by Zhou, and personally approved all the Chinese decisions. The principal decision was for the Chinese to invite Nixon to visit the mainland the following year, which was what Kissinger came to seek, once he and Zhou had worked out a formula under which the United States would recognize that Taiwan was part of China and its future fate would be settled among the Chinese. The Nixon administration was prepared to ditch the Nationalists on Taiwan in favor of a full-fledged relationship with the People's Republic and its (then) eight hundred million inhabitants. It was realistic, and it was belated. The Vietnam War was not a factor in the Beijing talks despite continuing American involvement.

Though Zhou was too well mannered to show it, Kissinger's visit to him eased his memory of John Foster Dulles's refusal to shake his hand in Geneva in 1954. (Zhou and Kissinger were intellectually delighted with each other, and they remained each other's fans until the premier's death in 1975.) Kissinger then reappeared in Rawalpindi, flew to Paris for a day, and went on to San Clemente to give Nixon a minute-by-minute account of his mission. Secretary of State Rogers was the only Cabinet member who knew beforehand about Kissinger's Beijing foray. On July 15 the President went on national television to tell Americans about the Kissinger China visit, his own plans to go there before May of the following year, and his conviction that "all nations will gain from a reduction of tensions and a better relationship" between the two countries. It was Nixon's biggest foreign policy coup in two and a half years in the White House.

The next step was for the administration to help Beijing gain membership in the United Nations (a move the United States had successfully opposed for more than twenty years when the Soviets were sponsoring it) while, for the sake of appearances, seeming to be fighting to prevent Taiwan from being expelled. This looked like a two-Chinas policy, which Nixon and Kissinger knew the Communists did not accept and which really made no sense in the context of the developing new relationship between Washington and Beijing. The White House therefore devised a diplomatic shell game: The United States would support seating Beijing in both the Security Council and the General Assembly but would pretend it opposed expelling Taiwan from the General Assembly.

Kissinger flew to Beijing in October to be with Zhou when the vote came in the United Nations and to assure him privately that the President would not mind at all being defeated on the pro-Taiwan part of the membership proposition. Secretary of State Rogers and the new American chief delegate to the United Nations, a former congressman from Texas and oil millionaire named George Bush, were not told the truth about the shell game although they were in charge of marshaling votes in the General Assembly for the dual membership resolution. Bush was having trouble finding friendly governments, most of whom were understandably confused by what was happening, to cosponsor the resolution, but as usual, he was indefatigable. I was covering the story for the *Times*, and this was the first time I had the opportunity of meeting the future President of the United States; I thought he was most impressive. In the space of less than one month he conferred with ninety-four delegations in search of support for the resolution in which he personally believed, and I remember one of his associates' remarking that it was "a quantitative track record."

In the end Nixon and Kissinger had their way, that is, the United States lost on the resolution that would have preserved Taiwan's seat in the General Assembly; then it joined the majority in awarding full membership to Beijing. When the final vote was taken shortly before midnight on October 25, a conga line of Third World delegates danced in triumph across the General Assembly hall on New York's First Avenue. Now the People's Republic of China was no longer an international pariah and Richard Nixon could announce that he would travel to Beijing next February 21 (two years later Henry Kissinger, the new secretary of state, appointed George Bush the chief of the U.S. diplomatic liaison office in China).

The Security Council and the General Assembly took one more major action in the autumn of 1971; It chose Austria's former foreign minister Kurt Waldheim to be secretary-general of the United Nations to replace Burma's U Thant. Waldheim, who campaigned so hard for the job that he kept visiting press offices at the United Nations to obtain favorable coverage, served two five-year terms before running for president of Austria. Interestingly, no diplomat, no journalist, and no intelligence agent—as far as it is known—came at any time during those years across documents in United Nations files revealing that Waldheim was an intelligence officer in Hitler's army in Yugoslavia during World War II. This detail was also missing from Waldheim's official biography.

As planned, President Nixon (with a vast entourage) arrived in Beijing on February 21, 1972. No American President had ever set foot in China, and Nixon was a glutton for firsts.

An apparent attempt to oust Mao Zedong by his designated successor and defense minister Lin Piao the previous September did not interfere with Nixon's trip because the plot was discovered in time. Lin Piao died when the jet airliner aboard which he was fleeing to the Soviet Union somehow crashed in Soviet Mongolia; that, at any rate, was the official version.

Though the Cultural Revolution was still very much in progress in China, Mao saw to it that his American guest was spared any exposure to its manifestation. In fact, Beijing's streets were empty as the Nixon motorcade sped from the airport to the quarters he was to occupy in the city.

The Chinese, for their part, seemed to have no interest in American military operations in Indochina as they welcomed Nixon. And although Nixon was continuing to withdraw troops from Vietnam (forty-five thousand additional men were ordered home in November 1971, and seventy thousand more in January 1972) he was escalating the war through other means. Heavy air bombardment of North Vietnam was resumed just before Christmas 1971, the justification being Communist preparations for an offensive early in 1972 that American intelligence was beginning to pick up. In his State of the Union message a month before he flew to China, the President warned that if the war could not be ended through negotiations, it would be ended through Vietnamization, which meant indefinite arming of the South Vietnamese and indefinite American air support. At the same time Nixon and Kissinger did not deem it necessary to confide fully in the Chinese all aspects of secret peace negotiations with Hanoi. These, they hoped, were about to resume after an unexplained pause forced by the Communists.

Nixon spent seven days in China that were immensely fascinating to him as he later recounted. Mao honored and surprised the President by receiving him within an hour of his arrival (Kissinger was asked to come along while Secretary of State Rogers was not). The meeting with the seventy-eight-year-old chairman lasted ninety minutes, with Nixon deferring conversationally to his host; there was no attempt at negotiations, simply a joint *tour d'horizon* of the world and future Chinese-American relations. The President also concluded, as he said later, that Mao was true to the original Marxist-Leninist gospel, that "he was like an early Christian basically. . . . He considered the Russians, on the other hand, to be deviationists." Evidently, the chairman was conveying in his special way the reasons for his split with Moscow more than a decade before and for continuing his Cultural Revolution six years after launching it. Perhaps Mao even knew intuitively that a Mikhail Gorbachev would appear in Russia one day to throw doctrinaire communism into toil and trouble.

Apart from banquets (during which a Chinese army band played "America the Beautiful" and "Home on the Range") and sight-seeing, Nixon and Kissinger spent most of the time negotiating the precise outlines of the new Chinese-American relationship that would be spelled out in the Shanghai communique on the last day of the visit. Defining their respective attitudes on the still-controversial issue of Taiwan, Nixon and Zhou agreed that it should be resolved peacefully by the Chinese themselves and that in the meantime, the United States would progressively remove its military forces from the island. The Shanghai document, pleasantly ambiguous, served as the basis of relations between Washington and Beijing until full diplomatic relations were established seven years later. Nixon went home, delighted with his diplomatic triumph (he regarded it as such) and ready to launch his next great diplomatic enterprise. The Chinese were just as pleased; now they enjoyed complete international acceptance.

The new objective was Moscow—another first for an American President—and the expectation of signing the SALT package on nuclear arms with Leonid Brezhnev. Nixon had gone to Russia as Vice President in the fifties, and it would be a triumphal return. He had known Khrushchev (and argued with him in public), and he was anxious to meet Brezhnev. With the gradual but inexorable windup of the Indochina War and with the progress made over the past two years by Soviet and American SALT negotiators, Nixon believed that his first term would surely constitute a victorious peace crusade. The year had opened auspiciously with the China journey. May 22, 1972, was selected as the date for the Moscow summit to open, and the President was exceedingly optimistic.

Although North Vietnam had asked that the next secret peace negotiating session be delayed well into April (it was initially set for March 20), the administration thought that diplomacy with Hanoi was safely back on track, and it was not overly concerned with continuing intelligence reports of a major Communist military buildup. Under Vietnamization, the American forces in Vietnam were down to just under seventy thousand, Nixon having brought home nearly a half million men since taking office. Americans were no longer an effective combat presence. The President intended to make this point to Brezhnev in hope of enlisting his cooperation in pushing Hanoi into a rapid peace agreement—preferably before the November presidential elections. Nixon, of course, was shooting for a second term.

Then, at first light of April 1, the North Vietnamese and the Vietcong launched coordinated attacks across the demilitarized zone (DMZ) in the north and over the western borders from Laos and Cambodia. At the White House Nixon and Kissinger puzzled over Hanoi's decision to strike in force after having agreed to a new round of peace talks. To be sure, the Communists may have chosen to imitate the American strategy of fighting and negotiating aggressively; they may have wished to take military advantage of the departure of the bulk of American combat units to strike a better cease-fire-in-place deal; or they may have wished to embarrass Brezhnev on the eve of the Nixon visit—or all of the above. The only clear thing seventy-two hours into the offensive was that the ARVN was being massacred.

The attack was a textbook example of the use of conventional and guerrilla forces along multiple fronts. General Vo Nguyen Giap, the commander in chief who had defeated the French at Dien Bien Phu almost twenty years earlier, committed approximately two hundred thousand troops, including tank units, artillery, and mortars. The South Vietnamese had—theoretically—more than one million men in their armies, and General Abrams had advised Nixon only a week earlier that there was no way the

Communists could smash through ARVN lines. But they did—quickly. Vietnamization had not worked.

The North Vietnamese were advancing so successfully that by April 3 the White House knew it had a disaster on its hands. Tactical strikes by American planes were ineffective in stemming the Communists, and it was evident that only massive bombings could turn the tide. Nearly 1,000 warplanes, including 170 B-52 jet bombers, were urgently assembled for missions against North Vietnam, but Nixon and Kissinger chose to wait briefly. They hoped to avoid actions likely to do away with the approaching Moscow summit, yet they could not passively watch the destruction of the ARVN. On April 6 fighter-bombers hit military targets north of the DMZ— chiefly as a warning—and on April 8 Nixon ordered the B-52's to strike in North Vietnam, the first time since November 1968 that the huge bombers were sent into action there. Two days later the North Vietnamese port of city of Vinh was hit by the B-52's.

Still, the South Vietnamese were being mauled, and now Nixon (still thinking, along with Kissinger, that a "fourth-rate industrial power" could not withstand sustained carpet bombings) ordered B-52 raids against Hanoi and Haiphong for April 15. The reason for not doing it earlier was that the President was visiting Ottawa on April 13–14, and it seemed that this trip should not be overshadowed by the war's escalation. Besides, Canadians were antiwar-minded. Hanoi and Haiphong were bombed for three days in succession after Nixon decided that if necessary, the Soviet journey would be sacrificed to the defense of South Vietnam. He took the view that since the offensive was fought with Soviet weapons, the Russians had no business complaining about American responses. Indeed, they did not complain, advising Kissinger, instead, that he was still expected in Moscow for a secret preparatory visit on April 20.

The North Vietnamese offensive was rolling faster and faster across South Vietnam when Kissinger arrived in Moscow and surprised Brezhnev with a brand-new secret proposal: The United States would accept a cease-fire in place if the North Vietnamese withdrew to their positions before the April 1 assault. This was the first time the United States was willing to agree— explicitly—to allow some hundred thousand North Vietnamese who were in South Vietnam prior to the offensive to stay there, and Kissinger asked Brezhnev to pass on this offer to Hanoi (the offer was not revealed publicly for more than a year after the war ended). Brezhnev recognized that this was a concession of immense magnitude because the Americans no longer insisted on "mutual withdrawals" by all foreign forces from South Vietnam, and he immediately dispatched a senior Soviet official to Hanoi to communicate Kissinger's offer.

The ploy seemed to work, and Nixon could announce that Paris peace meetings with the North Vietnamese would resume on April 27 and that he would withdraw twenty thousand more Americans from Vietnam by July 1. But the Communists kept pushing forward, capturing the important city of

Quang Tri on May 1, and Nixon resolved to mine the Haiphong harbor. In Paris, Le Duc Tho, the chief North Vietnamese delegate, told Kissinger that the price for a cease-fire would be the removal of President Thieu (who had been "reelected" the previous year) and the creation of a coalition government. Back in Washington, the administration had to face the reality that Hanoi was out for total victory—at once—and all options were reviewed for saving South Vietnam. They included heavy bombing and mining, recommitment of American combat troops, and even the use of tactical nuclear weapons. This was the measure of desperation at the White House as the Communists were on the verge of severing South Vietnam along an east-west line.

On May 8, after a series of agonizing debates within the administration, Nixon announced that all North Vietnamese ports would be mined to prevent access to them (mainly by Soviet ships delivering arms and fuel) and rail and other communications would be cut off by bombing. This amounted to a blockade (Senator Fulbright commented that it was illegal because the Senate had repealed the Tonkin Gulf resolution), and Nixon's conditions for lifting it were the release of all American prisoners of war and an internationally supervised cease-fire.

That Vietnam had ceased to be relevant to the Kremlin (as had happened in the case of China in February) became obvious when the Russians virtually ignored the bombings and the blockade and went on with the preparations for Nixon's impending arrival on May 22. To Brezhnev and his associates, it was only a matter of a short time before the Vietnam War was liquidated in a predictable fashion, and they reasoned that the final spasms of heavy fighting needed not complicate long-range American-Soviet relations. Pragmatism again was prevailing over Marxist-Leninist and Third World solidarity, and Hanoi was discovering it painfully. The battleground began to stabilize, with the Communists retaining their gains but running out of steam.

The Soviet visit, extremely warm under the circumstances, lasted eight days, and its high point was the signing by Nixon and Brezhnev of the Strategic Arms Limitation Treaty (known as SALT I), the first superpower agreement on controlling the spread of nuclear weapons.

It had two parts: an agreement of indefinite duration on antiballistic missiles (ABM), under which each country would limit defensive ABM deployments to one single site, and a five-year agreement on qualitative and quantitative restrictions on new offensive strategic weapons—land-based and carried by submarines and manned bombers.

In the defensive realm the United States chose an ABM system already under construction to protect its Minuteman ICBM launching sites in North Dakota, and the Russians opted to stay with the ABM system they already had around Moscow. Concerning offensive weapons, SALT I provided for specific limits in each category.

The ABM agreement illustrated perfectly the pervasively strange psychology and philosophy of the nuclear age, and it was the best expression of the basic paradox in superpower relationships. The reasoning, which went under the cold-blooded definition of "mutual assured destruction" (aptly enough, MAD in its English-language acronym), was that so long as cities as well as missile-launching sites on each side had no antinuclear defenses, neither would hit the other out of fear of instant retaliation.

In other words, the theory developing in the seventies was that leaving great populated metropolitan areas open to enemy attack was actually a deterrent because such a strike would result in a retaliatory second strike (for which both sides would have adequate weapons, mainly aboard submarines). This was the MAD logic in the nuclear world, and the principal reason for the one-site ABM accord was that investments had already been made around North Dakota and Moscow. Later the United States accused the Russians of illegally deploying ABM types of defensive radars around other strategic sites, and the Soviets acknowledged it after Gorbachev took power.

During the fifties and the sixties, the American nuclear targeting plan against the Soviet Union—SIOP, an acronym for "single integrated operations plan"—aimed at a first-strike destruction of its warmaking capability, which did not necessarily spare the cities. By definition, SIOP is a highly classified planning document, but it is known that in the seventies and the eighties both the Joint Chiefs of Staff and the Strategic Air Command (which controls the ICBMs as well as manned bombers) began to emphasize much more precisely the targeting of Soviet missile silos and the known (or suspected) command, control, and intelligence centers (the C^3 in military parlance). American intelligence also came up with useful information about the alternate command sites where Soviet leadership would escape in the event of nuclear war (hardened underground locations in the countryside or command-and-control aircraft), and these data have been added to SIOP.

Negotiating over nuclear weapons requires not only military and strategic mastery of the subject and considerable diplomatic talents but also the acquisition and possession of first-rate intelligence and the correct interpretation of this intelligence. This is where Nixon and Kissinger appear to have committed a colossal negotiating error because intelligence at their disposal was inadequate and downright faulty. It resulted in their agreeing to drop their original proposal for strategic arms parity (nineteen hundred nuclear launchers) when Brezhnev and his excellently prepared advisers argued that this was unfair because the United States already had a MIRV advantage.

MIRV stands for "multiple independent reentry vehicle"—more than one nuclear warhead on a missile, each capable of being independently guided to target—and it represents the most lethal nuclear technology in existence (there may be as many as fourteen warheads on a missile with limitless explosive megatonnage for each).

MIRV had been developed by the United States some years before the start of the SALT I negotiations, and even as Nixon and Brezhnev met at the Kremlin, the Soviets had not yet matched this technological breakthrough. In preparing the American negotiating position, Kissinger was given a CIA assessment that the Soviets would not be able to develop their MIRV systems for long years (similar assessments in the mid-forties had indicated that the Russians would not have an atomic bomb for ten years or more). Trusting this intelligence, he and Nixon accepted the Soviet counterproposal that the number of ICBMs be frozen at 1,054 in the United States and at 1,618 in the Soviet Union (the United States was no longer building ICBMs, and the Russians would stop at this limit).

Catastrophically, the Americans, feeling secure in their technological superiority, expected to last until the next SALT accord would be negotiated within five years or even longer, also agreed that both sides could develop and test MIRVs and more advanced systems. The problem turned out to be, however, that the Soviets were almost on the verge of unveiling their MIRV though Brezhnev certainly was not about to tell it to Nixon. Actually the Soviets were ready with MIRV warheads in 1975 before SALT II negotiations. John Newhouse, former counselor to the Arms Control and Disarmament Agency, writes in his book *War and Peace in the Nuclear Age* that in Moscow in 1972 Nixon and Kissinger "ignored the opportunity to kill MIRV" because they let MIRV developments continue. Had intelligence been of better quality, nuclear arms today might have been under much stricter controls. The House Select Committee on Intelligence reported in 1976 that "it is clear that, in the final stages of the SALT talks, U.S. negotiators did not fully consult or inform intelligence experts. . . . Only Russian technical experts were on hand. Dr. Kissinger's private talks with Soviet leaders in this period were not disseminated."

The SALT negotiations in all their aspects were immensely complex, and they neared collapse several times. Vietnam was discussed at considerable length by Nixon and Brezhnev and by Kissinger and Foreign Minister Andrei Gromyko. Again, the Americans surprised the Russians by their private flexibility and their sudden willingness to accept a tripartite electoral commission for South Vietnam, a Communist idea they had rejected for a long time. Again, a senior Soviet envoy flew to Hanoi to inform the South Vietnamese. The Russians were eager mediators in the Vietnam peace quest.

Nixon wound up his Soviet visit with short trips to Leningrad and Kiev, where he paid homage at monuments to the victims of World War II. All in all, the journey had been another great success for the President.

Secret diplomacy and the start of new American covert actions in the Third World occupied Nixon and Kissinger as they stopped in Teheran to confer with the shah of Iran on their way home from Moscow.

The first agreement they made with the shah provided for CIA assistance in money and weapons for Kurdish tribal rebels against the radical Iraqi regime next door. Kurds living in both Iran and Iraq had long dreamed of an independent Kurdistan, but the shah chose to support the Iraqi tribesmen because of a running dispute with Iraq's government. In short, he wished to help the Kurds overthrow the Baghdad regime, and he wanted the CIA to help *him*. Though the State Department had earlier rejected Iranian requests for such covert aid, Nixon now promised it to the shah.

That Iraq was an ally of the Soviet Union, where he had just negotiated a series of propeace accords, did not seem to bother Nixon. Iran was America's new ally in the region following Britain's decision the previous year to withdraw from the Persian Gulf, and the President was anxious to please the shah. Consequently, a separate secret accord reached in Teheran assured Iran of unrestricted sales of *all* conventional weapons systems by the United States, an open-ended arrangement. The shah argued convincingly that Soviet arms deliveries to Iraq posed a threat to the stability in this petroleum-rich area and that in effect, the Iranians had to act as the policeman in the Persian Gulf. Nixon never informed the Congress of this agreement, but according to the State Department, Iran suddenly became in 1974 the world's leading weapons importer—ahead of Israel, Saudi Arabia, Syria, and Vietnam.

In 1975 the Nixon administration and the shah joined in betraying the trusting Kurds in Iraq. Following a settlement with Iraq arranged by Algeria, Iran—and the CIA—withdrew their support from the tribesmen almost overnight. The insurgency collapsed, and thousands of Kurds were killed. A decade later Iraq embarked on killing and exiling other thousands of Kurdish citizens; some died from poison gas. As the shah was to find out, nothing should ever be taken for granted in his part of the world—except, perhaps, poetic justice in that land of Omar Khayyam. In July 1972, however, Nixon and the shah received good news: Egypt's new president, Anwar al-Sadat, suddenly expelled the Soviets from his territory—the combat troops, the SAM missile batteries, the warplanes, and the warships. The Middle East was finally stabilizing, it would seem.

Richard Nixon returned home on June 1, 1972, his final stop on the flight from the Soviet Union having been Warsaw, which he had visited once as Vice President. He believed the new détente should be expanded to Poland, too. From Andrews Air Force Base the President hurried to Capitol Hill to deliver a dramatic evening address to Congress. He said: "Everywhere new hopes are rising for a world no longer shadowed by fear and want and war. . . ." A standing ovation was the response to his words.

At dawn on Saturday, June 17, as Nixon rested in Key Biscayne, three Cuban exiles directed by two former CIA officers broke into the offices of the Democratic National Committee in the Watergate office building in Washington. One of the ex-CIA men, a Latin American specialist named E. Howard Hunt, turned out to be employed by a secret investigative unit at the White House. When Nixon flew back to Washington two days later, his press secretary dismissed the incident as a "third-rate burglary" despite the participants' CIA and White House links. The shadow of Cuban connections was once again falling over American politics and history.

IV

On November 7, 1972, Richard Nixon was reelected to a second presidential term by a landslide, defeating the Democrats' "peace candidate," Senator George McGovern of South Dakota. That the war in Vietnam still had not ended was clearly not a matter of concern to the electorate. Neither was Watergate—at that point.

The balance of the year in Vietnam was talk and bomb, talk and bomb. Both sides knew that peace was inevitable—and soon—and now it was only a matter of the terms on which it would be attained. The secret negotiations in Paris between Kissinger and Le Duc Tho, a member of the North Vietnamese Politburo and himself a policymaker, had resumed on July 19, after the Americans had sent their new offers through Brezhnev and Hanoi had brought the offensive in South Vietnam to a halt.

Both the United States and North Vietnam hoped to end the conflict in a way in which their interests would be served the best. Nixon and Kissinger desired a solution—"peace with honor"—that would leave Saigon strong enough to survive indefinitely following the final American withdrawal. Hanoi, not surprisingly, wished for a deal that, in effect, would permit it to seize South Vietnam after what diplomats were already calling a "decent interval." The spring offensive had failed to produce a new Dien Bien Phu because of Nixon's tough reaction, but the Communists were in a vastly improved military position as the new diplomatic phase opened in the secluded villa on the outskirts of Paris where Kissinger and Le Duc Tho usually met.

As a counter to the freshly acquired North Vietnamese military strength in South Vietnam, the United States was maintaining its heavy bombings of the North, with the big B-52's flying from Guam and bases in Thailand and light fighter-bombers from aircraft carriers in the Tonkin Gulf and fields in South Vietnam. Having initially linked the bombardment of the North to the Communist offensive in the South, Nixon now promised to keep up the raids until Hanoi accepted his peace terms. But these raids were no longer sufficient reason for Le Duc Tho to break off his talks with Kissinger; both men sensed this was the home stretch.

As fully expected by the administration, the American bombings in the North were violently criticized all over the world (including famous Americans ranging from Norman Mailer to Jane Fonda), but the White House was mildly surprised when UN Secretary-General Kurt Waldheim joined the chorus of condemnation. At that stage, of course, Washington knew nothing about Waldheim's inner secrets and could not appreciate his need for righteous public attitudes. Still, Nixon had no compunctions about including him in his denunciation of those applying a "hypocritical double standard" to the United States, ignoring the fact that, as he said, the Communist spring offensive had caused forty-five thousand civilian casualties in the South. There is no record of Waldheim's response to Nixon.

In the meantime, Mao Zedong made his contribution to a settlement by convincing North Vietnamese and Vietcong leaders (contrary to what the United States believed all along, there were two separate Communist leaderships waging the war in the South) to abandon their insistence on President Thieu's resignation in Saigon as a precondition to a peace settlement. He reminded them that in the 1940's, when it was necessary, he had made a deal with Chiang Kai-shek, emphasizing that at this stage the Vietnamese Communists had to put up with Thieu. This was one of the milestones on the road to peace. Thieu had not yet been told about it by the Americans, but in the course of Kissinger-Le Duc Tho meetings during August 1972 the question of a total North Vietnamese withdrawal from South Vietnam was no longer being mentioned by Kissinger.

Now Thieu had to be sold on the odious notion that the North Vietnamese would stay in his country after the cease-fire and that Washington and Hanoi had agreed, in effect, on a tripartite electoral commission to define the future government in Saigon. It should not have been a surprise, but Thieu, fighting to survive, turned out to be an extremely difficult interlocutor when Kissinger flew to meet with him in Saigon in late August. His mission was to soften Thieu up for a settlement he never thought he would be asked to accept, and he tried to sweeten it by suggesting that the South Vietnamese president plan an invasion of North Vietnam before signing the peace treaty. It is hard to say whether Kissinger was serious about it and whether Thieu was taking him seriously. Thieu, in fact, was learning that Westerners could be as devious as Asians. Flying home from Saigon, Kissinger told his aides: "We cannot stand another four years of this. . . . So let's finish it brutally once and for all."

During the closing weeks of the campaign Nixon said that by December 1 there would be only twenty-seven thousand American ground troops left in Vietnam—5 percent of the number there when he had become President less than four years earlier. This fact, he knew, was his ticket to reelection, and he added an emotional element by saying that these troops would stay there until the last American prisoner of war (POW) had been released by the Communists. He also said that he would not place any time limit on American bombings of the North, now going on for four months. CIA and Defense Intelligence Agency reports to the White House that despite the bombings, Hanoi could go on fighting "at the present rate" for two years failed to affect the President's strategy; he was counting on the psychological and political effects of the bombardment, not on logistical damage. That eight hundred thousand tons of "air ammunition" had been dropped on Indochina in the first nine months of 1972 seemed like a statistical detail. Bomb tonnage was no longer related to the loss of human lives or destruction; no such ratios appeared in after-mission reports.

On October 19 Kissinger was back in Saigon with the final draft of a peace agreement he and the North Vietnamese had hammered out in Paris the previous week. The plan was for him to obtain Thieu's accord, then fly to Hanoi on October 24 to initial the agreement with the North Vietnamese, and finally go to Paris to watch the four foreign ministers sign the actual peace treaty on October 31. The idea was that it would all be accomplished a week before the American presidential elections. It was a marvelous scenario—except that Thieu was not ready to capitulate to help Nixon's reelection. He was so opposed to the Kissinger draft that Nixon had to cable Hanoi that there could be no signing there on the thirty-first. Instead, an exhausted Kissinger flew home to see how the situation could be salvaged.

Few major diplomatic negotiations in modern annals were as complex and frustrating as Kissinger's simultaneous dealings with Hanoi and Saigon, with the United States suddenly becoming, in effect, the mediator between the two Vietnamese bands and Kissinger having to sell Nixon and a number of White House doubters on the correctness of his strategies. The lesson that presumably should be drawn from this exhausting and distracting diplomatic and political performance is that negotiations affecting the life or death—or at least the destiny—of other nations should not be tied to the reelection deadline of a superpower leader. This was not the case in the United States in 1972.

In any event, North Vietnam was not inclined to play this game either. On October 26 Hanoi radio broadcast the highlights of the agreement the North Vietnamese thought they had reached with Kissinger in Paris. It was clearly intended to embarrass the Americans and make them live up to the secret deal. At noon Kissinger held a news conference, confirming Hanoi's disclosures and announcing—perhaps prematurely at that stage—that "peace is at hand." At that moment the White House's overwhelming concern was that the elections were twelve days away—and Nixon was taking no chances. Kissinger used the news conference to urge all concerned to cool it, saying that a few more meetings with the North Vietnamese were needed to nail down final details. Thieu had really no options but to keep silent, and he obliged. Kissinger's worry on that beautiful Washington autumn day, however, was that after the election Nixon might tear up the Paris agreements and proceed to bomb North Vietnam to death to exact a Communist capitulation—not a likely prospect in his opinion.

The President, instead, ordered a bombing halt. Under the Enhance program, the United States was now shipping military equipment—F-5 jet aircraft, tanks, helicopters, artillery, mortars, infantry weapons, radios—and food, and clothing as quickly as it could to beat a cease-fire deadline, after which arms from abroad could no longer be supplied to either side. The idea was to make South Vietnam as militarily powerful as possible when the cease-fire came; the only problem was whether given its appalling track record of the past ten years, the ARVN would wish to use these weapons intelligently. The corollary in Washington's mind was to weaken North Vietnam as much as possible before the moment of disengagement, and this would be the assigned mission of B-52 and aircraft carrier pilots. The United States had already lost more than three thousand aircraft in Vietnam in the ten years of war, but this was no deterrent to new raids. Astoundingly, friend and foe—the Russians and the Chinese and the British and the French—were willing to let nature take its course in Vietnam, that "rotten country," as Charles de Gaulle had called it a generation before.

Within days of the election Nixon and Kissinger decided that the United States would sign a peace agreement whether Thieu liked it or not. The American commitment made by John Kennedy had to end. But America still wanted Thieu to survive, or, at least, to have it appear so. Thus Enhance Plus was launched, handing Thieu between November 1972 and January 27, 1973, a huge arsenal: 266 aircraft, 277 helicopters, and masses of lesser ordnance. The Enhance deliveries were valued by the Pentagon at $1.23 billion, but military bookkeeping had a way of undervaluing equipment for friends.

Kissinger and the North Vietnamese met in Paris late in November, and Hanoi agreed that the old DMZ would be the temporary dividing line between the two Vietnams. It should be noted at this point that Vietnam was taking up so much of Nixon's and Kissinger's time that they could pay no attention to other worrisome situations developing elsewhere, such as in the Middle East. And the President went on disregarding an increasingly nagging domestic problem known as Watergate. They would discover again the curse of big government: that you can really live with only one man-size problem at a time.

On December 14 and 15 the Americans and the North Vietnamese had another session in Paris, and suddenly peace prospects crumbled. Hanoi demanded so many changes in the text that had been approved by both sides in October that Kissinger went public to accuse the North Vietnamese of "perfidy." Whether or not this was a reaction to the Enhance programs, the diplomatic process was paralyzed (nothing being said about the massive North Vietnamese reinforcements of their armies in South Vietnam). Perplexed, Nixon sent a secret cable to Hanoi on December 15, announcing that B-52 bombings would be resumed within seventy-two hours if the North Vietnamese did not return to the negotiating table.

What remains unclear almost twenty years later is whether the Hanoi leadership had split between hawks and doves, something of a mirror image of what had existed more visibly on the American side for long years. In any case, Hanoi seemed to be politically paralyzed, and it was Nixon's turn to decide that *he* had no more time to play diplomatic games. Actually the differences introduced by Hanoi in the peace text were not insurmountable. The President concluded, however, that the situation was again getting out of hand, and on December 18 he ordered heavy bombings of Hanoi, Haiphong, and the rest of North Vietnam. This was Operation Linebacker II, the Christmas bombings. The situation had become so strange that, as a senior official told me that day, "We are bombing them to force them to accept our concessions." I found this line too surreal to include it in my *New York Times* story.

While the B-52's were hitting North Vietnam around the clock, Nixon flew south to Florida to spend Christmas in the sun at his Key Biscayne home. He believed that his landslide electoral victory in November had given him a mandate to conduct war and peace in Vietnam according to his rights, and he was not perturbed by the new situation that had just developed. He had told Kissinger that Hanoi would "cry uncle" any day now, and he was right. On December 27 Nixon received a message that Hanoi was ready to resume talks with Kissinger in Paris on January 8, 1973. On December 30 the White House announced that "all bombing will be discontinued above the 20th parallel as long as serious negotiations are under way."

The Christmas bombings added up over twelve days to ten times the tonnage dropped over North Vietnam between 1969 and 1971, caused the death of twenty-two hundred civilians in Hanoi alone (according to North Vietnamese figures), and may have cost as many as thirty-four downed B-52's (the Hanoi figure). There is no way of determining, however, whether it took the bombings to force the warring sides to accept peace. The American war in Indochina had lasted roughly twelve years, and all participants demonstrated extraordinary savagery in combat. But in hindsight, almost thirty years after the first U.S. involvement in Vietnam, that sad and beautiful country, it is time to ask whether that terrible effort was justified.

Frances FitzGerald, who knows Vietnam well, writes in *Estrangement: America and the World*, a collection of essays published in 1985: "Now that it was over, no American politician seemed able to explain why the United States had sent troops to Vietnam in the first place, or what it had lost by failing to win. . . . The defeat had no effect on national security as defined by real assets such as sea-lanes or markets—or even allies in Southeast Asia. . . . The United States was now in a better position in Asia, militarily, economically, and politically, than it had ever been before."

This may not have been apparent when Kissinger and Tho initialed the Vietnam peace agreement at a private meeting near Paris on January 23, 1973, and when Secretary of State Rogers and the foreign ministers of South Vietnam, North Vietnam, and the South Vietnamese Provisional Revolutionary Government (the Vietcong) signed the full text in Paris on January 27.

Richard Nixon hailed the agreement in a televised address to announce that "we today have concluded an agreement to end the war and bring peace with honor in Vietnam and in Southeast Asia." He went on to say that "ending the war is only the first step toward building the peace" and that "all parties must now see to it that this is a peace that lasts, and also a peace that heals." He surely meant it, but it is not certain that he believed what he said.

Again, realities asserted themselves in Indochina in a sequence of events that followed logically the Paris peace treaties. The American-supported regimes in Cambodia and South Vietnam could not survive the Communist thrusts: Pnom Penh fell to the Khmer Rouge rebels on April 17, 1975, and Saigon fell to the Vietcong and the North Vietnamese two weeks later, on April 30, 1975. Richard Nixon, though no longer in office, must have known that it was an inevitable outcome—once the Americans were gone.

The War Powers Act passed by the Congress over Nixon's veto during 1973, largely as a result of the Tonkin Gulf deception, made it virtually impossible for the United States to go on protecting its Indochinese clients. The legislation strictly defined the conditions under which American forces could be committed in "hostile environments" without congressional consent. Lyndon Johnson, the prophet of the massive American intervention in Vietnam, was spared the pain of watching the collapse of his hopes; he had died in January 1973.

As the years went by, Southeast Asian politics developed in the most unexpected fashion, confirming Frances FitzGerald's judgment that the United States had really lost nothing as a result of the defeat in the Indochina war—except, of course, in terms of American lives, American wounded, and the cruel reception given returning veterans and their subsequent reincorporation in the ungrateful society at home. There were no falling dominoes in the region, no Soviet or Chinese thrusts in the region, and no Communist conquests anywhere. Kennedy, Johnson, Nixon, and Gerald Ford (who observed from the Oval Office the debacle of American client regimes in the area) all were horribly wrong about Indochina—to say nothing of the military commanders.

For the horrors came from within. Led by the fantasmagoric figure of Pol Pot, the Cambodian Communists—the Khmer Rouge—established a murderous reign over the once-gentle kingdom. Perhaps one million, perhaps more Cambodians were murdered by the Khmer Rouge as they forced urban dwellers into the countryside to turn them into peasants at gunpoint and killed whole families in the rural areas in a crazed attempt to impose an unreal primitive Marxist-Leninist society. The country became known as the Killing Fields.

In January 1978 Communist Vietnam invaded Communist Cambodia (using captured American aircraft and arms) to impose *its* rule over that ancient kingdom and to try to do away with Pol Pot. After ten years of civil war the Vietnamese troops began departing in 1989, though the old ethnic enmities with the Cambodians remained as alive as ever.

In Vietnam itself (where the North and South became unified as a socialist republic in 1976, and Saigon was renamed Ho Chi Minh City), the great "bloodbath" of non-Communists, confidently predicted by successive American administrations, never occurred. Former Thieu officials and ARVN officers were sent to "reeducation" camps for a few years (Thieu himself fled abroad); then the country bogged down in austerity and misery and big-city black marketing. Since the Japanese occupation in 1942 Vietnam had been continuously at war for almost a half century, longer than any nation on Earth.

More than a million and a half Vietnamese from a total population of 53 million left, legally or as "boat people" in junks and sampans and fishing vessels, in the thirteen years after the end of the war. Except for the United States (where 850,000 Vietnamese settled and generally prospered), the refugees were simply unwanted. The boat people, a grippingly pathetic by-product of the long war, were kept out of Thailand, Malaysia, the Philippines, and Hong Kong because—supposedly—there was no room for them and left to drift on the seas, where they were frequently attacked and murdered by Thai pirates. But families went on escaping from Indochina; in July 1989 alone, 5,268 Indochinese refugees were resettled by international organizations. Nobody knows how many just vanished.

Politically Vietnam posed no postwar problems for the United States.

In 1978 it joined Comecon, the Communist bloc common market, to become eligible for large-scale Soviet economic aid. The Russians took over the huge Cam Ranh Bay air and naval base built by the Americans in South Vietnam, but this was militarily unthreatening to Washington. Hanoi sought for years to establish diplomatic and economic relations with the United States—the Vietnamese were now concerned with the future more than with the past and its war—but Washington went on saying, "No." No clear reason has been given, and at a Geneva conference on Indochina refugees in July 1989, sixteen years after the peace treaties, Deputy Secretary of State Lawrence Eagleburger, representing the young Bush administration, pointedly refused to meet with Vietnamese Foreign Minister Nguyen Co Thach. It seemed like an echo from 1954, when John Foster Dulles refused to shake hands with Zhou Enlai. Meanwhile, Vietnam began moving toward a market economy and a quiet acceptance of some of the Gorbachev reform ideas.

The pro-Communist Pathet Lao formed a quiet socialist regime that from the outset had formal ties with the United States. It minds its own business.

Before Cambodia was decimated by the Khmer Rouge, President Ford demonstrated American machismo in May 1975 by dispatching military force to free the cargo ship *Mayaguez* captured by Cambodian pirates following the fall of Pnom Penh (the crew aboard the U.S. vessel was unharmed, but this exercise cost the lives of forty-one American servicemen).

In February 1979 China invaded Vietnam to fight an inconclusive—and unexplained—border war. Mao Zedong had died in September 1976, his demise ostensibly marking the end of the decadelong Cultural Revolution that destroyed a whole generation of Chinese intellectuals, but why his successors chose to attack Vietnam, supposedly an ideological ally, remains a mystery.

The settlement of the American war in Indochina was hailed in 1973, by a joint award of the Nobel Peace Prize to Henry Kissinger and Hanoi's chief negotiator, Le Duc Tho. Kissinger accepted his half; Tho declined his half. Young Americans who refused to serve in the Vietnam War were pardoned only in 1977 by President Carter. The memory of Americans who gave their lives in Vietnam was honored on November 11, 1982, Veterans Day, with the unveiling of the Vietnam War Memorial hard by the Lincoln Memorial in Washington, D.C. It lists on black marble the names of all those known to have died in a war most of them never understood. This was their homecoming, at last. As late as 1989 more remains arrived from Vietnam as jungle graves were located, so new names were added to the marble. Survivors, now middle-aged men, some invalids and some victims of the Agent Orange chemical defoliant used by the United States to destroy the jungles of Indochina, come to visit the memorial, bringing their families, often weeping in silence. This is the monument to the longest, most tragic, most unnecessary and divisive war in American history.

V

No sooner was the world freed of the Indochina War than a new conflict—and an extremely dangerous one—erupted in the Middle East on October 6, 1973. It was the Arab-Israeli Yom Kippur War, which brought Washington and Moscow back to the brink of confrontation, possibly even a nuclear one, for the first time since the 1962 Cuban crisis. Strangely, much of what happened behind the scenes during that war in terms of superpower moves remains swathed in mystery more than fifteen years later. The United States was crippled in the conduct of its policies because at that stage President Nixon was swamped by the Watergate scandal. And the Arab oil embargo against America and the West hit their economies hard.

Kissinger, elevated by Nixon to the exalted post of secretary of state (the number one Cabinet post) after liquidating Vietnam, had planned to make 1973 the "Year of Europe." In fact, he announced it grandiloquently in a New York speech that Western European statesmen—especially French Foreign Minister Michel Jobert—found irritating and patronizing, like a busy parent telling neglected children, "Now, I have a little time to pay attention to you . . ." Actually Western Europe was doing well on its own, the European Economic Community being enlarged during 1973 by the accession of Britain (which had resisted it for nearly twenty years), Ireland, and Denmark to become a powerful nine-nation trading bloc.

In any event, Europe as a stage for Kissingerian virtuoso performances of setting the world straight (he was, after all, an admirer of Metternich and Bismarck, who had tried to do just that with no insignificant success) was rapidly set aside when black clouds of war rolled once more across the Middle East.

The Yom Kippur War and the extent of the Soviet involvement in it came as a surprise to the Nixon administration. The United States had been delighted the previous year, when Sadat expelled the Soviet military establishment from Egypt, and it did not believe that the Russians would try to stage a comeback so quickly and stealthily. Soviet-American relations were excellent in the aftermath of the 1972 Moscow summit and the détente spirit it generated. The termination of the American participation in the Indochina conflict (the last American soldiers left in March 1973) contributed to the happy climate. The Soviets were buying billions of dollars' worth of American grain, enriching American farmers, storage silo owners, railroad operators, and shipowners (and making quite a profit for themselves in the process). Finally, Leonid Brezhnev came to the United States in June 1973, to return Nixon's visit, and the President entertained him lovingly at San Clemente. The Arab-Israeli issue was barely mentioned in their communiqué. Why, then, a war in the Middle East four months later?

In the spring of 1973 neither American intelligence nor Israel's famed Mossad had any inkling that a war was being planned by the Arabs in collusion with the Soviets. Abba Eban, then Israeli foreign minister, wrote later in his autobiography that Israel's intelligence chiefs were adamant on the subject: "The Arabs would not risk an attack which they knew would be suicidal; and even if they did, they would be flung back so quickly and with such violence that Israel's deterrent power would, if anything, become even stronger than before."

So sure of themselves were the Israelis early in 1973, Eban adds, that they could cross into Egypt "to bring back a new Soviet tank or radar installation," enter Beirut "to make a street-by-street search for terrorist leaders, and inflict heavy casualties on Arab aircraft which they met on patrol." Eban comments that "whenever the Israeli army or air force moved, there was always a sense of mastery and command." Israelis were not particularly disturbed over the death of passengers on a Libyan airliner "mistakenly shot down by the Israeli air force on the unlikely assumption that the plane was on its way to attack the Dimona research reactor." Dimona, of course, was where Israel was assembling its nuclear weapons, a fact to which Eban did not directly allude.

Both President Nixon and Henry Kissinger have stressed in their memoirs that the surprise onset of the October war represented massive intelligence failures by the United States as well as Israel, concurring with Abba Eban's judgment about the fiasco of his country's intelligence services. Large-scale Egyptian and Syrian troop movements and concentrations had been detected since mid-spring, but the CIA, the Defense Intelligence Agency, and Israeli intelligence insisted that they represented nothing more sinister than regular maneuvers. All intelligence experts were operating on the assumption that the Arabs would not start a war because there was no way they could win it militarily. Because Syria had lost thirteen MiG jets in dogfights with Israeli pilots on September 13 (in the Middle East air combat is a common occurrence even in the absence of war), the State Department's intelligence specialists acknowledged in the first days of October that a retaliatory but "limited" Syrian strike could not be excluded.

Even as the Egyptian-Syrian attack began on the afternoon of Saturday, October 6 (it was morning in Washington), and a top-level meeting was getting under way at the White House—it had been urgently called after Israel passed on at dawn information it had just obtained that war would start within hours—the American intelligence agencies advised the group that they could find "[n]o hard evidence of a major, coordinated Egyptian Syrian offensive across the Canal and in the Golan Heights area."

But the most significant aspect of the joint Israeli-American intelligence failure was, in Kissinger's word, "intellectual." Accepting his share of the blame, he has written that it simply had not occurred to anybody that President Sadat would hurl Egypt into a war he probably could not win in order to create a profound crisis in the Middle East. Such a crisis, in turn, would result in serious negotiations that theretofore had been impossible "while Israel considered itself militarily supreme and Egypt was paralyzed by humiliation."

Under the circumstances, all the intelligence estimates were distorted by the inability to understand Sadat's mind; as Kissinger puts it, "Our definition of rationality did not take seriously the notion of starting an unwinnable war to restore self-respect." That intelligence collectors and interpreters are not psychologists and philosophers is a fact of life that policymakers do not take adequately into consideration although the art of deception and disinformation dates back to Sun-tzu, the Medici of Florence, Talleyrand, Bismarck, and the KGB. There is something magic and mystical about secret intelligence data that seem to discourage surgical scrutiny by "producers" and "consumers" alike. However, historical memory should have played a role in evaluating the onrushing and confusing events of those first October days. Not only had there already been three full-fledged wars around Israel in the preceding twenty-five years (plus raids, bombings, terrorism, and permanent turbulence), but the Middle East and Palestine in particular have been a big power battleground since the Ottoman Empire (to say nothing of the Crusades). Napoleon went to the Pyramids, the British fought the French and Russians throughout most of the nineteenth century, then the British and the Russians built up Arab leaders against the Ottoman Empire during the First World War, the World War II Western Allies quarreled with the Russians over Iran after 1945, the French armed Israel and the Soviets armed the Arabs for the 1967 war, and the Soviets gained a solid foothold in Egypt under Nasser. For the early history of the Middle Eastern contests, policymakers of today should learn about the "Great Game" that is most instructively described in David Fromkin's A Peace to End All Peace; it may come in handy the next time there are intelligence misunderstandings in those lands of sui generis logic.

In our time "intellectual" intelligence interpretation and policy breakdowns happen almost exclusively with Third World countries and the assessment of their mental and psychological processes and responses along with their capability to stand up to the big boys on the block.

Just since World War II, the French were wrong about Indochina and Algeria, the Americans were wrong about Vietnam and Cuba, the Israelis and the Americans were wrong about Egypt and Syria in 1973 and thereafter, the British and the Americans (and the shah himself) were wrong about Iran, and the Soviets (including the KGB) were wrong about Afghanistan.

In the case of the Yom Kippur War, nobody in authority foresaw the Arab use of the oil weapon; it might have been foretold if thought had been given in Washington and elsewhere to the personal religious sentiments of King Faisal ibn Abd al-Aziz al Sa'ud of Saudia Arabia and to the conditions of the world petroleum market at that time. Sometimes it is useful to keep up with both religion and petroleum, but nothing seemed to have been remembered from the oil embargo lessons of 1973 when the Iranian Revolution burst forth in 1978. Taken together, these two events altered fundamentally world economics in such ways that the lifting of embargoes no longer mattered.

The October war, known as the Yom Kippur War because it was launched by the Arabs on Yom Kippur, the Day of Atonement, which is the Jews' holiest day, lasted eighteen days. It started out with Israel's and America's certainty that Egypt and Syria would be smashed militarily within seventy-two hours (another intelligence error of vast proportions), suddenly turned into the danger of an Israeli rout (Israel was losing aircraft and tanks at a staggering rate because Arabs had state-of-the-art equipment the Soviets had managed to introduce secretly), then became an astonishing Israeli triumph when, with fresh American weapons and munitions, the tide shifted and entire Egyptian armies found themselves encircled by Israeli tanks with their backs to the Suez Canal.

At that stage Leonid Brezhnev, who had obviously encouraged the war (though probably for less subtle reasons than Sadat) and went on airlifting matériel to Syria around the clock, realized the extent of the Arab disaster and faced that terrible big power dilemma of how to save client states in mortal trouble. The Soviet-American maneuvering during the final week of the 1973 war, including considerable brinksmanship with nuclear overtones, is a most complex story that remains full of gaps and contradictions although many of the top players, including Nixon, Kissinger, and Eban, have written about it in considerable detail (so far there are no Soviet contributions to this literature).

Wars by nature are cynical, especially in this sophisticated world of crisscrossing interests and influences. Once the 1973 conflict had broken out, nobody felt great urgency to end it prematurely (we speak of governments, not ordinary human beings). In the first phase, Israel was not ready for a cease-fire in place because it might have left Arab troops indefinitely in territories Israel had controlled since the 1967 war, or even deeper, and the United States certainly supported Prime Minister Golda Meir in this stance. In the second phase, when Israeli tanks had surrounded the Egyptian Second and Third armies and stood 101 kilometers from Cairo, Israel was in no great hurry either—this time to gain maximal political advantage from its sensational counteroffensive.

At this juncture the United States—which meant, primarily, Henry Kissinger because of Nixon's increasing concern with the Watergate drama—initially kept its own counsel, then began pressing Mrs. Meir for a cease-fire order. The pressure stemmed from Kissinger's correct conclusion that an exaggerated Israeli victory would exclude lasting peace settlements for years, if not decades (there was the Arab self-respect problem to bear in mind), as well as from Brezhnev's warnings that if Israel did not halt operations at once, the Soviets would land airborne troops to save the Egyptians. The Arabs, naturally, were not urging cease-fires when they were winning, and neither was Brezhnev.

It is pointless to speculate which was the prevailing motivation in Kissinger's mind as he advised the Israelis to quit when they were actually ahead. Most likely the two reasons overlapped. Moreover, Kissinger had made a thirty-eight-hour visit to Moscow on October 21 to confer with Brezhnev at his invitation just as the Israelis were completing the isolation of Egyptian forces on the east bank of the Suez Canal. The Russians and the Americans had agreed on a cease-fire formula to be approved by the UN Security Council and on making their "auspices" available to all combatants, for peace negotiations, and Kissinger knew that Brezhnev was serious about putting a stop to the war. He stopped in Israel en route home from Moscow to impress his conclusions on Mrs. Meir, and he believed that the military and diplomatic situations were now in balance and propitious for a cease-fire with the potential to bring about a political settlement before too long.

The big power theory of war and peace in regional situations is that war must not be allowed to race out of control and threaten worldwide peace (and the superpowers' special interests) and that when sufficient exhaustion has been reached by the warring parties, they must be forced (or helped) to settlement. In the meantime, superpowers tend not to interfere unnecessarily with each other or each other's client states. This was why the Indochina War and Soviet-American relations were always kept separate as far as Washington was concerned and why Nixon was warmly received by Mao and Brezhnev while fighting still raged in Vietnam. The same principles were now being applied in the Middle East with all the required fine-tuning although the danger of a slipup and an unplanned confrontation always remained.

Astrology through the observation of constellations and the relative position of stars proclaims certain years, months, and days as auspicious or inauspicious for the welfare and success of people and nations. Whether or not one believes in astrology, no month could have been more inauspicious for the felicity of the United States than October 1973 and no day during that month could have matched Saturday, October 20 for the sheer convergence of evil forces and shattering events.

First, Watergate was overshadowing all else in America, with talk of Nixon's possible impeachment growing in serious political circles. Although Watergate had not been a problem for him when he was reelected the previous November—very little was known publicly at the time—it had exploded into an unprecedented presidential scandal during the spring and summer of 1973. Nixon was being accused of foreknowledge of the break-in and obstruction of justice. By September it was revealed that the President had secretly tape-recorded conversations in the Oval Office, and a U.S. court of appeals was deciding whether the tapes should be surrendered to investigators. John Ehrlichman, one of Nixon's closest aides, was among the first group of officials indicted by a federal grand jury. Vice President Spiro Agnew was on the verge of resigning over payoffs he allegedly made when he was governor of Maryland and over alleged tax fraud (none of which had any connection with Watergate).

It was hard to imagine a worse moment for the United States to face a major war in the Middle East where its most vital interests—from strategic balance vis-à-vis the Soviet Union to the access to oil—were at stake. Nixon has written in his memoirs that the Yom Kippur War took the United States "completely by surprise" and that he was "disappointed" by "our own intelligence shortcomings." In understatement, he remarks that "the immensely volatile situation created by the unexpected outbreak of this war could not have come at a more complicated domestic juncture." Not only was Agnew preparing to resign and a successor had to be found, Nixon writes, but he had to review his subpoenaed tapes and "the media were slamming us with daily Watergate charges." And the Congress had passed earlier in the year the "far-reaching" War Powers Act, which restricted the presidential freedom to act in an international crisis. However, it had not yet become law.

Agnew resigned on October 10, when the Middle Eastern war was in its fourth day and the Israeli situation looked grave. Nixon had to select a Vice President (he chose House Majority Leader Gerald Ford of Michigan on October 12) and to decide to order a military airlift of war equipment to Israel (which was becoming desperate for it) for October 13. The administration had barely weathered the storm of criticism that followed the army revolution in Chile the month before that had resulted in the ouster and death of President Allende. The "minicrisis" over the possible installation of a Soviet nuclear submarine base in Cuba had brought foreign censure for "overreaction." And from the moment the Arabs attacked in the Middle East, America's Western European allies became struck with panic over its repercussions on them.

As this fatal October unfolded, the Arabs unsheathed the oil weapon, and suddenly the United States had to face a crisis within a crisis. Decision making was urgently required almost every hour on the hour on an infinity of topics, but in the international sphere Nixon, in Kissinger's words, "was too distracted to shape the decisions before they reached him." The secretary of state adds, "That responsibility now descended on me," perhaps a touch of overstatement. But in the case of oil there was nothing he or Nixon could do.

The Arab move on oil was made in stages, starting on October 17, and unquestionably it was orchestrated by Saudi Arabia, the most important producer. King Faisal was a moderate force in the Middle East, and his kingdom and the United States traditionally enjoyed good relations; most of the Saudi petroleum was pumped, refined, and merchandised by American oil companies.

Faisal, however, was consumed with hatred for Israel for having established its state at the expense of Palestinians, he believed, and especially for having occupied East Jerusalem in the 1967 war and with it the al-Aqsa Mosque, the third holiest site for Sunni Moslems. From there, the prophet Muhammad is said to have flown to heaven on his steed. Faisal had dreamed of praying at least once more at al-Aqsa (which is just above the Jews' holy Western Wall) before dying, and this powerful religious sentiment was behind his actions in 1973.

In Saudi Arabia Islam dominates lives. A visit to Mecca, where the Kaaba (holy stone) is located, is the most important pilgrimage for Muslims. Among the five worship duties of Islam, the hajj (pilgrimage to Mecca) is the fifth. The hajj is the central event in the life of Saudi Arabia; close to two million pilgrims from all over the world appear in Mecca every year, many of them staying for months. As religious fervor has mounted in the Islamic world since the early seventies, perhaps as a reaction to the onrush of modernity, more and more people from the growing Muslim populations from Indonesia and the Philippines to Morocco and Nigeria pour each year into Mecca. It takes jumbo jets to fly them to Saudi Arabia in the never-ending contrasts of shifting cultures and civilizations. The hajj is the largest commercial (nonoil) source of revenue for the country.

And the depth of emotions generated by Faisal's beloved al-Aqsa Mosque was demonstrated, among many other manifestations of faith, when it was set on fire by a deranged visiting Australian sheep rancher in August 1969. I was in Jerusalem on a *Times* assignment that month, and awakened by a friend's telephone call at dawn, I rushed to the Old City to see the seventh-century mosque burning. Thousands or tens of thousands of Jerusalem Arabs had already gathered around the site, the men ready for revenge for the horrible sacrilege, the women ullulating wildly, their heads thrown back in despair. I was certain a terrible riot and carnage would occur—the Arabs automatically assumed the fire was the work of an Israeli or a Jew—but the day was saved by the gentle handling of the situation by Jerusalem's mayor, Teddy Kollek, and his police officers (in those days Arabs and Jews in Jerusalem had contacts, talked to each other).

It was over al-Aqsa that Faisal resolved to punish the United States during the 1973 war. Specifically, he was retaliating for the airlifting of military equipment to Israel with the operation launched on October 13, designed to forestall an Israeli defeat, and for Nixon's request to Congress for $2.2 billion to pay for it. The U.S. Air Force airlift was ordered after five days of deep divisions within the U.S. government on how quickly and through what channels the deliveries should begin (foot-dragging charges and countercharges flew across Washington on the highest level in discreet but understandable fashion for nearly a week, and the controversy was never resolved), and to Faisal this was formal American identification with Israel.

In a communication to Nixon on October 18, Faisal emphasized that the war would end only when Israel returned to the 1967 borders (that is, surrendered East Jerusalem) and warned that "if the United States continues to stand by the side of Israel, the friendship will risk being diminished." He was referring to the American-Saudi friendship. Memoirs by the central American players in the 1973 affray create the impression that the U.S. government had fully taken into account the risk of the Arab use of the oil weapon, but this impression seems to be incorrect. The Arabs had not proclaimed an oil embargo or even cuts in production during or after the 1967 war (a halfhearted attempt failed when Iran and the United States raised output), and the conventional wisdom in October 1973, to the extent that the topic was considered in depth, was that it would not happen. For one thing, the reasoning was that the Arabs had no alternate markets and could not do without oil revenues.

This was where conventional policy planning showed its weakness in ignoring or underestimating religious and cultural factors in non-Western civilizations, a weakness that does not appear to have been greatly remedied in the American government even after all the Middle Eastern shocks of the seventies and the eighties.

The six Arab oil producers, meeting in Kuwait on the ministerial level, started the pressure by announcing on October 17 an immediate 5 percent cutback in production, to be increased by 5 more percents every month until Israel pulled back its lines to the 1967 frontiers. The next day Saudi Arabia announced that *its* monthly cuts would be 10 percent and warned that it might halt all deliveries to the United States if there were no quick and tangible responses to its action. Cutbacks turned out to be even more of a surprise than an embargo would have been, and a still greater shock was the Arabs' simultaneous moves to raise the price of crude oil by 70 percent. Oil was still cheap, but the increase erased the losses from the cutbacks. Iran, which is Muslim but not Arab, did not join the embargo (it was busy planning huge world price hikes).

The month of October became an absolute tragedy for the U.S. government two days after the Saudi thrust. On Saturday, the twentieth, as Kissinger flew to Moscow to confer with Brezhnev, Saudi Arabia and the five other Arab producers announced they were halting all sales of petroleum to the United States. To the Saudis, "quick and tangible" results evidently meant no more than forty-eight hours, and the American airlift was not being canceled. It is unclear whether Saudi Arabia really expected to force America to abandon Israel—and whether it realized that this would not happen as a matter of principle, American self-interest, and rejection of blackmail—but the embargo was not lifted until March 18, 1974. The five months of the embargo nevertheless helped to change the West's economic structure in a fundamental fashion. As for King Faisal, he was assassinated by a demented nephew a year later. David Ben-Gurion, the first prime minister of Israel and the king's anathema, died at the age of eighty-seven, on December 1, 1973, in the knowledge that his nation had survived once more.

But the oil embargo was not the only event of October 20. That evening Nixon ordered Watergate Special Prosecutor Archibald Cox fired in a dispute over the Oval Office tapes. Within hours Attorney General Elliot Richardson and Deputy Attorney General William D. Ruckelshaus resigned in protest. That was the "Saturday Night Massacre" in Washington, executed as men went on killing each other in the continuing Yom Kippur War.

Always jealous of his prerogatives, Nixon vetoed on October 24 the War Powers Act on the grounds that it was unconstitutional and "would seriously undermine this Nation's ability to act decisively and convincingly in times of international crisis." For example, the President said, "our recent actions to bring about a peaceful settlement of the hostilities in the Middle East would have been seriously impaired if this resolution had been in force." On November 7 the House and the Senate overrode the veto, and the War Powers Act became law without Nixon's signature.

*   *   *

The cease-fire in the Middle East had finally gone into effect on October 23, but the worst—and the most dangerous—was still to come in terms of the superpowers' relations. The next day Egypt and the Soviet Union accused Israel of violating the cease-fire in attempts to cut off all escape (or supply) routes of the Egyptian Third Army in the southwestern corner of the Sinai. Israeli armor was already well west of the Suez Canal, controlling the Cairo–Suez highway and deploying units less than a hundred kilometers from the Egyptian capital. An urgent message from Brezhnev to Kissinger called Israeli actions a "flagrant deceit" though Americans were still uncertain what was really happening on the ground. A few hours later Brezhnev cabled Nixon to propose "joint" actions "without delay." Then a third message from Brezhnev that day reached Washington, suggesting that the Third Army must be coming apart.

Though the United States and Egypt had had no formal diplomatic relations since 1967, an urgent message from Sadat to Nixon arrived in the late afternoon, proposing American action, even with force, to implement the cease-fire. The cease-fire was resumed on October 24, but within hours Sadat was again demanding American intervention; it did look as if Israeli commanders just could not bring themselves to leave the beaten Egyptians in peace. By nightfall Kissinger had concluded that a confrontation with the Russians was in the making. When Egypt requested a joint Soviet-American military force to enforce the cease-fire, the assumption in Washington was that the Russians were behind the idea. And the decision was to prevent them from placing troops in the Middle East.

Then Brezhnev sent Nixon the message that if the United States would not join in a peace force, he would take "appropriate steps unilaterally." To Kissinger, this was "one of the most serious challenges to an American President by a Soviet leader." The CIA reported that Soviet transport aircraft were being readied in Hungary to lift airborne divisions and that now there were eighty-five Soviet warships in the Mediterranean. It was late evening in Washington, and Nixon had already retired for the night; General Alexander Haig, his chief of staff, refused to wake him up, apparently because he believed that the President was too overwrought by Watergate pressures to become involved at midnight in a superpower crisis. In his memoirs Nixon does not allude to this episode, making it clear that he was not personally involved in the dramatic events of that night.

According to Kissinger, the consensus at the meeting he chaired at the White House throughout the night—it included Defense Secretary Schlesinger, Chairman of the Joint Chiefs of Staff Admiral Thomas Moorer, CIA Director William Colby, and Haig—was that the Soviet airlift would start at dawn. The group decided that the best response was to place American forces around the world on DefCon III (Defense Condition I is war; DefCon III is increased readiness) mainly as a ploy to dissuade the Soviets from precipitate action. The idea was that Soviet intelligence would instantly pick up the orders and inform the Kremlin. To make American moves even more obvious, the Eighty-second Airborne Division was alerted for movement, and additional aircraft carriers were ordered to steam to the Mediterranean. Guam-based B-52 jet bombers were recalled home. There was no way the Russians could miss this display. Then, around six o'clock in the morning, a message was sent to Brezhnev warning him against unilateral action. It was *almost* the Cuban missile crisis all over again.

The next day, October 25, the crisis was suddenly over. Whether the alert maneuver had worked or Brezhnev had simply decided that the confrontation had gone far enough now that the cease-fire was again in force, the Soviets turned off the pressure. It was probably inevitable that Nixon and Kissinger would be accused of manufacturing the crisis to turn attention away from Watergate—so charged was the political atmosphere—and indeed, such accusations flew to and fro. In retrospect, it does appear likely that if the crisis had not been resolved by October 25, the whole national political fabric might have been torn asunder with horrifying consequences.

On October 28 Israeli and Egyptian generals met in a tent at Kilometer 101 of the Suez–Cairo road to discuss the modalities of springing free the Third Army and withdrawing Israelis forces from Egypt. United Nations observers were on hand to assist, but the rival generals handled it just fine. Their sessions were the prelude to an extraordinary breakthrough in Middle Eastern history that came four years later.

Although all the texts of high-level exchanges among the principals during the Yom Kippur War and minutes of secret Washington meetings have not been made public (the Soviets had released nothing by late 1989), there is no question that it was an extremely serious superpower confrontation. The great difference between the Cuban crisis of 1962 and the Middle Eastern affair in 1973 was that neither side engaged in nuclear posturing or threats. Both sides now had SALT I behind them and evidently a new sense of nuclear reality. As McGeorge Bundy puts it, the 1973 alert helped "demonstrate the weakness of atomic diplomacy and the essentially secondary role of nuclear weapons in the regional conflicts."

The Yom Kippur War was the last serious Soviet-American confrontation on any level of danger. It may have marked the end of a postwar era of open hostility between the United States and the Soviet Union.

VI

The new era in postwar world economics, with the restructuring of all the past relationships among the industrial democracies and between them and the Third World, opened in the early seventies. Nearly twenty years later changes and readjustments—some of them of immense importance even for the approaching new century—were still occurring as a result of rapidly evolving social, economic, and political conditions everywhere and of the impact of new technologies.

The Second World War distorted and paralyzed previous existing relationships and for this reason buried economic arrangements that had prevailed, by and large, since the beginning of the twentieth century. The 1914–18 conflict had, of course, brought changes of its own, including the birth of the Soviet Union after the collapse of the czardom, but it was World War II that marked a greater historical turning point. This was the emergence of the United States as the unquestioned leader and arbiter in international economics. The Western European nations were exhausted and grievously damaged by the war, all of them (except neutral Portugal and Spain) losing their overseas colonies. Germany and Japan were prostrate. The Soviet Union was bled white by the struggle. And a new phenomenon appeared with the birth of the infant sovereign nations of the Third World.

The first postwar era ran roughly from 1945 to the early 1970's, with the United States still preeminent, but with Western Europe and Japan rising triumphantly from the ashes of war and with the Third World acquiring new importance as an expanding market for the industrial West (its goods and its capital) and new leverage as owners and producers of strategic commodities.

The second postwar economic era grew out of the shaping of these new trends and forces at the very outset of the decade of the seventies although the transformation was gradual. When the great shocks came in the mid-1970's, governments, economists, and corporate managers were not really aware that the crisis was happening. In the long run it may turn out that the seventies marked the most fundamental economic revolution of this century—before the Soviet Union and Eastern Europe abandoned Communist economics and started on the path of neo-capitalism in the early nineties.

Many people believed that these epochal changes resulted directly and overwhelmingly from the "petroshocks," specifically from the 1973 Arab oil embargo. In truth, the broader process began earlier and had deeper and more complex origins.

The first and foremost fact was the astonishingly rapid recovery of Western Europe (triggered by the Marshall Plan), reflected in unprecedented growth rates between 1948 and 1973. As a result, total Western European production nearly equaled that of the United States; in northern European countries per capita incomes began to approach American levels. Japan had a slower start, but at the outset of the seventies it was catching up quickly. Whereas in 1948 the United States provided one half of the world's gross national product (GNP), it had fallen to approximately 30 percent in the early seventies.

Actually the quarter century between 1948 and 1973 was a golden age for the American economy, too. Civilian jobs increased from fifty-seven to eighty-two million, the nation was optimistic, and Americans had great personal expectations for the future. The economy slowed down after 1973, in part because of the inflation induced by the jump in oil prices and in part, many economists believe, because of wrong corporate strategies at home in the face of the new challenges coming from Western Europe and Japan and because of the expansion of multinational corporations, many of them American-led, that shifted jobs abroad where labor was cheaper.

A tendency has developed in the late eighties to regard as calamitous this shrinking of the American slice of the world economic pie. In every sense the United States *statistically* is not doing anywhere as well as it did at the end of the war, when its domestic economy had tripled in size. But the immediate postwar situation abroad was catastrophic, and no planner in his right mind wished to see it perpetrated. Hence the massive American aid. Violent population rise in the Third World likewise altered the shape of the cake. By the early 1970's, therefore, adjustments were required in the posture of the American economy and its relations—monetary and trade—with the rest of the world.

This was the start of the economic revolution of the 1970's, which was simply inevitable as a historical process and must not be regarded as the twilight of American influence in the world, as fashionable "declinist" writers have propounded. The new economic revolution has recognized and accentuated economic—and environmental—interdependence on the eve of the new century; if intelligently managed, interdependence benefits all. This has not always been the case, but generally the approach in the West has been constructive.

On December 12, 1971, Richard Nixon landed at Lajes Air Force Base on Terceira Island in the Portuguese Azores in the mid-Atlantic to do nothing less than dismantle the international monetary system created at Bretton Woods during World War II. He did this in concert with France's President Georges Pompidou, who came to meet him in the Azores as a representative of the European Community because it had become evident that new conditions required new systems. As Air Force One, a Boeing 707 passenger jet, touched down at Lajes, the President was seized with envy, if not lust. As I remember him bantering about it during the Azores stay, it was galling to see that Pompidou had flown from Paris aboard a supersonic Concorde, which awaited the 707 on the tarmac, when the Congress had refused to finance the construction of supersonic planes for U.S. airlines (the Congress was proved right; the Concorde was a commercial flop).

The Azores conference was made necessary by rising pressures on the dollar since early in the year by Western Europe (especially West Germany) and Japan, which desired to see the U.S. currency devalued by perhaps 10 percent to make their growing trade more competitive internationally. America's dollar liabilities to foreign official institutions rose from twelve billion dollars in 1969 to forty-one billion dollars in mid-1971. Washington, worried by the falling dollar, tended to accept a devaluation, but at a set rate, not subject to new pressures and speculation; it also wanted European concessions on free trade with the removal of various obstacles to American exports. The Europeans preferred free floating rates and were reluctant to make trade concessions. Nixon, concerned about domestic inflation and the mounting international problems, stunned America's allies (and everybody else) with an announcement, on August 15, of a ninety-day freeze on wages and prices, a 10 percent surcharge on all imports, and the suspension of the convertibility of the dollar into gold. This was the "Nixon shock," and it really shook the world.

Financial news rarely made front pages in those days, but this time the implications at home in day-to-day terms and abroad in terms of a possible trade war among the Western allies were obvious. The immediate problem was what to do next in dealing with shocked and furious Europeans and Japanese, but the Nixon administration was not equipped to handle it. Nobody was responsible for tying together the financial, trade, and foreign policy aspects of the "Nixon shock," and top officials in the administration were in disarray, each representing different constituencies at home and different interests. The post of special assistant to the President for International Economic Affairs had been created just a few months earlier; the State Department and Kissinger as national security adviser were out of the picture altogether.

The next three months were spent in interallied squabbles, with the Americans pointedly reminding the Europeans that apart from the Marshall Plan, the United States was spending billions of dollars annually on the stationing of more than three hundred thousand troops on the European continent to protect it from the Russians, and all it was finding was ingratitude. Such arguments normally do not produce harmony, and in their renewed nationalisms the Europeans responded with charges of an "American hegemony" oppressing them. It was becoming ridiculous, and Kissinger, with no responsibility and little experience in this area, had the sense to convince Nixon to sit and negotiate with the Europeans; Pompidou agreed to speak for the Common Market countries.

As so often happens when great decisions are made, the Azores accord was concluded hastily and sloppily. Nixon and Kissinger had their minds on foreign wars—the secret Vietnam negotiations were in high gear, and the India-Pakistan conflict over Bangladesh was at its climactic point—when the two-day Azores conference began. Secretary of State Rogers and Treasury Secretary John Connally were on the island, but in the end it was Kissinger who ironed out a deal in secret meetings with Pompidou. While Kissinger acknowledges in *White House Years* that his expertise was minimal, he and the French president found an essentially political solution.

In brief, new exchange relationships between the dollar and other major currencies were established (the dollar's official value went down 9 percent), the dollar again became convertible, and the Europeans made vague trade concessions. This implied a change in the price of gold, which Nixon had initially opposed, but as the presidents adjourned at lunchtime and rushed back to their airplanes, White House press aides circulated among American reporters assuring them that a great victory had been achieved. When I asked for a clarification—and I really did not understand what happened—I was told, "Oh, just take my word for it. . . . And hurry up with your story. The press plane for Washington is ready to go."

On December 17 the Group of Ten (the major industrial nations of Western Europe plus the United States, Canada, and Japan) met at the red-brick "Castle" of the Smithsonian Institution in Washington to ratify the Azores deal. The new system of exchange rates was approved, and the price of gold was fixed at thirty-eight dollars per ounce (up from the thirty-five-dollar peg established in 1933). Nixon, never at a loss for hyperbole, announced that the Smithsonian agreement was the "most significant monetary agreement in the history of the world." Before too long the new fixed exchange rates were dropped in favor of the free float of the dollar, all the other currencies, and gold. Ever since, chaos and crisis have plagued the world's financial markets (gold in the late 1970's reached more than eight-hundred dollars per ounce; in the late eighties it somewhat stabilized around four hundred dollars). The Azores and the Smithsonian clearly were not the most significant agreements in history, but they helped set in motion the new economic revolution.

This revolution continued with the unexpected self-assertion by Middle Eastern petroleum producers in 1971, though at the outset neither the Western governments nor the oil companies comprehended what they were facing. Since before the Second World War petroleum production levels and prices had been set by the companies. Because Middle Eastern oil was so incredibly cheap—a dollar per barrel—the United States kept the imports down through a quota system to protect the domestic production price, more than twice as high. Even at the end of the sixties nobody in authority thought that oil might become scarce—albeit American imports had risen from 8 percent of national consumption in 1947 to 33 percent in 1969—or that the price might go up significantly. Decision making was centered in New York and Houston, London, The Hague, and Paris, not in dusty Arab or Persian Gulf capitals.

At this stage Colonel Qaddafi, not yet thirty years old, entered the picture as the new ruler of Libya (he and a group of other young officers had seized power on September 1, 1969) and as an extraordinary irritant to the United States and much of the West, a role he still played twenty years later. His name will go down in the annals of the world oil industry as the man who forced its radical metamorphosis. Qaddafi belonged to the new breed of nationalists who began emerging across the Third World in the aftermath of decolonization with wholly fresh ideas about the destiny of their countries. Before the war Libya was an Italian colony. Given independence by the United Nations, it survived on an annual five-million-pound-sterling—just over $1 million—British subsidy, limited revenue from the cheap oil it produced, and rentals from the United States for Wheelus Air Base, which was used for training jet pilots over the desert and the Mediterranean. King Idris, installed by the British, was perfectly happy with this state of affairs though Libya was one of the world's poorest nations.

Qaddafi had other ideas. He resented the foreign domination of Libyan oil and economy, and as a Muslim fundamentalist he was viscerally opposed to the West, whose values he despised. If the West had taken the trouble to try to understand Qaddafi in 1969, it might have better understood Iran's Ayatollah Khomeini in 1979. In those days, however, religious-minded radicals and self-proclaimed social reformers (Qaddafi was a champion of social justice, developing a complicated system of social equality in Libya) were not taken seriously. Kissinger, who was concerned about losing Wheelus, which happened soon, regarded the colonel as a dangerous fellow. He writes in *Years of Upheaval* that two months after Qaddafi captured power, Kissinger raised the possibility of "covert action" in Libya (presumably meaning the new regime's overthrow), "but the agencies did not have their heart in it." Later they probably wished they had.

In any event, early in 1970, Qaddafi asked the oil companies for an increase of forty cents per barrel for Libyan oil, which sounds ridiculous twenty years later, but no country had ever before demanded so much (it amounted to a 20 percent hike). The companies agreed when the Libyans ordered a cutback in production—Qaddafi had embraced the embargo notion, too—and this was the end of the epoch of cheap oil and Western control of resources.

Seeing Libya's success, Persian Gulf producers (including Iran and Saudi Arabia) held out for increases as well. Then Libya upped the ante again in what became known as the leapfrogging game. But oil still cost only around three dollars per barrel, and the West remained essentially passive. OPEC, put together by Venezuela in the early sixties and consisting of thirteen members around the world, discovered it had potential clout, demanding across-the-board negotiations with all the producers. Higher prices resulted from Libyan and Iranian agreements in 1971, but even then the consumer nations were contemptuous of OPEC.

By 1972 the big oil companies had finally formed a united front, but it was too late to recoup their former influence. Now OPEC was insisting on its governments' participation in the ownership of oil on their territories; the companies that had held production concessions for decades thought this radical and cheeky. OPEC, however, had rapidly mastered the art of pressure, and Saudi Arabia became the first producer to obtain 51 percent of equity in its own oil. The shah, who the previous year was promised by Nixon unlimited weapons and CIA assistance in his anti-Iraqi campaign, asked in mid-1973 for equal treatment for Iran. The West had effectively lost control of the world production; with 51 percent ownership, the producers now set the prices.

The Yom Kippur War in October 1973 first kicked up the prices, then led to the total Arab embargo against oil shipments to the United States. Although oil was plentiful in the world and available from non-Arabs, the market panicked, and prices soared for spot (immediate-delivery) crude to around $10 per barrel, almost double of the Arab price set just a few weeks earlier. In December OPEC ministers raised the price of crude to $11.65. This was nearly 400 *percent* since October, and the oil market was never the same again.

America was now hit directly by the world economic revolution. Traditional low oil production prices at home had not encouraged greater domestic output, turning the impact of Arab embargo into a psychological crisis. With consumption in the industrialized countries in 1973 virtually double of that a decade earlier, the panic grew. For the first time in history Americans had to endure long lines to buy gasoline and fuel, if they could find them at all. There was hoarding, there was nastiness, and there was helplessness. The government imposed in 1974 a national fifty-five-mile-per-hour speed limit on American highways to conserve fuel (it also turned out to save lives), the first time such a measure was invoked. There had been strict rationing during the war; but this was peacetime, and Americans could not understand it. Foreign policy, normally an abstraction for most citizens, abruptly invaded their daily lives.

The lifting of the Arab embargo on March 18, after Kissinger had completed the disengagement of Egyptian and Israeli forces in the Sinai (they were now separated by a demilitarized zone supervised by American observers), and an increase in the Saudi production helped stabilize the prices; but there was no return to the happy days of one-dollar oil. A Washington conference of Western consumer nations to plan against future emergencies through the creation of "safety net" reserve systems resulted in no real progress; when it came to economics, Western unity was elusive. And OPEC kept squeezing and squeezing, aware that this was a seller's market and that its leverage could not be broken. In 1975 oil cost more than twenty dollars per barrel; in 1979 the Iranian Revolution raised it to an incredible forty dollars.

The continuing economic revolution of the seventies and the eighties with all the realignments and structural changes it was causing was intimately tied to Third World events—from the Arab-Israeli War and the Iranian Revolution to the still-rolling waves of nationalism—but it instantly affected the Third World itself as well.

Now the mass of money in the hands of the producers was raising fears that such excess capital might wreck the international financial system as governments and bankers did not know at first how to recycle or invest these immense funds. Then it became clear that the high oil prices would deeply injure most of the developing nations. Third World countries that did not produce much oil—Brazil was the best example—were destroying their economies trying to pay for the imports, going deep into debt.

An idea of how petrodollars were amassed by the producers during the boom period can be formed from the fact that the gross domestic product (GDP) of twenty-one Arab countries plus Iran leaped from $41 billion in 1970 to $461 billion in 1980; the revenues of Venezuela, Mexico, Ecuador,

Indonesia, and Nigeria must be added to it. More than a half trillion dollars were sloshing around the world during the seventies, distorting all the economic structures, domestic and international. One of the immediate results was dangerously high inflation in the United States and most of the Western countries (West Germany with the memories of the catastrophic inflation of the 1920's somehow managed to control it) as well as in the Third World. Then came the huge capital transfers, still another aspect of the revolution of the seventies.

The recycling of petrodollars resulted in investments running into hundreds of billions of dollars, mainly from the Arab countries, in the United States and to a lesser extent in Western Europe. Arab money went into American real estate and into corporate equity as direct foreign investment and into government securities such as treasury bills and bonds. In the latter case Saudi and Kuwaiti funds became significant in helping finance the growing federal deficit. In Western Europe the Arabs seemed to prefer showier investments such the Ritz Hotel in Paris and the Dorchester in London and villas in Monte Carlo along with equity in British enterprises.

Moreover, the enormous sums in the hands of oil producers encouraged them to import billions of dollars in sophisticated weapons from the United States and Western Europe, along with Rolls-Royces, Maseratis, Ferraris, and Mercedes cars and every imaginable item of luxury. In this fashion some of the oil money came back to the West. But other money, mainly through Western banks, went into loans to the Third World, causing the next revolutionary dimension. By the late 1980's the Third World debt approached one *trillion* dollars to become a source of concern about the stability of lender banks that might not be able to collect much of it and about the political stability of the nations forced into austerity programs to be able to repay what they owed.

The United States, too, was damaged by the flood of foreign money. Flushed with the oil bonanza, Iran and Saudi Arabia in particular developed a hunger for the most advanced defense systems, and contractors in the United States as well as the Pentagon rushed to meet the demand.

On the one hand, fortunes were made, chiefly by Iranian and Saudi middlemen, on huge commissions on defense contracts they were negotiating in Washington, and inevitably payoffs and corruption tainted much of this trade. Some of the same characters reappeared in the Iran-Contra scandal of the 1980's. The Lockheed Corporation became entangled in scandals involving illegal payments to high government officials in Japan, Italy, and Turkey to help along competitive sales (with other U.S. and foreign aircraft builders) of C-130 military transports and civilian airliners. On one occasion Nixon spoke on Lockheed's behalf with Japan's prime minister.

When the Congress proposed legislation against such illegal payments, the industry protested on the ground that they constituted a necessary aspect of doing business abroad; thus morality at home was being corroded as vast profits were made. In the eighties similar irregularities involving Pentagon officials and U.S. defense contractors were discovered, a legacy from the happy seventies.

On the other hand, the United States was becoming dangerously dependent on Saudi Arabia, Iran, and several Arab nations for financing basic research and development (R&D) in the design of weapons systems. Advance payments on military purchases paid for much R&D that otherwise might not have been undertaken. Contractors argued that this foreign money helped improve America's defenses; the saner among Pentagon officials thought the United States should not be put in a position of gearing its defense industry to the oil producers' needs and, in the end, fall into excessive reliance on such funding.

The astonishing capacity of Second World War losers—West Germany and Japan—to rebuild their economies through exports to the United States, Western European countries, and the Third World created other new flows of capital. Japanese direct investments in the United States have reached unprecedented levels since the seventies, including automotive plants producing for the American market. And America's huge imports from Japan already in the 1970's pushed the United States into a painfully adverse trade balance position, making it a net debtor in the world for the first time since the First World War.

The reason for the Japanese car boom in the United States (which was even bigger late in the eighties than in the early 1970's) was that in the wake of oil embargo the American public was thirsting for small fuel efficient automobiles and Japan already manufactured them. It is one of the great postwar economic and industrial mysteries why Detroit failed to understand the fundamental change affecting automotive markets worldwide. U.S. automakers either assumed (without any data pointing in such a direction) that oil would soon again be cheap and plentiful or that Americans would never sacrifice their pride in the big American cars to buy the small Japanese vehicles—or both. When it finally dawned on Detroit that it faced a very different new world, its design of compacts and retooling for them simply came too late.

The public had developed a loyalty to the Japanese product, which was well built and efficient, superbly advertised in the media and elsewhere, and supported by an impressive network of service departments and spare parts; unlike most American manufacturers (and the dealers who reflected their philosophy), the Japanese understood that it is vital to care for the customer. Bashing of Japanese cars with sledgehammers on the steps of the Capitol in Washington, as several congressmen did on occasions for TV cameras, or imposing mandatory import quotas twenty years after the Japanese had run away with the American market for reasons of quality will not affect the preference of the consumer for the Japanese cars (and television sets and tape recorders). They like them. It is astounding how the great minds of American captains of industry never perceived this simple fact.

Japan leads the world in automotive and electronic exports, and ten of the world's thirteen largest banks are Japanese. The world's largest is the Dai-Ichi Kangyo Bank with $312 billion in deposits. But it may come as a surprise that the world's two biggest *piano* manufacturers and exporters are Japanese: Yamaha and Kawai. I have unsuccessfully sought to find an explanation for this phenomenon, Japan not being in the great tradition of Artur Rubinstein or Robert Casadesus. But it has occurred to me that contrary to what one may have thought about it (the humorist James Thurber once proclaimed in writing that "there are no pianos in Japan" in order to provide an example of what he thought was a truism), there must be a domestic market for pianos there. I once mentioned this topic to Byron Janis, a distinguished American pianist who has played in concerts for forty years, and he further astonished me with the information that in the postwar years Japan has developed an impressive number of highly talented musicians, principally pianists and violinists. Further inquiry revealed that young Japanese turned to the piano immediately after the war as part of the influence exercised by the American occupation.

The war and the occupation have evidently had immensely variegated and even bizarre impacts on Japan. They have stimulated inventiveness in industry, chiefly the art of absorbing and refining American technology, which may be one reason why the United States has developed in 1986 only 50 percent of the world's advanced technology, down from 70 percent in 1974. We now know that the Japanese count importantly in classical music, but they have copied other aspects of American life and mores as well. During six years in the eighties, seventy million Japanese visited the Disneyland theme park in Maihama, a site near Tokyo that once was submerged beneath Tokyo Bay. The attraction—and the financial value—of the American concept of entertainment were proved overwhelmingly when the Sony Corporation purchased CBS Records for $2 billion in 1987 and Columbia Pictures Entertainment, Inc., the owner of one of Hollywood's most famous studios, for $3.4 billion in 1989. This made Sony, whose sales were over $16 billion during 1989, one of the world's leading entertainment firms, producing video and audio equipment, television cameras and TV sets, records—and now movies. Also in 1989, Japanese investors purchased controlling interest in New York's Rockefeller Complex of office and entertainment buildings, including the famous Radio City Music Hall. Seemingly unnoticed, however, is the fact that British interests represent the largest single foreign direct investment in the United States. And in the late eighties sex scandals have popped up at the highest level of Japanese politics, costing Cabinet ministers their jobs. The interesting question about the American-Japanese symbiosis is, then, To what extent *is* imitation the most sincere form of flattery?

A possible answer lies in the story of General Minoru Genda, the planner of the Japanese air attack on Pearl Harbor, who died in 1989 at the age of eighty-five—a hero to both nations. Genda was a fighter pilot at the time of the invasion of China in the thirties, the creator of the Genda's Circuses flying acrobatic teams, and the naval officer assigned to plan the strike of December 7, 1941. My knowledge of Genda's career comes from his obituary in a New York newspaper, in which I learned (without further explanation) that he became a general in the new Japanese Defense Force (army) and chief of staff of the air force in 1959. At the age of fifty-six, he became a jet pilot, logging a thousand hours in F-104 Starfighters (built by the controversial Lockheed).

Clearly a very outspoken gentleman, Genda said during a 1969 visit to the United States that if he had been commander in chief of the Japanese armed forces during the war, he would have kept bombing Pearl Harbor and would have occupied Hawaii in order to invade the American mainland. General Genda was then awarded the Legion of Merit, the highest U.S. decoration given to foreigners, for rebuilding the Japanese Air Force after the 1945 defeat.

West Germany, the other postwar economic "miracle," has similarly absorbed great American influences and has sought to buy its way, so to speak, into American culture. The leading West German publishing house, for example, has purchased several major American book publishing houses, book clubs, and magazines. A stroll through the giant Frankfurt airport, to say nothing of the streets of German cities from Hamburg to West Berlin, makes one think of a strange overlay of American ways on a society that seems to want to act American: the gestures, the blue jeans, American words, advertisements for American cigarettes, and Visit America posters. Sex scandals, of course, are not new to German politics; but Germans are Europeans, and this practice is not as astonishing as in Tokyo.

Japan's and Germany's great economic strengths have become during the seventies—the time of transition—crucial elements in the latest postwar revolution. After Richard Nixon decoupled the gold, the West German deutsche mark (DM) and the Japanese yen became the benchmark currencies in relation to the dollar, leaving behind the pound sterling and the Swiss franc.

But the Japanese and West German "miracles" may face a disturbing future: Demographic projections show that the populations of these countries are both shrinking and aging and that they will be smaller in absolute numbers at the start of the next century. In year 2008, according to the projections, Japan and West Germany will be the oldest societies in terms of median age in the entire world.

IX

The Nixon presidency spanned some of the gravest events of the postwar period—from the windup of the American war in Indochina to the Yom Kippur War and the energy crisis—as well as the moments of triumph of his visits to Beijing and Moscow, the signing of SALT I, and the landing of the American astronauts on the moon.

It ended on August 9, 1974, when Richard Nixon resigned after four and a half years in the White House as the principal victim of the Watergate scandal mounted by his overzealous aides and compounded by his own efforts to obstruct justice through a senseless cover-up. He wept as he left the White House, and America was emotionally drained. The next two presidents of the decade of the seventies, Gerald Ford and Jimmy Carter, were to have their share of drama and challenge.

For President Ford, an amiable and noncontroversial figure, the immediate responsibility was to restore confidence at home and abroad in American institutions so wrenched by Vietnam and Watergate. The first nonelected President in American history, he acquitted himself well. He was criticized for pardoning Nixon a month after the resignation, but in retrospect this was a wise move. It spared the nation more agony and left Watergate behind, allowing America to concentrate on the present and the future. Americans had never really lost faith in themselves, and opinion abroad quickly absorbed the changeover in the White House; what mattered were American policies, not American politics.

In foreign matters Ford maintained the Nixon stance. He appointed Nelson Rockefeller as Vice President, showing his partiality to the more liberal wing of Repubicanism, and he kept Kissinger as secretary of state. Toward the Soviet Union the policy was to strengthen détente, which was already coming under criticism. A congressional amendment, for example, had linked trade with Moscow to the Soviet willingness to let Jews emigrate—a form of pressure Brezhnev angrily denounced. The expulsion of Nobel Prizewinner Aleksandr Solzhenitsyn to Paris added criticism. Nixon's last major foreign enterprise was a visit to Moscow and the Crimea late in June, continuing the pattern of annual summits he and Brezhnev had inaugurated in 1972. (Earlier in June he had also gone to Egypt, Saudi Arabia, Syria, Israel, and Jordan to shore up Middle Eastern peace prospects.)

Ford's concern, therefore, was to keep the momentum in Soviet-American relations, and in November 1974 he flew to Vladivostok for a meeting with Brezhnev to pursue talks on SALT II, which Nixon had begun in June. The Soviets had by then developed the MIRV technology for their missiles, and the hope was for a deal limiting MIRVed warheads. Kissinger believes that Brezhnev's willingness in Vladivostok to place equal ceilings on MIRVs could have led to the halt of this particular arms race, but no agreement was reached. McGeorge Bundy has written that Ford "had too little time, and he did not seize his one big chance to lead in finishing SALT II and taking it to the country."

Ford continued Nixon's policy toward China as well: Americans had already come to accept it. He flew to Beijing on December 1, 1975, for a five-day visit, paying a long call on the eighty-two-year-old Mao Zedong, whom he had never met. Ford found him in fine shape and with a sharp mind. He regretted he was unable to see Zhou Enlai, who was in a hospital with cancer (he died the following month), but he believed that his conversation with Mao had cemented the relationship established by Nixon in 1972; Mao himself was dead ten months after Ford's visit.

During his two and a half years in the White House Ford had a full plate of foreign crises and problems. In 1974, apart from SALT II, he had to deal with inherited crises and with new ones.

The most important one was Portugal. There the fifty-year right-wing dictatorship was overthrown on April 25, by a revolution organized by young military officers in order to establish democracy at home and liquidate the debilitating colonial war in Africa. Most of the leaders were troop commanders who had served and fought in the African territories, acquiring sympathy for the independence movement and becoming convinced that time had come to halt the combat.

Antônio de Oliveira Salazar, the ascetic financial specialist who had been put in power by a right-wing military junta in 1926, had been disabled by a stroke in 1968, to be replaced as prime minister by a nonentity named Marcello Caetano. What Salazar had constructed was a classic fascist dictatorship, with a secret police called PIDE, a rubber-stamp president of the republic and legislature, and a quasi-medieval approach to public morality and mores.

I remember interviewing Salazar in the austere living room of his house in downtown Lisbon sometime in 1967, and what I heard was one long tirade in elegant, old-fashioned Portuguese by this lifelong bachelor against the "licentiousness" of the young people and against U.S. sympathy for the colonial uprisings. Salazar had kept Portugal neutral in World War II, greatly helping the Allies (although Nazi agents also had a free run of Lisbon), and had subsequently granted the United States military bases in the Azores. For this, he argued angrily, Portugal deserved gratitude, not hostility, from America.

Caetano was younger and more open-minded, but he maintained both the dictatorial regime and the African war. It was Caetano who was ousted by the idealistic captains and majors that April day in Lisbon, and the atmosphere in the ancient streets was one of unrelieved joy. It was called the Carnations' Revolution because people filled the barrels of tanks' cannons and soldiers' rifles with flowers in something bordering on a spiritual communion between the troops and most of the population. The victorious Movement of the Armed Forces (MFA) named General Antônio de Spínola to be Portugal's provisional president. He was a political moderate, had commanded in Africa, and a year before had published a book denouncing the colonial wars.

But after Ford took over from Nixon months after the Portuguese Revolution, concern began to grow in Washington that dangerous radicalism—and powerful Communist infiltration—were infecting the new regime. Portugal was a NATO member, and the United States had bases in the Azores. The

West could not afford to lose Portugal to neutralism, to say nothing of communism. Kissinger became a crusading spirit in machinations to save Portugal for the West, being darkly convinced that the Portuguese were unable to do it for themselves. It took a year before the crisis in Portugal would be finally resolved—in favor of democracy.

What helped Portuguese democrats save the day was, in the first place, the determination of non-Communist leaders to wrest the controls of government away from leftist extremists. They succeeded when the Socialist party garnered the highest vote in 1975 elections with 37.9 percent, the Communists coming in third with only 12.5 percent. Discreet financial and organizational support from Western European Socialist and Christian Democratic parties helped defeat the Communists and extreme leftist groups. Mario Soarès, whom I knew when he was exiled in Western Europe as a foe of the Salazar dictatorship, became the Socialist prime minister (he was elected president of the republic in the mid-eighties), and Portugal relaxed.

On the American side the hero was Ambassador Frank Carlucci (later secretary of defense), who convinced a doubting Kissinger in a face-to-face confrontation that democracy had a chance in Portugal, that the United States should remain cool and refrain from foolish enterprises. We had many conversations in Lisbon during those difficult days, and my recollection is that Carlucci, a fluent Portuguese-language speaker, was always on top of events.

The next crisis Ford inherited also involved NATO allies, Greece and Turkey. The United States had military bases and nuclear weapons in both countries, and it was faced with a maddening dilemma when Turkey invaded Cyprus on July 20, 1974, allegedly to protect Turkish minorities from the Greek majority on that Mediterranean island. The Turks landed in Cyprus after the Cypriot president, Orthodox Archbishop Makarios III, regarded as his country's liberator from British colonialism, was overthrown by a coup d'état apparently orchestrated by the right-wing military junta then in power in Athens. This led Turkey to conclude that Cyprus would be forcibly united with Greece, a prospect it would not tolerate. In his final days in office Nixon could hardly concentrate on Cyprus, but Kissinger and the State Department were able to force a cease-fire two days after the Turks had invaded with overwhelming force.

Taking sides between two NATO allies was abhorrent to the United States, but when the Greek junta was in turn overthrown on July 22, public sympathies at home went out to the Greek Cypriots and Greece. Because of Cypriot resistance, the Turks launched a second invasion three days after Ford became President in Washington, making Cyprus his top priority before he could even move into the White House. The invasion resulted in a partition of Cyprus and a protective presence of United Nations forces that was still maintained fifteen years later. The Congress voted an embargo on deliveries of arms to Turkey, which did not prevent Greece, the beneficiary of this action, from becoming stridently anti-American when a leftist regime was elected in Athens the following year. Turkey, naturally, resented the embargo. The end result of this crisis was permanent paralysis of NATO in the eastern Mediterranean.

On May 18, 1974, India had exploded an atomic device, becoming the sixth nation in the world in the nuclear club (Israel was the real sixth member, but it had never admitted to nuclear capability). The Indian explosion, the result of years of secret work and clandestine transfers of fuels and equipment from Canada and Western Europe, dealt a lethal blow to the nonproliferation policies propounded by the United States, Britain, and the Soviet Union (France and China have not signed the Nuclear Nonproliferation Treaty). It has encouraged Pakistan, the perennial rival, to follow India's example, and in all probability the Pakistanis, notwithstanding denials, have at least a nuclear industrial capability, if not the weapon itself. South Africa, Sweden, Argentina, and Brazil, advanced in nuclear physics and with access to uranium ore, are regarded as nuclear-threshhold countries. Libya may have a bomb.

During the Ford presidency the Congress wrote stringent legislation linking American foreign aid and arms sales to nuclear efforts by recipient countries. In the end, however, the big power nuclear monopoly had been broken once and for all. It is pointless to wax indignant over the fact that India, with its immense needs in the realm of human welfare, has devoted so much of its resources to a nuclear program. Nations tend to do what they perceive as their sovereign interest, and they resent interference. They know that reprisals will not be lasting on the part of the United States, which remains both moralistic and pragmatic about nuclear proliferation because it cannot really afford to antagonize offenders (whether it is Israel, India, or Pakistan) in the light of other policy interests it has.

When I interviewed Pakistan's late President Mohammad Zia ul-Haq at his residence in Rawalpindi in 1984, he told me, "We do *not* have an atomic bomb, but why shouldn't we, if we want it?" Zia's key role in channeling American, Saudi, and Chinese military aid to the Afghanistan guerrillas after the Soviet invasion in 1979 deprived the United States of serious leverage in pursuing the nuclear issue. Indira Gandhi, the Indian prime minister, acknowledged when I interviewed her in New Delhi in 1981 that her country had nuclear capabilities, and she forcefully defended India's right to them though insisting Indian nuclear device was for peaceful purposes. In Israel, officials do not discuss nuclear capabilities with newsmen; it is a taboo topic.

Naturally this worldwide proliferation increases the threat of nuclear terrorism, if terrorists of whatever persuasion succeed in getting their hands on plutonium. There is not much that can be done to prevent it apart from standard security precautions, and potential terrorists have probably read enough novels and seen enough motion pictures dealing with nuclear terror to know exactly how to proceed.

A problem with immense implications for the stability of Africa and even East-West relations appeared in Ethiopia when young leftist army officers deposed Emperor Haile Selassie on September 8, 1974, a month after Ford became President. The emperor had been crowned in 1916, and his rule had been interrupted by the Italian conquest in 1936, to be restored after the Allied victory. His feudal state was replaced by a brutal military junta headed by Lieutenant Colonel Mengistu Haile Mariam. Ethiopia was declared a socialist state three weeks after the coup and became a Marxist-Leninist state in the mid-1980's. Under Mengistu, it has fought wars with Somalia, and it has battled secession rebels in Eritrea and Tigre Province, who launched their uprisings in 1961. At least a half million people died in Ethiopian wars and famines between 1974 and 1990; refugees are estimated to be in the millions. Under the Carter administration a dispute over the rising Soviet influence in the Horn of Africa—around Ethiopia—seriously undermined relations between Washington and Moscow. What Ford learned very quickly in the Oval Office was that no foreign problem is truly alien to the United States; none can be ignored.

The year 1974 removed a great number of outstanding personalities from the world scene, people who in their special, individual ways have affected contemporary life.

Richard Nixon resigned as President of the United States. French President Georges Pompidou died of cancer, ending the Gaullist era. Valéry Giscard d'Estaing, the former minister of finance, was elected to the Élysée Palace. And famous figures in fields other than politics also vanished in 1974. In music, one of them was Duke Ellington, the extraordinary jazz composer and pianist, beloved the world over. In the cinema it was the death of Warsaw-born Hollywood producer Sam Goldwyn, who made some of the most quintessentially American pictures in movie history, like *The Best Years of Our Lives*. And television, and American viewers, lost Chet Huntley, who with David Brinkley had pioneered the best and most honest news coverage since the advent of the tube (and probably unequaled since).

Francisco Franco Bahamonde, the generalissimo and head of state of Spain, died the following year after thirty-six years in power—since his 1939 victory in the savage and unbelievably emotional Spanish Civil War. An aloof, solitary personage, he presided over a fascist dictatorship (though he had declared Spain to be a monarchy), but he kept Hitler out of the Iberian Peninsula during World War II (thereby helping the Allies) and quietly saved uncounted Jewish lives in Nazi-occupied Europe—and later in the Middle East.

When I arrived in Madrid in mid-1968 as *The New York Times* correspondent, Franco was celebrating his "Thirty Years of Peace," a time of recovery and modernization that allowed Spain to build up its economy and—after his death—to join the European Community and NATO. I met him only once, at a ceremonial reception at El Pardo Palace, and I had the impression I was shaking hands with a mummy. Yet he manipulated Spain and its politics until almost his last day. The final verdict about Franco will be as complex and contradictory as Spain herself, and it may be a long time before history can render it with absolute impartiality. It is probably relevant that Franco was succeeded by one of the most admirable experiences in democracy in postwar Europe, not by bloodshed and dissension, as so many had predicted. This was accomplished by the young prince, Juan Carlos, personally picked by the old generalissimo to be king.

China's Mao Zedong died in 1976.

The mid-1970's were another dividing line in postwar history. The Nixon, Pompidou, Franco, and Mao disappearances ended political periods with roots in World War II—Nixon being Eisenhower's successor, Pompidou having succeeded de Gaulle, and Franco personifying the prewar, wartime, and postwar eras.

World War II itself was formally ended—in the absence of Versailles-type peace treaties and notably in the absence of a German peace treaty—with the signing on August 1, 1975, by thirty-three European nations, the United States, and Canada of the Helsinki Final Act, which confirmed the borders drawn after 1945. The Helsinki document, signed by President Ford for the United States and General Secretary Brezhnev for the Soviet Union, was the culmination of the Conference on Security and Cooperation in Europe that was one of the outcomes of the Soviet-American détente.

For the future, Helsinki's crucial accomplishment was the so-called "Basket Three" of the agreement, the first time a collective commitment having been made for the observance of human rights. It was the beginning of the process of political relaxation in Eastern Europe and even the Soviet Union as Western governments, human rights organizations, and domestic Helsinki monitor groups (even in Moscow until Brezhnev disbanded them) could invoke the Final Act to protest violations by Communist regimes. That same year Andrei Sakharov, the Soviet physicist and father of the Soviet hydrogen bomb, was awarded the Nobel Peace Prize in recognition of his struggle for human rights as a dissident in his country. He was not allowed to go to Oslo to receive the prize; a little more than a decade later he was elected an opposition member of the new Soviet parliament under *perestroika*. When he died on December 14, 1989, at the age of sixty-eight, Gorbachev led the deputies in tribute to his memory.

In April 1975 more wars ended. The Cambodian regime of General Lon Nol, supported by the United States, was vanquished by the Communist Khmer Rouge movement when Pnom Penh fell on the sixteenth. This was five years after Lon Nol's original coup and the American incursion that followed it, enlarging the Indochina War. The Khmer Rouge rule that followed resulted in the killings of millions; in 1989 the return of the Khmer Rouge to power as part of a coalition was discussed with utter seriousness by an international conference in Paris. Some evils simply do not die.

On April 30 Saigon fell to the North Vietnamese and the Vietcong after a sudden offensive that the Americans were no longer there to deter. The U.S. ambassador and staff were evacuated aboard helicopters from the roof of the embassy to Navy warships offshore. Pictures of this evacuation illustrate the real end of the American war in Vietnam, begun in 1960 by John Kennedy and pursued by three succeeding Presidents. Apart from the "rescue" operation of the American freighter *Mayaguez* off Cambodia in mid-May, there was nothing more the United States could do in Indochina, symbolically or otherwise.

Still another war cycle ran its course on November 11, 1975, when the revolutionary government of Portugal granted independence to Angola, the richest of the old colonies. The others had been liberated the previous year. Power was assumed by the Soviet-armed Popular Movement for the Liberation of Angola (MPLA), which had defeated American-, South African-, and Chinese-backed rival guerrilla groups; in past years all of them had fought the Portuguese.

As South African military units entered southern Angola to prevent the MPLA victory, Cuban forces were airlifted to Luanda to tilt the balance in the final moments of the civil war, followed by sea transports of more troops from Cuba and war matériel from the Soviet Union.

Kissinger's instant reaction was to activate the CIA in covert operations to reopen the civil war and dislodge the MPLA and the still-limited contingents of Cuban troops. But word leaked out, and the Congress passed specific legislation barring American intelligence involvement in southern Africa; the War Powers Act barred military action. To Kissinger and others in the government, this was the first alarming manifestation of the "Vietnam syndrome," the refusal by Congress and the media (supposedly representing public opinion) to allow America to be drawn into new foreign adventures.

As for Angola, the Cuban presence was to reach fifty thousand men as part of a new war with South Africa and the UNITA guerrilla movement it sponsored, and this new war was to last nearly fifteen years. As far as Fidel Castro was concerned, Angola and then Ethiopia (where he also sent sizable military units in support of the Mengistu regime against Somalia) awarded him a preeminent position as a Third World leader. In 1979 he was chosen chairman of the nonaligned movement of nearly a hundred nations. But most Cuban troops left in 1989, under an agreement with South Africa, brokered by the United States and the Soviet Union.

The congressional ban on covert CIA operations in Angola coincided with a broader—and very critical—review of all U.S. intelligence activities. This was the first time that the sanctity of the CIA and sister intelligence agencies was violated by an open inquiry. Until then intelligence operations were free from any form of meaningful oversight although there was much public knowledge, disseminated by the press, of their activities involving Iran, Guatemala, and the Bay of Pigs.

The inquiry, which marked the end of the Cold War freedom enjoyed by the CIA, was triggered by disclosures in *The New York Times* that the agency had been involved in domestic surveillance operations against antiwar and other radical groups. Such operations are illegal under the National Security Act, which bars the CIA from any domestic projects, and President Ford appointed a commission headed by Vice President Rockefeller to look into the accusations. Soon investigators came across other undisclosed CIA operations, such as assassination attempts against Castro and other foreign leaders.

When the Rockefeller Commission completed its work, confirming most of the charges of domestic CIA operations, a Senate Select Committee on Intelligence was formed to launch a two-year across-the-board study of American intelligence operations since World War II. It was part of the new mood in the nation, one that led to a sea change in national politics.

VIII

This sea change was the 1976 election of Jimmy Carter, the former governor of Georgia (and a Naval Academy graduate who specialized in nuclear engineering), as President of the United States on the Democratic party ticket, defeating Gerald Ford.

To the extent that the decisions of the electorate can be correctly analyzed, Carter appears to have won principally because he represented a fresh beginning after the woes of Indochina and Watergate. There was no animosity against Ford—he was a well-liked man—but the nation evidently wished a break with the Nixon years. Ford, after all, had retained many top Nixon administration officials, notably Henry Kissinger, and it seemed to be time for new faces.

The one-term Carter presidency would complete the decade of the seventies amid American triumphs and defeats, notable achievements and painful failures. It was one of the great postwar paradoxes.

Carter entered the White House with an all-consuming interest in foreign affairs and a reasonable background in this field of policy. Like all postwar Presidents, regardless of their subsequent actions, he vowed to be a man of peace when he was inaugurated; by postwar standards, he did remarkably well in this endeavor notwithstanding much bad luck stacked up against him.

Carter had four major concerns in world politics. One was to preserve the détente, building on the foundations first Nixon and then Ford had erected in dealing with Brezhnev. Carter was keen on negotiating the SALT II treaty that had eluded Ford, aware that the five-year agreement covering the limitation of strategic nuclear weapons that Nixon had signed in Moscow was due to expire in 1977. During the Ford administration Washington and Moscow had signed a treaty banning underground nuclear testing of weapons above 150 kilotons (aboveground testing was banned by the 1963 Kennedy-Khrushchev pact), with the unprecedented Soviet agreement to on-site verification. The decay of the détente, however, had prevented its ratification over the fifteen years that followed. Negotiations over a pact to control chemical weapons also opened during Ford's tenure. Carter's notion was that he could advance along all these arms control fronts. But in 1976, before he was in the Oval Office, the Russians—quite surprisingly—began deploying new intermediate-range SS-20 missiles aimed at Western Europe.

The second Carter foreign affairs interest was the Middle East. Formal peace had returned to the region with Kissinger's disengagement accord in May 1974 between Israeli and Syrian forces. With the Yom Kippur War now behind all parties, Carter thought that the time had come to seek permanent peace settlements actively. This view was reinforced by the eruption of a political-religious civil war in Lebanon in 1975, nearly two years before he took office. Carter quickly realized that this little country of three million inhabitants wedged between Israel, Syria, and the Mediterranean had a potential for immense trouble.

The Lebanese Civil War broke out when the Muslim majority finally tired of the wartime arrangement, worked out by the French in 1943, which gave the Maronite Christian minority—two fifths of the population—a strong presidency. Carter remembered that an earlier Lebanese crisis, in 1958, had led to a pointless landing of American Marines, and he wanted to be especially careful about U.S. involvements there. However, Syria's President Assad, freshly humiliated by the Israelis, had no such compunctions. In 1976 he dispatched a forty-thousand-man "peacekeeping" force that went on controlling about 70 percent of Lebanese territory, including parts of the capital of Beirut, for the next fifteen years. Suleiman Franjieh, a Christian warlord, was then president of Lebanon.

Lebanon also served as refuge for thousands of Palestinian guerrillas, and the Carter administration made the correct assumption that sooner or later Israel would enter the Lebanese maelstrom to protect *its* interests. But when Carter became President in 1977, nobody could imagine that the civil war would reach such point of suicidal savagery that Beirut, once a jewel of a Mediterranean city, would become the new Stalingrad, almost leveled to the ground.

Finally, Carter accepted the idea that Palestinians could not go on being ignored by everybody forever and that some solution for them must be found in conjunction with Israel. For this view, expressed publicly, Carter was roundly condemned by Americans who thought the United States should never deal with the Palestine Liberation Organization (they were unaware that Kissinger had dispatched General Vernon Walters, then deputy CIA director, on a secret mission to meet PLO leaders in Morocco in 1973).

Carter's third interest abroad was normalizing relations with China. Since Nixon's 1972 trip and the Shanghai communiqué, the formal relationship was limited to diplomatic liaison missions in the two capitals, which complicated diplomatic and economic relations. Mao Zedong's death in September 1976 brought nearer the end of the ten-year-long Cultural Revolution and the incessant internal struggles and purges, and Carter believed that before long it would be propitious to deal with a permanent post-Mao leadership.

All these three objectives were generally consistent with American foreign policy since the start of the seventies, when the Cold War began to abate. In postwar history there has been much more true bipartisanship in foreign policy than outsiders realized; on basic issues of American interest (well or ill defined) Democratic and Republican Presidents and legislators never have had basic differences. In the case of the Indochina War, most of the opposition came from *outside* the government, until antiwar sentiment coalesced. Every President since Eisenhower had sought forms of détente with the Soviets through summits and other channels. In this sense, then, Carter was continuing, refining, and streamlining policies of the past.

The fourth area of Carter's international concerns, however, was an innovation: his energetic and determined policy of seeking and promoting the observance and enforcement of human rights everywhere in the world. Endless rhetoric notwithstanding, the United States had never before created or conducted a comprehensive human rights policy—except in denouncing the very real and enormous abuses and violations in the Communist countries. This was done before and after the Helsinki "Third Basket" agreement, and important as it was, its value lay also in anti-Communist propaganda. Massive and ever-increasing violations of human rights under right-wing dictatorships in Europe and Latin America and in the new Third World countries failed to arouse much official interest.

Postwar administrations had no time for this subject, and human rights in those days had a limited domestic constituency; only in the sixties did the United States act to protect legally the civil rights (which also are human rights) of its own citizens. As prisons filled up and tortures mounted from Argentina to Cuba and from Greece and South Africa to Syria and Iran, the tendency was to avoid antagonizing offender regimes with nit-picking about human rights. The usual excuse was that "quiet diplomacy" worked better to serve the cause of the victims than did public denunciations, a view that was absolutely untrue from what is known nowadays about the wholesale butcheries, imprisonments, and harassments of opponents of any strong-arm regime anywhere.

Interestingly, it was the Congress that opened the human rights policy door in Washington when it passed legislation during the Ford administration requesting reports on this situation in countries receiving American economic and military aid. Later the Congress enlarged this requirement to cover human rights situations everywhere in the world; American embassies now are mandated by law to report annually on the human rights situation in the countries where they are located. No other government, and not the United Nations' feeble Human Rights Commission, has ever attempted a comparable effort. When Jimmy Carter arrived on the scene, therefore, the climate already existed for a coordinated human rights policy, and the administration created the new post of assistant secretary of state for human rights.

That even generals and colonels forming part of military dictatorships will listen to human rights arguments and participate in a reasonable discussion was a discovery I made in Lima, Peru, in 1978, when I was asked by the United States Information Agency to deliver lectures on the subject in several Latin American countries. On this particular occasion I spent a week lecturing (with two American colleagues) at the Center of Superior Military Studies (CAEM), the equivalent of the National Defense University in Washington. At first I found my uniformed and bemedaled audience cold, skeptical, and possibly resentful that a gringo had the temerity to tell *them* about human rights.

At the week's end the mood had changed altogether. The officers began raising questions about the reasons for the Carter policy and human rights in the United States. I found that being truthful about problems in America is appreciated, and soon we had a Spanish rapid-fire dialogue on politics, foreign policy—and human rights. I went home with a copper ashtray with the CAEM insignia, a present from my audience; it was delivered to me over pisco sour drinks toasting the observance of human rights. I am not sure, however, my technique would have worked in Cuba, North Korea, or South Africa.

I imagine that it was the idealistic aspect of Carter's personality that inspired him to make human rights such an important priority. It was the kind of idealism that made 120,000 Americans (including Carter's mother, "Miss Lillian") serve in the Peace Corps. On the whole, however, Carter was a puzzling figure. He seemed cold and looked tight-lipped; his smiles appeared forced. He was generally ill at ease with people other than his closest personal friends (his top advisers were always kept at a distance). His attempts at a populist image—such as his decision to walk, not ride, down Pennsylvania Avenue from Capitol Hill to the White House after his inauguration—never caught on. During the campaign he presented himself as an "outsider" in terms of the Washington establishment.

In policy-making, his scientist's and professional politician's pragmatism blended well with his idealism in peacemaking and human rights. He worked extremely hard and was superbly well read and informed, and almost obsessively Carter personally looked after small White House details, such as the allocation of tennis courts. Despite so many qualities, he never infused the nation with a sense of leadership. He was neither liked nor disliked. His defeat for reelection in 1980 stemmed basically from the fact that Ronald Reagan was more likable and persuasive, not that he had a better program.

To assist and advise him on foreign policy, Carter picked Cyrus Vance, a New York lawyer with reasonable international exposure and some government experience to be secretary of state. He was a man of high integrity and limited imagination and daring who left little impact on America's foreign policy, especially following men like Acheson, Foster Dulles, and Kissinger. The national security adviser was Polish-born Zbigniew Brzezinski, who taught at Columbia University in New York and who had become a foreign policy tutor of sorts to Jimmy Carter. A very intense and rather humorless man, Brzezinski had the talent for spinning new ideas, policies, and judgments one after another—not all wholly felicitous.

Admiral Stansfield Turner, a sailor with a well-rounded intellectual background, became CIA director with the unenviable task of trimming drastically the agency's clandestine operations as a result of the continuing Senate investigations of intelligence activities. His other unenviable task was competing with Brzezinski in the interpretation of foreign intelligence, the national security adviser holding at the time firm ideas on such crucial situations as Iran and shying away from other experts' views. Carter's best Cabinet choice was secretary of defense, Dr. Harold Brown, a physicist who had served as Secretary of the Air Force and as a university president and was the possessor of one of the most interesting minds in Washington.

With this team Jimmy Carter set out in January 1977 to make the world a safer and happier place.

In fact, with Carter the United States soared beyond this world. It was during his presidency—and with his assent—that the spacecraft *Voyager 2* was launched on what became the greatest space odyssey since the moon landing. An unmanned spacecraft, *Voyager 2* soared into the sky on August 20, 1977, to pursue American spatial programs. The Skylab space station had been sent up in June 1973 as part of manned flights, but American scientists' minds were already on the outer frontiers of the solar system.

Voyager 2's objective was the planet Neptune, 4.4 billion miles away and four times bigger than the Earth. In Homer's epic poem *Odyssey* Odysseus (also known as Ulysses) wanders for ten years on his journey. The American spacecraft took *twelve* years and five days to reach Neptune (after photographing Jupiter, Saturn, and Uranus on its way through outer space), hovering at 3,000 miles over this fourth-largest planet to photograph it with its television and still cameras.

Voyager 2 arrived at its preassigned spot on August 24, 1989, *four minutes* earlier than had been predicted at the time of launch and 21 miles wide of the mark; scientists explained this "error" on astronomy's uncertainty in 1977 about where precisely Neptune was located. The spacecraft then flew at 330,000 miles over Triton, the largest of Neptune's four moons, taking more pictures and scientific data that it radioed continuously down to Earth. The ability to study pink-and-blue Triton was an unexpected bonus; it turned out to be the coldest "object" in the solar system, with icy volcanoes and lakes, and at least four active volcanoes spewing nitrogen ice and gas five miles high and ninety miles downwind.

Having explored Neptune and Triton from above (and discovering Neptune's moons and rings), *Voyager* 2 hurtled at its cruising speed of thirty-eight thousand miles per hour on its way out of the solar system, the second man-made object to try to penetrate interstellar space, *Voyager* 1 having been sent up earlier to Jupiter. *Pioneer 10* and *Pioneer 11* were launched in the early seventies, and they are probably approaching the boundary of the solar system. Actually nobody knows where this boundary is located; it could be between five and fourteen billion miles from Earth.

The one-ton *Voyager* 2 has a plutonium-powered electrical generator, and it may travel forever—even after its fuel is spent in twenty-five years. The solar system's boundary is known as the heliopause, and scientists at the Jet Propulsion Laboratory in Pasadena, California, thought that *Voyager* 2 might reach it in the year 2012, when radio transmissions will most likely end. Then, scientists explained, it will soar past Pluto, the outermost planet, fly through the Milky Way, passing Barnard's Star in 6,500 years, Proxima Centauri star 11,500 years later, and possibly arriving near Sirius in the year 296036—this will be roughly two thousand centuries from now. Because scientists do not like to be unprepared, they have outfitted *Voyager* 2 with records of earthly music—from Beethoven and Bach to American rock 'n' roll—in case the spacecraft encounters an intelligent civilization. Saluting *Voyager* 2 as it vanished past Neptune and Triton, Dr. Edward C. Stone, who heads the project, quoted from T. S. Eliot: "Not fare well, /But fare forward, voyagers."

The extraordinary thing about *Voyager* 2 was that it has been functioning on the basis of the technology of the 1960's. Its radio has only twenty watts of power, and the images it sends are encoded into binary numbers by on-board computers and then reconstituted by computers in Pasadena. Scientists had high hopes for *Voyager* 2, but the Neptune-Triton harvest exceeded their wildest dreams. In terms of scientific achievement, the flight was considered the most significant in the thirty-two-year history of space exploration, providing astounding new data about the solar system and its history. The 1969 moon landing was spectacular, but it added relatively little to the sum of human scientific knowledge. *Voyager* 2 opened totally new horizons, including the discovery from radioed images that Neptune is swept by 1,500 mile-an-hour winds, the fastest known in the solar system.

Carl Sagan, the astronomer, wrote after examining the *Voyager 2* pictures that what has already been learned about Triton seems to make "very clear that we see a record of changes occurring on time scales between centuries and billions of years, and possible clues to the origin of life on Earth." Sagan also concluded that "the Voyagers . . . have found evidence of the first stirrings and intimations of life—a rich and diverse organic chemistry, but not life itself." He went on to point out that the spacecrafts found that "Saturn's clouded moon Titan is generating in its atmosphere complex organic molecules, which give Titan its reddish-brown color. The molecules rain down on the ground, where a layer of organic sediment hundreds of feet thick or more may be covering the ground. There may be an ocean of liquid hydrocarbons."

For the United States, it was the event that finally began to erase the memories of the space shuttle *Challenger*, which exploded after launch in January 1986, killing its crew of seven (at that moment *Voyager 2* was nearing Uranus). There were successful shuttle flights when the manned program was resumed in 1989, but it was *Voyager 2* that earned the recognition of American scientific genius. And, not to be forgotten, this spacecraft, too, was a descendant of World War II's primitive rocketry.

John Kennedy did not live to see the moon landing that he had promised his fellow citizens. Jimmy Carter had the quiet satisfaction of seeing the success of *Voyager 2*, launched during his watch.

Problem solving in the international arena was a Carter passion, if this term can be used, and the first one he addressed was the question of the Panama Canal, long a bone of contention between Panama and the United States and increasingly a theme of Latin American pressures. Panama, pure and simple, wished the Americans out of the Canal Zone while the United States, invoking security reasons, for decades refused to entertain this notion.

The Canal between the Atlantic and the Pacific was built by the United States in the expansive "Manifest Destiny" days of Theodore Roosevelt across the narrow isthmus linking Central and South America. In order to build the Canal and maintain indefinite control over it, the United States detached the province of Panama from Colombia in 1902, creating an "independent" republic from it. A 1903 treaty vested in the United States the jurisdiction over the 552-square-mile Canal Zone and its inhabitants; in time the "Zonians," mainly American citizens, totaled forty thousand, living in the comfort of their enclave. American troops were stationed in the zone to protect the canal.

During World War II the Canal was vital for U.S. troop movement between the two oceans, and the security concern continued in the postwar years. The seizure of the Canal by Communists (Russians or Cubans) or its blockage became a nightmare for Pentagon planners as the Cold War developed—especially after Castro seized power in nearby Cuba—and Washington turned a deaf ear to Panamanian demands for revising the Canal treaties. By the 1960's, however, pressures had begun to rise dangerously as anti-American sentiment and riots developed, and it began to dawn on the United States that if some concessions were not made, the Canal could become endangered from within Panama.

President Johnson opened negotiations with Panama in 1965, but no serious progress was made over the ensuing decade. Sensitive to Panamanian and Latin American feelings and unwilling to see the United States practice colonialism of sorts in the Canal Zone, Carter started new talks almost immediately after taking office. Panama's strongman General Omar Torrijos Herrera was a reasonable negotiator, and a new treaty was signed on September 7, 1977, in a remarkably short period of negotiations. It provided for the end of U.S. jurisdiction over the Canal Zone (which was formally incorporated into Panama two years later), the transfer of the Canal itself to Panama on the last day of 1999, and the withdrawal of all American armed forces. However, the United States was granted the "perpetual right" to defend the Canal's neutrality.

It cost the Carter administration an immense effort to obtain Senate ratification of the treaty; critics saw it as the crumbling of American defenses in the Western Hemisphere, concessions to communism, and the betrayal of the rights of the American Zonians, many of whom were third-generation inhabitants of the area. Finally, the Senate gave the treaty its consent in 1978, by the required two thirds majority, with one vote to spare. The treaty went far to improve the image of the United States throughout Latin America.

Carter's next venture into problem solving and peacemaking was centered on the Middle East. But it took amazing initiatives in that region by the parties themselves to create the conditions that allowed the United States to contribute its mediatory efforts. And it was a scenario that defied all imagination.

It started, absolutely improbably, with the victory of the right-wing Likud party in national elections in Israel in May 1977. Likud's leader, Menachem Begin, became prime minister with the religious parties backing him as well. Begin, who was born in Poland and emigrated to Palestine, where he joined anti-British terrorist organizations, represented the antithesis of any peace settlement with the Arabs, other than by their acceptance of the territorial status quo, which they would never do.

This was a time in Israel when, as Abba Eban has written, "there had been a sharp swing toward political militance and social conservatism," and now the Likud leadership was bringing "overtones of religious dogmatism and rigidity on territorial issues." Begin, indeed, was riding a wave of nationalism and rightist populism, with his electorate composed largely of Sephardic Jews from North Africa and the Middle East rather than Israelis of Eastern European descent—more sophisticated and conciliatory—as the Labor party had been during its nearly thirty years in power.

Begin personally was inflexible about Greater Israel, the country inside the enlarged 1967 boundaries. He spoke prophetlike of the West Bank as the Judea and Samaria of biblical times, organically part of Israel. Together with the Likud, he wholeheartedly and emotionally supported religious organizations like Gush Emunim, whose members fought the army in the mid-seventies for the right to build settlements on the West Bank in defiance of official policy. Driving near Ramallah on the West Bank one day in the autumn of 1974, I was stunned to see young Israeli soldiers use physical force against other Israelis, many of them just as young, who had gathered in that spot to start erecting a village. Thus, with Begin in power, the possibility of any settlement in the Middle East seemed to be out of the question.

Watching Begin's ascent to power in Jerusalem was Anwar al-Sadat in Cairo. The Egyptian president, too, was a man of strong convictions, having launched the Yom Kippur War three years earlier to assert the Arab pride and irredentism. In Washington, the assumption was that Begin and Sadat would never find common ground. Yet Sadat was a surprising statesman, with a long-range view of events and history. Henry Kissinger was right in claiming that Sadat had gone to war in 1973 to defend Arab prestige; though Egypt lost the war, Israel had first come to the edge of defeat and suffered huge losses in men and equipment in fighting the Egyptians. The Egyptian Army had performed better than ever before, and Sadat, a military man as well as a politician, had made his philosophical point. From there on everything made sense, if one stopped to ponder.

At the end of October, five months after Begin's election, Sadat stood before the National Assembly in Cairo to announce that he was ready to travel to Jerusalem to meet with Begin and join him in a search for peace. This was an absolutely electrifying moment. As soon as Begin digested the incredible news, he responded in kind, likewise surprising the world, by inviting Sadat to come. On November 9, 1977, Sadat was the first Arab chief of state to set foot on the territory of the state of Israel; on December 9 Begin returned the visit, going to Sadat's villa in Ismailia and becoming the first Israeli chief of government to be received in an Arab country. For his temerity (some said betrayal), Sadat was read out of the Arab community. Most Arab governments broke diplomatic relations with Egypt; it was also suspended from the Arab league. But the Sadat-Begin dialogues planted not only seeds of peace but ideas in Carter's mind how to go about helping this incipient process. In February 1978, for example, Carter visited Sadat in Aswan (he was on his way to Paris) to sound him out.

A half year of preparations and secret three-way communications preceded the arrival in Washington in September 1978 of the Egyptian and Israeli leaders to negotiate Middle Eastern peace under U.S. auspices. To assure quiet and isolation, Carter took Sadat and Begin on September 5 to Camp David, twenty minutes away from Washington by helicopter, installing them and their advisers in comfortable cabins. The talks were held in the presidential lodge.

There was a particularly mysterious element in the secret dealings between Carter and Sadat that may have influenced the Egyptian president's actions toward the peace process. In his memoirs former French President Giscard d'Estaing has described a dinner conversation with Sadat at the Élysée Palace in Paris on February 12, 1977, during which Sadat had strongly hinted that he had considered military action to overthrow Qaddafi in Libya. Both Egypt and France regarded Qaddafi with enormous disgust, Egypt because the Libyan accused Sadat of being an American "tool" (and he probably plotted against Sadat) and France because of his continuing efforts to take over Chad, the neighboring desert republic that the French regarded as their domain and where they kept sending arms and troops to defend the local regime.

Giscard, as he told the story, strongly urged Sadat to act against Qaddafi, but the Egyptian said he could not make a decision until the end of the following month. In March, however, an Egyptian helicopter crashed near the Libyan border, killing several high-ranking Egyptian army officers. Giscard writes: "I understood that they constituted the staff to whom Sadat had entrusted the preparations of the operation" against Qaddafi. When Sadat next visited Giscard on July 24, he told him that "concerning the operation I was planning for March, the Americans intervened to demand insistently that I renounce it." According to Giscard, Sadat did not explain what the American intervention meant. But Carter was already busy planning his Middle East peacemaking, Menachem Begin had been elected, and Washington may have wished to avoid additional turmoil in the region.

In any event, Carter was able to produce an Egyptian-Israeli framework peace agreement on September 17, 1978, after exceedingly difficult negotiations that lasted twelve days and nights and often came to the brink of collapse. It provided for the return to Egypt of the Sinai Peninsula (with its oilfields), which Israel had captured in the 1967 war, the stationing of United Nations forces near the new border areas, and the guarantee of freedom of navigation for Israeli shipping in the Red Sea and the Gulf of Aqaba. Full diplomatic relations would be established, and Egypt would refrain from economic boycott against Israel.

A separate agreement set forth the foundations for a comprehensive Middle Eastern peace settlement through the conclusion of peace treaties between Israel and the other Arab countries. It proposed that Egypt, Israel, Jordan, and the "representations of the Palestinian people" should negotiate the resolution of all the aspects of the Palestine problem, with transitional arrangements for the West Bank and Gaza for the election of self-governing authorities. Israeli military forces would be withdrawn from these two areas after the elections, which, according to the document, should occur within five years. Finally, negotiations would be conducted to work out the "final status" of these territories.

The Camp David agreement was a fabulous coup and diplomatic triumph for Sadat and Begin as well as for Jimmy Carter. This was the first peace treaty between Israel and an Arab nation in the thirty years of the existence of the Jewish state. And it pointed the way toward a comprehensive Palestinian settlement, which had eluded all parties since 1948 and through four successive wars and generations of suffering on both sides. The documents were signed by the three men (Carter signing as witness) at a White House ceremony, rich in smiles, warm feeling, and hope. Sadat and Begin were awarded jointly the Nobel Peace Prize that same year by the fast-moving committee of the Norwegian parliament. Egypt and Israel signed the actual peace treaty in Washington on March 26, 1979, but Carter had to rush to Cairo, to Jerusalem, and back to Cairo in early March to prevent a last-minute breakdown. Jews who had left Egypt in 1948 were allowed to return freely.

It was a spectacular first step toward peace in the tortured Middle East. Then there would be frustration, violence, and death again.

In 1978, as world peace looked more promising than at any time since the Second World War had ended, the mood in America was optimistic and upbeat. Inflation was mounting, but employment remained plentiful, and only a few Cassandras warned of an approaching recession. There was hope even in the inner cities as fresh social programs were inaugurated. For the young, there was excitement in music and sports.

The new popular idol was twenty-four-year-old John Travolta. Since his *Saturday Night Fever* appeared on the nation's screens in December 1977, he became the hottest new movie star of the seventies. Elvis Presley had died earlier that year, and Travolta, the king of disco, was the pop culture icon. He graced the cover of *Time* in April 1978, and he dined with the Carters at the White House in October. His first picture had grossed $350 million. The album of the sound track had sales of twenty-five million, seemingly one album for each American in nine. His second picture— *Grease*—grossed $400 million as the most profitable movie musical ever.

Travolta was living proof that when you make it in America, you make it big, very big—from the millions in earnings to sharing dinner with the President of the United States. Before a decade elapsed, Travolta became proof that in America you can be forgotten just as rapidly. The early eighties would be the time of Michael Jackson, then Madonna, then . . .

There was new talent, too, on America's tennis courts—always a matter of great interest and curiosity. Tennis bred its own national idols. In the seventies some of the best fresh talent came from Europe, from Communist Czechoslovakia, of all places. Martina Navratilova, who came to the United States in 1973 at the age of sixteen, quickly became a star. So did her fellow Czech Ivan Lendl. They remained champions throughout the eighties. America's Chris Evert, sixteen in 1971, was Navratilova's top rival; she won 157 tournaments in her career, a world record. On the gridiron, the new celebrity was O.J. ("Orange Juice") Simpson, and the Washington Redskins were the team to watch.

*   *   *

In 1979 dark clouds were gathering once more over the world, and President Carter began living from problem to problem, from crisis to crisis.

The first bad news actually appeared during 1978, when Carter was concentrating on Middle East diplomacy. Hardly any attention was paid in Washington, for example, when President Mohammad Daud Khan of Afghanistan was dislodged by a military coup d'état on April 27, 1978. The new ruler was the secretary-general of the Afghan Communist party, Noor Mohammad Taraki, but neither the White House nor the State Department seemed particularly exercised by this event. Afghanistan was too remote; very little was known about it. "Your government is making a very serious mistake ignoring what is happening in Afghanistan," the Pakistani ambassador, Sahabzada Yaqub Khan, said to me at lunch in Washington several days later. He went on to explain that Taraki was Moscow's man, adding, "if you don't watch out, you will lose Afghanistan, which is very strategic." Yaqub was a former army general, and Pakistan had excellent intelligence about Afghanistan. He turned out to be right, of course, a fact he modestly mentioned in passing when he became Pakistani foreign minister a few years later.

Also during 1978, danger signs were discernible elsewhere across the Third World, each situation portending serious trouble: South Africa, the Horn of Africa, Nicaragua, El Salvador, and Iran. Preoccupied with the Middle East, busy with SALT II negotiations with the Soviet Union, and normalization with China, and distracted by the reorganization of the U.S. intelligence community, the principal foreign policy planners in the Carter administration simply had neither time nor desire to think very deeply about all these Third World side issues.

South Africa, of course, had been festering for a very long time. In 1960 the first massive antiapartheid demonstration occurred in the black township of Sharpeville; many were killed by white security forces. This was during the Eisenhower administration, which had no definable policy toward South Africa and its racist posture. The South African regime was regarded as a stout ally in the anti-Communist struggle as fears arose over Soviet infiltrations into southern Africa. Under Kennedy the United States helped win votes for a United Nations arms sales embargo against Pretoria, but it was rather ineffective.

Under Nixon, U.S. policy was one of neglect, not even benign—just simply indifference. Kissinger and the British were active in defusing the threat of civil war in Southern Rhodesia, subsequently to gain full independence as the republic of Zimbabwe, but when it came to South Africa, U.S. policy was based on a National Security Council finding that the five million whites would be indefinitely in control of South Africa's twenty-three million nonwhites. (This policy was known as "Tar Baby" among administration officials) and it proclaimed that "a selective relaxation of our stance toward the white regimes . . . can encourage some modification of their current racial and colonial policies."

In mid-1976, a half year before Carter assumed office, ten thousand demonstrators marched in protest against apartheid in the huge black township of Soweto, outside Johannesburg. It was the biggest demonstration since Sharpeville, launching the new wave of militant opposition to apartheid. The Ford administration lamented that the police had brutally dispersed the crowd but did nothing more. With Carter in the White House, domestic pressures mounted for a sterner policy against South African racism, but again there was no sense of urgency about it. When I met black protest leaders in Soweto in 1984, I was asked why the Carter administration had seemed to care so little about racial oppression in South Africa despite its official human rights policy.

In the Horn of Africa Ethiopia and Somalia were at war, ostensibly over the possession of the empty vastness of the Ogaden Desert, which occupies most of eastern Ethiopia and to which the Somalis had historic claims. Actually it was much more of a political and ideological war. In one of those bizarre reversals of allegiances that occasionally occur in the Third World, Ethiopia and Somalia switched sides in terms of the broad East-West alignments.

Prior to the Marxist officers' coup in 1974, Ethiopia was closely allied with the United States (which maintained vitally important intelligence communications intercept facilities in Ethiopian mountains) while Somalia was virtually a Soviet client state, with Soviet naval installations on its coast. After the coup the new Ethiopian regime established intimate relations with Moscow, which evidently judged that Ethiopia, a major African power on the Red Sea and with strategic frontiers with Sudan and Kenya, was a more valuable asset than primitive Somalia. Somali President Major General Muhammad Siad Barre, the head of the Somali Revolutionary Socialist party (but clearly no ideologue), reacted by going over to the American side, particularly after being assured of economic and military aid.

It is unclear how the Ogaden war started late in 1977, but it became vicious and savage during 1978, and the Carter administration decided that the Soviets were behind it in an attempt to control all of the Horn of Africa, Ethiopia's Red Sea coast in the north and Somalia's Indian Ocean coast in the south. With modern Soviet equipment being airlifted into Ethiopia and thousands of Cubans in combat units fighting in the Ogaden Desert and flying the MiG jets, the United States concluded that it was facing a strategic challenge from the Soviet Union.

Matters reached the point where National Security Adviser Brzezinski warned Moscow that SALT II negotiations would be suspended until the Soviets abandoned their involvement in the Horn region. Brzezinski noted in a memorandum to Carter that the Russians sought "a selective détente." It was a period of sudden Soviet-American tension; but after a while the administration reconsidered its position, and the strategic talks were resumed even though the Cubans kept fighting in the Ogaden and the desert war went on.

In 1979 another war erupted in the same region, this time between Marxist-led North Yemen (where the Soviets had a naval base in Aden) and Saudi-supported South Yemen, both on the Arabian Peninsula, east of the Red Sea. This war—inconclusive—did not spill over into East-West relations, but it underscored the permanent warmaking potential in the huge arc stretching from East Africa to the Persian Gulf, a point the United States understood well as it proceeded with the expansion of its air and naval base on Britain's Diego Garcia Island in the Indian Ocean.

A situation to which the Carter administration paid absolutely no high-level attention in 1978 was the spreading civil war in Nicaragua, the Central American republic whose attitudes and travails were to haunt the United States for the whole decade of the eighties. The administration's failure to act intelligently—or to act at all—while the national uprising against General Anastasio Somoza Debayle was in progress and the United States still could influence future events stands out as a classic example of mismanaging foreign policy. The sad story of Nicaragua also serves as a reminder that the United States should *never* take for granted Latin America and its problems and that historically it seems condemned to keep repeating the same errors of judgment and response. The pattern over this whole century has been to ignore Latin America, be caught by surprise and indignation when events damaging to the United States suddenly happen (or the *Yankees* realize that something has happened), react through attempted subornation or covert actions, and, in final despair, engage in direct intervention.

In Nicaragua's case the first American intervention occurred with the landing of the U.S. Marines in 1912; they remained until 1925, turning the little republic into a U.S. fief. They were back a year later, when things appeared to be getting out of hand; this time they stayed until 1933. During the occupation the Marine Corps organized a National Guard, and the original Anastasio Somoza, a professional military man, was named to command it; he started the Somoza dynasty. In 1934 the Guard killed General Augusto César Sandino, a guerrilla leader who fought for years against the Marine Corps and Somoza's National Guard. The Sandinista movement, which launched the anti-Somoza revolution and has held power in Nicaragua since 1979, until its electoral defeat in February 1990, is named after Sandino.

After World War II no U.S. administration attempted to impress the ruling Somoza family with the virtues of democracy. Along with the rest of Central America (except for Costa Rica, which in 1948 *did* create a lasting democracy at home), Nicaragua was a safe and friendly dictatorship. The American ambassador in the 1950's was a poker crony of Luis Somoza, the second Somoza president. The third Somoza (Luis's brother) was a West Point graduate; he was known as Tacho. In 1961 the CIA used the Nicaraguan port of Puerto Cabezas to embark aboard ships the Cuban exiles' brigade destined for the Bay of Pigs. In December 1972 a powerful earthquake destroyed much of Managua, the capital. President Tacho Somoza succeeded in diverting American assistance away from the population; the fortunes of the Somoza family and their friends kept augmenting.

The Nixon administration was prepared to lend economic aid to the earthquake-ravaged country, but it had no interest in Nicaraguan politics. Nor was it particularly aware that a revolutionary organization had been formed by a group of young Nicaraguans in the mid-sixties to seek Somoza's ouster; they named it the Sandinista Front of National Liberation (FSLN). Carlos Fonseca Amador and Tomás Borge were among the principal founders. By the mid-seventies the anti-Somoza movement had spread to professionals, businessmen, and intellectuals (Rubén Darío, one of Latin America's most famous poets, came from Nicaragua's rich cultural tradition). Somoza and the National Guard reacted with brutal repression, and Fonesca Amador was killed by the *Guardia* in November 1976, along with a number of his associates.

Thus, when Carter became President two months later, the Sandinista rebellion, running parallel with active anti-Somoza efforts by the Nicaraguan middle class, was in full swing. Somehow it did not evoke any special interest at the White House. There Cuba was the only Latin American situation that commanded the attention of National Security Adviser Brzezinski—and only in the East-West context. In his book *Power and Principle* Brzezinski relates his concerns (and his advice to Carter) over the Cuban involvement in Ethiopia and Angola and the reported presence of new Soviet MiG-23's and of a Soviet combat brigade in Cuba. Though the book was written after the Sandinistas won the revolution in 1979, the word "Nicaragua" appears only three times in the text; writing about events late in 1978, Brzezinski remarks, in passing, that "the crisis in Nicaragua was beginning to preoccupy and absorb us," but he does not explain how or why.

At that point the United States should have been very deeply involved in monitoring the Nicaraguan Revolution, much beyond the very limited interest conveyed by that sentence in Brzezinski's book. Managua was in the midst of urban guerrilla warfare during the summer, and men and women were killed every day in rebel confrontations with the National Guard and the secret police. For reasons that totally escape comprehension, Carter chose that moment to praise Somoza for improving his human rights record, a remark that was guaranteed to magnify the Nicaraguans' latent resentments against the United States.

The Sandinistas showed their mettle on August 22, 1978, when a handful of rebels led by Edén Pastora, a guerrilla leader known as Comandante Cero (Zero), captured Managua's National Palace, where the rubber-stamp National Assembly was in session, making into hostages several hundred top officials, including sixty deputies, several ministers, and Somoza's relatives. Pastora and his team held the palace for two days. Then the regime agreed to their demands: the liberation from prison of the FSLN's cofounder Tomás Borge (who had spent eight years in a tiny cell, hooded much of the time) and eighty-two other rebels, five million dollars in cash, and the publication of the front's statement denouncing the dictatorship and giving the reasons for the attack on the palace.

On August 24 a Panamanian Air Force plane few the Sandinistas to Panama, where General Torrijos gave them comfortable shelter in the barracks of his National Guard on the outskirts of the capital. Torrijos had been supporting the Nicaraguan rebels from the beginning, and now he was ready to help the team resume combat after a short rest as his guests. In the meantime, Torrijos arranged for me to meet the Sandinista leaders the afternoon after their arrival in Panama. I happened to be in Panama when the Nicaraguan palace coup occurred, and I had asked Torrijos what were my chances for a "first" interview. The general told me to be at the Guard barracks the following day. The first writer to see the Sandinistas was my friend Gabriel García Márquez; I was the second.

Borge, then already in his fifties and a Marxist with considerable intellectual credentials, was the most impressive in the group (the others were Cero, a young woman guerrilla, and a young guerrilla commander), outlining calmly the FSLN's revolutionary program. My interview with them was published in the Sunday editions of the Washington Post (I had become by then an independent writer), but I was astounded at the lack of interest in the Sandinistas on the part of my friends in the Carter administration. I felt strongly that the administration should learn more about them, but my offer of a loan of my tape recording of the interview was politely declined. A young National Security Council official listened skeptically to my comments about the importance of the Sandinistas and had nothing to say when I suggested that the administration should establish discreet contacts with them. Later I discovered that in a follow-up to my recommendation, Edén Pastora (Commander Zero) had been approached by the CIA deputy station chief in Honduras. Pastora told me that he refused the meeting "because I don't discuss politics with policemen."

By 1979 the civil war in Nicaragua had turned into something resembling a conventional warfare as rebel units (with arms from Cuba, Panama, and Venezuela) fought the National Guard for the control of provincial towns. Latin American sympathies were firmly on the rebels' side, but only on February 8 did Washington halt economic and military aid to Somoza. In Latin American terms, continuing support of a dictatorship is often seen as intervention in its favor, and that was how American actions were perceived. When Secretary of State Vance proposed late in June an inter-American peacekeeping force for Nicaragua to halt the civil war, the Latin Americans turned it down; the majority now demanded Somoza's resignation. And State Department officials who had long urged an open anti-Somoza stance by the United States (this would be an acceptable form of intervention in Latin American legal minds) were chastised by their superiors.

On July 19, 1979, it was all over: Somoza fled, and the Sandinistas took over Managua and Nicaragua. Their ideological anti-American sentiments were now reinforced by the behavior of the United States during the Revolution. Whatever the winners might have done in any case, they should not have been given an excuse by the Carter administration for their hard-line policies.

Ex post facto, the Carter people have invoked their overwhelming preoccupation with the simultaneously unfolding revolution in Iran to justify the lack of attention for Nicaragua (and for El Salvador, where a civil war also was getting under way). So incredibly that even political science-fiction writers could not have imagined it, Nicaragua and Iran merged before too long into a single scandal that seared American foreign policy as few scandals had done before.

President and Mrs. Carter spent New Year's Eve, December 31, 1977, in Teheran with the shah of Iran and his empress. The Carters had visited Warsaw after Christmas, and they decided to take up the shah, that close ally of the United States, on his invitation to come to the capital of ancient Persia. The shah had traveled to Washington in November 1977 for policy discussions with the President, and they had agreed on a social get-together for the following month in Teheran since the Carters were going abroad anyway.

It may strain credulity, but as they clicked champagne glasses at midnight in the Imperial Palace, Carter appeared to have no inkling that a frightful crisis was brewing in Iran behind the bland facade of official smiles and mutual congratulations. Brzezinski was absolutely right when he wrote in his White House memoirs that "Iran was the Carter Administration's greatest setback." Though history might well have taken the course we have seen regardless of American policies, the fact remains that the Carter administration was the victim of first a colossal intelligence failure (notwithstanding that former CIA Director Richard Helms was U.S. ambassador in Teheran in 1977 and early in 1978, when the anti-shah revolution was inexorably taking shape) and then a policy management disaster.

The intelligence failure stemmed from the administration's bizarre policy of deliberately depriving itself of direct acquisition of intelligence in Iran in order to please the shah. This policy had actually gone into effect during the Nixon administration, when the shah requested the United States to refrain from political contacts with the opposition in the country. The SAVAK, his secret police, the shah said at the time, was magnificently equipped to keep the Americans informed, and it would be unfriendly to go behind its back in quest of political information. The American Embassy and the CIA station were therefore paralyzed when it came to intelligence gathering, a situation verging on the grotesque. Moreover, only very few embassy and CIA officers at the Teheran Embassy, understood, read or spoke Farsi, the language of Iran.

That the shah chose to keep himself and his American friends insulated from political reality is probably best explained by National Security Adviser Brzezinski, who had dealt with him and subsequently tried to save him. Brzezinski remarks in his book that the shah "displayed megalomaniacal tendencies" and that he "clearly seemed to enjoy being a traditional Oriental despot, accustomed to instant and total obedience from his courtiers." It is harder to understand, however, the willingness of the United States to act as a courtier to the shah, showing him, in effect, such instant and total obedience. It also calls into question, if Brzezinski really felt that way in those days, the wisdom of the administration's attitude in trusting the shah and his judgment of Iranian affairs.

Yet this was one more instance in which a Third World country had the power and the leverage to influence American decisions and policies. The shah never let Americans forget—he communicated his views in a pleasant, courteous fashion—that Iran had *not* joined the Arab oil embargo, that some of the most sensitive U.S. intelligence facilities monitoring Soviet nuclear strategic missile deployments were in Iranian mountains, that he had been guaranteeing stability in the Persian Gulf since the British departed almost a decade ago, and, finally, that he was a leading customer of the U.S. defense industry. The saying in the Pentagon at the time was that "What the shah wants, the shah gets," and Brzezinski acknowledges that the Carter administration had approved "major sales of arms" to Iran during 1978 (when the rot was spreading in the regime's foundations), along with admonitions for "more rapid progress toward constitutional rule." The shah, of course, had already made it clear that he was not interested in American meddling in Persian politics.

In mid-1978 French intelligence began to warn the United States against taking too lightly Ayatollah Ruhollah Khomeini, the Muslim fundamentalist leader who had recently moved from twelve years of exile in Iraq to a house in the environs of Paris, from which he was directing the anti-shah revolutionary activities at home. My French friends, puzzled over the apparent lack of American interest in Iranian events, told me the same thing. It was the shah who had exiled Khomeini to Iraq to punish him for his thunderous denunciations of the ways in which Iran was being modernized (he was appalled by the immorality of the ruling classes, women's uncovered faces, the drinking of scotch and cognac, and rock music), and the bearded mullah had sworn revenge.

I had been tipped off by a friend that the CIA had obtained and translated into English a collection of the ayatollah's speeches and sermons from his days in Iraq, offering a reasonably complete outline of his plans to oust the emperor he so hated, an Islamic *Mein Kampf*. It took no more than a telephone call to the CIA's technical translations section (it has an innocuous-sounding official name) in suburban Washington to obtain a copy; I wondered whether any policymaker had taken the time to read it (or knew it existed).

Even as late as October 1978 the American Embassy in Iran was reporting that the shah had the situation in hand, that he could "restrain" the military and that he was flexible enough to accept a transition to "a truly democratic regime." William Sullivan, the career ambassador who had replaced Helms, was opposed to any dealings with Khomeini although the ayatollah was flooding Iran with cassettes of his speeches and was developing a vast following. It is not easy to reconstruct how the Carter administration handled the shah and his crisis; the great tragedy is that it could never get its act together. Brzezinski and his staff had one set of analyses, while Secretary of State Vance and his specialists had another, as did Ambassador Sullivan, the CIA headquarters in Langley, Virginia, and its Teheran station, the civilians and the military at the Pentagon, and the defense attachés in the Iranian capital.

It would be pointless to try to match all those contradictory and backbiting accounts, many of them already in public print, but what the shah thought during those dramatic days about American behavior and varying pieces of advice is relevant. Perhaps as illuminating as any American account (and less self-serving) was the confidential report to French President Giscard d'Estaing by Interior Minister Michel Poniatowski, who was dispatched immediately after Christmas 1978 on a personal mission to the shah. Poniatowski first described what he called a virtual "state of siege" in Teheran, the riots, the battles between the opposition and the army, the absence of gasoline, heating and cooking gas, and electricity (cut everywhere except at hospitals and the French Embassy).

Writing on his return to Paris on December 29, 1978, Poniatowski recounts his lengthy meeting with the shah, who complained that "I am almost alone . . . I have been abandoned by many [friends]" and wondered aloud whether there was "a Western plot against me . . . [whether] it has been decided to abandon me?" Sad and exhausted, the shah told the French minister that "most dangerous are these ambiguities that conceal a decision that [they] dare not confess to me." Though Ambassador Sullivan and the British ambassador saw him almost every day, the shah no longer trusted his allies, saying to Poniatowski that "the Americans tell me that they will support me to the end, but I know that some of them already have serious hesitations."

This was the shah's own analysis, as expressed to Poniatowski, of the causes of the revolution he was facing: "An excessively rapid modernization: Iran was not ready to absorb an accelerated Westernization and a lay policy. . . . A strong religious renaissance that allowed the long conflict that has existed for 50 years between the Shiite clergy and our dynasty to turn into a test of strength. . . . External influences: certainly Russian ones but limited, Libyan ones when it came to the financing, and American ones when it came to the mishandling. . . ."

On January 16, 1979, three weeks after he had described his dilemma to the French envoy (and slightly over a year after he had drunk New Year's toasts with Jimmy Carter), the shah and his family fled Teheran for exile in Cairo as the imperial regime finally collapsed. The armed forces no longer were willing to support him against an aroused nation and to execute a bloodbath. The Americans ran out of ideas for the shah, to the extent that they had any useful ones in the first place (the use of the army to crush the revolution was suggested from the White House, but the shah himself refused to order it).

At the end of January the ayatollah arrived triumphantly in Teheran aboard an Air France jet airliner. Though the government was still in the hands of moderate civilians, Khomeini instantly began to erect a theocratic state in Iran. The monarchic system was transformed into an Islamic republic. The fall of the shah was the end of another postwar period and the start of a new one.

Parallel with his concerns over Middle East peacemaking and the revolution in Iran, Carter concentrated on strengthening relations with the principal Communist nations.

He had believed from the time he entered the White House that America's relations with China should be normalized. The system of liaison missions in the two capitals, established by Nixon and Mao in 1972, no longer met the requirements of the late seventies. The scope of diplomatic and trade activity between China and the United States demanded a more satisfactory relationship, and much of 1978 was spent in quiet diplomacy, mainly by Brzezinski, to remove the obstacles to it.

The question of Taiwan was still unresolved. Under the Nixon-Mao formula, the disposition of the island was left to the Chinese themselves, but six years later the two sets of Chinese had not come up with solutions (and they were not looking for them very hard). When the question of upgrading the relationship between Beijing and Washington came up in 1977 and 1978, Deng Xiaoping, the post-Mao leader in Beijing, made an issue of the continued sale of arms to Taiwan. Carter took the position that the sales were an American commitment, a matter of principle, and they would continue until the Chinese had decided what they wished done about the island they all claimed was part of China. Besides, the administration argued, these arms were no threat to the mainland; the Taiwanese obviously had no means of attacking China and certainly no desire; they were too busy getting rich as the latest Asian newly industrialized "tiger" country.

In the end Deng compromised. On December 15, 1978, Carter went on national television to announce the establishment of full diplomatic relations between China and the United States, thirty years after they had been broken as a result of the Communist victory. Late in January 1979 Deng arrived in Washington on his first visit to the United States. First, Brzezinski entertained him at dinner at his suburban home, toasting the Chinese visitor in Soviet vodka that (Brzezinski recounts) had been sent by the Soviet Embassy. Then Carter offered a state dinner at the White House, making a point of inviting former President Nixon in recognition of his 1972 breakthrough in Beijing. This was the first time Nixon had set foot at the White House since his resignation four and a half years earlier.

Deng was a fascinating visitor. He was interested in modernizing China in every possible way. He had just launched a far-reaching agricultural reform, making Chinese peasants, in effect, landowners, free to sell their products on the open market while paying only nominal rent to the state for the land they tilled. When I toured western China six years after the Deng reform, the most impressive sights were smiling farmers building new, comfortable houses and the abundance of food in shops and open-air markets. Having just completed long visits to Poland and Cuba, I found this a startling socialist contrast.

Deng's other interest was in purchasing advanced American weapons, an idea to which the Carter administration was less than receptive—especially after a quarter million Chinese troops invaded Vietnam on February 17, 1979, two weeks after Deng's Washington visit. It was an obscure war in terms of motivations, but casualties were high on both sides before the Chinese withdrew a month later. Subsequently China became a buyer of American arms, and an active relationship developed between the general staffs of the two countries.

With the Soviet Union, Carter negotiated the SALT II treaty covering offensive strategic weapons. He flew to Vienna on June 15 for three days of meetings with Brezhnev (this was their first summit though Carter had already been in office two and a half years) and for the signing of the SALT pact, after which two men exchanged kisses on both cheeks. In their discussions Brezhnev complained about China, and Carter about Soviet-Cuban conspiracies around the world. The Americans came home with the impression that Brezhnev had turned senile and that it was not really clear who was in charge of policy-making in the Kremlin.

Indeed, the Soviet behavior during 1979 was peculiar. They signed the SALT II agreement, which granted the United States some important concessions, such as a limit on new offensive weapons, technical sharing of information for treaty verification purposes, and a promise to keep low the production of the new Soviet manned strategic bomber Backfire. At the same time, however, they continued deploying the SS-20 intermediate-range nuclear missiles in western Russia and Eastern Europe, fully realizing that it was a major irritant to the United States and its NATO allies. The SS-20 deployments played a role in the Senate's reluctance to ratify SALT II—senators were also unconvinced that the pact provided adequate verification safeguards against Soviet cheating—and the Carter administration concluded it lacked votes for passage. The sudden emergence of reports about a Soviet combat brigade in Cuba (the same one that had been stationed there in 1962, with soldiers periodically rotated over the past seventeen years) made the Senate even more antagonistic toward Moscow. SALT II was never submitted for ratification.

In sum, 1979 was a depressing year for the Carter administration. At times it seemed catastrophic. In January the shah fell in Iran. On February 18 the American Embassy in Teheran was briefly seized by a hostile crowd, presaging the subsequent tragedy. On February 19 American Ambassador to Afghanistan Adolph "Spike" Dubs, the friend of many journalists, was killed by unidentified terrorists in Kabul, and the administration suspected, as Brzezinski puts it, "either Soviet ineptitude or collusion." In July the Sandinistas won the civil war in Nicaragua, marking the beginning of a hostile relationship with the United States that lasted for a decade. About the same time a desert war over the former Spanish Sahara broke out between the Polisario independence guerrillas, backed by Algeria, and Mauritania, backed by Morocco. Then the Senate, in effect, shelved SALT II.

The only encouraging events during the year were the signing by Sadat and Begin of the Egyptian-Israeli peace agreement, brokered by Carter, and a NATO decision to deploy a new generation of intermediate-range nuclear weapons in Western Europe if the Soviets refused to remove their SS-20's.

Tragedy came on November 4 in Teheran. There Revolutionary Guards attacked the American Embassy, taking over the building and seizing sixty-six American hostages inside. Ambassador Sullivan had already left Iran, but Chargé d'Affaires Bruce Laingen was among the hostages along with diplomats, secretaries, and the small Marine Corps guard detail. Unquestionably inspired by Khomeini (who portrayed America as Satan), the young Iranians demanded that the shah be returned home to stand trial as a condition for releasing the hostages. Fourteen of the hostages, including the women, were released quickly. The fifty-two others were held for fifteen months—until the end of Carter's term. The Carter administration and the President never recovered politically from the Teheran humiliation. For months Americans could watch on television the padlocked embassy gates with Revolutionary Guards behind the fence and chanting crowds parading in front of the embassy.

An event with extraordinary repercussions in world politics occurred at Christmas in Kabul. Babrak Karmal, an Afghan Communist leader, had staged a coup against the eighteen-month-old leftist regime installed by the military, but he encountered unexpected resistance. The coup had been orchestrated by the Soviets. On December 25 Soviet troops invaded Afghanistan in an action that bogged the Kremlin in an exhausting guerrilla war that lasted a decade despite the Soviet tanks, jets, and helicopters—it became known after a time as the Soviet Vietnam—and had immense consequences for the entire Soviet system. It is entirely possible that without the disastrous Afghanistan War, there would be no Mikhail Gorbachev in power in the Soviet Union today.

Jimmy Carter's response to the invasion was to impose an economic embargo on the Soviet Union and to declare in a personal message to Brezhnev that the invasion "could mark a fundamental and long-lasting turning point in our relations." There was deep concern in the administration that with Iran no longer in the Western camp, the Soviets would have a free hand in the Persian Gulf region; there was speculation that the attack on Afghanistan was a prelude to a Soviet march toward the shores of the Persian Gulf. It was a danger to the United States, but not then and not ten years later have the Soviet reasons for the Afghan intervention been made fully clear.

The decade had begun with a superpower fighting in a Third World nation in Asia. It ended with another superpower fighting in a Third World nation in Asia. In the meantime, there were at least *twelve* full-fledged regional wars on four continents, plus countless revolutions. Thirty years after the world war there was still no peace.

BOOK SEVEN

THE EIGHTIES

The new phase . . . [is] de-ideologizing relations among states. We are not abandoning our convictions, our philosophy or traditions, nor do we urge anyone to abandon theirs. . . . Let everyone show the advantages of their social system, way of life or values—and not just by words or propaganda, but by real deeds.

—MIKHAIL S. GORBACHEV,
　　Address before the United Nations General
　　Assembly, December 7, 1988

I

*T*he fiftieth anniversary of the outbreak of the Second World War was commemorated on September 1, 1989, in a mood of both hope and hopelessness.

It was the first time since the 1940's that no full-scale international war was being fought anywhere in the world. But at least fifteen civil wars, some of them lasting so long as to appear to have become permanent, were raging around the globe. There were revolutions apace throughout the ever-restless Third World.

Democracy was in ascendance, stronger and more widespread than ever, and the decomposition of the Marxist-Leninist systems during the eighties was a new milestone in the history of the century. Rightist dictatorships were withering away as well. On the other hand, human rights were still being violated massively in the countries where neither democracy nor modernity had been able to flourish. There were executions, imprisonments, tortures, and beatings.

The superpowers made great strides in the course of the decade to limit and control nuclear weapons though they failed to safeguard their populations from lethal accidents in nuclear reactors producing for peaceful uses and from radioactive contamination.

Arts and culture in the 1980's were experiencing a renaissance. Paris gloried in an architectural spree not seen since Louis XIV and Napoleon. London, New York, and Washington were beautified. A Van Gogh painting fetched close to sixty million dollars and a Monet close to thirty million dollars at frantic art auctions.

But unresolved conflicts and political, ideological, ethnic, and religious antagonisms—and pure hatred—had made the eighties the decade of uncontrollable terrorism on the land, in the air, and on the seas.

Racial and religious prejudice was likewise—and incredibly—returning in many countries, including the United States, when it had been assumed that tolerance of color and faith had finally been firmly established. The war, of course, had been fought against the intolerance that sent millions of Jews, Catholics, and Gypsies to Nazi death camps.

Thirty-five years after the Supreme Court handed down its historic ruling on school segregation—the start of major civil rights legislation in this country—America was increasingly dividing itself into separate white, black, Hispanic, and Asian societies. The economic, social, cultural, and educational gap between whites and blacks kept growing, instead of shrinking. A 1989 congressional study found that 45.1 percent of all black children in America lived below the poverty line; the figure for black children in households headed by women living in poverty was 68.3 percent. Nearly one-half of black families were headed by women, with an income of $11,000 annually. There were racially motivated killings of blacks and Asians in New York City and the Southwest during the eighties, and racial hatreds were mounting in the streets of the inner cities and on the campuses of great American universities. I live in Washington, where the population is 75 percent black, and I can report there is virtually no social contact between blacks and whites. Ironically, the end of the rigid Communist controls in the Soviet Union and Eastern Europe—the return of the freedom of speech—unleashed other anti-Semitism in the region.

Synagogues have been firebombed and defaced during the decade, and Jewish organizations claim there has been a resurgence of anti-Semitic talk and attitudes.

The most sordid episode in the postwar history of Christian-Jewish relations was the 1989 dispute—on the fiftieth anniversary of the start of World War II—over the Carmelite nuns' convent located outside the walls of the Oświęcim concentration camp in a structure where the Nazis used to store lethal Zyklon-B gas. It was a dispute of indescribable ugliness, in which all the principals behaved about as badly as can be imagined.

In 1987 Franciszek Cardinal Macharski of Kraków, near Oświęcim, and one Belgian and two French cardinals signed in Geneva an agreement with Jewish organizations providing for the removal of the convent to an interfaith prayer and dialogue center to be built by Christians and Jews. This was done in good faith to meet Jewish sensitivities over the presence of the few Roman Catholic sisters next to the shrine where nearly three million Jews out of a total of five million had been murdered by the Germans. In 1989, however, Cardinal Macharski and Józef Cardinal Glemp, the primate of Poland, unilaterally canceled the accord for unconvincing reasons; they said the Carmelite nuns were praying for Jews, too.

The move had been scheduled for February of that year, but when the Polish cardinals changed their minds, many Jews responded angrily and even violently. In July a group of American Jews scaled the iron fence of the convent to deposit a box of protest leaflets, but Polish construction workers chased them away, pouring pails of dirty water on them from a scaffolding. In horrifying fashion all these incidents led to bitter charges and countercharges, reviving all the memories of anti-Semitism, real and imagined, in Polish history. There are only five or six thousand Jews remaining in Poland, but the Oświęcim dispute immediately turned into a world cause célèbre.

Cardinal Glemp, who should have known better, not only denounced the American Jews' actions (on this point he was right) but accused the world media of being owned, dominated, or influenced against Poland by Jews; his comments in a press interview touched off another storm. Israel's Prime Minister Yitzhak Shamir, who also should have known better, countered gratuitously with charges that Poles "drink anti-Semitism in their mothers' milk." French moviemaker Claude Lanzmann, who produced the nine-hour film *Shoah* about the Holocaust, told journalists that "the Poles have absorbed anti-Semitism together with the teachings of the Church."

Perhaps the most guilty of all was the Polish pope, John Paul II, who maintained a studied silence until late September, when the Carmelite issue took over front pages everywhere. Only then did the Vatican declare that the Geneva accord should be fulfilled. Cardinal Glemp reacted instantly by saying that he now agreed and that the church had made "mistakes." In the end, the convent was torn down, and a new one erected farther away.

Naturally so much of the harm could have been avoided by Vatican intervention at the very outset. For the nascent Polish democracy, the dispute and the resulting controversy over anti-Semitism were immensely embarrassing. Though Solidarity has close church links, its daily newspaper forcefully denounced the whole affair and anti-Semitism in particular. Then forty-six leading Polish intellectuals (including Jews and Roman Catholic priests) published a manifesto demanding that the Geneva agreement be respected, acknowledging past "shameful" anti-Semitism in the country, and proclaiming, "We are entering a new political and social reality. Let us try, Poles and Jews, to greet the prospects of freedom in a spirit of love and truth."

Why did it all have to happen in the first place?

Medicine and science and technology made new quantum leaps. In the most futuristic vistas—and they rapidly become present-day realities—scientists have been working on adapting the human brain's neural networks to virtually automatic solutions and decision making in investments and economic planning. It is the marriage of the brain and the computer through the harnessing of artificial intelligence. Only twenty years had elapsed since Dr. Christian Barnard had performed the first human heart transplant in Cape Town, South Africa, on December 2, 1967, and it seemed as if a century had gone by in terms of medical and precision surgery advances. Heart, liver, and other organ transplants have become routine operations, and there is virtually no limit to medical virtuosity with the availability of lasers, computers, and a whole array of hi tech facilities to treat people.

Yet the entire world has been hit by the calamity of narcotic drugs—from cocaine to heroin to marijuana to chemical compounds—to such a degree that in the eighties it was shaping up as the century's gravest societal crisis. We seemed helpless. The traffic in narcotics knew no borders, hundreds of billions of dollars in drug money flooded international financial channels, governments could be corrupted and controlled by drug dealers operating on the scale of multinational corporations, and thousands and thousands everywhere were dying from drug overdoses and drug-related crime and terrorism. Millions of families were shattered. The U.S. Department of Health and Human Services has estimated that cocaine and crack addiction was rising in the United States across all social and class lines; the number of once-a-week-or-more addicts (as known to the authorities) went up from 647,000 in 1985 to 862,000 in 1988. There were 8 million users in 1988. The General Motors Corporation has calculated that abuse of all drugs costs it more than one billion dollars annually for treatment and worker absenteeism. In September 1989 twenty *tons* of cocaine, worth around ten billion dollars in the street, were seized by agents in Los Angeles, the biggest such haul in history. In Colombia the so-called Medellín cartel of cocaine producers and exporters became a virtual sovereign state within that South American nation, which is the source of most of the cocaine consumed in the United States.

Acquired immune deficiency syndrome (AIDS) became the health plague of the century during the decade, having killed tens of thousands since it spread from Africa to the United States and much of the industrialized world and infecting possibly millions through sexual practices and narcotics injections. There was hope for a breakthrough in cancer research, but very little hope for a cure for AIDS in the foreseeable future.

The economy in the Western world was strong and resilient, feeding on the technological revolution. The twelve members of the European Community set January 1, 1993, as the date for establishing a fully integrated common market that would be the world's largest trading bloc. Already in the eighties, Western Europeans could travel on European passports, and individual European regions traded directly with each other. The United States and Canada established in 1988 the great North American trading bloc.

But the Third World remained the domain of frightening poverty, hunger, disease, infant mortality, and unemployment as nations in Asia, the Middle East, Africa, and Latin America could not even begin to cope with the immensity of the basic human needs of their still-skyrocketing populations. Third World nations owed nearly one *trillion* dollars in debts to Western banks; they paralyzed their economies and triggered social explosions when they imposed austerity programs to be able to start repaying the billions in principal and interest; if they could not pay, they risked losing access to new credits without which they could not develop.

It was a world of slums and misery, from Mexico City, Lima, and São Paulo to Calcutta, Bombay, Karachi, Cairo, and Lagos, where urban populations wasted away, and it was a world of absolute resignation in the villages of India, Pakistan, and Bangladesh, where tree bark and insects were often the only available food; in the vastness of the Brazilian northeast and the Peruvian Andean altiplano, where people, mostly children, die silently under the eternally burning sun (or occasionally from flash floods); and in the refugee camps of East Africa and the Middle East, where there simply is no future for anybody.

Both economic progress and development and primitive efforts to survive in the Third World (slashing and burning forests, for example, to plant in the shallow soil in order to produce enough to eat) have resulted in ecological and environmental catastrophes. Seas, lakes, and rivers have become polluted on all continents from industrial, medical, and human waste. In Eastern Europe the water table is sinking and disappearing because of maltreatment of the soil.

The air has become unbreathable from smog and pollution in Los Angeles, Mexico City (which novelist Carlos Fuentes calls Makesicko Seedy in his latest novel, *Christopher Unborn*, about his hometown of eighteen million inhabitants), Tokyo, Kraków and Katowice (the steel towns of Poland), Belgrade, and Ankara. During the eighties we learned about the "greenhouse effect," the predicted rise in world temperatures because of idioxide filling the air as pollution grows and as natural "lungs" like the jungles of Brazil, Indonesia, and West Africa are sacrificed to the slashers.

This, then, was the state of the world—for better and for worse—a half century after World War II ravaged the planet and its people and moved on to influence the greatest, deepest, and most rapid process of change in human history.

Men and women, of course, define history and the fate of people and nations. Hitler and Stalin nearly destroyed the world as we knew it. Franklin Roosevelt, Winston Churchill, and Charles de Gaulle helped save it in World War II and afterward.

The postwar years produced a generation of leaders responsible for reconstructing the world and giving it new visions and dimensions. They ran the gamut from Harry Truman, Dwight Eisenhower, and John Kennedy in the United States to Konrad Adenauer and Jean Monnet in Western Europe, Jawaharlal Nehru (and his daughter, Indira Gandhi) in India, Juscelino Kubitschek in Brazil, Anwar el-Sadat in Egypt, and Julius Nyerere in Tanzania. In the Communist world, Mao Zedong transformed China forever through violence and fervor, and in the Soviet Union, Nikita Khrushchev slowly began the process of change. In the world of revolutions Fidel Castro in Cuba had a magnificent vision but let it erode and deteriorate into an ineffectual tyranny.

In the eighties a curious panoply of leaders, often totally different in outlook, ideology, and style—but astonishingly capable of dialogue and often common purpose—came on the scene everywhere. Taken together, they formed the transition generation to the next century.

In the United States Ronald Reagan, exuding bonhomie, anticommunism, and an emotional dedication to free enterprise and the deregulation of every aspect of the American economy, was elected in 1980 and went on to serve two terms. George Bush, his loyal Vice President for eight years, was chosen to succeed Reagan in 1988 and in his first year provided freshness, and a sense of happy honesty that had been lacking throughout the decade.

Reagan beat Jimmy Carter principally because he had greater personal appeal to the electorate and because Americans were disappointed in Carter—especially with the onset of first inflation, then recession, his indecisiveness, and his astoundingly bad luck, emphasized by the seizure of American hostages at the Teheran Embassy and his failure to liberate them. It does not follow that the voters really understood whatever Reagan meant by his "revolution," apart from the fact that he was against new taxes and social programs (strangely, blue-collar voters who had benefited from some of the social programs voted for him). But his appeals to patriotism and his pledge to rebuild America's defenses did strike a powerful response.

At the same time Reagan and his wife, Nancy, were genuinely liked by vast numbers of Americans, who admired the style and the elegance in the White House and the President's seemingly homespun attitudes. Only intellectuals criticized Reagan, the oldest President in history, for his passionate taste for telling and retelling Hollywood stories; most Americans did not care if he napped during Cabinet meetings or appeared confused and ill informed at the news conferences he staged in a royal fashion, walking down a red carpet to the lectern in the East Room of the White House.

And if Americans did realize that the Reagan administration was largely responsible for the immense federal budget deficit and bureaucratic and stock market scandals, it was too late to do much about it. Even the Iran-contra scandal—his wild secret scheme in 1985 to sell weapons to Iran to obtain freedom for American hostages in Lebanon and to use illegally the Iranian money to finance the contras in Nicaragua—did not truly tarnish his reputation (Richard Nixon might have been impeached for it). Americans are funny about their presidents.

On the world scene Reagan's passage was extraordinary in every conceivable way. It was, in fact, perplexing—until one realized that Reagan went through a personal process of evolution and learning that coincided with the appearance of his Soviet partner, Mikhail S. Gorbachev.

The Reagan presidency began with strident anticommunism and clarion calls for American superiority over the Soviet "evil empire"; it was punctuated with muscle flexing and American interventions—open and covert—in Lebanon, Libya, Angola, Grenada, Afghanistan, Nicaragua, and Panama; and it ended with far-reaching agreements with the Soviet Union. Paradoxically, it was under Ronald Reagan that in the true sense the Cold War began to end for the United States. But it took both Reagan and Gorbachev to bury it.

Historically, Gorbachev's rise to power in March 1985 and his determination to reform the Soviet Union and the Communist world were the most significant event of the eighties in terms of new world leadership. In Soviet and Communist history Gorbachev's presence became the next great turning point since the 1917 Russian Revolution; it may have marked its end.

In China the eighties brought to power Deng Xiaoping, a veteran of every Chinese Communist move, adventure, war, and revolution since the 1920's—including the Long March across the length of China under Mao

Zedong—as another leader of vision. Deng was elected on September 13, 1982, to chair the party's Central Advisory Committee. He helped end the Cultural Revolution that Mao had launched in the sixties (being personally victimized by it, too), and he set in motion a spectacular program of economic reforms. He strengthened ties with the United States, taking up where Mao had left off with Nixon in 1972, and was the first Chinese leader in almost thirty years ready to make peace with the Soviet Union—but only after Gorbachev emerged as a fellow Communist reformer. Unhappily Deng, the tiny, endlessly energetic, chain-smoking and bridge-playing professional revolutionary, may in the end be remembered by history mainly for the massacre of prodemocracy students in Beijing in June 1989.

In Poland the amazing leadership team to emerge in 1989 from nearly a decade of unrelenting battle between the Communist regime and the democratic opposition represented by the Solidarity free trade union were President Wojciech Jaruzelski, the Communist, and Lech Wałęsa and Prime Minister Mazowiecki, the Solidarity leaders.

In Western Europe the march toward economic unity—and a European political identity—was led by a group of people who basically dislike each other and have wholly different personalities and viewpoints.

In Britain it was Prime Minister Margaret Thatcher, the "Iron Lady," who began in 1989 her second decade at 10 Downing Street, the longest period anyone has held this post in British history. Her determination to improve the economy through privatization, the destruction of the labor unions' power to dictate economic decisions, and building up British exports has evidently worked as a pragmatic proposition. Mrs. Thatcher's great battle with the rest of Western Europe in the late eighties was to oppose too much European Community decision making in the approaching unified Common Market in 1993. The British sometimes do not seem to wish to become part of the Continent.

In France the advocate of greater European unity was the dour, imperious, and intellectually brilliant François Mitterrand, the first member of the Socialist party ever to be elected president (there have been numerous Socialist prime ministers), a particular accomplishment because under the constitution of the Fifth Republic vast powers are vested in this post. Mitterrand (who is not an ideological Marxist) was elected in 1981 and reelected in 1988. With its royalist traditions, France has a seven-year presidential term, and Mitterrand, who is in his seventies, may serve a total of fourteen years at the Élysée Palace, health permitting. Over the years Mitterrand has evolved a quasi-Gaullist style of majestic demeanor. It was under his inspiration that Paris gained in the eighties its great new architectural monuments, notably the underground museum at the Louvre, topped by a tall glass pyramid, the design of the Chinese-American architect I. M. Pei, whom Mitterrand chose arbitrarily over French architects.

In West Germany Chancellor Helmut Kohl, a Christian Democrat, has been in office most of the decade. A colorless but effective politician, he has fought for increasing German independence within NATO and the European Community in nuclear weapons' deployments and trade and monetary policies. In an increasingly articulate fashion, West Germany has been asserting its voice in the eighties, rejecting its wartime guilts and refusing to behave as if it still were under Allied military occupation.

The breakdown of communism in East Germany and the high probability of German reunification has created an entirely new and basic dimension of the "German Question" at the start of the 1990's. But even apart from this central problem, adjustments must be made to redefine West Germany's political role in the new Europe—regardless of reunification—in light of the reality that it is *already* economically dominant in the European Community. And the 1989 events in East Germany and Eastern Europe served to highlight new trends in West German politics. With a strong resurgence of extreme right-wing sentiment in West Germany in the eighties, political attitudes are changing on the part of men like Chancellor Kohl. It was under his pressure that Ronald Reagan visited the Bitburg cemetery, containing the remains of some SS troops, when he came to Germany in May 1985, the fortieth anniversary of V-E Day, and saved himself from total embarrassment at home by a hasty decision to visit the site of a Nazi concentration camp as well.

When the fiftieth anniversary of the 1939 war was commemorated, West German President Richard von Weizsäcker, a respected philosopher, had to cancel his visit to Poland, a form of penance, because of a growing Polish-German dispute over postwar borders. Following the end of the war, Stalin had annexed to the Soviet Union the eastern provinces of Poland and had prevailed on the Western Allies to compensate the Poles with territories in the easternmost part of Germany, up to the Elbe and Oder rivers and including the city of Wrocław (formerly Breslau) and the port of Szczecin (formerly Stettin). This resulted in population shifts involving millions, as to make room for the Russians, Poles from eastern Poland were transported west to the "reconquered" German territories while to make room for the Poles, the German inhabitants of eastern Germany were thrown westward, losing their homes and properties.

Although the 1985 Helsinki European Security Conference reaffirmed all postwar borders, presumably including the new Polish-German border, the Germans (both West and East) would like to reopen this whole matter, especially after the 1989 collapse of East German Communist rule. On the eve of the war's fiftieth anniversary President von Weizsäcker wrote Poland's President Jaruzelski that West Germany had renounced all its claims over these territories. But Kohl's center-right coalition killed in parliament a resolution confirming the renunciation, and Weizsäcker, who as a young soldier had marched into Poland in Hitler's army, decided not to go back among the Poles—in embarrassment. Even in 1990, Kohl refused to accept definitely the new borders, deepening the dispute with democratic Poland. To compound matters, Poland also had a dispute with Communist East Germany over North Sea and Baltic territorial waters; their navies had even fired at each other.

Disturbingly, the end of Communist supremacy in Poland and East Germany has accentuated and brought into the open all these disputes; in the old days, Communist regimes did not allow public criticism of one another. The East German–Polish border, closed to East Germans and Poles after Solidarity's birth in 1980, had not been reopened two months after the Berlin Wall was pierced. Rolf Henrich, a founder of the prodemocracy New Forum movement in East Germany, complained in December 1989 that "I have friends in Poland, but it would be more difficult to visit them than to travel to Frankfurt (in West Germany). And at the same time, the Roman Catholic weekly *Tygodnik Powszechny* protested against "the explosion of anti-Polish attitudes" in Germany and "anti-German attitudes" in Poland.

The German future became a burning issue for all Europe (and obviously for the United States as well) when Communist power suddenly ended in East Germany in November. Instantly German reunification became a theme of speculation in all major capitals. With the fall of the hard-line Communist regime headed by the aging Erich Honecker, why should not East and West Germany reunite? And if they did, would this new power (already increasingly nationalistic) pose a real or perceived economic and political threat to the European Community—and to the Soviet Union? Would a united Germany emerge a half century after the world war it had started in 1939, as Europe's greatest power, just as Japan has done in the Pacific? Those were the sudden and immense questions appearing at the dawn of the nineties.

There was new-generation leadership in the ancient lands of Asia with a history of ancient hatreds. In India Prime Minister Indira Gandhi was killed by her Sikh bodyguards in 1984, to be replaced by her son, Rajiv (the third generation of prime ministers in the line started by his grandfather Jawaharlal Nehru at independence).

In Pakistan President Zia was killed in an unexplained aircraft crash on August 17, 1988, bringing to an end the long cycle of military dictatorships in the country. On November 16 the opposition Pakistan People's party won the parliamentary elections, and its leader, Benazir Bhutto, was sworn in as premier. Her father, Zulfikar Ali Bhutto, Pakistan's president and premier before the 1971 Bangladesh War, had been executed on Zia's orders after a dubious trial for an alleged political assassination, and Benazir Bhutto had been held in Zia's prisons. Yet the transition was peaceful and smooth, with the premier careful not to offend the religious sensitivities of the Pakistani Muslims; Zia had turned the country into a nearly theocratic state, codifying Islamic laws and imposing national prohibition on the consumption of alcohol. The American-educated Premier Bhutto had accepted a traditional arranged Muslim wedding (she did not know the groom beforehand) even before General Zia's death.

The children of the dead rulers found it easier to move toward each other than had their parents, encumbered by the living memory of their respective countries' wars, the killings, and the horrors of expulsions. Benazir Bhutto and Rajiv Gandhi met in Islamabad, the Pakistani capital, less than a month after she became premier; they started out agreeing not to attack each other's nuclear facilities. That same week, in December 1988, Rajiv Gandhi flew to Beijing, the first Indian prime minister to visit China in thirty-four years—twenty-six years after their Himalayan border war—to participate in the creation of working groups charged with resolving frontier disputes. But in the general elections in November 1989, Rajiv Gandhi and his Congress party were defeated by the National Front, a coalition of all the opposition parties. The Nehru-Gandhi dynasty vanished after forty-two years in power through a display of democracy at the polls.

The new face in the Philippines was President Corazón Aquino, who replaced the dictatorial Ferdinand Marcos (and his wife, Imelda, of the thousand pairs of shoes) on August 25, 1986, after tens of thousands of demonstrators supported by most of the army demanded that power be handed to her. In elections held ten days earlier, Marcos claimed victory over Mrs. Aquino—her husband, Benigno Aquino, the longtime opposition leader, had been assassinated by Marcos's agents the previous year at the Manila airport—but election fraud was declared, and the pro-Aquino movement erupted.

Interestingly, the Reagan administration helped push Marcos into resigning; it realized that the dictatorship had become intolerable to the nation and that continued American support for it would create problems for Washington over the retention of vital air and naval bases in the Philippines. Therefore, the Marcoses, who in the past had been regally entertained at the White House (and had sung duets for the Reagans), fled Manila to exile in Hawaii; the administration would not allow them to come to the U.S. mainland. Subsequently suits against the Marcoses were brought by the federal government in New York City over millions of dollars in U.S. funds illegally diverted into real estate the Marcoses had secretly purchased on the mainland. Shortly after Marcos died in 1989 (the Manila government refused to allow his body to be brought home for burial), an extremely dangerous coup attempt against Mrs. Aquino was launched by a military faction, the sixth such attempt. The Aquino democracy was saved when President Bush ordered two U.S. Phantom jet fighter-bombers to circle over the capital to prevent rebel aircraft from taking off from the airfield they controlled, depriving the attackers of air superiority.

The Reagan administration also played a key role in encouraging Haiti's army to dislodge President Jean-Claude Duvalier on February 7, 1986. Known as Baby Doc (his father, François Duvalier, a voodoo-worshiping physician nicknamed Papa Doc, had started the dictatorial dynasty), Duvalier ran a repressive, corrupt regime that helped destroy even more completely the economy of Haiti, one of the world's poorest (and most beautiful) countries.

Baby Doc fled to France, but Haiti was soon back under a dictatorship. A civilian president had been elected in 1988; but he was overthrown by a military coup within months, and lethal silence returned to that tortured Caribbean island republic. The Tontons Macoute, militia gangsters of the Duvalier era, were back in control, beating and terrorizing opponents.

Having gone to Haiti as a reporter on many occasions since the early 1960's, I could never shake off the impression that this black republic of immensely artistically gifted people (the first nation in the Western Hemisphere after the United States to win independence—in 1802—from colonial rule) was cursed by the gods; there simply does not seem to be any economic or social or political future for the Haitians, no matter how hard they try or how much foreign aid they receive. This is perhaps why so many Haitians risk their lives to flee to the United States in fishing boats and inner tubes.

In Iran Ayatollah Khomeini died on June 3, 1989, after being the supreme leader of the Islamic Republic for ten years. It was on his orders that the American Embassy hostages were kept until the exact moment Carter's term had expired and Ronald Reagan was sworn in as President. Khomeini's ire against Carter, supposedly for supporting the shah more or less until the end, was aggravated when the United States dispatched an air rescue mission to Iran to retrieve the hostages. The complex operation, involving aircraft carriers, planes and helicopters, and elite assault troops, failed as the craft collided in sandstorms at their Iranian desert rendezvous spot. Eight American servicemen died. Secretary of State Vance resigned in protest over the rescue operation, which he opposed, and his place was taken by former Senator Edmund Muskie of Maine.

Khomeini's successor as the top leader of Iran was Ali Akbar Hashemi Rafsanjani, also a mullah but regarded as a fairly moderate leader. He was speaker of parliament. Rafsanjani inherited power almost exactly a year after the cease-fire in the nine-year-long Persian Gulf war between Iran and Iraq that cost close to a million Iranian lives (and hundreds of thousands of Iraqi lives) and dealt a body blow to the shaky postrevolutionary Iranian economy. The war was launched in September 1980 by Iraq's President Saddam Hussein, an Arab "socialist" dictator and army general, who feared that Khomeini would attempt to impose his brand of fundamentalist Shiite Islamic faith on the Iraqis and other Persian Gulf countries.

The assumption was that Iran's demoralized army would collapse and the young Revolutionary Guards would not be a match for the professional Iraqi Army, but Pakistani President Zia, himself a general, told me in Washington later that year that the gulf war would last indefinitely. He had been asked to mediate in the conflict and had visited both Teheran and Baghdad, but he concluded that no mediation was possible. To the surprise of experts, Iran not only did not lose but in the end invaded Iraq and forced the cease-fire. Iranian pilots flew American-built Phantoms with great efficiency, shooting down Iraq's MiGs, and Khomeini-inspired youths, sometimes children, were sent into battle in human waves.

Inevitably the United States feared that the gulf war would become internationalized: Saudi Arabia supported Iraq, and Syria supported Iran; the position of the Soviet Union, already deeply mired in Afghanistan, was unclear. Later Iranians (and occasionally Iraqis) began attacking foreign-flag oil tankers sailing the gulf and attempting to block the Strait of Hormuz leading into the Indian Ocean. In 1987 the United States decided to fly the American flag on Kuwaiti ships as a form of protection; soon thereafter the U.S. Navy was moved into the gulf to assure safe passage for navigation. In one of the most horrifying mistaken-identity accidents in recent warfare, the USS *Vincennes*, a guided-missile cruiser, shot down an Iranian airliner on July 3, 1988, mistaking it for an Iranian fighter preparing to attack it; 290 civilian passengers and crew were killed.

There had been other such disasters. On September 1, 1983 (the forty-fourth anniversary of World War II), a Soviet fighter jet aircraft shot down a Korean Airlines Boeing 747 with more than three hundred passengers aboard over the Sea of Japan after the plane had penetrated Soviet airspace; it passed over highly sensitive Soviet defense areas around Khabarovsk and Petropavlovsk. There has never been a full explanation of what happened— or why. Moscow claimed that the MiG pilot, who had asked for instructions from air force headquarters before firing the fatal air-to-air missile, had assumed that the Korean 747 was an electronics aircraft on a spy mission for the United States, not responding to radioed orders to turn back or land. A real American electronics plane had been reported about the same time near Soviet airspace.

Subsequent investigations and U.S. court rulings suggested that the jumbo jet, flying from Anchorage, Alaska, to Tokyo, had gone considerably off its course in a western direction, thus entering Soviet airspace. The pilots may have done it through inattention or on receipt of incorrect data in the on-board navigational computers upon leaving Anchorage or may have been obeying airline management orders to take a shortcut over Soviet territory to economize on fuel. The truth will never be known; there were no survivors, and no flight recorders were recovered.

On another occasion Israeli jets intercepted a Libyan jet airliner, which it forced to land because of suspicion that it was a disguised bomber on its way to strike at Israel.

Governments and air defenses guard their territories around the clock with radar and jet air patrols against penetration by unknown aircraft, and contemporary technology is highly advanced. The United States, for example, protects its East Coast from flights by Soviet long-range reconnaissance aircraft based in Cuba as well as from small craft bringing narcotics into the country from South America and the Caribbean. But Soviet technology or air defenses failed completely in May 1987, when a twenty-one-year-old West German amateur pilot named Mathias Rust flew undetected below radar coverage aboard a single-engine Cessna from Helsinki to Moscow and landed on the cobblestones of Red Square between the walls of the Kremlin and the GUM department store. It was spectacular—and hugely embarrassing to the Soviet military—and the bespectacled Rust served one year of a three-year sentence for illegally entering the Soviet Union. But it was a boon for Gorbachev. He used the Rust conquest of the Soviet airspace as an excuse for firing most of the top military command, including many generals known to oppose *perestroika*, replacing them with younger—and trusted—officers.

The cease-fire in the Gulf war, negotiated by a United Nations mediator when both parties asked for it, resulted from the sheer exhaustion of the combatants. The new Iranian president thus faced the immense task of economic, military, and political reconstruction of his once-rich country at a time when oil prices were relatively low and foreign capitalists were wary about investing in revolutionary Iran. Still, Rafsanjani's Cabinet, approved by the Iranian parliament in August 1989, was the most moderate leadership group in a decade, and the assumption was that the new government would sooner or later restore ties with the West, notably the United States, which had frozen billions of dollars in Iranian assets.

II

The end of the Iran-Iraq War in August 1988 and the withdrawal of the Soviet troops from Afghanistan, completed in mid-1989, marked the first time in more than four decades that the world was free of full-fledged wars.

The French Indochina War erupted within less than two years of V-J Day in 1945 and lasted until 1954, overlapping with the Korean War. The Indochina conflict resumed in a low-intensity fashion in 1955, with the arrival of the first American advisers in Vietnam. The American war in Indochina ended in 1973; four Middle East wars, two India-Pakistan wars, an Indian-Chinese war, and several colonial and postcolonial African wars were fought during that same time. The East African wars came in 1974 and lasted past the end of the decade. Then the Soviets invaded Afghanistan and Iraq attacked Iran; these two wars spanned the eighties. Israel invaded Lebanon in 1982. The same year Argentina seized the Falkland Islands in the South Atlantic from the British (the Argentines call the islands the Malvinas) but were rapidly dislodged and defeated by Britain's sea and air power.

When the fiftieth anniversary of the start of the Second World II was

commemorated in September 1989, the world was at peace—as far as organized wars were concerned. But it was witnessing (or ignoring) the fifteen or
more civil wars in progress.

The worst civil wars were in Lebanon, Afghanistan, Ethiopia, and Sri
Lanka.

The conflict in once-bucolic Lebanon was in its fifteenth year, and Beirut,
its capital, had been almost razed. As a result of six months of artillery battles
between Christian and Muslim militias in and around the city during 1989—
the worst carnage of the civil war with over 900 people killed and 5,000
wounded between March and October—Beirut's population was reduced
from its normal 1.5 million to 150,000 as 90 percent of the inhabitants simply
fled for their lives. Essentially, this political-religious civil war stemmed from
the insistence of the Muslim majority on seizing the powers—such as the
right to the nation's presidency—vested in the Christian Maronite minority
since the 1943 independence from France and from the Christians' refusal to
yield them. But Lebanese Muslims were also fighting each other (they were
split into pro-Syrian and pro-Iranian factions), and, inevitably, outside interests were deeply involved as well. Syria, often switching sides, has maintained
40,000 "peacekeeping" troops in Lebanon since 1976. Israel invaded
Lebanon in 1982 in order to destroy the Palestinian guerrillas of Yassir Arafat
who had established their headquarters in West Beirut and in the refugee
camps, but it retained control over an enclave in the Lebanese south even
after Arafat escaped, and it continues to support the Christian militias. Over
300 Americans died in 1983 when Muslim terrorists blew up the U.S. Embassy in Beirut and the headquarters of a Marine force President Reagan had
dispatched to Lebanon in a misguided attempt to impose peace. And a score
of American hostages were taken by obscure Muslim factions. Fates seemed
determined to destroy that nation of three million, so long prosperous and
happy, an oasis in the war-engulfed Middle East—or else Lebanon, as a
country, simply became suicidal.

The eighties were an uninterrupted tragedy for Lebanon. Its Maronite
president-elect, Bashir Gemayel, was assassinated in a bombing, presumably
by Muslim groups, in September 1982; then Christian militiamen
massacred hundreds of Palestinian civilians in Beirut's Sabra and Shatila
refugee districts administered by Israeli occupation forces, and the civil war
turned into a permanent state of affairs in Lebanon. The fighting during
1989 was described as "horrific" by foreign newsmen who had seen other
wars and revolutions, with the first week of September being the wildest
ever, with point-blank artillery duels. A new hope for peace appeared in
October when Saudi Arabia and the Arab League produced a settlement
plan that reduced Christian political power though still reserving the presidency for the Maronites. General Michel Aoun, the Christian army commander, rejected the Arab peace plan, demanding that all the Syrian troops
leave Lebanon as a prerequisite for a political solution. On November 5, the
Lebanese parliament met in a rump session under Syrian military protection

to elect a new Maronite president, René Moawad. General Aoun continued his opposition, and on November 22, after seventeen days in office, President Moawad was assassinated when a remote-controlled, four hundred-pound bomb blew up his motorcade on the way back from a Lebanese independence-day celebration; twenty-three others died along with him. He was the second Lebanese president murdered in seven years. It was unknown who killed Moawad, and the next day Elias Hrawi, another Maronite, was chosen as president. The Christians and pro-Syrian Muslims had barely suspended their battle when pro-Iranian Party of God militias and pro-Syrian Amal militias, both Muslim, engaged in murderous combat two days before Christmas, again emptying Beirut of its civilian population. As the Lebanese civil war spilled over into the 1990's, proxies for Iran and Syria fought over the control of the wretched country—as did rival Christian factions.

The Soviet army withdrew from Afghanistan in February 1989, having, in effect, lost the ten-year war against the Muslim Afghan guerrillas equipped militarily by the United States, Saudi Arabia, and China. Gorbachev had decided to pull out the 120,000 Soviet troops to cut Moscow's losses (like Nixon in Vietnam in 1973, he had concluded that the Afghanistan war was unwinnable for him and too costly) and to start doing away with the regional conflicts around the world fought, by and large, by Soviet and American surrogates.

However, the Afghan civil war did not cease when the Russians left. It was in its twelfth year at the end of 1989 (having started two years before the Soviet intervention) with the cost in Afghan lives estimated at 1.3 million and with nearly 5 million Afghans as refugees aboard, mostly in camps in Pakistan and Iran. The civil conflict continued, with no solution in sight, because the United States and its friends were determined to see the *muhajaheddin* guerrillas overthrow the Soviet-supported regime of President Najibullah in Kabul, and the Russians were just as determined to keep him in power. With American and Egyptian missiles and other arms steadily flowing to the guerrillas and with the Soviets delivering war matériel and food to their Kabul friends—Ilyushin-76 transport jets were making 250 weekly supply flights to Afghanistan—the civil war had turned into a proxy war. It was a cruel and essentially pointless confrontation (over 1,000 people were killed in Kabul in 1989 by guerrilla rockets) in which the Bush administration had engaged American prestige and thus forced Gorbachev to engage *his* prestige. At the end of 1989, not only were the guerrillas unable to oust Najibullah, but the seven principal *muhajeddin* organizations were busy fighting each other as well—thereby embarrassing the United States. The split was mainly among Islamic fundamentalists and nonfundamentalists, with numbers of the fighters switching sides and even joining Kabul-sponsored militias. In the words of a Western diplomat in Kabul, Afghanistan had ceased to exist as an organized country and it slid into the 1990's in a state of murderous chaos and national decomposition.

In Sri Lanka, once a peaceful island in the Indian Ocean known as Ceylon and famous for its tea and elephants, outsiders could not be blamed for the terrible civil war that cost at least 20,000 lives between its start in 1983 and the closing days of 1989. During that year the violence in Sri Lanka had escalated to the point where more than 1,000 people were killed each month in massacres resulting from ethnic, religious, and political hatreds. The worst day came on December 21: At least 200 young men were shot or hacked to death during a single 24-hour period in a series of fighting engaging various factions. Bodies were hanging from trees and lampposts, and others were burning on car tires. The killings were carried out by Tamil Tiger rebels belonging to the Tamil ethnic minority against the Sinhalese ethnic majority and against Muslims, by Tamil factions battling each other, by Sinhalese majority armed squads against the Tamils, by the left-wing extremist Sinhalese People's Liberation Front against Sri Lankan government troops and civilians, and by the national armed forces and progovernment paramilitary units against all opponents.

In an overwhelming majority of cases, people were murdered in the most atrocious ways imaginable, and Amnesty International said in a report issued in December 1989 that "violence is so widespread that it is often difficult to establish with certainty who the agents of specific killings were." India sent nearly 50,000 troops to Sri Lanka in 1987 on a "peacekeeping" mission (over 50 million Tamils live in the southern Indian state of Tamil Nadu, across a narrow strait from Sri Lanka, and favor their fellow Tamils on the island), but it accomplished nothing and the local government demanded their withdrawal. By the end of 1989, about 25,000 Indian troops were still in Sri Lanka. During a visit to New Delhi at that time, a senior Indian government official told me, "Let's face it: Sri Lanka has collapsed as a nation."

That three countries—Lebanon, Afghanistan, and Sri Lanka—have been virtually obliterated by internecine wars was a warning for the nineties of the immense pressures rising across the Third World that may well become one of the central problems in the new decade. Such conflicts not only paralyze comprehensive economic development (or destroy the economy as was the case in Lebanon), but they spawn mass starvation, hunger, and disease, and generate millions of new refugees for whom nobody can afford to care.

Ethiopia and Sudan are examples of this kind of danger. In Ethiopia, the central government—first under Emperor Haile Selassie and then under Marxist President Mengistu Haile Mariam—has fought separatist rebels from the northeastern provinces of Eritrea and Tigre for twenty-eight years. Nobody knows how many people died in combat or from famines directly related to the fighting, but the numbers surely run into millions—and at the end of 1989, the Addis Ababa regime was as far from victory as ever. Unable to win militarily, and warned by Moscow not to expect further arms deliveries, Mengistu seemed to have decided to starve out the rebels. As a result of a new drought in 1989 (the 1984–85 drought brought death to millions), four million people in rebel territory were faced with famine, but the Ethiopian government blocked the deliveries of relief supplies for the northeastern provinces, threatening more mass starvation in 1990 and beyond.

In Sudan, where a civil war between Muslim majorities and Christian minorities has been going on since 1983, as many as one million refugees displaced by the fighting may have died from hunger. The United Nations estimated that 250,000 people died of hunger there in 1989 alone. At the end of the year there were about 2.2 million refugees in southern Sudan, Ethiopia, Eritrea, and Chad. There were no resources available to guarantee them even the most primitive form of survival; moreover, farm production in this huge region kept decreasing, and the menace of new droughts held sinister prospects.

As for Cambodia, its civil war was a quarter century old at the end of the eighties, having gone through every imaginable cycle. Between 1964 and 1970, the war was between the Khmer Rouge Communists led by Pol Pot and the neutralist government of Prince Norodom Sihanouk. In 1970, Cambodia was drawn fully into the Indochina War (and bombed and invaded by the United States); then—in 1975—it was taken over by Pol Pot's murderous troops, who killed well over one million of their fellow citizens to impose their brand of ideological purity. In 1979, Vietnam invaded Cambodia, removing Pol Pot from power but triggering a war against Vietnamese occupation. When the Vietnamese pulled out in 1989, (in part under pressure from Gorbachev), still another civil war broke out, this time between the Pnom Penh regime that Vietnam continued to support from afar and Pol Pot's Khmer Rouge backed by China and by the sixty-seven-year-old Sihanouk, the eternal survivor of all the Cambodian conflicts. A Cambodian peace conference in Paris collapsed in August 1989, and full-fledged fighting followed it immediately. At the end of 1989, Pol Pot appeared to be winning—and there was nothing and nobody to stop the man of the Killing Fields. History in Cambodia jumped back fifteen years.

In Angola, the Cubans and the South Africans removed their forces under an agreement signed early in 1989, but the civil war between the Marxist government in Luanda and rightist UNITA guerrillas supported by the United States and South Africa spurted along almost a year later. The Bush administration could not bring itself to end clandestine support for UNITA (a CIA aircraft carrying weapons was shot down over Angola in December) although the chances of its victory appeared nil.

Mozambique, another former Portuguese colony, is being gradually destroyed by the civil war between the leftist government in Maputo and the right-wing RENAMO guerrillas, a conflict that began in 1976. RENAMO (which stands for the Portuguese name of the movement, the National Resistance of Mozambique) was launched by South Africa next door to oust the local regime, and this support has continued despite a South African–Mozambique peace agreement signed in 1984. The United States, which has good relations with the Maputo government, estimates that RENAMO guerrillas have killed 100,000 people between 1987 and 1989 in an effort to terrorize the population and that they have smashed the economy by burning farms and towns. There was starvation in Mozambique, too, but nobody outside seemed to care about that unhappy land.

Parallel religious and ideological civil wars—one waged by Muslims, one by Communists, and both against the central government in Manila—had gone on in the Philippines since the Huk rebellion of the 1940's. They were the chief preoccupation for President Aquino as she strove to keep her country together. In December 1989, she survived—with U.S. aid—the sixth coup attempt by unhappy army factions.

Iraq and its autonomy-minded Kurdish tribesmen have fought for a quarter century. In 1988 Iraq (then still fighting Iran) was accused of using poison gas against the Kurds; thousands fled to Turkey to be hospitalized.

In South America Colombia and Peru were enduring merciless civil wars in which ideology and politics acquired an added dimension with the struggle between the authorities and powerful drug warlords. In Colombia the civil war in one form or another has been fought since 1948. First, it was a war between the Conservative and Liberal parties. Then leftist guerrillas of the M-19 Movement, supported by Cuba, entered the fray. Nonpolitical bandit gangs took advantage of this war chaos that Colombians called *chusma*. Since the mid-1980's the violence has been between the authorities and the private armies of the drug networks, some trained by British and Israeli mercenaries. In mid-1989 the United States dispatched military equipment and advisers to help Colombia fight the battle of narcotics.

In Peru an extremist and mystical movement calling itself the Shining Path, claiming to trace its inspirational origins to the Incas and the Indian tribes that followed them in history, savagely fought against the democratic government of the left-of-center President Alan García, perpetrating hundreds of assassinations and becoming protectors of the Indian peasants who grow coca leaf in their mountain valleys; cocaine is processed from it.

An American-financed civil war against the Marxist regime in Nicaragua (launched in the early eighties by the Reagan administration after the Carter administration failed to pay adequate attention to the earlier Nicaraguan Revolution) spanned practically the entire decade. Between the actions of the Americans and its contra clients and the government in Managua, the impoverished Central American republic was simply ruined.

The fighting between the CIA-organized contras and the Nicaraguan army was halted in 1988 as a result of a Central American peace plan presented by Costa Rica—and relative peace was maintained while efforts were made in many capitals to achieve a lasting political settlement. Mikhail Gorbachev, increasingly determined to wind up regional conflicts in which Moscow was pitted through proxies against Washington, helped to stabilize the Central American situation by making it clear that the Soviet Union was washing its hands of Nicaragua and phasing out shipments of arms to the Sandinistas. The Managua regime then agreed to free elections, monitored by foreign observers. On February 25, 1990, the Sandinista president Daniel Ortega Saavedra was stunningly defeated by the opposition candidate, Mrs. Violeta Chamorro, and Nicaragua moved toward democracy.

In El Salvador the civil war between leftist guerrillas and the rightist re-gime had erupted in the late seventies and continued ten years later, with Cuba and Nicaragua supporting their ideological clients and the United States spending hundreds of millions of dollars to save the country from communism. The cost in lives was 70,000. After a decade of warfare in which the army used bombs and napalm against the guerrillas and the rebels sowed land mines that crippled peasants and children on both sides, the stalemate in El Salvador was total late in 1989. Though the Marxist threat in El Salvador appeared so great to the Reagan administration after it took office in 1981 (and nearly two years after Nicaragua had gone the wrong way) that Secretary of State Alexander M. Haig, Jr., pronounced it to be a main battleline in the basic East-West dispute, he subsequently had to re-think this evaluation. El Salvador was disturbing and painful, but in the end it was a marginal issue. The guerrillas failed to win not only because of U.S. support for the government, but basically because they could never gain national enthusiasm for their cause. By the end of the 1980's, revolu-tionary solutions no longer had the appeal of a generation ago.

In Israel and its occupied territories in the former Palestine, the *intifada*—the uprising—by the Palestinians demanding their own state erupted in December 1987. Two years later, it had acquired the form of an institutionalized civil war in which Arabs continued to hurl stones and Mo-lotov cocktails at Israeli soldiers, who responded with extraordinary brutality, killing and maiming the demonstrators (over four hundred were killed) and destroying their homes. Palestinians also executed fellow Arabs they sus-pected of collaborating with Israel, staged strikes, and employed many forms of passive resistance.

What was unclear, however, after two years was whether the *intifada* helped or hindered a Palestinian peace process. In December 1988 Palestine Liberation Organization Chairman Arafat formally declared that the PLO was "renouncing terrorism" and recognizing the existence of the state of Israel—alongside a Palestinian homeland state. This led to the establish-ment of direct diplomatic contacts between the United States and the PLO and new hopes of a permanent Middle Eastern settlement. When I visited Arafat at his Tunis headquarters a month later, he told me that it was the *intifada*—he claimed that uprising leaders were, in effect, taking orders from him—that had made it possible for his PLO faction to move to more moderate positions and accept Israel's existence because now he could act from a position of strength. He seemed very anxious for the peace process to move forward; during a dinner in Algiers (where I had flown with him on a private jet for an overnight visit) Arafat exclaimed, "I wish Israel had a De Gaulle," a reference to the Frenchman's decision to grant Algeria indepen-dence and end the war.

Intifada and the prospects of peace reopened the "land for peace" argu-ment in Israel—the question of whether territories should be given Palestin-ians on the West Bank of the Jordan and in Gaza in exchange for a formal peace settlement—and divided the country right down the middle. When I traveled to Israel in September 1989, I found hardening attitudes among Israelis on this subject, but also a sense of growing isolation in the world. Trust in Arafat, limited as it was, had diminished, and the Israelis pointed to the executions of alleged Palestinian collaborationists as proof that the Arabs and the PLO could not be trusted. Though the diplomatic peace process remained alive at the end of the year, the situation again seemed as stale-mated as ever. Meanwhile, *intifada* violence and counterviolence were an accepted part of daily life; Christmas of 1989 could not be traditionally celebrated in Bethlehem and Nazareth on the West Bank by visitors from around the world because of security concerns, with the Israeli authorities refusing to risk incidents. And matters, it appeared, could be worse: Arafat and the Tunis-based PLO began during the year to lose influence in Gaza and the West Bank to the extremely hard-line Islamic Hamas fundamen-talists, who do not accept the notion of the Israeli state. (Arafat may have been right when he told me, "The Israelis and the Americans should deal with me now; the next guy will be much tougher.") I found Israel to be a depressing place as I revisited it that year after a long absence.

On the other hand, a continent away in South Africa, pessimism was turning for the first time into very cautious optimism. When I went there in 1984, the tensions between the ruling white minority and the nonwhite majority were so enormous that the country was clearly being pushed toward a full-fledged civil war. In the ensuing years, these tensions grew even more with the proclamation of a state of emergency. But the situation changed in a dramatic fashion in 1989, when Frederik W. de Klerk became South Africa's president after forcing out P. W. Botha, a man who never grasped the process of change. Though de Klerk was never suspected of progressive thought, he moved instantly to defuse the pressures, surprising friend and foe. He released from prison three top leaders of the African National Con-gress (long regarded officially as a Communist subversive organization) and, just before Christmas, received at his home Nelson Mandela, the ANC's principal figure, who had been imprisoned for a quarter century. Mandela was freed in February 1990, opening the way for a dialogue between the white government and the ANC. While apartheid obviously was not abol-ished, public beaches and many other facilities were desegregated and non-whites were permitted to hold public demonstrations. When I visited Johannesburg in 1984, I learned that blacks could be admitted only to black hospitals, and that a black would be left to die in the street after an accident if a black ambulance was not available. Moreover, hospital facilities at the vast Soweto township there were grossly insufficient for the black popula-tion. In 1989, however, this policy was suddenly altered: White hospitals opened their doors to nonwhites. By South African standards, these were revolutionary events.

In Northern Ireland, there was no good news in the eighties. In 1979, Earl Mountbatten of Burma, former viceroy of India and a beloved British hero, was killed when Irish Republican Army (IRA) terrorists blew up his yacht with a bomb. The religious and economic conflicts between Catholics and Protestants in the Ulster counties was well into the second decade as a full-scale civil war, with British troops unable to impose peace. And IRA terrorists kept striking at British military installations in Northern Ireland, Britain, and West Germany.

Civil wars and revolutions and all the pent-up hatreds and resentments spawned in the eighties a wave of political terrorism on a scale the world had never known. It was impossible to determine what were isolated, individual acts, such as assassination attempts, and what were organized political, ideological, or religious deeds of violence and vengeance. And the world was basically defenseless against terrorism; nobody could guess who or what would be struck by whom, when, and where.

In 1981 there were three assassination attempts against world leaders. On March 30 President Reagan was shot in front of the Hilton Hotel in Washington, D.C., by a demented young man, hoping to impress an actress he loved from afar, never having met her. Reagan recovered, but with the history of political murders in the United States since the sixties, anyone with a gun shooting at a President had to be regarded as a terrorist—however this is defined. On May 13 Pope John Paul II was shot and seriously injured on St. Peter's Square in Rome by a young Turk with a bizarre political and criminal past, named Mehmet Ali Agca. He was arrested and tried, but the motivation and Agca's connections remain mysterious. Low-level Bulgarian officials were charged with plotting the shooting—there was a theory the KGB wanted the pope dead because of his support for Solidarity in Poland—but nothing was ever proved. On October 10 Egypt's President Sadat was killed, apparently by Muslim fundamentalists, as he reviewed a military parade in Cairo. It is entirely possible that he was murdered as vengeance for making peace with Israel.

Mozambique's President Samora Moises Machel, a Marxist who had established working relations with the United States after visits to Presidents Carter and Reagan, was killed on October 19, 1986, in an unexplained plane crash near the South African border; the 1988 midair explosion of President Zia's plane in Pakistan likewise lacked explanation (a quarter century later nobody knows why Dag Hammarskjöld's plane crashed in Africa). Two Lebanese presidents were murdered during the decade as was President Ahmed Abdallah Abderemane of the Comoro Islands.

The Middle East was the most horrific battlefield of terrorism, stemming from the Lebanese Civil War, the Arab-Israeli conflict over Palestine, and Syrian, Iranian, and PLO involvements. Mass killings with car bombs had become routine in Beirut, and the catalog of terrorist strikes against Israel or its Lebanese friends and Israeli retaliation with commando raids, air strikes, and secret service operations is endless. Assassinations and bombings related to Middle Eastern tensions have spread to Western European cities and airports.

Americans were badly victimized by Middle Eastern terrorism, in part because they made themselves vulnerable—in actions that were not always wise. Thus, in August 1982, a force of U.S. Marines landed in Lebanon (for the first time since 1958) as part of a multinational peacekeeping operation, following Israel's invasion of that country on June 6. This invasion, undertaken to protect northern Israel from Palestinian guerrilla incursions, turned into a nightmare for Israel—and everybody else. The Marines were withdrawn after two weeks, but Reagan sent them back on September 29, to rejoin French and Italian units there; this was done in the aftermath of the massacre of more than eight hundred Palestinian refugees—including women and children—by the Lebanese Christian militia (operating with Israel's knowledge) at the Sabra and Shatila refugee camps near Beirut. The camps were PLO guerrilla centers, according to the Israelis.

Then Arab reprisals began. The United States being regarded as an ally of Israel, on April 18, 1983, the American Embassy in Beirut was hit by a car bomb, and 50 Americans were killed, including the CIA's principal officer for the Middle East. In a crescendo of horror, another car bomb struck the quarters occupied by the Marines in Beirut, and 241 Marines were killed. The same day 58 French soldiers died when a car bomb hit their barracks. The United States responded with air and battleship gun bombing against presumed terrorist concentrations on the Lebanese coast; it lost an airplane. The Marines were soon withdrawn, but the new American Embassy in Beirut was bombed on December 20, 1984.

The kidnappings of Americans in Beirut—American University professors, journalists, businessmen, and intelligence officers—started about the same time. Nobody ever knew the identity of the captors. They could be Lebanese or Syrians or Iranian-supported Muslim fundamentalists. It was to win the release of these hostages (there were always demands for freeing Arab and Muslim prisoners in Israel and elsewhere) that President Reagan authorized his former National Security Adviser Robert McFarlane to undertake a secret trip to Iran to seek to exchange them for American Hawk antiaircraft batteries.

Then came terrorism in the air. On June 14, 1985, a TWA airliner was hijacked over the Mediterranean by Lebanese Shiite Muslims and forced to land in Beirut. The 145 passengers and crew were held hostage for two weeks aboard the jet as negotiations went on under terrible tension; a U.S. Navy serviceman, traveling as a passenger, was killed by the kidnappers. Finally, the hostages were let go in exchange for 31 Lebanese Shiites held in Israeli prisons. (In 1985 Israel traded 1,550 Palestinian and Lebanese prisoners in exchange for 3 Israeli soldiers held since 1982 by Palestinian guerrillas.)

On April 2, 1986, 4 passengers were killed when a bomb exploded aboard a TWA airliner approaching Athens for a landing. In the summer of 1986 a Pan Am jet was hijacked in Pakistan. On December 12, 1988, Pan American Flight 103, en route from London to New York, exploded in midair over Scotland, killing all the 259 aboard and 22 on the ground as it plummeted down on the village of Lockerbie. A sophisticated device in a cassette player had apparently been placed in luggage that was transferred from a connecting flight from Frankfurt.

Nobody was safe from airborne terror. An Indian Boeing 747 flying between Canada and London exploded in midair off the Irish coast in June 1985; it was assumed to be the work of Sikh terrorists (Sikhs had killed Indira Gandhi in 1984 and have maintained over the years an ever-growing terror campaign in the Punjab and main Indian cities in support of an independent Sikh state, Kalistan). In November 1985 an Egyptian airliner was hijacked to Malta, and a bloody rescue followed. In April 1986 security guards in London prevented the bombing of an Israeli El Al airliner. In April 1988 a Kuwaiti airliner was hijacked to Iran; two passengers were killed. Passengers and bypassers were killed in airline terminal buildings in Rome, Vienna, and Madrid. Powerful Semtex explosives blew up a French DC-10 airliner over Niger in September 1989, killing 171 people. And 107 people died when a Colombian Boeing 727 exploded in November.

A new dimension in terror appeared in October 1985, when extremist Palestinian guerrillas led by Muhammad "Abu" Abbas hijacked the Italian cruise ship *Achille Lauro*. An elderly Jewish American was killed when the terrorists threw him overboard in his wheelchair. (In 1961 a former Portuguese colonial official named Henrique Galvão had captured the Portuguese cruise liner *Santamaria* with hundreds of American tourists aboard in protest against the African war, but nobody was hurt.)

Convinced that Libya was behind much of the new terrorism, the United States decided to punish it. On March 24, 1986, a U.S. naval task force deliberately cruised in the Gulf of Sidra, claimed by Libya; when Libyans fired missiles at American carrier jets, the planes bombed the missile base ashore and Libyan patrol boats.

On April 5, 1986, a discotheque in West Berlin where American servicemen congregated was bombed, and many suffered injuries. The Reagan administration announced it had evidence that the attack had been planned by Libyans, and on April 15 American carrier jets and F-111 fighter-bombers from British bases hit Tripoli and Benghazi in retaliation. Colonel Qaddafi's family quarters were hit, and an adopted daughter was said to have been killed. In apparent counterretaliation, one American and two British hostages were killed in Lebanon, and a Libyan team attempted to blow up a U.S. officers' club in Ankara, Turkey.

And it went on and on. Jews praying at a synagogue in Istanbul were massacred in 1986, and there was a two-week Arab bombing campaign in the streets of Paris. In 1987 Israeli aircraft hit PLO headquarters in Tunis in a high-precision raid, killing Chairman Yassir Arafat's deputy Khalil Wazir, known as Abu Jihad. In July 1989 two bombs exploded in Mecca during the holy pilgrimage; Saudi Arabia accused a group of pro-Iranian Kuwaitis of terrorism, and sixteen of them were beheaded in public in September. On October 4, the president of the principal Jewish organization in Belgium was shot dead in Brussels. On November 30, Alfred Herrhausen, the chairman of Deutsche Bank, the largest bank in West Germany, died when his car was blown up by a bomb in Bad Homburg by the Red Army Faction, a West German terrorist organization of long standing. On December 6, thirty-five people were killed and hundreds injured when a truck bomb with a half-ton of dynamite exploded in front of a police office on a street in the Colombian capital of Bogotá. As in the case of the airliner explosion in November, the assumption was that the blast was ordered by the Colombian cocaine cartel in reprisal for the extraditions of its leaders to the United States. On December 15, Colombian police killed in a shootout one of the top leaders of the cartel, Gonzálo Rodríguez Gacha, who was believed to have ordered the bombing of the airliner and of the Bogotá Federal Investigative Police headquarters. In Colombia, fifty judges were killed by bombs in 1989 for prosecuting drug-running cases.

The horrible irony of the world in the eighties was that this level of blind violence was rising just as great forces of history were bringing a promise of new hope and peace and freedom.

III

The triumph of democracy in much of the world during the eighties had truly historical dimensions. It manifested itself through the process of an astonishingly accelerated breakup of the Marxist-Leninist systems around the world as well as through the fall of a half dozen rightist dictatorships.

Between the inauguration of the first postwar non-Communist prime minister in Poland in August 1989 and the end of that year, hard-line Communist regimes were ousted by overwhelming public pressure in Hungary, East Germany, Bulgaria, Czechoslovakia, and Romania. The transfer was peaceful except in Romania, where street battles between prodemocracy groups aided by the army and President Nicolae Ceaușescu's private security forces cost between 7,000 and 10,000 lives. At the climax of the Christmastime revolution, Ceaușescu and his wife, Elena, were captured by the rebels, sentenced to death in a secret trial, and executed immediately. In Europe, only Albania, self-isolated even from the rest of the Communist world for decades, was the last remaining stronghold of totally repressive hard-line communism, but the little mountain republic on the Adriatic had no relevance to global ideological trends. Yugoslavia, torn asunder by internal ethnic tensions, retained its ostensible Communist ideological identity, though it no longer had any meaning.

The transformations in the Communist world, especially in the Soviet Union, had immensely beneficial effects on superpower relations as well. Thus Washington and Moscow took a major step toward limiting and controlling nuclear weapons when Ronald Reagan and Mikhail Gorbachev signed at the Kremlin on June 1, 1988, the Intermediate Nuclear Forces (INF) Treaty, eliminating all intermediate-range launchers from Europe and the Far East. Then the two men stood smilingly in the center of the Red Square, waving at the cameras. Within months both the United States and the Soviets had begun to remove and destroy their Pershing and SS-20 missiles, the first such public demonstration of détente making in the postwar era.

Then the two sides embarked on negotiations for a new agreement on offensive strategic weapons (the Nixon-Brezhnev pact had expired in 1977, but both governments went on observing it in the interval) and for pacts on prohibiting chemical weapons and defining the size of NATO and Warsaw Pact conventional military forces in Europe.

Gorbachev's ascent to power on March 11, 1985, signified for all practical purposes the closing of the Bolshevik cycle initiated by Lenin almost seventy years earlier. Even before he completed five years in power, this son of peasants from a village in the northern Caucasus had already entered history books as one of the most crucial figures of the century. In terms of the Soviet Union and communism, Gorbachev already ranked along Lenin and Stalin; in the long run, he could quite conceivably eclipse them, if orthodox Marxism-Leninism goes down the drain under his direction. In less than five years on the world scene, he had achieved—and changed—more than any Soviet leader since Stalin, who died thirty-two years earlier. Clearly an outstanding statesman in the last half century, Gorbachev created a new relationship with the United States—and helped to end the Cold War.

Gorbachev, then fifty-four (graduated as a lawyer, he was the first Soviet leader with a university education), replaced the seventy-three-year-old President Konstantin Chernenko, a party old-timer who died of emphysema that same day. Chernenko had won brief power at the death of Yuri Andropov, the former KGB chief, who had succeeded Brezhnev. Gorbachev was regarded as a Andropov protégé, and there are reasons to believe the two men shared their views on the need for basic reform for the Soviet Union if the country was to survive as a viable entity in the age of technological revolution. Andropov, as it developed later, was a man of considerable learning and cultural background (this was not generally known at the time because Kremlin leaders traditionally concealed all information about their private personalities), and it made sense for him to select Gorbachev as the Soviet Union's man of the future. (Gorbachev, by the way, does not try to conceal everything about his past or his tastes, another departure from the old practice.)

Five years after he launched his *perestroika*—restructuring—program, Gorbachev has succeeded in a variety of stunning and controversial endeavors, and no matter what happens to him, the Soviet Union is not likely to revert to the repressive stagnation policies of the Brezhnev years. Most significantly, as one becomes aware even after a few days in Moscow, the Soviet Union is no longer an ideological police state. Gorbachev's obvious conclusion was that economic reform and *perestroika* would be impossible without a relatively open (if not altogether free) society because only social and political pressures can force in time the fundamental changes he hopes to achieve. This led him to proclaim *glasnost*—openness—and for the first time in Soviet history, national issues were frankly discussed in the press, on radio and television, and in public debates at Communist party headquarters, government offices, factories, and farms.

By allowing and encouraging in 1988 virtually free elections to the new Soviet parliament—no longer a rubber-stamp instrument, but a body that has already flexed its muscles by rejecting official nominees for posts of deputy premiers and Cabinet ministers—Gorbachev has, in effect, done away with Lenin's concept of democratic centralism, which was power flowing from the top down, in favor of what amounts to the opposite notion of representative democracy. The Soviet Union was not a democracy in 1989, but the trend was clearly in that direction. After five years the economic results of *perestroika* were not yet visible, and Gorbachev had to face Western types of challenges like workers' strikes; but common sense suggested that the Soviet Union has no alternative to patience, education, and hard work. As Aleksandr Yakovlev, his closest adviser, explained to me in Moscow in 1988, Gorbachev's idea is that people must begin to understand the issues affecting them before they can behave accordingly.

Inevitably Gorbachev opened every conceivable Pandora's box in the Soviet Union, from ethnic tensions in the Central Asian republics to separatist and nationalist pressures in the Baltic states, Georgia, Armenia, and even Moldavia and the Ukraine. Again his view has been that the Soviet Union must ride out these pressures, because otherwise it cannot function as a modern nation.

By the end of 1989, however, Gorbachev began facing the danger of an actual breakup of the Soviet Union, a previously unthinkable notion. Parliaments in Lithuania and Latvia, once docile assemblies, voted in December to excise from the constitutions of their republics the crucial Article Six, which established the Communist party's monopoly on political power; only days earlier, Gorbachev had barely prevented the Congress of People's Deputies in Moscow from doing away with Article Six for all of the Soviet Union. In stripping the Communist party of its supremacy, the Baltic republics were following the example of the Eastern European nations where Gorbachev had facilitated, if not encouraged, the process of change. Then the Lithuanian Communist party, controlled by reformers, moved to declare its independence from the Soviet Communist party at the Kremlin. To

Gorbachev, this was a prologue to actual secession of the Baltic states (Latvia was already planning to reinstate its old flag and national anthem) and a powerful threat to his own reform program; in one of his angriest speeches, he warned that continued separatist moves would "sow discord, bloodshed, and death." Indeed, Gorbachev was caught in a terrifying dilemma as the 1990's opened: On the one hand, he could not allow the Soviet Union to come apart; on the other hand, he could not use military force without risking the creation of an uncontrollable situation in the country, as well as damaging the new Soviet image of a peace-loving superpower no longer engaging in military interventions.

The nationalities crisis also threatened Gorbachev's own leadership position, raising the possibility that the armed forces, the KGB, and *perestroika*'s conservative foes in the power hierarchy would overthrow him, invoking the need to maintain the integrity of the Soviet Union as the reason to act. Simultaneously, the overall Soviet economic situation had deteriorated to such an extent during 1989 that Gorbachev was vulnerable in this context as well—only his extraordinary personality, and the very basic reality that none of his rivals offered better solutions than *perestroika* and patience, maintained his hold on the national destiny. While Gorbachev continued to insist that his policies were designed to improve and modernize the Marxist-Leninist system—and the assumption must be that he meant it, at least at the outset—the question of whether in truth the system was reformable at all began emerging with increasing sharpness. If it became absolutely clear that the answer was in the negative, the only Soviet option (short of stagnation, paralysis, and social disorder) was a transition toward forms of a market economy and multiparty political democracy. By the end of 1989, Poland, Hungary, and Czechoslovakia had already embarked on that road. For Gorbachev, the fundamental challenge in the nineties (and when no longer for him, for his successors, because political dynamics are irrepressible) was whether the Soviet Union, the mother of modern communism, was prepared to abandon it once for all. Under *glasnost*, this was the real debate in the Soviet Union.

In February 1990, Gorbachev, always on the offensive, stunned his nation and the world by proposing that the Soviet Communist Party abandon its monopoly on power—exercised since 1918—and accept the principle of political pluralism, a Western-type presidency and limited return to private property. The party's Central Committee, fully controlled by Gorbachev, voted on February 7 to repeal the Soviet Constitution's famous Article Six (that he was not prepared to do three months earlier), which proclaimed that "the leading and guiding force of Soviet society and the nucleus of its political system . . . is the Communist Party of the Soviet Union."

Parliament was to reaffirm this decision formally, but, for all practical purposes, the Marxist-Leninist era had ended; February 7, 1990, marked the death of the political system implanted by Lenin on November 7, 1917, the start of the great Russian Revolution. It was a date that would live in history. Two weeks later, the Communist party was roundly defeated in the elections for parliament in Lithuania, the first free regional vote in Soviet history.

In foreign policy Gorbachev's proclaimed desire to deideologize international relations—the centerpiece of his speech before the United Nations General Assembly in New York in December 1988—removed the Soviet Union from traditional Marxist-Leninist world revolution ambitions. He seemed to have realized that world revolution, if attainable, is an extremely expensive proposition that the Soviet Union cannot afford and does not really need. The cost of subsidizing revolutionary friends like Cuba, Vietnam, Afghanistan, and Nicaragua—approximately ten billion dollars annually—was no longer justified by foreign policy ambitions, and Gorbachev was retrenching.

Finally, his readiness to pursue and reach arms control agreements with the United States and NATO demonstrated that Gorbachev wished to avoid an exorbitantly expensive arms race with the West. Curiously, Ronald Reagan's concept of the Strategic Defense Initiative ("Star Wars"), announced by the President in 1983, two years before Gorbachev became boss in the Kremlin, may have shocked Gorbachev into arms limitation negotiations. He knew, even better than the Congress in Washington, that Reagan was talking hundreds of billions of dollars that the Soviets simply did not have to spend on arms. Just as curiously, Reagan, the great anti-Communist, turned into an admirer of Gorbachev just as the Soviet leader's two visits to the United States triggered "Gorbymania" among Americans. The two men held five summit meetings in fewer than five years, culminating in their meeting with President-Elect George Bush on Governors Island in New York Harbor in December 1988, and their being photographed against the background of the Statue of Liberty. Less than a year later, Bush and Gorbachev held their "get acquainted" summit meeting aboard a Soviet liner in Valetta, Malta, in what a Kremlin spokesman described as the way "from Yalta to Malta."

In China, too, Marxism-Leninism was cracking in the eighties, but there was no Chinese equivalent of Gorbachev in the Beijing leadership; events developed differently and much more tragically.

Under the octogenarian Deng Xiaoping, China had made impressive advances in economic reform, moving increasingly toward a market economy not only in the rural areas where the experiment had begun in 1979 but also in urban trade and gradually in industry. China opened its doors to foreign investment, know-how, and arms (chiefly from the United States) and to foreign education. Tens of thousands of students were sent to study abroad—twenty-six thousand were studying in the United States in 1988—and foreign visitors to China numbered millions in the late 1980's.

One of the sights that struck me the most during a visit to Beijing in 1985 was the forest of construction cranes rising over the capital's skyline; they were building hotels for tourists and office buildings for businessmen. One of the new hotels, the Fragrance, was designed by I. M. Pei. And not too far from the Great Hall of the People, I discovered Maxim's Beijing restaurant, an exact replica of Maxim's in Paris, complete with waiters (Chinese) in white tie and tails and a superb French menu (no Chinese food served). It was established as a lark by Pierre Cardin, the French designer, whose clothes are produced on a large scale under contracts with Chinese textile plants and who thought it was a neat way of gaining still more Chinese goodwill. And the Great Wall Hotel, I discovered, had venison flown from Paris twice a week (it was the autumn).

The Chinese leadership, however, was not prepared for political reforms or political freedoms. It was flying in the face of reality to insist on the ideological status quo and Marxist purity with the masses of foreign visitors bringing their ways and ideas to China and, even more so, with the returning students, who had observed and tasted American and Western European freedoms and consumer societies' life-styles. More and more young Chinese were listening to shortwave radio broadcasts from the Voice of America, the British Broadcasting Corporation, Radio Japan, and Radio Australia and watching Chinese-language television programs from Hong Kong. The desire of the Chinese for their own freedoms could not be bottled up forever.

Not surprisingly it began erupting. Student demonstrations in favor of democracy started in Beijing on December 20, 1986, with marches, speeches, and wall posters demanding liberalization. During the week the demonstrations spread to Shanghai and other cities. Deng and his associates ordered a crackdown, and the police were able to discourage the protests without much violence. But the spirit of change could not be dampened altogether; it was a question of a new opportunity to protest.

Deng, the uncontested ruler, thought at the same time that the party leadership itself must be purged of those who might be overly sympathetic to political liberalization. Communist Party General Secretary Hu Yaobang, whom Deng suspected of planning a Gorbachev-like coup, was dismissed from his post early in 1988, without a clear explanation, suggesting that it was the octogenarian who really controlled the Central Committee.

Hu had already antagonized the People's Liberation Army (PLA) in April 1985 by announcing that the Chinese armed forces would be cut by one million men—25 percent of the total. It so happened that Deng was chairman of the party's Military Commission. In September ten Politburo and sixty-four Central Committee members were retired, supposedly because of age, but only six new members were elevated to the Politburo, reducing the total number. It was unclear whether this was engineered by Deng or Hu; there was speculation that the general secretary was trying to pack the Politburo with his own people. In March 1986 Premier Zhao Ziyang, whose role in this shadow theater of Chinese politics was at best confusing, announced that China would conduct no more atmospheric nuclear tests. Again it was hard to determine whether he spoke for Deng as well.

In removing Hu, a friendly personage with Western tastes in dress, Deng may have remembered that the general secretary had sent a message of congratulations to Gorbachev upon his election by the Soviet Politburo in 1985. In the wake of the student demonstrations in the winter of 1986, and Hu's reluctance to criticize the students publicly, the telegram to Moscow may have been the equivalent of a smoking gun in the Forbidden City.

Having won the power struggle with Hu in 1988, Deng gave the job of general secretary to Premier Zhao, presumably regarding him at that point as a reliable functionary. Li Peng, an economist, became premier, and the Cabinet was reorganized in April 1988, supposedly to speed up reforms. In September, however, Premier Li Peng changed his mind, announcing after a weeklong party conference that the program for decentralizing the economy would be slowed down.

The next chapter in the Chinese drama opened when Gorbachev arrived in Beijing on May 15, 1989, the first Soviet leader to come to China since Khrushchev's visit in 1959. This was the new opportunity for protest awaited by the prodemocracy students. The first demonstrations actually began after Hu Yaobang died on April 15, and the Soviet leader's arrival was an occasion to continue them. As Gorbachev landed in Beijing, thousands of students began gathering at Tienanmen Square, the vast and usually empty area in front of the Great Hall of the People. Mao's statue is visible from there. The young crowd was friendly, and Gorbachev appeared pleased, but his hosts could not open passage among the students to lead him into the hall through the front door; embarrassingly a side door was used.

Though the students were greeting Gorbachev as a symbol of political reforms, he could not respond except in generalities without offending his official hosts. As he left Beijing for home, the student crowd grew and grew, and similar demonstrations erupted in scores of Chinese cities, from Shanghai to Xian and Chengdu. The rest is tragic history. After a week of student defiance Deng was able to muster a majority in the Politburo to order an army attack on the students to dislodge them from the square. Television pictures and press photographs have shown the world how the tanks and infantrymen with automatic weapons cleared the area, attacking it in battle formation, armor running over the students' bodies. Perhaps one, perhaps ten thousand students were killed or maimed. The same happened in the other cities. Troops were used to disperse students. Then came the massive arrests and executions. Nobody knows how many students were executed; Amnesty International has reported that there were secret executions as well. And the regime cut back drastically on the number of students it would send overseas.

Zhao, who sided with the students and opposed armed action, was naturally fired as general secretary. Premier Li, who turned out to be a hardliner by conviction or opportunism, was named to take his place. Deng reappeared in public view when Chinese television broadcast film of ceremonies at which he congratulated white-gloved army commanders for their dedication and loyalty.

The massacre of June 1989 and the executions and imprisonments were not likely to arrest the march of history. Deng and his colleagues surely understood history when they fought as revolutionaries against reactionary power more than a half century earlier. They may have forgotten it in their old age, but again, it was only a question of another opportunity for the new generations to reassert themselves. Sadly, President Bush appeared to ignore this reality too. Though the Chinese prodemocracy movement was profoundly inspired by American traditions—the students at Tienanmen Square had erected a small Statue of Liberty as their symbol—Bush in effect turned his back on them. Not only did the President drag his feet in imposing sanctions on the Deng regime after the massacre (Congress finally pushed him to act), but, as it later turned out, he immediately sent two of his top advisers on a secret mission to Beijing to assure the Chinese of the U.S. desire to preserve a good relationship. National Security Adviser Brent Scowcroft and Deputy Secretary of State Lawrence Eagleburger, the secret emissaries, returned to Beijing in December to brief the local leadership on the Bush-Gorbachev summit meeting off Malta—and press photographs showed them clinking glasses at a reception with Deng and his associates. Bush responded to the storm of national criticism by explaining that he understood China better than most people, having served there as the first American diplomatic representative in the early seventies.

The Polish story—the story that really began in 1956—resumed its logical course in July 1980, with the birth of the Solidarity free trade union in Gdańsk at the shipyard named after V. I. Lenin.

In the usual Polish way this event was not planned; there were no plots, no conspiracies. It just happened because the time was ripe, the right people appeared at the right time and right place out of nowhere, and the rest was improvised hour by hour, day by day, week by week, and month by month. It could not go on from year to year because on a wintry dawn in 1981 the Polish Communist Army, moved to liquidate Solidarity, fearing that the free union had achieved its objective. Eight years later, of course, Solidarity and the Communists were sharing power in the most astounding outcome of the struggle over the fate of Poland. In this story, too, the figure of Mikhail Gorbachev stands in the wings, benignly observing the Polish phenomenon.

Strikes broke out in various Polish cities in the latter part of July 1980 in an uncoordinated fashion as a result of rising prices, food and consumer goods shortages, and dissatisfaction with the general state of affairs. With Edward Gierek now in his tenth year as the first secretary of the Communist party, the economy was going from bad to worse, as were official corruption and the overall condition of the society. For example, public health, once the pride of socialist Poland, had broken down almost completely. There were accidents in industrial plants and coal mines, and the national structure was rapidly deteriorating. The regime, however, stubbornly ignored the situation, and official propaganda insisted that a new Poland was being built with foreign loans. Gierek, in fact, seemed to believe it himself—an illustration of his isolation from reality. The secret police harassed, beat, or arrested dissidents from KOR—the principal opposition group formed chiefly by intellectuals—and from illegal WZZ free trade unions that had been organized in 1978 in the steel town of Katowice in the southwest and in Gdańsk. The port city, of course, already had its tradition of antiregime struggles; in addition to the WZZ union, a student movement known as Young Poland (RMP) was created there in mid-1979.

Visiting Warsaw in the autumn of 1979, I had dinner with Mieczysław Rakowski, a maverick member of the Communist party's Central Committee, and editor of the surprisingly liberal and outspoken weekly *Polityka*, published by the Central Committee but regarded in the peculiar Polish political milieu as a virtual opposition organ. Rakowski, whom I had known well for many years, went into considerable detail to explain to me that the situation in Poland was not simply difficult but downright untenable. He talked about the economy, the corruption, the rot inside the party's leadership, and the demoralized state of the citizenry, concluding with the remark "This just can't go on much longer; something has to give. . . ." My friends in KOR, notably the young historian Adam Michnik, who was in and out of jail all the time, took the same view.

So when the strikes erupted in July 1980 with demands for pay increases and the establishment of free trade unions, the climate in the country was ripe for a major confrontation. Still, there were no plans afoot for any follow-up to the strikes that at first were in central and southern Poland as well as among Warsaw transportation workers. At the Lenin Shipyard in Gdańsk the management fired a crane operator named Anna Walentynowicz, a jolly middle-aged woman who was active in illegal trade union activities, and in response thousands of her fellow workers went on strike on August 14. A thirty-seven-year-old electrician with an impressive mustache, named Lech Wałęsa, who belonged to the WZZ illegal union, had been fired a few days earlier.

When the strike appeared to lose steam, Wałęsa climbed over the fence of the shipyard to join the strikers and urge them not to give up; he suddenly became the principal leader of the strike. The government temporized over the strikers' demands, insisted that they be halted before concessions were made, and surrounded the shipyard with units of the gray-uniformed ZOMO riot police (ZOMO is the Polish acronym for "motorized detachments of the citizens' militia," and it became world-famous for its tear gas and baton charges as the disturbances spread). But other shipyards in Gdańsk, Gdynia, and Szczecin joined the Lenin plant strike, as did, one after another, scores of industries across Poland. Gdańsk strikers used the telephone and telex to urge workers throughout the country to support them, and they asked for a show of solidarity. From the use of that word the idea occurred to one of the strike leaders that this would be a fine name for the new free trade unions they were organizing inside the shipyard.

Solidarność—Solidarity—caught on instantly, and someone else wrote it out in script in red on white (Polish national colors) with a Polish flag atop the letter *n*. It quickly became one of the best-known symbols in the world.

By late August it became evident to the regime that it had to deal with Solidarity and Wałęsa, who now assumed the chairmanship of the nationwide Inter-Enterprise Strike Committee. Negotiations opened between a deputy prime minister and the strikers' leadership, assisted by KOR intellectuals who rushed from Warsaw to Gdańsk to be on hand with professional advice. There were lawyers, historians, writers, and journalists. Among them were Tadeusz Mazowiecki, the journalist who soon became the editor of the weekly *Solidarność* and, nine years later, the first non-Communist prime minister of Poland since the war, and pipe-smoking historian Bronisław Geremek, who has been Solidarity's chief strategist over all these years. Their deep friendship with Wałęsa goes back to the Gdańsk shipyard days.

Agreements that met most of the strikers' demands, including legal status for Solidarity, were reached in Szczecin on August 30, in Gdańsk on August 31, and elsewhere a few days later. Nothing of the kind had happened before in a Communist country, where labor unions, like everything else, are run by the party. The negotiations were televised by the government network and broadcast on radio and over loudspeakers. It was an explosion of freedom that Poland had been denied when the war had ended thirty-five years earlier, and the nation was gripped with excitement. Gierek resigned as first secretary of the Communist party, to be replaced by a party hack named Stanisław Kania; General Wojciech Jaruzelski, the defense minister and a Politburo member, was named prime minister. Virtually unknown in the country, he was a quiet man, often wearing dark glasses because of an eye affliction. In November Solidarity was formally legalized. It had a little more than a year's free life ahead.

When I came to Poland in June 1981 on a magazine assignment, I found joy and excitement, and I found concern that the Soviets would not tolerate Solidarity and freedom much longer. Brezhnev's invasion of Czechoslovakia in 1968 was very well remembered, and the question I often heard was "When?" rather than "Whether?" The collapsing Communist party held a special congress in July, with newly elected delegates, many of them liberals. Jaruzelski was chosen the party's first secretary (Kania simply vanished) while remaining prime minister and defense minister. In September Solidarity held its first congress. It named Wałęsa as its president and presented a program of economic and social reforms for Poland that proposed, in effect, a social democracy and market economy.

Now the end was approaching. Wałęsa spent most of his time negotiating reform proposals with Rakowski, my journalist friend, whom Jaruzelski appointed a deputy prime minister, while Solidarity and other emerging opposition groups turned increasingly anti-Communist and anti-Soviet. There were more and more incidents between Solidarity members and the police. At one point a Solidarity rally urged workers in other Communist countries to rise and form free labor unions as well. As Wałęsa told me many years later, he was losing control of Solidarity to an extremist leadership group. When I had visited him at Solidarity headquarters in Gdańsk late in June 1981—the first time we met—I heard his rivals criticizing him openly for being too soft and too moderate. Even Anna Walentynowicz told me that she was disappointed in Wałęsa.

At dawn of Sunday, December 13, 1981, the Polish military struck. Army troops, tanks, ZOMO, and secret police were deployed in all the key locations across the country as part of a carefully prepared contingency plan. At least ten thousand Solidarity leaders and militants were arrested and placed in jails and detention camps (Solidarity said the actual figure was much higher). Wałęsa was detained in Gdańsk and flown by helicopter to a countryside villa, where he was kept under house arrest. Martial law was declared, and Solidarity was deprived of its legal status. The military coup was staged by a junta of generals headed by Jaruzelski.

The real truth behind what happened may never be fully known. When I met Jaruzelski in May 1982, six months after the coup, he told me that the alternative was a civil war, and he hinted that there would have been a Soviet invasion if the Polish military had not acted themselves to prevent the destruction of the Communist system in Poland that Moscow was known to fear. With Brezhnev still in power in the Kremlin, I find Jaruzelski's explanation credible. Many people in Poland did not believe that the general was anything other than a Soviet tool; with one's patriotism at stake, this is a very touchy subject in Poland. But I thought that Jaruzelski was prepared for massive national resentment, if not worse, and he knew that time must elapse before the situation could change.

What was left of Solidarity went underground, and new opposition groups—mainly the youth—began working in clandestinity. Actors boycotted national television and radio in order not to work for the "occupiers." Lifelong personal friendships were broken. Jaruzelski, however, was not interested in a permanent system of complete repression (in contrast with President Gustav Husák in Czechoslovakia), and he lifted martial law in July 1983, although most Solidarity leaders remained in confinement. Wałęsa was freed and declared a nonperson, a claim that totally underestimated his continued popularity. Pope John Paul II returned to his homeland after martial law was lifted (this was his second visit to Poland after his elevation to the papacy) and was allowed to meet with Wałęsa. This alone was a huge concession made by the regime. In Washington the Reagan administration simplemindedly maintained the sanctions it had imposed against Poland after the December coup, and Defense Secretary Caspar Weinberger described Jaruzelski (whom he had never met) on television as a "Soviet general in a Polish uniform." Wałęsa was given the Nobel Peace Prize, which his wife accepted in Oslo.

Perhaps the most important change came in March 1985, when Gorbachev assumed power in the Kremlin. As Jaruzelski told me the story years later, the first sign was a different attitude. Brezhnev, he said, would insult him and his military colleagues when they visited Moscow. Gorbachev, according to Jaruzelski, went out of his way to show friendship and an understanding of Poland's problems. The general told me that over the years he and Gorbachev began exchanging their respective experiences in fighting the inertia of their Communist bureaucracies in the face of the reforms they both urged on their nations.

My next trip to Poland was in 1987, and I found a changed nation. Jaruzelski told me that everybody in Poland, including himself, had learned a lot in recent years and that he welcomed conversations with "moderate opposition." Wałęsa surprised me by telling me when I went to see him in Gdańsk that he and Jaruzelski would meet "on the road to reform." I had long dinner chats with Geremek about possible cooperation between the regime and the opposition and similar chats with Rakowski, who remained a close adviser to Jaruzelski. The pope was back in Poland, again conferring with the general and Wałęsa. There were still arrests and censorship, but they seemed to be more for effect than for real—certainly as compared with situations in Czechoslovakia, East Germany, or Romania.

In 1988 the breakthrough came with the "round table" sessions between the regime and the opposition. On June 3, 1989, the freest elections since the war were held in Poland with a stunning Solidarity victory (the same day the Chinese army massacred prodemocracy students in Beijing's Tienanmen Square). Rakowski, now prime minister, orchestrated the political transition, then resigned to make room for an opposition prime minister (it was to be Mazowiecki, the sixty-two-year-old Warsaw editor.) Then, in an extraordinary reversal, Wałęsa, Geremek, and Mazowiecki maneuvered the new parliament to elect Jaruzelski president of Poland—with one vote to spare—against the opposition of hard-line Communists who regarded the general as a traitor to Marxism-Leninism.

Wałęsa was right when he predicted that he and Jaruzelski would meet on the way to reform. A remarkable degree of mutual respect had developed between the general and the Solidarity leaders whom he had once imprisoned. The opposition respected him especially for agreeing with Gorbachev to disclose the truth about the murder of thousands of Polish officers by the Soviets in 1941 and other Stalinist crimes against the Poles. As for Gorbachev, he telephoned the Communist party leadership in Warsaw during August 1989 to recommend that they cooperate with Prime Minister Mazowiecki in forming the coalition government; Mazowiecki was approved by parliament with one solitary voice against him.

Adam Michnik, the rebel historian (and now a member of parliament and editor of the prodemocracy *Gazeta Wyborcza*, the most widely read newspaper in Poland), took the view that the Poles had successfully adapted the "Spanish model" of peaceful transition from dictatorship to democracy; in Spain, dictator Franco had been replaced at his death by King Juan Carlos I, who instantly installed a fully democratic political system. Other analysts concluded that the two groups in Poland, the opposition and the Communists, had produced a "historic compromise" through a joint decision to phase out Communist rule in a gradual fashion: This was the "Polish way away from socialism." It would soon be followed elsewhere in Eastern Europe.

The "Polish Summer" led directly to the "Eastern European Autumn," now also known as the "Autumn of the People," and it was an incredible sequence of spectacular events that surprised the world and changed forever the international equation.

Hungary came right after Poland—as it had done in 1956—because their internal dynamics were the closest in Eastern Europe. Though the Hungarians had produced nothing resembling Solidarity, nor did they live through Polish-type confrontations in the course of the eighties, they embarked on their own low-profile process of change with Communist party reformers leading the way. When I visited Budapest on the twentieth anniversary of the 1956 uprising, Hungary was a most relaxed society by Communist standards, and it even seemed relatively successful under János Kadár's "goulash communism," as it was then popularly called. It was not a free country by any means—the media were fully controlled and the Communist party was fully in charge of daily life—but the Hungarian regime was not as harshly repressive as, say, that of Romania, East Germany, or Czechoslovakia. Unlike Poland, Hungary had no cohesive opposition groups (such as KOR, which preceded Solidarity), but mild dissent was tolerated. The economy, much more liberalized than elsewhere in Eastern Europe as a result of a series of quiet reforms, was performing reasonably well: There was a small private sector in trade, farming, and small construction, and the more affluent were building weekend homes in the countryside. In conversations with Hungarian friends, I found mild contentment, the assumption that Kadárism in some form would survive in perpetuity, and something of a consensus that confrontations were undesirable. The year 1956 had not been forgotten.

Hungary, however, began to stir politically in the late eighties, as Gorbachev already held power in Moscow—suggesting that Soviet thinking about Marxism-Leninism, and therefore about controls over Eastern Europe, was evolving—and as more and more political opposition was being tolerated by the Jaruzelski regime in Warsaw, with a new national dialogue about to start there. At that juncture, the initiative for change was assumed by the younger reformists in the leadership of the Hungarian Communist party. In 1988, Kadár was ousted by his Politburo colleagues from the chairmanship of the party, thirty-two years after he had welcomed Soviet tanks into Budapest. He was replaced by Premier Karolý Grosz. Kadár was treated gently—despite 1956, he was not detested by Hungarians—and no effort was made to charge him with any past sins. Kadár died the following year, at the age of seventy-seven, as the wave of liberalization swept the country.

The Hungarian transition toward democracy, launched in earnest early in 1989, was the handiwork of the reformist Communist faction in the Politburo led by Grosz, Rezso Nyers, Imre Pozsgay, and the new prime minister, Miklos Nemeth, and foreign minister, Gyula Horn. These men were convinced that rising trends against orthodox communism were irreversible, that the nation demanded a basic change, and that Hungarians wanted their sovereignty reaffirmed and respected. Playing the reform role within the Communist party that Dubček and his associates in Czechoslovakia had pioneered in 1968, the Hungarian Communist progressives concluded that confrontations should be averted as unnecessary and that they should take the country down the road to political and economic freedom. Inasmuch as no organized opposition existed in Hungary, the regime was not faced with the type of negotiations the Polish Communist leadership had to conduct with Solidarity and the Citizens' Committee. In fact, the Hungarian changeover happened virtually by national consensus. Whether or not events in Hungary were directly inspired by the Polish experience of 1988–89, Poland unquestionably helped to set the mood—and Gorbachev's assurances to Grosz in March 1989 that the Soviets would not interfere with reforms in Eastern Europe became a significant encouragement for the Hungarians.

But first, the ghost of 1956 had to be exorcised. The Communist-dominated Hungarian parliament declared that the great uprising had *not* been a "counterrevolution," as originally charged, and that Premier Imre Nagy, who had been secretly executed at the time, was not a traitor. In June 1989, Nagy and four of his murdered colleagues were reburied in a formal ceremony attended by a quarter-million Hungarians.

In the political realm, parliament had already voted in January to legalize freedom of assembly and freedom of association; it did so at the initiative of the Politburo reformers, and it marked for all practical purposes the end of the Communist dictatorship. In February, the Socialist Workers' party, which was the Communist party's official name, announced that it approved the creation of independent political parties, opening the way for a democratic multiparty system. In this sense, the Hungarian evolution was smoother than Poland's, as no negotiations with anybody were required. Meanwhile, Gorbachev, as part of his broader foreign-policy offensive, began withdrawing Soviet troops from Eastern Europe, even in the absence of a conventional forces agreement with NATO, choosing Hungary to be the first country in the removal (with the exception of Romania, Soviet troops were permanently stationed in all the Warsaw Pact countries, with nearly a half million in East Germany alone).

Early in May, the Hungarian regime ordered the dismantling of barbed-wire fences along the Austrian frontier, becoming the first Communist nation with an open border to the West. In the most literal sense, the iron curtain was torn down at that moment, four decades after, in Winston Churchill's words, it had descended from the Baltic to the Adriatic. When President Bush visited Budapest in July as part of his trip to Poland and Hungary, he was presented with a strand of that barbed wire, proudly displaying it to the crowds as the symbol of the end of the iron curtain era. But the opening of the Hungarian frontier would soon have much more palpable and politically significant effects.

Now internal reform dynamics in Hungary accelerated rapidly. Imre Pozsgay and Rezso Nyers, the top Politburo progressives, published a manifesto calling for fundamental economic changes and for a dialogue with the emerging political opposition groups. In June, senior Communist leaders and spokesmen for the opposition met to discuss the creation of a multiparty system in Hungary, a step reminiscent of Poland's 1988 "round table" negotiations. At the end of the month, as the next step in the transition process, the regime established a collective presidency of Hungary led by Rezso Nyers. The Communists were still very much in power, but they appeared to be presiding over the liquidation of the ancien régime, and they obviously commanded wide national support. By September, the Communists and the opposition put together the framework for the inauguration of a multiparty system during 1990. In October, Rezso Nyers became chairman of the Socialist Workers' party, and this organization formally renounced Marxism-Leninism as its ideology, to adopt instead democratic socialism on the Scandinavian model. It also renamed itself the Hungarian Socialist party. Two weeks later, on the anniversary of the 1956 uprising, the regime proclaimed Hungary a free republic, dropping the former name, the Hungarian People's Republic, which over the decades had identified the country as part of the Communist bloc.

At that juncture, the reformist Communist leadership made it clear that it would like to keep power in the context of the new Hungary, an idea that Communists elsewhere in Eastern Europe were beginning to develop quietly as well. The leadership's idea was to hold presidential elections in January 1990, ostensibly to demonstrate that Hungary had become a full-fledged democracy. It was a very subtle maneuver based on the assumption that Nyers, the head of the reorganized and renamed Communist party, would probably be elected because of his personal popularity, and also, more to the point, because the new democratic parties—such as the infant Hungarian Democratic Forum—had no time to organize after forty years in wilderness and would be unable to conduct effective campaigns and field candidates with a winning potential. To the Communists' credit, however, they readily agreed to a referendum on the subject, and they accepted the defeat of their idea with equanimity when the voters went to the polls on November 26—the first free election in forty-four years. The plan approved in the referendum provided for the election of a new parliament in the spring of 1990, and then the choice of the president by the legislature. All the signs were that during the first year of the new decade, Hungary would become a full-fledged representative democracy, with the Communists probably becoming the opposition party.

East Germany's fate was the product of a very special kind of political dynamics and political chemistry, a collective shift in national behavior that remains extremely difficult to explain scientifically—perhaps because people's decisions on how they act are not scientific propositions. This point, by the way, was never understood by orthodox Communist leaders weaned on notions of "scientific Marxism," and inevitably led to their demise, to their great surprise.

Historically, East Germany did not seem a likely prospect for a revolt, certainly not so soon. By Eastern European standards, this German Democratic Republic (GDR) seemed reasonably well off economically, and it was quiescent politically. There had been no violent protests in East Germany since June 1953, and political opposition was confined to a small group of intellectuals and artists and to factions of the Lutheran Evangelical Church, the dominant religion. Erich Honecker, the seventy-seven-year-old East German president and Communist party chief, had no trouble controlling this limited political dissent, and Honecker himself was a leading European opponent of Mikhail Gorbachev's *perestroika*. The old man had no use for it and made no bones about it, knowing that the Soviets would not use their massive military presence in East Germany to enforce democratic change, of all things. But Honecker did not understand his own people any better than he understood *perestroika*.

It is virtually impossible to explain what happened in East Germany in the summer of 1989, other than by falling back on the mysteries of political dynamics and what became known in Eastern Europe that incredible year as "People's Power." Whether or not Poland and Hungary—and the persona of Gorbachev—had anything to do with the inspiration of the movement, East Germans suddenly started to flee their homeland. Under Honecker, GDR citizens were rarely permitted to visit the West, but they were free to spend their vacations in Eastern European countries (except Poland, which was put on the blacklist with the advent of the bad example of Solidarity). It was normal, therefore, for thousands and thousands of East Germans to turn up in Czechoslovakia and Hungary during the summer, many families driving their little Trabant cars built in East Germany, as they have done in the past. They could easily cross the East German border to Czechoslovakia, and from there proceed to Hungary.

What was not normal, however, was that many of these East Germans had suddenly resolved they did not wish to return home, but wanted to go to West Germany instead. This was the start of the unraveling of the Honecker system, although nobody realized it at first when hundreds of these East German tourists took refuge in West German embassies in Prague and Budapest and demanded political asylum in West Germany. Again, it is not known who originally came up with the idea, or why, or when; there is nothing to suggest that this was a planned movement. It was entirely spontaneous, which is presumably why it worked as splendidly as it did.

Now that Hungary had opened its border with Austria, the East German visitors started crossing into the Austrian territory, but their departures were technically illegal because of a 1969 Hungarian-GDR agreement under which East Germans could not proceed to any third country without valid travel papers issued by East German authorities. But East Germans kept streaming into Hungary clandestinely through Czechoslovakia, while others, returning from Black Sea vacations in Romania and Bulgaria, simply dug in their heels on Hungarian territory. By the first week of September, there were close to fifteen thousand East Germans in Hungary demanding to go west, and the Budapest regime had to choose between letting them do so in violation of the 1969 accord, or forcing them back to East Germany in violation of what the Hungarians regarded as their human rights. East Germany naturally insisted that its Warsaw Pact ally live up to its legal obligations, but the Hungarian government concluded that human rights came first (it did not wish, among other considerations, to face the certain ire of its own public if it repatriated the refugees) and that it would let the agreement lapse on September 10, because of changed conditions. Within ten days, over twenty thousand East Germans crossed from Hungary into Austria and then to West Germany. The Hungarian decision, as it turned out, was the death sentence for East German Communist hard-liners.

Now the scene shifted to Prague, where thousands of East Germans who had illegally crossed the border into Czechoslovakia sought asylum at the West German embassy; others did likewise in Warsaw. For the East German regime (which had erected the Berlin Wall in 1961 to keep its population from fleeing west), the new exodus instantly became a grave political crisis. Though this growing movement—the spectacle of East Germans escaping from communism under their very noses—posed potential dangers for Czechoslovakia's hard-liners, the regime made no effort to stem the flow to the West German Embassy. It feared that a repression of the refugees might trigger a domestic revolt against the status quo; but, unlike Hungary, Czechoslovakia was not ready to let the East Germans go west.

Inside East Germany, powerful pressures were rising. On September 10, the New Forum, the first organized opposition group, came into being, and two weeks later over ten thousand East Germans demonstrated in the streets of the ancient city of Leipzig to demand basic reforms and a legal status for the New Forum. At this stage, the Soviet Union again intervened directly in the Eastern European rebellion (Gorbachev's July call to Rakowski in Warsaw had been the first such involvement)—on the side of the rebels. At a meeting at the United Nations in New York on September 27, Soviet Foreign Minister Eduard A. Shevardnadze persuaded East German Foreign Minister Oskar Fischer (in the presence of West German Foreign Minister Hans-Dietrich Genscher) that the refugees in the West German embassies in Prague and Warsaw should be permitted to emigrate west. On September 30, Genscher appeared at his Prague embassy to announce the deal, and more than ten thousand refugees were finally free to rush west. Compounding the irony of the situation, they were transported from Czechoslovakia to West Germany across East Germany in East German trains. At Dresden and other towns, East Germans fought to board the westbound trains; they had to be held back by riot policemen. By October 4, over twenty thousand East Germans had reached the West from Prague and Warsaw, and the GDR regime closed the border into Czechoslovakia, believing that it had stopped the hemorrhage.

But now the real challenge was in East Germany. For the first time since 1953, protesters demonstrated across the country—in Leipzig, Dresden and other cities. And Gorbachev decided the time had come for personal intervention, flying to East Berlin on October 5—most ironically—for the celebration of the fortieth anniversary of the creation of the German Democratic Republic. On arrival, he expressed his faith in the East German future in a way that clearly invited the hard-liners' ouster: "We know our German friends very well, as well as their ability to recognize and to learn from life and to forecast the political road ahead and to introduce corrections if necessary. They have our full confidence." The next day Gorbachev met for three hours with the ailing Honecker; the substance of their conversations was not disclosed, but Gorbachev remarked afterward that he hoped the East German government would work "with all the forces in society." There was no question that he had read the Soviet riot act to Honecker.

Honecker, however, was not about to listen to Gorbachev, whom he despised, or about to quit. He continued to order his riot police to beat demonstrators, and, as it developed later, he planned to use military force if matters got out of hand. In a public comment, Honecker compared what he called the "present campaign of defamation" against his regime to the "counter-revolutionary rebellion" in Beijing the past spring, and he issued instructions for security forces to be equipped with live ammunition—and to use it. His associates realized that Honecker was prepared to stage a massacre comparable to Tienanmen Square when the opposition held the mass demonstration it had called for Leipzig for October 9. They also saw the potential for a civil war in the likely event that the Regular Army took the side of the rebels. It is unclear how Honecker was talked out of his determination to use force, but credit was claimed mostly by Egon Krenz, the Politburo member in charge of security and (incongruously) youth affairs, who may even have countermanded Honecker's orders. There are also reasons to believe that the Soviets, with their vast armies stationed in East Germany, undertook to talk sense to the old leader. In any event, the demonstration that evening by seventy thousand citizens in Leipzig was held peacefully.

But the end was near. Honecker had lost his grip on power, and at a Politburo session on October 10, the regime decided "to open discussions" with outsiders on a whole range of issues, including the sensitive question of free travel. Honecker was told repeatedly that the crisis was beyond the point of a solution by police action, but he still had trouble understanding the situation; it was a classic case of the dictator isolated from reality (for the eighteen years in power, in Honecker's case). On October 16, over one hundred thousand prodemocracy citizens marched in Leipzig. On October 18, Honecker was forced by his colleagues to resign from the Politburo and the presidency of GDR. The fifty-two-year-old Egon Krenz, a new-generation Communist, was picked to replace Honecker as the head of the Communist party and East Germany's president. Willi Stoph, seventy-five, the prime minister and a party hack, resigned too. This was the end of the first phase of the East German saga.

A second phase was necessary because Honecker's ouster did not solve the basic problems posed by the new revolutionary dynamics, and Krenz, given his former security-chief post, was clearly a transitional figure. Demonstrations went on in all the East German cities; on November 4, one million demonstrated in East Berlin in favor of free elections, and the situation was wholly out of control. Krenz tried to curry favor by reopening the Czechoslovakian border (ten thousand East Germans crossed it that weekend on their way to West Germany), then reorganized the Politburo.

The great moment in history came on November 9. The revamped Politburo's first step was to announce that East Germans could cross to West Germany without any permits through any crossing of their choice. At that instant the Berlin Wall ceased to exist as an obstacle to free movement, twenty-eight years and three months after its erection. Starting that Thursday night, at least two million East Germans rushed to West Berlin and beyond, with the whole city chanting, "The Wall is gone, the Wall is gone!," people embracing and kissing each other, and champagne, wine, and beer bottles appearing in the streets in overwhelming numbers. Young people from both sides climbed on the Wall to cheer and chant and sing. Others chipped off bits of the Wall. East German guards watched it all with happy smiles. Yet the fall of the Wall was not simply a German event: It was a powerful symbol of the end of the Cold War—and it immediately raised the question of what further justification remained for a divided Germany.

In the meantime, East German political dynamics required further solutions. On November 20, the Politburo appointed Hans Modrow, a former mayor of Dresden and a popular progressive new Politburo member, to be prime minister. Modrow instantly picked non-Communists for almost one half of his Cabinet seats and opened discussions with New Forum and Lutheran church leaders. The press and radio and television were now free to report what they pleased. On December 4, Krenz, in his capacity of East German president and party chairman, flew to Moscow for a Warsaw Pact summit at which Gorbachev reported on his Malta summit meeting with President Bush earlier that week (Poland was represented by non-Communist Prime Minister Mazowiecki, the Solidarity leader). Modrow came along and he was the only East German to meet with Gorbachev, presumably because the Russians knew that Krenz's brief leadership career was over. Two days later, Krenz was removed as president, and Manfred Gerlach, sixty-one, a non-Communist, became the head of state. Three days later, Krenz lost the party leadership to the forty-one-year-old Gregor Gysi, a lawyer and Communist party member. Gysi was not only the youngest Communist Politburo chief, he was also of Jewish descent. Honecker was expelled from the Communist party and placed under house arrest, where he would remain for a month while the new government investigated his involvement in what turned out to be extraordinary corruption in his leadership, including life in luxurious villas in a heavily guarded enclave, hunting lodges, costly cars, and access to a super-capitalist life-style.

But East Germany had to move ahead. The GDR People's Chamber (the hand-picked Communist parliament) voted to end the Communist party's monopoly in power, to write a new constitution, and to set May 6, 1990, as the date for multiparty elections. It also passed a resolution "sincerely deploring" East Germany's participation in the 1968 invasion of Czechoslovakia and apologizing "to the peoples of Czechoslovakia on behalf of the GDR people." (The Warsaw Pact summit issued a declaration on December 4, describing the invasion as "an interference in the internal affairs of sovereign Czechoslovakia" that "disrupted the process of democratic renewal in Czechoslovakia.")

All of these changes and initiatives were extremely promising, but at the start of 1990, it was also evident that the political road ahead was very difficult—and that East German Communists, like Communists elsewhere, were prepared to fight for their place in the sun, if not for significant participation in the new power structures. Though East German President Gerlach was a non-Communist, his post became largely ceremonial, with power being exercised by Prime Minister Modrow and party chairman Gysi, a progressive Communist, but a Communist nonetheless. And months after the process of change began in East Germany, no credible or even identifiable leader had emerged in the opposition groups.

For nearly forty-five years, Bulgaria had been the Soviet Union's most obedient ally, virtually a Soviet republic, where Bulgarians tended to like Russians more than other Eastern Europeans. They had never been invaded by the Soviets, they had cultural ties with the Russians (sharing the Cyrillic alphabet with their fellow Slavs to the northeast and across the Black Sea), and their top Communist leaders never questioned Moscow's orders.

The principal figure among the latter was the Bulgarian president and party chairman, Todor I. Zhivkov, who had been in power since 1954, longer than any other Eastern European Communist party head. Under Zhivkov, there were no opposition groups or dissidents of any type, and no independent action was expected in Bulgaria in any direction. This was so until the wave of rebellion rolled over the region in the autumn of 1989, when it suddenly developed that Zhivkov had powerful enemies in his own backyard. Chief among them was Politburo member and Foreign Minister Petar T. Mladenov, a postwar-generation Communist who knew that time had come for a change, and his quiet allies were Defense Minister Dobri Dzhurov, Prime Minister Georgy Atanasov, and foreign trade chief Andrey Lukanov. All personally picked by Zhivkov, the ministers had been quiescent so long as Eastern Europe, apart from Poland and her Solidarity problems, was tranquil on the surface. But when the other Communist monoliths began to crack, with Gorbachev encouraging the process, the Bulgarian regime personalities, who regarded themselves as progressive, took the opportunity to act.

The seventy-eight-year-old Zhivkov fell because, like his fellow geriatric Communist rulers in Eastern Europe, he did not grasp the process of change. When members of an emerging opposition group—the Euro-Glasnost—held a prodemocracy march in Sofia in October during an international environmental conference, Zhivkov committed the classic dictatorial error of responding with naked force. He had his riot police club the demonstrators, then he blamed Mladenov for creating conditions auspicious for opposition manifestations. But it was already a different Bulgaria, and Mladenov countered by accusing Zhivkov of destroying the Bulgarian economy through the expulsion of hundreds of thousands of ethnic Turks as part of his policy of "Bulgarization." He also submitted his resignation, which Zhivkov refused.

Now the moment of confrontation had come. Knowing that Defense Minister Dzhurov assured the loyalty of the armed forces against Zhivkov's police, the foreign minister flew to Moscow on November 5 to ask the Soviets for support in the planned attempt to oust the old dictator. Evidently the Kremlin made its sympathies for Mladenov known among its influential Bulgarian friends, and the Politburo met on November 9 to expel Zhivkov from power. This was the day the Berlin Wall collapsed in that other hardline Communist state, East Germany. Not surprisingly, Mladenov became Zhivkov's successor and immediately received a telegram of congratulations from Gorbachev. Now Bulgaria followed the new Eastern European Communist scenario: Mladenov proposed the end of the Communist monopoly on political power and promised elections for the spring of 1990.

But new tragedy came soon. The Mladenov regime had moved rapidly to revoke the repressive measures against the Turkish Muslim minority in Bulgaria that Zhivkov had enforced since the mid-1980's, because the new leader thought they were wrong and because he was concerned about Bulgaria's international image in human rights. Instantly, the Slavic Bulgarian majority rose against the new policy, demanding through strikes and riots that the Muslims be pushed back to their inferior status and prevented from using Turkish names and speaking the Turkish language. As the new decade opened, Bulgaria was faced with a horrifying ethnic dilemma—largely inherited from the hard-line Communists, who saw a political advantage in ethnic discrimination and accustomed Slav bigots to the idea—that no outside force could help it solve. And Bulgaria was an example of painful ethnic and nationalist tensions that so ironically were brought into the open by the removal of orthodox communism. These tensions loomed as some of the gravest post-Communist problems in Eastern Europe.

The chain reaction triggered by the Polish events of spring and summer was rolling across Eastern Europe as the autumn of 1989 advanced toward the winter. Hungary, East Germany, and Bulgaria were now free of Stalinist communism and poised on the road toward democracy. By mid-November, Czechoslovakia and Romania were the last hard-line holdouts, and both looked like hard nuts to crack.

Czechoslovakia, to be sure, had a small but active dissident movement, the illegal Charter '77 group organized in 1977 by intellectuals and artists to defend the human rights of the citizenry living under the oppression of the

Communist regime that had been installed in the aftermath of the Warsaw Pact invasion. Its leading activists included the playwright Václav Havel, the journalist Jiři Dienstbier, and the former foreign minister Jiři Hájek, all of whom had played key roles in the 1968 Prague Spring and refused to go into exile after the "fraternal assistance" attack launched by Leonid Brezhnev. They were courageous and dedicated, but they lacked the kind of mass support that Solidarity leaders enjoyed in Poland and the Communist reformers had in Hungary, and they did not appear to be a threat to the regime and its powerful security services. This, at least, was the view held by the Prague leaders—and by most foreign experts.

Romania looked even more hopeless in terms of an imminent liberation from the tyranny of President Nicolae Ceauşescu, Europe's nearest equivalent to such genocidal maniacs in the former colonial world as Pol Pot in Cambodia or Idi Amin in Uganda. Romanians had absolutely nothing in the way of an organized or even loosely knit opposition, not even a human rights committee like Czechoslovakia's Charter '77. There were no known intellectual dissenters like Andrei Sakharov in the pre-Gorbachev Soviet Union or Havel in Prague. Securitate, the enormous secret-service apparatus, tolerated no critical conversations among Romanians, let alone plotting or protesting. When six former senior Communist party and government officials wrote Ceauşescu a respectful but firm letter urging domestic reforms in 1989, they were placed under house arrest. Romanians were not allowed to have any contacts with foreigners; owners of typewriters had to register the machines' numbers with the secret police so that no clandestine tracts could be typed and circulated. There appeared to be no chance whatsoever that Romanians could rise successfully against the regime—at least in the opinion of Nicolae Ceauşescu and of most experts abroad.

The problem was that dictators and experts alike were prisoners of conventional wisdom. Besides, none of them understood the new phenomenon of "people power" that was spreading like contagion across Eastern Europe. It had already manifested itself in Poland and, more recently, in East Germany, but it was not expected to burst forth in Czechoslovakia and Romania. There had been prodemocracy demonstrations in Prague in 1988 involving several thousand participants, mostly students and intellectuals (Havel was arrested at a demonstration in January 1989 for the fifth time in a decade), but these protests were not catching fire. In Romania, hungry coal miners near the city of Braşov rioted in 1987, and, according to unverified reports, many were killed by security forces putting down the protest. Nobody expected a repeat performance by Romanians.

But autumn 1989 brought extraordinary surprises from "people power."

On October 28, ten days after Honecker fell in East Germany, some ten thousand young Czechs demonstrated in Prague, demanding freedom for their country too. Police dispersed them easily. On November 17, a Friday, Charles University students received official permission to gather to commemorate the killing by the Nazis of a resistance fighter. This was after the piercing of the Berlin Wall in East Germany and Zhivkov's fall in Bulgaria, but the authorities decided to take a chance—not suspecting that the Czechoslovakian chain reaction was being set in motion. As it turned out, however, the students marched after the university ceremony to Wenceslas Square downtown, the traditional site of demonstrations and the area where students of an earlier generation had fought barehanded against Soviet tanks on August 21, 1968, to shout freedom slogans. There were about fifteen thousand of them, and the police committed the usual error of reacting with force. This time, they did so with shocking brutality, gassing, clubbing, kicking, and bloodying scores of the youths.

The turning point had been reached. It was simply the decision by a great many citizens that henceforth they would no longer be afraid of the police, the brutality, the imprisonments, or anything else. Such decisions are spontaneous and it is impossible to determine by whom or when they were first taken. This is the stuff of revolutions throughout history, and in the immediate past this decision had been taken by the Poles and East Germans. However, this decision could not be comprehended by Czechoslovakia's two top hard-liners, President Gustav Husák and Communist party chairman Milŏs Jakeš. Husák, a seventy-six-year-old Slovak Communist lawyer, had been put in power by the Soviets to replace Alexander Dubček in the aftermath of the invasion, and he proved to be a merciless executor of the Moscow-mandated "normalization" of Czechoslovakia. In 1988, he turned over the party leadership to Jakeš, retaining the largely ceremonial but still quite influential post of president and the historical residence at Hradčany Castle. Jakeš was a career Communist bureaucrat who, representing the conservative faction in the Communist leadership of the Prague Spring, had been in charge of the Central Committee's Control and Auditing Commission; it was a security post within the party, and he was permanently in touch with the KGB. Thus Jakeš had been one of the three hard-line Communist officials who "requested" the Soviet invasion, supposedly in the name of a party in need of "fraternal assistance." Over the years, he had become one of the country's most despised men, and he was just as tough when he became party chairman as he had been in 1968. To Husák and Jakeš, the person and the ideas of Gorbachev were anathema, and they cold-shouldered him as much as they could during his few visits to Prague.

Husák and Jakeš evidently assumed that their show of force on November 17 had put a halt to the burgeoning rebellion. This seemed to be confirmed the following evening when some fifteen hundred students, a relatively small crowd, tried to gather at Wenceslas Square and were easily dispersed by the police. That same evening, however, a Jakeš emissary—the party's ideological chief, Jan Fojtik—returned from a mission to Moscow, where senior Kremlin figures told him that time had come for the Czechoslovakian leadership to reexamine the events of 1968. It was an invitation to political suicide for Husák and Jakeš, who had always presented the invasion as a great patriotic act on the part of Communists. The two hard-liners may have resented Gorbachev and his *perestroika,* but they knew the limits of opposition to the Russians—who had turned into liberals and *mea culpa* breastbeaters. Obviously, the Soviets would not invade to impose democracy (Gorbachev had now left such gestures to George Bush), but they had the power to inflict economic pain on Prague, and they still had loyal friends in Czechoslovakia. It was a surreal situation, and all sides knew it.

On Sunday, November 19, over one hundred thousand Czechoslovakians demonstrated peacefully on Wenceslas Square, and this time the regime had the sense to let it happen. Now the opposition was able to orchestrate the events; the new leadership emerged from Charter '77 in the same way Solidarity in Poland nine years earlier had drawn on the intellectual support of KOR (the Committee for the Defense of Workers), a conglomeration of philosophers, historians, lawyers, writers, and journalists. In fact, KOR and Charter '77 maintained secret contacts for twelve years. In Prague, Havel and Dienstbier were the natural leaders, given their trajectory—and courage—over the past twenty years, and they were instantly accepted by fellow intellectuals, as well as students and workers. On November 20, the dissidents organized the regime's opponents into the Civic Forum, a national unity front rather than a political party. Its first move was to demand Jakeš's resignation and the investigation of police violence against the students. It also called a two-hour general strike for the following week. In the evening, two hundred thousand citizens gathered on the square to listen to Havel (who was allowed to use a public address system) and to jingle their key rings in unison as a sign of victory. Czechoslovakia's "velvet revolution," as Havel called it, was well under way.

Now the regime realized it had to deal with the opposition. On November 21, Prime Minister Ladislav Adamec, a Communist nonentity, met with Havel and his Civic Forum colleagues. For the fifty-four-year-old Havel this was a moment of vindication: Only in May he had been released from prison after serving his latest sentence for antiregime activities, and suddenly he was the coequal of a Communist prime minister. Jakeš attempted one last end run by mobilizing the party's People's Militia to turn industrial plants in the Prague area into the regime's strongholds, but the workers would not have it, and the militiamen withdrew quietly. At that stage, prodemocracy leaders assumed control of the state television network from within, allowing the nation to watch the "gentle revolution" develop step by step. On November 22, the Soviet ambassador called on Jakeš with "fraternal" advice to resign. In the afternoon, 250,000 prodemocracy citizens were back in Wenceslas Square.

Friday, November 24, was the day of victory for Czechoslovakia.

Alexander Dubček, gaunt at the age of sixty-seven, returned to Prague to be greeted as a hero as he addressed 350,000 adoring people at Wenceslas Square and in adjoining streets—he was back with his ideals after twenty-one years of enforced silence as a nonperson tucked away in a corner of his native Slovakia. Smiling and crying for joy, Dubček told the crowd: "An old wise man said, 'If there once was light, why should there be darkness again?' Let us act in such a way to bring the light back again.''

It was an astounding irony of history that three hours after Dubček spoke downtown, Miloš Jakeš, the man who had invited Brezhnev's tanks in 1968, resigned at a session of the Communist party's Central Committee at its headquarters on the Vltava River. His farewell words to the Central Committee summed up in masterful understatement the disaster the Communist hard-liners in Czechoslovakia had brought upon themselves: "We have underestimated completely the processes taking place in Poland, Hungary, and especially recently in East Germany and their effect and influence on our society." He might have added that the regime simply could not cope with daily protest demonstrations by hundreds of thousands of aroused citizens who were ready to paralyze the nation to get rid of the existing leadership; the day Jakeš finally resigned, Prague demonstrations were in their eighth consecutive evening. But there was no violence by the prodemocracy forces, not even against the hated secret police—this was the "gentle revolution."

Jakeš was replaced as general secretary of the Communist party by forty-eight-year-old Karel Urbanek, a Politburo bureaucrat whose principal strength lay in the fact that he was too young to have played an objectionable role in 1968. Adamec was retained as prime minister, but the new Communist cast was clearly a caretaker presence. The Civic Forum was pressing for greater changes and for the end of the Communist monopoly on power, although it was not entirely clear what the opposition had in mind as a plausible long-term solution. The white-haired Dubček, who spoke to one million Czechs at Letenske Gardens in Prague on Sunday, November 26, to support the Civic Forum's demands, suddenly emerged as the crowds' candidate for president, the post still held by Gustav Husák, his other archenemy. But other forces were pushing in other directions as normal political life in Czechoslovakia was resuming after nearly forty-two years of Communist domination implanted by the Soviet-backed coup d'état in 1948.

A two-hour general strike by millions of Czechs and Slovaks was held on November 27, as part of the opposition's continuing demands for even more basic changes. The regime was in absolute disarray when Prime Minister Adamec met with Havel and other Civic Forum leaders to negotiate the country's political future. Two days later, the Communist-controlled National Assembly voted to end the Communist party's leading role in Czechoslovak politics, but Communists were still in power in Prague. It was a wearying process to dislodge them.

On December 1, another extraordinary event of this extraordinary year occurred in Rome, further quickening the process of change. Mikhail Gorbachev called on the Polish pope, John Paul II, at the Vatican, the first time a Soviet Communist leader had met with a Roman Catholic pontiff. The two men conversed alone for several hours (the pope speaks Russian) and both appeared highly pleased with their encounter; the next step was to be the establishment of diplomatic relations between the Kremlin and the Vatican, a theretofore unthinkable notion. Gorbachev's gesture symbolized the end of the Soviet Union's ideological war on religion stemming from Lenin's dictum that religion is "the opium of the people," and it followed a broad relaxation on religious observances in the Soviet Union, where a revival of the Russian Orthodox faith was already well under way. From Rome, Gorbachev flew to Malta for a summit with George Bush, another step in the liquidation of the Cold War. There was no more question as to the path chosen by the Soviets in their domestic and foreign policies.

In Czechoslovakia, however, the old-line Communists were still playing for time. On December 3, Husák, Urbanek, and Adamec named a new Cabinet composed of sixteen Communists and five non-Communists, but the Civic Forum saw it as a sham, and 150,000 protesters went back into the streets of Prague. Negotiations were resumed between the regime and the opposition, leading to the creation of a new Cabinet headed by Marian Calfa, a Slovak Communist, and a much more equitable distribution of seats between the Communists and the opposition. The Civic Forum's Jiři Dienstbier, for example, became foreign minister, and a grass-roots movement of support for Havel for the presidency spread across the country. Dubček was still admired, but the sentiment grew that the new president should not be a Communist—which Dubček had been most of his life. The presidency became vacant on December 10, when Husák belatedly gave up the post, his last act being to swear in the Calfa-Dienstbier government. Then Urbanek resigned from the party chairmanship to be replaced by Adamec, a much more flexible politician with good contacts with the Civic Forum. But the party split into the liberal-minded Democratic Forum of Communists and what was left of the traditional Communist party, after the expulsion in mid-December of all the hard-liners.

The Czechoslovakian year of liberation culminated in an agreement between the Communist leadership and the Civic Forum that Václav Havel would be chosen president of the republic and Alexander Dubček chairman of the National Assembly, an arrangement that seemed to delight the nation. On December 28, Dubček was elected unanimously by the National Assembly, and Havel was elected five days later, though he said he would not serve past the general elections set for June 1990. For Dubček, this was the personal vindication of his efforts to give his country "Marxism with a Human Face" in 1968, and of the sacrifices and punishment he had had to endure subsequently. For Havel, the fighting playwright and author of *Protest* and *The Strength of the Helpless*, it was literally poetic justice. On invasion day, he had been arrested by Soviet troops at the headquarters of the Writers' Union, which Brezhnev and his associates regarded as one of the most dangerous and strategic objectives in Czechoslovakia; it was the home of the ideas that the Kremlin then so feared.

While euphoria reigned in Czechoslovakia, a totally unexpected and bloody revolution broke out in Romania on December 16. Curiously, it was Ceaușescu who apparently brought it upon himself. In power since 1965, he seemed to dismiss contemptuously the wave of change and liberalization in Eastern Europe and the Soviet Union, confident of his place and authority. On November 24, after Honecker had already fallen in East Germany, Zhivkov in Bulgaria, and Jakeš in Czechoslovakia, the Congress of the Romanian Communist party reelected Ceauşescu to another five-year term as general secretary (and his wife, Elena, as his deputy), and he poured scorn on his fellow Eastern European Communists. "What can we say about those who are declaring now that they do not want socialism anymore, that they would like to take the path to capitalism though they used to hold high offices in this or that country?" he asked in the course of a five-hour speech that was madly applauded by the three thousand congress delegates and later by tens of thousands of followers in front of the presidential palace in Bucharest.

Few leaders, however, had earned as much silent hatred as the seventy-one-year-old Ceauşescu, a victim of clinical megalomania who insisted on being called "the genius of the Carpathians," "the helmsman who guides," and "the brilliant genius of the nation." I had occasion to interview him in Bucharest in 1976, and it was a grotesque scene, during which Ceauşescu grandly read in Romanian a series of wholly vacuous written answers to my written questions (this procedure was a requirement), but refused to reply to oral follow-up queries. He was surrounded by fawning courtiers and security agents, and when I asked his chief of staff for appointments with government ministers, I was told, "But the president has already told you everything. . . . Nobody can add anything."

On a much more tragic level, Ceauşescu's manias virtually destroyed the nation over the past decade. Hundreds of thousands of peasants were forcibly moved out of their villages under the "agricultural modernization program," in part to make room for dams and spillways. Nearly forty-five hundred villages were earmarked for destruction. The Bucharest downtown was razed to allow the construction of regal buildings for the Communist party headquarters and for the palace. Because of his obsession with the repayment of Romania's foreign debt, which he accomplished, Ceauşescu ordered that most of the country's food production be exported; this caused virtual starvation among the twenty-three million Romanians. There was no heat for dwellings in the winter and minimal amounts of electricity; even television broadcasts were curtailed, with Ceauşescu's explanation that he did not wish his people to be "fatigued." Romanians could not travel abroad, invite foreigners, or read anything except the mind-dulling official press with multiple daily articles about the Ceauşescu family. And this paragon of socialism, as it developed later, lived in majestic luxury in a heavily guarded compound in Bucharest's lake district.

Depressingly, the West, including the United States, long courted Ceauşescu because of his foreign policies, which defied the Soviet Union under Khrushchev and Brezhnev. He refused to let the Soviets station troops in Romania, banned Warsaw Pact maneuvers on his territory, and barred his armies from joining in the invasion of Czechoslovakia. In the anti-Soviet

Cold War mood of the 1960's and 1970's, Romania was regarded as almost an ally by the United States: President Nixon visited Bucharest in 1969, and Ceauşescu was feted at the White House the following year. Nobody seemed to be troubled by the fact that he operated the most oppressive Stalinist dictatorship in Europe, with the possible exception of Albania; this dawned on the West only in the late eighties when Gorbachev brought the new détente and the Romanians became internationally irrelevant.

One of Ceauşescu's obsessions was the 1.6 million members of the Hungarian minority in Transylvania, whom he treated with stunning cruelty as third-class citizens, though that too was long disregarded by the West. Yet the Hungarian minority became his undoing. His "agricultural modernization program" was believed to be aimed chiefly at the ethnic Hungarians, whom he wanted to push off the land. After twenty-seven thousand of them fled to Hungary during 1989, Ceauşescu commented haughtily, "Now that we have achieved happiness, I cannot understand why anyone would want to leave this country." One man who would not agree with him, however, was the Reverend Laszlo Tokes, the thirty-seven-year-old pastor of the Protestant Reformed Church of Romania in Timişoara, a western Romanian city of 325,000 inhabitants and an ethnic Hungarian center. When his growing criticism of the regime's policies caught the attention of Securitate, the decision was taken to transfer him away from Timişoara. On Friday, December 15, secret police agents attempted to seize the Reverend Tokes— and this triggered the revolutionary explosion that ten days later resulted in Ceauşescu's ouster and death by firing squad. Timişoara became a textbook example of what happens when dictators let themselves underestimate their own people.

To Ceauşescu's immense surprise, not only ethnic Hungarians but Romanians of all ages and backgrounds—a great many of them students—rallied to the pastor's defense, staging protest rallies on Saturday, December 16. The security forces put down the demonstration with a brutal use of force, and large numbers were killed by police fire. On Sunday, Ceauşescu issued orders to all the top Communist officials in the country to kill protesters wherever they dared to challenge the public order: "Anyone who does not obey orders should be shot," he said over a closed-circuit television hookup. Confident that no real danger faced him, the president and his wife flew the next day to Iran on a scheduled three-day official visit; Ceauşescu was among the few friends the fundamentalist and intolerant Muslim regime had anywhere in the world.

In Timişoara, Ceauşescu's orders were obeyed and mass killings began: Several thousand protesters were murdered (the exact figure may never be known) as Securitate troops, which were units totally independent from the Regular Army, sprayed crowds with automatic weapons fire on the ground and from helicopters, and with tank cannon. Wounded protesters were executed in a hospital ward invaded by Securitate men with guns blazing. Simultaneously, the Reverend Tokes was taken away by police agents to a hiding place, where he was pressed to sign a declaration admitting that he had been acting as a Western intelligence agent. The plan was for Ceauşescu to read it at a mass rally in Bucharest on his return from Iran. Tokes refused to sign it—and miraculously, he was spared.

Battles in Timişoara between Securitate and the people of the city continued on Monday and Tuesday, December 18 and 19. The death toll was rising sharply. Ceauşescu returned from Iran on Wednesday, December 20, and instantly went on nationwide television to denounce the events in Timişoara as a "Fascist" conspiracy organized abroad. He was angry, aggressive, and arrogant, certain of victory.

That same day, however, world attention was shifted from the Romanian revolution and bloodshed to the American invasion of Panama, ordered by President Bush to overthrow and capture the local dictator, General Manuel Antonio Noriega, a domestic tyrant and allegedly a key figure in narcotics traffic between Colombia and the United States. Hundreds of civilians were killed as American forces used heavy weapons to demolish Noriega's Panama Defense Forces headquarters, and there were military casualties on both sides as Noriega loyalists fought back for days. Capping the astounding year 1989, the Christmas season brought the heaviest fighting in Europe since the end of the Second World War and the biggest American military involvement abroad—over twenty-five thousand troops—since the Vietnam War.

In Bucharest, Ceauşescu was possessed on Thursday, December 21, by the idea of addressing a mass rally of what he assumed were his faithful followers in front of the Communist party headquarters building. It was a megalomaniac's idea and, in effect, an invitation to a full-fledged revolution. With Elena at his side, Ceauşescu proceeded to deliver a rambling speech from the building's balcony, calling the Timişoara protesters "hooligans" and again charging "Fascist" plots. At that point, he turned into the emperor with no clothes: For the first time in his twenty-four years in power, Ceauşescu was booed by hundreds of university students gathered at the far end of the plaza. At first he was speechless; then he disappeared from television screens as the live broadcast was suddenly ended. Now the people knew their emperor was vulnerable.

The crowds stayed on the plaza, now openly demonstrating against Ceauşescu. Hundreds were killed by the security forces in a night of bloodshed. On Friday morning, December 22, the revolutionary mob stormed the Communist party headquarters and the presidential palace, overcoming Securitate and the withering fire of its weapons. Now the Regular Army entered the battle on the side of the rebels, tipping the scale. At 12:15 P.M., the Ceauşescus fled aboard a small helicopter from the roof of the Communist party headquarters building, trying to reach a Securitate base outside of the capital, either to direct further resistance or to try to escape Romania by plane for a country unknown. Landing near Tîrgovişte, Ceauşescu and his wife were spotted by civilian and military rebels and captured. Placed inside an armored car, they were driven around Tîrgovişte for three days to avoid a rescue attack by Securitate—and to await a decision on their fate.

In Bucharest, a Council of National Salvation assumed power as the provisional government, moments after the dictator fled. The council was an amorphous combination of former senior Communist officials, high military officers, professionals, intellectuals, and student leaders. Ion Iliescu, a former Communist party figure who had broken with Ceauşescu, became the head of the council in a way that remains unclear; a young engineer named Petre Roman was chosen as the prime minister, and Silviu Brucan, once a brilliant diplomat and a signer of the protest letter to Ceauşescu in March 1989, emerged as the spokesman for the new government. The new leadership tended to be rather secretive and vague about its origins and the way it had so rapidly assumed political power, most of its members being generally unknown. There were indications that its hard-core group was a conspiracy started in utmost secrecy six months earlier and that it included army generals resentful of Securitate's sway, but no confirmation was forthcoming. I found it intriguing that Corneliu Bogdan, a former ambassador to the United States and a highly respected Romanian figure who had fallen into disfavor with Ceauşescu, returned to Bucharest just days before the Timişoara explosion after spending a year in Washington at an academic institution. When Bogdan was named a council member and deputy foreign minister in the new government, I wondered whether he had gone back because he had advance knowledge that a revolution was in the making. We were neighbors in Washington and knew each other for many years, but I never heard him allude to it. Bogdan died of a heart attack ten days after Ceauşescu's fall, taking his secrets to the grave.

The council's immediate concern was to stop the carnage resulting from the continuing attacks by the ever loyal Securitate forces (there even was worry that the superbly equipped and trained police might win the upper hand), and its decision on December 24 was to put the Ceauşescus on secret military trial. They were charged with the genocide of sixty thousand Romanians (it is unclear how this figure was obtained) and the removal of billions of dollars to private bank accounts abroad. The sentence by the military tribunal—its membership was not disclosed to avoid Securitate revenge— was death and it was carried out by an army firing squad on Christmas Day. Videotapes broadcast by Romanian television showed the defiant Ceauşescus refusing to be judged by anyone except "the working class," and then the couple lying dead in the snow after the execution. The death toll in the horribly bloody December revolution was believed to exceed ten thousand— mainly Securitate victims—but the exact number may never be known.

The trial and the death sentence came under much criticism abroad, where there was strong sentiment against such cavalier procedures, but the Council of National Salvation took the view that a civil war could be averted only by doing away with the Ceauşescus. But there were no other acts of vengeance against the dictatorship; detained Securitate officials and agents were held pending future trials. By the end of December, all fighting ended and Romania turned to the monumental task of reconstructing its political life, its economy, and the emotional health of the nation. Elections were scheduled for April 1990, amid uncertainty as to who stands for what in the post-Ceauşescu era.

Traditional communism was liquidated in Eastern Europe over a six-month span of time in the second half of 1989, one of the most important periods in the history of the past half century. Only Albania remained hermetically sealed as a Stalinist fief; the old dictator, Enver Hoxha, had died in 1985 after forty years in power, but his successors carried on the policy of total isolation from the outside world. Yugoslavia remained a fairly repressive state, practicing its own often disconcerting brand of communism (mixed with free enterprise and a market economy), and the survival of the Yugoslav federation was threatened by mounting ethnic tensions involving its six republics and two autonomous regions.

The decade of the eighties opened with the violence of the Soviet war in Afghanistan, the Iran-Iraq War, the civil wars in El Salvador and Nicaragua, and bloody internal conflicts raging from Lebanon to Angola and Mozambique and Cambodia. It ended with violence and bloodshed in Romania and Panama, but, on balance, the world looked better than a decade earlier.

The end of Communist hard-line rule in Eastern Europe—and its great relaxation in the Soviet Union—marked the dawn of a new epoch, although vast problems lay ahead. But the curious phenomenon after the "Autumn of the People" was that throughout the region, countries lived under what have been called "Communists without communism." The old regimes had been consigned to oblivion, but their bureaucracies remained basically intact.

Poland had a Communist president in Wojciech Jaruzelski, a Solidarity prime minister, and a government with a Communist minority, but it had to depend on Communists to make the machinery of state function. "After forty years of communism, we just don't have enough of our own people to run the country," a Solidarity leader told me a few months after Tadeusz Mazowiecki became prime minister. For example, all the new governments maintained most of the ambassadors abroad who had been named by previous regimes, because nobody was available to replace them during the first months. The foreign ministries remained intact below the highest level, and this was true of all other government agencies, including the interior ministries in charge of the secret police. Besides, there was no thought anywhere of purges in the bureaucracies; this was commendable in a way, because most of the lesser officials could not be blamed for political decisions and they had had to have Communist party membership or approval to keep their jobs, but it also posed the danger of quiet sabotage of reforms by those who had enjoyed privileges under the past status quo. Clearly, the denazification concepts of 1945 in Germany could not be applied to the Communist bureaucracies in Eastern Europe, though there was much resistance and foot dragging vis-à-vis the new democratic order.

And the democratic forces in Poland were increasingly divided, Solidarity was splitting, and the Mazowiecki regime was publicly criticized for its economic recovery program—not only by the Communists, but by its closest ideological associates as well. Meanwhile, the Communist party was changing its name to the Polish Socialist party, hoping to be very much in the running in the 1990 elections. In Czechoslovakia, power was shared by a democratic president—Václav Havel—and a Communist prime minister heading a mixed Cabinet; the democratic groups had a difficult time preparing for the 1990 elections. In Hungary, all key posts were in the hands of reform-minded Communists with no serious challenge from the democratic opposition. In East Germany, the prime minister was a progressive Communist (the president, a non-Communist, was a figurehead) as were most of the other ministers; the Communist party was reorganizing itself under a dynamic young leader, while democratic groups produced no promising leaders and, to make matters worse, were unable to maintain a united front. In Romania, students and more and more intellectuals were deeply disenchanted that the Council of National Salvation was packed with former Communists.

Across Eastern Europe, the new reality following the euphoria of victory was that it was easier to demolish the Communist monopoly on power than to build democratic structures. To do so was the priority task for the nineties in this early dawn period between totalitarianism and democracy.

Marxism-Leninism was not faring much better in Cuba and Nicaragua, its sad outposts in the Western Hemisphere.

In Cuba the decade opened on a note of despair and official madness. In April 1980 the Peruvian Embassy on Havana's tree-shaded Quinta Avenida was invaded by thousands of Cubans demanding asylum and permission to leave. Fidel Castro's first reaction after being caught unawares was to let special evacuation planes take most of them to Costa Rica, then on to Peru. His second reaction was to announce that the port of Mariel near Havana could be used by anyone wishing to depart from Cuba. Flotillas of small boats from Cuba and others from Florida began plying the straits back and forth, transporting tens of thousands to the United States. Then Castro added a touch of malevolence: He released inmates from psychiatric hospitals and prisons for habitual criminals, and boat captains were told they could not sail without this extra human cargo.

Between the end of April and the end of September 1980 close to 125,000 Cubans left the island. Castro managed to portray it to some extent as a blessing for the Revolution: Cuba did not need enemies of the regime, idle miscreants, criminals, and madmen; they were consuming Cuban food and resources while offering the nation nothing in exchange. Moreover, this sudden emigration alleviated what was already developing as an unemployment problem.

For President Carter, the Mariel exodus was the final blow, coming after the taking of the hostages in Teheran. There were no facilities in Florida and no funds to care for these refugees, and the state was being swamped by them. At first the administration attempted to have the Navy and the Coast Guard turn back the flow; it quickly realized how politically untenable was this idea. Americans could not participate in preventing patriotic Cubans from fleeing communism.

Castro nevertheless knew that Mariel was a politican problem; no matter what he said, the exodus was a slap at the Revolution. To defuse internal pressures, he allowed farmers' markets to function in Cuba for the first time since the nationalizations of the 1960's, selling meat and produce directly to consumers. With Cuba's horrendous shortages, this was a popular move. At the same time he encouraged visits to the island by Cubans who had left at the start of the Revolution; they could visit their relatives and, above all, bring dollars and appliances and clothing and everything else that could not be found in Cuba. To buy imported goods (like television sets, designer shirts, and scotch whiskey), Cubans had to have dollars, and this was a good way to obtain them; the dollars then went to the government, which kept the profits from the transactions. It was called internal export.

When I spent most of 1985 in Cuba, gathering material for an earlier book, there were growing signs that the economy, never in good shape, was in bad trouble despite Soviet aid running close to five billion dollars annually. Not enough sugar could be produced to meet export commitments to the Soviet Union, the quality of local industrial production was appalling, there were perennial housing and food shortages, and nothing seemed to work properly. In his speeches Castro castigated his fellow citizens for being lazy and unproductive, but in the absence of incentives, many people simply lapsed into lethargy.

Castro had traveled to Moscow for Brezhnev's and Andropov's funerals, but chose not to attend Chernenko's burial, sending his brother Raúl in his place. He never explained it, but in retrospect, it is interesting to speculate whether he wished to avoid an immediate contact with Gorbachev, the new general secretary (they had met casually during Castro's past visits to Moscow, but the Cuban barely remembered him and may have felt unprepared for a meeting).

Castro's political and ideological attitudes hardened in inverse proportion to the new relaxation developing in the Soviet Union. In foreign policy he remained committed to Cuban support for the regimes in Angola and Nicaragua. He detested Reagan, a sentiment compounded by the U.S. invasion of the tiny island of Grenada in the eastern Caribbean on October 25, 1983. Reagan ordered the invasion rather hastily three weeks after the killing of the marines in Beirut, perhaps as a way of salvaging American prestige. Grenada had been ruled since a revolution in 1979 by a Marxist regime headed by Prime Minister Maurice Bishop, a man of great personal attraction and intelligence. Bishop, however, had brought Cuban military advisers and a small combat unit to train *his* revolutionary army—he always did fear an American invasion—and to protect Cuban workers who were building a modern airport for Grenada, including a long runway for large jet aircraft.

The Reagan administration concluded that this was a military base for Cuba and the Soviet Union, a dangerous installation that would be astride maritime lanes between the United States and South America (including oil tanker lanes from Venezuela and Curaçao) and between the United States and Europe, endangering American naval movements in the event of a major war. Fortunately for Washington, Bishop was killed in a coup by his extreme leftist rivals in mid-October, and the administration became convinced that nearly one thousand American students at a medical college in Grenada might be in danger. Right or wrong, in his assessment, Reagan did not want to risk one more hostage situation for Americans, and the invasion was on.

It became a messy affair in which U.S. forces suffered unnecessary and excessive losses because of command and control confusion, poor planning, and underestimating the fighting prowess of the Grenadians and the Cuban guards and airport workers. In the end American power prevailed; the Cubans were defeated, captured, and sent home. The United States helped organize an election in Grenada the following year, and then forgot about this very lovely and very impoverished island in the sun.

At home Castro imposed increasing rigidity. He liquidated the farmers' markets in 1986 on the ground that the peasants were becoming rich and "bourgeois" from "selling garlic," and Cuba returned to a Stalinist command economy. He saw Gorbachev in Moscow briefly during the midyear Twenty-seventh Congress of the Soviet Communist party—he could not stay away without insulting the Russians—but he made his orthodox Communist point by then visiting Kim Il Sung in Pyongyang; he took his son, Fidelito, a physicist, presumably to meet the son and anointed successor of the North Korean leader.

By 1988 Castro was openly critical of *perestroika*; his speeches made it clear that Gorbachev's reforms were not meant for Cuba and that he intended to remain loyal to ideological tradition. "Marxism-Leninism or Death!" he shouted in one of the more bizarre modern political slogans. Gorbachev was scheduled to visit Cuba after his New York and Washington tour in December 1988, but the devastating earthquake in Armenia forced him to rush home. He made a special trip to Cuba in April 1989, the first Soviet leader in Havana since Brezhnev's visit a quarter century earlier. By then the lines had been drawn. Castro had made more speeches to remind his listeners that Cuba, being next to the United States, not in the Black Sea next to the Russians, could not experiment with *perestroika* types of policies. It is not known whether Gorbachev had specifically complained about the waste of the Soviet aid on the part of the Cubans, but Castro clearly did all he could to upstage him. His introduction of Gorbachev before the National Assembly lasted fifty-three minutes—it was mainly an attack on the United

States (therefore on the new Soviet-American détente) while the visitor spoke only three minutes longer.

In midsummer Castro formally announced that Cuba would go on practicing Marxism-Leninism no matter what happened in the Soviet Union. Then he launched an extraordinary purge on his own regime. General Arnaldo Ochoa Sánchez, the first commander of Cuban troops in Angola and a national hero (he had just been named head of the crucial Western Army in Cuba), was accused of having organized and protected a drug-smuggling ring to the United States, and he was denounced as a "traitor." He was arrested, tried by forty-seven generals and admirals, found guilty, and executed, along with four alleged associates (including one of Castro's closest personal friends). The interior minister, who had the rank of general, was dismissed, arrested, and sentenced to twenty years in prison for failing in his duties. Scores of other senior officials were fired; many were arrested.

Although Castro had been accused by the United States in the past of encouraging cocaine traffic from Colombia to the United States over Cuba and of working closely with Panama's strongman General Manuel Antonio Noriega (indicted by U.S. grand juries), the Ochoa conspiracy scenario was far from credible. It was hard to believe that Castro, supposedly in total control of everything on his island, was unaware of such a cocaine operation run by his top generals if it had really happened. And if it did not happen, what had Ochoa done to deserve the firing squad? Was he conspiring against Castro over the lack of reforms in Cuba, as some observers had alleged, or was he simply becoming too popular? Of course, Ochoa confessed to everything, but in his televised explanations Castro had not really answered any of the fundamental questions concerning the situation of Cuba and its future.

Interestingly Castro chose not to attend the September 1989 Belgrade summit of the nonaligned movement over which he had presided a decade earlier; he sent his brother Raúl to speak for Cuba. It was a sign of the times that the Belgrade conference's resolutions lacked the traditional anti-American pronouncements, being confined to banalities. Both the nonaligned and Castro seemed to become irrelevant.

Later during the autumn, as Communist regimes began faltering and collapsing across Eastern Europe, Castro made the final decision to oppose actively *perestroika*-type reforms in general and in Cuba in particular. He also recognized that under the new conditions, Cuba may suffer in terms of reduced economic assistance from the Soviet Union.

In a Havana speech on December 7, Castro proceeded, in effect, to lecture Gorbachev and Eastern European Communists: "Capitalism, its market economy, its values, its categories [sic] and its methods can never pull socialism out of its present difficulties or rectify whatever mistakes have been made. . . . We shouldn't blame Lenin now for having chosen Czarist Russia as the place for the biggest revolution in history. Thus we didn't hesitate to stop the circulation [in Cuba] of certain Soviet publications that are full of poison against the USSR itself and socialism. . . . Some of those publications have already started calling for an end to the fair and equitable trade relations that were established between the USSR and Cuba during the Cuban revolutionary process. . . . In short, they want the USSR to join the U.S. blockade against Cuba. . . . Can socialism be improved by foresaking Marxism-Leninism's most basic principles? Why must the so-called reforms be along capitalist lines? . . . If fate were to decree it, we would be among the last defenders of socialism in a world in which U.S. imperialism has realized Hitler's dreams of world domination—we would defend this bulwark to the last drop of our blood."

With Ceauşescu's death, Castro and North Korea's Kim Il Sung were the last two strongmen of orthodox communism (Albania being internationally irrelevant). Both were close to the Romanian dictator, and his fall was a painful blow to Havana as well as Pyongyang. Almost immediately, Castro started turning to China, with which he had had only the most superficial relations for the past quarter century because of his Soviet alliance. In December, after his great speech in defense of traditional "socialism," Castro signed a half-billion-dollar trade agreement with the visiting Chinese foreign-trade minister, Zheng Tuobin—the first high-level visit to Cuba from Beijing in many years. Then Castro was invited to come to China early in 1990, as if to forge a new alliance of hard-line Communists. The Romanian revolution also deeply shook the Beijing leadership, not only because of China's traditional ties with Ceauşescu, the anti-Moscow maverick, but because it had demonstrated to the authors of the Tienanmen Square massacre that violence can work either way—and that Communist parties cannot blindly depend on military loyalties. The same thought must have occurred to Castro, who had executed his top army general only a half year earlier.

Nicaragua was an absolute disaster because the Sandinistas had believed at the outset in Marxism-Leninism and counted on more Soviet and Cuban aid than could have possibly been given them. Then they proceeded to construct a strange dictatorship of the left but without forsaking private enterprise altogether.

They built an extremely powerful army by Central American standards that the Soviets and the Cubans equipped although it was unclear whether this militarization was undertaken as a defense against the United States, as the regime claimed, or because Nicaragua wished to be a regional power. Either way the Sandinistas handed the Reagan administration every excuse—including providing arms to leftist guerrillas in El Salvador—to try to overthrow them, as the administration wanted to do anyway.

Though Daniel Ortega Saavedra, one of the principal Sandinista leaders, was made president in 1984 in an uncontested election, the regime remained essentially a collective group of ten *comandantes*—a singularly inept leadership in every way. Not only did it bring upon Nicaragua the American-financed contras and a war which has ruined the country, but Ortega helped to make Nicaragua ridiculous as well. In September 1989, for example, he joined the PLO's Arafat and Syria's President Assad at ceremonies in Tripoli where Qaddafi celebrated his twenty years in power, hardly a proper occasion for a Latin American president who claims he believes in real democracy and who hopes for help from the West. He rode a white horse there.

For Reagan, Nicaragua became an obsession, leading him into illegal as well as thoughtless policies and threatening his presidency halfway through his second term. Having instructed the CIA to create the contras' army in Honduras and to do everything possible to undermine the Sandinistas (the CIA began secretly mining Nicaraguan harbors in April 1984), Reagan chose to violate the law to keep these operations going. After the Congress had banned aid for the contras, the White House and the CIA embarked on exceedingly imaginative enterprises to get around the legal prohibition. It was at that point that Lieutenant Colonel Oliver North, a National Security Council aide, joined with Robert McFarlane and Admiral John Poindexter, the new national security adviser, to produce the Iran-contra conspiracy. McFarlane was selling the arms to Iran through Israel to obtain the release of American hostages in Lebanon while North was using the money to buy other arms for the contras.

What finally brought the Nicaraguan war to an end was the Arias Peace Plan, which President Oscar Arias Sánchez of Costa Rica, the only democratic nation in Central America, forced upon his fellow presidents at a conference in Guatemala on August 7, 1987. As Arias explained to me when I visited him subsequently in San José, Ortega had to be convinced that his only choice was to accept democracy in Nicaragua or be destroyed by the United States—one way or another. His other task was to persuade a skeptical Reagan administration that the plan would work and that the United States should "give peace a chance."

Fighting ended in mid-1988, and the Sandinistas committed themselves to free elections in 1990 and Ortega, seeking reelection was crushed by the opposition's Violeta Chamorro on February 25. And this was the end of the Marxist enterprise in Nicaragua.

In El Salvador, Marxist guerrillas lost their last chance for victory when their attack on San Salvador, the capital, in November 1989 failed to trigger the great national uprising they had expected. But the American-supported Salvadoran Army behaved as senselessly and criminally as the guerrillas. On November 16, six Jesuit priests, including the rector of the University of Central America, were murdered by members of the elite, U.S.-trained Atlacatl battalion, for reasons that defied comprehension. And it was Salvador's rightist president, Alfredo Cristiani, who announced that the killings had been perpetrated by the military; given his regime's absolute dependence on American aid, he had to protect his own credibility.

Communism was faring poorly elsewhere in the Third World. In Africa, the "revolutionary" regime in tiny Benin announced in December it was dropping its Marxist-Leninist identity.

IV

In a world beset with civil wars, dictatorships, ideological and political struggles, and endless violence, the human rights of millions were being violated in every conceivable fashion—notwithstanding efforts by the United States, France, and many other committed governments. Unquestionably the situation in 1989 was vastly better than a decade earlier, before Gorbachev came to power in the Soviet Union and before rightist dictatorships began disappearing in Latin America, Asia, and Europe. But it still was a shocking state of affairs.

Forty-one years after the General Assembly of the United Nations approved the Universal Declaration of Human Rights on December 10, 1948, the lack of serious respect for human rights remained appalling. The worst offenders were among Middle Eastern, African, and Latin American governments, as well as many Communist regimes in Eastern Europe until the great changes in the autumn of 1989. It is doubtful that we even begin to know the full truth concerning the magnitude of human rights violations, inasmuch as situations in countries like Albania, North Korea, or Cuba cannot be verified. Naturally, political freedoms are nonexistent where human rights are torn to shreds as a matter of national policy.

In a 1988 report on North Korea the Minnesota Lawyers International Human Rights Committee charged that the Pyongyang regime "has established a comprehensive system which consistently deprives its citizens of basic human rights and freedoms." It said that "the Government preserves this system by erecting walls of fear around its borders and around each of its citizens. . . . There appears to be little individuality, spontaneity, or social interaction. . . . Political surveillance is pervasive at the workplace, in the neighborhood, and in housing units as small as twenty families." According to this report, "all North Koreans are classified as to their actual loyalty to the Kims," and a 1989 United Nations field study said that "nearly every citizen wears over his or her heart a small lacquered portrait of President Kim Il Sung." The lawyers committee reported that "the Ministry of State

Security has used a special team of 15 to 20 members trained to assassinate the political opponents of Kim Il Sung and his son, Kim Jung Il."

Much of the recent improvement consisted, of course, of lip service or efforts at greater discretion in practicing human rights violations. Tom J. Farer, an international law expert, has commented that "to the extent that an oppressive government feigns cooperation with the U.N. Human Rights Commission's confidential scrutiny, it can escape public inquiry and political shame." Still, it *was* becoming harder to hide, particularly since the U.S. Congress mandated the State Department in 1974 to prepare and issue detailed annual reports on human rights practices in all the countries in the world. These reports are painfully frank about the state of affairs from Afghanistan to Zaire and from South Africa to the Soviet Union; the report for 1988 was a 1,560-page volume, dealing with situations in 169 individual countries. And private organizations were increasingly publishing their own studies and reports.

For reasons of political or ideological views, religious faith, ethnic origin, family ties, sex, or color, people in various countries may be summarily sentenced to death by bullet, beheading, hanging, stoning, or crucifixion; murdered out of sight by local soldiers and policemen; thrown without explanation into prison cells to be kept sometimes for years in total darkness and isolation; tortured physically in prisons with ancient and state-of-the-art devices and psychologically in mental hospitals, where mind-destroying drugs are administered; savagely beaten and flogged; and submitted to mutilation or amputation of limbs.

In most cases, maximal cruelty was applied to political opponents and religious and ethnic minorities (sometimes the fact of religious or national identity was regarded as a political threat), but medieval punishment was meted out, too, for minor criminal infractions, usually in countries where Shari'a Islamic law prevails. In Saudi Arabia, for example, Shari'a provides for amputation of the hand as punishment for repeated theft. Alcohol offenses are punished by flogging—up to three hundred lashes for drinking. To be sure, these are human rights violations, covered by such legal instruments as the United Nations Declaration on the Protection of All Persons from Being Subjected to Torture and Other Cruel, Inhuman or Degrading Treatment or Punishment. Most nations are signatories of the Universal Declaration of Human Rights and related covenants and declarations; but none of the documents is binding, and they are usually observed in the breach.

It was also impossible to be precise about human rights violations. The best-educated guess was that during the 1980's there must have been thousands (perhaps tens of thousands) of executions of human beings whom their governments hated or feared, with or without reason. Millions were killed in Asian and African genocide waves in the previous decade. The gallery of Third World mad tyrants included Uganda's Idi Amin, Cambodia's Pol Pot, Burma's Ne Win, Iran's Ayatollah Khomeini, Central African Empire's Jean Bocassa and Haiti's François "Papa Doc" Duvalier.

In the eighties the number of men and women tortured, often in the most atrocious manner, must have been in the hundreds of thousands. Amnesty International, the most important human rights organization and a Nobel Peace Prizewinner, says in a special report on "Torture in the Eighties" that "more than a third of the world's governments have used or tolerated torture or ill-treatment of prisoners."

I have heard and read scores of accounts that defy the imagination by victims of imprisonments and tortures and by witnesses to executions. Reflecting on torture and the character of torturers—frequently, in this day and age, men with a reasonable degree of education and decent family backgrounds—I could not help remembering my conversation about Adolf Eichmann with an Israeli psychiatrist years ago. He had remarked that "if you scratch long and deep enough, you will remove the veneer of civilization from any human being—and Eichmann will come out," and I began thinking of the pleasant and worldly Brazilian Air Force and Navy officers and Argentine and Chilean Army officers whom I knew so well before they suddenly turned out to be torturers, and of Arab and African Cabinet ministers, many with Sorbonne doctorates, who ordered and enjoyed the torturing of their enemies.

And I thought that Eichmann's ghost must be haunting Israel when I read in the Amnesty International report that long before the Palestinian riots in the Occupied Territories broke out in 1987, "some Palestinians . . . arrested for security reasons and interrogated by the *Shin Beth* intelligence services have been hooded, handcuffed and forced to stand without moving for many hours at a time for several days, and have been exposed while naked to cold showers or cold air ventilators for long periods of time."

The State Department's human rights report for 1988 said that there had been "a substantial increase in human rights violations" as a result of Israel's response to the *intifada*, the Arab uprising in the Occupied Territories that erupted in December 1987 and continued with wildly escalating violence throughout 1989.

Israel asserts that it is impossible to distinguish between its vital security measures and acts that are seen as human rights violations of its Arabs. In two years over 570 Palestinians, including children, were killed by the Israeli Army for throwing Molotov cocktails and stones at soldiers and Jewish settlers; the State Department said that in 1988 alone "over 20,000 Palestinians were wounded or injured" by the Israeli Army. The Israelis also demolish the houses of Palestinians suspected in involvement in the *intifada*, and severe beatings by soldiers are routine.

Strolling through Jerusalem's Jewish Quarter in September 1989, I came upon three young Israeli border patrol soldiers slapping a young Palestinian across the face while examining his identity papers. The most awful, of course, are the mutual hatreds stirred between young Israelis and young Palestinians, "children killing children," as a friend of mine put it.

During 1989 Palestinians began assassinating and maiming large numbers of Palestinians and Israeli Arabs believed to be collaborating with the Israeli

authorities. Israel's President Chaim Herzog told me in September that Israeli security services had informed him that they never heard of most of
them; Herzog thinks that the Palestinians are also battling among themselves
over power in the Occupied Territories. Palestine Liberation Organization
Chairman Yassir Arafat told me in Tunis in February 1989 that thus far he
had forbidden the use of firearms by the Arabs in the *intifada* but that this
may soon change if there is no political settlement. In this quickening cycle
of political violence, everybody's human rights were shattered.

Cruelty is limitless. There were reports from Marxist Ethiopia of victims
hung upside down for long hours by the knees and wrists from a horizontal
pole, the raping of women prisoners, the tying of a heavy weight to a man's
testicles, the burning of parts of the body with hot water or oil, and the
crushing of the hands or feet.

From Zaire there were accounts of political detainees made to drink their
own urine, of the infliction of electric shocks to genitals, of the insertion of
sticks between the victim's fingers, which were then crushed together, and
of victims' being held in leg irons in total darkness.

In Paraguay the secret police in the days of General Alfredo Stroessner
(ousted in 1989 after thirty-five years in power) favored the method of
plunging a victim's head into a tank of water, sometimes polluted with ex-
crement, until a sense of suffocation was induced or of wrapping a victim in
a plastic sheet and placing him (or her) in a metal cylinder for prolonged
periods.

Accounts from Syria described the "Black Slave," the strapping of the
seated victim to an apparatus that inserts a heated metal skewer into the
anus. The Syrians were also partial to the pouring of boiling or cold water
over the victim alternately.

The most popular torture instrument in the world appeared to be the
electric prod (normally used on cattle) that policemen liked to apply to genitals, male and female, breasts, and mouths. Prods are cheap and require
minimal training in their application.

And torture is steeped in tradition. An Amnesty International official in
Washington told me of visiting an exhibit on "Ancient Techniques of Torture" in a museum in Toledo, Spain, near Madrid, where "almost all the
instruments of torture were the same instruments that are being used today
in the countries from which Amnesty is reporting torture." She added that
"the only difference was that the new ones are more sophisticated" and that
"today the instrument would be made of metal whereas in the thirteenth or
fourteenth century it was made of wood."

Formal executions and what human rights organizations euphemistically
call extra-judicial executions, which simply mean quiet murders by the authorities, were another grim dimension of cruelty. And often it was not
enough just to kill. In Iran, where there were more than seven thousand
executions between 1979 and 1986 as part of the ongoing Islamic fundamentalist revolution (the figure was reported by the UN Commission on

Human Rights), relatives of executed members of the Baha'i religious faith told of being ordered by the authorities to pay for the bullets that killed their loved ones before they could take the bodies away for burial.

According to a United Nations report, Iran during the second half of 1988 executed at least a thousand people, including women and clergymen. Ten women were hanged in January 1989 on charges of adultery and corruption. A subsequent United Nations report said that the government of President Hojatolislam Hashemi Rafsanjani violated the basic human rights of Iranians on the same large scale as during the rule of the Ayatollah Khomeini who died in June 1989.

There were reports from a dozen Middle Eastern, African, and Asian countries of parents being executed in front of their children as well as of the killing of children in the presence of their parents to punish or intimidate them (torture or rape of men and women before the eyes of their spouses is commonplace in many countries). And increasingly, children became direct targets of imprisonment, tortures, and murder.

In South Africa as many as 11,000 nonwhite children were detained without trial between 1984 and 1986—and 312 children were killed by police gunfire, and 1,000 wounded. At a conference of doctors and social workers in Johannesburg in 1985 a lawyer told the group that "one of the most awful memories I have is of children screaming through the night." The conference dealt with long-term effects of detention and ill-treatment on children, and Amnesty International has reported that "immediately after arrest, children may be beaten for several hours while being continuously interrogated." They have been hit with fists, whips, or rifle butts and kicked, Amnesty International says, and "attempted strangulation, electric shock torture and beatings on the soles of the feet have all been reported." South African authorities presumably arrest children to extract information about clandestine opposition organizations or to terrorize their parents.

Between 1983 and 1989 more than 700 persons, mostly blacks, were executed in South Africa. In the first nine months of 1989 there were 39 hangings, including of two mixed-race political activists sentenced for the murder of a teacher who had violated a school boycott. The new South African president, Frederik W. de Klerk, believed to be in favor of great racial tolerance, ordered these two executions in September despite an international appeal for clemency.

Although the UN General Assembly approved a Declaration on the Rights of the Child in 1959—three decades ago—children across the world continued to be exposed to extreme sadism and cruelty. Reports by private groups covering 1987 alone dealt with an eight-year-old-boy in the Napo Province in Ecuador who was thrown over a roll of barbed wire and beaten by soldiers looking for a stolen rifle; a three-year-old boy shot dead in his mother's arms in a village in eastern Suriname in South America; four small boys in a Kurdish village in Turkey who were given electric shocks to their mouths by gendarmes looking for insurgent ethnic guerrillas; a seven-year-old boy born in 1980 in the Central Prison in Addis Ababa, Ethiopia, after the detention of his mother, an ethnic political activist, who has never set foot outside his cell; and several two-year-old children massacred by Marcos government troops in Lupao in the Philippines. General Ramón Camps, former Buenos Aires police chief who is now serving a prison sentence once explained that "subversive parents teach their children subversion."

On November 20, 1989, the UN General Assembly adopted by consensus the International Convention on the Rights of the Child, exactly thirty years after passing the nonbinding Declaration on the Rights of the Child. The new convention, which was negotiated over ten years, will become binding when ratified by the legislatures of at least twenty nations. The fifty-four-article convention covers every possible contingency—from the right to a name to freedom from child labor and abuse—and its timeliness was emphasized by a UN report that more than one hundred million children are abandoned on the streets of the world's cities. As in all other human rights situations, however, compliance with the convention's provisions may be extremely hard to monitor and enforce.

Arbitrary imprisonment for longer or shorter periods was the most common form of politically motivated human rights violations (sometimes the victims were put through the motions of a "trial" with no witnesses or defense lawyers), and it is probably accurate to say that many millions have gone through prisons on all continents since the signing of the Universal Declaration of Human Rights in 1948.

Among them were the inmates of the Soviet gulag, (before Gorbachev), Chinese prisons and "reeducation" camps after the Communist "liberation" and the Cultural Revolution, Cuban prisons before and after Fidel Castro's victorious revolution, Chilean prisons after the 1973 military coup d'état, and jails from Iran and Iraq to Vietnam and Indonesia.

It is a fair estimate that at least one hundred thousand people remained imprisoned on political, religious, ethnic, and related grounds as the 1980's drew to a close. Except for political celebrities—like Nelson Mandela in South Africa—the bulk are nameless, faceless, forgotten prisoners for whom the world cares little. Amnesty International describes those detained for reasons of political principle as "prisoners of conscience," and it tries to keep track of their fate.

Prison conditions, almost as a rule, were deplorable everywhere in the world. The worst were in the Third World, where populations have skyrocketed and political prisoners were often held together with common criminals in unspeakable overcrowding—mostly in prisons built as far back as the last century by British, French, Dutch, or Belgian colonialists. At the Pul-i-charkhi fortress in Afghanistan, 11,000 prisoners were killed after the Communist coup in 1978.

There is a vast literature on political prisoners' treatment—from the Siberian gulags to prison camps on Chile's Tierra del Fuego and fortresses like Havana's La Cabaña—and this outpouring by inmate writers grows and grows, year after year, from the Soviet Union's Aleksandr Solzhenitsyn to Cuba's Jorge Vals. I happened to see Beethoven's opera *Fidelio* not long ago, and I was shocked to realize how the haggard prisoners, crawling out of the dungeon into fresh air and sunlight in the courtyard of the prison near Seville at the outset of the nineteenth century, reminded me of inmates I have seen in prisons in the Third World and Eastern Europe some 185 years later. The prisoner singing, "We still trust in God's help. . . . We will be free, we will find peace!" could be sung today in Beijing, Teheran, Havana, or Rangoon.

Denial of political freedoms, arbitrary imprisonment, torture, and even executions represented *individual* violations of human rights—no matter how many thousands or millions of individuals were affected. Still more frightening because cruelty and savagery operate blindly were the mass killings and mass deracinations of populations from their natural and traditional habitats and surroundings.

Thus, in the last twenty years, millions of civilians have been murdered in systematic programs of genocide. Genocide is defined in international law as the deliberate destruction of national, ethnic, or religious groups, and the UN General Assembly approved in 1948 the Convention on the Prevention and Punishment of the Crime of Genocide. It was signed and ratified by an overwhelming number of UN member states, but the civilized world has tolerated unbelievable acts of genocide with hardly a protest.

In Cambodia the Khmer Rouge regime of Pol Pot, a demented revolutionary despot, murdered between one and three million people after the U.S. withdrawal in 1975 (the total population was around fifteen million) as he attempted to set up a visionary peasant state; other millions were chased out of the capital, Pnom Penh, and other cities into the countryside. But the UN Commission on Human Rights, the only international organ dealing globally with rights violations (though lacking enforcement powers), did not address itself to the fact of the Cambodian genocide until 1983—four years *after* Pol Pot had been overthrown by the Vietnam-backed People's Republic of Kampuchea and its Khmer Communist party.

The government established following the Vietnamese invasion engaged in killings on a much lesser scale than the Pol Pot genocide as well as in mass imprisonments; the Human Rights Commission, dominated by Third World votes, chose to limit itself to a condemnation of "the persistent occurrence of gross and flagrant violations of human rights" in Cambodia, but naming no names. In 1986 there were several thousand political prisoners held without charges in Cambodia, many tortured and some buried alive.

In Uganda more than three hundred thousand citizens (including Anglican Archbishop Janani Luwum) were killed between 1971 and 1979 by the forces of Idi Amin, the former British army sergeant and boxing champion. His troops massacred additional thousands of Tanzanian civilians across the border. But only in 1978, shortly before he was ousted by the invading Tanzanian Army and Ugandan guerrillas, did the UN Commission act at all: It requested the UN secretary-general to appoint a special representative to Uganda. It took Amnesty International to report that Idi Amin had "whole villages massacred" and that in the numerous torture centers thousands of prisoners were routinely subjected to "flogging, electric shocks, physical mutilation, drownings, arbitrary shootings," and chaining and burning to death in the presence of senior security officials.

The reign of terror in Uganda resumed under the succeeding regimes of President Milton Obote and Major General Tito Okello—tens of thousands of murders occurred during that period—and a semblance of normality returned only in 1986, with the installation of still another regime. But a low-grade civil war persisted in Uganda, and the State Department has said that the authorities continued to use the "three-piece tie" modality of torture, apparently invented by Idi Amin. This entails tying a person's arms behind his back until the elbows meet, a very painful procedure that can lead to gangrenous infections of the hands and arms as well as rupture of the breastbone and asphyxiation. United Nations bodies looked the other way while Uganda lived through fifteen years of steady horror; as Professor Farer remarked in a recent study on the role of the United Nations in this field, "they talk softly and carry a twig."

In Equatorial Guinea, a tiny country on the west coast of Africa and a former Spanish colony, a crazed ruler named Francisco Macías Nguema had at least six hundred prisoners assassinated, quote a number in a total population of three hundred thousand between 1968 and 1979, when he was overthrown. The State Department called it a "state-sanctioned policy of terror," and Tom Farer described Equatorial Guinea as "another of the great abattoirs of our time."

In the Islamic world there have been wholesale massacres, too. Before and during the 1971 war when Bangladesh broke away from Pakistan, the Pakistani military engaged in a campaign to liquidate Hindus and elite Bengali Muslims in what was East Pakistan. Thousands were killed, and millions fled to India. But in independent Bangladesh things were not going well either. The army fought tribal insurgents in the Chittagong Hill Tracts, and in this poorest and most densely inhabited country in the world, too many resources flowed into the control of rebellions and political opponents.

Total repression reigned in Iran and Iraq, and in neither country was there any mercy for political or religious opponents. There have been thousands of executions in Iran since the 1979 Islamic Revolution. A State Department report notes that in the prisons, "stories of tortures are rampant and cover a wide range of inhuman practices, ranging from mock executions to the beating of prisoners on the soles of their feet until they can no longer walk." Followers of the Baha'i faith, the largest non-Muslim religious minority in Iran, which numbered around 350,000 when the Revolution came, are a special target of hate for the fundamentalists in power. Formal banning of all Baha'i religious activity in 1983 provided the legal foundation for charging Baha'is with crimes simply because of their beliefs. The State Department estimated that approximately 200 Baha'is "have died following torture" since the Revolution.

In Iraq, where, in the words of the State Department, "execution has been an established method for dealing with perceived political and military opponents of the government," the principal enemies were militant and separatist-minded Kurdish minorities, and Iran-backed Shi'ite Muslims, whose Da'wa party is illegal. Large numbers of Kurdish villages were razed by the army to contain the insurgency, and Amnesty International estimated that hundreds of Kurds were executed and killed in 1986.

In 1988 Iraqi forces used poison gas against Kurdish villages; some fifty thousand Kurds fled into Turkey, another tragic migration hardly noticed by the outside world. The Kurds, who aspire to their own independent state, are also engaged in guerrilla warfare against Turkey next door. The State Department ascribed most of the bloody violence to the rebels, but the Human Rights Watch organization in New York indicated that there is "denial of human rights to the Kurdish minority in eastern Turkey," including torture.

President Assad, who runs a brutal dictatorship in Syria, was held responsible by human rights organizations for ordering the massacre of twenty thousand defiant Islamic fundamentalists in the city of Hama in 1982; in December 1986 some two hundred political opponents were killed by Syrian troops in Tripoli.

Indonesia, too, comes under the bloodbath chapter in the postwar annals of massive human rights violations. An abortive uprising there in 1966 led to the deaths of hundreds of thousands of leftists and alleged leftists at the hands of the military; nobody knows the exact figure. In 1989, there were several hundred prisoners held in Indonesian prisons for their involvement in the attempted Communist coup twenty-three years ago.

In Burma, for decades isolated from the outside world, the army turned to mass killings and jailings and to brutal torture to liquidate a prodemocracy movement led by students and intellectuals in 1988 and 1989. After the military coup in September 1988 the country's name was changed to Myanmar, and the capital's name to Yangon (from Rangoon).

According to the State Department, three thousand unarmed Burmese were killed by the army in July 1988, and thousands were arrested in July 1989. The arrests encompassed the entire leadership of the prodemocracy groups, including Daw Aung San Suu Kyi and U Tin Oo of the National League for Democracy. The American Embassy in Yangon reported in mid-1989 that it had "credible" reports of torture, including the crowding of prisoners in small cells in knee-deep water. Some five hundred prisoners, most of them naked, were forced to carry heavy loads of rice and munitions for the army over twenty-five-mile stretches of rough terrain; they were bound together by ropes in a chain, hand to hand, foot to foot.

Though Ne Win, the army general who ruled Burma for twenty-six years as a most ruthless dictator, formally resigned in 1988, all indications were that he continued to pull the strings and insist on total repression. During his presidency, uncounted thousands of Burmese were killed by the army and police. Burma, however, has all along been virtually closed to outsiders and there are no comprehensive records on the killings and human rights violations.

Apart from massacres and extreme oppression applied by governments to destroy opponents challenging, really or potentially, their political, ideological, or religious power, there were staggering instances of the physical elimination of huge numbers of human beings to impose the national and ethnic sway of one group over another.

Thus, in Tibet, which Communist armies forcibly incorporated into China in 1950, hundreds of thousands of inhabitants have been killed in the process, while others died from related causes. The New York-based Asia Watch Committee says in a recent report that "it is estimated by Tibetan exiles that over one million Tibetans died from unnatural causes in the thirty years between 1950 and 1980," a startling figure considering that Tibet's present population is barely in excess of two million. The committee concedes that this figure could not be verified, but it comments that "it is rare to meet a Tibetan who hasn't lost at least one relative in the turmoil of those years. . . . Population statistics reveal a disproportionate dearth of males in Tibet, particularly in the eastern part of the plateau, where fighting in the 1950s was said to have been extremely heavy." The report adds that "despite liberalization in some areas, political imprisonment, torture and discrimination are also characteristic of the current situation in Tibet."

As part of liberalization the Chinese government allowed in 1986 the resumption of public celebrations surrounding the annual eight-day Tibetan Great Prayer Festival, the most important Buddhist observance there, but this gesture simply proved that neither nationalism nor religious sentiment can be erased no matter what actions to achieve it are taken by the occupying power and for how long. In October 1987 a violent anti-Chinese protest broke out in Lhasa, the capital of Tibet, in connection with a religious feast as thousands of Tibetans, including Buddhist monks, rushed into the streets to claim for independence from China, which considers such demands to be a crime. Twelve Tibetans were killed by police gunfire. In March 1988, on the last day of the prayer festival, pro-independence rioting broke out anew after observances at the Jokhang Temple, the holiest shrine in Tibetan Buddhism, despite an enormous Chinese police presence; at least nine persons were killed. Tibetans seemed to be proclaiming their continued loyalty to the Dalai Lama, their spiritual leader, who has lived in exile in India since 1950, and the Chinese central government clearly face a major nationalism problem in that legendary land.

Eight Tibetans, including monks, were killed by the Chinese police on December 10, 1988, as the authorities quelled still another pro-independence demonstration. Visiting the kingdom of Bhutan, south of Tibet, in 1989, I learned that a new wave of Tibetan refugees had crossed the high Himalayas border earlier that year, fleeing Chinese persecution. The refugees brought word that eight hundred Tibetans were killed in March of that year by Chinese security forces. In October 1989 the Dalai Lama, the spiritual Buddhist ruler of Tibet, exiled in India since 1950, was awarded the Nobel Peace Prize.

In Burundi, a tiny, impoverished country of five million in the heart of Africa, more than a hundred thousand members of the Hutu tribal majority were massacred in May 1972 by the forces of the ruling Tutsi tribe minority under the republic's first president, Michel Micombero (who had replaced King Ntare V and who was ousted himself in 1976). It was a grisly affair, a dramatic reminder that tribal politics and loyalties still loom high in African life, affecting the course of national events. In oil-rich Nigeria, which has 250 separate ethnic groups, well over one million died in battle and from starvation and disease during the savage war in the late 1960's and the early 1970's when the tribes in Biafra rose in secession. And all these tensions have continued in Nigeria under successive military regimes; Amnesty International reported at least sixty executions there in 1986.

Nationalistic obsession possessed the Communist government of Bulgaria in the 1980's, as it used army tanks and police dogs to force 1.2 million ethnic Turks, roughly 10 percent of the total population, to change their names to Bulgarian names and, in effect, to shed their allegiance to Islam as a religion. Turks began settling in what today is Bulgaria toward the end of the fourteenth century, but it took the Communist regime to decide that ethnic Turks must be forcibly assimilated. The violent assimilation campaign, certainly without precedent in Europe, was carried out in 1984 and 1985, and according to Amnesty International, "over 100 ethnic Turks were allegedly killed by the security forces." The campaign was resumed in 1989, before the fall of the Zhivkov regime.

The official explanation for the attempts to destroy Turkish identity in Bulgaria, attempts the regime sought to conceal from the outside world, was that "a unified Bulgarian socialist nation" was desirable. But the real reason appeared to be concern in Sofia that "Islamic fanaticism" (a phrase used in an official publication in the late 1970's) may pose a challenge to absolute Communist rule. Moreover, the majority Bulgarian population was decreasing while minority ethnic and Muslim populations were increasing, and the regime must be worried that problems of control of power may arise in the next generation.

Bulgarian troops began surrounding ethnic Turkish villages early in 1984 to force the inhabitants to change their traditional names to "official" Bulgarian names. By the end of the year this had become a nationwide campaign. Troops with tanks and police with dogs occupied villages early in the morning, and officials rushed into households and forced the inhabitants to accept new identity cards, often at gunpoint. Those who refused to sign "petitions" for new names, Amnesty International reports, were imprisoned. When villagers marched in peaceful protest against the assimilation campaign, security forces used tear gas and dogs on the people and opened fire on them. In some instances ethnic Turks were shot on the spot for refusing to accept new identity cards. Barricades were erected in a number of villages to keep out the name-changing officials; but tanks were brought up to smash the barricades, and the houses of those declining to cooperate were blown up with explosives or destroyed with bulldozers. Some villagers were summarily executed.

Under the new regulations, not only must ethnic Turks change names, but most of the mosques have been closed down or destroyed. Those speaking Turkish in public are subject to fines. Parents who circumcised their children according to Islamic precepts were prosecuted and faced up to three years of imprisonment. The Islamic custom of washing the body of the deceased prior to burial has been forbidden by the authorities.

After the campaign against Turkish minorities resumed in 1989—as usual, there was no official explanation—310,000 ethnic Turks fled Bulgaria to Turkey during June and July alone. In August, Turkey closed its border both to force the Bulgarians to end the anti-Turkish campaign and to protect the Turkish economy already suffering from high unemployment. In all, nearly 500,000 Turks had fled Bulgaria in the 1980's in one of the largest European migrations since World War II.

Ironically, it was the great exodus of 1989 that appears to have forced the ouster in November of Bulgarian President Zhivkov after thirty-five years in power. The seventy-eight-year-old Zhivkov and his hard-line associates came under powerful pressures from reformers when the prodemocracy movement began sweeping Eastern Europe in the autumn, but it was the Turkish issue that ultimately brought him down. He had personally ordered the Turks' departure, but the immediate result was a virtual paralysis of the Bulgarian economy—and the old Communist was made to pay for it by his erstwhile colleagues. But the cruelest irony was that when the new regime abolished the anti-Muslim measures, a savage backlash developed among the Slavs, who wanted to see the Turks in submission—or gone.

Still another glaring violation of human rights was the forcible removal of populations for alleged "national security" or "counterinsurgency" reasons, invoked by leftist and rightist regimes alike, and millions of people have been affected. These removals were reminiscent of deportations of whole national groups by the Nazis and the Soviets during the Second World War. During the Mau Mau rebellion in Kenya in the 1950's, the British forced nearly one million Kikuyu tribesmen out of their villages and farms, and settled them in enclaves surrounded by barbed wire and armed guards. Americans in Indochina had deracinated probably one million or more villagers to make room for battle zones, and the Soviets did likewise in Afghanistan. Iraq was doing it with the Kurds. Regimes in leftist Nicaragua and rightist Guatemala and El Salvador forcibly removed hundreds of thousands of rural dwellers in the midst of their respective civil wars. Romania expelled tens of thousands of peasants from their homes to make room for power dams. The Marxist government in Ethiopia moved around five million half-starved peasants into strategic villages it controls.

An exceedingly painful and controversial situation developed in Hong Kong in December 1989 when the British authorities forcibly repatriated fifty-one Vietnamese boat people, the vanguard of the forty-four thousand refugees from Vietnam who have streamed into the colony since mid-1988 and now face expulsion. The British action provoked cries of outrage from foreign governments (the United States called it "odious"), Pope John Paul II, and human rights' groups, but for Britain this was not a simple matter. The Thatcher government took the view that immensely overcrowded Hong Kong could not cope with the Vietnamese, most of whom were regarded as "economic refugees"—people who seek to better their economic status rather than to escape political oppression. It feared that other thousands of Vietnamese boat people would sail to Hong Kong if the expulsions were not carried out, and by the year's end the British decision was to repatriate the refugees held in camps on small islands off the colony.

V

Hunger, starvation, disease, and death in the Third World stem in the first place from the sheer size of its populations. The Third World now accounts for 75 percent of humanity; it was only 50 percent in 1914. But it will be 85 percent in year 2008.

During the last half century the global population has more than *doubled* from 2.3 billion in 1940 (the start of the Second World War) to 5.5 billion at the end of 1989. The wartime growth was extremely limited (war conditions, including dispersals of families and nations, the physical destruction of countries, the absence of men from home environments as well as the immense casualties kept down population increases), but it exploded with a vengeance just before 1950. The postwar world, caught up in crises of reconstruction, decolonization and nation building, was completely unprepared for such a surge. Nobody had predicted it during the tranquil colonial days prior to 1939, when even the notion of the Third World did not exist, and thus there were no resources and no experience to deal with this phenomenon.

An immense effort has been undertaken by international organizations, governments, and individual communities across the world to bring down birthrates as well as infant mortality rates. Birthrates tend to go down when infant mortality decreases; there is less need for replacements of children in families that need their labor to survive.

The problem has been studied in depth for many years, producing volumes of statistics and analysis. But when I visited India in 1988, it occurred to me that the best way to understand the problems of population and poverty was to go out and look at it. I chose a village here and there at random, and the material I gathered probably speaks for itself.

Savitri Yadan came to live in dusty, hot Manethi from another village of Haryana State in India as a teenage bride sixteen or seventeen years ago (she can no longer fix the exact date), and what she remembers the most poignantly is that in those days approximately twenty to twenty-two infants out of a hundred died there before their first birthday every year. But today, Savitri says, no more than ten infants are lost to their parents in this fashion in Manethi, and she beams as other village mothers sitting around her on the dirt floor of the community center nod vigorously.

That this has happened in Manethi and is gradually happening nowadays in much of India—that the atrocious infant and child mortality rates are finally beginning to go down—represents the first piece of fundamental positive news from the Third World in contemporary history. To be sure, the exceedingly high childhood mortality rates are dropping elsewhere, too, but India is such an enormous portion of humanity that Indian patterns correspondingly affect the global picture, showing how the battle against baby deaths may someday be really won, excruciatingly slow and difficult as the advances appear to be.

Manethi is one of India's 570,000 villages, and it is located in the Mahendragarh district in the southernmost tip of Haryana on a tongue of land jutting into the arid desert state of Rajasthan. With its 15 million people, Haryana is a relatively small state in the immensity of India's population of 810 million. It is overshadowed politically by the majestic presence of New Delhi, the Indian capital, and Uttar Pradesh, the country's largest state, to the east, and by the Punjab (with its bloody strife engaging autonomy-seeking Sikhs against Hindus, Muslims, and others in the state) to the north.

But the state of Haryana, with more than 80 percent of its inhabitants vegetating in the rural areas (the figure for India is 74 percent) and with the endemic problems of very high birthrates, overall bad health, malnutrition, and shocking illiteracy, is fairly illustrative of the Indian nation, especially as it concerns the impact on the youngest segment of the population.

Overall projections for India are that despite an improvement in birthrate ratios, the demographic situation remains out of hand—the population growth rate is 2.1 percent annually (almost seventeen million people born in 1989)—and that at the start of the new century the country will have six hundred million illiterates, six hundred million homeless and four hundred million unemployed. This would make the world's largest democracy the world's poorest nation, even though the Indian economy has grown remarkably since the 1970's, becoming self-sufficient in grain and creating a modern industry. It is a terrible contradiction in the world's second most populous nation.

Manethi and its eight or nine thousand dwellers are, as I discovered, reasonably typical of the life and hardships of Haryana although the Mahendragarh district is said by local officials to be "the poorest of the poor" in the state. On the average, a family's *annual* income is 3,500 rupees, which is well below India's national figure; it translates into $230, but this is entirely meaningless in terms of economic values, and it is probably more to the point that the cost of a water buffalo or a camel is around 4,000 rupees. People in Manethi and the Mahendragarh district in general make their living from agriculture (some own parcels of land; others are landless peasants employed by neighbors), and to them buffaloes and camels are vital for tilling and transportation. In other words, the whole family must work all year to earn the equivalent of the price of an animal, but of course, this is illusory, too, because a family spends everything it earns just to stay alive.

Actually, the state of Haryana is rather well off economically by Indian standards even though, as I saw during my tour, quality of life in its most elementary sense leaves much to be desired. Virtually no village, for example, has running water or sewers, and septic-tank latrines are only now being introduced here and there. In the villages of Dighal and Dimana, as well as in Manethi, raw sewage runs down the center of the main street, and children often play in it under the scorching sun.

Being relatively wealthier than most other states, Haryana is not a better place to live for that reason alone. Curiously, some of the most economically depressed states in India display enviable progress in education and social institutions while many of the richer ones fail appallingly to look properly after their people, very much including women and children. Thus the impoverished southwestern state of Kerala is an astounding example of social achievement, and by contrast, Haryana still is something of a disaster in this realm. The infant mortality rate in Kerala stands at an impressively low thirty per one thousand live births, but it is ninety-nine in Haryana, slightly higher than the figure for all India (for comparison, the U.S. rate is ten). Kerala is an internationally admired phenomenon in the Third World, resulting from the state's strong political activism and a long tradition of education and literacy. Unfortunately Kerala is not representative of India.

The only analogy with Kerala I know in the Third World is Costa Rica. Likewise lacking in natural resources (and, moreover, surrounded by rapacious and dictatorial neighbors), that little Central American republic is a showcase of what a democratic government with correct social instincts can accomplish. I revisited Costa Rica after a decade's absence in 1988, immediately after my return from India, and I was immensely impressed with public health and education services, the relatively high living standards, the cleanliness, and the high employment.

All this had been achieved over forty years of political peace—a Latin American record—in a successful mix of public-sector and free-enterprise economy, a vociferously free press, and regular quadrennial elections. Costa Rica abolished its army altogether in 1948, and President Arias told me that "we can afford social progress because we don't waste money on defense budgets."

In Manethi the infant mortality rate, based on the numbers given me by the smiling Savitri Yadan, works out approximately to a ratio of a hundred per one thousand live births. To this woman in her early thirties, and a mother of three, the improvement in her village since the days of her girlhood has obviously been spectacular; the infant mortality rate then used to be over *two hundred*. I was introduced to Savitri at the Manethi community center, a dark but cool room in a brick structure where the grammar school is also located, and where thirty or forty grandmothers, mothers, and young wives gathered for a hurriedly organized session of questions-and-answers with me.

Dr. Sunder Lal, a member of the staff of the Medical College of Rohtak, one of Haryana's largest towns, came along as my guide (he has served there for nearly six years, and he seems to know everybody in every village in the area), and he volunteered to be my interpreter as well as we traveled around the state. Speaking in Haryanvi language through Dr. Lal, Savitri now explained to me that the reduction in the deaths of infants and children under the age of five in her village was largely due to the immunization through vaccination programs conducted aggressively these days by the Indian government with the crucial support of UNICEF (United Nations Children's Fund). UNICEF, of course, is the leader in the worldwide campaign of immunizing the great majority of Third World children against the six killer diseases—tuberculosis, smallpox, diphtheria, polio, measles, and tetanus—by 1990. Along with UNICEF, India is similarly endeavoring to control diarrhea, the leading cause of child deaths (four million worldwide in 1987), by providing safe drinking water to its hundreds of millions of inhabitants, and oral rehydration salts (ORS) packets of salt and sugar to death-brink children dehydrated by diarrhea.

I asked Savitri lots of questions about immunization programs, and Dr. Lal told me that "she says that immunization has affected the lives of children in such a dramatic and such a positive way that the people here feel that since there are injections available, which save the lives of children from diseases, why shouldn't our children live?"

And if children do survive, Savitri went on, then parents who otherwise—and traditionally—would have five or more offspring nowadays have rarely more than three, like herself. Birth control is mainly practiced through the rhythm method and increasingly through the use of condoms. However, as women become more educated, they tend to avert pregnancies and to space them better. Unquestionably, she added, the ever-rising cost of bringing up children, even in Manethi, is an equally important reason for limiting childbearing. The grandmothers in the back of the community center room nodded approvingly as Savitri spoke, but several of them burst out giggling. I inquired about the giggles, and Dr. Lal said, "Oh, they say that in the old days, it was different for them; they would each have ten, eleven, or twelve kids. . . ."

Savitri's enthusiastic report was, of course, a great oversimplification because India's—and even Manethi's future—cannot be resolved by immunizations alone. I had recently gone to Manethi and to other villages of Haryana to see and try to understand how rural India, forty years after independence from Britain and still in the midst of a population explosion, is coping with the scourge of infant and child mortality as well as with the eternal cycles of poverty, disease, and hunger. Taken together, these are the greatest obstacles in the way of India's social and economic development.

Inevitably there is an intimate link between infant and child deaths, and the birthrates. Classically in India, as elsewhere in the Third World, parents (chiefly in the countryside) compensate for the premature deaths of their babies by procreating more and more. It is a sad and pathetic form of insurance against a family's finding itself short of labor in the fields—agricultural child labor is a fact of life in India along with women's labor in the fields—particularly when the father and the mother begin to age and can hardly breathe. I already knew that for many reasons India's birthrates were now less steep.

First, however, I had to place India in a world context, turning to population statistics. According to UNICEF, close to *fifteen million* children die annually in the Third World, mainly from preventable causes. Preventable in this sense means prevention of disease, weakening, and death through immunizations of mothers, infants, and children; access to potable water to avoid contagion and gastric illness; proper nutrition of pregnant mothers, infants, and children; and spacing of pregnancies so that babies are not born underweight—i.e., under the minimal 2.5 kilograms considered safe by the World Health Organization.

India, I was informed, currently accounts for about one quarter of these preventable global deaths—well over 3 million annually, of which some 2.3 million are infants under one year of age and more than 1 million between the ages of one and four. With around 26 million children born in India last year, the cumulative deaths accounted for close to 15 percent, an abomination for a modern society. And it is demonstrably true, as noted above, that *fewer* children would be born if *fewer* were dying.

Still, figures and statistics are an abstraction. What *does* it mean in human terms that fifteen million children are condemned to death annually? James P. Grant, UNICEF's executive director, prefers to translate it into the notion that *forty thousand* children die *every day* in the Third World. During my stay in India I heard Grant proclaim indignantly in a speech in New

Delhi that "it is obscene that nearly forty thousand kids must die daily" and insist that this state of affairs is internationally "severe enough" to warrant the kind of "creative action" taken in the United States at the time of the Great Depression and in World War II.

But even to speak of the forty thousand daily deaths remains an abstraction, and I have asked myself how the world press would react if every day of the year a town of forty thousand inhabitants were systematically destroyed somewhere because of some calamity. As a reporter I know that such news would command front-page banners in the United States and elsewhere in the West until the calamity had run its course—in Bhopal, India, the explosion in a chemical plant in 1984 caused *only* twenty-five hundred deaths, it was front page for days, and it continues to be reported because of spreading cancer among survivors (another 1,700 died later from injuries related to gas leakage). But I also realize that forty thousand individual anonymous daily deaths, distributed over three or four continents, simply do not make news in, say, New York or London or Paris. They are too remote and monotonous.

Driving through India is marvelously deceptive. Along Haryana highways, the proudly moving camels, pulling or carrying great loads, give the flat landscape a dimension of dignity. Incredibly plumed wild peacocks float low over the road, and the traveler suddenly (if inaccurately) thinks of imperial India of yore. The wheat, millet, and rice fields are a symphony of colors (at least in western Haryana, where the killer drought has not yet reached in this period of the late 1980's) not only composed by the crops but even more so by the graceful figures of Indian women in their many-hued saris, working in the furrows or advancing along the road's edge with clay water vessels or loads of firewood. It all looks lovely and romantic from the car's window—until the visitor spends time in a village, looking closely and listening carefully to the sights and sounds of Indian rural life, asking questions and absorbing the answers. Then the illusion vanishes.

The Indian chain of misery begins with the drama of its social and economic status. According to figures for 1985, the latest complete data, the gross national product (GNP) *per capita* in India was $270. This was the average income generated annually by each inhabitant or, for that matter, *earned* annually, placing the country in the "low-income" group. While Zaire was at the lowest end of the scale with a $170 GNP, Argentina, in the middle, had $2,130, and Japan and the United States, at the highest end, had $11,300 and $16,690, respectively. Considering that India's population is five times larger than the United States' the extent of Indian poverty is strikingly evident.

Again, statistics translate dramatically into the human condition of India. There 51 percent of the rural population and 40 percent of the urban population live below what is officially described as the absolute poverty level, which is defined by the daily caloric supply per person; in India the caloric intake is only 96 percent of the required minimum for healthy survival (in the United States it is 140 percent). This means hunger in the most literal sense in the villages and in the vast urban slums of Bombay, Calcutta, and New Delhi, the skeletal adults and the malformed children, the meager rations extracted from the fields and from animal products in the countryside, and the scavenging for food in the huge garbage and waste dumps of the great cities.

These are the daily sights of India, and nightmarishly they follow the visitor the length and the breadth of the subcontinent. And when drought hits India, as it did in 1987, continuing in mid-1988 in the central belt as the worst one in a half century, then the hunger worsens. Between 1980 and 1986 about 33 percent of children under five suffered from mild malnutrition, and 5 percent from severe malnutrition.

Children under the age of fifteen constitute approximately one third of India's population; they are the survivors. But it is so tough to go on surviving in India because of malnutrition, disease, and harrowingly hard work (especially for women) that an Indian child's life expectancy at birth in 1986 was only fifty-seven years (it is seventy in Argentina and seventy-eight in the United States). A basic precondition for health—and child survival—in the Third World is access to safe drinking water (polluted water is the worst disease and contagion carrier); but in India only 47 percent of the rural population enjoys such access, and the majority of Indians do live in villages. On the plus side of this depressing ledger, however, it must be noted that in 1988 one third of urban inhabitants already had safe water; an enormous effort is being made to improve the water situation.

Education, even in the most primitive form, is the key to everything from national economic development to the survival of infants. When it comes to basic child care and the prevention of infant death, the crucial difference is the mother's knowledge and understanding of the first precepts of health, the rejection of awesomely unhygienic practices, and breaching millennial traditions. To possess such knowledge, it is necessary for the woman in pregnancy and the mother to be able to read. But in the continuing Indian tradition in the rural areas, it is much less important for girls than for boys to be educated—in fact, it is better to have boys than girls anyway, another aspect of the Indian tragedy—and therefore, only 29 percent of women in the countryside are literate (men's literacy stands at 57 percent). And only 38 percent of all Indian children completed grade school in 1986.

In Manethi, the Haryana village where infant mortality has dropped so greatly, Savitri Yadan let me in on the secret of the local success, perhaps unaware of the implications of her own life's story. I had asked the interpreter how Savitri had been treated as a little girl, and this was the reply: "She says that when she was a little girl, she was sent to school, and that was because her father was enlightened enough to want to educate girls, and she went up right through high school. . . . Yes, it is unusual. . . . Her brother also studied up to high school, and he got a job as an inspector of schools. She says that because of the fact that her brother, who was older than his sisters, got his education, the girls were sent to school, too—and she married into a family where her father-in-law, and her husband, and her husband's younger brother have also been educated. So she says that she feels that her family's attitude that everyone in a family must be educated does influence the others in the village."

But what does education mean in the sense of ameliorating life quality and eluding premature death in an Indian village? The best answer was provided in a UNICEF-supported study of Haryana villages by a young Indian scholar, Purnima Mankekar, who sums up her findings with the observation that "the most crucial obstacle with regard to improvement in the health status of a community was the unsanitary conditions in which they lived and their absolute apathy towards environmental hygiene . . . a majority of the people, for instance, persist in drinking water from wells fed by filthy ponds." They prefer it to piped chlorinated water available in a number of Haryana villages from nearby hydroelectric projects because, as Miss Mankekar reports, most villagers believe that "tapwater is 'lifeless' and tastes bad." She quotes a mother asking, "What life can be left in [the water] after electricity has been extracted from it?" Her conclusion was that the first priority in Indian life must be *educating* people about their health environment and practices.

A common sight along Indian highways are villagers bathing in slime-edged ponds and washing their buffaloes and cows in them, a daily rite. Often wells from which villagers draw water to drink and wash their utensils are next to these ponds; Indian doctors say the wells contain "seepage water," and inevitably it is dangerously polluted, responsible for gastric infections. In a related fashion the habit of outdoor defecation persists in tens of thousands of villages as well as in urban slums, where hundreds of thousands of India's poor live and sleep on sidewalks with no access to latrines.

Outdoor defecation may be the single greatest health hazard in India; it occurs even in the ponds where people bathe. Writing about Dighal, a village of some thirteen thousand inhabitants I visited on my first day in Haryana, Elizabeth Cherian, another Indian researcher, comments that "a child who defecates at the doorstep of the house is not chided, and the faeces remains there, sometimes for days." Miss Cherian found in Dighal exactly what I did five or six years after her survey: "The dirty streets clogged with rain water, the flies collecting over open piles of garbage—do not bother the villagers and they continue to live in apparent ignorance of the threat to health that these things pose." In another village she discovered that "the people continue to house their cattle in the same part of the house where cooking is done, flies abound in the houses, and dirty habits are not frowned upon."

In Basantpur, a grim, old village of 350 houses and some four thousand inhabitants in Haryana's drought belt, the headman with a grizzly beard showed me several indoor latrines built after the government had supplied septic tanks and connecting tubes, and said, yes, people were beginning to use them. Dr. Lal, my guide, told me that this was progress: "You know, this is doing away with customs of centuries and centuries—getting up in the morning and strolling over to one's fields to relieve oneself in nature's surroundings. . . . And villagers think that it is healthier than being confined in a latrine."

Both the Indian government and UNICEF are engaged in a vast campaign, employing everything from cartoons and comic strips to puppetry, radio, and television, to spread the gospel of cleanliness and hygiene. A strip shows a small boy defecating in a field, then a dog putting his nose in the feces, running to the house in the village, and drinking water from a vessel that the inhabitants may use later for eating. This is disgusting, all right, but it also is highly effective in a largely illiterate society.

Indian health workers, such as Miss Mankekar, believe that while younger generations of women increasingly attend school and are taught the basics of hygiene and proper child care, it is still necessary to educate village mothers-in-law—known as *dadi*—who are the great social force in the families. The word of a *dadi* is usually obeyed, and the mothers-in-law (some of whom I met in Manethi) are encouraged to come to the community center to listen to the weekly hourlong broadcast in the local language or dialect. These radio programs deal with every subject relevant to women and mothers, from the need to immunize children to the importance of pregnant women's eating well (there is widespread belief in rural India that if a woman eats too much, she becomes "heavy" and has difficult labor along with a belief that water must be poured on a mother's head to make her breast milk run).

But as I learned in Haryana, education has to go beyond village mothers to the Indian society at large to assure the creation of a healthy environment in the place of today's chain reaction of disease and death—in childhood and otherwise. It is urgent to deal with religion, tradition, and ancient customs to bury superstitions and fears that paralyze a nation striving for modernity. And in this context one of India's great tragedies is the awesome pollution of its rivers by industrial waste and human religious waste.

Describing the holy river Ganges, a report by the New Delhi Centre for Science and Environment emphasizes that a stretch near the city of Varanasi "where six million devotees bathe every year is contaminated by incredible amounts of biological and chemical filth." And it presents this tetric scene: "About 40 thousand human bodies are burnt at two cremation ghats and their ash dumped into the river . . . [and] about 10,000 half-burnt bodies are pushed into the river every year. In accordance with tradition, unburnt bodies of saints, lepers and animals are thrown into the river—an estimated 60,000 carcasses of cows, dogs and buffaloes are dumped annually into the Ganges at Varanasi."

In the heartbreaking equation of Indian life and death, the fate of women remains most dramatic. Aside from moral aspects of the treatment of women in India, their condition affects directly the health and the survival of children. A sickly woman, one would imagine, cannot deliver or rear a healthy child, but this verity is still lost on the Indian society. A recent study of *Infant Mortality in India*, edited by population experts Anrudh K. Jain and Pravin Visaria, insists that "conscious efforts should be made towards education of the community," adding that "education, to have the necessary impact, must be supplemented with measures for a more equitable environment for females in terms of intra-household distribution of food and the drudgery of work performed by them."

To put it bluntly, Indian women are treated like beasts of burden. In Haryana I saw only a sample of it. In Manethi, for example, I was taken to a small textile center where local women earned additional cash working on looms to produce floor-cover mats and sewing hosiery and T-shirts. I thought this was an admirable undertaking—until I asked my guide how often and how long the women could perform this activity in the period of, say, a week. "Oh," my guide replied, "they can only spend a few hours a week here—you know, when they're finished their domestic work and their field work." Even my smiling Savitri Yadan confirmed that Manethi women, like women elsewhere in rural India, rise before dawn to collect scarce firewood, cook breakfast for the family, labor all day in the fields in backbending work, return home to cook the evening meal, clean up—and the rest of the time is free to play or to earn a few extra rupees at the textile shop.

Ironically, economic growth condemns women to an even worse lot. I was told at the Rohtak Medical College that when industrial jobs opened up in Haryana towns, men from the villages rushed to take them—and the women's farm labor increased proportionally. Also in relatively prosperous Haryana, women must pick an acre of cotton on a landlord's farm to be allowed to take home cotton stalks for use as fuel; no wages are paid. Most Indian researchers agree that women in the rural areas work at least fourteen hours a day every day and sometimes more, even if they are pregnant.

The following account of a woman's life in a village in the state of Uttar Pradesh tells the story: "This is the seventh month of my pregnancy. I am the only adult in the household to take care of my children, two buffaloes, and a calf. My husband is a petty trader in a nearby town. The entire responsibility of the house is on my shoulders. I have to cook, fetch water, and provide fodder for the animals. In the evening I take them for grazing and collect green fodder. I also have to supervise the plowing. . . . I usually resume my normal activities just four or five days after delivery."

In the great cities of India—New Delhi, Calcutta, or Bombay—tens of thousands of women work as laborers on construction sites along with their husbands (or without husbands) and try to care for their children at the same time. When I was doing my research in New Delhi, I was taken to the headquarters of Mobile Créches, an organization providing care for the children of construction workers, by William J. Cousins, an American sociologist who has been engaged in Indian urban problems on and off for the last thirty years. As we walked through the Mobile Créches office, Bill Cousins pointed to a poster on the wall, which he urged me to read. I copied it:

> To Women Construction Workers:
> Woman worker in construction industry carries a three-fold burden in harsh and subhuman conditions—A ceaseless load carrier, she is given only hard physical labor throughout the day with no shelter or room for respite—All doors to learning skilled jobs are closed—A harassed mother, she gets no maternity relief, no leave, no place to keep her children except on the dangerous work site—There is no way to educate her older children—A struggling home-maker, she has a hovel for a home, no drinking water for her family, no latrines or drains, no ration facilities or health services nearby—No respite from morning to night—Mobile Créches is a response to some of these needs. . . .

Bill Cousins, a 1944 Yale graduate, is one of the most remarkable Americans I have ever met in the Third World: totally knowledgeable, dedicated, compassionate, and good-natured to the point where one forgets that he is a childhood polio victim. To Indians with whom he has worked all these years as an adviser on urban development, Cousins is the personification of what they like to think America is all about.

Talking about New Delhi slums, Cousins remarked that "this area draws people from all over India" and that in terms of child health, it was more difficult to immunize children in the teeming cities than in the rural regions, where people were generally fixed in the villages. It was hard, he said; but it had to be done, and it was being done.

Shortly after I left Bill Cousins, my car stopped at a traffic light in midtown New Delhi, a horribly teeming neighborhood, and suddenly the whole story of India's children was thrust at me. An emaciated young man in a torn shirt and ragged trousers leaned toward me, proffering a newspaper from a batch he held in his hand—he was selling them—and I saw that cradled in his other arm was a baby, hardly a few months old. Two huge deep brown eyes stared at me unblinkingly from a tiny head. The baby was silent. Its face was covered with a reddish rash. Three flies sat on its left cheek. The traffic light changed. We departed. The young man and the baby remained in place.

VI

High technology, developed over the last half century as a direct result of World War II research, has been a blessing, and it has been a lethal threat.

This became painfully evident when on April 26, 1986, the nuclear power plant at Chernobyl near Kiev in the Soviet Union released a radioactive cloud over the Ukrainian region and over much of Europe.

It was the worst nuclear power plant accident in the atomic age. At least 250 persons who were at the plant at the time or who worked in rescue and cleanup operations have died. People had to be evacuated from a eighteen-mile radius around the reactor. More than 130,000 people were evacuated at the time, leaving behind thirty-six thousand acres of land, twenty large collective farms, and 170 villages. Three years later it became evident that radiation had not been entirely cleared from the area, and plans were made to evacuate another 100,000 people. And the health of 100,000 people who lived near Chernobyl will be monitored for life; there are no guesses on what may be found and when.

In the United States a disaster was barely avoided at Pennsylvania's Three-Mile-Island power plant in 1979. Subsequently Americans learned the extent of the risk that results from our nuclear industry, civilian and military.

It has been known for a long time, though in little detail, that accidents, possibly with leakage of radiation, had occurred in 1952 at the Chalk River plant in Canada engaged in processing uranium and, also in 1952, at the plant in Harwell, England, where nuclear weapons are produced for the British nuclear force. The problem in Harwell was apparently quite serious.

But only in 1988 did we discover that the deterioration of the entire nuclear weapons production establishment in the United States had forced the shutdown of *all* three plants processing weapons-grade material for national defense and has posed immense and still not fully assessed health hazards.

Athough the whole nuclear weapons complex, consisting of forty-nine major facilities in twenty-three states, was over forty years old (going back to the dawn of the atomic age) and disturbingly obsolete, neither the U.S. Department of Energy, which supervises nuclear production, nor the big private corporations actually operating the plants had voluntarily admitted this condition. Nor did they apprise the workers and the surrounding populations of radiation and toxic dangers threatening them.

It was an unbelievable state of affairs that only under pressure did the government finally acknowledge publicly that the United States was out of the business of producing nuclear weapons, at least temporarily, and that for long years some of its nuclear plants had been releasing radiation into the air and water and contaminating the soil. National security secrecy should, of course, rank high in government concerns, but not higher than the health and welfare of Americans—and not higher than a decent standard of national morality.

Without any announcement, the reactors at the plant in Hanford, Washington, where plutonium triggers for thermonuclear weapons were manufactured, were shut down in 1987 for safety reasons. There may have been accidents. The only other plants for weapons-grade materials processing— the Savannah River plant near Aiken, South Carolina, and the Rocky Flats plant on the outskirts of Denver—suspended production during 1988. Moreover, the Savannah River plant was the sole facility for the production of tritium gas, the key explosive substance for thermonuclear weapons. Tritium is perishable, and it was customary to replace it regularly in hydrogen bomb warheads. The government has not explained how it would maintain its arsenal operational without the availability of fresh tritium.

We ignore whether any of the old nuclear plants has come close to a major accident with potential dire consequences in recent years (though cracks in the reactors' walls were reported at the Savannah River plant) and whether management and operators are properly trained. But we *now* know something about health and environmental damage and danger created by the nuclear plants, and even the government finally agrees that they must be urgently remedied.

At Hanford more than 440,000 cubic yards of highly radioactive waste have accumulated over the decades, and nobody has any idea how to dispose of them. The Energy Department acknowledged in 1989 that it would take fifty-seven *billion* dollars—a huge chunk of the national budget—for a cleanup at Hanford alone.

At the plant at Fernald, Ohio, where uranium is processed into fuel for nuclear reactors, an estimated thirteen million pounds of radioactive waste have been buried or stored in the thirty-seven years since the plant opened. Uranium and thorium salts are buried in pits, and the latest plan was to cover them with sand (which would increase the volume of radioactive emissions if these sand domes were to collapse). At the Savannah River plant, millions of gallons of irradiated water from the reactors have been poured into unlined seepage pools on the three-hundred-square-mile reservation, presumably endangering the water table under much of South Carolina.

Documents declassified by the government and disclosed in newspaper articles and in lawsuits starting in the late 1970's suggest that the United States nuclear industry was operated with shocking disregard of the workers' health just as the military had done with troops at atomic tests. The best estimates are that 600,000 Americans have worked at nuclear weapons facilities between 1943 and the mid-1980's, and 220,000 servicemen were exposed to test radiation between 1945 and 1962. It is obviously impossible to determine the impact on their health or, in most cases, their causes of death, but some indications are available to show the scope of danger. A lawsuit filed in 1989 alleged, according to *The New York Times*, that radiation from Nevada atomic bomb tests between 1951 and 1981 caused the cancer deaths of 200 employees.

VII

At the threshold of the nineties, humanity was suspended between the astonishing scientific and technological achievements of the past half century—along with the perils they represented side by side with their positive aspects—and its inability to cope with social challenges in the Third World and in the most affluent industrial nations.

The two opposite poles were space travel and nuclear medicine and Chernobyl and Hanford on one side and the frightening demographics of India and Africa as well the life in Western urban ghettos, with all their attending problems and suffering, on the other side.

Fifty years later, the fundamental question is, of course, whether humanity is safer, healthier, and happier today. Naturally there is no flat, across-the-board assessment—not political, not ideological, not economic, not social and cultural, not even scientific. As in all things human, there is a multitude of answers, not always complete, not always logical and understandable, not always satisfying. And there are vast contradictions.

Painted on the broad canvas—though some are still being sketched—are the great events occurring between 1939 and 1989, especially the stunning political and human transformations of the 1980's.

The central reality is world peace reigning since the end of the Second World War in 1945, notwithstanding superpower nuclear temptations and near confrontations, and all indications that it will be maintained indefinitely. There were only twenty-one years of peace between the two world wars; now it has been forty-five years since the last war.

Nevertheless, the East-West Cold War in all its dimensions did dominate four postwar decades—roughly until 1986—with the nuclear arms race, the Korea and Indochina wars, the crises over Berlin and Cuba, and the exhausting competition across the Third World. The Cold War produced regional wars and proxy wars under the umbrella of ostensible world peace.

That the Cold War finally ended during the late eighties was as remarkable in contemporary history as the fact that World War III, so often invoked, had been avoided. New thinking by the superpowers, other immense challenges to human survival, and generational changes in attitudes combined to create a fresh climate that appears to make world wars obsolete. The Palme Commission on Disarmament and Security Issues summed up well this state of affairs when it reported in April 1989 that we have now entered "a time when reason and common sense seem at last to be taking hold in the world."

Lord Zuckerman, a wartime adviser to Winston Churchill and a world authority on nuclear issues, put it this way in October 1989:

> The East-West military confrontation is all but becoming an anachronism in the face of the vast political, ethnic, and economic problems that are now plaguing the USSR and its allies, of the difficulties with which the countries of Western Europe contend as they move toward economic and, as some hope, a form of political union, and of the upheavals and disasters that are occurring in China and the Third World. The US and the USSR now have far less to fear from each other than they have to fear not only from their internal problems, but from events over which they can have little control—from the repercussions of the unrestrained growth of population in large parts of the world, from the changing age and ethnic structure of their own populations, from the global environmental changes that have become so serious a threat, from the likely emergence of new nuclear weapons states. . . .

The end of the Cold War is no longer a matter of semantic debate or wishful thinking. It has happened, tangibly. To wit, the Intermediate Nuclear Forces (INF) Treaty was signed by Presidents Reagan and Gorbachev in 1988, and in the ensuing year nearly thirteen hundred American and Soviet missiles of this type were destroyed under the eyes of American inspectors in the Soviet Union (after the Russians unprecedentedly agreed to on-site inspections in their country) and Soviet inspectors in the United States. The INF Treaty has mandated the removal of all Soviet and American intermediate-range nuclear missiles from Europe, the most spectacular breakthrough in postwar disarmament efforts. New talks on strategic nuclear forces (START, to follow up on the 1972 and 1979 SALT agreements) and on the limitation of conventional NATO and Warsaw Pact armies have been seriously under way since the autumn of 1989. Both sides had agreed beforehand on sizable troop cuts, and the Soviets captured headlines and evening television news programs with their public removals of the first tank regiments from Eastern Europe. In January 1989 thirty-five nations, including all NATO and Warsaw Pact members, signed their most ambitious security accord, in which they pledged themselves to strengthen and observe human rights through new international mechanisms.

The world has emerged from the Cold War for the simple reason that both superpowers finally took the political decision to do so. As Lord Zuckerman has remarked, "one salient lesson that can be drawn from the history of arms control talks in the postwar years is that it is a waste of time to negotiate on major arms control issues unless the leaders of the two sides are determined to reach the same goal, and begin by instructing their officials to discuss matters to a solution rather than arguing them to an impasse."

In the late eighties such a decision was taken by Mikhail Gorbachev in Moscow and Ronald Reagan and George Bush in Washington, and then everything fell into place. Clearly it was not a miracle, but the result of historical processes that are continuing.

Great new trends emerged during the 1980's. The most significant among them was the disappearance of Marxism-Leninism as a great political and ideological force and phenomenon. The immense transformations in Soviet life at home and in Soviet foreign policies—as well as Soviet acceptance of political democratization of Poland, Hungary, and Czechoslovakia through a peaceful abandonment of communism as a system of government—are a direct consequence of the recognition of the fact that the Marxist-Leninist cycle has run its course. Gorbachev has not formulated it in exactly these words, but his actions since his advent to power in 1985 obviously reflect this conclusion.

Indeed, Gorbachev's entrance on the Kremlin stage may historically equal Lenin's launching of the Soviet state in the aftermath of the Russian Revolution seven decades earlier. Whatever Gorbachev's personal and political fortunes turn out to be, the Soviet Union and Eastern Europe cannot return to Stalinism (or even the Brezhnevian stagnation and repression) and remain a viable group of nations. In this sense Gorbachev's *perestroika* and *glasnost* are not genies that can be forced back into the bottle. Too much has happened, too much freedom has been tasted in the former Communist empire, and too much needs to be done with extraordinary dispatch to improve living standards there to allow any meaningful change in the new course already taken in Moscow, Warsaw, Budapest, East Berlin, Sofia, Prague, and Bucharest.

In foreign policy the same pressures led Gorbachev to move to an accommodation with the West, an act of remarkable political courage he first displayed at his summit meeting with Reagan in Reykjavik in October 1986 with his proposal for a nuclear-free world by the end of the century. Reagan's willingness to respond positively notwithstanding his powerful ideological penchant against the "evil empire" made possible the amazing achievements in reducing international tensions everywhere, from arms pacts to American-Soviet collaboration in seeking to wind down regional wars. George Bush has pursued this policy because it suits the national interest of the United States.

The other great trend of the eighties was the return of democracy to nations in Latin America and Asia after long nights of dictatorship. On December 14, 1989, the first free elections in sixteen years were held in Chile: Patricio Aylwin, a Christian Democrat heading a coalition of opposition parties handily defeated the official candidate for the presidency put up by General Augusto Pinochet, the dictator. Pinochet captured power when the Chilean armed forces under his command overthrew in a bloody revolution in 1973 the freely elected Marxist President Salvador Allende. Allende had been chosen in 1970. That Pinochet was a highly unpopular figure was demonstrated in 1988 as Chileans voted in a plebiscite against his proposal to keep the presidency for eight additional years. The aging general was then forced by public opinion at home and abroad to call presidential elections, but he assured himself of continued influence by staying on as commander in chief of the armed forces. In Brazil, the first direct presidential elections in twenty-eight years took place on December 17, 1989, marking the end of a long period of dictatorial rule and then of semidemocratic government— the previous president had been chosen by the Congress, where the military carried much weight—following the armed forces' revolution that in 1964 ousted the constitutional regime elected three years earlier. The winner was the centrist candidate Fernando Collor de Mello, who narrowly defeated a quasi-Marxist leftist candidate and now must cope with inflation that was running over 1,000 percent annually. Both Argentina and Uruguay had free elections for the second time in a row during the eighties after lengthy military dictatorships. Paraguay's President Stroessner was finally thrown out of office after thirty-five years, but full-fledged democracy had not returned by the end of 1989.

Democracy fared less well in Panama. General Manuel Noriega, the head of the armed forces and the de facto ruler for a decade, annulled presidential elections in May 1989 when his figurehead candidate appeared to be losing. Noriega was indicted in the United States for his alleged involvement in international narcotics traffic, and both the Reagan and Bush administrations tried repeatedly to have him overthrown through American-aided Panamanian conspiracies against him. These attempts kept failing, and in December 1989, Noriega had his handpicked legislature name him chief of government. No foreign leader since Fidel Castro had frustrated United States governments as much as Noriega had.

In fact, Noriega and Castro, along with Nicaragua's Daniel Ortega and Libya's Colonel Qadaffi, were men who literally obsessed Reagan and then Bush: They were personal affronts to the American Presidents (Iran's Ayatollah Khomeini dropped from the obsession list when he died in 1989).

To be sure, Noriega was a singularly repugnant personage: He was a killer and torturer, a secret agent in the pay of both the CIA and Cuban intelligence, a thief on a colossal scale who stole millions from the national treasury, and allegedly a partner of Colombian drug lords. By any standards, he had no business running any country.

The pity of it, however, was that George Bush made Noriega into a personal and emotional issue, instead of handling him as a foreign policy or even a national security problem. When an anti-Noriega military conspiracy failed in October 1989, Bush was attacked at home by conservative opinion for his failure to provide direct armed aid to the rebels, using U.S. troops permanently stationed along the Canal. He took it as a challenge to his personal and presidential machismo (Reagan, after all, had unleashed the contra war in Nicaragua, invaded Grenada, and twice bombed Libya) and awaited the opportunity to show his mettle in Panama. Bush must also have been greatly annoyed by frequently published press photographs showing him as a cordial vice-presidential caller on Noriega at his Panamanian headquarters, and reminders that the pockmarked dictator had been on the CIA's payroll during Bush's tenure as director of central intelligence.

In any event, Noriega handed Bush the opportunity to do away with him. On December 15, for mysterious reasons, he had his rubber-stamp legislature formally name him head of state and declare that Panama was in a state of war with the United States—whatever that meant. The next evening, a U.S. Marine officer was killed in a shootout with Panamanian troops near Noriega's headquarters, and the wife of an American serviceman was molested by Panamanians. Now Bush had the justification he needed to hit Noriega. After the October conspiracy, the CIA was instructed to find ways to oust or capture the dictator (three million dollars was earmarked for the project), and both the Pentagon and the Southern Command in Panama drafted fresh invasion plans. The time to apply them had come.

In the small hours of Wednesday, December 20, an invasion force of fourteen thousand troops, including paratroops, marines, light infantry units, military police detachments, Navy Seals and Ranger commandos, landed in and around Panama City by air and sea. They joined the ten thousand U.S. troops permanently stationed in Panama under the terms of the Canal Treaty; tanks and armored vehicles had been secretly prepositioned there earlier in the month. Even two F-117A Stealth bombers, the supermodern radar-evading jet aircraft, was assigned to the anti-Noriega operation. Bush proclaimed that the invasion had been launched to protect American lives in Panama as well as the Canal, to restore democracy in Panama, and to grab Noriega to deliver him for trial before courts in Florida, where he had been indicted in absentia on charges of organizing drug running to the United States. But clearly, the capture of Noriega was foremost in Bush's mind.

This goal, however, eluded the Americans at the outset because of their faulty intelligence and ill-conceived battle plans. When Noriega's Panama

Defense Forces headquarters in Panama City fell to the invading forces, the general was not there to await his foes. He had vanished in the night. But the headquarters is located in the midst of a densely populated, working-class district of the capital, and at least three hundred civilians in the neighborhood were killed when U.S. armor and artillery opened fire on the building (the number of civilian casualties was never disclosed by the U.S. command and there was no Panamanian government in existence at the outset to count victims).

No reason was given by the United States for the obvious overkill—in the end the total force was twenty-six thousand—even if Noriega's loyalists (like Ceauşescu's Securitate) fought on for several days. The Panama Defense Forces had sixteen thousand men. It was not explained why Noriega's capture, ostensibly Bush's greatest wish, could not have been accomplished by commando teams without destroying parts of a city, considering the effort that has gone into the creation of special operations units. Indeed, it was a mystery why the United States had initiated an armed conflict if the object was to catch a thief and reward Panama with democracy, and why it sacrificed 23 American lives (there were 330 servicemen wounded) to accomplish these goals of "Operation Just Cause." Panamanian forces had 293 killed. Damage resulting from the invasion was estimated at $500 million, from destruction in combat to looting by Panamanian bands.

The Panama invasion was a test of military medical practices developed since the Vietam War, the last major involvement in combat by American military forces. The lessons of Vietnam led to an emphasis on mobility and speed of evacuation from the combat zone. Air Force transport planes carrying the troops for the invasion were instantly reconfigured into flying hospitals for the return flight, with room for thirty soldiers on stretchers and for medical teams. The Air Force's Wilford Hall Medical Center in San Antonio, Texas, had been designated as the main receiving facility for the wounded from Panama, and the first Starlifter transport carrying forty-three casualties (four died en route) reached San Antonio fourteen hours after the invasion started. Most of them were paratroopers who had been among the first to land in Panama City. The second evacuation jet arrived two and a half hours later in San Antonio. The majority of the wounded had been hit by high-velocity bullets, which cause tremendous damage to the body, and others had suffered from complex bone fractures. That so many of the seriously wounded servicemen were able to survive was principally because of the speed and efficiency of the Air Force medical operations in the Panamanian emergency.

Democracy was implanted when Guillermo Endara, who had won the 1988 elections that Noriega subsequently annulled, was inaugurated as Panama's new president at a ceremony at a United States military base near the capital. Noriega went into asylum at the papal nunciature on Christmas Eve; he would turn himself over to the American authorities ten days later to be flown to Miami and arraigned in federal district court.

The invasion of Panama, the ninth American military intervention in Latin America in this century (including the *indirect* invasions in Guatemala and the Bay of Pigs), had the inevitable effect of raising the question of whether the United States had embarked on a long-range policy of the use of force in the Western Hemisphere whenever it seemed to suit its interests. Bush would say that this was certainly not the case, but the Latin Americans remained quite skeptical; they knew, for example, that since December the administration had been contemplating the assignment of warships and aircraft to Colombian coasts to interdict the flow of drugs to the United States (uncannily, this scenario had been carefully outlined in Tom Clancy's bestselling thriller *Clear and Present Danger*, published late in 1989).

Democracy also triumphed during the eighties in the Philippines, South Korea, and Pakistan, where elected presidents replaced dictators. In Manila, Cory Aquino was chosen over Marcos after "people power" in the streets forced him to call free elections. In Seoul, years of street confrontations with students and the opposition led to democratic elections when the military finally agreed to step down. In both situations the United States supported the democratic forces, another major change during the 1980's, especially under Republican administrations (as was the case with the Duvalier dictatorship in Haiti). Late in 1989, President Bush ordered American jet aircraft to patrol the skies over Manila to keep anti-Aquino military rebels from victory in their coup attempt. Bush's action raised the interesting question of whether it was proper for the United States to intervene militarily in a foreign country in the "good" cause of defending democracy.

The events of the eighties—especially the 1989 happenings—have developed with such dizzying speed that there has been really no time to absorb them fully—intellectually, ideologically, and historically. But they have proved beyond any doubt that life pays no attention to academic predictions, projections, and analyses—especially Western masochistic analyses. Only a few years ago a huge tonnage of paper was devoted to the printing of prophecies about the coming decline of the West and notably of the "American Empire" in ways that would make Spengler sound like an optimist, and it was disturbing to see how seriously this literature was being taken. Reality very quickly disproved these arcane theories, and it should have taught the lesson that it is not prudent for intellectuals and historians to rush into the limelight with grandiose conclusions about the fate and nature of civilization before things actually take shape and happen. It would seem to be just as arrogantly facile to claim today that the West has "won" as it was to affirm yesterday that it had "lost." Processes of history are much more complex, frequently unexpected, and certainly more interesting than current intellectual games.

The demise of the Cold War has had truly mind-shaking effects in terms of new human and international relations. It looked as if people on all sides could barely wait for the Cold War to end officially and for all iron curtains to be raised to hurl themselves into each other's arms, as it were. After a half century of bitterly poisoned propaganda emitted from East and West, people everywhere demonstrated that they had paid very little attention to it, that everybody wanted to be friends.

On the official level, American and Soviet civilian and military defense chiefs of the highest rank visit each other, inspect the most secret facilities (which the hosts show with pride), and compare notes and experiences. Late in 1989 retired top CIA and KGB intelligence officers had something of a class reunion in San Francisco, talking over food and drink about past adventures and conspiracies and having a marvelous time of it. Historians have been meeting to reconstruct what really happened in the great crises of the Cold War.

On the human level, the activity and exchanges were limitless. The Soviets authorized emigration, notably of Soviet Jews, to such an extent that the United States, which had been righteously demanding such emigration for decades, discovered that it could not absorb a large portion of those free to leave. 1989 was the record year for Jewish emigration. But for months and months there were moving scenes of reunions between Jews arriving in New York—or in Israel—and their families. Nothing of the kind on such a scale had happened since the end of the war.

Miss Soviet Union flew to Washington to attend a Soviet Embassy party with Miss America. Soviet writers and journalists flocked to the United States on university grants, and mutual curiosity was endless. American businessmen, lawyers, bankers, and carpetbaggers stormed Moscow and Leningrad in rising waves to the point that it was virtually impossible to get a hotel room in the Soviet Union or a seat on a plane on flights between the two countries. Boris Yeltsin, the Communist populist who thinks Gorbachev is a conservative, barnstormed America. It was an explosion of pent-up empathy after a half century of silence, and obviously Americans and Russians (and Ukrainians, Latvians, Estonians, Lithuanians, and Armenians) liked each other a lot.

Soviet and American musicians played for each other's audiences, from classical music to rock, rock having become the greatest of all international languages; even Jewish American rock stars turned up in the Soviet Union. With a touch of incredulity, I read in Jerusalem in September 1989 that a "folk-rock-Jewish-soul" concert was being held in Leningrad, to be followed by nineteen other concerts in the Soviet Union. The Promised Land Rock Band from Los Angeles and Hassidic folk singer Shlomo Carlebach had sold out a hundred thousand tickets ahead of time, I learned from the Jerusalem *Post*, and the band's guitarist, Jerry (Yehuda) Katz, proclaimed that "we consider ourselves as emissaries for the Jewish people in what is the first authentic Jewish cultural exchange of this magnitude since the Russian Revolution."

And there was much human goodwill. Though Israel and the Soviet Union still had no diplomatic relations, El Al airline jets landed at Soviet airports for the first time in twenty-two years to fly victims of the Armenian earthquake for specialized treatment at Israeli hospitals. A few months later the El Al jets flew the Armenians home, the men, women, and children now equipped with artificial limbs and other state-of-the-art medical devices. It was touching to see the smiling Armenians walk down the ramp from the big Boeing.

Though all was better and better between the superpowers, the tragedy of the Third World—from its wars and revolutions to its social conditions and the murderous financial debt burden—was worsening from year to year.

The terrible violence went unabated albeit some of the regional conflicts were being settled. The refugee population remained over 17 million, with the refugees concentrated in eighteen African countries (Malawi with 720,000 and the Sudan with 690,000 leading the list); five Asian countries (450,000 refugees in Thailand, mainly from Cambodia); ten South Asian and Middle Eastern countries and territories (led by Pakistan with 3.7 million Afghans and Iran with 3 million Afghans—plus 2.3 million Palestinians in the Gaza Strip, Jordan, Lebanon, Syria, and the Israeli-occupied West Bank); and four Latin American countries. Most of them had no future whatsoever; a great many were second- and third-generation refugees.

A disturbing trend developing in the eighties was the sharp rise in religious fundamentalism and religion-related conflicts. Islamic fundamentalism became a powerful political force not only in Iran in the aftermath of the Ayatollah Khomeini's 1979 revolution, but also in Egypt and Jordan. Before his death, Khomeini issued orders for the murder of Salman Rushdie, the Indian-born author of *The Satanic Verses*, on the grounds that he had demeaned Islam. Rushdie has been in hiding ever since. Jewish fundamentalism propounding restrictive social behavior by Jews and the permanent occupation by Israel of the territories conquered in the 1967 war was steadily gaining strength during the decade. Hindu fundamentalism appeared in India, not only threatening a new period of hostility against Muslim populations, but acquiring a political dimension as well; in the general elections in November 1989, a Hindu fundamentalist political party did surprisingly well at the polls as part of the opposition's National Front against Prime Minister Gandhi's Congress party, helping to defeat him. Between October and December 1989, nearly fifteen hundred Muslims and Hindus were killed in communal fighting in the Indian state of Bihar—the worst religious conflict since the 1947 partition. In many countries, religious prejudice on the part of the ruling majorities took the form of human rights violations: The Sudan, Syria, and Bulgaria were among the examples.

Third World countries have made immense efforts to improve their lot, but they always seem to be backsliding. India and Brazil, for example, are virtually self-sufficient in food production, but they are unable to distribute foodstuffs as well as national wealth equitably; this is why *net* poverty grows along with the size of the populations. Mexico exports appliances and petroleum to the United States, but it still has to export people—illegally—because the economy could not sustain the ever-growing population. The huge external debts carried by most of the Third World countries—the total in 1989 was in excess of $1 trillion—further paralyzed economic development.

Health standards are dropping despite vast international and local efforts to improve it. In 1989 well over 1 billion people in the Third World were seriously ill or malnourished; malaria, measles, diarrhea, and respiratory diseases take the greatest toll, and infant mortality in most countries is not being diminished as effectively as it should. About 160 *million* Africans (30 percent of the African population) were affected by malnutrition and disease, including AIDS. The World Health Organization estimates that at least 17 million people in the Third World die annually from preventable diseases. There are 100 million annual malaria cases, 10 million new cases annually of tuberculosis, 200 million cases of schistosomiasis, and in 1989 between 6 and 8 million people were believed to be infected with the AIDS virus. It is impossible to visualize the full human extent of this health catastrophe. The World Health Organization said in December that "the epidemic is still out of control."

Nature (or God), too, seems to conspire against the battered Third World. Thus Bangladesh, one of the world's poorest and most densely inhabited countries, suffers awesome floods at least once a year when heavy rains swell the Brahmaputra, Ganges, and Meghna rivers, which are among the mightiest on the globe. In September 1989 two thirds of Bangladesh were inundated, with two thousand people drowning, agriculture destroyed, and millions of dollars lost in buildings and roads. Brazil's vast northeast region, one of the world's poorest, lives between drought and flood cycles. Hurricanes smash Caribbean islands (in the autumn of 1989 it was Puerto Rico, the Virgin Islands, and Guadeloupe), and typhoons flatten the Philippines and Malaysia. What sins are being so terribly punished?

Then there is the deepening conflict between technology and tradition in ancient lands, with technology often surpassing people's capability of using it. I spent some time in 1989 in the Himalayan kingdom of Bhutan to discover that while the overwhelming majority of the population (less than one million) was illiterate and the nation lacked a generally understood national language, investments were made in producing software in the Dzong-ka written language (descended from Tibetan scripts and spoken only in western Bhutan) for computer terminals. In Israel computers are used to store Hebrew inscriptions from ancient tombs, but Orthodox Jews insist on quasi-medieval practices in daily life. Brazil has the world's most active and extensive television network and its own computer and data industry while in the north Indian tribes are losing the battle to survive against the onrushing settlers who want their lands.

For the nineties and for the new century, the Third World and its numbing problems are certain to dominate the attentions of the more affluent societies, much in self-defense against the spread of disease, new wars, and the threat to the international financial system posed by the trillion-dollar debt owed by the poor of this universe.

And what about America as it enters the 1990's?

Basically the nation and the economy are resilient, but the contrasts in the society are too glaring and the contradictions too profound.

As usual, extremes tell the story. There were 58 Americans among the world's 157 *billionaires* on *Fortune* magazine's 1989 list (nobody counts millionaires anymore). But the National League of Cities reported at the same time that poverty in America was the worst since 1970; it had risen in two decades from 12 to 15 percent of the population—around 30 million Americans. The league also concluded that the new poor was younger (the rate among children jumped from 16 percent in 1979 to 21 percent in 1986) and increasingly concentrated in the inner cities. Homelessness, too, was on the rise, the most shameful visible aspect of poverty in rich America.

The most alarming of all, however, was the soaring rate of infant mortality in Washington, D.C., the capital of the free world, as it is called. In 1989 the infant mortality rate (death under the age of one) had jumped to 32.3 per 1,000 live births from 23.2 in 1988. This was the triple of the national average, placing Washington in the ranks of medium-income Third World countries. And the chilling explanation was that infant mortality had exploded so drastically because of a surge in babies born to cocaine-addicted women. Can America tolerate a social scandal on such a scale?

Aging Americans were not faring too well either. The United States is an aging society, but it refuses to accept this demographic fact out of what is essentially selfishness and greed on the part of the more affluent Americans. The jolting example is that in November 1989 the Congress repealed the Medicare Catastrophic Coverage Act it had passed only a year earlier. Basically the Congress responded to the complaints of older Americans who refused to pay larger insurance premiums, even if they could afford them. The result was that thirty-three million Americans covered by Medicare were back to the earlier level of benefits even though the cost of nursing home care, hospital stays, care at home, doctor bills, and prescription drugs keeps mounting.

This adds up to one of the most gripping postwar ironies and contradictions. The technology and quality of medicine and health services have improved spectacularly in the last half century—virtual miracles have become possible—but a growing number of aging Americans probably cannot afford them to prolong their lives and make them more bearable, if not joyful.

At the end of the 1980's younger and healthier Americans—and the more affluent ones—were having the time of their lives, insulated from other American realities. Large disposable incomes, especially with both men and women working in more and more households, made possible in unprecedented numbers domestic and international travel as well as massive purchases of appliances and marvels of technology. The cachet of distinction was the fax machine at home as well as at the office ("What is your fax number?" became a routine question of new acquaintances), and it was even more classy to have a cellular phone in the car (especially in a convertible) and a mobile phone in hand or in the pocket.

The National Golf Foundation announced in 1989 that golf was the fastest-growing sport in America, double what it was four years earlier. Americans spent around eight billion dollars in 1988 on golf-related travel and lodging and nearly one billion dollars on club memberships, fees, and equipment. Twenty-four million Americans played 487 million rounds of golf, which is rather hard to visualize, and for the first time blacks and women accounted for an important segment of this activity. President Bush was the nation's best-known golfer (as Eisenhower had been thirty years earlier), dividing his sport time equally between golf and tennis.

Yuppie Americans (and older ones) bought sports cars and convertibles in a return to the immediate postwar years, and they spent more on expensive clothes than ever before. In 1989 Americans spent five billion dollars on cinema tickets, a 20 percent increase over the previous year, and *Batman* was the biggest box-office success for reasons that it is probably idle to explore.

How long and in what shape would American prosperity continue were questions that could not be easily answered. At the end of the 1980's the nation was emerging from the postindustrial era, which had characterized the postwar period, to enter the high technology and service economy era, and there were still too many unknowns in this evolutionary process to project a clear picture ahead.

Lester C. Thurow of the Massachusetts Institute of Technology was probably right in foreseeing a sharp expansion in U.S. industrial production to make up for the loss of most of our agriculture markets abroad and for our immense trade deficit. High technology and robotics, however, will most likely account for much of this production although in Thurow's view, workers will have to be attracted from the service sector as well because of anticipated labor shortages. This is an optimistic but credible scenario for the transformation of the American society and its work habits in the next century—if nothing unexpected appears to upset it. The shift away from the defense industry expected to result from the new world political climate will inevitably affect the changing economic structure. But the key point is that America—again—is in the midst of an epochal process of evolution.

The year and the decade ended amid unbelievable juxtapositions.

December sadly saw the death of two great men of our century: the Soviet Union's Andrei Sakharov, sixty-eight, who in the tradition of Gandhi and Martin Luther King, Jr., symbolized resistance to oppression, devotion to human rights, and amazing personal courage; and Samuel Beckett, eighty-three, the Irish-born Nobel Prize–winning playwright and poet, one of the most powerful voices in contemporary English-language (and French) literature, and the author of *Waiting for Godot*, the play that changed forever all concepts of modern theater.

During the Christmas season, we saw bloody street battles in Bucharest and Panama City, but on Christmas Day we could see and hear Leonard Bernstein conducting Beethoven's Ninth Symphony in East Berlin, near the skeleton of the Berlin Wall. Bernstein substituted the word "freedom" for "joy" in the choir's triumphal rendition of the "Ode to Joy." On New Year's Eve, the East German conductor Kurt Masur directed the Ninth Symphony at a concert in Leipzig in tribute to "the revolution . . . of the spirit of freedom." At midnight, the historic Brandenburg Gate, which had separated East and West Berlin for twenty-eight years, was opened to passage at the climax of the greatest postwar New Year's celebration in Germany. In Panama, the U.S. Army played acid rock music at top volume at the papal nunciature to drive Noriega—and the nuncio—mad from the noise (Noriega is an opera lover).

Over Bucharest television, a Romanian artist sang Christmas carols, the first time they could be sung publicly in forty-five years. A few hours later, Romanian television broadcast videotapes of the executed Nicolae Ceauşescu and his wife, Elena—and Secretary of State James Baker said on American television that the United States would approve if the Soviet Union sent troops to Romania in support of the prodemocracy rebels. Poland and Hungary announced they had invited the Peace Corps to send volunteers to help them rebuild their economies, an impressive show of confidence in American goodwill and know-how. Hawkers in Berlin sold chunks of the Wall. Susan Eisenhower, Ike's granddaughter, announced that she was marrying leading Soviet space scientist and Gorbachev adviser Roald Z. Sagdeyev. The Italian Communist party dropped the word "Communist" from its name.

It was an astonishing new world spawned by the 1980's.

A half century after the start of the Second World War, humanity is at a crossroads. The world war and the Cold War in all its manifestations are behind us. New political and economic solutions are required—and are beginning to emerge—in the dying Communist world as well as in the new Western Europe of the integrated common market and in Japan and the other newly prosperous nations of the Pacific Rim. America is redefining its purpose. The Third World strives to survive—in the most literal sense.

With full caution and in awareness of the problems and challenges facing the world on the eve of the twenty-first century, there are reasons for optimism that we have entered a time of "common sense and reason." The international climate should remain fairly favorable to peace and peaceful endeavors though shocks and dramas and tragedies are inevitable. The astounding advances in science, technology, and medicine since 1939 should be made to serve humanity as fully as possible. New thinkers and philosophers must contribute to a more sublime human condition.

Fifty years after the outbreak of the most terrible war in human history, the world is embarking on a new era. The promise that it will be a hopeful era is very much before us. These concluding words are being written on December 31, 1989, at the end of one of the most extraordinary years in the last half century. Tomorrow is the dawn of the next age.

BIBLIOGRAPHY

I. BOOKS

Acheson, Dean. *Present at the Creation*. New York: W. W. Norton, 1969.

Bernstein, Jeremy. *Einstein*. New York: Viking, 1973.

Blight, James G., and David A. Welch. *On the Brink*. New York: Hill & Wang, 1989.

Bloom, Allan. *The Closing of the American Mind*. New York: Simon & Schuster, 1987.

Brzezinski, Zbigniew. *Power and Principle*. New York: Farrar Straus Giroux, 1983.

Bundy, McGeorge. *Danger and Survival*. New York: Random House, 1988.

Clodfelter, Mark. *The Limits of Air Power*. New York: The Free Press, 1989.

Coles, James S., ed. *Technological Innovation in the 80's*. Englewood Cliffs, N.J.: Prentice-Hall, 1984.

Collins, Larry, and Dominique La Pierre. *Freedom at Midnight*. New York: Simon & Schuster, 1975.

Djilas, Milovan. *Conversations with Stalin*. New York: Harcourt, Brace & World, 1962.

————. *The Unperfect Society*. New York: Harcourt, Brace & World, 1969.

Eban, Abba. *An Autobiography*. New York: Random House, 1977.

Eisenhower, David. *Eisenhower at War 1943–1945*. New York: Random House, 1986.

Ford, Gerald R. *A Time to Heal*. New York: Harper & Row and Reader's Digest Association, 1979.

Freedman, Lawrence. *The Price of Peace.* New York: Henry Holt, 1986.

Fromkin, David. *A Peace to End All Peace.* New York: Henry Holt, 1989.

Gaddis, John Lewis. *The Long Peace.* New York: Oxford University Press, 1987.

Giscard d'Estaing, Valéry. *Le Pouvoir et la Vie.* Hérissey à Evreux: Compagnie 12, 1988.

Gutman, Roy. *Banana Diplomacy.* New York: Simon & Schuster, 1988.

Haig, Alexander M., Jr. *Caveat.* New York: Macmillan, 1984.

Halecki, Oscar. *Borderlands of Western Civilization.* New York: Ronald Press, 1952.

Hamilton, Edward K., ed. *America's Global Interests.* New York: W. W. Norton, 1989.

Hart, Alan. *Arafat.* London: Sedgwick & Jackson, 1984.

Hastings, Max. *The Korean War.* New York: Simon & Schuster, 1987.

Herzstein, Robert Edwin. *Waldheim.* New York: Arbor House/William Morrow, 1988.

Jobert, Michel. *Les Américains.* Paris: Éditions Albin Michel S.A., 1987.

Jones, R. V. *Most Secret War.* London: Hamish Hamilton, 1978.

Karnow, Stanley. *Vietnam: A History.* New York: Viking, 1983.

———. *In Our Image.* New York: Random House, 1989.

Kennan, George F. *Memoirs 1925–1950.* Boston: Little, Brown, 1967.

———. *From Prague After Munich.* Princeton, N.J.: Princeton University Press, 1968.

———. *Memoirs 1950–1963.* Boston: Little, Brown, 1972.

———. *The Fateful Alliance.* New York: Pantheon Books, 1984.

Klass, Philip J. *Secret Sentries in Space.* New York: Random House, 1971.

Kissinger, Henry. *White House Years.* Boston: Little, Brown, 1979.

———. *Years of Upheaval.* Boston: Little, Brown, 1982.

Krishan, S., senior contributor. *A Common Faith*. Bombay: U.S. Information Service, 1988.

Krock, Arthur. *In the Nation: 1932–1966*. New York: McGraw-Hill, 1966.

Lacouture, Jean. *Pierre Mendès-France*. Paris: Éditions du Seuil, 1981.

———. *De Gaulle*, Vol. 1, *Le Rebelle*. Paris: Éditions du Seuil, 1984.

———. *De Gaulle*, Vol. 2, *Le Politique*. Paris: Éditions du Seuil, 1985.

———. *De Gaulle*, Vol. 3, *Le Souverain*. Paris: Éditions du Seuil, 1986.

Lattimore, Owen. *Ordeal by Slander*. Boston: Little, Brown, 1950.

Malraux, André. *La Condition Humaine*. Paris: Éditions Gallimard, 1946.

Marchetti, Victor, and John D. Marks. *The CIA and the Cult of Intelligence*. New York: Alfred A. Knopf, 1974.

Maxwell, Neville. *India's China War*. New York: Pantheon Books, 1970.

Medvedev, Roy. *Khrushchev*. Garden City, N.Y.: Anchor Books, 1984.

Minnesota Lawyers International Human Rights Committee. *Human Rights in the Democratic People's Republic of Korea*. Washington: Asia Watch, 1988.

Newhouse, John, *Cold Dawn: The Story of SALT*. New York: Holt, Rinehart & Winston, 1973.

———. *War and Peace in the Nuclear Age*. New York: Knopf, 1989.

Nicolson, Harold. *Diaries & Letters: 1930–1939*. New York: Atheneum, 1966.

Nixon, Richard. *R.N.: The Memoirs of Richard Nixon*. New York: Grosset & Dunlap, 1978.

———. *No More Vietnams*. New York: Arbor House, 1985.

O'Reilly, Kenneth. *Racial Matters—The FBI's Secret File on Black America*. New York: The Free Press, 1989.

Osmańczyk, Edmund Jan. *Był rok 1945*. . . . Warsaw: Państwowy Instytut Wydawniczy, 1977.

———. *Encyclopedia of the United Nations*. Philadelphia-London: Taylor and Francis, 1985.

Phillips, Cabell. *From the Crash to the Blitz 1929–1939.* New York: Macmillan, 1969.

Pogue, Forrest C. *George C. Marshall.* New York: Viking, 1987.

Public Papers of the Presidents of the United States. *Richard Nixon 1973.* Washington: U.S. Government Printing Office, 1975.

———. *Richard Nixon 1974.* Washington: U.S. Government Printing Office, 1975.

Rakowski, Mieczysław F. *Przesilenie Grudniowe.* Warsaw: Państwowy Instytut Wydawniczy, 1981.

Ranelagh, John. *The Agency: The Rise and Decline of the CIA.* New York: Simon & Schuster, 1986.

Rhodes, Richard. *The Making of the Atomic Bomb.* New York: Simon & Schuster, 1986.

Roosevelt, Kermit. *Counter Coup.* New York: McGraw-Hill, 1979.

Rosset, Peter, and John Vandemeer, eds. *The Nicaragua Reader.* New York: Grove Press, 1983.

Schlesinger, Arthur M., Jr. *A Thousand Days.* Boston: Houghton Mifflin, 1965.

Sheehan, Neil. *A Bright Shining Lie.* New York: Random House, 1988.

Shtasel, Philip. *Speak to Me on Nuclear Medicine.* Hagerstown, Md.: Harper & Row, 1976.

Smith, Bradley F. *The War's Long Shadow.* New York: Simon & Schuster, 1986.

Talbott, Strobe, ed. and trans. *Khrushchev Remembers.* Boston: Little, Brown, 1976.

———. *Deadly Gambit.* New York: Alfred A. Knopf, 1984.

Taylor, A. J. P. *The Origins of the Second World War.* New York: Atheneum, 1962.

Thomas, Hugh. *Armed Truce.* New York: Atheneum, 1987.

Truman, Harry S. *Memoirs.* Vol. 1, *Year of Decisions.* Vol. 2, *Years of Trial and Hope.* Garden City, N.Y.: Doubleday, 1955–56.

Ulam, Adam B. *Stalin.* New York: Viking, 1973.

Ungar, Sanford J., ed. *Estrangement.* New York: Oxford University Press, 1985.

Wałęsa, Lech. *A Way of Hope.* New York: Henry Holt, 1987.

Weisskopf, Kurt. *The Agony of Czechoslovakia '38/'68.* London: Elek, 1968.

Zachariah, K. C., and My T. Vu. *World Population Projections 1987–88 Edition.* (World Bank.) Baltimore: Johns Hopkins University Press, 1988.

Zawodny, J. K. *Death in the Forest.* New York: Hippocrene Books, 1962.

II. REPORTS, PAMPHLETS, PERIODICALS

Carnegie Endowment for International Peace. *Foreign Policy Summer 1987.* Washington, D.C.: 1987.

———. *Foreign Policy Winter 1987–88.* Washington, D.C.: 1987.

———. *Foreign Policy Spring 1988.* Washington, D.C.: 1988.

———. *Foreign Policy Fall 1988.* Washington, D.C.: 1988.

———. *Foreign Policy Spring 1989.* Washington, D.C.: 1989.

———. *Foreign Policy Fall 1989.* Washington, D.C.: 1989.

Council on Foreign Relations. *Foreign Affairs—Spring 1987.* New York: Council on Foreign Relations, 1987.

———. *Foreign Affairs—Fall 1987.* New York: Council on Foreign Relations, 1987.

———. *Foreign Affairs—Winter 1987/1988.* New York: Council on Foreign Relations, 1987.

———. *Foreign Affairs—America and the World 1987/88.* New York: Council on Foreign Relations, 1988.

———. *Foreign Affairs—Winter 1988/89.* New York: Council on Foreign Relations, 1989.

———. *Foreign Affairs—Summer 1989.* New York: Council on Foreign Relations, 1989.

Dunbar, William. "India in Transition." *Washington Papers,* vol. III, no. 31. Beverly Hills and London: Sage Publications, 1976.

German Foreign Affairs Review. *Aussen Politik*. Hamburg: Interpress, 1988.

Halperin, Ernst. "Terrorism in Latin America." *Washington Papers*, vol. III, no. 33. Beverly Hills and London: Sage Publications, 1976.

Harsgor, Michael. "Portugal in Revolution." *Washington Papers*, vol. III, no. 32. Beverly Hills and London: Sage Publications, 1976.

Human Rights Watch. *The Reagan Administration's Record on Human Rights in 1988*. United States of America: Human Rights Watch and the Lawyers Committee for Human Rights, 1989.

International Institute for Strategic Studies. *Strategic Survey 1988–1989*. London: Brassey's, 1989.

———. *The Changing Strategic Landscape*. London: Brassey's, 1989.

———. *Strategic Survey 1985–1986*. London: International Institute for Strategic Studies, 1986.

———. *Strategic Survey 1986–1987*. London: International Institute for Strategic Studies, 1987.

International Monetary Fund. *Annual Report, 1989*. Washington: International Monetary Fund, 1989.

Larrabee, F. Stephen, ed. *Technology and Change in East-West Relations*. New York: Institute for East-West Security Studies, 1988.

Long, David E. "Saudi Arabia." *Washington Papers*, vol. IV, no. 39. Beverly Hills and London: Sage Publications, 1976.

Menges, Constantine Christopher. *Spain: The Struggle for Democracy Today*. Beverly Hills and London: Sage Publications, 1978.

Ministry of Foreign Affairs of the U.S.S.R. *Documents and Materials Relating to the Eve of the Second World War, Volume II (1938–1939)*. Moscow: Foreign Languages Publishing House, 1948.

Nobel Foundation Directory 1985–1986. Stockholm: Nobel Foundation, 1985.

U.S. Army Medical Department. *Two Hundred Years of Military Medicine*. Frederick, Md.: Historical Unit, U.S. Army Medical Department, 1974.

The World Bank. *Annual Report 1989 Washington, D.C. The World Resources Institute: World Resources 1988–89*. New York: Basic Books, 1989.

INDEX